The Measurement of Productive Efficiency and Productivity Growth

The Measurement of Productive Efficiency and Productivity Growth

Edited by

Harold O. Fried
C. A. Knox Lovell
Shelton S. Schmidt

UNIVERSITY PRESS
2008

OXFORD
UNIVERSITY PRESS

Oxford University Press, Inc., publishes works that further
Oxford University's objective of excellence
in research, scholarship, and education.

Oxford New York
Auckland Cape Town Dar es Salaam Hong Kong Karachi
Kuala Lumpur Madrid Melbourne Mexico City Nairobi
New Delhi Shanghai Taipei Toronto

With offices in
Argentina Austria Brazil Chile Czech Republic France Greece
Guatemala Hungary Italy Japan Poland Portugal Singapore
South Korea Switzerland Thailand Turkey Ukraine Vietnam

Published by Oxford University Press, Inc.
198 Madison Avenue, New York, New York 10016

www.oup.com

Library of Congress Cataloging-in-Publication Data

The measurement of productive efficiency and productivity growth/edited by
  Harold O. Fried, C.A. Knox Lovell, and Shelton S. Schmidt.
    p. cm.
  Includes bibliographical references and index.
  ISBN 978-0-19-518352-8
  1. Industrial efficiency—Measurement. 2. Industrial productivity—Measurement.
  I. Fried, Harold O. II. Lovell, C. A. Knox.
  III. Schmidt, Shelton S.
  HD56.25.M4356 2007
  338.5—dc22   2007015061

We extend thanks to our many friends and colleagues around the world; your research and stimulating conversations have inspired the material in this book.

Preface

Some individuals are more productive than others; some small businesses find and exploit a lucrative market niche that others miss; some large corporations are more profitable than others; and some public agencies provide more efficient service than others. In each case, performance, both absolute and relative to the competition, can improve through time or lag behind. Success in the short run can be associated with failure in the long run; failure in the short run can lead to death, or it may be the precursor of success in the long run.

What do we mean by business performance? Surely it is multidimensional, but for most producers, the ultimate yardstick is profit. However, we take the view that profit, or any other financial indicator, is a reflection, rather than a measure, of business performance. Performance itself means doing the right things right. This involves solving the purely technical problem of avoiding waste, by producing maximum outputs from available inputs or by using minimum inputs required to produce desired outputs. It also involves solving the allocative problems of using inputs in the right proportion and producing outputs in the right proportion, where "right" generally respects prevailing input prices and output prices. Technical and allocative efficiency in the use of inputs leads to cost efficiency. Technical and allocative efficiency in the production of outputs leads to revenue efficiency. Overall technical and allocative efficiency leads to profit efficiency, the generation of maximum possible profit under the circumstances.

However, circumstances change through time, and so changes in business performance involve changes in technical and allocative efficiency. But they also involve changes in productivity arising from development or adoption of new technologies that bring improvements in efficiency of both types. Thus, business performance has both static and dynamic aspects.

Why does business performance vary? Ultimate responsibility for performance rests with management. We believe that inefficiency arises from the varying abilities of managers and that firms with varying degrees of inefficiency that operate in overlapping markets can coexist for some period of time. Our belief comes from observing the real world, in which reported quarterly earnings vary across similar firms and through time, and in which these same firms provide employment opportunities for myriad business consulting gurus armed with their buzzwords and their remedies for a host of economic ailments.

Managerial ability is unobservable. Consequently, we infer it from technical efficiency relative to the competition, which involves construction of a best practice production frontier and measurement of distance to it for each entity. We also infer it from cost, revenue, or profit efficiency relative to the competition, which involves construction of a best practice cost, revenue, or profit frontier and measurement of distance to it for each entity. In a dynamic context, we are interested in the progressive entities that push the envelope and in which entities keep pace or fall behind. In all circumstances, we attempt to level the playing field by distinguishing variation in business performance from variation in the operating environment.

This is a relatively new, and to some a heretical, approach to business performance evaluation. The notions of best practice and benchmarking are firmly entrenched in the business world, but they are inconsistent with the economics textbook world in which all firms optimize all the time. The objective of this book is to merge the two strands of thought by developing analytically rigorous models of failure to optimize and of failure to be progressive. We do not dispense with the time-honored paradigm of optimizing behavior. Rather, we build on the paradigm by allowing for varying degrees of success in the pursuit of conventional economic objectives. The objective is to bring economic analysis closer to a framework useful for the evaluation of business performance. Call it economically and analytically rigorous benchmarking.

Two approaches to business performance evaluation have been developed, one in economics and the other in management science. The former uses parametric econometric techniques, and the latter uses nonparametric mathematical programming techniques. They share a common objective, that of benchmarking the performance of the rest against that of the best. We take an eclectic approach by reporting both, and mixtures and extensions of the two, as well. For the novice reader, chapter 1 provides a broad-ranging introduction to the field that provides preparation and motivation for continuing. Distinguished experts who have developed and extended the field of efficiency and productivity analysis contribute subsequent chapters. For open-minded and agnostic readers, chapters 2 and 3 provide in-depth expositions of the two approaches. For readers already committed to an approach, chapters 2 and 3 provide the opportunity to broaden their perspective by an exposure to an alternative approach. For all readers, chapter 4 advances both approaches by providing a nonparametric statistical approach to performance evaluation. Again for all readers, chapter 5 extends and combines the two approaches to develop a dynamic approach to performance evaluation in which the measurement of productivity growth and the identification of its sources occupy center stage.

The contributors to this book work hard and play hard. In fact, we believe there is no clear distinction between work and play. Although we are all getting older (some more advanced than others), there remains a freshness and excitement toward the material, much of which is new. The field is young; many challenging problems have been solved, but many others remain. It is our hope that this book will inspire the jaded and recruit the novices. There are discoveries to be made, at the office and at the bar. This was all too apparent when we gathered in Athens, Georgia, to share early drafts of the chapters. Enjoy reading what we have enjoyed writing.

Harold O. Fried
C. A. Knox Lovell
Shelton S. Schmidt

Contents

Contributors

Ozren Despić
Aston Business School
Aston University
Birmingham, UK
o.despic@aston.ac.uk

Rolf Färe
Department of Agricultural
    & Resource Economics
    & Department of Economics
Oregon State University
Corvallis, OR
rolf.fare@orst.edu

Harold O. Fried
Department of Economics
Union College
Schenectady, NY
friedh@union.edu

William H. Greene
Department of Economics

Stern School of Business
New York University
New York, NY
wgreene@stern.nyu.edu

Shawna Grosskopf
Department of Economics
Oregon State University
Corvallis, OR
shawna.grosskopf@orst.edu

C. A. Knox Lovell
Emeritus Professor
Department of Economics
University of Georgia
Athens, GA
knox@terry.uga.edu
and
Honorary Professor
School of Economics
University of Queensland
Brisbane, Australia

Dimitri Margaritis
Finance Department
Auckland University of
    Technology Auckland,
    New Zealand
dimitri.margaritis@aut.ac.nz

Maria C. S. Portela
Faculdade de Economia e Gestão
Universidade Católica Portuguesa
Porto, Portugal
csilva@porto.ucp.pt

Shelton S. Schmidt
Department of Economics
Union College
Schenectady, NY
schmidts@union.edu

Léopold Simar
Institut de Statistique
Université Catholique de Louvain
Louvain-la-Neuve, Belgium
simar@stat.ucl.ac.be

Emmanuel Thanassoulis
Aston Business School
Aston University
Birmingham, UK
e.thanassoulis@aston.ac.uk

Paul W. Wilson
The John E. Walker
    Department of Economics
Clemson University
Clemson, SC
pww@clemson.edu

The Measurement of Productive Efficiency and Productivity Growth

1

Efficiency and Productivity

Harold O. Fried, C. A. Knox Lovell,
and Shelton S. Schmidt

1.1 Introduction

Airlines in the United States have encountered difficulties since September
11, 2001, particularly on domestic routes. Figure 1.1 plots quarterly operating
profit margins (profit from domestic operations as a percentage of operating
revenue) for three segments of the industry: the small regional airlines; the
medium-size, low-cost airlines; and the large network airlines. The regional
airlines have performed relatively well, earning more than a 10% profit margin,
and the low-cost airlines have performed adequately, earning a considerably
smaller but nonetheless positive profit margin. However, the network airlines
have performed poorly, earning a large negative profit margin. Some have
sought bankruptcy protection.

When we ask why airline performance has varied so much, we naturally
think of revenues and costs. Figure 1.2 plots quarterly operating revenue per
available seat-mile (a measure of average revenue), and figure 1.3 plots quarterly operating expense per available seat-mile (a measure of average cost). On
the revenue side, the regional airlines earned the highest operating revenue per
available seat-mile, trailed in order by the network airlines and the low-cost
airlines. On the cost side, the low-cost airlines incurred the lowest operating cost per available seat-mile, appropriately enough, trailed by the network
airlines and the regional airlines.

It appears that the regional airlines have been the most profitable segment
of the domestic airline industry despite having had the highest unit costs.
The low-cost airlines have been marginally profitable because their low unit

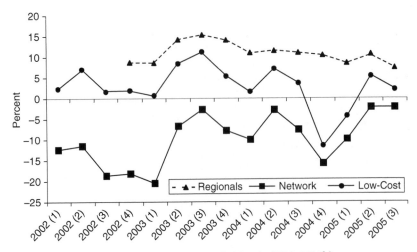

Figure 1.1. Airline Domestic Operating Profit Margin (BLS, 2005b)

revenues have been offset by even lower unit costs. Finally, the network airlines have lost money primarily because of their high unit costs.

On the cost side, three hypotheses spring quickly to mind, each inspired by conventional economic theory. First, the pattern of unit operating costs may reflect a pattern of scale economies that generates a U-shaped minimum average cost function favoring the medium-size low-cost airlines. Second, it may reflect higher input prices paid by the regional and network airlines. This hypothesis rings true for the older network airlines, which at the time were

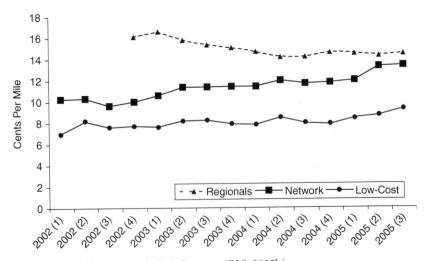

Figure 1.2. Airline Domestic Unit Revenue (BLS, 2005b)

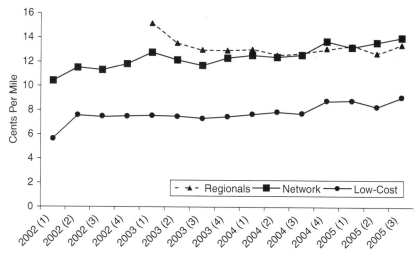

Figure 1.3. Airline Domestic Unit Cost (BLS, 2005b)

burdened by high labor costs attributable in large part to onerous pension obligations. Third, it may reflect different technologies embedded in a "low-cost business model" employed by the low-cost airlines and an inefficient "hub-and-spoke" system employed by the network airlines. Support for this hypothesis comes from the network airlines themselves, which predict efficiency gains and cost savings as they gradually abandon the system they adopted three decades ago.

On the revenue side, differential pricing power is a possible explanation, although it is not clear why the small regional airlines would have such an advantage. A more likely explanation is variation in rates of capacity utilization as measured by load factors (the percentage of available seats actually sold), which might have favored the regional airlines and penalized the low-cost airlines.

Each of these hypotheses is suggested by economic theory and may or may not be refuted by the evidence. We now put forth an additional pair of refutable hypotheses that, although not suggested by conventional economic theory, should not be dismissed a priori.

One hypothesis concerns the cost side and posits that part of the observed pattern of unit operating cost may be a consequence of cost inefficiency at the regional and network airlines. Cost inefficiency can be "technical," arising from excessive resource use given the amount of traffic, or "allocative," arising from resources being employed in the wrong mix, given their prices. Perhaps the low-cost airlines had relatively low unit costs because they utilized part-time labor and because they leased, rather than purchased, aircraft. Either strategy would reduce idleness and down time. More generally, perhaps the low-cost airlines had relatively low unit costs because their resources, human and physical, were well managed. This would place them on the minimum average cost function, whereas cost inefficiency at the regional and network airlines would place them above the minimum average cost function.

The second hypothesis concerns the revenue side and posits that part of the observed pattern of unit operating revenue may be a consequence of revenue inefficiency at the network and low-cost airlines. Revenue inefficiency can be "technical," arising from a failure to provide maximum service from the available resources, or "allocative," arising from the provision of services in the wrong mix, given their prices. Perhaps the regional airlines were nimble enough to adjust their route structures to respond quickly to fluctuations in passenger demand. Perhaps the regional airlines have faster gate turnaround times than the network airlines, whose hub-and-spoke technology leaves aircraft and crew idle and sacrifices revenue. This would place the regional airlines on the maximum average revenue function, whereas revenue inefficiency at the network and low-cost airlines would place them beneath the maximum average revenue function.

The point of the foregoing discussion is not to engage in a deep exploration into airline economics, about which we are blissfully ignorant. We are merely frequent fliers who happen to be curious economists wondering what might explain the observed variation in the recent domestic performance of U.S. airlines. The point is to suggest that variation in productive efficiency, in both the management of resources and the management of services, may be a potentially significant source of variation in financial performance. Inefficient behavior is assumed away in conventional economic theory, in which first-order and second-order optimizing conditions are satisfied. But it exists in the real world, as a perusal of almost any trade publication will verify, and as the hordes of consultants armed with their buzzwords will testify.

Productive inefficiency exists, and it deserves to be included in our analytical toolkit because it can generate refutable hypotheses concerning the sources of variation in business performance. This book is devoted to the study of inefficiency in production and its impact on economic and financial performance. The study ranges from the underlying theory to the analytical foundations, and then to the quantitative techniques and the empirical evidence.

Chapter 1 sets the stage. Section 1.2 provides background material and focuses on hypotheses that have been proposed in the literature that would explain variation in producer performance. This section also provides a glimpse at the empirical literature and demonstrates that the search for variation in producer performance has been conducted in a wide variety of settings. Section 1.3 lays the theoretical foundation for the measurement of productive efficiency. It provides definitions of alternative notions of productive efficiency, and it provides corresponding measures of efficiency. Section 1.4 offers a brief introduction to alternative techniques that have been developed to quantify inefficiency empirically. Section 1.5 introduces various econometric approaches to efficiency estimation, while section 1.6 introduces variants of the mathematical programming approach to efficiency estimation. Section 1.7

introduces the Malmquist productivity index and shows how to decompose it into various sources of productivity change, including variation in productive efficiency. Section 1.8 describes three ways of approximating a Malmquist productivity index: the use of superlative index numbers, the use of econometric techniques, and the use of mathematical programming techniques. Section 1.9 offers some concluding observations.

Chapter 2 extends section 1.5 by providing a detailed survey of the econometric approach to efficiency estimation. Chapter 3 extends section 1.6 by providing a detailed survey of the mathematical programming approach to efficiency estimation. Chapter 4 recasts the parametric and statistical approach of chapter 2, and the nonparametric and deterministic approach of chapter 3, into a nonparametric and statistical approach. Chapter 5 extends sections 1.7 and 1.8 by discussing alternative approaches to the measurement of productivity change, with special emphasis on efficiency change as a source of productivity change.

1.2 Background

When discussing the economic performance of producers, it is common to describe them as being more or less "efficient" or more or less "productive." In this section, we discuss the relationship between these two concepts. We consider some hypotheses concerning the *determinants* of producer performance, and we consider some hypotheses concerning the financial *consequences* of producer performance.

By the *productivity* of a producer, we mean the ratio of its output to its input. This ratio is easy to calculate if the producer uses a single input to produce a single output. In the more likely event that the producer uses several inputs to produce several outputs, the outputs in the numerator must be aggregated in some economically sensible fashion, as must the inputs in the denominator, so that productivity remains the ratio of two scalars. Productivity growth then becomes the difference between output growth and input growth, and the aggregation requirement applies here, as well.

Variation in productivity, either across producers or through time, is thus a residual, which Abramovitz (1956) famously characterized as "a measure of our ignorance." Beginning perhaps with Solow (1957), much effort has been devoted to dispelling our ignorance by "whittling away at the residual" (Stone, 1980). Much of the whittling has involved minimizing measurement error in the construction of output and input quantity indexes. The conversion of raw data into variables consistent with economic theory is a complex undertaking. Griliches (1996) surveys the economic history of the residual, and state-of-the-art procedures for whittling away at it are outlined by the Organisation for Economic Co-operation and Development (OECD, 2001). When the whittling is finished, we have a residual suitable for analysis.

In principle, the residual can be attributed to differences in production technology, differences in the scale of operation, differences in operating efficiency, and differences in the operating environment in which production occurs. The U.S. Department of Labor's Bureau of Labor Statistics (BLS 2005) and the OECD (2001) attribute variation in productivity through time to these same sources. Proper attribution is important for the adoption of private managerial practices and the design of public policies intended to improve productivity performance. We are naturally interested in isolating the first three components, which are under the control of management, from the fourth, which is not. Among the three endogenous components, our interest centers on the efficiency component and on measuring both its cross-sectional contribution to variation in productivity and its intertemporal contribution to productivity change.

By the *efficiency* of a producer, we have in mind a comparison between observed and optimal values of its output and input. The exercise can involve comparing observed output to maximum potential output obtainable from the input, or comparing observed input to minimum potential input required to produce the output, or some combination of the two. In these two comparisons, the optimum is defined in terms of production possibilities, and efficiency is technical. It is also possible to define the optimum in terms of the behavioral goal of the producer. In this event, efficiency is measured by comparing observed and optimum cost, revenue, profit, or whatever goal the producer is assumed to pursue, subject, of course, to any appropriate constraints on quantities and prices. In these comparisons, the optimum is expressed in value terms, and efficiency is economic.

Even at this early stage, three problems arise, and much of this section is devoted to exploring ways each has been addressed. First, which outputs and inputs are to be included in the comparison? Second, how are multiple outputs and multiple inputs to be weighted in the comparison? And third, how is the technical or economic potential of the producer to be determined?

Many years ago, Knight (1933/1965) addressed the first question by noting that if all outputs and all inputs are included, then since neither matter nor energy can be created or destroyed, all producers would achieve the same unitary productivity evaluation. In this circumstance, Knight proposed to redefine productivity as the ratio of useful output to input. Extending Knight's redefinition to the ratio of useful output to useful input, and representing usefulness with weights incorporating market prices, generates a modern economic productivity index. As a practical matter, however, the first problem is not how to proceed when all outputs and all inputs are included, but rather how to proceed when not enough outputs and inputs are included.

As Stigler (1976) has observed, measured inefficiency may be a reflection of the analyst's failure to incorporate all relevant variables and, complicating the first problem, to specify the right economic objectives and the right constraints. Stigler was criticizing the work of Leibenstein (1966, 1976), who focused on inadequate motivation, information asymmetries, incomplete contracts, agency problems, and the attendant monitoring difficulties within the firm, and who lumped all these features together and called the mix "X-inefficiency." When the agents' actions are not aligned with the principal's objective, potential output is sacrificed. Thus, what appears as inefficiency to Leibenstein is evidence of an incomplete model to Stigler (1976), who called it waste and concluded that "waste is not a useful economic concept. Waste is error within the framework of modern economic analysis" (p. 216). The practical significance of this exchange is that if Stigler's wish is not granted, and not all variables reflecting the objectives and constraints of the principal and the agents are incorporated into the model, agency and related problems become potential sources of measured (if not actual) inefficiency.

Leibenstein was not writing in a vacuum. His approach fits nicely into the agency literature. The recognition of agency problems goes back at least as far as the pioneering Berle and Means (1932) study of the consequences of the separation of ownership from control, in which owners are the principals and managers are the agents. Leibenstein's notion of X-inefficiency also has much in common with Simon's (1955) belief that in a world of limited information processing ability, managers exhibit "bounded rationality" and engage in "satisficing" behavior. Along similar lines, Williamson (1975, 1985) viewed firms as seeking to economize on transaction costs, which in his view boiled down to economizing on bounded rationality. Bounded rationality and the costs of transacting also become potential sources of measured inefficiency.

It would be desirable, if extraordinarily difficult, to construct and implement Stigler's complete model involving all the complexities mentioned above. We have not seen such a model. What we have seen are simplified (if not simple) models of the firm in which measured performance differentials presumably reflect variation in the ability to deal with the complexities of the real world. Indeed, performance measures based on simplified models of the firm are often useful, and sometimes necessary. They are useful when the objectives of producers, or the constraints facing them, are either unknown or unconventional or subject to debate. In this case, a popular research strategy has been to model producers as unconstrained optimizers of some conventional objective and to test the hypothesis that inefficiency in this environment is consistent with efficiency in the constrained environment. The use of such incomplete measures has proved necessary in a number of contexts for lack of relevant data. One example of considerable policy import occurs when the production of desirable (and measured and priced) outputs is recorded, but the generation of undesirable (and frequently unmeasured and more frequently unpriced) byproducts is not. Another occurs when the use of public infrastructure enhances private performance, but its use goes unrecorded. In each case, the measure of efficiency or productivity that is obtained may be very different from the measure one would like to have.

Even when all relevant outputs and inputs are included, there remains the formidable second problem of assigning weights to variables. Market prices provide a natural set of weights, but two types of question arise. First, suppose market prices exist. If market prices change through time, or vary across producers, is it possible to disentangle the effects of price changes and quantity changes in a relative performance evaluation? Alternatively, if market prices reflect monopoly or monopsony power, or cross-subsidy, or the determination of a regulator, do they still provide appropriate weights in a relative performance evaluation? Second, suppose some market prices do not exist. In the cases of environmental impacts and public infrastructure mentioned above, the unpriced variables are externalities either generated by or received by market sector producers. How do we value these externalities? However, the weighting problem is more pervasive than the case of externalities. The nonmarket sector is growing relative to the market sector in most advanced economies, and by definition, the outputs in this sector are not sold on markets. How, then, do we value outputs such as law enforcement and fire protection services, or even public education services, each of which is publicly funded rather than privately purchased? Is it possible to develop proxies for missing prices that would provide appropriate weights in a performance evaluation? The presence of distorted or missing prices complicates the problem of determining what is meant by "relevant."

The third problem makes the first two seem easy. It is as difficult for the analyst to determine a producer's potential as it is for the producer to achieve that potential. It is perhaps for this reason that for many years the productivity literature ignored the efficiency component identified by the BLS and the OECD. Only recently, with the development of a separate literature devoted to the study of efficiency in production, has the problem of determining productive potential been seriously addressed. Resolution of this problem makes it possible to integrate the two literatures. Integration is important for policy purposes, since action taken to enhance productivity performance requires an accurate attribution of observed performance to its components.

By way of analogy, we do not know, and cannot know, how fast a human can run 100 meters. But we do observe best practice and its improvement through time, and we do observe variation in actual performance among runners. The world of sport is full of statistics, and we have all-star teams whose members are judged to be the best at what they do. Away from the world of sports, we use multiple criteria to rank cities on the basis of quality-of-life indicators (Zurich and Geneva are at the top). At the macro level, we use multiple criteria to rank countries on the basis of economic freedom (Norway, Sweden, and Australia are at the top), environmental sustainability (Finland and Norway are at the top), business risk (Iraq and Zimbabwe pose the most risk), and corruption (Finland and New Zealand are the least corrupt), among many others. The United Nation's Human Development Index is perhaps the best-known and most widely studied macroeconomic performance indicator (Norway and Sweden are at the top). In each of these cases, we face the three problems mentioned at the outset of this section: what indicators to include, how to weight them, and how to define potential. The selection and weighting of indicators are controversial by our standards, although comparisons are appropriately made relative to best practice rather than to some ideal standard.

The same reasoning applies to the evaluation of business performance. We cannot know "true" potential, whatever the economic objective. But we do observe best practice and its change through time, and we also observe variation in performance among producers operating beneath best practice. This leads to the association of "efficient" performance with undominated performance, or operation on a best-practice "frontier," and of inefficient performance with dominated performance, or operation on the wrong side of a best-practice frontier. Interest naturally focuses on the identification of best-practice producers and on benchmarking the performance of the rest against that of the best. Businesses themselves routinely benchmark their performance against that of their peers, and academic interest in benchmarking is widespread, although potential synergies between the approaches adopted by the two communities have yet to be fully exploited. Davies and Kochhar (2002) offer an interesting academic critique of business benchmarking.

Why the interest in measuring efficiency and productivity? We can think of three reasons. First, only by measuring efficiency and productivity, and by separating their effects from those of the operating environment so as to level the playing field, can we explore hypotheses concerning the sources of efficiency or productivity differentials. Identification and separation of controllable and uncontrollable sources of performance variation are essential to the institution of private practices and public policies designed to improve performance. Zeitsch et al. (1994) provide an empirical application showing how important it is to disentangle variation in the operating environment (in this case, customer density) from variation in controllable sources of productivity growth in Australian electricity distribution.

Second, macro performance depends on micro performance, and so the same reasoning applies to the study of the growth of nations. Lewis (2004) provides a compelling summary of McKinsey Global Institute (MGI) productivity studies of 13 nations over 12 years, the main findings being that micro performance drives macro performance, and that a host of institutional impediments to strong micro performance can be identified. This book, and the studies on which it is based, make it clear that there are potential synergies, as yet sadly unexploited, between the MGI approach and the academic approach to performance evaluation.

Third, efficiency and productivity measures are success indicators, performance metrics, by which producers are evaluated. However, for most producers the ultimate success indicator is financial performance, and the ultimate metric is the bottom line. Miller's (1984) clever title, "Profitability = Productivity + Price Recovery," encapsulates the relationship between productivity and financial performance. It follows that productivity growth leads to improved financial performance, provided it is not offset by declining price recovery attributable to falling product prices and/or rising input prices. Grifell-Tatjé and Lovell (1999) examine the relationship for Spanish banks facing increasing competition as a consequence of European monetary union. Salerian (2003) explores the relationship for Australian railroads, for which increasing intermodal competition has contributed to declining price recovery that has swamped the financial benefits of impressive productivity gains. This study also demonstrates that, although the bottom line may be paramount in the private sector, it is not irrelevant in the public sector; indeed, many governments monitor the financial performance as well as the nonfinancial performance of their public service providers.

Many other studies, primarily in the business literature, adopt alternative notions of financial performance, such as return on assets or return on equity. These studies typically begin with the "DuPont triangle," which decomposes return on assets as $\pi/A = (\pi/R)(R/A) =$ (return on sales)(investment turnover), where π = profit, A = assets, and R = revenue. The next step is to decompose the first leg of the DuPont triangle as $(\pi/R) = [(R - C)/R] = [1 - (R/C)^{-1}]$, where C is cost and R/C is profitability. The final step is to decompose profitability into productivity and price recovery, a multiplicative alternative to Miller's additive relationship. The objective is to trace the contribution of productivity change up the triangle to change in financial performance. Horrigan (1968) provides a short history of the DuPont triangle as an integral part of financial ratio analysis, and Eilon (1984) offers an accessible survey of alternative decomposition strategies. Banker et al. (1993) illustrate the decomposition technique with an application to the U.S. telecommunications industry, in which deregulation led to productivity gains that were offset by deteriorating price recovery brought on by increased competition.

In some cases, measurement enables us to quantify performance differentials that are predicted qualitatively by economic theory. An example is provided by the effect of market structure on performance. There is a common belief that productive efficiency is a survival condition in a competitive environment, and that its importance diminishes as competitive pressure subsides. Hicks (1935) gave eloquent expression to this belief by asserting that producers possessing market power "are likely to exploit their advantage much more by not bothering to get very near the position of maximum profit, than by straining themselves to get very close to it. The best of all monopoly profits is a quiet life" (p. 8). Berger and Hannan (1998) provide a test of the quiet life hypothesis in U.S. banking and find evidence that banks in relatively concentrated markets exhibit relatively low cost efficiency.

Continuing the line of reasoning that firms with market power might not be "pure" profit maximizers, Alchian and Kessel (1962) replaced the narrow profit maximization hypothesis with a broader utility maximization hypothesis, in which case monopolists and competitors might be expected to be equally proficient in the pursuit of utility. The ostensible efficiency differential is then explained by the selection of more (observed) profit by the competitor and more (unobserved) leisure by the monopolist, which of course recalls the analyst's problem of determining the relevant outputs and inputs of the production process. Alchian and Kessel offer an alternative explanation for the apparent superior performance of competitive producers. This is that monopolies are either regulated, and thereby constrained in their pursuit of efficiency, or unregulated but threatened by regulation (or by antitrust action) and consequently similarly constrained. If these producers are capable of earning more than the regulated profit, and if their property rights to the profit are attenuated by the regulatory or antitrust environment, then inefficiency becomes a free good to producers subject to, or threatened by, regulation or antitrust action. As Alchian and Kessel put it, "The cardinal sin of a monopolist … is to be too profitable" (p. 166).

Baumol (1959), Gordon (1961), and Williamson (1964) argued along similar lines. An operating environment characterized by market power and separation of ownership from control leaves room for "managerial discretion." Given the freedom to choose, managers would seek to maximize a utility function in which profit was either one of several arguments or, more likely, a constraint on the pursuit of alternative objectives. This idea, and variants of it, recurs frequently in the agency literature.

Thus, competition is expected to enhance performance either because it forces producers to concentrate on "observable" profit-generating activities at the expense of Hicks's quiet life, or because it frees producers from the actual or potential constraints imposed by the regulatory and antitrust processes. One interesting illustration of the market structure hypothesis is the measurement of the impact of international trade barriers on domestic industrial performance. Many years ago, Carlsson (1972) used primitive frontier techniques to uncover a statistically significant inverse relationship between the performance of Swedish industries and various measures of their protection from international competition. More recently, Tybout and Westbrook (1995), Pavcnik (2002), and Schor (2004) have applied modern frontier techniques to longitudinal micro data in an effort to shed light on the linkage between openness and productivity in Mexico, Chile, and Brazil. Specific findings vary, but a general theme emerges. Trade liberalization brings aggregate productivity gains attributable among other factors to improvements in productivity among continuing firms, and to entry of relatively productive firms and exit of relatively unproductive firms.

A second situation in which measurement enables the quantification of efficiency or productivity differentials predicted fairly consistently by theory is in the area of economic regulation. The most commonly cited example is rate-of-return regulation, to which many utilities have been subjected for many years, and for which there exists a familiar and tractable analytical paradigm developed by Averch and Johnson (1962). Access to a tractable model and to data supplied by regulatory agencies has spawned numerous empirical studies, virtually all of which have found rate-of-return regulation to have led to overcapitalization that has had an adverse impact on utility performance and therefore on consumer prices. These findings have motivated a movement toward incentive regulation in which utilities are reimbursed on the basis of a price cap or revenue cap formula RPI – X, with X being a productivity (or efficiency) offset to movements in an appropriate price index RPI. The reimbursement formula allows utilities to pass along any cost increases incorporated in RPI, less any expected performance improvements embodied in the offset X. Since X is a performance indicator, this trend has spawned a huge theoretical and empirical literature using efficiency and productivity measurement techniques to benchmark the performance of regulated utilities. Bogetoft (2000, and references cited therein) has developed the theory within a frontier context, in which X can be interpreted as the outcome of a game played between a principal (the regulator) and multiple agents (the utilities). The Netherlands Bureau for Economic Policy Analysis (2000) provides a detailed exposition of the techniques. Kinnunen (2005) reports either declining or stable trends in customer electricity prices in Finland, Norway, and Sweden, where variants of incentive regulation have been in place for some time. Since enormous amounts of money are involved, the specification and weighting of relevant variables and the sample selection criteria become important, and frequently contentious, issues in regulatory proceedings.

Another regulatory context in which theoretical predictions have been quantified by empirical investigation is the impact of environmental controls on producer performance. In this context, however, the private cost of reduced efficiency or productivity must be balanced against the social benefits of environmental protection. Of course, the standard paradigm that hypothesizes private costs of environmental constraints may be wrong; Porter (1991) has argued that well-designed environmental regulations can stimulate innovation, enhance productivity, and thus be privately profitable. Ambec and Barla (2002) develop a theory that predicts the Porter hypothesis. In any event, the problem of specifying and measuring the relevant variables crops up once again. Färe et al. (1989, 1993) have developed the theory within a frontier context. Reinhard et al. (1999) examined a panel of Dutch dairy farms that generate surplus manure, the nitrogen content of which contaminates groundwater and surface water and contributes to acid rain. They calculated a mean shadow price of the nitrogen surplus of just greater than 3 Netherlands guilders (NLG) per kilogram, slightly higher than a politically constrained levy actually imposed of NLG1.5 per kilogram of surplus. Ball et al. (2004) calculated exclusive and inclusive productivity indexes for U.S. agriculture, in which pesticide use causes water pollution. They found that inclusive productivity growth initially lagged behind exclusive productivity growth. However, when the U.S. Environmental Protection Agency began regulating the manufacture of pesticides, inclusive productivity growth caught up with, and eventually surpassed, exclusive productivity growth, as would be expected. Consistent with these findings, Ball et al. found an inverted U-shaped pattern of shadow prices, reflecting a period of lax regulation followed by tightened regulation that eventually led to the discovery and use of relatively benign and more effective pesticides.

A third situation in which measurement can quantify theoretical proposi-tions is the effect of ownership on performance. Alchian (1965) noted that the inability of public-sector owners to influence performance by trading shares in public-sector producers means that public-sector managers worry less about bearing the costs of their decisions than do their private-sector counterparts. Hence, they are contractually constrained in their decision-making latitude, given less freedom to choose, so to speak. "Because of these extra constraints—or because of the 'costs' of them—the public arrangement becomes a higher cost (in the sense of 'less efficient') than that for private property agencies" (p. 828). A literature has developed based on the supposition that public man-agers have greater freedom to pursue their own objectives, at the expense of conventional objectives. Niskanen (1971) viewed public managers as budget maximizers, de Alessi (1974) viewed public managers as preferring capital-intensive budgets, and Lindsay (1976) viewed public managers as preferring "visible" variables. Each of these hypotheses suggests that measured perfor-mance is lower in the public sector than in the private sector. Holmstrom and Tirole (1989) survey much of the theoretical literature, as does Hansmann (1988), who introduces private not-for-profit producers as a third category. Empirical tests of the public/private performance differential hypothesis are numerous. Many of the comparisons have been conducted using regulated utility data, because public and private firms frequently compete in these industries, because of the global trend toward privatization of public utilities, and because regulatory agencies collect and provide data. Jamash and Pollitt (2001) survey the empirical evidence for electricity distribution. Education and health care are two additional areas in which numerous public/private performance comparisons have been conducted.

In any public/private performance comparison, one confronts the prob-lem of how to measure their performance. Pestieau and Tulkens (1993) offer a spirited defense of a narrow focus on technical efficiency, so as to level the play-ing field. They argue that public enterprises have objectives and constraints (e.g., fiscal balance and universal service, uniform price requirements, but at the same time a soft budget constraint) different from those of private enter-prises, and the only common ground on which to compare their performance is on the basis of their technical efficiency.

In some cases, theory gives no guidance, or provides conflicting signals, concerning the impact on performance of some phenomenon. In such cases, empirical measurement provides qualitative, as well as quantitative, evidence. Four examples illustrate the point. Are profit-maximizing firms more efficient than cooperatives? Is one form of sharecropping more efficient than another? Is slavery an efficient way of organizing production? Is organized crime effi-ciently organized? The answer to each question seems to be "it depends," and so empirical measurement is called for. Theory and evidence are offered by Pencavel (2001) for cooperatives, by Otsuka et al. (1992) and Garrett and Xu (2003) for sharecropping, by Fogel and Engerman (1974) for slavery, and by Fiorentini and Peltzman (1995) for organized crime.

Table 1.1
Empirical Applications of Efficiency and Productivity Analysis

Application	Analysis
Accounting, advertising, auditing, and law firms	Banker et al. (2005) Luo and Donthu (2005) Dopuch et al. (2003) Wang (2000)
Airports	Oum and Yu (2004) Sarkis and Talluri (2004) Yoshida and Fujimoto (2004) Yu (2004)
Air transport	Coelli et al. (2002) Sickles et al. (2002) Scheraga (2004) Duke and Torres (2005)
Bank branches	Davis and Albright (2004) Camanho and Dyson (2005) Porembski et al. (2005) Silva Portela and Thanassoulis (2005)
Bankruptcy prediction	Wheelock and Wilson (2000) Becchetti and Sierra (2003) Cielen et al. (2004)
Benefit–cost analysis	Goldar and Misra (2001) Hofler and List (2004) Chien et al. (2005)
Community and rural health care	Birman et al. (2003) Dervaux et al. (2003) Jiménez et al. (2003) Kirigia et al. (2004)
Correctional facilities	Gyimah-Brempong (2000) Nyhan (2002)
Credit risk evaluation	Emel et al. (2003) Paradi et al. (2004)
Dentistry	Buck (2000) Grytten and Rongen (2000) Linna et al. (2003) Widstrom et al. (2004)
Discrimination	Croppenstedt and Meschi (2000) Bowlin et al. (2003) Mohan and Ruggiero (2003)
Education: primary and secondary	Dolton et al. (2003) Mayston (2003) Ammar et al. (2004) Dodson and Garrett (2004)
Education: tertiary	Bonaccorsi and Daraio (2003) Mensah and Werner (2003) Guan and Wang (2004) Warning (2004)

Application	Analysis
Elections	Obata and Ishii (2003)
	Foroughi et al. (2005)
Electricity distribution	Agrell et al. (2005)
	Delmas and Tokat (2005)
	Pollitt (2005)
	Edvardsen et al. (2006)
Electricity generation	Arocena and Waddams Price (2003)
	Korhonen and Luptacik (2004)
	Atkinson and Halabi (2005)
	Cook and Green (2005)
Environment: macro applications	Jeon and Sickles (2004)
	Zaim (2004)
	Arcelus and Arocena (2005)
	Henderson and Millimet (2005)
Environment: micro applications	Gang and Felmingham (2004)
	Banzhaf (2005)
	Shadbegian and Gray (2005)
	Wagner (2005)
Financial statement analysis	Chen and Zhu (2003)
	Feroz et al. (2003)
Fishing	Chiang et al. (2004)
	Herrero (2004)
	Martinez-Cordero and Leung (2004)
	Kompas and Che (2005)
Forestry	Otsuki et al. (2002)
	Bi (2004)
	Hof et al. (2004)
	Liu and Yin (2004)
Gas distribution	Rossi (2001)
	Carrington et al. (2002)
	Hammond et al. (2002)
	Hawdon (2003)
Hospitals	Chang et al. (2004)
	Stanford (2004)
	Ventura et al. (2004)
	Gao et al. (2006)
Hotels	Hwang and Chang (2003)
	Chiang et al. (2004)
	Barros (2005)
	Sigala et al. (2005)
Inequality and Poverty	Deutsch and Silber (2005)
Insurance	Greene and Segal (2004)
	Cummins et al. (2005)
	Jeng and Lai (2005)
	Tone and Sahoo (2005)

(Continued)

Table 1.1
(Continued)

Application	Analysis
Internet commerce	Wen et al. (2003)
	Barua et al. (2004)
	Chen et al. (2004)
	Serrano-Cinca et al. (2005)
Labor markets	Sheldon (2003)
	Ibourk et al. (2004)
	Lang (2005)
	Millimet (2005)
Libraries	Hammond (2002)
	Shim (2003)
	Kao and Lin (2004)
	Reichmann and Sommersguter-Reichmann (2006)
Location	Thomas et al. (2002)
	Cook and Green (2003)
	Takamura and Tone (2003)
Macroeconomics	Cherchye et al. (2004)
	Despotis (2005)
	Ravallion (2005)
	Yörük and Zaim (2005)
Mergers	Cuesta and Orea (2002)
	Ferrier and Valdmanis (2004)
	Bogetoft and Wang (2005)
	Sherman and Rupert (2006)
Military	Barros (2002)
	Bowlin (2004)
	Brockett et al. (2004)
	Sun (2004)
Municipal services	Hughes and Edwards (2000)
	Moore et al. (2001)
	Prieto and Zofio (2001)
	Southwick (2005)
Museums	Mairesse and Vanden Eeckaut (2002)
	Bishop and Brand (2003)
	Basso and Funari (2004)
Nursing homes	Farsi and Filippini (2004)
	Hougaard et al. (2004)
	Laine et al. (2005)
	Dervaux et al. (2006)
Physicians and physician practices	Wagner et al. (2003)
	Rosenman and Friesner (2004)
Police	Spottiswoode (2000)
	Wisniewski and Dickson (2001)
	Stone (2002)
	Drake and Simper (2004)
Ports	Clark et al. (2004)
	Lawrence and Richards (2004)

Application	Analysis
	Park and De (2004)
	Cullinane et al. (2005)
Postal services	Pimenta et al. (2000)
	Maruyama and Nakajima (2002)
	Borenstein et al. (2004)
Public infrastructure	Mamatzakis (2003)
	Martiin et al. (2004)
	Paul et al. (2004)
	Salinas-Jiminez (2004)
Rail transport	Kennedy and Smith (2004)
	Loizides and Tsionas (2004)
	Farsi et al. (2005)
	Smith (2005)
Real estate investment trusts	Lewis et al. (2003)
	Anderson et al. (2004)
Refuse collection and recycling	Bosch et al. (2000)
	Worthington and Dollery (2001)
	Lozano et al. (2004)
Sports	Haas (2003)
	Lins et al. (2003)
	Fried et al. (2004)
	Amos et al. (2005)
Stocks, mutual funds, and hedge funds	Basso and Funari (2003)
	Abad et al. (2004)
	Chang (2004)
	Troutt et al. (2005)
Tax administration	Serra (2003)
Telecommunications	Guedes de Avellar et al. (2002)
	Uri (2004)
	Lam and Lam (2005)
	Resende and Façanha (2005)
Urban transit	De Borger et al. (2002)
	Dalen and Gómez-Lobo (2003)
	Jörss et al. (2004)
	Odeck (2006)
Water distribution	Corton (2003)
	Tupper and Resende (2004)
	Aubert and Reynaud (2005)
	Cubbin (2005)
World Health Organization	Hollingsworth and Wildman (2003)
	Richardson et al. (2003)
	Greene (2004)
	Lauer et al. (2004)

Finally, the ability to quantify efficiency and productivity provides management with a control mechanism with which to monitor the performance of production units under its control. The economics, management science, and operations research literatures contain numerous examples of the use of efficiency and productivity measurement techniques for this and related purposes. However, interest in these techniques has spread far beyond their origins, as evidenced by the empirical applications referenced in table 1.1. The recent dates of these studies and the journals in which they appear demonstrate that the techniques are currently in use in fields far removed from their origins. In each of these applications, interesting and challenging issues concerning appropriate behavioral objectives and constraints, and the specification of relevant variables and their measurement, arise. These applications also illustrate the rich variety of analytical techniques that can be used in making efficiency and productivity comparisons. It is worth pondering how each of these examples deals with the long list of problems discussed in this section.

1.3 Definitions and Measures of Economic Efficiency

Economic efficiency has technical and allocative components. The technical component refers to the ability to avoid waste, either by producing as much output as technology and input usage allow or by using as little input as required by technology and output production. Thus, the analysis of technical efficiency can have an output-augmenting orientation or an input-conserving orientation. The allocative component refers to the ability to combine inputs and/or outputs in optimal proportions in light of prevailing prices. Optimal proportions satisfy the first-order conditions for the optimization problem assigned to the production unit.

Koopmans (1951) provided a formal *definition* of technical efficiency: A producer is technically efficient if an increase in any output requires a reduction in at least one other output or an increase in at least one input, and if a reduction in any input requires an increase in at least one other input or a reduction in at least one output. Thus, a technically inefficient producer could produce the same outputs with less of at least one input or could use the same inputs to produce more of at least one output.

Debreu (1951) and Farrell (1957) introduced a *measure* of technical efficiency. With an input-conserving orientation, their measure is defined as (one minus) the maximum equiproportionate (i.e., radial) reduction in all inputs that is feasible with given technology and outputs. With an output-augmenting orientation, their measure is defined as the maximum radial expansion in all outputs that is feasible with given technology and inputs. In both orientations, a value of unity indicates technical efficiency because no radial adjustment is feasible, and a value different from unity indicates the severity of technical inefficiency.

In order to relate the Debreu-Farrell measures to the Koopmans definition, and to relate both to the structure of production technology, it is useful to introduce some notation and terminology. Let producers use inputs $x = (x_1, \ldots, x_N) \in R_+^N$ to produce outputs $y = (y_1, \ldots, y_M) \in R_+^M$. Production technology can be represented by the production set

$$T = \{(y, x) : x \text{ can produce } y\}. \tag{1.1}$$

Koopmans's definition of technical efficiency can now be stated formally as $(y, x) \in T$ is technically efficient if, and only if, $(y', x') \notin T$ for $(y', -x') \geq (y, -x)$.

Technology can also be represented by input sets

$$L(y) = \{x : (y, x) \in T\}, \tag{1.2}$$

which for every $y \in R_+^M$ have input isoquants

$$I(y) = \{x : x \in L(y), \lambda x \notin L(y), \lambda < 1\} \tag{1.3}$$

and input efficient subsets

$$E(y) = \{x : x \in L(y), x' \notin L(y), x' \leq x\}, \tag{1.4}$$

and the three sets satisfy $E(y) \subseteq I(y) \subseteq L(y)$.

Shephard (1953) introduced the input distance function to provide a functional representation of production technology. The input distance function is

$$D_I(y, x) = \max\{\lambda : (x/\lambda) \in L(y)\}. \tag{1.5}$$

For $x \in L(y), D_I(y, x) \geq 1$, and for $x \in I(y), D_I(y, x) = 1$. Given standard assumptions on T, the input distance function $D_I(y, x)$ is nonincreasing in y and is nondecreasing, homogeneous of degree $+1$, and concave in x.

The Debreu-Farrell input-oriented measure of technical efficiency TE_I can now be given a somewhat more formal interpretation as the value of the function

$$TE_I(y, x) = \min\{\theta : \theta x \in L(y)\}, \tag{1.6}$$

and it follows from (1.5) that

$$TE_I(y, x) = 1/D_I(y, x). \tag{1.7}$$

For $x \in L(y), TE_I(y, x) \leq 1$, and for $x \in I(y), TE_I(y, x) = 1$.

Since so much of efficiency measurement is oriented toward output augmentation, it is useful to replicate the above development in that direction. Production technology can be represented by output sets

$$P(x) = \{y : (x, y) \in T\}, \tag{1.8}$$

which for every $x \in R_+^N$ has output isoquants

$$I(x) = \{y : y \in P(x), \lambda y \notin P(x), \lambda > 1\} \qquad (1.9)$$

and output efficient subsets

$$E(x) = \{y : y \in P(x), y' \notin P(x), y' \geq y\}, \qquad (1.10)$$

and the three sets satisfy $E(x) \subseteq I(x) \subseteq P(x)$.

Shephard's (1970) output distance function provides another functional representation of production technology. The output distance function is

$$D_o(x, y) = \min\{\lambda : (y/\lambda) \in P(x)\}. \qquad (1.11)$$

For $y \in P(x)$, $D_o(x, y) \leq 1$, and for $y \in I(x)$, $D_o(x, y) = 1$. Given standard assumptions on T, the output distance function $D_o(x, y)$ is nonincreasing in x and is nondecreasing, homogeneous of degree $+1$, and convex in y.

The Debreu-Farrell output-oriented measure of technical efficiency TE_o can now be given a somewhat more formal interpretation as the value of the function

$$TE_o(x, y) = \max\{\phi : \phi y \in P(x)\}, \qquad (1.12)$$

and it follows from (1.11) that

$$TE_o(x, y) = [D_o(x, y)]^{-1}. \qquad (1.13)$$

For $y \in P(x)$, $TE_o(x, y) \geq 1$, and for $y \in I(x)$, $TE_o(x, y) = 1$. [Caution: some authors replace (1.12) and (1.13) with $TE_o(x, y) = [\max\{\phi : \phi y \in P(x)\}]^{-1} = D_o(x, y)$, so that $TE_o(x, y) \leq 1$ just as $TE_I(y, x) \leq 1$. We follow the convention of defining efficiency of any sort as the ratio of optimal to actual. Consequently, $TE_I(y, x) \leq 1$ and $TE_o(x, y) \geq 1$.]

The foregoing analysis presumes that $M > 1$, $N > 1$. In the single input case,

$$D_I(y, x) = x/g(y) \geq 1 \iff x \geq g(y), \qquad (1.14)$$

where $g(y) = \min\{x : x \in L(y)\}$ is an input requirement frontier that defines the minimum amount of scalar input x required to produce output vector y. In this case, the input-oriented measure of technical efficiency (1.7) becomes the ratio of minimum to actual input

$$TE_I(y, x) = 1/D_I(y, x) = g(y)/x \leq 1. \qquad (1.15)$$

In the single output case,

$$D_o(x, y) = y/f(x) \leq 1 \iff y \leq f(x), \qquad (1.16)$$

where $f(x) = \max\{y : y \in P(x)\}$ is a production frontier that defines the maximum amount of scalar output that can be produced with input vector x. In this

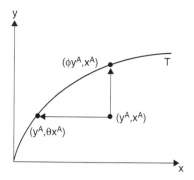

Figure 1.4. Technical Efficiency

case, the output-oriented measure of technical efficiency in (1.13) becomes the ratio of maximum to actual output

$$TE_o(x, y) = [D_o(x, y)]^{-1} = f(x)/y \geqq 1. \qquad (1.17)$$

The two technical efficiency measures are illustrated in figures 1.4–1.6. As a preview of things to come, technology is smooth in figure 1.4 and piecewise linear in figures 1.5 and 1.6. This reflects different approaches to using data to estimate technology. The econometric approach introduced in section 1.5 and developed in chapter 2 estimates smooth parametric frontiers, while the mathematical programming approach introduced in section 1.6 and developed in chapter 3 estimates piecewise linear nonparametric frontiers.

In figure 1.4, producer A is located on the interior of T, and its efficiency can be measured horizontally with an input-conserving orientation using (1.6) or vertically with an output-augmenting orientation using (1.12). If an input orientation is selected, $TE_I(y^A, x^A) = \theta x^A/x^A \leqq 1$, while if an output orientation is selected, $TE_o(x^A, y^A) = \phi y^A/y^A \geqq 1$.

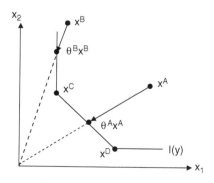

Figure 1.5. Input-Oriented Technical Efficiency

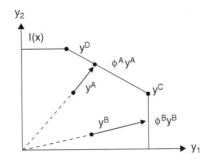

Figure 1.6. Output-Oriented Technical Efficiency

It is also possible to combine the two directions by simultaneously expanding outputs and contracting inputs, either hyperbolically or along a right angle, to arrive at an efficient point on the surface of T between $(y^A, \theta x^A)$ and $(\phi y^A, x^A)$. A hyperbolic measure of technical efficiency TE is defined as

$$\mathrm{TE_H}(y, x) = \max\{\alpha : (\alpha y, x/\alpha) \in T\} \geq 1, \tag{1.18}$$

and $\mathrm{TE_H}(y, x)$ is the reciprocal of a hyperbolic distance function $D_H(y, x)$. Under constant returns to scale, $\mathrm{TE_H}(y, x) = [\mathrm{TE_o}(x, y)]^2 = [\mathrm{TE_I}(y, x)]^{-2}$, and $\mathrm{TE_H}(y, x)$ is dual to a profitability function. One version of a directional measure of technical efficiency is defined as

$$\mathrm{TE_D}(y, x) = \max\{\beta : [(1 + \beta)x] \in T\} \geq 0, \tag{1.19}$$

and $\mathrm{TE_D}(y, x)$ is equal to a directional distance function $D_D(y, x)$. Even without constant returns to scale, $\mathrm{TE_D}(y, x)$ can be related to $\mathrm{TE_o}(x, y)$ and $\mathrm{TE_I}(y, x)$ and is dual to a profit function. The directional measure and its underlying directional distance function are employed to good advantage in chapter 5.

In figure 1.5, input vectors x^A and x^B are on the interior of $L(y)$, and both can be contracted radially and still remain capable of producing output vector y. Input vectors x^C and x^D cannot be contracted radially and still remain capable of producing output vector y because they are located on the input isoquant $I(y)$. Consequently, $\mathrm{TE_I}(y, x^C) = \mathrm{TE_I}(y, x^D) = 1 > \max\{\mathrm{TE_I}(y, x^A), \mathrm{TE_I}(y, x^B)\}$. Since the radially scaled input vector $\theta^B x^B$ contains slack in input x_2, there may be some hesitancy in describing input vector $\theta^B x^B$ as being technically efficient in the production of output vector y. No such problem occurs with radially scaled input vector $\theta^A x^A$. Thus, $\mathrm{TE_I}(y, \theta^A x^A) = \mathrm{TE_I}(y, \theta^B x^B) = 1$ even though $\theta^A x^A \in E(y)$ but $\theta^B x^B \notin E(y)$.

Figure 1.6 tells exactly the same story, but with an output orientation. Output vectors y^C and y^D are technically efficient given input usage x, and output vectors y^A and y^B are not. Radially scaled output vectors $\phi^A y^A$ and $\phi^B y^B$

are technically efficient, even though slack in output y_2 remains at $\phi^B y^B$. Thus, $TE_o(x, \phi^A y^A) = TE_o(x, \phi^B y^B) = 1$ even though $\phi^A y^A \in E(x)$ but $\phi^B y^B \notin E(x)$.

The Debreu-Farrell measures of technical efficiency are widely used. Since they are reciprocals of distance functions, they satisfy several nice properties [as noted first by Shephard (1970) and most thoroughly by Russell (1988, 1990)]. Among these properties are the following:

- $TE_I(y, x)$ is homogeneous of degree -1 in inputs, and $TE_o(x, y)$ is homogeneous of degree -1 in outputs.
- $TE_I(y, x)$ is weakly monotonically decreasing in inputs, and $TE_o(x, y)$ is weakly monotonically decreasing in outputs.
- $TE_I(y, x)$ and $TE_o(x, y)$ are invariant with respect to changes in units of measurement.

On the other hand, they are not perfect. A notable feature of the Debreu-Farrell measures of technical efficiency is that they do not coincide with Koopmans's definition of technical efficiency. Koopmans's definition is demanding, requiring the absence of coordinatewise improvements (simultaneous membership in both efficient subsets), while the Debreu-Farrell measures require only the absence of radial improvements (membership in isoquants). Thus, although the Debreu-Farrell measures correctly identify all Koopmans-efficient producers as being technically efficient, they also identify as being technically efficient any other producers located on an isoquant outside the efficient subset. Consequently, Debreu-Farrell technical efficiency is necessary, but not sufficient, for Koopmans technical efficiency. The possibilities are illustrated in figures 1.5 and 1.6, where $\theta^B x^B$ and $\phi^B y^B$ satisfy the Debreu-Farrell conditions but not the Koopmans requirement because slacks remain at the optimal radial projections.

Much has been made of this property of the Debreu-Farrell measures, but we think the problem is exaggerated. The practical significance of the problem depends on how many observations lie outside the cone spanned by the relevant efficient subset. Hence, the problem disappears in much econometric analysis, in which the parametric form of the function used to estimate production technology (e.g., Cobb-Douglas, but not flexible functional forms such as translog) imposes equality between isoquants and efficient subsets, thereby eliminating slack by assuming it away. The problem assumes greater significance in the mathematical programming approach, in which the nonparametric form of the frontier used to estimate the boundary of the production set imposes slack by a strong (or free) disposability assumption. If the problem is deemed significant in practice, then it is possible to report Debreu-Farrell efficiency scores and slacks separately, side by side. This is rarely done. Instead, much effort has been directed toward finding a "solution" to the problem. Three strategies have been proposed:

- Replace the radial Debreu-Farrell measure with a nonradial measure that projects to efficient subsets (Färe and Lovell, 1978). This guarantees that an observation (or its projection) is technically efficient if, and only if, it is efficient in Koopmans's sense. However nonradial measures gain this "indication" property at the considerable cost of failing the homogeneity property.

- Develop a measure that incorporates slack and the radial component into an inclusive measure of technical efficiency (Cooper et al., 1999). This measure also gains the indication property, but it has its own problems, including the possibility of negative values.
- Eliminate slack altogether by enforcing strictly positive marginal rates of substitution and transformation. We return to this possibility in section 1.6.4, in a different setting.

Happily, there is no such distinction between definitions and measures of economic efficiency. Defining and measuring economic efficiency require the specification of an economic objective and information on relevant prices. If the objective of a production unit (or the objective assigned to it by the analyst) is cost minimization, then a measure of cost efficiency is provided by the ratio of minimum feasible cost to actual cost. This measure depends on input prices. It attains a maximum value of unity if the producer is cost efficient, and a value less than unity indicates the degree of cost inefficiency. A measure of input-allocative efficiency is obtained residually as the ratio of the measure of cost efficiency to the input-oriented measure of technical efficiency. The modification of this Farrell decomposition of cost efficiency to the output-oriented problem of decomposing revenue efficiency is straightforward. Modifying the procedure to accommodate alternative behavioral objectives is sometimes straightforward and occasionally challenging. So is the incorporation of regulatory and other nontechnological constraints that impede the pursuit of some economic objective.

Suppose that producers face input prices $w = (w_1, \ldots, w_N) \in R_{++}^N$ and seek to minimize cost. Then, a minimum cost function, or a cost frontier, is defined as

$$c(y, w) = \min_x \{w^T x : D_I(y, x) \geq 1\}. \tag{1.20}$$

If the input sets $L(y)$ are closed and convex, and if inputs are freely disposable, the cost frontier is dual to the input distance function in the sense of (1.20) and

$$D_I(y, x) = \min_w \{w^T x : c(y, w) \geq 1\}. \tag{1.21}$$

A measure of cost efficiency CE is provided by the ratio of minimum cost to actual cost:

$$CE(x, y, w) = c(y, w)/w^T x \tag{1.22}$$

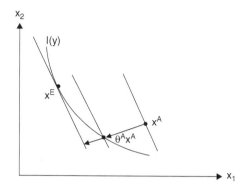

Figure 1.7. Cost Efficiency I

A measure of input-allocative efficiency AE_I is obtained from (1.6) and (1.22) as

$$AE_I(x, y, w) = CE(x, y, w)/TE_I(y, x). \qquad (1.23)$$

$CE(x, y, w)$ and its two components are bounded above by unity, and $CE(x, y, w) = TE_I(y, x) \times AE_I(x, y, w)$.

The measurement and decomposition of cost efficiency is illustrated in figures 1.7 and 1.8. In figure 1.7, the input vector x^E minimizes the cost of producing output vector y at input prices w, so $w^T x^E = c(y, w)$. The cost efficiency of x^A is given by the ratio $w^T x^E / w^T x^A = c(y, w)/w^T x^A$. The Debreu-Farrell measure of the technical efficiency of x^A is given by $\theta^A = \theta^A x^A / x^A = w^T(\theta^A x^A)/w^T x^A$. The allocative efficiency of x^A is determined residually as the ratio of cost efficiency to technical efficiency, or by the ratio $w^T x^E / w^T(\theta^A x^A)$. The magnitudes of technical, allocative, and cost inefficiency are all measured by ratios of price-weighted input vectors. The

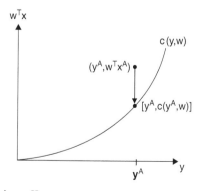

Figure 1.8. Cost Efficiency II

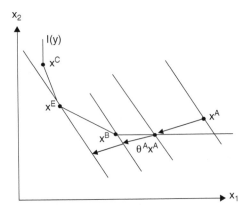

Figure 1.9. Cost Efficiency III

direction of allocative inefficiency is revealed by the input vector difference $(x^E - \theta^A x^A)$. An alternative view of cost efficiency is provided by figure 1.8, in which $CE(x^A, y^A, w) = c(y^A, w)/w^T x^A$.

The measurement and decomposition of cost efficiency are illustrated again in figure 1.9, for the case in which the efficient subset is a proper subset of the isoquant. The analysis proceeds as above, with a twist. The cost efficiency of input vector x^A now has three components, a radial technical component $[w^T(\theta^A x^A)/w^T x^A]$, an input slack component $[w^T x^B/w^T(\theta^A x^A)]$, and an allocative component $(w^T x^E/w^T x^B)$. With input price data, all three components can be identified, although they rarely are. The slack component is routinely assigned to the allocative component.

Suppose next that producers face output prices $p = (p_1, \ldots, p_M) \in R_{++}^M$ and seek to maximize revenue. Then, a maximum revenue function, or a revenue frontier, is defined as

$$r(x, p) = \max_y \{p^T y : D_o(x, y) \leqq 1\}. \tag{1.24}$$

If the output sets $P(x)$ are closed and convex, and if outputs are freely disposable, the revenue frontier is dual to the output distance function in the sense of (1.24) and

$$D_o(x, y) = \max_p \{p^T y : r(x, p) \leqq 1\}. \tag{1.25}$$

A measure of revenue efficiency RE is provided by the ratio of maximum revenue to actual revenue:

$$RE(y, x, p) = r(x, p)/p^T y \tag{1.26}$$

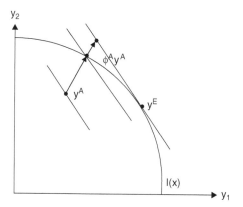

Figure 1.10. Revenue Efficiency I

A measure of output-allocative efficiency AE_o is obtained from (1.12) and (1.26) as

$$AE_o(y, x, p) = RE(y, x, p)/TE_o(x, y). \qquad (1.27)$$

$RE(y, x, p)$ and its two components are bounded below by unity, and $RE(y, x, p) = TE_o(x, y) \times AE_o(y, x, p)$.

The measurement and decomposition of revenue efficiency in figures 1.10 and 1.11 follow exactly the same steps. The measurement and decomposition of revenue efficiency in the presence of output slack follow along similar lines as in figure 1.9. Revenue loss attributable to output slack is typically assigned to the output-allocative efficiency component of revenue efficiency.

Cost efficiency and revenue efficiency are important performance indicators, but each reflects just one dimension of a firm's overall performance. A measure of profit efficiency captures both dimensions and relates directly to

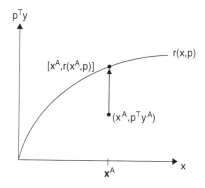

Figure 1.11. Revenue Efficiency II

the bottom line discussed in section 1.1. Suppose that producers face output prices $p \in R_{++}^M$ and input prices $w \in R_{++}^N$ and seek to maximize profit. The maximum profit function, or profit frontier, is defined as

$$\pi(p, w) = \max_{y,x} \left\{ (p^T y - w^T x) : (y, x) \in T \right\}. \tag{1.28}$$

If the production set T is closed and convex, and if outputs and inputs are freely disposable, the profit frontier is dual to T in the sense of (1.28) and

$$T = \{(y, x) : (p^T y - w^T x) \leqq \pi(p, w) \forall p \in R_{++}^M, w \in R_{++}^N\}. \tag{1.29}$$

A measure of profit efficiency is provided by the ratio of maximum profit to actual profit

$$\pi E(y, x, p, w) = \pi(p, w)/(p^T y - w^T x), \tag{1.30}$$

provided $(p^T y - w^T x) > 0$, in which case $\pi E(y, x, p, w)$ is bounded below by unity. The decomposition of profit efficiency is partially illustrated by figure 1.12, which builds on figure 1.4. Profit at (y^A, x^A) is less than maximum profit at (y^E, x^E), and two possible decompositions of profit efficiency are illustrated. One takes an input-conserving orientation to the measurement of technical efficiency, and the residual allocative component follows the path from $(y^A, \theta x^A)$ to (y^E, x^E). The other takes an output-augmenting orientation to the measurement of technical efficiency, with residual allocative component following the path from $(\phi y^A, x^A)$ to (y^E, x^E). In both approaches the residual allocative component contains an input-allocative efficiency component and an output-allocative efficiency component, although the magnitudes of each component can differ in the two approaches. These two components are hidden from view in the two-dimensional figure 1.12. In both approaches, the residual allocative efficiency component also includes a scale component, which is illustrated in figure 1.12. The direction of the scale component is sensitive to the orientation of the technical efficiency component, which imposes a burden on the analyst to get the orientation right. Because profit efficiency

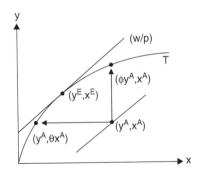

Figure 1.12. Profit Efficiency

involves adjustments to both outputs and inputs, hyperbolic and directional technical efficiency measures are appealing in this context. Whatever the orientation of the technical efficiency measure, profit inefficiency is attributable to technical inefficiency, to an inappropriate scale of operation, to the production of an inappropriate output mix, and to the selection of an inappropriate input mix.

We conclude this section with a brief discussion of dominance. Producer A dominates all other producers for which $(y^A, -x^A) \geq (y, -x)$. This notion is a direct application of Koopmans's definition of efficiency, in which producer A is "more efficient" than all other producers it dominates. Reversing the definition, producer A is dominated by all other producers for which $(y, -x) \geq (y^A, -x^A)$. In figure 1.4, producer A is dominated by all producers to the northwest $\in T$ because they use no more input to produce at least as much output. Similar dominance relationships can be constructed in figures 1.5 and 1.6. In each case, dominance is a physical, or technical, relationship. However, dominance can also be given a value interpretation. In figure 1.8, producer A is dominated (in a cost sense) by all other producers to the southeast on or above $c(y, w)$ because they produce at least as much output at no more cost, and in figure 1.11 producer A is dominated (in a revenue sense) by all other producers to the northwest on or beneath $r(x, p)$ because they use no more input to generate at least as much revenue.

Dominance is an underutilized concept in the field of producer performance evaluation, where the emphasis is on efficiency. This neglect is unfortunate, because dominance information offers a potentially useful complement to an efficiency evaluation, as Tulkens and Vanden Eeckaut (1995, 1999) have demonstrated. Inefficient producers can have many dominators and hence many potential role models from which to learn. To cite one example, Fried et al. (1993) report an average of 22 dominators for each of nearly 9,000 U.S. credit unions.

The identification of dominators can constitute the initial step in a benchmarking exercise. It is possible that dominators utilize superior business practices that are transferable to the benchmarking producer. However, it is also possible that dominance is due to a more favorable operating environment. Although this may be cold comfort to the benchmarking business, it can be very useful to the analyst who does not want to confuse variation in performance with variation in the operating environment. Incorporating variation in the operating environment is an important part of any performance evaluation exercise, and techniques for doing so are discussed below and in subsequent chapters.

1.4 Techniques for Efficiency Measurement

Efficiency measurement involves a comparison of actual performance with optimal performance located on the relevant frontier. Since the true frontier is unknown, an empirical approximation is needed. The approximation is frequently dubbed a "best-practice" frontier.

The economic theory of production is based on production frontiers and value duals such as cost, revenue, and profit frontiers and on envelope properties yielding cost-minimizing input demands, revenue-maximizing output supplies, and profit-maximizing output supplies and input demands. Emphasis is placed on optimizing behavior subject to constraint. However, for more than 75 years, at least since Cobb and Douglas started running regressions, the empirical analysis of production has been based on a least squares statistical methodology by which estimated functions of interest pass through the data and estimate mean performance. Thus, the frontiers of theory have become the functions of analysis, interest in enveloping data with frontiers has been replaced with the practice of intersecting data with functions, and unlikely efficient outcomes have been neglected in favor of more likely but less efficient outcomes, all as attention has shifted from extreme values to central tendency.

If econometric analysis is to be brought to bear on the investigation of the structure of economic frontiers, and on the measurement of efficiency relative to these frontiers, then conventional econometric techniques require modification. The modifications that have been developed, improved, and implemented in the last three decades run the gamut from trivial to sophisticated. Econometric techniques are introduced in section 1.5 and developed in detail in chapter 2.

In sharp contrast to econometric techniques, mathematical programming techniques are inherently enveloping techniques, and so they require little or no modification to be employed in the analysis of efficiency. This makes them appealing, but they went out of favor long ago in the economics profession. Their theoretical appeal has given way to a perceived practical disadvantage: their ostensible failure to incorporate the statistical noise that drives conventional econometric analysis. This apparent shortcoming notwithstanding, they remain popular in the fields of management science and operations research, and they are making a comeback in economics. Programming techniques are introduced in section 1.6 and developed in detail in chapter 3.

The econometric approach to the construction of frontiers and the estimation of efficiency relative to the constructed frontiers has similarities and differences with the mathematical programming approach. Both are analytically rigorous benchmarking exercises that exploit the distance functions introduced in section 1.3 to measure efficiency relative to a frontier. However, the two approaches use different techniques to envelop data more or less tightly in different ways. In doing so, they make different accommodations for statistical noise and for flexibility in the structure of production technology. It is these two different accommodations that have generated debate about the relative merits of the two approaches. At the risk of oversimplification, the differences between the two approaches boil down to two essential features:

- The econometric approach is stochastic. This enables it to attempt to distinguish the effects of noise from those of inefficiency, thereby providing the basis for statistical inference.
- The programming approach is nonparametric. This enables it to avoid confounding the effects of misspecification of the functional form (of both technology and inefficiency) with those of inefficiency.

A decade or more ago, the implication drawn from these two features was that the programming approach was nonstochastic and the econometric approach was parametric. This had a disturbing consequence. If efficiency analysis is to be taken seriously, producer performance evaluation must be robust to both statistical noise and specification error. Neither approach was thought to be robust to both.

Happily, knowledge has progressed and distinctions have blurred. To praise one approach as being stochastic is not to deny that the other is stochastic, as well, and to praise one approach as being nonparametric is not to damn the other as being rigidly parameterized. Recent explorations into the statistical foundations of the programming approach have provided the basis for statistical inference, and recent applications of flexible functional forms and semiparametric, nonparametric, and Bayesian techniques have freed the econometric approach from its parametric straitjacket. Both techniques are more robust than previously thought. The gap is no longer between one technique and the other, but between best-practice knowledge and average practice implementation. The challenge is to narrow the gap.

It is worth asking whether the two techniques tell consistent stories when applied to the same data. The answer seems to be that the higher the quality of the data, the greater the concordance between the two sets of efficiency estimates. Of the many comparisons available in the literature, we recommend Bauer et al. (1998), who use U.S. banking data, and Cummins and Zi (1998), who use U.S. life insurance company data. Both studies find strong positive rank correlations of point estimates of efficiency between alternative pairs of econometric models and between alternative pairs of programming models, and weaker but nonetheless positive rank correlations of point estimates of efficiency between alternative pairs of econometric and programming models.

Chapters 2 and 3 develop the two approaches, starting with their basic formulations and progressing to more advanced methods. Chapter 4 recasts the parametric econometric approach of chapter 2 into a nonparametric statistical framework and explores the statistical foundations of the programming approach of chapter 3. In addition to these chapters, we recommend comprehensive treatments of the econometric approach by Kumbhakar and Lovell (2000) and of the programming approach by Cooper et al. (2000). Both contain extensive references to analytical developments and empirical applications.

1.5 The Econometric Approach to Efficiency Measurement

Econometric models can be categorized according to the type of data they use (cross section or panel), the type of variables they use (quantities only, or quantities and prices), and the number of equations in the model. In section 1.5.1, we discuss the most widely used model: the single-equation cross-section model. In section 1.5.2, we progress to panel-data models. In both contexts, the efficiency being estimated can be either technical or economic. In section 1.5.3, we discuss multiple equation models, and in section 1.5.4, we discuss shadow price models, which typically involve multiple equations. In these two contexts, the efficiency being estimated is economic, with a focus on allocative inefficiency and its cost.

1.5.1 Single-equation cross-section models

Suppose producers use inputs $x \in R_+^N$ to produce scalar output $y \in R_+$, with technology

$$y_i \leq f(x_i; \beta) \exp\{v_i\}, \tag{1.31}$$

where β is a parameter vector characterizing the structure of production technology and $i = 1, \ldots, I$ indexes producers. The deterministic production frontier is $f(x_i; \beta)$. Observed output y_i is bounded above by the stochastic production frontier $[f(x_i; \beta) \exp\{v_i\}]$, with the random disturbance term $v_i \gtrless 0$ included to capture the effects of statistical noise on observed output. The stochastic production frontier reflects what is possible $[f(x_i; \beta)]$ in an environment influenced by external events, favorable and unfavorable, beyond the control of producers $[\exp\{v_i\}]$.

The weak inequality in (1.31) can be converted to an equality through the introduction of a second disturbance term to create

$$y_i = f(x_i; \beta) \exp\{v_i - u_i\}, \tag{1.32}$$

where the disturbance term $u_i \geq 0$ is included to capture the effect of technical inefficiency on observed output.

Recall from section 1.3 that the Debreu-Farrell output-oriented measure of technical efficiency is the ratio of maximum possible output to actual output (and that some authors use the reciprocal of this measure). Applying definition (1.17) to (1.32) yields

$$TE_o(x_i, y_i) = f(x_i; \beta) \exp\{v_i\}/y_i = \exp\{u_i\} \geq 1, \tag{1.33}$$

because $u_i \geq 0$. The problem is to estimate $TE_o(x_i, y_i)$. This requires estimation of (1.32), which is easy and can be accomplished in a number of ways depending on the assumptions one is willing to make. It also requires a decomposition of the residuals into separate estimates of v_i and u_i, which is not so easy.

One approach, first suggested by Winsten (1957) and now known as corrected ordinary least squares (COLS), is to assume that $u_i = 0, i = 1, \ldots, I$, and that $v_i \sim N(0, \sigma_v^2)$. In this case (1.32) collapses to a standard regression model that can be estimated consistently by OLS. The estimated production function, which intersects the data, is then shifted upward by adding the maximum positive residual to the estimated intercept, creating a production frontier that bounds the previous data. The residuals are corrected in the opposite direction and become $\hat{v}_i = v_i - v_i^{max} \leq 0, i = 1, \ldots, I$. The technical efficiency of each producer is estimated from

$$\hat{TE}_o(x_i, y_i) = \exp\{-\hat{v}_i\} \geq 1, \tag{1.34}$$

and $\hat{TE}_o(x_i, y_i) - 1 \geq 0$ indicates the percentage by which output can be expanded, on the assumption that $u_i = 0, i = 1, \ldots, I$.

The producer having the largest positive OLS residual supports the COLS production frontier. This makes COLS vulnerable to outliers, although ad hoc sensitivity tests have been proposed. In addition, the structure of the COLS frontier is identical to the structure of the OLS function, apart from the shifted intercept. This structural similarity rules out the possibility that efficient producers are efficient precisely because they exploit available economies and substitution possibilities that average producers do not. The assumption that best practice is just like average practice, but better, defies both common sense and much empirical evidence. Finally, it is troubling that efficiency estimates for all producers are obtained by suppressing the inefficiency error component u_i and are determined exclusively by the single producer having the most favorable noise v_i^{max}. The term $\exp\{u_i\}$ in (1.33) is proxied by the term $\exp\{-\hat{v}\}$ in (1.34). Despite these reservations, and additional concerns raised in chapters 2 and 4, COLS is widely used, presumably because it is easy.

A second approach, suggested by Aigner and Chu (1968), is to make the opposite assumption that $v_i = 0, i = 1, \ldots, I$. In this case, (1.32) collapses to a deterministic production frontier that can be estimated by linear or quadratic programming techniques that minimize either $\Sigma_i u_i$ or $\Sigma_i u_i^2$, subject to the constraint that $u_i = \ln[f(x_i; \beta)/y_i] \geq 0$ for all producers. The technical efficiency of each producer is estimated from

$$\hat{TE}_o(x_i, y_i) = \exp\{\hat{u}_i\} \geq 1, \tag{1.35}$$

and $\hat{TE}_o(x_i, y_i) - 1 \geq 0$ indicates the percentage by which output can be expanded, on the alternative assumption that $v_i = 0, i = 1, \ldots, I$. The $\hat{u}_i$ values are estimated from the slacks in the constraints $[\ln f(x_i; \beta) - \ln y_i \geq 0, i = 1, \ldots I]$ of the program. Although it appears that the term $\exp\{\hat{u}_i\}$ in (1.35) coincides with the term $\exp\{u_i\}$ in (1.33), the expression in (1.35) is conditioned on the assumption that $v_i = 0$, while the expression in (1.33) is not. In addition, since no distributional assumption is imposed on $u_i \geq 0$, statistical inference is precluded, and consistency cannot be verified. However, Schmidt (1976) showed that the linear programming "estimate" of β

is maximum likelihood (MLE) if the u_i values follow an exponential distribution, and that the quadratic programming "estimate" of β is maximum likelihood if the u_i values follow a half-normal distribution. Unfortunately, we know virtually nothing about the statistical properties of these estimators, even though they are maximum likelihood. However, Greene (1980) showed that an assumption that the u_i values follow a gamma distribution generates a well-behaved likelihood function that allows statistical inference, although this model does not correspond to any known programming problem. Despite the obvious statistical drawback resulting from its deterministic formulation, the programming approach is also widely used. One reason for its popularity is that it is easy to append monotonicity and curvature constraints to the program, as Hailu and Veeman (2000) have done in their study of water pollution in the Canadian pulp and paper industry.

The third approach, suggested independently by Aigner et al. (1977) and Meeusen and van den Broeck (1977), attempts to remedy the shortcomings of the first two approaches and is known as stochastic frontier analysis (SFA). In this approach, it is assumed that $v_i \sim N(0, \sigma_v^2)$ and that $u_i \geq 0$ follows either a half-normal or an exponential distribution. The motive behind these two distributional assumptions is to parsimoniously parameterize the notion that relatively high efficiency is more likely than relatively low efficiency. After all, the structure of production is parameterized, so we might as well parameterize the inefficiency distribution, too. In addition, it is assumed that the v_i and the u_i values are distributed independently of each other and of x_i. OLS can be used to obtain consistent estimates of the slope parameters but not the intercept, because $E(v_i - u_i) = E(-u_i) \leq 0$. However the OLS residuals can be used to test for negative skewness, which is a test for the presence of variation in technical inefficiency. If evidence of negative skewness is found, OLS slope estimates can be used as starting values in a maximum likelihood routine.

Armed with the distributional and independence assumptions, it is possible to derive the likelihood function, which can be maximized with respect to all parameters (β, σ_v^2, and σ_u^2) to obtain consistent estimates of β. However, even with this information, neither team was able to estimate $TE_o(x_i, y_i)$ in (1.33) because they were unable to disentangle the separate contributions of v_i and u_i to the residual. Jondrow et al. (1982) provided an initial solution, by deriving the conditional distribution of $[-u_i|(v_i - u_i)]$, which contains all the information $(v_i - u_i)$ contains about $-u_i$. This enabled them to derive the expected value of this conditional distribution, from which they proposed to estimate the technical efficiency of each producer from

$$\hat{TE}_o(x_i, y_i) = \{\exp\{E[-\hat{u}_i|(v_i - u_i)]\}\}^{-1} \geq 1, \qquad (1.36)$$

which is a function of the MLE parameter estimates. Later, Battese and Coelli (1988) proposed to estimate the technical efficiency of each producer from

$$\hat{TE}_o(x_i, y_i) = \{E[\exp\{-\hat{u}_i\}|(v_i - u_i)]\}^{-1} \geq 1, \qquad (1.37)$$

which is a slightly different function of the same MLE parameter estimates and is preferred because $-\hat{u}_i$ in (1.36) is only the first-order term in the power series approximation to $\exp\{-\hat{u}_i\}$ in (1.37).

Unlike the first two approaches, which suppress either u_i or v_i, SFA sensibly incorporates both noise and inefficiency into the model specification. The price paid is the need to impose distributional and independence assumptions, the prime benefit being the ability to disentangle the two error components. The single parameter half-normal and exponential distributions can be generalized to more flexible two-parameter truncated normal and gamma distributions, as suggested by Stevenson (1980) and Greene (1980), although they rarely are. The independence assumptions seem essential to the MLE procedure. The fact that they can be relaxed in the presence of panel data provides an initial appreciation of the value of panel data, to which we return in section 1.5.2.

The efficiency estimates obtained from (1.36) and (1.37) are unbiased, but their consistency has been questioned, not because they converge to the wrong values, but because in a cross section we get only one look at each producer, and the number of looks cannot increase. However, a new contrary claim of consistency is put forth in chapter 2. The argument is simple and runs as follows: The technical efficiency estimates in (1.36) and (1.37) are conditioned on MLEs of $(v_i - u_i) = \ln y_i - \ln f(x_i; \beta)$, and since β is estimated consistently by MLE, so is technical efficiency, even in a cross section.

For more than a decade, individual efficiencies were estimated using either (1.36) or (1.37). Hypothesis tests frequently were conducted on β and occasionally on σ_u^2/σ_v^2 (or some variant thereof) to test the statistical significance of efficiency variation. However, we did not test hypotheses on either estimator of $TE_o(x_i, y_i)$ because we did not realize that we had enough information to do so. We paid the price of imposing distributions on v_i and u_i, but we did not reap one of the benefits: We did not exploit the fact that distributions imposed on v_i and u_i create distributions for $[-u_i \mid (v_i - u_i)]$ and $[\exp\{-u_i\} \mid (v_i - u_i)]$, which can be used to construct confidence intervals and to test hypotheses on individual efficiencies. This should have been obvious all along, but Horrace and Schmidt (1996) and Bera and Sharma (1999) were the first to develop confidence intervals for efficiency estimators. The published confidence intervals we have seen are depressingly wide, presumably because estimates of σ_u^2/σ_v^2 are relatively small. In such circumstances, the information contained in a ranking of estimated efficiency scores is limited, frequently to the ability to distinguish stars from strugglers.

The preceding discussion has been based on a single output production frontier. However, multiple outputs can be incorporated in a number of ways:

- Estimate a stochastic revenue frontier, with $p^T y$ replacing y and (x, p) replacing x in (1.32). The one-sided error component provides the basis for a measure of revenue efficiency. Applications are rare.

- Estimate a stochastic profit frontier, with $(p^T y - w^T x)$ replacing y and (p, w) replacing x in (1.32). The one-sided error component provides the basis for a measure of profit efficiency. Estimation of profit frontiers is popular, especially in the financial institutions literature. Berger and Mester (1997) provide an extensive application to U.S. banks.
- Estimate a stochastic cost frontier, with $w^T x$ replacing y and (y, w) replacing x in (1.32). Since $w^T x \geq c(y, w; \beta) \exp\{v_i\}$, this requires changing the sign of the one-sided error component, which provides the basis for a measure of cost efficiency. Applications are numerous.
- Estimate a stochastic input requirement frontier, with the roles of x and y in (1.32) being reversed. This also requires changing the sign of the one-sided error component, which provides the basis for a measure of input use efficiency. Applications are limited to situations in which labor has a very large (variable?) cost share, or in which other inputs are not reported. Kumbhakar and Hjalmarsson (1995) provide an application to employment in Swedish social insurance offices.
- Estimate a stochastic output distance function $D_o(x, y) \exp\{v_i\} \leq 1 \Rightarrow D_o(x_i, y_i; \beta) \exp\{v_i - u_i\} = 1, u_i \geq 0$. The one-sided error component provides the basis for an output-oriented measure of technical efficiency. Unlike the models above, a distance function has no natural dependent variable, and at least three alternatives have been proposed. Fuentes et al. (2001) and Atkinson et al. (2003) illustrate alternative specifications and provide applications to Spanish insurance companies and U.S. railroads, respectively.
- Estimate a stochastic input distance function $D_I(y, x) \exp\{v_i\} \geq 1 \Rightarrow D_I(y_i, x_i; \beta) \exp\{v_i + u_i\} = 1, u_i \geq 0$. Note the sign change of the one-sided error component, which provides the basis for an input-oriented measure of technical efficiency, and proceed as above.

In the preceding discussion, interest has centered on the estimation of efficiency. A second concern, first raised in section 1.2, involves the incorporation of potential determinants of efficiency. The determinants can include characteristics of the operating environment and characteristics of the manager such as human capital endowments. The logic is that if efficiency is to be improved, we need to know what factors influence it, and this requires distinguishing the influences of the potential determinants from that of the inputs and outputs themselves. Two approaches have been developed:

(1) Let $z \in R^K$ be a vector of exogenous variables thought to be relevant to the production activity. One approach that has been used within and outside the frontier field is to replace $f(x_i; \beta)$ with $f(x_i, z_i; \beta, \gamma)$. The most popular example involves z serving as a proxy for technical change that shifts the production (or cost) frontier. Another popular example involves the inclusion of stage length and load factor in the analysis of airline performance; both are thought to influence operating cost. Although z is relevant in the sense that it is thought to

be an important characteristic of production activity, it does not influence the efficiency of production. The incorporation of potential influences on productive efficiency requires an alternative approach, in which z influences the distance of producers from the relevant frontier.

(2) In the old days, it was common practice to adopt a two-stage approach to the incorporation of potential determinants of productive efficiency. In this approach efficiency was estimated in the first stage using either (1.36) or (1.37), and estimated efficiencies were regressed against a vector of potential influences in the second stage. Deprins and Simar (1989) were perhaps the first to question the statistical validity of this two-stage approach. Later, Battese and Coelli (1995) proposed a single-stage model of general form

$$y_i = f(x_i; \beta) \exp\{v_i - u_i(z_i; \gamma)\}, \tag{1.38}$$

where $u_i(z_i; \gamma) \geqq 0$ and z is a vector of potential influences with parameter vector γ, and they showed how to estimate the model in SFA format. Later, Wang and Schmidt (2002) analyzed alternative specifications for $u_i(z_i; \gamma)$ in the single-stage approach; for example, either the mean or the variance of the distribution being truncated below at zero can be made a function of z_i. They also provided detailed theoretical arguments, supported by compelling Monte Carlo evidence, explaining why both stages of the old two-stage procedure are seriously biased. We hope to see no more two-stage SFA models.

1.5.2 Single-equation panel-data models

In a cross section, each producer is observed once. If each producer is observed over a period of time, panel-data techniques can be brought to bear on the problem. At the heart of the approach is the association of a "firm effect" from the panel-data literature with a one-sided inefficiency term from the frontier literature. How this association is formulated and how the model is estimated are what distinguish one model from another. Whatever the model, the principal advantage of having panel data is the ability to observe each producer more than once. It should be possible to parlay this ability into "better" estimates of efficiency than can be obtained from a single cross section.

Schmidt and Sickles (1984) were among the first to consider the use of conventional panel-data techniques in a frontier context. We follow them by writing the panel-data version of the production frontier model (1.32) as

$$y_{it} = f(x_{it}; \beta) \exp\{v_{it} - u_i\}, \tag{1.39}$$

where a time subscript $t = 1, \ldots, T$ has been added to y, x, and v, but not (yet) to u. We begin by assuming that technical efficiency is time invariant and not a function of exogenous influences. Four estimation strategies are available.

(1) It is straightforward to adapt the cross-section MLE procedures developed in section 1.5.1 to the panel-data context, as Pitt and Lee (1981) first showed. Allowing u_i to depend on potential influences is also straightforward, as Battese and Coelli (1995) demonstrated. Extending (1.39) by setting $u_{it} = u_{it}(z_{it}; \gamma)$ and specifying one of the elements of z_{it} as a time trend or a time dummy allows technical inefficiency to be time varying, which is especially desirable in long panels. Maximum likelihood estimators of technical efficiency obtained from (1.36) and (1.37) are consistent in T and I. However, MLE requires strong distributional and independence assumptions, and the availability of panel-data techniques enables us to relax some of these assumptions.

(2) The fixed-effects model is similar to cross-section COLS. It imposes no distributional assumption on u_i and allows the u_i values to be correlated with the v_{it} and the x_{it} values. Since the u_i values are treated as fixed, they become producer-specific intercepts $\beta_{0i} = (\beta_0 - u_i)$ in (1.39), which can be estimated consistently by OLS. After estimation, the normalization $\beta_0^* = \beta_{0i}^{max}$ generates estimates of $\hat{u}_i = \beta_0^* - \beta_{0i} \geq 0$, and estimates of producer-specific technical efficiencies are obtained from

$$\hat{TE}_o(x_i, y_i) = [\exp\{-\hat{u}_i\}]^{-1}. \tag{1.40}$$

These estimates are consistent in T and I, and they have the great virtue of allowing the u_i values to be correlated with the regressors. However, the desirable property of consistency in T is offset by the undesirability of assuming time invariance of inefficiency in long panels. In addition, the fixed-effects model has a potentially serious drawback: The firm effects are intended to capture variation in technical efficiency, but they also capture the effects of all phenomena that vary across producers but not through time, such as locational characteristics and regulatory regime.

(3) The random-effects model makes the opposite assumptions on the u_i values, which are allowed to be random, with unspecified distribution having constant mean and variance, but are assumed to be uncorrelated with the v_{it} and the x_{it} values. This allows the inclusion of time-invariant regressors in the model. Defining $\beta_0^{**} = \beta_0 - E(u_i)$ and $u_i^{**} = u_i - E(u_i)$, (1.39) can be estimated by generalized least squares (GLS). After estimation, firm-specific estimates of u_i^{**} are obtained from the temporal means of the residuals. Finally, these estimates are normalized to obtain estimates of $\hat{u}_i = u_i^{**max} - u_i^{**}$, from which producer-specific estimates of technical efficiency are obtained from

$$\hat{TE}_o(x_i, y_i) = [\exp\{-\hat{u}_i\}]^{-1}. \tag{1.41}$$

These estimates also are consistent in T and I. The main virtue of GLS is that it allows the inclusion of time-invariant regressors, whose impacts would be confounded with efficiency variation in a fixed-effects model.

(4) Finally, an estimator from Hausman and Taylor (1981) can be adapted to (1.39). It is a mixture of the fixed-effects and random-effects estimators that allows the u_i values to be correlated with some, but not all, regressors and can include time-invariant regressors.

We have explored the tip of the proverbial iceberg. Panel-data econometrics is expanding rapidly, as is its application to frontier models. Details are provided in chapter 2.

1.5.3 Multiple equation models

We begin by reproducing a model popularized long ago by Christensen and Greene (1976). The model is

$$\ln(w^T x)_i = c(\ln y_i, \ln w_i; \beta) + v_i,$$

$$(w_n x_n / w^T x)_i = s_n(\ln y_i, \ln w_i; \beta) + v_{ni}, n = 1, \ldots, N-1. \quad (1.42)$$

This system describes the behavior of a cost-minimizing producer, with the first equation being a cost function and the remaining equations exploiting Shephard's (1953) lemma to generate cost-minimizing input cost shares. The errors (v_i, v_{ni}) reflect statistical noise and are assumed to be distributed multivariate normal with zero means. The original motivation for appending the cost-share equations was to increase statistical efficiency in estimation, since they contain no parameters not appearing in the cost function. Variants on this multiple equation theme, applied to flexible functional forms such as translog, appear regularly in production (and consumption) economics.

The pursuit of statistical efficiency is laudable, but it causes difficulties when the objective of the exercise is the estimation of economic efficiency. We do not want to impose the assumption of cost minimization that drives Shephard's lemma, so we transform the Christensen-Greene model (1.42) into a stochastic cost frontier model as follows:

$$\ln(w^T x)_i = c(\ln y_i, \ln w_i; \beta) + v_i + T_i + A_i,$$

$$(w_n x_n / w^T x)_i = s_n(\ln y_i, \ln w_i; \beta) + v_{ni} + u_{ni}, n = 1, \ldots, N-1. \quad (1.43)$$

Here, v_i and the v_{ni} capture the effects of statistical noise. $T_i \geq 0$ reflects the cost of technical inefficiency, $A_i \geq 0$ reflects the cost of input-allocative inefficiency, and $(T_i + A_i) \geq 0$ is the cost of both. Finally, $u_{ni} \gtrless 0$ captures the departures of actual input cost shares from their cost-efficient magnitudes. Since technical inefficiency is measured radially, it maintains the observed input mix and has no impact on input share equations. However, allocative inefficiency represents an inappropriate input mix, so its cost must be linked to the input cost-share equations by means of a relationship between A_i and $u_{ni}, n = 1, \ldots, N-1$.

The linkage must respect the fact that cost is raised by allocative errors in any input in either direction. The formidable problem is to estimate the technology parameters β and the efficiency error components (T_i, A_i, and u_{ni}) for each producer.

The problem is both conceptual and statistical. The conceptual challenge is to establish a satisfactory linkage between allocative inefficiency (the u_{ni}) and its cost (A_i). The statistical challenge is to estimate a model with so many error components, each of which requires a distribution. The problem remained unresolved until Kumbhakar (1997) obtained analytical results, which Kumbhakar and Tsionas (2005) extended to estimate the model using Bayesian techniques. This is encouraging, because (1.42) remains a workhorse in the nonfrontier literature and, more important, because its extension (1.43) is capable of estimating and decomposing economic efficiency.

There is an appealing alternative. The solution is to remove the influence of allocative inefficiency from the error terms and parameterize it inside the cost frontier and its input cost shares. We turn to this approach below.

1.5.4 Shadow price models

The econometric techniques described in sections 1.5.1–1.5.3 are enveloping techniques. Each treats technical efficiency in terms of distance to a production frontier, economic efficiency in terms of distance to an appropriate economic frontier, and allocative efficiency as a ratio of economic efficiency to technical efficiency. They are in rough concordance on the fundamental notions of frontiers and distance, in keeping with the theoretical developments in section 1.3. They differ mainly in the techniques they employ to construct frontiers and to measure distance. However they all convert a weak inequality to an equality by introducing a one-sided error component.

There is a literature that seeks to measure efficiency without explicit recourse to frontiers, and indeed, it contains many papers in which the word "frontier" does not appear. In this literature, little attempt is made to envelop data or to associate efficiency with distance to an enveloping surface. Unlike most econometric efficiency analysis, the focus is on allocative efficiency. Instead of attempting to model allocative inefficiency by means of error components, as in (1.43), allocative inefficiency is modeled parametrically by means of additional parameters to be estimated.

The literature seems to have originated with Hopper (1965), who found subsistence agriculture in India to attain a high degree of allocative efficiency, supporting the "poor but efficient" hypothesis. He reached this conclusion by using OLS to estimate Cobb-Douglas production functions (not frontiers), then to calculate the value of the marginal product of each input, and then to make two comparisons: the value of an input's marginal product for different outputs, and the values of an input's marginal product with its price. In each comparison equality implies allocative efficiency, and the sign and magnitude of an inequality indicate the direction and severity (and the cost, which can be calculated since the production function parameters have been estimated) of the allocative inefficiency. Hopper's work was heavily criticized, and enormously influential.

In a nutshell, the shadow price models that have followed have simply parameterized Hopper's comparisons, with inequalities being replaced with parameters to be estimated. Thus, assuming $M = 1$ for simplicity and following Lau and Yotopoulos (1971) and Yotopoulos and Lau (1973), the inequality

$$y \leqq f(x; \beta) \tag{1.44}$$

is parameterized as

$$y = \phi f(x; \beta). \tag{1.45}$$

There is no notion of a production frontier here, since in moving from (1.44) to (1.45) the obvious requirement that $\max\{\phi\} \leq 1$ is ignored. Indeed, so far this is just a Hoch (1955)–Mundlak (1961) management bias production function model, in which different intercepts are intended to capture the effects of variation in the (unobserved) management input. But it gets better.

If producers seek to maximize profit, then the inequalities

$$\partial \phi f(x; \beta)/\partial x_n \gtreqless (w_n/p), n = 1, \dots, N \tag{1.46}$$

are parameterized as

$$\partial \phi f(x; \beta)/\partial x_n = \theta_n(w_n/p), \tag{1.47}$$

where $\theta_n \gtreqless 1$ indicate under- or overutilization of x_n relative to the profit-maximizing values. All that remains is to endow $f(x; \beta)$ with a functional form, and estimation of (β, ϕ, θ_n) provides a more sophisticated framework within which to implement Hopper's procedures. A host of hypotheses can be tested concerning the existence and nature of technical and allocative efficiency, without recourse to the notion of a frontier and error components.

The shadow price approach gained momentum following the popularity of the Averch-Johnson (1962) hypothesis. This hypothesis asserted that regulated utilities allowed to earn a "fair" rate of return on their invested capital would rationally overcapitalize, leading to higher than minimum cost and thus to customer rates that were higher than necessary.

The analysis proceeds roughly as above. A producer's cost

$$w^T x \geqq c(y, w; \beta) \tag{1.48}$$

is parameterized as

$$w^T x = (1/\phi)c(y, \theta w; \beta), \tag{1.49}$$

where θw is a vector of shadow prices. Now, $\phi \leq 1$ reflects technical inefficiency and $\theta_n \gtreqless 1$ reflects allocative inefficiency, and there is an explicit notion of a cost frontier. A producer's input demands

$$x_n \gtreqless x_n(y, w; \beta) \tag{1.50}$$

are parameterized as

$$x_n = (1/\phi)x_n(y, \theta w; \beta). \tag{1.51}$$

Although x_n may be allocatively inefficient for the input prices w that a producer actually pays, it is allocatively efficient for the shadow price vector θw.

The Averch-Johnson hypothesis asserts that rate-of-return regulation lowers the shadow price of capital beneath the cost of capital, leading to rational overcapitalization. The situation is depicted in figure 1.13. Given exogenous output y and input prices w_K and w_L, the cost-minimizing input combination occurs at x^E. The actual input combination occurs at x^A, which is technically efficient but allocatively inefficient, involving overcapitalization. Since the actual input combination must be allocatively efficient for some price ratio, the problem boils down to one of estimating the distortion factor θ along with the technology parameters β. In the two-input case illustrated in figure 1.13, there is one distortion parameter, while in the N input case there are $N - 1$ distortion parameters. The hypothesis of interest is that $\theta < 1$, the cost of which is given by the ratio $[c(y, \theta w; \beta)/c(y, w; \beta)] \geq 1$, which is the reciprocal of the cost-efficiency measure (1.22) translated to this analytical framework.

Comparing (1.49) and (1.51) with (1.43) makes it clear that in the shadow price approach both sources of cost inefficiency have been moved from error components to the functions to be estimated. Although the error components approach to estimation and decomposition of economic efficiency has proved intractable so far, the shadow price approach has proved successful and has become very popular. It is also possible to combine the two approaches, by modeling technical efficiency as an error component and modeling allocative

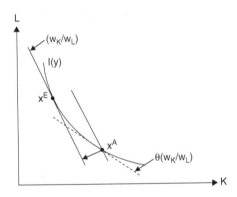

Figure 1.13. The Averch-Johnson Hypothesis

efficiency parametrically. Kumbhakar and Lovell (2000) discuss estimation strategies for the pure shadow price model and the combined model.

When modeling the behavior of producers who are constrained in their pursuit of a conventional objective, or who pursue an unconventional objective, analysts have two choices. The preferred choice is to model objective and constraint(s) correctly, derive the first-order conditions, and construct an estimating model based on the assumption that producers are efficient. This can be hard work, as Färe and Logan (1983) have demonstrated for the case of the profit-seeking rate-of-return–regulated producer. An easier alternative approach, illustrated above, is to model such producers as being unconstrained in their pursuit of a conventional objective, allow for failure to satisfy first-order conditions, and check to see if the direction of the estimated allocative inefficiency is consistent with what one would expect if in fact the producers were constrained or pursued some other objective. That is, use a model that is inappropriate but familiar, and look for allocative inefficiency by comparing shadow price ratios with actual price ratios.

In a related situation the analyst does not know the constraints or the objective of producers, perhaps because there are competing paradigms at hand. In this case, it is feasible to use the familiar model and use estimated shadow prices to provide an indirect test of the competing paradigms.

These are the two purposes that the shadow price approach most frequently serves. Thus, allocative inefficiency in the unconstrained pursuit of cost minimization or profit maximization suggests allocative efficiency in a more complicated environment, and departures of shadow price ratios from actual price ratios provide the basis for hypothesis tests. The model has been used frequently to test the Averch-Johnson hypothesis, and more generally as a framework for testing allocative efficiency hypotheses in a wide variety of contexts. Two other examples come to mind, primarily because they are current and have not yet been subjected to analysis using the shadow price approach. The impact of domestic content legislation could be explored within the shadow price framework. Another popular hypothesis that could be tested within this framework is that of discrimination, against minorities or immigrants or whatever group is of interest.

1.6 The Mathematical Programming Approach to Efficiency Measurement

The mathematical programming approach to the construction of frontiers and the measurement of efficiency relative to the constructed frontiers goes by the descriptive title of data envelopment analysis, with the interesting acronym DEA. It truly does envelop a data set; it makes no accommodation for noise and so does not "nearly" envelop a data set the way the deterministic kernel of a stochastic frontier does. Moreover, subject to certain assumptions about the structure of production technology, it envelops the data as tightly as possible.

Like the econometric approach, the programming approach can be categorized according to the type of data available (cross section or panel) and
according to the types of variables available (quantities only, or quantities and
prices). With quantities only, technical efficiency can be estimated, while with
quantities and prices economic efficiency can be estimated and decomposed
into its technical and allocative components. However, DEA was developed
in a public-sector, not-for-profit environment, in which prices are suspect at
best and missing at worst. Consequently, the vast majority of DEA studies use
quantity data only and estimate technical efficiency only, despite the fact that
the procedures are easily adapted to the estimation of economic efficiency in
a setting in which prices are available and reliable.

In section 1.6.1, we analyze plain vanilla DEA to estimate technical efficiency. In section 1.6.2, we discuss one of many possible DEA models of
economic efficiency. In section 1.6.3, we discuss the application of DEA to
panel data, although the most popular such application occurs in the analysis
of productivity change (which we discuss in section 1.8.3). In section 1.6.4,
we discuss a technical issue, the imposition of weight restrictions, which has
important economic implications. Finally, in section 1.6.5, we offer a brief
introduction to the statistical foundations of DEA, a subject covered more
fully in chapter 4.

1.6.1 Basic DEA

Producers use inputs $x \in R_+^N$ to produce outputs $y \in R_+^M$. The research objective
is to estimate the performance of each producer relative to best observed
practice in a sample of $i = 1, \ldots, I$ producers. To this end, weights are attached
to each producer's inputs and outputs so as to solve the problem

$$\begin{aligned}
&\text{Min}_{\upsilon,\mu} \, \upsilon^T x_0 / \mu^T y_0 \\
&\text{Subject to } \upsilon^T x_i / \mu^T y_i \geq 1, i = 1, \ldots, 0, \ldots, I \\
&\upsilon, \mu \geq 0
\end{aligned} \tag{1.52}$$

Here (x_0, y_0) are the vectors of inputs and outputs of the producer under evaluation, and (x_i, y_i) are the vectors of inputs and outputs of the ith producer
in the sample. The problem seeks a set of nonnegative weights, or multipliers,
that minimize the weighted input-to-output ratio of the producer under evaluation, subject to the constraints that when these weights are assigned to every
producer in the sample, their weighted input-to-output ratios are bounded
below by one. Associate the multipliers (υ, μ) with shadow prices, and think
of the objective in the problem as one of minimizing the ratio of shadow cost
to shadow revenue.

The nonlinear program (1.52) can be converted to a dual pair of linear
programs. The first DEA model is known as the CCR model, after Charnes,
Cooper, and Rhodes (1978). The "multiplier" program appears in the right
column of (1.53) below, where X is an $N \times I$ sample input matrix with columns

of producer input vectors x_i, and Y is an $M \times I$ sample output matrix with columns of producer output vectors y_i. Think of the multiplier program as one of minimizing shadow cost, subject to the constraint that shadow revenue is normalized to one, and subject to the constraints that when these multipliers are assigned to all producers in the sample, no producer earns positive shadow profit:

CCR Envelopment Program	CCR Multiplier Program	
$\text{Max}_{\phi,\lambda}\,\phi$	$\text{Min}_{\upsilon,\mu}\,\upsilon^T x_o$	
Subject to $X\lambda \leq x_o$	Subject to $\mu^T y_o = 1$	(1.53)
$\quad \phi y_o \leq Y\lambda$	$\quad \upsilon^T X - \mu^T Y \geq 0$	
$\quad \lambda \geq 0$	$\quad \upsilon, \mu \geq 0$	

Because the multiplier program is a linear program, it has a dual, which is also a linear program. The dual "envelopment" program appears in the left column of (1.53), where ϕ is a scalar and λ is an $I \times 1$ intensity vector. In the envelopment program, the performance of a producer is evaluated in terms of its ability to expand its output vector subject to the constraints imposed by best practice observed in the sample. If radial expansion is possible for a producer, its optimal $\phi > 1$, while if radial expansion is not possible, its optimal $\phi = 1$. Noting the output orientation of the envelopment program, it follows that ϕ is the DEA estimator of $TE_o(x, y)$ defined in (1.12). Noting that ϕ is a radial efficiency measure, and recalling the divergence between Koopmans's definition of technical efficiency and the Debreu-Farrell measure of technical efficiency, it follows that optimal $\phi = 1$ is necessary, but not sufficient, for technical efficiency since $(\phi y_o, x_o)$ may contain slack in any of its $M + N$ dimensions. At optimum, $\phi = 1$ characterizes technical efficiency in the sense of Debreu and Farrell, while $\{\phi = 1,\ X\lambda = x_o,\ \phi y_o = Y\lambda\}$ characterizes technical efficiency in the sense of Koopmans.

The output-oriented CCR model is partly illustrated in figure 1.14, for the $M = 2$ case. Producer A is technically inefficient, with optimal projection $\phi^A y^A$ occurring at a convex combination of efficient producers D and C on the output isoquant $I^{CCR}(x)$, so $\lambda^D > 0, \lambda^C > 0$, with all other elements of the intensity vector being zero. The efficient role models D and C are similar to, and a linear combination of them is better than, inefficient producer A being evaluated. The envelopment program provides this information. The multiplier program provides information on the trade-off between the two outputs at the optimal projection. The trade-off is given by the optimal shadow price ratio $-(\mu_1/\mu_2)$. The fact that this shadow price ratio might differ from the market price ratio, if one exists, plays a role in the DEA model of economic efficiency in section 1.6.2. The multiplier program also provides information on input trade-offs $-(\upsilon_n/\upsilon_k)$ and output–input trade-offs (μ_m/υ), although this information is not portrayed in figure 1.14.

Problem (1.53) is solved I times, once for each producer in the sample, to generate I optimal values of (ϕ, λ) and I optimal values of (υ, μ). It thus

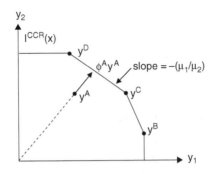

Figure 1.14. The Output-Oriented CCR Model

provides a wealth of information about the performance of each producer in the sample and about the structure of production technology.

The CCR production set corresponding to T in (1.1) is obtained from the envelopment problem in (1.53) as $T^{CCR} = \{(y, x) : y \leq Y\lambda,\ X\lambda \leq x,\ \lambda \geq 0\}$ and imposes three restrictions on the technology. These restrictions are constant returns to scale, strong disposability of outputs and inputs, and convexity. Each of these restrictions can be relaxed.

Constant returns to scale is the restriction that is most commonly relaxed. Variable returns to scale is modeled by adding a free variable v_0 to the multiplier program, which is equivalent to adding a convexity constraint $\Sigma_i\lambda_i = 1$ to the envelopment program. The variable returns to scale model was introduced by Afriat (1972), but is better known as the BCC model after Banker, Charnes, and Cooper (1984). The BCC envelopment and multiplier programs become

BCC Envelopment Program   *BCC Multiplier Program*

$$\text{Max}_{\phi,\lambda}\ \phi \qquad\qquad \text{Min}_{v,v_0,\mu}\ v^T x_0 + v_0$$
$$\text{Subject to } X\lambda \leq x_0 \qquad \text{Subject to } \mu^T y_0 = 1 \qquad\qquad (1.54)$$
$$\phi y_0 \leq Y\lambda \qquad\qquad v^T X + v_0 - \mu^T Y \geq 0$$
$$\lambda \geq 0,\ \Sigma_i\lambda_i = 1 \qquad\qquad v, \mu \geq 0,\ v_0 \text{ free}$$

The interpretation of the BCC envelopment and multiplier programs is essentially the same as for the CCR model, but the BCC production set shrinks, becoming $T^{BCC} = \{(y, x) : y \leq Y\lambda,\ X\lambda \leq x,\ \lambda \geq 0,\ \Sigma_i\lambda_i = 1\}$. T^{BCC} exhibits variable returns to scale, because only convex combinations of efficient producers form the best-practice frontier. For this reason, it envelops the data more tightly than T^{CCR} does.

The difference between the two production sets is illustrated in figure 1.15. Because T^{BCC} envelops the data more tightly than T^{CCR} does, efficiency estimates are generally higher with a BCC specification, and rankings can differ in the two specifications. As in the CCR model, the BCC envelopment program provides efficiency estimates and identifies efficient role models. Also as in the CCR model, the BCC multiplier program estimates optimal shadow

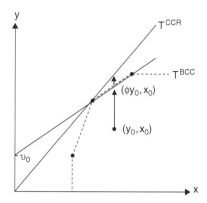

Figure 1.15. Returns to Scale in DEA

price ratios, but it also provides information on the nature of scale economies. The optimal projection to T^{BCC} occurs at $(\phi y_0, x_0)$. At this projection, the output–input trade-off is μ/υ. The vertical intercept of the supporting hyperplane $y = \upsilon_0 + \upsilon x_0$ at $(\phi y_0, x_0)$ is positive. This indicates decreasing returns to scale at $(\phi y_0, x_0)$, which should be apparent from figure 1.15. More generally, $\upsilon_0 \lessgtr 0$ signals that a producer is operating in a region of increasing, constant or decreasing returns to scale.

Notice the shape of T^{BCC} in figure 1.15. Requiring strictly positive input to produce nonzero output is a consequence of not allowing for the possibility of inactivity and of imposing convexity on T^{BCC}. This creates a somewhat strained notion of variable returns to scale, one that is well removed from the classical S-shaped production frontier that reflects Frisch's (1965) "ultrapassum" law. Petersen (1990) has attempted to introduce more flexibility into the DEA approach to measuring scale economies by dispensing with the assumption of convexity of T while maintaining the assumption of convexity of $L(y)$ and $P(x)$.

The CCR and BCC models differ in their treatment of scale economies, as reflected by the additional equality constraint $\Sigma_i \lambda_i = 1$ and free variable υ_0 in the BCC model. Just as (μ, υ) are shadow prices of outputs and inputs, υ_0 is the shadow value of the convexity constraint $\Sigma_i \lambda_i = 1$. It is possible to conduct a test of the null hypothesis that $\upsilon_0 = 0$, or that the convexity constraint $\Sigma_i \lambda_i = 1$ is redundant. This is a test for constant returns to scale and is discussed along with other hypothesis tests in chapter 4. However, a qualification is in order concerning the interpretation of the multipliers. Most efficient producers are located at vertices, and it is possible that some inefficient producers are projected to vertices. At vertices, shadow prices of variables (υ, μ) in the CCR and BCC models, and of the convexity constraint (υ_0) in the BCC model, are not unique.

The CCR and BCC envelopment programs are output oriented, just as the econometric problem (1.32) is. It is a simple matter to obtain analogous input-oriented envelopment programs, by converting the envelopment programs to minimization programs and converting the multiplier problems to maximization programs (details appear in chapter 3). The choice between the two orientations depends on the objective assigned to producers. If producers are required to meet market demands, and if they can freely adjust input usage, then an input orientation is appropriate.

The assumption of strong disposability is rarely relaxed, despite the obvious interest in relaxing the free disposability of surplus inputs or unwanted outputs. One popular exception occurs in environmental economics, in which producers use purchased inputs to produce marketed outputs and undesirable byproducts such as air or water pollution. In this case, the byproducts may or may not be *privately* freely disposable, depending on whether the regulator is watching, but they are surely *socially* weakly or expensively disposable. The value of relaxing the strong output disposability assumption lies in its potential to provide evidence on the marginal private cost of abatement. This evidence can be compared with estimates of the marginal social benefit of abatement to inform public policy.

Without going into details [which are provided by Färe et al. (1989, 1993) and a host of subsequent writers], the essence of weak disposability is captured in figure 1.16. Here, y_2 is a marketed output and y_1 is an undesirable byproduct. A conventional output set exhibiting strong disposability is bounded by the output isoquant $I^S(x)$ with solid line segments. The corresponding output set exhibiting weak disposability of the byproduct is bounded by the output isoquant $I^W(x)$ with dashed line segments. $L^W(x) \subseteq L^S(x)$, and that part of $L^S(x)$ not included in $L^W(x)$ provides an indication of the amount of marketed output foregone if the byproduct is not freely disposable. Disposal is free with technology $L^S(x)$, and abatement is costly with technology $L^W(x)$. For $y_1 < y_1^*$, the conventional strong disposal output set allows abatement of y_1 to be privately free, as indicated by the horizontal solid line segment along which $(\mu_1/\mu_2) = 0$. In contrast, the weak disposal output set makes abatement privately costly, as indicated by the positively sloped dashed line segments to the left of y_1^*. Moreover, increased abatement becomes increasingly costly, since the shadow price ratio $(\mu_1/\mu_2) > 0$ increases with additional abatement.

In figure 1.16, the marginal cost of abatement is reflected in the amount of y_2 (and hence revenue) that must be sacrificed to reduce the byproduct. With given inputs and technology, reducing air pollution requires a reduction in electricity generation. Allowing x or technology to vary would allow the cost of abatement to reflect the additional input or the new technology (and hence cost) required to abate with no loss in marketed output. With given electricity generation, reducing air pollution could be accomplished by installing scrubbers or by upgrading technology.

The assumption of convexity of output sets P(x) and input sets L(y) also is rarely relaxed, despite the belief of many, expressed by McFadden (1978, pp. 8–9), that its importance lies more in its analytical convenience than in its technological realism. In the previous context of scale economies, feasibility

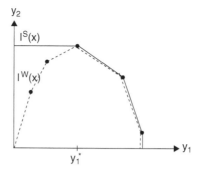

Figure 1.16. Weak Disposability of y_1

of an activity (y, x) does not necessarily imply feasibility of all scaled activities $(\lambda y, \lambda x)$, $\lambda > 0$, which motivates relaxing the assumption of constant returns to scale. In the present context, feasibility of two distinct activities (y^A, x^A) and (y^B, x^B) does not necessarily imply feasibility of all convex combinations of them, which motivates relaxing the assumption of convexity.

Deprins et al. (1984) were the first to relax convexity. They constructed a "free disposal hull" (FDH) of the data that relaxes convexity while maintaining strong disposability and allowing for variable returns to scale. An FDH output set is contrasted with a BCC output set in figure 1.17. The BCC output set is bounded by the output isoquant $I^{BCC}(x)$ as indicated by the solid line segments. The FDH output set dispenses with convexity but retains strong disposability, and is bounded by the output isoquant $I^{FDH}(x)$ as indicated by the dashed line segments. The contrast between FDH and DEA input sets and production sets is structurally identical. In each case, dispensing with convexity creates frontiers that have a staircase shape. This makes slacks a much more serious problem in FDH than in DEA, and it complicates the FDH multiplier program.

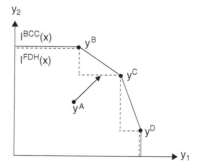

Figure 1.17. An FDH Output Set

The FDH envelopment program is identical to the BCC envelopment program in (1.54), apart from the addition of an integral constraint $\lambda_i \in \{0, 1\}, i = 1, \ldots, I$. Since all intensity variables are assigned values of zero or one, the convexity constraint $\Sigma_i \lambda_i = 1$ implies that exactly one intensity variable has a value of one. Thus, FDH identifies exactly one role model for an inefficient producer, and the role model is an actual efficient producer rather than a fictitious convex combination of efficient producers. In figure 1.17, inefficient producer A receives an FDH radial efficiency estimate (indicated by the arrow) and has efficient role model C rather than a convex combination of C and B as in DEA. The additional constraint in the FDH envelopment program causes $P^{FDH}(x) \subseteq P^{BCC}(x)$, so FDH efficiency estimates are generally higher than BCC efficiency estimates. Although the addition of an integral constraint converts (1.54) to a more complicated mixed integer program, it actually simplifies the computation of the envelopment program. In fact, programming techniques are not required to obtain FDH efficiency estimates. Tulkens (1993) provides details.

We closed section 1.3 by bemoaning the neglect of dominance. Although dominance information provides a useful complement to any type of efficiency analysis, it is popular only in FDH efficiency analysis. The vector comparison tools that are used to identify the single efficient role model also serve to identify all dominating producers for each inefficient producer, and all dominated producers for each efficient producer. Identifying dominating producers enhances the likelihood that an inefficient producer can find a useful role model, fully efficient or not. Identifying the number of dominated producers also offers a procedure for ranking ostensibly efficient producers, a problem that has engaged researchers ever since Andersen and Petersen (1993) first raised the issue. The problem is addressed in chapter 4.

At the end of section 1.5.1, we discussed procedures for incorporating potential determinants of efficiency in SFA. The same challenge arises in DEA, and at least two approaches have been developed. One approach is to add to the CCR envelopment program (1.53) or the BCC envelopment program (1.54) the additional constraints $Z\lambda \leq z_0$ or $Z\lambda \geq z_0$, or a combination of the two, depending on whether the potential determinants enhance or retard output. This, of course, requires appropriate modification of the dual multiplier programs. This approach is analogous to replacing $f(x_i; \beta)$ with $f(x_i, z_i; \beta, \gamma)$ in SFA. Two difficulties arise. First, unlike SFA, in which we simultaneously estimate both the magnitudes and the signs of the elements of γ, here we must know in advance the direction of the influence of the elements of z in order to set the inequalities. Second, in this formulation, elements of z either enhance or retard output, but they do not influence the efficiency with which x produces y. The other approach, far more popular, is to regress estimated efficiency scores against z in a second-stage regression. We have already warned of the sins committed by doing so in SFA, and the story is similar, but happily not quite so bleak, in DEA. Chapter 4 provides a detailed analysis of the use of second-stage regressions in DEA. The message is of bad news–good news form: (i) Statistical inference on the second-stage regressions you have seen (or conducted) is invalid, but (ii) it is possible to formulate the model in such a way that it provides a rational basis for regressing efficiency estimates in a second-stage analysis, and bootstrapping can provide valid inference.

1.6.2 A DEA model of economic efficiency

The DEA models in section 1.6.1 use quantity data only and so capture technical efficiency only. In this section, we show how to extend DEA models to provide measures of economic efficiency. We continue our output orientation by illustrating the extension with a problem of revenue maximization.

Producers are assumed to use inputs $x \in R_+^N$ to produce outputs $y \in R_+^M$ for sale at prices $p \in R_{++}^M$. Their objective is to maximize revenue, subject to the constraints imposed by output prices, input supplies, and the structure of production technology, which is allowed to exhibit variable returns to scale. This problem can be expressed in linear programming format as

Revenue Maximization Program

$$R(x, p) = \max_{y,\lambda} p^T y$$
$$\text{Subject to } X\lambda \leqq x_o \tag{1.55}$$
$$y \leqq Y\lambda$$
$$\lambda \geqq 0, \Sigma_i \lambda_i = 1$$

The production set can be recognized as T^{BCC}, so (1.55) is a straightforward extension of conventional DEA to an economic optimization problem. The problem is illustrated in figure 1.18. The revenue efficiency of producer A is estimated from (1.55) as $RE(y^A, x, p) = p^T y^{RM}/p^T y^A > 1$. The technical efficiency of A is estimated from (1.54) as $TE_o(x, y^A) = p^T(\phi y^A)/p^T y^A = \phi > 1$. The output-allocative efficiency of A is estimated residually as $AE_o(y^A, x, p) = p^T y^{RM}/p^T(\phi y^A) > 1$. Notice that at the optimal projection ϕy^A the estimated shadow price ratio $(\mu_1/\mu_2) < (p_1/p_2)$. This provides an indication of the existence, and the direction, of a misallocation of outputs; the output mix $(y_2/y_1)^A$ is too large, given (p_1/p_2). The cost of this misallocation, in terms of lost revenue, is estimated as $[p^T y^{RM} - p^T(\phi y^A)] > 0$.

Alternative objectives, and alternative or additional constraints, can be entertained within the same general linear programming format. All that is required is the requisite data and the ability to write down a linear programming problem analogous to (1.55) that captures the objective and the constraints of the economic problem of interest. Färe et al. (1985) analyze several economic optimization problems with linear programming techniques.

1.6.3 Panel data

Thus far in section 1.6, we have assumed that we have a single cross section of data with which to evaluate producer performance. Suppose now that we have

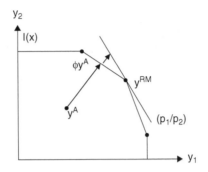

Figure 1.18. Revenue Maximization in DEA

a panel consisting of T time periods and I producers in each period. How does DEA exploit the ability to observe each producer multiple times? The available techniques are not as sophisticated as panel-data econometric techniques, but several options are available.

One option is to pool the data and estimate a single grand frontier. In doing so, this option assumes an unvarying best-practice technology, which may be untenable in long panels. It does, however, generate T efficiency estimates for each producer, all against the same standard, and trends in efficiency estimates of individual producers may be of interest.

At the other extreme, it is possible to estimate T separate frontiers, one for each period. This allows for technical progress and regress. It also allows for intersecting frontiers, which would signal local progress in a region of output–input space and local regress in another region. A danger of this approach is the possibility of excessive volatility in efficiency scores resulting from excessive variation in temporally independent period frontiers.

An intermediate option is to estimate a sequence of overlapping pooled panels, each consisting of a few time periods of arbitrary length. Known as "window analysis," this option tracks efficiency trends through successive over-lapping windows. One purpose of window analysis is to relieve degrees of freedom pressure when $M + N$ is large relative to I. As such, it provides a compromise between running DEA once on one large $I \times T$ pooled panel and running DEA T times on T small cross sections. Another objective of window analysis is to alleviate volatility in efficiency estimates.

A second intermediate option is to estimate a sequential frontier by continuously adding data from successive time periods. In the end, this procedure constructs a grand frontier, but prior to the terminal period, frontiers are estimated sequentially from current and all previous (but not subsequent) data. This option rules out the possibility of technical regress, presumably in the belief that techniques once known are not forgotten and remain available for adoption. A drawback of this option is that sample sizes increase sequentially, which complicates statistical inference.

A final option is to use two adjacent periods of data at a time, beginning with periods 1 and 2, continuing with periods 2 and 3, and so on. This option may look like two-period window analysis, but it is very different. It is used to estimate and decompose Malmquist indexes of productivity change, and we defer discussion of this option to section 1.7.

1.6.4 Weight restrictions

The multipliers (υ, μ) in the CCR problem (1.53) and the BCC problem (1.54) are not market prices. Indeed, a frequently touted virtue of DEA is that it is practical in situations in which market prices are missing, as in the environmental context illustrating weak disposability in section 1.6.1. The multipliers are in fact endogenously determined *shadow prices* revealed by individual producers in their effort to maximize their relative efficiency. The great Russian mathematician (and, together with Koopmans, the 1975 recipient of the Nobel Prize in Economic Sciences) Kantorovich (1939) referred to them as "resolving multipliers," ostensibly because they solve the dual linear programs. As figure 1.14 illustrates, different producers can choose different sets of shadow price ratios, and the freedom to choose is limited only by the nonnegativity constraints υ, $\mu \geq 0$. Consequently, the range of multipliers chosen by producers might differ markedly from market prices (when they exist), or might offend expert judgment on the relative values of the variables (when market prices are missing). This opens up the possibility of limiting the freedom to choose.

At the other extreme, many comparisons are based on fixed weights that give no freedom to choose. A recent example is provided by the World Health Organization (WHO, 2000), which somewhat controversially evaluated the ability of 191 member countries to provide health care to their citizens. WHO used five health care indicators y_m, to which they assigned fixed weights $\mu_m > 0$, $\Sigma_m \mu_m = 1$. These fixed weights were based on expert opinion, but they were common to all countries, regardless of their development status. To require Mali and Canada, for example, to assign equal importance to each indicator seems undesirably restrictive. Why not retain the five indicators, but give countries the freedom to choose their own weights, subject to the requirements that $\mu_m \geq 0$, $\Sigma_m \mu_m = 1$?

This is exactly what DEA does. Lauer et al. (2004) ran the output-oriented DEA program

$$
\begin{array}{ll}
\text{Max}_{\phi,\lambda}\,\phi & \text{Min}_{\mu,\omega}\,\omega \\
\text{Subject to} & \text{Subject to } \mu^T y_0 = 1 \\
\quad \phi y_0 \leq Y\lambda & \quad -\mu^T Y + \omega \geq 0 \\
\quad \lambda \geq 0, \Sigma_i \lambda_i = 1 & \quad \mu \geq 0, \Sigma_m \mu_m = 1, \omega \text{ free}
\end{array}
\tag{1.56}
$$

which is the BCC model (1.54) with scalar input with unit value for each country (each country is "itself"). Each country is allowed to select its own nonnegative health care indicator weights.

The results were unacceptable. More than one-third of the countries assigned a zero weight to four of five indicators, and nearly 90% of the countries assigned a zero weight to y_1 = population health, the defining goal of any health system. Only three countries assigned positive weights to all five indicators. The fixed positive weights common to all countries used by WHO are unappealing, but so is the excessive variability of self-assigned nonnegative weights allowed by DEA. A frequently touted virtue of DEA, that it is value-free in its selection of weights, can turn out to be a vice.

This is not an isolated incident. Imposing only the restrictions that output and input weights be nonnegative can, and frequently does, generate silly weights and implausible weight variability, both of which offend common sense. Fortunately, a remedy exists. It is possible to allow weight flexibility and, at the same time, to restrict weight flexibility. This was the fundamental insight of Thompson et al. (1986). They were forced to figure out how to impose weight restrictions in their DEA study of identifying an optimal site to place a high-energy physics facility. Their motivation was that sites have characteristics, and in the opinion of experts, no characteristic could be ignored by assigning it zero weight. Necessity is the mother of invention.

The DEA literature on imposing weight restrictions has come a long way since 1986, and there exist many ways of restricting weights. One appealing procedure is to append to the multiplier program of (1.56) the restrictions

$$\gamma_m \geq \mu_m y_m / \mu^T y \geq \beta_m, \quad m = 1, \ldots, 5, \qquad (1.57)$$

which place lower and upper bounds on the relative importance of each indicator in the evaluation of health care performance. Although these bounds are common to all countries, they do allow limited freedom to choose.

More generally, it is possible to impose restrictions on output weights, on input weights, and on the ratio of output weights to input weights, in the BCC model (1.54). The appeal of the procedure is that it offers a compromise between the arbitrary imposition of common weights and the excessively flexible DEA weights. Of course, we still need experts to set the bounds, and experts frequently disagree. A fascinating example, related by Takamura and Tone (2003), is occurring in Japan, whose government plans to move several agencies out of congested Tokyo. Ten candidate sites have been identified, and 18 criteria have been specified. Criteria vary in their importance; a committee of wise men has been named to establish bounds of the form (1.57) on each criterion, and these bounds must reflect differences of opinion among the wise men. DEA with weight restrictions is being used to solve a 12 trillion yen problem!

Of course, the problem of unreasonable shadow prices is not limited to DEA; it can arise in SFA, as well. The problem has received far more attention in DEA, where it is arguably easier to resolve. (For more on weight restrictions in DEA, see chapter 3.)

1.6.5 Statistical foundations of DEA

A distinguishing feature of the DEA models discussed above is that they do not contain a random error term that would incorporate the impacts of statistical noise; the DEA frontier is not stochastic as it is in SFA. This has led to two separate strands of research.

Land et al. (1993) and Olesen and Petersen (1995) sought to make DEA stochastic by introducing a chance that the constraints (on either the envelopment problem or the multiplier problem) in either (1.53) or (1.54) might be violated with some probability. This approach is an extension to DEA of chance-constrained programming developed by Charnes et al. (1958) and Charnes and Cooper (1959) and is known as "chance-constrained DEA."

We follow Land et al. (1993) by writing the CCR envelopment problem in (1.53) as

Chance-Constrained CCR Envelopment Program

$$\text{Max}_{\phi,\lambda}\,\phi$$
$$\text{Subject to } \Pr[X\lambda \leq x_o] \geq 0.95 \tag{1.58}$$
$$\Pr[y_o \leq Y\lambda] \geq 0.95$$
$$\lambda \geq 0$$

where the prespecified probabilities of satisfying each constraint are assumed equal at the popular 95% level to simplify the exposition. Program (1.58) asks producers to radially expand their output vector as far as possible, subject to the constraint that $(\phi y_o, x_o)$ "probably" is feasible.

Program (1.58) is not operational. It can be made operational by making assumptions on the distributions of the sample data. If it is assumed that each output y_{im} is a normally distributed random variable with expected value Ey_{im} and variance–covariance matrix $Vy_{im}y_{jm}$, and that each input is a normally distributed random variable with expected value Ex_{in} and variance–covariance matrix $Vx_{in}x_{jn}$, then (1.58) can be expressed in modified certainty-equivalent form as

Chance-Constrained CCR Envelopment Program: Certainty Equivalent Form

$$\text{Max}_{\phi,\lambda}\,\phi$$
$$\text{Subject to } \Sigma_i x_{in}\lambda_i + \Sigma_i(Ex_{in}-x_{in})\lambda_i + 1.645\left[\Sigma_i\Sigma_j\lambda_i\lambda_j Vx_{in}x_{jn}\right]^{1/2} \leq x_{on},$$
$$n = 1,\ldots,N$$
$$\phi y_{om} \leq \Sigma_i y_{im}\lambda_i + \Sigma_i(Ey_{im}-y_{im})\lambda_i - 1.645\left[\Sigma_i\Sigma_j\lambda_i\lambda_j Vy_{im}y_{jm}\right]^{1/2},$$
$$m = 1,\ldots,M$$
$$\lambda_I \geq 0, i = 1,\ldots,I \tag{1.59}$$

where $1.645 = F^{-1}(0.95)$ is the prespecified value of the distribution function of a standard normal variate. If $x_{in} - Ex_{in} = y_{im} - Ey_{im} = Vx_{in}x_{jn} = Vy_{im}y_{jm} = 0$ for all producers i and j and for all variables m and n, the nonlinear program (1.59) collapses to the linear program (1.53). However, if we have reason to believe that a sample data point departs from its expected value, perhaps due to unusually good weather or unexpected supply disruption, then this information is fed into the chance-constrained program. The desired outcome is that, unlike program (1.53), good or bad fortune does not distort efficiency measures for any producer. Similarly, if we have reason to believe that any pair of inputs or outputs is correlated across producers, perhaps because farmers in the same region experience similar weather patterns, this information is also fed into the program.

The data requirements of chance-constrained efficiency measurement are severe. In addition to the data matrices X and Y, we require information on expected values of all variables for all producers, and variance–covariance matrices for each variable across all producers. The idea is neat, and developments continue, but serious applications are few and far between.

There is another way of dealing with the absence of an explicit random error term in DEA. This is to acknowledge at the outset that DEA efficiency scores are estimators of true, but unknown, efficiencies. The properties of these estimators depend on the structure of the true, but unknown, technology and also on the process by which the sample data have been generated, the data generating process (DGP).

We know the DEA assumptions on the structure of the true technology. In a series of papers, Simar and Wilson (see chapter 4) and their colleagues have introduced assumptions on the DGP. This enables them to interpret the DEA efficiency measure as an estimator with statistical properties, thus endowing DEA with statistical foundations. In addition to convexity and strong disposability of the true, but unknown, technology, they make the following assumptions on the DGP:

- The sample data (x_i, y_i), $I = 1, \ldots, I$, are realizations of independent and identically distributed random variables with probability density function $f(x, y)$.
- The probability of observing an efficient unit $[\phi(x, y) = 1]$ approaches unity as the sample size increases.
- For all (x, y) in the interior of T, $\phi(x, y)$ is differentiable in (x, y).

Armed with these assumptions on the DGP, it is possible to prove that

- the DEA efficiency estimator $\phi^{DEA}(x, y)$ is biased toward unity,
- but $\phi^{DEA}(x, y)$ is a consistent estimator,
- although convergence is slow, reflecting the curse of dimensionality.

A closed form for the density of $\phi^{DEA}(x, y)$ has yet to be derived. Consequently, bootstrapping techniques must be used to approximate it in order to conduct statistical inference. A sobering message emerges from the bootstrapping exercises, we have shown previously. DEA efficiency estimates are frequently used to compare the performance of one producer, or one group of producers, to another. However, bootstrapping tends to generate confidence intervals that are sufficiently wide to question the reliability of inferences drawn from such comparisons. This message mirrors that of the relatively wide confidence intervals surrounding SFA efficiency estimates.

In chapter 4, Simar and Wilson provide the analytical details, explain why and how to bootstrap, and discuss hypothesis testing.

1.7 Malmquist Productivity Indexes

Throughout this chapter, and particularly in section 1.3, we associate distance functions with efficiency measures. Here we show how distance functions also constitute the building blocks for a measure of productivity change. The story begins with Malmquist (1953), who introduced the input distance function in the context of consumption analysis. His objective was to compare alternative consumption bundles. He did so by developing a standard of living (or consumption quantity) index as the ratio of a pair of input distance functions. In the context of production analysis, Malmquist's standard of living index becomes an input quantity index. An analogous output quantity index is expressed as the ratio of a pair of output distance functions.

An obvious extension is to define a productivity index based on distance functions. Two such indexes have been developed, both bearing Malmquist's name even though he proposed neither one. One index is defined as the ratio of an output quantity index to an input quantity index. The output quantity index is a ratio of output distance functions, and the input quantity index is a ratio of input distance functions. It provides a rigorous extension to multiple outputs and multiple inputs of the fundamental notion of productivity as the ratio of output to input discussed in section 1.2. Caves et al. (1982b) mentioned and dismissed this index, which subsequently was introduced by Bjurek (1996). The other index uses only output distance functions or only input distance functions. In its output-oriented form it defines a productivity index as the ratio of a pair of output distance functions, and in its input-oriented form it defines a productivity index as the ratio of a pair of input distance functions. Caves et al. introduced this version of the Malmquist productivity index, and it is the subject of this section because it is more popular than the Bjurek version.

Intuition is provided by figure 1.19, in which a producer's input and output are depicted in two adjacent periods. It is obvious that productivity has increased, since $(y^{t+1}/x^{t+1}) > (y^t/x^t)$ or, equivalently, $(y^{t+1}/y^t) > (x^{t+1}/x^t)$. The challenge is to quantify productivity growth. A Malmquist productivity index does so by introducing the period t technology T_c^t as a benchmark and by comparing the distances of (y^{t+1}, x^{t+1}) and (y^t, x^t) to T_c^t. Distance can be measured vertically, with an output expanding orientation, or horizontally, with an input-conserving orientation, depending on the orientation of producers. The ratio of these two distances provides a quantitative measure of productivity change, which in figure 1.19 is greater than unity with either orientation.

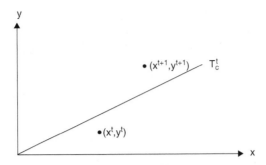

Figure 1.19. The Malmquist Productivity Index I

This raises the question of how to specify the period t technology. Caves et al. (1982b) defined their index on a technology that allowed for varying returns to scale. However Grifell-Tatjé and Lovell (1995) showed, by way of a simple numerical example, that this convention creates an index that ignores the contribution of scale economies to productivity growth. Färe and Grosskopf (1996) proved that if $M = N = 1$, the Caves et al. index provides an accurate measure of productivity change in the sense that it equals $(y^{t+1}/y^t)/(x^{t+1}/x^t)$ if, and only if, the index is defined on a technology exhibiting constant returns to scale. In light of these results, we follow what is now common practice by defining the Caves et al. index on a *benchmark* technology satisfying constant returns to scale, which is to be distinguished from a *best-practice* technology allowing for variable returns to scale. This convention enables the Malmquist productivity index to incorporate the influence of scale economies on productivity change, as a departure of the best-practice technology from the benchmark technology. In the general $M > 1, N > 1$ case, the influence of scale economies can be broadened to include the influence of changes in the output mix and changes in the input mix.

1.7.1 Definitions and properties

As in section 1.3, let inputs $x \in R_+^N$ be used to produce outputs $y \in R_+^M$. The benchmark technology $T_c = \{(y, x) : x \text{ can produce } y\}$ is the set of all technologically feasible output–input combinations and is assumed to satisfy global constant returns to scale. The output set $P_c(x) = \{y : (x, y) \in T_c\}$ is the set of all technologically feasible output vectors given inputs x, with outer boundary given by the output isoquant $I_c(x) = \{y \in P_c(x), \lambda y \notin P_c(x) \; \forall \lambda > 1\}$. The output distance function is defined on $P_c(x)$ as $D_{oc}(x, y) = \min\{\lambda : (y/\lambda) \in P_c(x)\}$.

Using the period t benchmark technology, the period t output-oriented Malmquist productivity index is written as

$$M_{oc}^t(x^t, y^t, x^{t+1}, y^{t+1}) = \frac{D_{oc}^t(x^{t+1}, y^{t+1})}{D_{oc}^t(x^t, y^t)}. \tag{1.60}$$

$M_{oc}^t(x^t, y^t, x^{t+1}, y^{t+1})$ compares (x^{t+1}, y^{t+1}) to (x^t, y^t) by comparing their distances to the benchmark technology T_c^t. Although $D_{oc}^t(x^t, y^t) \leq 1$ because (x^t, y^t) must be feasible for T_c^t, $D_{oc}^t(x^{t+1}, y^{t+1}) \gtreqless 1$ because (x^{t+1}, y^{t+1}) may or may not be feasible for T_c^t. Hence, $M_{oc}^t(x^t, y^t, x^{t+1}, y^{t+1}) \gtreqless 1$ according as productivity growth, stagnation, or decline has occurred between periods t and t + 1, from the forward-looking perspective of period t benchmark technology.

Using the period t + 1 benchmark technology, the period t + 1 output-oriented Malmquist productivity index is written as

$$M_{oc}^{t+1}(x^t, y^t, x^{t+1}, y^{t+1}) = \frac{D_{oc}^{t+1}(x^{t+1}, y^{t+1})}{D_{oc}^{t+1}(x^t, y^t)}. \tag{1.61}$$

$M_{oc}^{t+1}(x^t, y^t, x^{t+1}, y^{t+1})$ compares (x^{t+1}, y^{t+1}) to (x^t, y^t) by comparing their distances to the benchmark technology T_c^{t+1}. Although $D_{oc}^{t+1}(x^{t+1}, y^{t+1}) \leq 1$ because (x^{t+1}, y^{t+1}) must be feasible for T_c^{t+1}, $D_{oc}^{t+1}(x^t, y^t) \gtreqless 1$ because (x^t, y^t) may or may not be feasible for T_c^{t+1}. Hence, $M_{oc}^{t+1}(x^t, y^t, x^{t+1}, y^{t+1}) \gtreqless 1$ according as productivity growth, stagnation, or decline has occurred between periods t and t + 1, from the backward-looking perspective of period t + 1 benchmark technology.

Both indexes compare (x^{t+1}, y^{t+1}) to (x^t, y^t), but they use benchmark technologies from different periods. The choice of benchmark technology is arbitrary, and the two indexes are not necessarily equal except under restrictive neutrality conditions on technical change. Indeed, one index may signal productivity growth and the other productivity decline. Consequently, it is conventional to define the Malmquist productivity index as the geometric mean of the two, and to write it as

$$M_{oc}(x^t, y^t, x^{t+1}, y^{t+1}) = \left\{ \left[M_{oc}^t(x^t, y^t, x^{t+1}, y^{t+1}) \times M_{oc}^{t+1}(x^t, y^t, x^{t+1}, y^{t+1}) \right] \right\}^{1/2}$$

$$= \left[\frac{D_{oc}^t(x^{t+1}, y^{t+1})}{D_{oc}^t(x^t, y^t)} \times \frac{D_{oc}^{t+1}(x^{t+1}, y^{t+1})}{D_{oc}^{t+1}(x^t, y^t)} \right]^{1/2}. \tag{1.62}$$

$M_{oc}(x^t, y^t, x^{t+1}, y^{t+1}) \gtreqless 1$ according as productivity growth, stagnation, or decline has occurred between periods t and t + 1.

The two Malmquist productivity indexes are illustrated in figure 1.20, with $M = N = 1$. $M_{oc}^t(x^t, y^t, x^{t+1}, y^{t+1}) > 1$ (indicated by the solid arrows) because output has increased faster than input relative to the period t benchmark technology. This shows up in (1.60) as $D_{oc}^t(x^t, y^t) < 1$ and $D_{oc}^t(x^{t+1}, y^{t+1}) > 1$. $M_{oc}^{t+1}(x^t, y^t, x^{t+1}, y^{t+1}) > 1$ (indicated by the dotted arrows) because output has increased faster than input relative to the period t + 1 benchmark technology. This shows up in (1.61) as $D_{oc}^{t+1}(x^t, y^t) < D_{oc}^{t+1}(x^{t+1}, y^{t+1}) < 1$. Consequently, $M_{oc}(x^t, y^t, x^{t+1}, y^{t+1}) > 1$.

Because it is based on output distance functions, which satisfy a number of desirable properties, $M_{oc}(x^t, y^t, x^{t+1}, y^{t+1})$ also satisfies a number of

Figure 1.20. The Malmquist Productivity Index II

properties. The Malmquist productivity index satisfies most of the following desirable properties, with failure indicated by an inequality:

M1: Weak Monotonicity

$$y'' \geq y' \Rightarrow M_{oc}(x^t, y^t, x^{t+1}, y'') \geq M_{oc}(x^t, y^t, x^{t+1}, y')$$
$$y'' \geq y'' \Rightarrow M_{oc}(x^t, y'', x^{t+1}, y^{t+1}) \leq M_{oc}(x^t, y', x^{t+1}, y^{t+1})$$
$$x'' \geq x' \Rightarrow M_{oc}(x^t, y^t, x'', y^{t+1}) \leq M_{oc}(x^t, y^t, x', y^{t+1})$$
$$x'' \geq x' \Rightarrow M_{oc}(x'', y^t, x^{t+1}, y^{t+1}) \geq M_{oc}(x', y^t, x^{t+1}, y^{t+1})$$

M2: Homogeneity

$$M_{oc}(x^t, y^t, x^{t+1}, \lambda y^{t+1}) = \lambda M_{oc}(x^t, y^t, x^{t+1}, y^{t+1}), \lambda > 0$$
$$M_{oc}(x^t, \lambda y^t, x^{t+1}, y^{t+1}) = \lambda^{-1} M_{oc}(x^t, y^t, x^{t+1}, y^{t+1}), \lambda > 0$$
$$M_{oc}(x^t, \lambda y^t, x^{t+1}, \lambda y^{t+1}) = M_{oc}(x^t, y^t, x^{t+1}, y^{t+1}), \lambda > 0$$
$$M_{oc}(x^t, y^t, \lambda x^{t+1}, y^{t+1}) = \lambda^{-1} M_{oc}(x^t, y^t, x^{t+1}, y^{t+1}), \lambda > 0$$
$$M_{oc}(\lambda x^t, y^t, x^{t+1}, y^{t+1}) = \lambda M_{oc}(x^t, y^t, x^{t+1}, y^{t+1}), \lambda > 0$$
$$M_{oc}(\lambda x^t, y^t, \lambda x^{t+1}, y^{t+1}) = M_{oc}(x^t, y^t, x^{t+1}, y^{t+1}), \lambda > 0$$

M3: Proportionality

$$M_{oc}(x^t, y^t, x^{t+1}, \mu y^t) \neq \mu, \mu > 0$$
$$M_{oc}(x^t, y^t, \lambda x^t, y^{t+1}) \neq \lambda^{-1}, \lambda > 0$$
$$M_{oc}(x^t, y^t, \lambda x^t, \mu y^t) = \mu/\lambda, \mu, \lambda > 0$$

M4: Identity

$$M_{oc}(x, y, x, y) = 1$$

M5: Commensurability (independence of units of measurement)

$$M_{oc}(\mu_1 x_1^t, \ldots, \mu_N x_N^t, \lambda_1 y_1^t, \ldots, \lambda_M y_M^t, \mu_1 x_1^{t+1}, \ldots, \mu_N x_N^{t+1},$$
$$\lambda_1 y_1^{t+1}, \ldots, \lambda_M y_M^{t+1}) = M_{oc}(x^t, y^t, x^{t+1}, y^{t+1}), \lambda_m > 0,$$
$$m = 1, \ldots, M, \mu_n > 0, n = 1, \ldots, N$$

M6: Circularity

$$M_{oc}(x^t, y^t, x^{t+1}, y^{t+1}) \cdot M_{oc}(x^{t+1}, y^{t+1}, x^{t+2}, y^{t+2})$$
$$\neq M_{oc}(x^t, y^t, x^{t+2}, y^{t+2})$$

M7: Time Reversal

$$M_{oc}(x^t, y^t, x^{t+1}, y^{t+1}) = [M_{oc}(x^{t+1}, y^{t+1}, x^t, y^t)]^{-1}$$

Although the Malmquist productivity index does not satisfy the proportionality test in either outputs or inputs separately, it does satisfy the proportionality test in outputs and inputs simultaneously. In addition, it is not circular except under restrictive neutrality conditions on technical change. The seriousness of the failure to satisfy the circularity test depends on the persuasiveness of the arguments of Fisher (1922), who rejected the test, and of Frisch (1936), who endorsed it. We leave this evaluation to the reader, who may seek guidance from Samuelson and Swamy (1974).

In section 1.3, we note that distance to a production frontier can be measured hyperbolically or directionally. The two distance functions $D_H(y, x)$ and $D_D(y, x)$ can be used to derive hyperbolic and directional Malmquist productivity indexes analogous to the output-oriented Malmquist productivity index discussed in this section. A Malmquist productivity index based on directional distance functions is used extensively in chapter 5.

1.7.2 Decomposing the Malmquist productivity index

In section 1.2, we note that the BLS and the OECD attribute productivity change to technical change, efficiency change, scale economies, and changes in the operating environment in which production occurs. It is possible to decompose the Malmquist productivity index (1.62) into the first three of these sources. Thus, this index is capable not just of quantifying productivity change, but also of quantifying its three principal sources.

Färe et al. (1992) obtained an initial decomposition of (1.62). The mathematics is straightforward, and the economics is enlightening. Extracting the term $[D_{oc}^{t+1}(x^{t+1}, y^{t+1})/D_{oc}^t(x^t, y^t)]$ from the right side of (1.62) yields

$$M_{oc}(x^t, y^t, x^{t+1}, y^{t+1}) = \frac{D_{oc}^{t+1}(x^{t+1}, y^{t+1})}{D_{oc}^t(x^t, y^t)}$$

$$\times \left[\frac{D_{oc}^t(x^t, y^t)}{D_{oc}^{t+1}(x^t, y^t)} \times \frac{D_{oc}^t(x^{t+1}, y^{t+1})}{D_{oc}^{t+1}(x^{t+1}, y^{t+1})} \right]^{1/2}$$

$$= TE\Delta_{oc}(x^t, y^t, x^{t+1}, y^{t+1}) \times T\Delta_{oc}(x^t, y^t, x^{t+1}, y^{t+1}). \tag{1.63}$$

Recalling from section 1.3 that $TE_o(x, y) = [D_o(x, y)]^{-1}$, the first term on the right side of (1.63) measures the contribution of technical efficiency change to productivity change. $\text{TE}\Delta_{oc}(x^t, y^t, x^{t+1}, y^{t+1}) \gtreqless 1$ according as technical efficiency improves, remains unchanged, or deteriorates between periods t and t + 1. The second term on the right side of (1.63) measures the contribution of technical change to productivity change. It is the geometric mean of two terms, one comparing period t technology to period t + 1 technology from the perspective of period t data, and the other comparing the two technologies from the perspective of period t + 1 data. $\text{T}\Delta_{oc}(x^t, y^t, x^{t+1}, y^{t+1}) \gtreqless 1$ according as technical progress, stagnation, or regress has occurred between periods t and t + 1. In figure 1.20, it is apparent that productivity growth has occurred between periods t and t + 1 because technical efficiency has improved and because technical progress has occurred.

There is, however, a problem with decomposition (1.63), which is why we refer to it as an initial decomposition. Productivity change is properly measured relative to the benchmark technologies T_c^t and T_c^{t+1}. Unfortunately, so are its technical efficiency change and technical change components. They should be measured relative to the best-practice technologies T^t and T^{t+1} that are not constrained to satisfy global constant returns to scale. In addition, (1.63) attributes productivity change exclusively to technical efficiency change and technical change. Introducing a term capturing the contribution of scale economies requires introducing the best-practice technologies.

Figure 1.21 illustrates a subsequent decomposition. The middle row corresponds to the initial decomposition in (1.63). The bottom row describes a generic decomposition of productivity change into a technical efficiency change component $\text{TE}\Delta_o(x^t, y^t, x^{t+1}, y^{t+1})$ measured relative to the best-practice technologies, a technical change component $\text{T}\Delta_o(x^t, y^t, x^{t+1}, y^{t+1})$ characterizing the shift in the best-practice technologies, and a third component $\text{S}\Delta_o(x^t, y^t, x^{t+1}, y^{t+1})$ measuring the contribution of scale economies to productivity change. However, there is more than one way to implement this subsequent decomposition mathematically, and different mathematical decompositions have different economic interpretations. All appear to agree that a subsequent decomposition is needed, but disagreement over the nature of the subsequent decomposition persists. Grosskopf (2003) and Lovell (2003) survey the landscape, and the decomposition issue is revisited in chapter 5.

1.7.3 Evaluating Malmquist

The Malmquist productivity index has several nice theoretical features. Because it is based on distance functions, it inherits several desirable properties from them. Again, because it is based on distance functions, it readily accommodates multiple outputs as well as multiple inputs. The output expanding orientation can be reversed to generate an input-oriented Malmquist productivity index based on input distance functions, and nothing of substance would change.

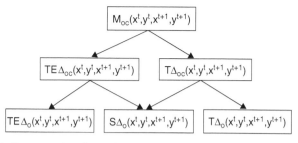

Figure 1.21. Decomposing the Malmquist Productivity Index

The Malmquist productivity index also has a very nice practical feature. Once again, because it is based on distance functions, it requires information on quantities but not prices. This makes it suitable for productivity measurement in situations in which prices are distorted or missing. We mention several such situations in section 1.2, and we revisit the issue in section 1.8.

The Malmquist productivity index can be decomposed into economically meaningful sources of productivity change, as figure 1.21 suggests. However, its decomposition requires a number of producers sufficiently large to enable one to construct benchmark and best-practice technologies for each period. Construction can be based on either SFA techniques introduced in section 1.5 or DEA techniques introduced in section 1.6, as we indicate in section 1.8. Particularly in the widely used DEA approach, however, the statistical significance of the contributions of the "economically meaningful" components is rarely investigated.

One potential source of productivity change is the vector z of exogenous variables previously discussed in the context of SFA and DEA. The pros and cons of alternative approaches to incorporating z in SFA and DEA efficiency analysis apply with equal force to the use of SFA and DEA to implement a Malmquist productivity analysis, a topic to which we now turn.

1.8 Approximating Malmquist

The Malmquist productivity index is a theoretical index, expressed in terms of distance functions defined on the true, but unknown, technology. If the index is to be implemented empirically, it must be approximated. Two philosophically different approaches have emerged. The older approach, which is far more popular, uses price information in place of technology information to *compute* productivity index numbers that provide empirical approximations to the theoretical Malmquist productivity index. This is the approach adopted by government statistical agencies around the world. The newer approach eschews price information and uses either econometric or mathematical programming techniques to *estimate* the theoretical Malmquist productivity index itself, by estimating its component distance functions that characterize the structure of the underlying technology. Balk (1998), Diewert (1981, 1987), and Diewert and Nakamura (2003, 2006) survey the literature.

1.8.1 Superlative index numbers: Fisher and Törnqvist

Suppose that producers use inputs $x \in R^N_+$ available at prices $w \in R^N_{++}$ to produce outputs $y \in R^M_+$ for sale at prices $p \in R^M_{++}$.

Laspeyres output quantity and input quantity indexes use base period prices to weight quantity changes:

$$Y_L = p^{tT}y^{t+1}/p^{tT}y^t,$$
$$X_L = w^{tT}x^{t+1}/w^{tT}x^t. \tag{1.64}$$

Paasche output quantity and input quantity indexes use comparison period prices to weight quantity changes:

$$Y_P = p^{t+1T}y^{t+1}/p^{t+1T}y^t,$$
$$X_P = w^{t+1T}x^{t+1}/w^{t+1T}x^t. \tag{1.65}$$

Fisher (1922) output quantity and input quantity indexes are geometric means of Laspeyres and Paasche indexes:

$$Y_F = (Y_L \times Y_P)^{1/2} = [(p^{tT}y^{t+1}/p^{tT}y^t) \times (p^{t+1T}y^{t+1}/p^{t+1T}y^t)]^{1/2},$$
$$X_F = (X_L \times X_P)^{1/2} = [(w^{tT}x^{t+1}/w^{tT}x^t) \times (w^{t+1T}x^{t+1}/w^{t+1T}x^t)]^{1/2}. \tag{1.66}$$

Fisher quantity indexes use both base period and comparison period prices to weight quantity changes. A Fisher productivity index is defined as

$$\Pi_F = \frac{Y_F}{X_F} = \frac{[(p^{tT}y^{t+1}/p^{tT}y^t) \times (p^{t+1T}y^{t+1}/p^{t+1T}y^t)]^{1/2}}{[(w^{tT}x^{t+1}/w^{tT}x^t) \times (w^{t+1T}x^{t+1}/w^{t+1T}x^t)]^{1/2}}. \tag{1.67}$$

Π_F makes no use of the true but unobserved technology and does not estimate it. It is computed from observable information on prices and quantities in base and comparison periods. What sort of approximation to the truth does it provide?

Diewert (1992) proved that, under certain conditions, $\Pi_F = M_{oc}(x^t, y^t, x^{t+1}, y^{t+1})$, so that there is no approximation error at all. However, these conditions are restrictive, collectively if not individually, and require the following:

- The output distance functions must be defined on the benchmark technologies exhibiting constant returns to scale.
- The output distance functions must have a flexible functional form that is not reproduced here.

- The period t and period t + 1 output distance functions must have certain coefficients identical, which limits the extent to which technology can differ from one period to the next.
- Production in both periods must be allocatively efficient in competitive output markets and competitive input markets.

The first three requirements are not terribly restrictive, but the final requirement is, since it precludes precisely what this book is concerned with, a failure to optimize. Unfortunately, we do not know the extent to which the performance of Π_F deteriorates as allocative inefficiency increases.

Törnqvist (1936) output and input quantity indexes are given (in logarithmic form) by

$$\ln Y_T = (1/2)\Sigma_m[(p_m^t y_m^t / \Sigma_m p_m^t y_m^t) + (p_m^{t+1} y_m^{t+1} / \Sigma_m p_m^{t+1} y_m^{t+1})]\ln(y_m^{t+1}/y_m^t),$$
$$\ln X_T = (1/2)\Sigma_n[(w_n^t x_n^t / \Sigma_n w_n^t x_n^t) + (w_n^{t+1} x_n^{t+1} / \Sigma_n w_n^{t+1} x_n^{t+1})]\ln(x_n^{t+1}/x_n^t).$$
$$(1.68)$$

The output quantity index uses the arithmetic mean of adjacent period revenue shares to weight output quantity changes, and the input quantity index uses the arithmetic mean of adjacent period cost shares to weight input quantity changes. A Törnqvist productivity index is defined as

$$\Pi_T = \frac{Y_T}{X_T} = \exp\{\ln Y_T - \ln X_T\}$$
$$= \exp\{(1/2)\Sigma_m[(p_m^t y_m^t / \Sigma_m p_m^t y_m^t) + (p_m^{t+1} y_m^{t+1} / \Sigma_m p_m^{t+1} y_m^{t+1})]\ln(y_m^{t+1}/y_m^t)$$
$$- (1/2)\Sigma_n[(w_n^t x_n^t / \Sigma_n w_n^t x_n^t) + (w_n^{t+1} x_n^{t+1} / \Sigma_n w_n^{t+1} x_n^{t+1})]\ln(x_n^{t+1}/x_n^t)\}.$$
$$(1.69)$$

Like the Fisher productivity index, the Törnqvist productivity index makes no use of the true but unobserved technology and does not estimate it. It is computed from observable information on shares and quantities in base and comparison periods. What sort of approximation to the truth does it provide?

Caves et al. (1982b) proved that, under certain conditions, $\Pi_T = M_{oc}(x^t, y^t, x^{t+1}, y^{t+1})$, so that there is no approximation error at all. However, these conditions are restrictive, collectively if not individually, and require the following:

- All output quantities and all input quantities must be strictly positive.
- The output distance functions must be defined on the benchmark technologies exhibiting constant returns to scale.
- The output distance functions must have flexible translog functional form.
- The period t and period t + 1 output distance functions must have identical second-order coefficients, which limits the extent to which technology can differ from one period to the next.

• Production in both periods must be allocatively efficient in competitive output markets and competitive input markets.

Our evaluation of the Törnqvist productivity index parallels our evaluation of the Fisher productivity index. The first four requirements are not terribly restrictive, although the first does rule out corner solutions. However, the final requirement is restrictive, since it precludes a failure to optimize. Unfortunately, we do not know the extent to which the performance of Π_T deteriorates as allocative inefficiency increases.

In the economic approach to index numbers Fisher and Törnqvist productivity indexes are called *superlative* because, under the conditions stated previously, each provides a close approximation to the truth as given by the theoretical Malmquist productivity index. If production technology is characterized by a flexible functional form (either Diewert or translog output distance functions), and if producers are allocatively efficient in competitive markets, then subject to some provisos, $\Pi_F = M_{oc}(x^t, y^t, x^{t+1}, y^{t+1}) = \Pi_T$. However, we do not yet have a good sense of the performance of either Π_F or Π_T in the presence of scale economies, market power, or allocative inefficiency. In addition, like the Malmquist productivity index itself, Π_F and Π_T are bilateral indexes that fail the circularity test. Both can be converted to circular multilateral indexes, but at a cost: The weights applied to quantity changes depend on the data of all producers, not just on the data of the producer whose productivity change is being measured. Caves et al. (1982a) provide the details for Π_T and references for Π_F.

1.8.2 An econometric approach

The econometric tools summarized in section 1.5 can be adapted to the estimation and decomposition of a Malmquist productivity index. We summarize an approach suggested by Orea (2002). This approach extends previous analyses of Denny et al. (1981) and Nishimizu and Page (1982) and exploits the Caves et al. (1982b) analysis of the relationship between a Malmquist productivity index and a translog specification of the underlying distance functions. Suppose the output distance functions in the Malmquist productivity index have translog functional form in (x, y, t), such that

$$\ln D_o(x, y, t) = \alpha_o + \Sigma_n \alpha_n \ln x_n + \Sigma_m \beta_m \ln y_m + (1/2)\Sigma_n \Sigma_k \alpha_{nk} \ln x_n \ln x_k$$
$$+ (1/2)\Sigma_m \Sigma_q \beta_{mq} \ln y_m \ln y_q + \Sigma_n \Sigma_m \gamma_{nm} \ln x_n \ln y_m + \delta_t t$$
$$+ (1/2)\delta_{tt} t^2 + \Sigma_n \delta_{tn} t \ln x_n + \Sigma_m \delta_{tm} t \ln y_m. \qquad (1.70)$$

Since this function is quadratic in (x, y, t), the change in the value of the distance function from period t to period t + 1 can be decomposed into the impacts of changes in outputs, changes in inputs, and the passage of time by means of

$$\ln D_o(x^{t+1}, y^{t+1}, t+1) - \ln D_o(x^t, y^t, t)$$

$$= (1/2)\Sigma_m \left[\frac{\partial \ln D_o(x^{t+1}, y^{t+1}, t+1)}{\partial \ln y_m} + \frac{\partial \ln D_o(x^t, y^t, t)}{\partial \ln y_m} \right] \cdot \ln(y_m^{t+1}/y_m^t)$$

$$+ (1/2)\Sigma_n \left[\frac{\partial \ln D_o(x^{t+1}, y^{t+1}, t+1)}{\partial \ln x_n} + \frac{\partial \ln D_o(x^t, y^t, t)}{\partial \ln x_n} \right] \cdot \ln(x_n^{t+1}/x_n^t)$$

$$+ (1/2) \left[\frac{\partial \ln D_o(x^{t+1}, y^{t+1}, t+1)}{\partial t} + \frac{\partial \ln D_o(x^t, y^t, t)}{\partial t} \right]. \tag{1.71}$$

If we define a logarithmic Malmquist productivity index $M_o(x, y, t)$ as the difference between weighted average rates of growth of outputs and inputs, with distance function elasticities as weights, (1.70) and (1.71) yield

$$\ln M_o(x, y, t) = (1/2)\Sigma_m \left[\frac{\partial \ln D_o(x^{t+1}, y^{t+1}, t+1)}{\partial \ln y_m} + \frac{\partial \ln D_o(x^t, y^t, t)}{\partial \ln y_m} \right] \cdot \ln(y_m^{t+1}/y_m^t)$$

$$- (1/2)\Sigma_n \left[\frac{-\partial \ln D_o(x^{t+1}, y^{t+1}, t+1)}{\partial \ln x_n} + \frac{\partial \ln D_o(x^t, y^t, t)}{\partial \ln x_n} \right] \cdot \ln(x_n^{t+1}/x_n^t),$$

$$\tag{1.72}$$

from which it follows that

$$\ln M_o(x, y, t) = [\ln D_o(x^{t+1}, y^{t+1}, t+1) - \ln D_o(x^t, y^t, t)]$$

$$- (1/2) \left[\frac{\partial \ln D_o(x^{t+1}, y^{t+1}, t+1)}{\partial t} + \frac{\partial \ln D_o(x^t, y^t, t)}{\partial t} \right]. $$

$$\tag{1.73}$$

Expression (1.73) decomposes the logarithmic Malmquist productivity index $\ln M_o(x, y, t)$ into a term capturing the impact of technical efficiency change and a term capturing the impact of technical change. However, because we did not impose constant returns to scale on $\ln D_o(x, y, t)$ in (1.70), the input weights in (1.72) do not necessarily sum to unity, and consequently, $\ln M_o(x, y, t)$ in (1.73) ignores the contribution of scale economies to productivity change. The two terms on the right side of (1.73) are correct, but $\ln M_o(x, y, t)$ is not a proper productivity index, as we note in section 1.7. The two components on the right side of (1.73) correspond to $TE\Delta_o(x^t, y^t, x^{t+1}, y^{t+1})$ and $T\Delta_o(x^t, y^t, x^{t+1}, y^{t+1})$ in figure 1.20, but a scale economies component corresponding to $S\Delta_o(x^t, y^t, x^{t+1}, y^{t+1})$ is missing.

Expression (1.72) decomposes $M_o(x, y, t)$ by aggregating outputs and inputs using distance function elasticities. Decomposing $M_o(x, y, t)$ by aggregating outputs and inputs using distance function elasticity *shares* instead gives

$$\ln M_o(x, y, t) = (1/2)\Sigma_m[\varepsilon_m(x^{t+1}, y^{t+1}, t+1) + \varepsilon_m(x^t, y^t, t)] \cdot \ln(y_m^{t+1}/y_m^t)$$
$$- (1/2)\Sigma_n[\varepsilon_n(x^{t+1}, y^{t+1}, t+1)$$
$$+ \varepsilon_n(x^t, y^t, t)] \cdot \ln(x_n^{t+1}/x_n^t), \tag{1.74}$$

where

$$\varepsilon_m(x^s, y^s, s) = \frac{\partial \ln D_o(x^s, y^s, s)}{\partial \ln y_m},$$

$$\varepsilon_n(x^s, y^s, s) = \frac{\partial \ln D_o(x^s, y^s, s)/\partial \ln x_n}{\Sigma_n \partial \ln D_o(x^s, y^s, s)/\partial \ln x_n},$$

for $s = t, t+1$.

$\ln M_{oc}(x, y, t)$ in (1.74) is a proper productivity index because its input weights sum to unity. Consequently, it corresponds to a benchmark technology satisfying constant returns to scale, as is required if it is to provide an accurate measure of productivity change. Finally, substituting (1.73) into (1.74) yields

$$\ln M_o(x, y, t) = [\ln D_o(x^{t+1}, y^{t+1}, t+1) - \ln D_o(x^t, y^t, t)]$$

$$- (1/2)\left[\frac{\partial \ln D_o(x^{t+1}, y^{t+1}, t+1}{\partial t} + \frac{\partial \ln D_o(x^t, y^t, t)}{\partial t}\right]$$

$$+(1/2)\Sigma_n \left[\begin{array}{l} \left(-\Sigma\dfrac{\partial \ln D_o(x^{t+1}, y^{t+1}, t+1)}{\partial \ln x_n} - 1\right) \cdot \varepsilon_n(x^{t+1}, y^{t+1}, t+1) \\ + \left(-\Sigma\dfrac{\partial \ln D_o(x^t, y^t, t)}{\partial \ln x_n} - 1\right) \cdot \varepsilon_n(x^t, y^t, t) \end{array}\right] \cdot \ln(x_n^{t+1}/x_n^t).$$

$$\tag{1.75}$$

Expression (1.75) attributes productivity change to technical efficiency change and technical change, both from $\ln M_o(x, y, t)$, and to scale economies, expressed as the logarithmic difference between $\ln M_{oc}(x, y, t)$ and $\ln M_o(x, y, t)$. The three terms on the right side of (1.75) provide empirical approximations to the components $TE\Delta_o(x^t, y^t, x^{t+1}, y^{t+1})$, $TA_o(x^t, y^t, x^{t+1}, y^{t+1})$, and $SA_o(x^t, y^t, x^{t+1}, y^{t+1})$ in figure 1.20, so their sum provides an empirical approximation to $M_{oc}(x^t, y^t, x^{t+1}, y^{t+1})$.

All that is required to implement (1.75) is to estimate the translog output distance function (1.70), imposing linear homogeneity in outputs and making an assumption about the error structure. After estimation, parameter estimates can be used to estimate the elasticities involved in the second and third components of the right side of (1.75). Estimation of the first component requires frontier techniques described in section 1.5 and employed by Orea (2002).

1.8.3 A mathematical programming approach

The mathematical programming tools summarized in section 1.6 also can be adapted to the estimation and decomposition of a Malmquist productivity index. We summarize an approach that originated with Färe et al. (1992) and that has been refined by many authors since.

The Malmquist productivity index given by (1.62) in section 1.7 contains four output distance functions, each defined on a benchmark technology satisfying constant returns to scale. The within-period distance functions are estimated using the CCR DEA envelopment program given by (1.53) in section 1.6:

$$D_{oc}^s(x^s, y^s), s = t, t + 1$$
$$\text{Max}_{\phi,\lambda} \phi$$
$$\text{Subject to } X^s\lambda \leqq x_o^s$$
$$\phi y_o^s \leqq Y^s\lambda$$
$$\lambda \geqq 0 \tag{1.76}$$

The adjacent-period distance functions are estimated using similar CCR DEA programs

$$D_{oc}^s(x^r, y^r), s, r = t, t + 1, s \neq r$$
$$\text{Max}_{\phi,\lambda} \phi$$
$$\text{Subject to } X^s\lambda \leqq x_o^r$$
$$\phi y_o^r \leqq Y^s\lambda$$
$$\lambda \geqq 0 \tag{1.77}$$

Substituting the solutions to these four programs into (1.62) generates a Malmquist productivity index estimated using mathematical programming techniques.

Decomposing the Malmquist productivity index requires the estimation of distance functions defined on a best-practice technology allowing for variable returns to scale. This requires use of the BCC DEA envelopment program given by (1.54) in section 1.6. $TE\Delta_o(x^t, y^t, x^{t+1}, y^{t+1})$ is estimated as the ratio of the following distance functions

$$D_o^s(x^s, y^s), s = t, t + 1$$
$$\text{Max}_{\phi,\lambda} \phi$$
$$\text{Subject to } X^s\lambda \leqq x_o^s$$
$$\phi y_o^s \leqq Y^s\lambda$$
$$\lambda \geqq 0, \Sigma_i\lambda_i = 1 \tag{1.78}$$

$T\Delta_0(x^t, y^t, x^{t+1}, y^{t+1})$ involves these two distance functions, and the two following distance functions, as well:

$$D_{oc}^s(x^r, y^r), s, r = t, t+1, s \neq r$$
$$\text{Max}_{\phi, \lambda} \phi$$
$$\text{Subject to } X^s \lambda \leqq x_o^r$$
$$\phi y_o^r \leqq Y^s \lambda$$
$$\lambda \geqq 0, \Sigma_i \lambda_i = 1 \tag{1.79}$$

Programs (1.79) evaluate the performance of producers in period r against best-practice technology prevailing in adjacent period s. Because best-practice technologies allow for variable returns to scale, it is possible that not all programs have feasible solutions, as Ray and Desli (1997) discovered. This possibility notwithstanding, once $M_{oc}(x^t, y^t, x^{t+1}, y^{t+1})$ has been estimated using the CCR programs, and $TE\Delta_0(x^t, y^t, x^{t+1}, y^{t+1})$ and $T\Delta_0(x^t, y^t, x^{t+1}, y^{t+1})$ have been estimated using the BCC programs, the contribution of scale economies to productivity change is estimated residually by means of

$$S\Delta_0(x^t, y^t, x^{t+1}, y^{t+1}) = M_{oc}(x^t, y^t, x^{t+1}, y^{t+1})/[TE\Delta_0(x^t, y^t, x^{t+1}, y^{t+1})$$
$$\cdot T\Delta_0(x^t, y^t, x^{t+1}, y^{t+1})]. \tag{1.80}$$

1.8.4 Evaluating the approximations

Since the truth is unknown, it is difficult to judge the accuracy of the econometric estimate of the Malmquist productivity index discussed in section 1.8.2 and the mathematical programming estimate of the Malmquist productivity index discussed in section 1.8.3. It is similarly difficult to judge whether an empirical Malmquist productivity index, estimated from either econometric or mathematical programming techniques, provides a better or worse approximation to the truth than a computed Fisher or Törnqvist productivity index does. In both cases, statistical inference is required.

We can, however, make some relevant observations:

- First and foremost, Fisher and Törnqvist indexes are superlative only under restrictive assumptions. Among them are allocative efficiency, which we believe should be treated as a hypothesis to be tested rather than as a maintained assumption. The econometric and mathematical programming approaches do not assume allocative efficiency. They are capable of testing the hypothesis, by comparing market price ratios with estimated shadow price ratios.
- Second, Fisher and Törnqvist indexes require price or share information in their computation. But prices (and therefore shares) can be distorted by market power, by cross-subsidy, and by regulation. In addition, prices

are missing in large parts of the nonmarket sector of the economy. The econometric and mathematical programming approaches do not require price information.

- Third, the econometric and mathematical programming approaches generate the same structural decomposition of the Malmquist productivity index, enabling one to attribute productivity change to technical efficiency change, technical change, and the contribution of scale economies. These are the sources identified by the U.S. BLS and the OECD. Ray and Mukherjee (1996) and Kuosmanen and Sipiläinen (2004) have obtained similar decompositions of the Fisher index, but the Törnqvist index has resisted similar efforts. The Fisher and Törnqvist productivity indexes have much more natural decompositions in terms of identifying the contributions of individual variables. Balk (2004) surveys the literature, and Salerian (2003) provides an application to Australian railroads.

1.9 Concluding Remarks

We began this chapter with an investigation into the recent variation in the economic and financial performance of U.S. airlines. Variation in efficiency and productivity is commonplace, and examples are reported regularly in the business press. Since business performance variation exists, it is incumbent on the profession to develop the analytical tools and the empirical techniques needed to study it. If we can quantify it, and if we can identify its sources, we have a chance of adopting private practices and public policies designed to improve it.

We have provided motivation for the study of efficiency and productivity, and we have referred to a wide range of empirical applications. We have laid out the basics of the underlying theory and the empirical techniques. The reader is now properly motivated and adequately prepared to continue on to the more extensive analyses provided in subsequent chapters.

References

Abad, C., S. A. Thore, and J. Laffarga (2004), "Fundamental Analysis of Stocks by Two-Stage DEA," *Managerial and Decision Economics* 25:5 (July-August), 231–41.

Abramovitz, M. (1956), "Resource and Output Trends in the United States Since 1870," *American Economic Review* 46:2 (May), 5–23.

Afriat, S. N. (1972), "Efficiency Estimation of Production Functions," *International Economic Review* 13:3 (October), 568–98.

Agrell, P., P. Bogetoft, and J. Tind (2005), "DEA and Dynamic Yardstick Competition in Scandinavian Electricity Distribution," *Journal of Productivity Analysis* 23:2 (March), 173–201.

Aigner, D. J., and S.-F. Chu (1968), "On Estimating the Industry Production Function," *American Economic Review* 58:4 (September), 826–39.

Aigner, D. J., C. A. K. Lovell, and P. Schmidt (1977), "Formulation and Estimation of Stochastic Frontier Production Function Models," *Journal of Econometrics* 6:1 (July), 21–37.

Alchian, A. A. (1965), "Some Economics of Property Rights," *Il Politico* 30:4 (December), 816–29.

Alchian, A. A., and R. A. Kessel (1962), "Competition, Monopoly, and the Pursuit of Money," in *Aspects of Labor Economics*. Princeton, NJ: Princeton University Press for the National Bureau of Economic Research.

Ambec, S., and P. Barla (2002), "A Theoretical Foundation of the Porter Hypothesis," *Economics Letters* 75:3 (May), 355–60.

Ammar, S., W. Duncombe, B. Jump, et al. (2004), "Constructing a Fuzzy-Knowledge-Based System: An Application for Assessing the Financial Condition of Public Schools," *Expert Systems with Applications* 27:3 (October), 349–64.

Amos, D., T. R. Beard, and S. B. Caudill (2005), "A Statistical Analysis of the Handling Characteristics of Certain Sporting Arms: Frontier Regression, the Moment of Inertia, and the Radius of Gyration," *Journal of Applied Statistics* 32:1 (January), 3–16.

Andersen, P., and Petersen, N. C. (1993), "A Procedure for Ranking Efficient Units in DEA," *Management Science* 39:10 (October), 1261–64.

Anderson, R. I., C. M. Brockman, C. Giannikos, and R. W. McLeod (2004), "A Non-Parametric Examination of Real Estate Mutual Fund Efficiency," *International Journal of Business and Economics* 3:3 (December), 225–38.

Arcelus, F. J., and P. Arocena (2005), "Productivity Differences across OECD Countries in the Presence of Environmental Constraints," *Journal of the Operational Research Society* 56:12 (December), 1352–62.

Arocena, P., and C. Waddams Price (2003), "Generating Efficiency: Economic and Environmental Regulation of Public and Private Electricity Generators in Spain," *International Journal of Industrial Organization* 20:1 (January), 41–69.

Atkinson, S. E., R. Färe, and D. Primont (2003), "Stochastic Estimation of Firm Inefficiency Using Distance Functions," *Southern Economic Journal* 69:3 (January), 596–611.

Atkinson, S. E., and C. E. Halabi (2005), "Economic Efficiency and Productivity Growth in the Post-privatization Chilean Hydroelectric Industry," *Journal of Productivity Analysis* 23:2 (March), 245–73.

Aubert, C., and A. Reynaud (2005), "The Impact of Regulation on Cost Efficiency: An Empirical Analysis of Wisconsin Water Utilities," *Journal of Productivity Analysis* 23:3 (July), 383–409.

Averch, H., and L. L. Johnson (1962), "Behavior of the Firm under Regulatory Constraint," *American Economic Review* 52:5 (December), 1052–69.

Balk, B. M. (1998), *Industrial Price, Quantity and Productivity Indexes*. Boston: Kluwer Academic Publishers.

Balk, B. M. (2004), "Decompositions of Fisher Indexes," *Economics Letters* 82:1 (January), 107–13.

Ball, V. E., C. A. K. Lovell, R. Nehring, and H. Luu (2004), "Incorporating Environmental Impacts in the Measurement of Agricultural Productivity Growth," *Journal of Agricultural and Resource Economics* 29:3 (December), 436–60.

Banker, R. D., H.-H. Chang, and S. K. Majumdar (1993), "Analyzing the Underlying Dimensions of Firm Profitability," *Managerial and Decision Economics* 14:1 (January-February), 25–36.

Banker, R. D., H. Chang, and R. Natarajan (2005), "Productivity Change, Technical Progress, and Relative Efficiency Change in the Public Accounting Industry," *Management Science* 51:2 (February), 291–304.

Banker, R. D., A. Charnes, and W. W. Cooper (1984), "Some Models for Estimating Technical and Scale Inefficiencies in Data Envelopment Analysis," *Management Science* 30:9 (September), 1078–92.

Banzhaf, H. S. (2005), "Green Price Indices," *Journal of Environmental Economics and Management* 49:2 (March), 262–80.

Barros, C. P. (2002), "Development and Conflict in the Balkans: Catch-up and Military Expenditure," *Defence and Peace Economics* 13:5, 353–63.

Barros, C. P. (2005), "Measuring Efficiency in the Hotel Industry," *Annals of Tourism Research* 32:2 (April), 456–77.

Barua, A., P. L. Brockett, W. W. Cooper, H. Deng, B. R. Parker, T. W. Ruefli, and A. Whinston (2004), "DEA Evaluations of Long- and Short-Run Efficiencies of Digital vs. Physical Product 'Dot Com' Companies," *Socio-economic Planning Sciences* 38:4 (December), 233–53.

Basso, A., and S. Funari (2003), "Measuring the Performance of Ethical Mutual Funds: A DEA Approach," *Journal of the Operational Research Society* 54:5 (May), 521–31.

Basso, A., and S. Funari (2004), "A Quantitative Approach to Evaluate the Relative Efficiency of Museums," *Journal of Cultural Economics* 28:3 (August), 195–216.

Battese, G. E., and T. Coelli (1988), "Prediction of Firm-Level Technical Efficiencies with a Generalized Frontier Production Function and Panel Data," *Journal of Econometrics* 38:3 (July), 387–99.

Battese, G. E., and T. J. Coelli (1995), "A Model for Technical Inefficiency Effects in a Stochastic Frontier Production Function for Panel Data," *Empirical Economics* 20, 325–32.

Bauer, P. W., A. N. Berger, G. D. Ferrier, and D. B. Humphrey (1998), "Consistency Conditions for Regulatory Analysis of Financial Institutions: A Comparison of Frontier Methods," *Journal of Economics and Business* 50:2 (March/April), 85–114.

Baumol, W. J. (1959), *Business Behavior, Value and Growth*. New York: Macmillan.

Becchetti, L., and J. Sierra (2003), "Bankruptcy Risk and Productive Efficiency in Manufacturing Firms," *Journal of Banking and Finance* 27:11 (November), 2099–120.

Bera, A. K., and S. C. Sharma (1999), "Estimating Production Uncertainty in Stochastic Frontier Production Function Models," *Journal of Productivity Analysis* 12:3 (November), 187–210.

Berger, A. N., and T. H. Hannan (1998), "The Efficiency Cost of Market Power in the Banking Industry: A Test of the 'Quiet Life' and Related Hypotheses," *Review of Economics and Statistics* 80:3 (August), 454–65.

Berger, A. N., and L. J. Mester (1997), "Inside the Black Box: What Explains Differences in the Efficiencies of Financial Institutions?" *Journal of Banking and Finance* 21:7 (July), 895–947.

Berle, A. A., and G. C. Means (1932), *The Modern Corporation and Private Property*. New York: Macmillan.

Bi, H. Q. (2004), "Stochastic Frrontier Analysis of a Classic Self-Thinning Experiment," *Austral Ecology* 29:4 (August), 408–17.

Birman, S. V., P. E. Pirondi, and E. Y. Rodin (2003), "Application of DEA to Medical Clinics," *Mathematical and Computer Modeling* 37:9–10 (May), 923–36.

Bishop, P., and S. Brand (2003), "The Efficiency of Museums: A Stochastic Frontier Production Function Approach," *Applied Economics* 35:17 (November), 1853–58.

Bjurek, H. (1996), "The Malmquist Total Factor Productivity Index," *Scandinavian Journal of Economics* 98:2, 303–13.

Bogetoft, P. (2000), "DEA and Activity Planning under Asymmetric Information," *Journal of Productivity Analysis* 13:1 (January), 7–48.

Bogetoft, P., and D. Wang (2005), "Estimating the Potential Gains from Mergers," *Journal of Productivity Analysis* 23:2 (March), 145–71.

Bonaccorsi, A., and C. Daraio (2003), "A Robust Nonparametric Approach to the Analysis of Scientific Productivity," *Research Evaluation* 12:1 (April), 47–69.

Borenstein, D., J. L. Becker, and V. J. do Prado (2004), "Measuring the Efficiency of Brazilian Post Office Stores Using Data Envelopment Analysis," *International Journal of Operations and Production Management* 24:9–10, 1055–78.

Bosch, N., F. Pedraja, and J. Suarez-Pandiello (2000), "Measuring the Efficiency of Spanish Municipal Refuse Collection Services," *Local Government Studies* 26:3 (Fall), 71–90.

Bowlin, W. F. (2004), "Financial Analysis of Civil Reserve Air Fleet Participants Using Data Envelopment Analysis," *European Journal of Operational Research* 154:3 (May), 691–709.

Bowlin, W. F., C. J. Renner, and J. M. Reeves (2003), "A DEA Study of Gender Equity in Executive Compensation," *Journal of the Operational Research Society* 54:7 (July), 751–57.

Brockett, P. L., W. W. Cooper, S. C. Kumbhakar, M. J. Kwinn, Jr., and D. McCarthy (2004), "Alternative Statistical Regression Studies of the Effects of Joint and Service Specific Advertising on Military Recruitment," *Journal of the Operational Research Society* 55:10 (October), 1039–48.

Buck, D. (2000), "The Efficiency of the Community Dental Service in England: A Data Envelopment Analysis," *Community Dentistry and Oral Epidemiology* 26:4 (August), 274–80.

BLS (2005), "Multifactor Productivity Trends, 2002." Bureau of Labor Statistics, U.S. Department of Labor. Available at http://www.bls.gov/news.release/pdf/prod3.pdf.

BTS (2007), "First Quarter 2007 System Airline Financial Data." Bureau of Transportation Statistics, U.S. Department of Transportation. Available at http://www.bts.gov/press_releases/2007/bts029_07/html/bts029_07.html.

Camanho, A. S., and R. G. Dyson (2005), "Cost Efficiency, Production and Value-Added Models in the Analysis of Bank Branch Performance," *Journal of the Operational Research Society* 56:5 (May), 483–94.

Carlsson, B. (1972), "The Measurement of Efficiency in Production: An Application to Swedish Manufacturing Industries, 1968," *Swedish Journal of Economics* 74:4 (December), 468–85.

Carrington, R., T. Coelli, and E. Groom (2002), "International Benchmarking for Monopoly Price Regulation: The Case of Australian Gas Distribution," *Journal of Regulatory Economics* 21:2 (March), 191–216.

Caves, D. W., L. R. Christensen, and W. E. Diewert (1982a), "Multilateral Comparisons of Output, Input, and Productivity Using Superlative Index Numbers," *Economic Journal* 92:365 (March), 73–86.

Caves, D. W., L. R. Christensen, and W. E. Diewert (1982b), "The Economic Theory of Index Numbers and the Measurement of Input, Output, and Productivity," *Econometrica* 50:6 (November), 1393–414.

Chang, H., W.-J. Chang, S. Das, and S.-H. Li (2004), "Health Care Regulation and the Operating Efficiency of Hospitals: Evidence from Taiwan," *Journal of Accounting and Public Policy* 23:6 (November-December), 483–510.

Chang, K.-P. (2004), "Evaluating Mutual Fund Performance: An Application of Minimum Convex Input Requirement Set Approach," *Computers and Operations Research* 31:6 (May), 929–40.

Charnes, A., and W. W. Cooper (1959), "Chance Constrained Programming," *Management Science* 6:1 (October), 73–79.

Charnes, A., W. W. Cooper, and E. Rhodes (1978), "Measuring the Efficiency of Decision-Making Units," *European Journal of Operational Research* 2:6 (November), 429–44.

Charnes, A., W. W. Cooper, and G. H. Symonds (1958), "Cost Horizons and Certainty Equivalents: An Approach to Stochastic Programming of Heating Oil," *Management Science* 4:3 (April), 235–63.

Chen, Y., L. Motiwalla, and M. R. Khan (2004), "Using Super-efficiency DEA to Evaluate Financial Performance of E-Business Initiative in the Retail Industry," *International Journal of Information Technology and Decision Making* 3:2 (June), 337–51.

Chen, Y., and J. Zhu (2003), "DEA Models for Identifying Critical Performance Measures," *Annals of Operations Research* 124:1–4 (November), 225–44.

Cherchye, L., W. Moesen, and T. Van Puyenbroeck (2004), "Legitimately Diverse, Yet Comparable: On Synthesizing Social Inclusion Performance in the EU," *Journal of Common Market Studies* 42:5 (December), 919–55.

Chiang, F. S., C. H. Sun, and J. M. Yu (2004a), "Technical Efficiency Analysis of Milkfish (Chanos chanos) Production in Taiwan—an Application of the Stochastic Frontier Production Function," *Aquaculture* 230:1–4 (February), 99–116.

Chiang, W.-E., M.-H. Tsai, and L. S.-M. Wang (2004b), "A DEA Evaluation of Taipei Hotels," *Annals of Tourism Research* 31:3 (July), 712–15.

Chien, Y.-L., C. J. Huang, and D. Shaw (2005), "A General Model of Starting Point Bias in Double-Bounded Dichotomous Contingent Valuation Surveys," *Journal of Environmental Economics and Management* 50:2 (September), 362–77.

Christensen, L. R., and W. H. Greene (1976), "Economies of Scale in US Electric Power Generation," *Journal of Political Economy* 84:4, Part 1 (August), 655–76.

Cielen, A., L. Peeters, and K. Vanhoof (2004), "Bankruptcy Prediction Using a Data Envelopment Analysis," *European Journal of Operational Research* 154:2 (April), 526–32.

Clark, X., D. Dollar, and A. Micco (2004), "Port Efficiency, Maritime Transport Costs, and Bilateral Trade," *Journal of Development Economics* 75:2 (December), 417–50.

Coelli, T., E. Grifell-Tatjé, and S. Perelman (2002), "Capacity Utilisation and Profitability: A Decomposition of Short-Run Profit Efficiency," *International Journal of Production Economics* 79:3 (October), 261–78.

Cook, W. D., and R. H. Green (2003), "Selecting Sites for New Facilities Using Data Envelopment Analysis," *Journal of Productivity Analysis* 19:1 (January), 77–91.

Cook, W. D., and R. H. Green (2005), "Evaluating Power Plant Efficiency: A Hierarchical Model," *Computers and Operations Research* 32:4 (April), 813–23.

Cooper, W. W., K. S. Park, and J. T. Pastor (1999), "RAM: A Range Adjusted Measure of Inefficiency for Use with Additive Models, and Relations to Other Models and Measures in DEA," *Journal of Productivity Analysis* 11:1 (February), 5–42.

Cooper, W. W., L. M. Seiford, and K. Tone (2000), *Data Envelopment Analysis*. Boston: Kluwer Academic Publishers.

Corton, M. L. (2003), "Benchmarking in the Latin American Water Sector: The Case of Peru," *Utilities Policy* 11:3 (September), 133–42.

Croppenstedt, A., and M. M. Meschi (2000), "Measuring Wage Discrimination in Italy: A Random-Coefficient Approach," *Applied Economics* 32:8 (June), 1019–28.

Cubbin, J. (2005), "Efficiency in the Water Industry," *Utilities Policy* 13:4 (December), 289–93.

Cuesta, R. A., and L. Orea (2002), "Mergers and Technical Efficiency in Spanish Savings Banks: A Stochastic Distance Function Approach," *Journal of Banking and Finance* 26:12 (December), 2231–24.

Cullinane, K., D.-W. Song, and T. Wang (2005), "The Application of Mathematical Programming Approaches to Estimating Container Port Production Efficiency," *Journal of Productivity Analysis* 24:1 (September), 73–92.

Cummins, J. D., M. Rubio-Misas, and H. Zi (2005), "The Effect of Organizational Structure on Efficiency: Evidence from the Spanish Insurance Industry," *Journal of Banking and Finance* 28:12 (December), 3113–50.

Cummins, J. D., and H. Zi (1998), "Comparison of Frontier Efficiency Methods: An Application to the U.S. Life Insurance Industry," *Journal of Productivity Analysis* 10:2 (October), 131–52.

Dalen, D. M., and A. Gómez-Lobo (2003), "Yardsticks on the Road: Regulatory Contracts and Cost Efficiency in the Norwegian Bus Industry," *Transportation* 30:4 (November), 371–86.

Davies, A. J., and A. K. Kochhar (2002), "Manufacturing Best Practice and Performance Studies: A Critique," *International Journal of Operations and Production Management* 22:3, 289–305.

Davis, S., and T. Albright (2004), "An Investigation of the Effect of Balanced Scorecard Implementation on Financial Performance," *Management Accounting Research* 15:2 (June), 135–53.

de Alessi, L. (1974), "An Economic Analysis of Government Ownership and Regulation: Theory and the Evidence from the Electric Power Industry," *Public Choice* 19:1, 1–42.

De Borger, B., K. Kerstens, and A. Costa (2002), "Public Transit Performance: What Does One Learn from Frontier Studies?" *Transport Reviews* 22:1 (January), 1–38.

Debreu, G. (1951), "The Coefficient of Resource Utilization," *Econometrica* 19:3 (July), 273–92.

Delmas, M., and Y. Tokat (2005), "Deregulation, Governance Structures, and Efficiency: The U.S. Electric Utility Sector," *Strategic Management Journal* 26:5 (May), 441–60.

Denny, M., M. Fuss, and L. Waverman (1981), "The Measurement and Interpretation of Total Factor Productivity in Regulated Industries, with an Application to Canadian Telecommunications," in T. G. Cowing and R. Stevenson, eds., *Productivity Measurement in Regulated Industries*. New York: Academic Press.

Deprins, D., and L. Simar (1989), "Estimation de Frontières Déterministes avec Facteurs Exogènes d'Inefficacité," *Annales d'Economie et de Statistique* 14 (April-June), 117–50.

Deprins, D., L. Simar, and H. Tulkens (1984), "Measuring Labor-Efficiency in Post Offices," in M. Marchand, P. Pestieau, and H. Tulkens, eds., *The Performance of Public Enterprises: Concepts and Measurement.* Amsterdam: North-Holland.

Dervaux, B., H. Leleu, V. Valdmanis, and D. Walker (2003), "Parameters of Control when Facing Stochastic Demand: A DEA Approach Applied to Bangladeshi Vaccination Sites," *International Journal of Health Care Finance and Economics* 3:4 (December), 287–99.

Dervaux, B., H. Leleu, H. Nogues, and V. Valdmanis (2006), "Assessing French Nursing Home Efficiency: An Indirect Approach via Budget-Constrained DEA Models," *Socio-economic Planning Sciences* 40:1 (March), 70–91.

Despotis, D. K. (2005), "Measuring Human Development via Data Envelopment Analysis: The Case of Asia and the Pacific," *Omega* 33:5 (October), 385–90.

Deutsch, J., and J. Silber (2005), "Measuring Multidimensional Poverty: An Empirical Comparison of Various Approaches," *Review of Income and Wealth* 51:1 (March), 145–74.

Diewert, W. E. (1981), "The Economic Theory of Index Numbers: A Survey," Chapter 7 in A. Deaton, ed., *Essays in the Theory and Measurement of Consumer Behaviour in Honour of Sir Richard Stone.* New York: Cambridge University Press.

Diewert, W. E. (1987), "Index Numbers," in J. Eatwell, M. Milgate, and P. Newman, eds., *The New Palgrave: A Dictionary of Economics*, Volume 2. New York: Macmillan Press.

Diewert, W. E. (1992), "Fisher Ideal Output, Input and Productivity Indexes Revisited," *Journal of Productivity Analysis* 3:3 (September), 211–48.

Diewert, W. E., and A. O. Nakamura (2003), "Index Number Concepts, Measures and Decompositions of Productivity Growth," *Journal of Productivity Analysis* 19:2/3 (April), 127–59.

Diewert, W. E., and A. O. Nakamura (2006), "The Measurement of Aggregate Total Factor Productivity Growth," in J. J. Heckman and E. E. Leamer, eds., *Handbook of Econometrics*, Volume 6. Amsterdam: Elsevier.

Dodson, M. E., and T. A. Garrett (2004), "Inefficient Education Spending in Public School Districts: A Case for Consolidation?" *Contemporary Economic Policy* 22:2 (April), 270–80.

Dolton, P., O. D. Marcenaro, and L. Navarro (2003), "The Effective Use of Student Time: A Stochastic Frontier Production Function Case Study," *Economics of Education Review* 22:6 (December), 547–60.

Dopuch, N., M. Gupta, D. A. Simunic, et al. (2003), "Production Efficiency and the Pricing of Audit Services," *Contemporary Accounting Research* 20:1 (Spring), 47–77.

Drake, L. M., and R. Simper (2004), "The Economics of Managerialism and the Drive for Efficiency in Policing," *Managerial and Decision Economics* 25:8 (December), 509–23.

Duke, J., and V. Torres (2005), "Multifactor Productivity Change in the Air Transportation Industry," *Monthly Labor Review* 128:3 (March), 32–45.

Edvardsen, D. F., F. R. Førsund, W. Hansen, S. A. C. Kittelsen, and T. Neurauter (2006), "Productivity and Deregulation of Norwegian Electricity Distribution Utilities," in T. J. Coelli and D. Lawrence, eds., *Performance Measurement and Regulation of Network Utilities*. Cheltenham, UK: Edward Elgar.

Eilon, S. (1984), *The Art of Reckoning—Analysis of Performance Criteria*. London: Academic Press.

Emel, A. B., M. Oral, A. Reisman, and R. Yolalan (2003), "A Credit Scoring Approach for the Commercial Banking Sector," *Socio-economic Planning Sciences* 37:2 (June), 103–23.

Färe, R., and S. Grosskopf (1996), *Intertemporal Production Frontiers: With Dynamic DEA*. Boston: Kluwer Academic Publishers.

Färe, R., S. Grosskopf, B. Lindgren, and P. Roos (1992), "Productivity Changes in Swedish Pharmacies 1980–1989: A Nonparametric Malmquist Approach," *Journal of Productivity Analysis* 3:1/2 (June), 85–101.

Färe, R., S. Grosskopf, and C. A. K. Lovell (1985), *The Measurement of Efficiency of Production*. Boston: Kluwer-Nijhoff Publishing.

Färe, R., S. Grosskopf, C. A. K. Lovell, and C. Pasurka (1989), "Multilateral Productivity Comparisons When Some Outputs Are Undesirable: A Nonparametric Approach," *Review of Economics and Statistics* 71:1 (February), 90–98.

Färe, R., S. Grosskopf, C. A. K. Lovell, and S. Yaisawarng (1993), "Derivation of Shadow Prices for Undesirable Outputs: A Distance Function Approach," *Review of Economics and Statistics* 75:2 (May), 374–80.

Färe, R., and J. Logan (1983), "The Rate-of-Return Regulated Firm: Cost and Production Duality," *Bell Journal of Economics* 14:2 (Autumn), 405–14.

Färe, R., and C. A. K. Lovell (1978), "Measuring the Technical Efficiency of Production," *Journal of Economic Theory* 19:1 (October), 150–162.

Farrell, M. J. (1957), "The Measurement of Productive Efficiency," *Journal of the Royal Statistical Society, Series A, General* 120:3, 253–82.

Farsi, M., and M. Filippini (2004), "An Empirical Analysis of Cost Efficiency in Non-profit and Public Nursing Homes," *Annals of Public and Cooperative Economics* 75:3 (September), 339–65.

Farsi, M., M. Filippini, and W. Greene (2005), "Efficiency Measurement in Network Industries: Application to the Swiss Railway Companies," *Journal of Regulatory Economics* 28:1 (July), 69–90.

Feroz, E. H., S. Kim, and R. L. Raab (2003), "Financial Statement Analysis: A Data Envelopment Analysis Approach," *Journal of the Operational Research Society* 54:1 (January), 48–58.

Ferrier, G. D., and V. G. Valdmanis (2004), "Do Mergers Improve Hospital Productivity?" *Journal of the Operational Research Society* 55:10 (October), 1071–80.

Fiorentini, G., and S. Peltzman, eds. (1995), *The Economics of Organized Crime*. New York: Cambridge University Press.

Fisher, I. (1922), *The Making of Index Numbers*. Boston: Houghton Mifflin.

Fogel, R. W., and S. L. Engerman (1974), *Time on the Cross*. Boston: Little, Brown and Company.

Foroughi, A. A., D. F. Jones, and M. Tamiz (2005), "A Selection Method for a Preferential Election," *Applied Mathematics and Computation* 163:1 (April), 107–16.

Fried, H. O., J. Lambrinos, and J. Tyner (2004), "Evaluating the Performance of Professional Golfers on the PGA, LPGA and SPGA Tours," *European Journal of Operational Research* 154:2 (April), 548–61.

Fried, H. O., C. A. K. Lovell, and P. Vanden Eeckaut (1993), "Evaluating the Performance of U.S. Credit Unions," *Journal of Banking and Finance* 17:2/3 (April), 251–65.

Frisch, R. (1936), "Annual Survey of General Economic Theory: The Problem of Index Numbers," *Econometrica* 4:1 (January), 1–38.

Frisch, R. (1965), *Theory of Production.* Chicago: Rand McNally.

Fuentes, H. J., E. Grifell-Tatjé, and S. Perelman (2001), "A Parametric Distance Function Approach for Malmquist Productivity Index Estimation," *Journal of Productivity Analysis* 15:2 (March), 79–94.

Gang, L., and B. Felmingham (2004), "Environmental Efficiency of the Australian Irrigation Industry in Treating Salt Emissions," *Australian Economic Papers* 43:4 (December), 475–90.

Gao, J., J. Campbell, and C. A. K. Lovell (2006), "Equitable Resource Allocation and Operational Efficiency Evaluation," *International Journal of Healthcare Technology and Management* 7:1/2, 143–67.

Garrett, M. A., Jr., and Z. Xu (2003), "The Efficiency of Sharecropping: Evidence from the Postbellum South," *Southern Economic Journal* 69:3 (January), 578–95.

Goldar, B., and S. Misra (2001), "Valuation of Environmental Goods: Correcting for Bias in Contingent Valuation Studies Based on Willingness-to-Accept," *American Journal of Agricultural Economics* 83:1 (February), 150–56.

Gordon, R. A. (1961), *Business Leadership in the Large Corporation.* Berkeley: University of California Press.

Greene, W. H. (1980), "Maximum Likelihood Estimation of Econometric Frontier Functions," *Journal of Econometrics* 13:1 (May), 27–56.

Greene, W. H. (2004), "Distinguishing Between Heterogeneity and Inefficiency: Stochastic Frontier Analysis of the World Health Organization's Panel Data on National Health Care Systems," *Health Economics* 13:10 (October), 959–80.

Greene, W. H., and D. Segal (2004), "Profitability and Efficiency in the U.S. Life Insurance Industry," *Journal of Productivity Analysis* 21:3 (May), 229–47.

Grifell-Tatjé, E., and C. A. K. Lovell (1995), "A Note on the Malmquist Productivity Index," *Economics Letters* 47:2 (February), 169–75.

Grifell-Tatjé, E., and C. A. K. Lovell (1999), "Profits and Productivity," *Management Science* 45:9 (September), 1177–93.

Griliches, Z. (1996), "The Discovery of the Residual: A Historical Note," *Journal of Economic Literature* 34:3 (September), 1324–30.

Grosskopf, S. (2003), "Some Remarks on Productivity and Its Decomposition," *Journal of Productivity Analysis* 20:3 (November), 459–74.

Grytten, J., and G. Rongen (2000), "Efficiency in Provision of Public Dental Services in Norway," *Community Dentistry and Oral Epidemiology* 28:3 (June), 170–76.

Guan, J. C., and J. X. Wang (2004), "Evaluation and Interpretation of Knowledge Production Efficiency," *Scientometrics* 59:1 (January), 131–55.

Guedes de Avellar, J. V., A. O. D. Polezzi, and A. Z. Milioni (2002), "On the Evaluation of Brazilian Landline Telephone Services Companies," *Pesquisa Operacional* 22:2 (July-December), 231–46.

Gymah-Brempong, K. (2000), "Cost Efficiency in Florida Prisons," in J. L. T. Blank, ed., *Public Provision and Performance.* Amsterdam: North-Holland.

Haas, D. J. (2003), "Productive Efficiency of English Football Teams—a Data Envelopment Analysis Approach," *Managerial and Decision Economics* 24:5 (August), 403–10.

Hailu, A., and T. S. Veeman (2000), "Environmentally Sensitive Productivity Analysis of the Canadian Pulp and Paper Industry, 1959–1994: An Input Distance

Function Approach," *Journal of Environmental Economics and Management* 40:3 (November), 251–74.

Hammond, C. (2002), "Efficiency in the Provision of Public Services: A Data Envelopment Analysis of UK Public Library Systems," *Applied Economics* 34:5 (March), 649–57.

Hammond, C. J., G. Johnes, and T. Robinson (2002), "Technical Efficiency under Alternative Regulatory Regimes: Evidence from the Inter-war British Gas Industry," *Journal of Regulatory Economics* 22:3 (November), 251–70.

Hansmann, H. (1988), "Ownership of the Firm," *Journal of Law, Economics and Organization* 4:2 (Fall), 267–304.

Hausman, J. A., and W. E. Taylor (1981), "Panel Data and Unobservable Individual Effects," *Econometrica* 49:6 (November), 1377–98.

Hawdon, D. (2003), "Efficiency, Performance and Regulation of the International Gas Industry—a Bootstrap Approach," *Energy Policy* 31:11 (September), 1167–78.

Henderson, D. J., and D. L. Millimet (2005), "Environmental Regulation and US State-Level Production," *Economics Letters* 87:1 (April), 47–53.

Herrero, I. (2004), "Risk and Strategy of Fishers Alternatively Exploiting Sea Bream and Tuna in the Gibraltar Strait from an Efficiency Perspective," *ICES Journal of Marine Science* 61:2 (April), 211–17.

Hicks, J. R. (1935), "The Theory of Monopoly: A Survey," *Econometrica* 3:1 (January), 1–20.

Hoch, I. (1955), "Estimation of Production Function Parameters and Testing for Efficiency," *Econometrica* 23:3 (July), 325–26.

Hof, J., C. Flather, T. Baltic, and R. King (2004), "Forest and Rangeland Ecosystem Condition Indicators: Identifying National Areas of Opportunity Using Data Envelopment Analysis," *Forest Science* 50:4 (August), 473–94.

Hofler, R. A., and J. A. List (2004), "Valuation on the Frontier: Calibrating Actual and Hypothetical Statements of Value," *American Journal of Agricultural Economics* 86:1 (February), 213–21.

Hollingsworth, B., and J. Wildman (2003), "The Efficiency of Health Production: Re-estimating the WHO Panel Data Using Parametric and Non-parametric Approaches to Provide Additional Information," *Health Economics* 12:6 (June), 493–504.

Holmstrom, B. R., and J. Tirole (1989), "The Theory of the Firm," in R. Schmalensee and R. D. Willig, eds., *Handbook of Industrial Organization*, Volume 1. Amsterdam: Elsevier-Science Publishers.

Hopper, W. D. (1965), "Allocation Efficiency in a Traditional Indian Agriculture," *Journal of Farm Economics* 47:3 (August), 611–24.

Horrace, W. C., and P. Schmidt (1996), "Confidence Statements for Efficiency Estimates from Stochastic Frontier Models," *Journal of Productivity Analysis* 7:2/3 (July), 257–82.

Horrigan, J. O. (1968), "A Short History of Financial Ratio Analysis," *Accounting Review* 43:2 (April), 284–94.

Hougaard, J. L., D. Kronborg, and C. Overgård (2004), "Improvement Potential in Danish Elderly Care," *Health Care Management Science* 7:3 (August), 225–35.

Hughes, P. A. N., and M. E. Edwards (2000), "Leviathan vs. Lilliputian: A Data Envelopment Analysis of Government Efficiency," *Journal of Regional Science* 40:4 (November), 649–69.

Hwang, S.-N., and T.-Y. Chang (2003), "Using Data Envelopment Analysis to Measure Hotel Managerial Efficiency Change in Taiwan," *Tourism Management* 24:4 (August), 357–69.

Ibourk, A., B. Maillard, S. Perelman, and H. R. Sneesens (2004), "Aggregate Matching Efficiency: A Stochastic Production Frontier Approach, France 1990–1994," *Empirica* 31:1 (March), 1–25.

Jamash, T., and M. Pollitt (2001), "Benchmarking and Regulation: International Electricity Experience," *Utilities Policy* 9:3 (September), 107–30.

Jeng, V., and G. C. Lai (2005), "Ownership Structure, Agency Costs, Specialization, and Efficiency: Analysis of Keiretsu and Independent Insurers in the Japanese Nonlife Insurance Industry," *Journal of Risk and Insurance* 72:1 (March), 105–58.

Jeon, B. M., and R. C. Sickles (2004), "The Role of Environmental Factors in Growth Accounting: A Nonparametric Analysis," *Journal of Applied Econometrics* 19:5 (September-October), 567–91.

Jiménez, J. S., F. P. Chaparro, and P. C. Smith (2003), "Evaluating the Introduction of a Quasi-Market in Community Care," *Socio-economic Planning Sciences* 37:1 (March), 1–13.

Jondrow, J., C. A. K. Lovell, I. Materov, and P. Schmidt (1982), "On the Estimation of Technical Inefficiency in the Stochastic Frontier Production Model," *Journal of Econometrics* 19:2/3 (August), 233–38.

Jörss, M., D. E. Powell, and C. Wolff (2004), "A Streetcar Named Productivity," *McKinsey Quarterly* Number 3.

Kantorovich, L. V. (1939), *The Mathematical Method of Production Planning and Organization*, Leningrad: Leningrad University Press.

Kao, C., and Y.-C. Lin (2004), "Evaluation of the University Libraries in Taiwan: Total Measure *versus* Ratio Measure," *Journal of the Operational Research Society* 55:12 (December), 1256–65.

Kennedy, J., and A. S. J. Smith (2004), "Assessing the Efficient Cost of Sustaining Britain's Rail Network—Perspectives Based on Zonal Comparisons," *Journal of Transport Economics and Policy* 38:2 (May), 157–90.

Kinnunen, K. (2005), "Pricing of Electricity Distribution: An Empirical Efficiency Study of Finland, Norway and Sweden," *Utilities Policy* 13:1 (March), 15–25.

Kirigia, J. M., A. Emrouznejad, L. G. Sambo, N. Munguti, and W. Liambila (2004), "Using Data Envelopment Analysis to Measure the Technical Efficiency of Public Health Centers in Kenya," *Journal of Medical Systems* 28:2 (April), 155–66.

Knight, F. H. (1965), *The Economic Organization.* New York: Harper and Row. (Originally published in 1933)

Kompas, T., and T. N. Che (2005), "Efficiency Gains and Cost Reductions from Individual Transferable Quotas: A Stochastic Cost Frontier for the Australian South East Fishery," *Journal of Productivity Analysis* 23:3 (July), 285–307.

Koopmans, T. C. (1951), "An Analysis of Production as an Efficient Combination of Activities," in T. C. Koopmans, ed., *Activity Analysis of Production and Allocation*. Cowles Commission for Research in Economics Monograph No. 13. New York: John Wiley and Sons.

Korhonen, P. J., and M. Luptacik (2004), "Eco-efficiency Analysis of Power Plants: An Extension of Data Envelopment Analysis," *European Journal of Operational Research* 154:2 (April), 437–46.

Kumbhakar, S. C. (1997), "Modeling Allocative Inefficiency in a Translog Cost Function and Cost Share Equations: An Exact Relationship," *Journal of Econometrics* 76:1/2 (January/February), 351–56.

Kumbhakar, S. C., and L. Hjalmarsson (1995), "Labour-Use Efficiency in Swedish Social Insurance Offices," *Journal of Applied Econometrics* 10:1 (January-March), 33–47.

Kumbhakar, S. C., and C. A. K. Lovell (2000), *Stochastic Frontier Analysis.* New York: Cambridge University Press.

Kumbhakar, S. C., and E. G. Tsionas (2005), "Measuring Technical and Allocative Inefficiency in the Translog Cost System: A Bayesian Approach," *Journal of Econometrics* 126:2 (June), 355–84.

Kuosmanen, T., and T. Sipiläinen (2004), "On the Anatomy of Productivity Growth: A Decomposition of the Fisher Ideal TFP Index," Discussion Paper 2004:17, MTT Economic Research, Agrifood Research Finland, Helsinki, Finland.

Laine, J., M. Linna, A. Noro, and U. Häkkinen (2005), "The Cost Efficiency and Clinical Quality of Institutional Long-Term Care for the Elderly," *Health Care Management Science* 8:2 (May), 149–56.

Lam, P.-L., and T. Lam (2005), "Total Factor Productivity Measures for Hong Kong Telephone," *Telecommunications Policy* 29:1 (February), 53–68.

Land, K. C., C. A. K. Lovell, and S. Thore (1993), "Chance-Constrained Data Envelopment Analysis," *Managerial and Decision Economics* 14:6 (November/December), 541–54.

Lang, G. (2005), "The Difference Between Wages and Wage Potentials: Earnings Disadvantages of Immigrants in Germany," *Journal of Economic Inequality* 3:1 (April), 21–42.

Lau, L. J., and P. A. Yotopoulos (1971), "A Test for Relative Efficiency and Application to Indian Agriculture," *American Economic Review* 61:1 (March), 94–109.

Lauer, J. A., C. A. K. Lovell, D. B. Evans, and C. J. L. Murray (2004), "World Health System Performance Revisited: The Impact of Varying the Relative Importance of Health System Goals," *BMC Health Services Research* 4:19 (July).

Lawrence, D., and A. Richards (2004), "Distributing the Gains from Waterfront Productivity Improvements," *Economic Record* 80 Supplement (September), S43–52.

Leibenstein, H. (1966), "Allocative Efficiency vs. 'X-Efficiency'," *American Economic Review* 56:3 (June), 392–415.

Leibenstein, H. (1976), *Beyond Economic Man.* Cambridge, MA: Harvard University Press.

Lewis, D., T. M. Springer, and R. I. Anderson (2003), "The Cost Efficiency of Real Estate Investment Trusts: An Analysis with a Bayesian Stochastic Frontier Model," *Journal of Real Estate Finance and Economics* 26:1 (January), 65–80.

Lewis, W. W. (2004), *The Power of Productivity.* Chicago: University of Chicago Press.

Lindsay, C. M. (1976), "A Theory of Government Enterprise," *Journal of Political Economy* 84:5 (October), 1061–77.

Linna, M., A. Nordblad, and M. Koivu (2003), "Technical and Cost Efficiency of Oral Health Care Provision in Finnish Health Centres," *Social Science and Medicine* 56:2 (January), 343–53.

Lins, M. P. E., E. G. Gomes, J. C. C. B. Soares de Mello, and A. J. R. Soares de Mello (2003), "Olympic Ranking Based on a Zero Sum Gains DEA Model," *European Journal of Operational Research* 148:2 (July), 312–22.

Liu, C., and R. S. Yin (2004), "Poverty Dynamics Revealed in Production Performance and Forestry in Improving Livelihoods: The Case of West Anhui, China," *Forest Policy and Economics* 6:3–4 (June), 391–401.

Loizides, J., and E. Tsionas (2004), "Productivity Growth in European Railways," *Journal of Transport Economics and Policy* 38:1 (January), 45–76.

Lovell, C. A. K. (2003), "The Decomposition of Malmquist Productivity Indexes," *Journal of Productivity Analysis* 20:3 (November), 437–58.

Lozano, S., G. Villa, and B. Adenzo-Diaz (2004), "Centralised Target Setting for Regional Recycling Operations Using DEA," *Omega* 32:2 (April), 101–10.

Luo, X. M., and N. Donthu (2005), "Assessing Advertising Media Spending Inefficiencies in Generating Sales," *Journal of Business Research* 58:1 (January), 28–36.

Mairesse, F., and P. Vanden Eeckaut (2002), "Museum Assessment and FDH Technology: Towards a Global Approach," *Journal of Cultural Economics* 26:4 (November), 261–86.

Malmquist, S. (1953), "Index Numbers and Indifference Surfaces," *Trabajos de Estadística* 4, 209–42.

Mamatzakis, E. C. (2003), "Public Infrastructure and Productivity Growth in Greek Agriculture," *Agricultural Economics* 29:2 (August), 169–80.

Martín, J. C., J. Gutiérrez, and C. Román (2004), "Data Envelopment Analysis (DEA) Index to Measure the Accessibility Impacts of New Infrastructure Investments: The Case of the High-Speed Train Corridor Madrid-Barcelona-French Border," *Regional Studies* 38:6 (August), 697–712.

Martinez-Cordero, F. J., and P. S. Leung (2004), "Sustainable Aquaculture and Producer Performance: Measurement of Environmentally Adjusted Productivity and Efficiency of a Sample of Shrimp Farms in Mexico," *Aquaculture* 241:1–4 (November), 249–68.

Maruyama, S., and T. Nakajima (2002), "The Productivity Analysis of Postal Services," Chapter 7 in M. A. Crew and P. R. Kleindorfer, eds., *Postal and Delivery Services: Delivering on Competition*. Boston: Kluwer Academic Publishers.

Mayston, D. J. (2003), "Measuring and Managing Educational Performance," *Journal of the Operational Research Society* 54:7 (July), 679–91.

McFadden, D. (1978), "Cost, Revenue and Profit Functions," in M. Fuss and D. McFadden, eds., *Production Economics: A Dual Approach to Theory and Applications*, Volume 1. Amsterdam: North-Holland.

Meeusen, W., and J. van den Broeck (1977), "Efficiency Estimation from Cobb-Douglas Production Functions with Composed Error," *International Economic Review* 18:2 (June), 435–44.

Mensah, Y. M., and R. Werner (2003), "Cost Efficiency and Financial Flexibility in Institutions of Higher Education," *Journal of Accounting and Public Policy* 22:4 (July-August), 293–323.

Miller, D. M. (1984), "Profitability = Productivity + Price Recovery," *Harvard Business Review* 62:3 (May/June), 145–53.

Millimet, D. L. (2005), "Job Search Skills, Employer Size and Wages," *Applied Economics Letters* 12:2 (February), 95–100.

Mohan, N., and J. Ruggiero (2003), "Compensation Differences Between Male and Female CEOs for Publicly Traded Firms: A Nonparametric Analysis," *Journal of the Operational Research Society* 54:12 (December), 1242–48.

Moore, A. T., J. Nolan, G. F. Segal, and M. Taylor (2001), *Competitive Cities: A Report Card on Efficiency in Service Delivery in America's Largest Cities*. Reason Public Policy Institute. Available at http://www.rppi.org/ps282.pdf

Mundlak, Y. (1961), "Empirical Production Function Free of Management Bias," *Journal of Farm Economics* 43:1 (February), 44–56.

Netherlands Bureau for Economic Policy Analysis (2000), "Yardstick Competition: Theory, Design and Practice," Working Paper No. 133. Available at http://www.cpb.nl/eng/pub/cpbreeksen/werkdoc/.

Nishimizu, M., and J. M. Page (1982), "Total Factor Productivity Growth, Technological Progress and Technical Efficiency Change: Dimensions of Productivity Change in Yugoslavia 1965–78," *Economic Journal* 92:368 (December), 920–36.

Niskanen, W. A. (1971), *Bureaucracy and Representative Government*. Chicago: Aldine Publishing Co.

Nyhan, R. C. (2002), "Benchmarking Tools: An Application to Juvenile Justice Facility Performance," *Prison Journal* 82:4 (December), 423–39.

Obata, T., and H. Ishii (2003), "A Method for Discriminating Efficient Candidates with Ranked Voting Data," *European Journal of Operational Research* 151:1 (November), 233–37.

Odeck, J. (2006), "Identifying Traffic Safety Best Practices: An Application of DEA and Malmquist Indices," *Omega* 34:1 (January), 28–40.

OECD (2001), *OECD Productivity Manual: A Guide to the Measurement of Industry-Level and Aggregate Productivity Growth*. Paris: Organisation for Economic Co-operation and Development. Available at http://www.oecd.org/dataoecd/59/29/2352458.pdf.

Olesen, O. B., and N. C. Petersen (1995), "Chance Constrained Efficiency Evaluation," *Management Science* 41:3 (March), 442–57.

Orea, L. (2002), "Parametric Decomposition of a Generalized Malmquist Productivity Index," *Journal of Productivity Analysis* 18:1 (July), 5–22.

Otsuka, K., H. Chuma, and Y. Hayami (1992), "Land and Labor Contracts in Agrarian Economies: Theories and Facts," *Journal of Economic Literature* 30:4 (December), 1965–2018.

Otsuki, T., I. W. Hardie, and E. J. Reis (2002), "The Implication of Property Rights for Joint Agriculture—Timber Productivity in the Brazilian Amazon," *Environment and Development Economics* 7:2 (May), 299–323.

Oum, T. H., and C. Yu (2004), "Measuring Airports' Operating Efficiency: A Summary of the 2003 ATRS Global Airport Benchmarking Report," *Transportation Research Part E* 40:6 (November), 515–32.

Paradi, J. C., M. Asmild, and P. C. Simak (2004), "Using DEA and Worst Practice DEA in Credit Risk Evaluation," *Journal of Productivity Analysis* 21:2 (March), 153–65.

Park, R.-K., and P. De (2004), "An Alternative Approach to Efficiency Measurement of Seaports," *Maritime Economics and Logistics* 6:1 (March), 53–69.

Paul, S., B. S. Sahni, and B. Biswal (2004), "Public Infrastructure and the Performance of Canadian Manufacturing Industries," *Southern Economic Journal* 70:4 (April), 998–1011.

Pavcnik, N. (2002), "Trade Liberalization, Exit, and Productivity Improvements: Evidence from Chilean Plants," *Review of Economic Studies* 69:1 (January), 245–76.

Pencavel, J. (2001), *Worker Participation: Lessons from the Worker Co-ops of the Pacific Northwest*. New York: Russell Sage Foundation.

Pestieau, P., and H. Tulkens (1993), "Assessing and Explaining the Performance of Public Enterprises," *Finanz Archiv* 50:3, 293–323.

Petersen, N. C. (1990), "Data Envelopment Analysis on a Relaxed Set of Assumptions," *Management Science* 36:3 (March), 305–14.

Pimenta, A. A., R. G. Santos, and S. C. Lagoa (2000), "Technical Efficiency in CTT—Correios de Portugal," Chapter 12 in M. A. Crew and P. R. Kleindorfer, eds., *Current Directions in Postal Reform*. Boston: Kluwer Academic Publishers.

Pitt, M., and L.-F. Lee (1981), "The Measurement and Sources of Technical Inefficiency in the Indonesian Weaving Industry," *Journal of Development Economics* 9:1 (August), 43–64.

Pollitt, M. (2005), "The Role of Efficiency Estimates in Regulatory Price Reviews: Ofgem's Approach to Benchmarking Electricity Networks," *Utilities Policy* 13:4 (December), 279–88.

Porembski, M., K. Breitenstein, and P. Alpar (2005), "Visualizing Efficiency and Reference Relations in Data Envelopment Analysis with an Application to the Branches of a German Bank," *Journal of Productivity Analysis* 23:2 (March), 203–21.

Porter, M. E. (1991), "America's Green Strategy," *Scientific American* April.

Prieto, A. M., and J. L. Zofio (2001), "Evaluating Effectiveness in Public Provision of Infrastructure and Equipment: The Case of Spanish Municipalities," *Journal of Productivity Analysis* 15:1 (January), 41–58.

Ravallion, M. (2005), "On Measuring Aggregate 'Social Efficiency'," *Economic Development and Cultural Change* 53:2 (January), 273–92.

Ray, S. C., and E. Desli (1997), "Productivity Growth, Technical Progress and Efficiency Change in Industrialized Countries: Comment," *American Economic Review* 87:5 (December), 1033–39.

Ray, S. C., and K. Mukherjee (1996), "Decomposition of the Fisher Ideal Index of Productivity: A Non-parametric Dual Analysis of US Airlines Data," *Economic Journal* 106:439 (November), 1659–78.

Reichmann, G., and M. Sommersguter-Reichmann (2006), "University Library Benchmarking: An International Comparison Using DEA," *International Journal of Production Economics* 100:2 (April), 131–47.

Reinhard, S., C. A. K. Lovell, and G. Thijssen (1999), "Econometric Estimation of Technical and Environmental Efficiency: An Application to Dutch Dairy Farms," *American Journal of Agricultural Economics* 81:1 (February), 44–60.

Resende, M., and L. O. Façanha (2005), "Price-Cap Regulation and Service-Quality in Telecommunications: An Empirical Study," *Information Economics and Policy* 17:1 (January), 1–12.

Richardson, J., J. Wildman, and I. K. Robertson (2003), "A Critique of the World Health Organization's Evaluation of Health System Performance," *Health Economics* 12:5 (May), 355–66.

Rosenman, R., and D. Friesner (2004), "Scope and Scale Inefficiencies in Physician Practices," *Health Economics* 13:11 (November), 1091–116.

Rossi, M. A. (2001), "Technical Change and Efficiency Measures: The Post-privatization in the Gas Distribution Sector in Argentina," *Energy Economics* 23:3 (May), 295–304.

Russell, R. R. (1988), "On the Axiomatic Approach to the Measurement of Technical Efficiency," in W. Eichhorn, ed., *Measurement in Economics: Theory and Applications of Economic Indices*. Heidelberg: Physica-Verlag.

Russell, R. R. (1990), "Continuity of Measures of Technical Efficiency," *Journal of Economic Theory* 51:2 (August), 255–67.

Salerian, J. (2003), "Analysing the Performance of Firms Using a Decomposable Ideal Index Number to Link Profit, Prices and Productivity," *Australian Economic Review* 36:2 (June), 143–55.

Salinas-Jiminez, M. D. (2004), "Public Infrastructure and Private Productivity in the Spanish Regions," *Journal of Policy Modeling* 26:1 (January), 47–64.

Samuelson, P. A., and S. Swamy (1974), "Invariant Economic Index Numbers and Canonical Duality: Survey and Synthesis," *American Economic Review* 64:4 (September), 566–93.

Sarkis, J., and S. Talluri (2004), "Performance Based Clustering for Benchmarking of US Airports," *Transportation Research Part A* 38:5 (June), 329–46.

Scheraga, C. A. (2004), "Operational Efficiency Versus Financial Mobility in the Global Airline Industry: A Data Envelopment and Tobit Analysis," *Transportation Research Part A* 38:5 (June), 383–404.

Schmidt, P. (1976), "On the Statistical Estimation of Parametric Frontier Production Functions," *Review of Economics and Statistics* 58:2 (May), 238–39.

Schmidt, P., and R. Sickles (1984), "Production Frontiers and Panel Data," *Journal of Business and Economic Statistics* 2:4 (October), 367–74.

Schor, A. (2004), "Heterogeneous Productivity Response to Tariff Reduction: Evidence from Brazilian Manufacturing Firms," *Journal of Development Economics* 75:2 (December), 373–96.

Serra, P. (2003), "Measuring the Performance of Chile's Tax Administration," *National Tax Journal* 56:2 (June), 373–83.

Serrano-Cinca, C., Y. Fuertes-Callén, and C. Mar-Molinero (2005), "Measuring DEA Efficiency in Internet Companies," *Decision Support Systems* 38:4 (January), 557–73.

Shadbegian, R. J., and W. B. Gray (2005), "Pollution Abatement Expenditures and Plant-Level Productivity: A Production Function Approach," *Ecological Economics* 54:2–3 (August), 196–208.

Sheldon, G. M. (2003), "The Efficiency of Public Employment Services: A Nonparametric Matching Function Analysis for Switzerland," *Journal of Productivity Analysis* 20:1 (July), 49–70.

Shephard, R. W. (1953), *Cost and Production Functions*. Princeton, NJ: Princeton University Press.

Shephard, R. W. (1970), *Theory of Cost and Production Functions*. Princeton, NJ: Princeton University Press.

Sherman, H. D., and T. J. Rupert (2006), "Do Bank Mergers Have Hidden or Foregone Value? Realized and Unrealized Operating Synergies in One Bank Merger," *European Journal of Operational Research* 168:1 (January), 253–68.

Shim, W. (2003), "Applying DEA Technique to Library Evaluation in Academic Research Libraries," *Library Trends* 51:3 (Winter), 312–32.

Sickles, R. C., D. H. Good, and L. Getachew (2002), "Specification of Distance Functions Using Semi- and Non-parametric Methods with an Application to the Dynamic Performance of Eastern and Western European Air Carriers," *Journal of Productivity Analysis* 17:1/2 (January), 133–55.

Sigala, M., P. Jones, A. Lockwood, and D. Airey (2005), "Productivity in Hotels: A Stepwise Data Envelopment Analysis of Hotels' Rooms Division Processes," *Service Industries Journal* 25:1 (January), 61–82.

Silva Portela, M. C. A., and E. Thanassoulis (2005), "Profitability of a Sample of Portuguese Bank Branches and Its Decomposition into Technical and Allocative Components," *European Journal of Operational Research* 162:3 (May), 850–66.

Simon, H. A. (1955), "A Behavioral Model of Rational Choice," *Quarterly Journal of Economics* 69:1 (February), 99–118.

Smith, A. S. J. (2005), "The Role of Efficiency Estimates in UK Regulatory Price Reviews: The Case of Rail," *Utilities Policy* 13:4 (December), 294–301.

Solow, R. M. (1957), "Technical Change and the Aggregate Production Function," *Review of Economics and Statistics* 39:3 (August), 312–20.

Southwick, L., Jr. (2005), "Sewer Plant Operating Efficiency, Patronage and Competition," *Managerial and Decision Economics* 26:1 (January-February), 1–13.

Spottiswoode, C. (2000), *Improving Police Performance: A New Approach to Measuring Police Efficiency*. London: HM Treasury. Available at http://www.hm-treasury.gov.uk/media/e/F/242.pdf.

Stanford, R. E. (2004), "A Frontier Analysis Approach for Benchmarking Hospital Performance in the Treatment of Acute Myocardial Infarction," *Health Care Management Science* 7:2 (May), 145–54.

Stevenson, R. E. (1980), "Likelihood Functions for Generalized Stochastic Frontier Estimation," *Journal of Econometrics* 13:1 (May), 58–66.

Stigler, G. J. (1976), "The Xistence of X-Efficiency," *American Economic Review* 66:1 (March), 213–16.

Stone, M. (2002), "How Not to Measure the Efficiency of Public Services (and How One Might)," *Journal of the Royal Statistical Society Series A* 165, Part 3, 405–34.

Stone, R. (1980), "Whittling Away at the Residual: Some Thoughts on Denison's Growth Accounting," *Journal of Economic Literature* 18:4 (December), 1539–43.

Sun, S. (2004), "Assessing Joint Maintenance Shops in the Taiwanese Army Using Data Envelopment Analysis," *Journal of Operations Management* 22:3 (June), 233–45.

Takamura, Y., and K. Tone (2003), "A Comparative Site Evaluation Study for Relocating Japanese Government Agencies Out of Tokyo," *Socio-economic Planning Sciences* 37:2 (June), 85–102.

Thomas, P., Y. P. Chan, L. Lehmkuhl, and W. Nixon (2002), "Obnoxious-Facility Location and Data Envelopment Analysis: A Combined Distance-Based Formulation," *European Journal of Operational Research* 141:3 (September), 494–514.

Thompson, R. G., F. Singleton, R. Thrall, and B. Smith (1986), "Comparative Site Evaluations for Locating a High-Energy Physics Lab in Texas," *Interfaces* 16:6 (November-December), 35–49.

Tone, K., and B. K. Sahoo (2005), "Evaluating Cost Efficiency and Returns to Scale in the Life Insurance Corporation of India Using Data Envelopment Analysis," *Socio-economic Planning Sciences* 39:4 (December), 261–85.

Törnqvist, L. (1936), "The Bank of Finland's Consumption Price Index," *Bank of Finland Monthly Bulletin* 10, 1–8.

Troutt, M. D., M. Y. Hu, and M. S. Shanker (2005), "A Distribution-Free Approach to Estimating Best Response Values with Application to Mutual Fund Performance Modeling," *European Journal of Operational Research* 166:2 (October), 520–27.

Tulkens, H. (1993), "On FDH Efficiency Analysis: Some Methodological Issues and Applications to Retail Banking, Courts and Urban Transit," *Journal of Productivity Analysis* 4:1/2 (June), 183–210.

Tulkens, H., and P. Vanden Eeckaut (1995), "Non-parametric Efficiency, Progress and Regress Measures for Panel Data: Methodological Aspects," *European Journal of Operational Research* 80:3 (February), 474–99.

Tulkens, H., and P. Vanden Eeckaut (1999), "Mesurer l'efficacité: avec ou sans frontières?" Chapter 3 in P.-Y. Badillo and J. C. Paradi, eds., *La méthode DEA: analyse des performances.* Paris: Hermes Science Publications.

Tupper, H. C., and M. Resende (2004), "Efficiency and Regulatory Issues in the Brazilian Water and Sewage Sector: An Empirical Study," *Utilities Policy* 12:1 (March), 29–40.

Tybout, J. R., and M. D. Westbrook (1995), "Trade Liberalization and the Dimensions of Efficiency Change in Mexican Manufacturing Industries," *Journal of International Economics* 39:1–2 (August), 53–78.

Uri, N. D. (2004), "Measuring the Impact of Incentive Regulation on Technical Efficiency in Telecommunications in the United States," *Applied Mathematical Modeling* 28:3 (March), 255–71.

Ventura, J., E. González, and A. Cárcaba (2004), "Efficiency and Program-Contract Bargaining in Spanish Public Hospitals," *Annals of Public and Cooperative Economics* 75:4 (December), 549–73.

Wagner, J. M., D. G. Shimshak, and M. A. Novak (2003), "Advances in Physician Profiling: The Use of DEA," *Socio-economic Planning Sciences* 37:2 (June), 141–63.

Wagner, M. (2005), "How to Reconcile Environmental and Economic Performance to Improve Corporate Sustainability: Corporate Environmental Strategies in the European Paper Industry," *Journal of Environmental Management* 76:2 (July), 105–118.

Wang, H.-J., and P. Schmidt (2002), "One-Step and Two-Step Estimation of the Effects of Exogenous Variables on Technical Efficiency Levels," *Journal of Productivity Analysis* 18:2 (September), 129–44.

Wang, W. R. (2000), "Evaluating the Technical Efficiency of Large US Law Firms," *Applied Economics* 32:6 (May), 689–95.

Warning, S. (2004), "Performance Differences in German Higher Education: Empirical Analysis of Strategic Groups," *Review of Industrial Organization* 24:4 (June), 393–408.

Wen, H. J., B. Lim, and H. L. Huang (2003), "Measuring E-Commerce Efficiency: A Data Envelopment Analysis (DEA) Approach," *Industrial Management and Data Systems* 103:9 (November), 703–10.

Wheelock, D. C., and P. W. Wilson (2000), "Why Do Banks Disappear? The Determinants of U.S. Bank Failures and Acquisitions," *Review of Economics and Statistics* 82:1 (February), 127–38.

WHO (2000), *The World Health Report 2000. Health Systems: Improving Performance.* Geneva: World Health Organization.

Widstrom, E., M. Linna, and T. Niskanen (2004), "Productive Efficiency and Its Determinants in the Finnish Public Dental Service," *Community Dentistry and Oral Epidemiology* 32:1 (February), 31–40.

Williamson, O. E. (1964), *The Economics of Discretionary Behavior: Managerial Objectives in a Theory of the Firm.* Englewood Cliffs, NJ: Prentice-Hall.

Williamson, O. E. (1975), *Markets and Hierarchies.* New York: Free Press.

Williamson, O. E. (1985), *The Economic Institutions of Capitalism.* New York: Free Press.

Winsten, C. B. (1957), "Discussion of Mr. Farrell's Paper," *Journal of the Royal Statistical Society Series A, General* 120:3, 282–84.

Wisniewski, M., and A. Dickson (2001), "Measuring Performance in Dumfries and Galloway Constabulary with the Balanced Scorecard," *Journal of the Operational Research Society* 52:10 (October), 1057–66.

Worthington, A. C., and B. E. Dollery (2001), "Measuring Efficiency in Local Government: An Analysis of New South Wales Municipalities' Domestic Waste Management Function," *Policy Studies Journal* 29:2, 232–49.

Yörük, B. K., and O. Zaim (2005), "Productivity Growth in OECD Countries: A Comparison with Malmquist Indices," *Journal of Comparative Economics* 33:2 (June), 401–20.

Yoshida, Y., and H. Fujimoto (2004), "Japanese-Airport Benchmarking with the DEA and Endogenous-Weight TFP Methods: Testing the Criticism of Overinvestment in Japanese Regional Airports," *Transportation Research Part E* 40:6 (November), 533–46.

Yotopoulos, P. A., and L. J. Lau (1973), "A Test for Relative Economic Efficiency: Some Further Results," *American Economic Review* 63:1 (March), 214–23.

Yu, M.-M. (2004), "Measuring Physical Efficiency of Domestic Airports in Taiwan with Undesirable Outputs and Environmental Factors," *Journal of Air Transport Management* 10:5 (September), 295–303.

Zaim, O. (2004), "Measuring Environmental Performance of State Manufacturing Through Changes in Pollution Intensities: A DEA Framework," *Ecological Economics* 48:1 (January), 37–47.

Zeitsch, J., D. Lawrence, and J. Salerian (1994), "Comparing Like with Like in Productivity Studies: Apples, Oranges and Electricity," *Economic Record* 70:209 (June), 162–70.

2

The Econometric Approach to Efficiency Analysis

William H. Greene

2.1 Introduction

Chapter 1 describes two broad paradigms for measuring economic efficiency, one based on an essentially nonparametric, programming approach to analysis of observed outcomes, and one based on an econometric approach to estimation of theory-based models of production, cost, or profit. This chapter presents an overview of techniques for econometric analysis of technical (production) and economic (cost) efficiency. The stochastic frontier model of Aigner, Lovell, and Schmidt (1977) is now the standard econometric platform for this type of analysis. I survey the underlying models and econometric techniques that have been used in studying technical inefficiency in the stochastic frontier framework and present some of the recent developments in econometric methodology. Applications that illustrate some of the computations are presented in the final section.

2.1.1 Modeling production

The empirical estimation of production and cost functions is a standard exercise in econometrics. The *frontier production function* or *production frontier* is an extension of the familiar regression model based on the theoretical premise that a *production function*, or its dual, the *cost function*, or the convex conjugate of the two, the *profit function*, represents an ideal, the *maximum output* attainable given a set of inputs, the *minimum cost* of producing that output given the prices of the inputs, or the *maximum profit* attainable given the inputs, outputs, and prices of the inputs. The estimation of frontier functions is the econometric exercise of making the empirical implementation consistent with the underlying theoretical proposition that no observed agent can exceed the ideal. In practice, the frontier function *model* is (essentially) a regression model that is fit with the recognition of the theoretical constraint that all observations lie within the theoretical extreme. Measurement of (in)efficiency is, then, the empirical estimation of the extent to which observed agents (fail to) achieve the theoretical ideal. My interest in this chapter is in this latter function. The estimated model of production, cost, or profit is the means to the objective of measuring inefficiency. As intuition might suggest at this point, the exercise here is a formal analysis of the "residuals" from the production or cost model. The theory of optimization, production, and/or cost provides a description of the ultimate source of deviations from this theoretical ideal.

2.1.2 History of thought

The literature on frontier production and cost functions and the calculation of efficiency measures begins with Debreu (1951) and Farrell (1957) [though there are intellectual antecedents, e.g., Hicks's (1935) suggestion that monopolists would enjoy their position through the attainment of a quiet life rather than through the pursuit of economic profits, a conjecture formalized somewhat more by Leibenstein (1966, 1975)]. Farrell suggested that one could usefully analyze technical efficiency in terms of realized deviations from an idealized frontier isoquant. This approach falls naturally into an econometric approach in which the *inefficiency* is identified with disturbances in a regression model.

The empirical estimation of production functions had begun long before Farrell's work, arguably with Cobb and Douglas (1928). However, until the 1950s, production functions were largely used as devices for studying the functional distribution of income between capital and labor at the macroeconomic level. The celebrated contribution of Arrow et al. (1961) marks a milestone in this literature. The origins of empirical analysis of microeconomic production structures can be more reasonably identified with the work of Dean (1951, a leather belt shop), Johnston (1959, electricity generation), and, in his seminal work on electric power generation, Nerlove (1963). It is noteworthy that all three of these focus on costs rather than production, though Nerlove, following Samuelson (1938) and Shephard (1953), highlighted the dual relationship between cost and production.[1] Empirical attention to production functions at a disaggregated level is a literature that began to emerge in earnest in the 1960s (see, e.g., Hildebrand and Liu, 1965; Zellner and Revankar, 1969).

2.1.3 Empirical antecedents

The empirical literature on production and cost developed largely independently of the discourse on frontier modeling. Least squares or some variant was generally used to pass a function through the middle of a cloud of points, and residuals of both signs were, as in other areas of study, not singled out for special treatment. The focal points of the studies in this literature were the estimated parameters of the production structure, not the individual deviations from the estimated function. An argument was made that these "averaging" estimators were estimating the average, rather than the "best-practice" technology. Farrell's arguments provided an intellectual basis for redirecting attention from the production function specifically to the deviations from that function, and respecifying the model and the techniques accordingly. A series of papers including Aigner and Chu (1968) and Timmer (1971) proposed specific econometric models that were consistent with the frontier notions of Debreu (1951) and Farrell (1957). The contemporary line of research on econometric models begins with the nearly simultaneous appearance of the canonical papers of Aigner, Lovell, and Schmidt (1977) and Meeusen and van den Broeck (1977), who proposed the stochastic frontier models that applied researchers now use to combine the underlying theoretical propositions with a practical econometric framework. The current literature on production frontiers and efficiency estimation combines these two lines of research.

2.1.4 Organization of the survey

This survey presents an overview of this literature and proceeds as follows:

Section 2.2 presents the microeconomic theoretical underpinnings of the empirical models. As in the other parts of our presentation, this section gives only a cursory survey because of the very large literature on which it is based. The interested reader can find considerable additional detail in chapter 1 of this book and in a gateway to the larger literature, chapter 2 of Kumbhakar and Lovell (2000).

Section 2.3 constructs the basic econometric framework for the econometric analysis of efficiency. This section also presents some intermediate results on "deterministic" (orthodox) frontier models that adhere strictly to the microeconomic theory. This part is brief. It is of some historical interest and contains some useful perspective for the more recent work. However, with little exception, current research on the deterministic approach to efficiency analysis takes place in the environment of "data envelopment analysis" (DEA), which is the subject of chapter 3 of this book.[2] This section provides a bridge between the formulation of orthodox frontier models and the modern stochastic frontier models.

Section 2.4 introduces the stochastic production frontier model and presents results on formulation and estimation of this model. Section 2.5 extends the stochastic frontier model to the analysis of cost and profits and describes the important extension of the frontier concept to multiple-output technologies.

Section 2.6 turns to a major econometric issue, that of accommodating heterogeneity in the production model. The assumptions made in sections 2.4

and 2.5 regarding the stochastic nature of technical inefficiency are narrow and arguably unrealistic. Inefficiency is viewed as simply a random shock distributed homogeneously across firms. These assumptions are relaxed at the end of section 2.5 and in section 2.6. Here, I examine proposed models that allow the mean and variance of inefficiency to vary across firms, thus producing a richer, albeit considerably more complex, formulation. This part of the econometric model extends the theory to the practical consideration of observed and unobserved influences that are absent from the pure theory but are a crucial aspect of the real-world application.

The econometric analysis continues in section 2.7 with the development of models for panel data. Once again, this is a modeling issue that provides a means to stretch the theory to producer behavior as it evolves through time. The analysis pursued here goes beyond the econometric issue of how to exploit the useful features of longitudinal data. The literature on panel data estimation of frontier models also addresses the fundamental question of how and whether inefficiency varies over time, and how econometric models can be made to accommodate the theoretical propositions.

The formal measurement of inefficiency is considered in sections 2.8 and 2.9. The use of the frontier function model for estimating firm-level inefficiency that was suggested in sections 2.3 and 2.4 is formalized in the stochastic frontier model in section 2.8. Section 2.9 considers the separate issue of allocative inefficiency. In this area of study, the distinction between errors in optimization and the consequences of those errors for the goals or objectives of optimization is made explicit. Thus, for example, the effect of optimization errors in demand systems is viewed apart from the ultimate impact on the costs of production.

Section 2.10 describes contemporary software for frontier estimation and illustrates some of the computations with "live" data sets. Some conclusions are drawn in section 2.11.

2.1.5 Preface

The literature on stochastic frontier estimation was already large at the time of the 1993 edition of this survey and it has grown vastly in the decade plus since then. It is simply not possible to touch upon all aspects of all the research that has been done and is ongoing. [Even the book-length treatise Kumbhakar and Lovell (2000) leaves the reader to their own devices to explore the received empirical studies.] In this survey, I introduce a number of topics and present some of the most familiar econometric estimators and issues. Since the earlier rendition of this survey, two topics have received great attention in the literature are given correspondingly greater coverage here: the statistical analysis of the inefficiency estimators (the Jondrow et al., 1982, estimator and counterparts) and panel data estimation. A few topics are treated relatively superficially, not for lack of interest but because, for better or for worse, they have not yet had great influence on how empirical work is done in this area. These include Bayesian estimation and semi- and nonparametric estimation. Yet another topic falls somewhere between the mainstream and these. In the analysis of inefficiency, we recognize that, in terms of costs, inefficiency can arise from two sources: *technical inefficiency*, which arises when, given the chosen inputs, output falls short of the ideal; and *allocative inefficiency*, which arises from suboptimal input choices given prices and output. Technical inefficiency (the difference between output and maximal output) is, in some sense, "pure" in that we can single out the source. Cost inefficiency, in contrast, is a blend of the two sources, technical and allocative inefficiency. Decomposition of cost inefficiency into its two components in a theoretically appropriate manner (the so-called "Greene problem") has posed a vexing challenge in this literature (see Greene, 1993, 1997, 2003c). The estimation of "allocative" inefficiency has received some attention in the research of the past two decades, with some interesting and creative results. However, the estimation of allocative inefficiency and the decomposition have received much less attention than the more straightforward analysis of technical inefficiency on the production side and *economic* inefficiency (i.e., the blend) on the cost side. This is due partly to the very heavy data and analytical/technical requirements of the received approaches but mainly, when all is said and done, to the persistent absence of a practical theoretically consistent solution to the original problem. Formal analysis of allocative inefficiency requires estimation of both a cost or production function and a complete demand system. I introduce this topic below but spend less space on it than on the estimation of technical and "economic" (cost) efficiency.

Note, finally, that the range of applications of the techniques described here is also huge. Frontier analysis has been used to study inefficiency in hospital costs, electric power, commercial fishing, farming, manufacturing of many sorts, public provision of transportation and sewer services, education, labor markets, and a huge array of other settings.[3] Both space and time precludes any attempt to survey this side of the literature here. I hope the community of researchers whose work is not explicitly cited here can forgive the omission of their work, again, not for lack of interest, but for lack of space. My intent in this chapter is to survey methods; reluctantly, I leave it to the reader to explore the vast range of applications. The extensive table in chapter 1 (which unfortunately is limited to twenty-first century contributions) should be very helpful.

There have been numerous general survey-style studies of the frontiers literature, including, of course, the earlier editions of this work: Førsund et al. (1980) and Greene (1993, 1997). Notable among these surveys are Bauer (1990), Battese (1992), Schmidt (1985), Cornwell and Schmidt (1996), Kalirajan and Shand (1999), and Murillo-Zamorano (2004). There are book-length treatments, as well, including Kumbhakar and Lovell (2000) and Coelli, Rao, and Battese (1998).[4] Given all of these, I felt it necessary to give some thought to the end purpose of the present exercise. First, obviously, it is an opportunity to give some exposure to the last five or six years of innovative research in the area. Primarily, however, I see my purpose here as providing the interested entrant to the area a bridge from the basic principles of econometrics and microeconomics to the specialized literature in econometric estimation of inefficiency. As such, it is not necessary to provide a complete compendium of either the theory or the received empirical literature. (That is fortunate, given its volume.) Thus, my intent is to introduce the econometric practice of efficiency estimation to the newcomer to the field.

2.2 Production and Production Functions

Let's begin by defining a producer as an economic agent that takes a set of *inputs* and transforms them either in form or in location into a set of *outputs*. We keep the definition nonspecific because we desire to encompass service organizations such as travel agents or law or medical offices. Service businesses often rearrange or redistribute information or claims to resources, which is to say, move resources rather than transform them. The production of *public services* provides one of the more interesting and important applications of the techniques discussed in this study (see, e.g., Pestieau and Tulkens, 1993).

2.2.1 Production

It is useful to think in terms of a producer as a simple machine. An electric motor provides a good example. The inputs are easily definable, consisting of a lump of capital, the motor, itself, and electricity that flows into the motor as a precisely defined and measurable quantity of the energy input. The motor produces two likewise precisely measurable (at least in principle) outputs, "work," consisting of the rotation of a shaft, and heat due to friction, which might be viewed in economic terms as waste, or a negative or undesirable output (see, e.g., Atkinson and Dorfman, 2005). Thus, in this setting, we consider production to be the process of transforming the two inputs into the economically useful output, work. The question of "usefulness" is crucial to the analysis. Whether the byproducts of production are "useless" is less than obvious. Consider the production of electricity by steam generation. The excess steam from the process might or might not be economically useful (it is in some cities, e.g., New York and Moscow), depending, in the final analysis, on relative prices. Conceding the importance of the distinction, we depart at this point from the issue and focus our attention on the production of economic "goods" that have been agreed upon a priori to be "useful" in some sense.

The economic concept of production generalizes from a simple, well-defined engineering relationship to higher levels of aggregation such as farms, plants, firms, industries, or, for some purposes, whole economies that engage in the process of transforming labor and capital into gross domestic product by some ill-defined production process. Although this interpretation stretches the concept perhaps to its logical limit, it is worth noting that the first empirical analyses of production functions, by Cobb and Douglas (1928), were precisely studies of the functional distribution of income between capital and labor in the context of an aggregate (macroeconomic) production function.

2.2.2 Modeling production

The *production function* aspect of this area of study is a well-documented part of the model. The "function" itself is, as of the time of the observation, a relationship between inputs and outputs. It is most useful to think of it simply as a body of knowledge. The various technical aspects of production, such as factor substitution, economies of scale, or input demand elasticities, while interesting in their own right, are only of tangential interest in the present context. To the extent that a particular specification, Cobb-Douglas versus translog, for example, imposes restrictions on these features, which then distort our efficiency measures, we are interested in functional form. But, this is not the primary focus.

The Cobb-Douglas and translog models overwhelmingly dominate the applications literature in stochastic frontier and econometric inefficiency estimation. (In contrast, the received literature in DEA—by construction—is dominated by linear specifications.) The issue of functional form for the production or cost function (or distance, profit, etc.) is generally tangential to the analysis and not given much attention. There have been a number of studies specifically focused on the functional form of the model. In an early entry to this literature, Caves, Christensen (one of the creators of the translog model), and Trethaway (1980) employed a Box-Cox functional form in the translog model to accommodate zero values for some of the outputs.[5] The same consideration motivated Martinez-Budria, Jara-Diaz, and Ramos-Real (2003) in their choice of a quadratic cost function to study the Spanish electricity industry. Another proposal to generalize the functional form of the frontier model is the Fourier flexible function used by Huang and Wang (2004) and Tsionas (2004).

In a production (or cost) model, the choice of functional form brings a series of implications with respect to the shape of the implied isoquants and the values of elasticities of factor demand and factor substitution. In particular, the Cobb-Douglas production function has universally smooth and convex isoquants. The implied cost function is likewise well behaved. The price to be paid for this good behavior is the strong assumption that demand elasticities and factor shares are constant for given input prices (for all outputs), and that Allen elasticities of factor substitution are all −1. Cost functions are often used in efficiency analysis because they allow the analyst to specify a model with multiple inputs. This is not straightforward on the production side, though distance functions (see section 2.5.4) also provide an avenue. The Cobb-Douglas multiple-output cost function has the unfortunate implication that in output space, the output possibility frontiers are all convex instead of concave—thus implying output specialization. These considerations have generally motivated the choice of flexible (second-order) functional forms, and in this setting, the translog production model for one output and K inputs,

$$\ln y = \alpha + \sum_{k=1}^{K} \beta_k \ln x_k + \frac{1}{2} \sum_{k=1}^{K} \sum_{m=1}^{K} \gamma_{km} \ln x_k \ln x_m,$$

or the translog multiple-output cost function for K inputs and L outputs,

$$\ln C = \alpha + \sum_{k=1}^{K} \beta_k \ln w_k + \frac{1}{2} \sum_{k=1}^{K} \sum_{m=1}^{K} \gamma_{km} \ln w_k \ln w_m$$

$$+ \sum_{s=1}^{L} \delta_s \ln y_s + \frac{1}{2} \sum_{s=1}^{L} \sum_{t=1}^{L} \phi_{st} \ln y_s \ln y_t$$

$$+ \sum_{k=1}^{K} \sum_{s=1}^{L} \theta_{ks} \ln w_k \ln y_s,$$

is most commonly used (see, e.g., Kumbhakar, 1989). These models do relax the restrictions on demand elasticities and elasticities of substitution. However, the generality of the functional form produces a side effect: They are not monotonic or globally convex, as is the Cobb-Douglas model. Imposing the appropriate curvature on a translog model is a generally challenging problem. [See Salvanes and Tjotta (1998) for methodological commentary.] Researchers typically (one would hope) "check" the regularity conditions after estimation. Kleit and Terrell (2001) in an analysis of the U.S. electricity industry used a Bayesian estimator that directly imposes the necessary curvature requirements on a two-output translog cost function. The necessary conditions, which are data dependent—they will be a function of the specific observations—are (1) monotonicity: $s_k = \partial \ln C/\partial \ln w_k = \beta_k + \sum_m \gamma_{km} \ln w_m \geq 0$, $k = 1, \ldots, K$ (nonnegative factor shares); and (2) concavity: $\Gamma - S + ss^T$ negative semidefinite, where $\Gamma = [\gamma_{km}]$, $S = \text{diag}[s_k]$, and $s = [s_1, s_2, \ldots, s_k]^T$. Monotonicity in the outputs requires $\partial \ln C/\partial \ln y_s = \delta_s + \sum_r \phi_{sr} \ln y_r > 0$. As one might imagine, imposing data- and parameter-dependent constraints such as these during estimation poses a considerable challenge. In this study, Kleit and Terrell selectively cull the observations during estimation, retaining those that satisfy the restrictions. Another recent study, O'Donnell and Coelli (2005) also suggest a Bayesian estimator, theirs for a translog distance function in which they impose the necessary curvature restrictions a priori, parametrically. Finally, Griffiths, O'Donnell, Tan, and Cruz (2000) impose the regularity conditions on a system of cost and cost-share equations.

The preceding is an issue that receives relatively little attention in the stochastic frontier applications, though it is somewhat more frequently examined in the more conventional applications in production and cost modeling (e.g., Christensen and Greene, 1976).[6] I acknowledge this aspect of modeling production and cost at this point, but consistent with others, and in the interest of brevity, I do not return to it in what follows.

2.2.3 Defining efficiency

The analysis of economic inefficiency stands at the heart of this entire exercise. If one takes classical microeconomics at face value, this is a fruitless exercise, at least regarding "competitive" markets. Functioning markets and the survivor principle simply do not tolerate inefficiency. But, this clearly conflicts with even the most casual empiricism. Also note that analysis of regulated industries and government enterprises (including buses, trains, railroads, nursing homes, waste hauling services, sewage carriage, etc.) has been among the most frequent recent applications of frontier modeling. Because the orthodoxy of classical microeconomics plays a much lesser role here, the conflict between theory and practice is less compelling. I eschew a philosophical discussion of the *concept* of inefficiency, technical, allocative, or otherwise. (For a very readable, if somewhat glib discussion, the reader may begin with Førsund, Lovell, and Schmidt, 1980).[7] Alvarez, Arias, and Greene (2005) also pursue this issue from an econometric perspective. In what follows, producers are characterized as efficient if they have produced as much as possible with the inputs they have actually employed or if they have produced that output at minimum cost. I formalize the notions as we proceed.

By technical efficiency, I mean here to characterize the relationship between observed production and some ideal, or potential production. In the case of a single output, we can think in terms of *total factor productivity*, the ratio of actual output to the optimal value as specified by a "production function." Two crucial issues, which receive only occasional mention in this chapter, are the functional form of the production function and the appropriate list of inputs. In both cases, specification errors can bring systematic errors in the *measurement* of efficiency.

We define production as a process of transformation of a set of inputs, denoted $\mathbf{x} \in R_K^+$, into a set of outputs, $\mathbf{y} \in R_M^+$. Henceforth, the notation $\mathbf{z}$, in boldface, denotes a column vector of the variables in question, whereas the same symbol z, in italics and not boldface, denotes a scalar, or a single input or output. The process of transformation (rearrangement, etc.) takes place in the context of a body of knowledge called the *production function*. We denote this process of transformation by the equation $T(\mathbf{y}, \mathbf{x}) = 0$. (The use of 0 as the normalization seems natural if we take a broad view of production against a backdrop of the laws of conservation—if $\mathbf{y}$ is defined broadly enough: Neither energy nor matter can be created nor destroyed by the transformation.)

I should emphasize that the production function is not static; technical change is ongoing. It is interesting to reflect that, given the broadest definition, the force of technical change would be only to change the mix of outputs obtained from a given set of inputs, not the quantities in total. The electric motor provides a good example. A "more efficient" motor produces more work and less heat (at least by the yardstick that most people would use), but, in fact, the total amount of energy that flows from it will be the same before and after our hypothetical technical advance. The notion of greater efficiency in this setting is couched not in terms of total output, which must be constant, but in terms of a subset of the outputs that are judged as useful against the remaining outputs that arguably are less so.

The state of knowledge of a production process is characterized by an *input requirements set*

$$L(y) = \{x : (y, x) \text{ is producible}\}.$$

That is to say, for the vector of outputs y, any member of the input requirements set is *sufficient* to produce the output vector. Note that this makes no mention of efficiency, nor does it define the production function per se, except indirectly insofar as it also defines the set of inputs that is *insufficient* to produce y [the complement of $L(y)$ in R_K^+] and, therefore, defines the limits of the producer's abilities. The production function is defined by the *isoquant*

$$I(y) = \{x : x \in L(y) \text{ and } \lambda x \notin L(y) \text{ if } 0 \leq \lambda < 1\}.$$

The isoquant thus defines the boundary of the input requirement set. The isoquant is defined in terms of contraction of an input point. A more general definition is the *efficient subset*

$$ES(y) = \{x : x \in L(y) \text{ and } x' \notin L(y) \text{ for } x' \text{ when } x'_k \leq x_k \forall k$$
$$\text{and } x'_k < x_j \text{ for some } j\}.$$

The distinction between these two similar definitions is shown in figure 2.1. Note that $x^A = (x_1^A, x_2^A)'$ is on the isoquant but is not in the efficient subset, since there is slack in x_2^A. But x^B is in both $I(y)$ and $ES(y)$. When the input

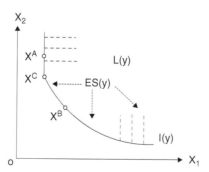

Figure 2.1. Input Requirements

requirements set is strictly convex, as is commonly assumed in econometric applications, the distinction disappears, but the distinction between these two sets is crucially important in DEA (discussed in chapter 3).

Shephard's (1953) *input distance function* is

$$D_I(y, x) = \max \left\{ \lambda : \left[\frac{1}{\lambda} \right] x \in L(y) \right\}.$$

It is clear that $D_I(y, x) \geq 1$ and that the isoquant is the set of x values for which $D_I(y, x) = 1$. The Debreu (1951)–Farrell (1957) input-based measure of technical efficiency is

$$TE(y, x) = \min\{\theta : \theta x \in L(y)\}.$$

From the definitions, it follows that $TE(y, x) \leq 1$ and that $TE(y, x) = 1/D_I(y, x)$. The Debreu-Farrell measure provides a natural starting point for the analysis of efficiency.

The Debreu-Farrell measure is strictly defined in terms of production and is a measure of *technical efficiency*. It does have a significant flaw in that it is wedded to radial contraction or expansion of the input vector. Consider, in figure 2.2, the implied inefficiency of input vector X^A. Figure 2.2 is a conventional isoquant/isocost graph for a single output being produced with two inputs, with price ratio represented by the slope of the isocost line, ww'. With the input vector X^A normalized to length one, the Debreu-Farrell measure of technical efficiency would be θ, but in economic terms, this measure clearly understates the degree of inefficiency. By scaling back both inputs by the proportion θ, the producer could reach the isoquant and thus achieve technical efficiency, but by reallocating production in favor of input x_1 and away from x_2, the same output could be produced at even lower cost. Thus, producer A is both technically inefficient and *allocatively inefficient*. The overall efficiency or economic efficiency of producer A is only α. Allocative inefficiency and

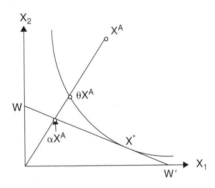

Figure 2.2. Technical and Allocative Inefficiency

its implications for econometric measurement of inefficiency are discussed in section 2.9. Empirically decomposing (observable) overall inefficiency, $1 - \alpha$, into its (theoretical, latent) components, technical inefficiency, $(1 - \theta)$, and allocative inefficiency, $(\theta - \alpha)$, is an ongoing and complex effort in the empirical literature on efficiency estimation.

2.3 Frontier Production and Cost Functions

The theoretical underpinnings of a model of production are suggested above.[8] Here we take as given the existence of a well-defined production structure characterized by smooth, continuous, continuously differentiable, quasi-concave production or transformation function. Producers are assumed to be price takers in their input markets, so input prices are treated as exogenous. The empirical measurement of TE(y, x) requires definition of a transformation function. For most of this analysis, we are concerned with a single-output production frontier. Let

$$y \le f(\mathbf{x})$$

denote the production function for the single output, y, using input vector $\mathbf{x}$. Then, an output-based Debreu-Farrell style measure of technical efficiency is.

$$\text{TE}(y, \mathbf{x}) = \frac{y}{f(\mathbf{x})} \le 1.$$

Note that the measure is the conventional measure of total factor productivity and that it need not equal the input-based measure defined earlier.

Our econometric framework embodies the Debreu-Farrell interpretation as well as the textbook definition of a production function. Thus, we begin with a model such as

$$y_i = f(\mathbf{x}_i, \boldsymbol{\beta}) \text{TE}_i,$$

where $0 < \text{TE}(y_i, \mathbf{x}_i) \le 1, \boldsymbol{\beta}$ is the vector of parameters of the production function to be estimated, and i indexes the ith of N firms in a sample to be analyzed. For present purposes, $\boldsymbol{\beta}$ is of secondary interest in the analysis. For example, in the setting of the translog model, parametric functions such as elasticities of substitution or economies of scale are of only marginal interest. The production model is usually linear in the logs of the variables, so the empirical counterpart takes the form

$$\ln y_i = \ln f(\mathbf{x}_i, \boldsymbol{\beta}) + \ln \text{TE}_i = \ln f(\mathbf{x}_i, \boldsymbol{\beta}) - u_i,$$

where $u_i \ge 0$ is a measure of *technical inefficiency* since $u_i = -\ln \text{TE}_i \approx 1 - \text{TE}_i$. Note that

$$\text{TE}_i = \exp(-u_i).$$

[See Jondrow et al. (1982) and Battese and Coelli (1992) for discussion and analysis of the distinction between these two measures.] The preceding provides the central pillar of the econometric models of production that are described below.

Formal econometric analysis of models of this sort as frontier production functions begins with Aigner and Chu's (1968) reformulation of a Cobb-Douglas model. A parallel literature is devoted to the subject of DEA. The centerpiece of DEA is the use of linear programming to wrap a quasi-convex hull around the data in essentially the fashion of Farrell's efficient unit isoquant. The hull delineates the efficient subset defined above, so, by implication, points observed inside the hull are deemed observations on inefficient producers. DEA differs fundamentally from the econometric approach in its interpretation of the data-generating mechanism but is close enough in its philosophical underpinnings to merit at least some consideration here. I turn to the *technique* of DEA in the discussion of deterministic frontiers below.[9]

2.3.1 Least squares regression–based estimation of frontier functions

In most applications, the production model, $f(x_i, \beta)$, is linear in the logs of the inputs or functions of them, and the log of the output variable appears on the left-hand side of the estimating equation. It is convenient to maintain that formulation and write

$$\ln y_i = \alpha + \beta^T x_i + \varepsilon_i,$$

where $\varepsilon_i = -u_i$, and x_i is the set of whatever functions of the inputs enter the empirical model. We assume that ε_i is randomly distributed across firms. An important assumption, to be dropped later, is that the distribution of ε_i is independent of all variables in the model. For present purposes, we assume that ε_i is a *nonzero* (negative) mean, constant variance, and otherwise ordinary regression disturbance. The assumptions thus far include $E[\varepsilon_i | x_i] \leq 0$, but absent any other special considerations, this is a classical linear regression model.[10] The model can thus be written

$$\ln y_i = (\alpha + E[\varepsilon_i]) + \beta^T x_i + (\varepsilon_i - E[\varepsilon_i]) = \alpha * + \beta^T x_i + \varepsilon_i^*.$$

This defines a classical linear regression model. Normality of the disturbance is precluded, since ε_i^* is the difference between a random variable that is always negative and its mean. Nonetheless, the model's parameters can be consistently estimated by ordinary least squares (OLS) since OLS is robust to nonnormality. Thus, the technical parameters of the production function, with the exception of the constant term, can be estimated consistently, if not efficiently by OLS. If the distribution of ε were known, the parameters could be estimated more efficiently by maximum likelihood (ML). Since the constant term usually reveals nothing more than the units of measurement of the left-hand side variable in this model, one might wonder whether all of this is much ado about nothing, or at least very little. But, one might argue that, in the present setting, the constant is the *only* parameter of interest. Remember, it is the residuals and, by construction, now $E[u_i|\mathbf{x}_i]$ that are the objects of estimation. Three approaches may be taken to examine these components.

(1) Since only the constant term in the model is inconsistent, any information useful for comparing firms to each other that would be conveyed by estimation of u_i from the residuals can be obtained directly from the OLS residuals,

$$e_i = \ln y_i - a^* - \mathbf{b}^\mathrm{T}\mathbf{x}_i = -u_i + E[u_i],$$

where $\mathbf{b}$ is the least squares coefficient vector in the regression of $\ln y_i$ on a constant and $\mathbf{x}_i$.

Thus, for example, $e_i - e_m$ is an unbiased and pointwise consistent estimator of $u_j - u_m$. Likewise, the ratio estimator $\exp(e_i)/\exp(e_m)$ estimates

$$\frac{\mathrm{TE}_i \exp(E[u_i])}{\mathrm{TE}_m \exp(E[u_m])} = \frac{\mathrm{TE}_i}{\mathrm{TE}_m}$$

consistently (albeit with a finite sample bias because of the nonlinearity of the function). For purposes of comparison of firms only, one could simply ignore the frontier aspect of the model in estimation and proceed with the results of OLS. This does preclude any sort of estimator of TE_i or of $E[u_i]$, but for now this is not consequential.

(2) Since the only deficiency in the OLS estimates is a displacement of the constant term, one might proceed simply by "fixing" the regression model. Two approaches have been suggested. Both are based on the result that the OLS estimator of the slope parameters is consistent and unbiased, so the OLS residuals are pointwise consistent estimators of linear translations of the original u_i values. One simple remedy is to shift the estimated production function upward until all residuals except one, on which we hang the function, are negative. The intercept is shifted to obtain the corrected OLS (COLS) constant,

$$a_{\mathrm{COLS}} = a^* + \max_i e_i.$$

All of the COLS residuals,

$$e_{i,\mathrm{COLS}} = e_i - \max_i e_i,$$

satisfy the theoretical restriction. Proofs of the consistency of this COLS estimator, which require only that, in a random sample drawn from the population u_i, $\mathrm{plim}\ \min_i u_i = 0$, appear in Gabrielsen (1975) and Greene (1980a). The logic of the estimator was first suggested much earlier by Winsten (1957). A lengthy application with an extension to panel data appears in Simar (1992).

In spite of the methodological problems to be noted below, this has been a popular approach in the analysis of panel data (see, e.g., Cornwell, Schmidt, and Sickles, 1990; Evans et al., 2000a, 2000b).

(3) An alternative approach that requires a parametric model of the distribution of u_i is modified OLS (MOLS). [The terminology was suggested by Lovell (1993, p. 21).] The OLS residuals, save for the constant displacement, are pointwise consistent estimates of their population counterparts, $-u_i$. The mean of the OLS residuals is useless—it is zero by construction. But, since the displacement is constant, the variance and any higher order *central* moment of (the negatives of) the OLS residuals will be a consistent estimator of the counterpart of u_i. Thus, if the parameters of $E[u_i]$ are identified through the variance or, perhaps, higher moments or other statistics, then consistent estimation of the deeper model parameters may be completed by using the method of moments. For a simple example, suppose that u_i has an exponential distribution with mean λ. Then, the variance of u_i is λ^2, so the standard deviation of the OLS residuals is a consistent estimator of $E[u_i] = \lambda$. Since this is a one-parameter distribution, the entire model for u_i can be characterized by this parameter and functions of it.[11] The estimated frontier function can now be displaced upward by this estimate of $E[u_i]$. This MOLS method is a bit less orthodox than the COLS approach described above since it is unlikely to result in a full set of negative residuals. The typical result is shown in figure 2.3.

A counterpart to the preceding is possible for analysis of the costs of production. In this case, the working assumption is that the estimated cost function lies under all the data, rather than above them.

The received literature contains discussion of the notion of an "average" frontier (an oxymoron, perhaps), as opposed to the "best-practice" frontier, based on the distinction between OLS and some technique, such as ML, which takes account of the frontier nature of the underlying model. One could argue that the former is being defined with respect to an estimator, OLS, rather than with respect to a definable, theoretically specified model. Whether the

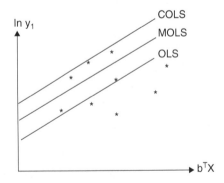

Figure 2.3. OLS Production Frontier Estimators

distinction is meaningful in an economic sense is questionable. There is some precedent for raising the question of whether the technology in use "at the frontier" differs from that in the middle of the pack, so to speak (see Klotz, Madoo, and Hansen, 1980), but the simple scaling of a loglinear production function is unlikely to reveal much about this possibility. Indeed, the implied radial expansion of the production function thus formulated might reveal nothing more than different rates of adoption of Hicks neutral technical innovations. But Førsund and Jansen (1977) argue that this difference or, more generally, differential rates of adjustment of capital stocks across firms in an industry *do* create a meaningful distinction between average and best-practice production frontiers. Some firms in an industry might be achieving the maximum output attainable, that is, be locating themselves on the frontier that applies to them, but might not have completely adjusted their capital stock to the most up-to-date, technically advanced available. Thus, the best-practice frontier for an industry that reflects this full adjustment would lie outside the frontiers applicable to some of the constituent firms (see Førsund and Hjalmarsson, 1974, for additional discussion). The description, as I show later, is akin to the motivation for the stochastic frontier model. However, the posited differences between firms are more systematic in this description.

2.3.2 Deterministic frontier models

Frontier functions as specified above, in which the deviation of an observation from the theoretical maximum is attributed solely to the inefficiency of the firm, are labeled *deterministic frontier functions*. This is in contrast to the specification of the frontier in which the maximum output that a producer can obtain is assumed to be determined both by the production function and by random external factors such as luck or unexpected disturbances in a related market. Under this second interpretation, the model is recast as a *stochastic frontier production function*, which is the subject of section 2.4.

Aigner and Chu (1968) suggested a loglinear (Cobb-Douglas) production function,

$$Y_i = AX_{1i}^{\beta_1} X_{2i}^{\beta_2} U_i,$$

in which U_i (which corresponds to TE_i) is a random disturbance between 0 and 1. Taking logs produces

$$\ln Y_i = \alpha + \sum_{k=1}^{K} \beta_k x_{ki} + \varepsilon_i$$

$$= \alpha + \sum_{k=1}^{K} \beta_k x_{ki} - u_i,$$

where $\alpha = \ln A, x_{ki} = \ln X_{ki}$, and $\varepsilon_i = \ln U_i$. The nonstochastic part of the right-hand side is viewed as the frontier. It is labeled "deterministic" because the stochastic component of the model is entirely contained in the (in)efficiency term, $-u_i$. Aigner and Chu (1968) suggested two methods of computing the parameters that would constrain the residuals u_i to be nonnegative, linear programming,

$$\min_{\alpha,\beta} \sum_{i=1}^{N} \varepsilon_i \text{ subject to } \ln y_i - \alpha - \beta^{\mathrm{T}} x_i \le 0 \forall i,$$

and quadratic programming,

$$\min_{\alpha,\beta} \sum_{i=1}^{N} \varepsilon_i^2 \text{ subject to } \ln y_i - \alpha - \beta^{\mathrm{T}} x_i \le 0 \forall i.$$

In both applications, the slack variables associated with the constraints produce the estimates of $-u_i$. A number of early applications, such as Førsund and Jansen (1977), built upon this approach both to study the technical aspects of production and to analyze technical efficiency.

The Aigner-Chu (1968) approach satisfies the original objective. One can compare the individual residuals based on the programming results,

$$\hat{u}_i = \hat{\alpha} + \hat{\beta}^{\mathrm{T}} x_i - \ln y_i,$$

to each other or to an absolute standard to assess the degree of technical (in)efficiency represented in the sample. A summary measure that could characterize the entire sample would be the

$$\text{average technical inefficiency} = \frac{1}{N} \sum_{i=1}^{N} \hat{u}_i.$$

Another useful statistic would be the

$$\text{average technical inefficiency} = \frac{1}{N} \sum_{i=1}^{N} e^{-\hat{u}_i} = \hat{E}[\text{TE}_i].$$

This semiparametric approach was applied in a series of studies including Førsund and Hjalmarsson (1979), Albriktsen and Førsund (1990), and Førsund (1992). In these studies, the authors specified the generalized production function proposed by Zellner and Revankar (1969),

$$\gamma_0 \ln y_i + \gamma_1 y_i = \alpha + \sum_{k=1}^{K} \beta_k x_{ki},$$

and minimized the sum of the residuals subject to the additional constraints $\sum_k \beta_k = 1$ and $(\gamma_0, \gamma_1, \beta_k, k = 1, \dots, K) > 0$. The foci of the applications are economies of scale and technical efficiency.

2.3.2.1 Statistical issues

The programming procedures are not based explicitly on an assumed statistical model. The properties of the "estimators" are therefore ambiguous—they would depend on what process actually did generate the data. (This is the logic of much of the contemporary discussion of how to bridge the econometric and DEA approaches to efficiency estimation. See, e.g., Simar and Wilson, 1998, 1999; see also chapter 4 of this volume.) The programming estimators have the notable disadvantage that they do not naturally produce standard errors for the coefficients, so inference is precluded. For present purposes, the main disadvantage is that absent a more detailed specification, consistency of the estimates cannot be verified, nor, as such, can consistency of the inefficiency estimates, $-u_i$. The programming procedures might, however, have the virtue of robustness to specification errors in the distribution of u_i, though this, too, remains to be verified and would depend on an underlying statistical specification (see Simar, 1996; Cazals, Florens, and Simar, 2002). Under the presumption that there is some common underlying stochastic process generating the observed data, one could proceed from here by using bootstrapping to attempt to deduce the properties of the estimators. (Again, this is an approach that has been employed to study the behavior of DEA techniques; see Simar and Wilson, 1998, 1999; see also chapter 4 this volume.) However, from a larger standpoint, it is a moot point, because the estimators themselves are no longer employed in estimating inefficiency. DEA has supplanted the linear programming approach, and the quadratic programming approach is now only of historical interest.

Schmidt (1976) observed that the Aigner-Chu optimization criteria could be construed as the log-likelihood functions for models in which one-sided residuals were distributed as exponential for the linear programming estimator, and half-normal for the quadratic programming approach. This would appear to endow the programming procedures with a statistical pedigree. However, neither log-likelihood function has a zero root, and the Hessians of both log-likelihoods are singular. The former contains a diagonal block of zeros, while the latter has a zero eigenvalue.[12] Therefore, one cannot base statistical inference on the standard results for ML estimators (MLEs) in these settings. The inference problem remains.

The statistical problem with Schmidt's estimators is a violation of the regularity conditions for MLE. This leaves the possibility that, for other distributions, the regularity conditions might be met, and as such, a well-behaved likelihood function for a one-sided disturbance might still be definable. Greene (1980a) proposed a model based on the gamma distribution,

$$h(u_i) = \frac{\theta^P}{\Gamma(P)} u_i^{P-1} e^{-\theta u_i}, \quad u_i \geq 0, \theta > 0, P > 2.$$

The density is defined for all $P > 0$, but $P > 2$ is required for a well-behaved log-likelihood function for the frontier model.[13] The gamma frontier model does produce a bona fide MLE, with all of the familiar properties. In principle, the log-likelihood,

$$\ln L(\alpha, \boldsymbol{\beta}, P, \theta) = P \ln \theta - N \ln \Gamma(P) + (P-1) \sum_{i=1}^{N} \ln u_i - \theta \sum_{i=1}^{N} u_i ,$$

$$\theta > 0, P > 2, u_i = \alpha + \boldsymbol{\beta}^\mathrm{T} \mathbf{x}_i - y_i > 0$$

can be maximized by conventional methods. The restriction that all sample residuals must be kept strictly positive for the estimator to be computable turns out to be a persistent and major complication for iterative search methods. However, inference can proceed as in more conventional problems. In spite of the practical complications, there have been several applications, including Greene (1980a, 1980b), Stevenson (1980), Aguilar (1988), Hunt, Kim, and Warren (1986), Chen and Tang (1989), and Hunt-McCool and Warren (1993). An extension that adds firm-specific effects to the efficiency term is described in Deprins and Simar (1989a). Like other deterministic frontiers, the gamma frontier model above is largely of historical interest. The contemporary work has focused on the stochastic frontier model as a preferable approach, for reasons discussed below. However, the gamma frontier model has retained some currency as the subject of several more recent studies and, in particular, as the platform for several Bayesian estimators (see Tsionas, 2000b, 2002; Huang, 2004; Koop et al., 1999; discussed below).

2.3.2.2 Deterministic cost frontiers

Førsund and Jansen (1977) formulated a hybrid of the linear programming approaches and the parametric model above to extend the analysis to costs of production. The Førsund and Jansen specification departs from a homothetic production function,[14]

$$y_i = F[f(\mathbf{x}_i)], F'[f(\mathbf{x}_i)] > 0, f(t\mathbf{x}_i) = tf(\mathbf{x}_i) \forall \mathbf{x}_i.$$

The empirical model is obtained by specifying

$$y_i = F[f(\mathbf{x}_i)v_i],$$

where v_i has a beta density (with parameters $\theta + 1$ and 1)

$$h(v_i) = (1+\theta)v_i^\theta, 0 < v_i < 1, \theta > 0.$$

The cost function that corresponds to this production function is

$$\ln C_i = \ln F^{-1}(y_i) + \ln c(\mathbf{w}_i) - \ln v_i,$$

where $\mathbf{w}_i$ is the vector of input prices, and $c(\mathbf{w}_i)$ is the unit cost function. The authors then derive the corresponding log-likelihood function. The parameters of the production function are obtained by using linear programming to minimize $\sum_{i=1}^{N} \ln C_i$ subject to the constraints that observed costs lie *on or above* the cost frontier.[15] There are three aspects of this approach that are of interest here. First, this construction is an alternative attempt to derive the linear programming criterion as the solution to an ML problem.[16] Second, this is one of the first applications to estimate a *cost frontier* instead of a production frontier. There is some controversy to this exercise owing to the possible contribution of allocative inefficiency to the observed estimates of firm inefficiency. Third, there is a subtle sleight-of-hand used in formulating the cost function. If the technical inefficiency component, v_i, were to enter the production function more naturally, *outside* the transformation of the core function, the form in which it entered the cost frontier would be far more complicated. On the other hand, if the inefficiency entered the production function in the place of $v_i x_i$, inside the homogeneous kernel function (in the form of input-oriented inefficiency), then its appearance in the cost function would be yet more complicated (see, e.g., Kumbhakar and Tsionas, 2005a; Kurkalova and Carriquiry, 2003).

2.3.2.3 COLS and MOLS estimators

The slope parameters in the deterministic frontier models can be estimated consistently by OLS. The constant term can be consistently estimated simply by shifting the least squares line upward sufficiently that the largest residual is zero. The resulting efficiency measures are $-\hat{u}_i = e_i - \max_i e_i$. Thus, absolute estimators of the efficiency measures in this model are directly computable using nothing more elaborate than OLS. In the gamma frontier model, a, the OLS estimate of α converges to plim $a = \alpha - E[u_i] = \alpha - (P/\theta)$. So, another approach would be to correct the constant term using estimates of P and θ. The gamma model also produces individual estimates of technical efficiency. A summary statistic that might also prove useful is $E[u_i] = P/\theta = \mu$, which can be estimated with the corrected residuals. Likewise, an estimate of var$[u_i] = P/\theta^2 = \sigma_u^2$ is produced by the least squares residual variance. Combining the two produces a standardized mean $\mu/\sigma_u = \sqrt{P}$. Here, as elsewhere, functions of the OLS parameter estimates and residuals can be used to obtain estimates of the underlying structural parameters. Consistent estimators of $\theta = P/\mu$ and $P = \theta\mu$ are easily computed. Using this correction to the least squares constant term produces the MOLS estimator. Another useful parameter to estimate is $E[\exp(-u_i)] = [\theta/(1+\theta)]^P$. A similar approach is taken by Afriat (1972), who suggests that u_i be assumed to have a one-parameter gamma distribution, with $\theta = 1$ in the preceding. Richmond (1974) builds on Afriat's model to obtain the distribution of e_i^{-u} and then derives $E[\exp(-u_i)]$ and other population moments.[17] Both authors suggest that the OLS residuals be used to estimate these parameters. As Richmond demonstrates, P can be consistently estimated simply by using the standard deviation of the OLS residuals.

2.3.2.4 Methodological questions

A fundamental practical problem with the gamma and all other deterministic frontiers is that any measurement error and any other outcome of stochastic variation in the dependent variable must be embedded in the one-sided disturbance. In any sample, a single errant observation can have profound effects on the estimates. Unlike measurement error in y_i, this outlier problem is not alleviated by resorting to large sample results.

There have been a number of other contributions to the econometrics literature on specification and estimation of deterministic frontier functions. Two important papers that anticipated the stochastic frontier model discussed in the next section are Timmer (1971), which proposed a probabilistic approach to frontier modeling that allowed *some* residuals to be positive, and Aigner, Amemiya, and Poirier (1976), who, in a precursor to Aigner et al. (1977), focused on asymmetry in the distribution of the disturbance as a reflection of technical inefficiency. Applications of the parametric form of the deterministic frontier model are relatively uncommon. The technical problems are quite surmountable, but the inherent problem with the stochastic specification and the implications of measurement error render it problematic. The nonparametric approach based on linear programming has an intuitive appeal and now dominates this part of the literature on frontier estimation.

2.3.3 Data envelopment analysis

DEA is a body of techniques for analyzing production, cost, revenue, and profit data, essentially, without parameterizing the technology. This constitutes a growth industry in the management science literature, and appears with some frequency in economics, as well.[18] We begin from the premise that *there exists a production frontier* that acts to constrain the producers in an industry. With heterogeneity across producers, they will be observed to array themselves at varying distances from the efficient frontier. By wrapping a hull around the observed data, we can reveal which among the set of observed producers are closest to that frontier (or farthest from it). Presumably, the larger the sample, the more precisely this information will be revealed. In principle, the DEA procedure constructs a piecewise linear, quasi-convex hull around the data points in the input space. As in our earlier discussions, technical efficiency requires production on the frontier, which in this case is the observed best practice. Thus, DEA is based fundamentally on a comparison among observed producers. Once again, to argue that this defines or estimates an ideal in any sense requires the analyst to assume, first, that there exists an ideal production point and, second, that producers strive to achieve that goal. Without belaboring the obvious, it is not difficult to construct situations in which the second of these would be difficult to maintain. The service sectors of the recently dismantled centrally planned economies of Eastern Europe come to mind as cases in point.

There are many survey-style treatments of DEA, including chapter 3 of this book. Because this chapter is devoted to econometric approaches to efficiency analysis, I eschew presentation of any of the mathematical details. Another brief (tight) and very readable sketch of the body of techniques is given in Murillo-Zamorano (2004, pp. 37–46).

The DEA method of modeling technical and allocative efficiency is largely atheoretical. Its main strength may be its lack of parameterization; it requires no assumptions about the form of the technology. The piecewise linearity of the efficient isoquant might be problematic from a theoretical viewpoint, but that is the price for the lack of parameterization. The main drawback is that shared with the other deterministic frontier estimators. Any deviation of an observation from the frontier must be attributed to inefficiency.[19] There is no provision for statistical noise or measurement error in the model. The problem is compounded in this setting by the absence of a definable set of statistical properties. Recent explorations in the use of bootstrapping methods has begun to suggest solutions to this particular shortcoming (see, e.g., Xue and Harker, 1999; Simar and Wilson, 1998, 1999; Tsionas, 2001b, which used efficiency measures produced by a DEA as priors for inefficiency in a hierarchical Bayes estimation of a stochastic frontier).

I do not return to the subject of DEA in this chapter, so at this point I note a few of the numerous comparisons that have been made between (nonparametric) DEA and statistics-based frontier methods, both deterministic and stochastic. Several studies have analyzed data with both DEA and parametric, deterministic frontier estimators. For example, Bjurek, Hjalmarsson, and Forsund (1990) used the techniques described above to study the Swedish social insurance system. Førsund (1992) did a similar analysis of Norwegian ferries. In both studies, the authors do not observe radical differences in the results with the various procedures. That is perhaps not surprising since the main differences in their specifications concerned functional form: Cobb-Douglas for the parametric models, and piecewise linear for the nonparametric ones. The differences in the inferences one draws often differ more sharply when the statistical underpinnings are made more detailed in the stochastic frontier model, but even here, the evidence is mixed. Ray and Mukherjee (1995), using the Christensen and Greene (1976) data on U.S. electricity generation, found good agreement between DEA and stochastic frontier-based estimates. Murillo-Zamorano and Vega-Cervera (2001) find similar results for a later (1990) sample of U.S. electricity generators. Cummins and Zi (1998) also found concordance in their analysis of the U.S. insurance industry. Finally, Chakraborty, Biswas, and Lewis (2001) found in analyzing public education in Utah that the empirical results using the various techniques are largely similar. These studies do stand in contrast to Ferrier and Lovell (1990), who found major differences between DEA and stochastic frontier-based inefficiency estimates in a multiple-out distance function fit in a large sample of American banks. Bauer et al. (1998) likewise found substantial differences between parametric and nonparametric efficiency estimates for a sample of U.S. banks. In sum, the evidence is mixed, but it does appear that, quite frequently, the overall pictures drawn by DEA and statistical frontier-based techniques are similar. That the two broad classes of techniques fail to produce the same pictures of inefficiencies poses a dilemma for regulators hoping to use the methods to evaluate their constituents (and, since they have the same theoretical underpinning, casts suspicion on both methods). As noted above, this has arisen in more than one study of the banking industry. Bauer et al. (1998) discuss specific conditions that should appear in efficiency methods to be used for evaluating financial institutions, with exactly this consideration in mind.

2.4 The Stochastic Frontier Model

The stochastic production frontier proposed by Aigner et al. (1977) and Meeusen and van den Broeck (1977)[20] is motivated by the idea that deviations from the production "frontier" might not be entirely under the control of the firm being studied. Under the interpretation of the deterministic frontier of the preceding section, some external events, for example, an unusually high number of random equipment failures, or even bad weather, might ultimately appear to the analyst as inefficiency. Worse yet, any error or imperfection in the specification of the model or measurement of its component variables, including the (log) output, could likewise translate into increased inefficiency measures. This is an unattractive feature of any deterministic frontier specification. A more appealing formulation holds that any particular firm faces its own production frontier, and that frontier is randomly placed by the whole collection of stochastic elements that might enter the model outside the control of the firm. [This is a similar argument to Førsund and Jansen's (1977) rationale for an average vs. best-practice frontier function.] An appropriate formulation is

$$y_i = f(\mathbf{x}_i)\text{TE}_i e^{v_i},$$

where all terms are as defined above and v_i is unrestricted. The latter term embodies measurement errors, any other statistical noise, and random variation of the frontier across firms. The reformulated model is

$$\ln y_i = \alpha + \boldsymbol{\beta}^T \mathbf{x}_i + v_i - u_i = \alpha + \boldsymbol{\beta}^T \mathbf{x}_i + \varepsilon_i.$$

(The issue of functional form was considered in section 2.2.2. I use the linear specification above generically here.) As before, $u_i > 0$, but v_i may take any value. A symmetric distribution, such as the normal distribution, is usually assumed for v_i. Thus, the *stochastic frontier* is $\alpha + \boldsymbol{\beta}^T \mathbf{x}_i + v_i$, and as before, u_i represents the inefficiency.

Note, before beginning this lengthy section, that the ultimate objective in the econometric estimation of frontier models is to construct an estimate of u_i or at least $u_i - \min_i u_i$. The first step, of course, is to compute the technology parameters, α, β, σ_u, and σ_v (and any other parameters). It does follow that, if the frontier model estimates are inappropriate or inconsistent, then estimation of the inefficiency component of ε_i, that is, u_i, is likely to be problematic, as well. So, we first consider estimation of the technology parameters. Estimation of u_i is considered in detail in section 2.8.

2.4.1 Implications of least squares

In the basic specification above, both components of the compound distur-bance are generally assumed to be independent and identically distributed (iid) across observations.[21] As long as $E[v_i - u_i]$ is constant, the OLS estimates of the slope parameters of the frontier function are unbiased and consistent. The average inefficiency present in the distribution is reflected in the asymme-try of the distribution, a quantity that is easily estimable, even with the results of OLS, with the third moment of the residuals,

$$m_3 = \frac{1}{N} \sum_{i=1}^{N} (\hat{\varepsilon}_i - \hat{E}[\varepsilon_i])^3,$$

however estimated, as long as the slope estimators are consistent. By expanding

$$\mu_3 = E[v_i - (u_i - E[u_i])]^3,$$

we see that, in fact, the skewness of the distribution of the estimable distur-bance, ε_i, is simply the negative of that of the latent inefficiency component, u_i. So, for example, regardless of the assumed underlying distribution, the negative of the third moment of the OLS residuals provides a consistent esti-mator of the skewness of the distribution of u_i. Since this statistic has units of measurement equal to the cube of those of the log of output, one might, as a useful first step in any analysis, examine the conventional normalized measure, $\sqrt{b_3} = -m_3/s^3$, where s is the sample standard deviation of the residuals. Values between 0 and 4 are typical. A Wald test of the hypothesis of no systematic inefficiency in the distribution could be based on the familiar chi-squared test,[22]

$$\chi_1^2 = \frac{1}{6}\left[\frac{-m_3}{s^3}\right]^2.$$

The skewness coefficient of the least squares residuals in any finite sample could have the "wrong" sign (positive in this case). This might cast doubt on the specification of the stochastic frontier model and suggest that the Wald test is meaningless.[23] Other tests of the stochastic frontier specification are presented in Schmidt and Lin (1984). The skewness of the residuals turns out to be an important indicator of the specification of the stochastic frontier model. I emphasize, however, that this is merely a sample statistic subject to sampling variability. The skewness is only suggestive—m_3 could be positive even if the stochastic frontier model is correct. Indeed, for a nonnormal specification of the random components, μ_3 could be positive in the population.

2.4.2 Forming the likelihood function

We begin with a general formulation of the model and then narrow the specification to the particular models that have been proposed in the contemporary literature. The generic form of the stochastic frontier is

$$\ln y_i = \alpha + \boldsymbol{\beta}^T \mathbf{x}_i + v_i - u_i$$
$$= \alpha + \boldsymbol{\beta}^T \mathbf{x}_i + \varepsilon_i.$$

It is convenient to start with the simplest assumptions, that

(a) $f_v(v_i)$ is a symmetric distribution;
(b) v_i and u_i are statistically independent of each other; and
(c) v_i and u_i are independent and identically distributed across observations.

Thus, our starting point has both error components with constant means 0 and μ and variances σ_v^2 and σ_u^2, respectively, over all observations. To form the density of $\ln y_i$ that underlies the likelihood function, we use these assumptions to obtain the joint density of the components,

$$f_{v,u}(v_i, u_i) = f_v(v_i)f_u(u_i).$$

Then, $\varepsilon_i = v_i - u_i$, so

$$f_{\varepsilon,u}(\varepsilon_i, u_i) = f_u(u_i)f_v(\varepsilon_i + u_i).$$

[The Jacobian of the transformation from (v, u) to (ε, u) is $\det \begin{bmatrix} 1 & 1 \\ 0 & 1 \end{bmatrix}^{-1} = 1.$]

Finally, to obtain the marginal density of ε_i, we integrate u_i out of the joint density:

$$f_\varepsilon(\varepsilon_i) = \int_0^\infty f_u(u_i)f_v(\varepsilon_i + u_i)du_i$$

The final step gives the contribution of observation i to the log-likelihood

$$\ln L_i(\alpha, \boldsymbol{\beta}, \sigma_u^2, \sigma_v^2 | \ln y_i, \mathbf{x}_i) = \ln f_\varepsilon(y_i - \alpha - \boldsymbol{\beta}^T \mathbf{x}_i | \sigma_u^2, \sigma_v^2).$$

In several important cases examined below, the integral has a convenient closed form so that estimation of the model by ML or through Bayesian methods based on the likelihood is straightforward. Note, however, that with current techniques of simulation-based estimation, closed forms for integrals such as this are not always necessary for estimation.[24]

The derivation above requires a trivial modification for a cost frontier. In this case,

$$\ln C_i = \alpha + \beta^\mathsf{T} x_i + v_i + u_i.$$

(For convenience here, we retain the symbol x for the variables in the frontier function, though in a cost function, they would be output and the input prices, not the inputs.) Then, $\varepsilon_i = v_i + u_i$ and $f_{\varepsilon,u}(\varepsilon_i, u_i) = f_u(u_i)f_v(\varepsilon_i - u_i)$. Since v_i is assumed to have a symmetric distribution, the second term may be written $f_v(\varepsilon_i - u_i) = f_v(u_i - \varepsilon_i)$. Making this simple change, we see that in order to form the density for log cost for a particular model in which observations lie above the frontier, it is necessary only to reverse the sign of ε_i where it appears in the functional form. An example below will illustrate.

2.4.3 The normal–half-normal model

The compound disturbance in the stochastic frontier model, while asymmetrically distributed, is, for most choices of the disturbance distributions, otherwise well behaved. MLE is generally straightforward. The literature on stochastic frontier models begins with Aigner et al.'s (1977) normal–half-normal model, in which

$$f_v(v_i) = N[0, \sigma_v^2] = (1/\sigma_v)\phi(v_i/\sigma_v), -\infty < v_i < \infty$$

and

$$u_i = |U_i| \text{ where } f_U(U_i) = N[0, \sigma_u^2] = (1/\sigma_u)\phi(U_i/\sigma_u), -\infty < U_i < \infty,$$

where $\phi(.)$ denotes the standard normal density. The resulting density for u_i is

$$f_u(u_i) = [1/\Phi(0)](1/\sigma_u)\phi(u_i/\sigma_u), 0 \leq u_i < \infty,$$

where $\Phi(.)$ is the standard normal cumulative distribution function (CDF). The symmetrically distributed v_i is usually to be assumed to be normal, which we denote $f(v_i) = N[0, \sigma_v^2]$. The distribution of the compound random variable $\varepsilon_i = (v_i - u_i)$ has been derived by Weinstein (1964) and is discussed in Aigner et al. (1977).[25] The end result, maintaining the form above, is

$$f_\varepsilon(\varepsilon_i) = \frac{2}{\sqrt{2\pi(\sigma_u^2 + \sigma_v^2)}}\left[\Phi\left(\frac{-\varepsilon_i(\sigma_u/\sigma_v)}{\sqrt{\sigma_u^2 + \sigma_v^2}}\right)\right]\exp\left(\frac{-\varepsilon_i^2}{2(\sigma_u^2 + \sigma_v^2)}\right).$$

A convenient parameterization that also produces a useful interpretation is $\sigma^2 = (\sigma_u^2 + \sigma_v^2)$ and $\lambda = \sigma_u/\sigma_v$.[26] Then,

$$f_\varepsilon(\varepsilon_i) = \frac{2}{\sigma\sqrt{2\pi}}\phi\left(\frac{\varepsilon_i}{\sigma}\right)\left[\Phi\left(\frac{-\varepsilon_i\lambda}{\sigma}\right)\right].$$

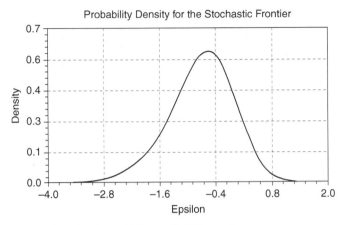

Figure 2.4. Density of a Normal Minus a Half-Normal

This density is skewed in the negative direction (see the above discussion). Figure 2.4 illustrates the shape of the distribution for $\lambda = 2$ and $\sigma = 1$. The constructed parameter $\lambda = \sigma_u/\sigma_v$ characterizes the distribution. If $\lambda \to +\infty$, the deterministic frontier results. If $\lambda \to 0$, the implication is that there is no inefficiency in the disturbance, and the model can be efficiently estimated by OLS.

With the assumption of a half-normal distribution, we obtain $E[u] = \sigma_u\sqrt{2/\pi}$ and $\mathrm{var}[u_i] = \sigma_u^2[(\pi - 2)/\pi]$. A common slip in applications is to treat σ_u^2 as the variance of u_i. In fact, this overstates the variance by a factor of nearly 3! Since σ_u is not the standard deviation of u_i, it gives a somewhat misleading picture of the amount of inefficiency that the estimates suggest is present in the data. Likewise, although λ is indicative of this aspect of the model, it is primarily a convenient normalization, not necessarily a directly interpretable parameter of the distribution. It might seem that the variance ratio σ_u^2/σ^2 would be a useful indicator of the influence of the inefficiency component in the overall variance. But again, the variance of the truncated-normal random variable u_i is $\mathrm{var}[U_i|U_i > 0] = [(\pi - 2)/\pi]\sigma_u^2$, not σ_u^2. In the decomposition of the total variance into two components, the contribution of u_i is

$$\frac{\mathrm{var}[u]}{\mathrm{var}[\varepsilon]} = \frac{[(\pi - 2)/\pi]\sigma_u^2}{[(\pi - 2)/\pi]\sigma_u^2 + \sigma_v^2}.$$

Further details on estimation of the half-normal model may be found in Aigner et al. (1977) and in Greene (2003a). The parameter λ is the inefficiency component of the model. The simple regression model results if λ equals zero. The implication would be that every firm operates on its frontier. This does not imply, however, that one can "test" for inefficiency by the usual means, because the polar value, $\lambda = 0$, is on the boundary of the parameter space, not in its interior. Standard tests, such as the Lagrange multiplier test, are likely to be problematic.[27]

The log-likelihood function for the normal–half-normal stochastic frontier model is

$$\text{Ln } L(\alpha, \beta, \sigma, \lambda) = -N \ln \sigma - \text{ constant} + \sum_{i=1}^{N} \left\{ \ln \Phi \left[\frac{-\varepsilon_i \lambda}{\sigma} \right] - \frac{1}{2} \left[\frac{\varepsilon_i}{\sigma} \right]^2 \right\},$$

where

$\varepsilon_i = \ln y_i - \alpha - \beta^T x_i, \lambda = \sigma_u/\sigma_v, \sigma^2 = \sigma_u^2 + \sigma_v^2,$ and $\Phi = $ the standard normal CDF.

The log-likelihood function is quite straightforward to maximize and has been integrated into several contemporary commercial computer packages, including *Frontier 4.1* (Coelli, 1996), *LIMDEP* (Greene, 2000), *Stata* (Stata, Inc., 2005), and *TSP* (TSP International, 2005; see also Greene, 2003a, for discussion of maximizing this log-likelihood). The normal–half-normal model has an intriguing and useful feature. Regarding an above point about the "incorrect" skewness of the least squares, Waldman (1982) has shown that in estimation of a stochastic production (cost) frontier with the normal–half-normal model, if the OLS residuals, ignoring the frontier function altogether, are positively (negatively) skewed (i.e., in the wrong direction), then the maximizers of the log-likelihood are OLS for $(\alpha, \beta, \sigma^2)$ and zero for λ.[28] This is a very useful self-diagnostic on specification and estimation of this frontier model.[29]

2.4.4 Normal–exponential and normal–gamma models

The assumption of half-normality has seemed unduly narrow, and numerous alternatives have been suggested. Meeusen and van den Broeck (1977) and Aigner et al. (1977) presented the log-likelihood and associated results for an exponentially distributed disturbance,[30]

$$f_u(u_i) = \theta \exp(-\theta u_i), \theta > 0, u_i \geq 0.$$

In the exponential model, $\sigma_u = 1/\theta$. To maintain continuity, it is helpful to use this parameterization. With this assumption,

$$\text{Ln } L(\alpha, \beta, \sigma_v, \sigma_u) = \sum_{i=1}^{N} \left[-\ln \sigma_u + \frac{1}{2} \left(\frac{\sigma_v}{\sigma_u} \right)^2 + \ln \Phi \left(\frac{-(\varepsilon_i + \sigma_v^2/\sigma_u)}{\sigma_v} \right) + \frac{\varepsilon_i}{\sigma_u} \right].$$

MLE with this distribution is straightforward, as well, although, as discussed below, there can be some complications involved with obtaining starting values.[31] The asymptotic covariance matrix of the estimated parameters is

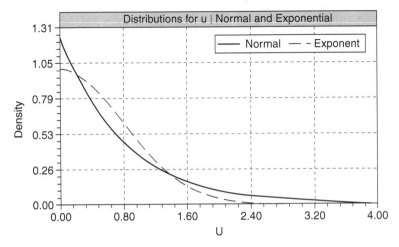

Figure 2.5. Half-Normal and Exponential Distributions

typically estimated by the Berndt, Hall, Hall and Hausman "outer product of gradients" method (Greene, 2003a), though the analytic Hessians are not overly burdensome (see Aigner et al., 1977).

The exponential model actually is qualitatively different from the half-normal. Figure 2.5 shows the half-normal distribution with $\sigma_u = 0.8$—this is the one that underlies figure 2.4—and the exponential distribution with $\theta = 1.659$, which implies the same standard deviation $[0.8(\pi - 2)/\pi = 0.603]$. As shown in figure 2.5, for a given value of the parameter, the exponential implies a tighter clustering of the values near zero. In practice, as explored below, this seems to make only a marginal difference in the estimated inefficiencies.

2.4.5 Bayesian estimation

Since van den Broeck et al. (1994) and Koop et al. (1994, 1995), there has been an active and rapid development of Bayesian estimators for stochastic frontier models.[32] Rather than treat this as a separate literature, which it is decidedly not, here I detail the basic form of the method and describe some of the numerous extensions in the different sections below, for example, on the gamma model and on multiple-output cost and distance functions. For reasons noted shortly, the basic platform for the Bayesian frontier estimator is the normal–exponential model. [I draw on Koop and Steel (2001) as a useful pedagogy for the interested reader.[33] Also, in the interest of readability, I deviate slightly from the conventional notation in Bayesian applications in which densities are usually formulated in terms of precision parameters (reciprocals of variances) rather than the natural parameters of the original model.]

The log of the likelihood function for the normal–exponential model is

$$\text{Ln } L(\text{data}; \alpha, \beta, \sigma_v, \sigma_u)$$

$$= \sum_{i=1}^{N} \left[-\ln \sigma_u + \frac{1}{2} \left(\frac{\sigma_v}{\sigma_u} \right)^2 + \ln \Phi \left(\frac{-((v_i - u_i) + \sigma_v^2/\sigma_u)}{\sigma_v} \right) + \frac{v_i - u_i}{\sigma_u} \right]$$

where $v_i - u_i = y_i - \alpha - \beta^{\mathsf{T}} x_i$. Estimation proceeds (in principle) by specifying priors over $\Theta = (\alpha, \beta, \sigma_v, \sigma_u)$ and then deriving inferences from the joint posterior $p(\Theta|\text{data})$. In general, the joint posterior for this model cannot be derived in closed form, so direct analysis is not feasible. Using Gibbs sampling and known conditional posteriors, it is possible use Markov chain Monte Carlo (MCMC) methods to sample from the marginal posteriors and use that device to learn about the parameters and inefficiencies. In particular, for the model parameters, we are interested in estimating $E[\Theta|\text{data}]$ and $\text{var}[\Theta|\text{data}]$ and perhaps even more fully characterizing the density $f(\Theta|\text{data})$. In addition, we are interested in estimating the posterior mean inefficiencies $E[u_i|\text{data}]$ and in constructing confidence intervals (or their Bayesian counterparts, highest posterior density [HPD] intervals), again, conditioned on the data.[34] The preceding does not include features of u_i in the estimation. One might, ex post, estimate $E[u_i|\text{data}]$ (see van den Broeck et al., 1994); however, it is more natural in this setting to include $(u_1, \ldots, u_N)$ with Θ and estimate the conditional means with those of the other parameters. (The method is known as *data augmentation*; see Albert and Chib, 1993.) We develop the priors for the model components, then the conditional posteriors, and, finally, the Gibbs sampler for inference based on the joint posterior.

Priors for the parameters are specified as follows: A diffuse (improper, uninformative) prior for (α, β) would have $p(\alpha, \beta) \propto 1$ over all of R^{K+1}. Another typical approach is to specify a proper, but relatively diffuse prior, $p(\alpha, \beta) \sim N[(\alpha^0, \beta^0), W]$ where (α^0, β^0) is generally $(0, 0)$ and W is large enough to avoid having an informative prior unduly influence the posterior.[35] For the stochastic elements of the frontier model, we specify $p(v_i|\sigma_v) \sim$ normal $(0, \sigma_v^2)$ and $p(u_i|\sigma_u) \sim$ exponential(σ_u) independent of v_i. [Note that this is the departure point for extensions such as the gamma model (see discussion in Koop and Steel, 2001, and the analysis below) or a Dirichlet process (see the discussion of semiparametric estimators below).] For specifying the priors over the variance parameters, Koop and Steel (2001) note that

> the researcher can, of course, use any prior in an attempt to reflect his/her prior beliefs. However, a proper prior for $1/\sigma_v$ and σ_u [maintaining our notation, not theirs] is advisable: Fernandez et al. (1997) show that Bayesian inference is not feasible (in the sense that

the posterior is not well defined) under the usual improper priors for $1/\sigma_v$ and σ_u. (p. 523)

Priors for assumed independent variance parameters in stochastic frontier models are usually assumed to follow gamma distributions:

$$p(1/\sigma_v) \sim G(1/\sigma_v|\phi_v, P_v) = \frac{\phi_v^{P_v}}{\Gamma(P_v)} \exp\left[-\phi_v(1/\sigma_v)\right](1/\sigma_v)^{P_v-1}, 1/\sigma_v \geq 0$$

The usual noninformative prior for $1/\sigma_v$ has $\phi_v = P_v = 0$ producing $p(1/\sigma_v) = (1/\sigma_v)^{-1}$, but use of this is precluded here. Different applications use different values—there is little uniformity as to how to choose these values, though in keeping with the aforementioned, values that produce more diffuse priors are preferred. For the parameter of the exponential inefficiency distribution, we likewise specify a gamma density:

$$p(\sigma_u) \sim G(\sigma_u|\phi_u, P_u) = \frac{\phi_v^{P_u}}{\Gamma(P_u)} \exp\left[-\phi_u\sigma_u\right]\sigma_u^{P_v-1}, \sigma_u \geq 0$$

Choice of the priors for the hyperparameters for the inefficiency distribution presents something of a difficulty, since, as above, a diffuse prior derails posterior inference. Many (possibly most) of the received applications have adopted a suggestion by Koop et al. (1997, and elsewhere). Setting $P_u = 1$ produces an exponential distribution for the prior over σ_u. We then set ϕ_u so that the prior median of efficiency, $\exp(-u_i)$, has a reasonable value. This involves setting $\phi_u = -\ln \tau^*$, where τ^* is the desired median. The value 0.875 is now conventional in the literature; hence, $\phi_u = 0.1335$. (Note that this is a fairly tight, quite informative prior. Koop et al. (1997, 2001) and subsequent researchers note that results seem not to be too dependent on this assumption.) The remaining detail is how to model the inefficiencies for the data augmentation. But that is already done in hierarchical fashion, since

$$p(u_i|\sigma_u) = \sigma_u \exp(-\sigma_u u_i).$$

We now have the joint prior for the parameters and $\mathbf{u} = (u_1, \ldots, u_N)$,

$$p(\Theta, \mathbf{u}) = p(\alpha, \beta)p(1/\sigma_v)p(\sigma_u)p(u_1, \ldots, u_N|\sigma_u)$$

$$= p(\alpha, \beta)p(1/\sigma_v)p(\sigma_u)\prod_{i=1}^{N} p(u_i|\sigma_u)$$

In order to draw inferences about the model components, we require information about the joint posterior

$$p(\Theta, \mathbf{u}|\text{data}) \propto p(\Theta, \mathbf{u})L(\text{data}; \Theta, \mathbf{u}).$$

The full posterior does not exist in closed form, so no analytic forms are available for the interesting characteristics, such as $E[\Theta, \mathbf{u}|\text{data}]$. The strategy to be adopted is to infer these values by random sampling from the posterior and, relying on the laws of large numbers, use statistics such as means and variances to infer the characteristics. However, no method exists for random sampling from this joint posterior. The Gibbs sampler provides the needed device. In broad terms, we desire to sample from

$$p(\Theta, \mathbf{u}|\text{data}) = p[(\alpha, \boldsymbol{\beta}), 1/\sigma_v, \sigma_u, u_1, \ldots, u_N|\text{data}].$$

As noted, this is not feasible. However, it has been shown (see Casella and George, 1992) that the following strategy, Gibbs sampling, produces a set of samples from the marginal posteriors, which is all we need: We construct the conditional posteriors

$$p[(\alpha, \boldsymbol{\beta})|1/\sigma_v, \sigma_u, u_1, \ldots, u_N, \text{data}],$$

$$p[1/\sigma_v|(\alpha, \boldsymbol{\beta}), \sigma_u, u_1, \ldots, u_N, \text{data}],$$

$$p[\sigma_u|(\alpha, \boldsymbol{\beta}), 1/\sigma_v, u_1, \ldots, u_N, \text{data}],$$

$$p[u_i|(\alpha, \boldsymbol{\beta}), 1/\sigma_v, \sigma_u|\text{data}], i = 1, \ldots, N.$$

Random samples from these, cycling in seriatim (an MCMC iteration), produces a set of random samples from the respective marginal posteriors. (The order of the draws does not matter.) The cycle begins at some value within the range of each variable. Many thousands of cycles are used, with the first several thousand discarded to eliminate the effects of the initial conditions— for example, received reported values range from 10,000 with the first 5,000 discarded to 75,000 with every fifth draw after 10,000 retained.

It remains to derive the conditional posteriors. For the stochastic frontier model, these are known: With all other values including $u_i, i = 1, \ldots, N$ known,

$$p[(\alpha, \boldsymbol{\beta})|1/\sigma_v, \sigma_u, u_1, \ldots, u_N, \text{data}] = p(\alpha, \boldsymbol{\beta}) \times N[(a, b), \sigma_v^2 A],$$

where (a, b) are the least squares coefficients in the linear regression of $y_i + u_i$ on a constant and x_i, and A is the inverse of the usual second moment matrix for $[1, x_i]$. Recall $p(\alpha, \boldsymbol{\beta}) = 1$ in our application. Random draws from the multivariate normal distribution are simple to draw; they can be built up from primitive draws from the standard normal with straightforward calculations (see Greene, 2003a, p. 922). The conditional densities for the variance parameters are a bit more complicated. For the symmetric distribution,

$$p[1/\sigma_v|(\alpha, \boldsymbol{\beta}), \sigma_u, u_1, \ldots, u_N, \text{data}] = \gamma(f, P^*),$$

where $f = \phi_v + \frac{1}{2N} \sum_{i=1}^{N} (y_i - \boldsymbol{\beta}^T x_i)^2$ and $P^* = P_v + N/2$. For the inefficiency parameter,

$$p[\sigma_u|(\alpha, \boldsymbol{\beta}), 1/\sigma_v, u_1, \ldots, u_N, \text{data}] = \gamma \left(\frac{1}{N} \sum_{i=1}^{N} u_i - \ln \tau^*, N + 1 \right).$$

Sampling from the gamma distribution is less straightforward than from the normal but can be done with published software, such as IMSL Libraries (Absoft, 2005). Finally, for the data augmentation step, we have

$$p[u_i|(\alpha, \beta), 1/\sigma_v, \sigma_u, \text{data}] = N^+[-(y_i - \beta^T x_i) + \sigma_v^2/\sigma_u, \sigma_v^2],$$

where $N^+[.]$ denotes the truncated normal distribution.[36] Sampling from a truncated normal distribution with a given underlying mean and standard deviation is also straightforward. Some authors (e.g., Tsionas, 2002) suggest acceptance/rejection—draw an observation, and either accept it if it is positive, or reject it and draw another. A simpler and smoother method requiring but a single draw is based on the inverse probability transform: $u_{i,r} = \mu + \sigma\Phi^{-1}[F_{i,r} + (1 - F_{i,r})\Phi(-\mu/\sigma)]$, where the subscript i, r denotes the rth draw for observation i, μ and σ are the mean and standard deviation noted above, $\Phi^{-1}(.)$ is the inverse function of the standard normal CDF, and $F_{i,r}$ is a single standard uniform, $U[0, 1]$ draw.

These equations define the Gibbs sampler, which can be used to produce samples from the desired marginal posterior distributions. Thus, after the iterations, the simple means and variances of the draws produce estimates of the means and variances of the conditional distributions, $f[(\alpha, \beta)|\text{data}]$, $f(1/\sigma_v|\text{data})$, $f(\sigma_u|\text{data})$, and $f(u_i|\text{data})$. (Note, again, that the last of these is not an estimator of u_i; it is an estimator of $E[u_i|\text{data}]$. No amount of data, manipulated in Bayesian or classical fashion, produces a convergent estimator of u_i; we only estimate the mean of the conditional distribution.)

2.4.6 The normal–gamma model

Stevenson (1980) and Greene (1980a, 1980b) also proposed results for the gamma/normal distribution. In this case,

$$f_u(u_i) = \frac{\sigma_u^{-P}}{\Gamma(P)} \exp(-u_i/\sigma_u)u_i^{P-1}, u_i \geq 0, P > 0.$$

Note that the exponential results if $P = 1$. Unlike the case of the deterministic gamma frontier model, this model only requires P to be positive. The convolution with v_i makes the resulting distribution of ε_i regular for all positive values of P. Stevenson limited his attention to the Erlang form (integer values of P, 1.0, and 2.0), which greatly restricts the model. Beckers and Hammond (1987) first formally derived the log-likelihood for the convolution of a normal and a gamma variate. The resulting functional form was intractable, however. Greene (1990) produced an alternative formulation that highlights the relationship of the gamma model to the exponential model considered above. The log-likelihood function with the normal–gamma mixture is

$$\text{Ln } L(\alpha, \beta, \sigma_v, \sigma_u) = \sum_{i=1}^{N} \left[\begin{array}{l} -P \ln \sigma_u - \ln \Gamma(P) + \ln q(P-1, \varepsilon_i) \\ + \frac{1}{2} \left(\frac{\sigma_v}{\sigma_u} \right)^2 + \ln \Phi \left(\frac{-\varepsilon_i + \sigma_v^2/\sigma_u}{\sigma_v} \right) + \frac{\varepsilon_i}{\sigma_u} \end{array} \right],$$

where
$$q(r, \varepsilon_i) = E\left[z^r | z > 0, \varepsilon_i \right], z \sim N[-\varepsilon_i + \sigma_v^2/\sigma_u, \sigma_v^2].$$

The log-likelihood function can be written

$$\text{Ln } L(\alpha, \beta, \sigma_v, \sigma_u) = \ln L_{\text{Exponential}} + \sum_{i=1}^{N} [-(P-1) \ln \sigma_u - \ln \Gamma(P)$$
$$+ \ln q(P-1, \varepsilon_i)].$$

The $q(r, \varepsilon)$ function is a (possibly) fractional moment of the truncated normal distribution.[37] The additional terms drop out if P equals 1, producing the exponential model.

The gamma formulation has some appeal in that it allows for different distributions of inefficiency. Figure 2.6 suggests the possibilities. The heaviest plot in figure 2.6 shows the distribution with $P = 0.8$. When $P < 1$, the distribution only asymptotes to the vertical axis, which implies that there is large mass near zero. The middle plot has $P = 1$, which is the exponential distribution shown in figure 2.5. The lower plot shows that, with $P > 1$, the distribution can be pulled away from zero, which is likely

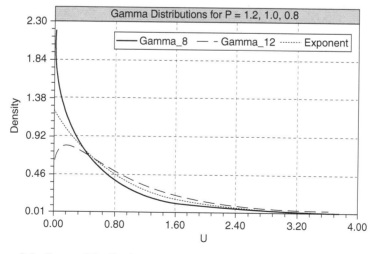

Figure 2.6. Gamma Distributions

to be a more reasonable characterization of inefficiency at least for some applications.

Greene's formulation of the gamma model brought some substantial differences from the half-normal specification in an empirical application.[38] However, the greatly increased complexity of the procedure has somewhat inhibited its application.[39] van den Broeck et al. (1994) and Koop et al. (1995) have taken a Bayesian approach to the specification of the inefficiency term in the stochastic frontier model. The former study considers several prior distributions for u_i including half- and truncated-normal, exponential, and the Erlang form of Greene's normal–gamma model.[40] Several other Bayesian applications (e.g., Tsionas, 2002; Huang, 2004) have employed the gamma model in stochastic frontier formulations—it provides a comfortable fit for the inverted gamma conjugate priors for variance parameters. Ritter and Simar (1997), however, have analyzed this model extensively and expressed considerable skepticism about its usability for classical formulation. They found that the parameters are very weakly identified, and estimation is exceedingly difficult. Accurate computation of the fractional moments is extremely difficult. Note, however, that the model that Ritter and Simar (1997) focus on has only a constant term, so their results may lack generality—they do stand as a caveat for researchers nonetheless. Greene (2000, 2003a, 2003b) proposes a more general approach than Ritter and Simar's, based on MSL that seems largely to overcome the previous problems of computation of the log-likelihood and its derivatives.

2.4.6.1 Classical estimation of the normal–gamma model

Several recent studies have resurrected the normal–gamma model. Greene (2003a) has produced an alternative approach to computing the complex part of the log-likelihood function, the expectations from the truncated normal distribution, using Monte Carlo simulation, rather than attempting to approximate the integrals directly. The method appears to produce more satisfactory results. The obstacle to estimation is accurate computation of $q(r, \varepsilon_i) = E[z^r | z > 0]$ where $z \sim N[\mu_i, \sigma_v^2], \mu_i = -(\varepsilon_i + \sigma_v^2/\sigma_u)$. Since it is an expectation, and an otherwise straightforward function, the function can be consistently (pointwise) estimated with $\hat{q}(r, \varepsilon_i) = (1/Q) \sum_{q=1}^{Q} z_{iq}^r$, where z_{iq} is a random draw from the indicated truncated normal distribution. The MSL estimator then replaces $q(r, \varepsilon_i)$ with $\hat{q}(r, \varepsilon_i)$. The remaining complication is how to obtain the random draws. Acceptance/rejection of a sample of draws from the untruncated normal population is unacceptable, since the resulting function is no longer smooth and continuous (different observations will be rejected depending on the parameters), it will take huge numbers of draws, and it will be very inaccurate in the tails. The alternative is to use the inverse probability transform, which translates random draws one for one. The strategy is implemented by using the generic formula for sampling from the truncated normal distribution,

$$z_{iq} = \mu_i + \sigma\Phi^{-1}[(1 - F_q)P_L + F_q],$$

where $\varepsilon_i = y_i - \beta^T x_i, \mu_i = -\varepsilon_i - \sigma_v^2/\sigma_u, \sigma = \sigma_v$, and $P_L = \Phi(-\mu_i/\sigma)$, and F_q is a draw from the continuous uniform $(0, 1)$ distribution. Combining all terms, then,

$\text{Ln } L_S(\alpha, \beta, \sigma_v, \sigma_u)$

$$= \sum_{i=1}^{N} \left[\begin{array}{l} -P\ln\sigma_u - \ln\Gamma(P) + \dfrac{1}{2}\left(\dfrac{\sigma_v}{\sigma_u}\right)^2 + \ln\Phi\left(\dfrac{-\varepsilon_i + \sigma_v^2/\sigma_u}{\sigma_v}\right) + \dfrac{\varepsilon_i}{\sigma_u} \\ + \ln\left\{ \dfrac{1}{Q}\sum_{q=1}^{Q}\left(\mu_i + \sigma_v\Phi^{-1}(F_{iq} + (1 - F_{iq})\Phi(-\mu_i/\sigma_v))\right)^{P-1} \right\} \end{array} \right].$$

As complicated as it is, this form is vastly simpler than the Pochammer function invoked by Beckers and Hammond (1987) or the direct integration in Greene (1990). The function and its derivatives are smooth and continuous in all the parameters of the model. Further details appear in Greene (2003b, 2004a). Vitaliano (2003) is a recent application.

2.4.6.2 Bayesian estimation of the normal–gamma model

Owing to its flexibility and its natural similarity to familiar forms of priors, the gamma model has also attracted researchers employing Bayesian methods to estimate stochastic frontier models. Tsionas (2002) begins with a normal–exponential model and an assumed panel-data setting. Each unit has its own parameter vector, β_i, which is assumed to be generated by a prior normal density, $N[\beta^0, \Omega]$. Posterior means are derived for all the production parameters using the MCMC simulation method that is now standard in Bayesian applications. Finally, the posterior distribution for the inefficiencies, u_{it} is obtained as a truncated normal variable with a specified mean and variance that is a function of the other parameters in his model. Thus, estimates of u_{it} are obtained after obtaining posterior estimates of the other parameters.[41] (The estimation of u_{it} and the use of panel data are both subjects of later sections of this chapter, but the use of the normal–gamma model remains somewhat out of the mainstream of empirical applications, so it seems appropriate to continue the thread of the discussion here rather than later, because this model does not figure prominently in most of the rest of the discussion.) Interestingly enough, after developing the model for panel-data applications, Tsionas (2002) applied it to a cross section—the Christensen and Greene (1976) electricity data. It seems likely that some of the fairly extreme empirical results in his paper were a consequence of stretching the panel-data estimator to samples of one in a cross section—his results appear to imply an average efficiency in the sample of more than 99%, which is considerably at odds with earlier findings with the same data set.) Tsionas proceeded to extend his model to half-normal and Erlang (gamma with $P = 1, 2, 3$) distributions, employing similar methodologies in each case.

Van den Broeck et al. (1994) and Koop et al. (1995) have also examined the normal–Erlang model using Bayesian MCMC techniques. Surprisingly, in an *earlier* paper, Tsionas (2000b), again employing MCMC techniques, examined the implications of a noninteger value of P in the normal–gamma model. Suggestions elsewhere notwithstanding, he found that variation to noninteger values of P, even within a fairly narrow range, does produce substantive differences in the appearance of the inefficiency distribution. He continues to examine the model with various values of P. In an indicator of the complexity of the estimation problem, in his analysis, it becomes necessary to fix one of the other model parameters at an assumed value to proceed with estimation. In their Capital Asset Pricing Model (CAPM) study of mutual fund performance, Annaert et al. (2001) also fit the Erlang model with $P = 1, 2$, and 3 and then probabilistically pooled the three sets of estimates. With P fixed in each case, the estimator itself is easily fit using the straightforward MCMC methods mentioned above. In sum, the normal–gamma model with a free shape parameter has posed an ongoing challenge in the Bayesian literature, but one that has attracted a fair amount of attention. Ultimately, the flexibility of the two-parameter distribution and the variety of shapes that it can accommodate do have an appeal. (One might surmise that the convenience of the conjugate prior with the flexibility of the two-parameter gamma model make it an irresistible target in this literature.) In the most recent attack on this vexing estimation problem, Huang (2004) develops a full likelihood-based Bayesian estimator for the normal–gamma model without the Erlang restriction. His results on inefficiency estimates are essentially the same as Tsionas's; in his full model with parameter heterogeneity, the modal efficiency is roughly 0.99 (Huang's figure 4). The estimates presented in Huang's table 1 suggest that the overall distribution of inefficiency is roughly exponential with a mean and standard deviation of $1/77.4337 = 0.0129$. Both of these sets of implausible results are considerably at odds with other evidence of inefficiency in the Christensen and Greene data.[42] Finally, Griffin and Steel (2004) propose a Dirichlet (semiparametric) specification for the inefficiencies in a semiparametric formulation of a Bayesian model. In passing, they also fit the normal–gamma (fully parametric) model. The application is based on Koop et al.'s (1997) hospital data, so we cannot compare the results to the foregoing. They do (apparently) find that for most of their sample the normal–gamma model tracks the semiparametric model fairly well, and far better than the normal–exponential model, which might be expected. Migon and Medici (2001) also propose methodology for the normal–gamma model but do not use it in their applications. (Unlike most other studies, they ultimately gravitated to a normal–lognormal model.)

In summary, then, it would appear that Greene (2003b) and Tsionas (2002)/Huang (2004) have reported considerable progress in the 20-plus year development of this strand of literature. Both estimation strategies based on simulation—the former in the classical tradition, the latter in the Bayesian paradigm—appear to be reasonably (not extremely) straightforward to implement.[43] What remains unsettled, at least as a caveat, is the Ritter and Simar (1997) argument that the model is difficult to identify. The applications seem to suggest otherwise, but extensive analysis remains to be done.

There have been numerous Bayesian applications in the stochastic frontier literature. A significant proportion of them are listed above, and nearly all of the remainder (that I have located) appear at one point or another below.[44] As in most applications, since the specifications are stringent in their specification of noninformative (diffuse) priors, the results usually differ marginally, if at all, from MLEs derived from the classical approach.[45] There are, however, some aspects of Bayesian estimation in the stochastic frontier literature that are worthy of note. First, there are now Bayesian applications to problems that have not received much attention in the classical literature, for example, O'Donnell and Coelli's (2005) application in which they imposed the theoretical curvature conditions on a translog distance function. The estimation of technical or cost inefficiency poses an unusual challenge for Bayesian estimators, however. Since estimates of inefficiency (technical or cost) are individual observation specific, it is not possible to obtain them without assuming an informative prior. Thus, Koop et al. (1994), Tsionas (2002), and Huang (2004) all assume a gamma prior for $\ln u_i$ with a known mean (and variance). Obviously, the results are sensitive to the assumption. The technique of data augmentation (Albert and Chib, 1993) is often used as a means to the end of posterior parameter mean estimation in models with missing data (e.g., the probit model). The estimates of the missing data values are generally of no intrinsic interest and are not analyzed at any length in the posterior analysis. The same technique is used in estimating u_i in stochastic frontier models, but in this setting, the augmented data are not a means to an end—they are the end. However, it is here that it is necessary to assume a fairly strongly informative prior in order to have a tractable posterior with finite variance. I return to this issue in some detail below.

In sum, some of the Bayesian applications merely demonstrate the existence of counterparts to classical estimators. Given diffuse priors, this produces little more than an alternative method (MCMC) of maximizing the likelihood function and then calling the new "estimate" something with a different name. (See Kim and Schmidt, 2000, for some evidence on this point.) But, at the same time, innovative applications that extend the model, such as Tsionas's (2003) dynamic model and Atkinson and Dorfman's (2005) distance function model, have begun to appear, as well. As of this writing, this strand of the literature remains a significant minority. I revisit it at various points below, but my treatment, like the literature it surveys, focuses primarily on classical, ML-based applications.

2.4.7 The truncated-normal model

Stevenson (1980) argued that the zero mean assumed in the Aigner et al. (1977) model was an unnecessary restriction. He produced results for a *truncated* as opposed to *half-normal* distribution. That is, the one-sided error term, u_i is obtained by truncating at zero the distribution of a variable with possibly nonzero mean. The complete parameterization is

$$v_i \sim N[0, \sigma_v^2],$$

$$U_i \sim N[\mu, \sigma_u^2], u_i = |U_i|.$$

For convenience, let us use the parameterizations given above for λ and σ. Then, the log-likelihood is

$$\mathrm{Ln}\, L(\alpha, \beta, \sigma, \lambda, \mu) = -N \left[\ln \sigma + \frac{1}{2} \ln 2\pi + \ln \Phi(\mu/\sigma_u) \right]$$

$$+ \sum_{i=1}^{N} \left[-\frac{1}{2} \left(\frac{\varepsilon_i + \mu}{\sigma} \right)^2 + \ln \Phi \left(\frac{\mu}{\sigma \lambda} - \frac{\varepsilon_i \lambda}{\sigma} \right) \right],$$

where $\sigma_u = \lambda \sigma / \sqrt{1 + \lambda^2}$ (a derivation appears in Kumbhakar and Lovell, 2000). Starting values for the iterations in the stochastic frontier models are typically obtained by manipulating the results of OLS to obtain method-of-moments estimators for the parameters of the underlying distribution. There does not appear to be a convenient method-of-moments estimator for the mean of the truncated normal distribution. But MLE presents no unusual difficulty. The obvious starting value for the iterations would be the estimates for a half-normal model and zero for μ. The benefit of this additional level of generality is the relaxation of a possibly erroneous restriction. A cost appears to be that the log-likelihood is sometimes ill-behaved when μ is unrestricted. As such, estimation of a nonzero μ often inflates the standard errors of the other parameter estimators considerably, sometimes attends extreme values of the other parameters, and quite frequently impedes or prevents convergence of the iterations. It is also unclear how the restriction of μ to zero, as is usually done, would affect efficiency estimates. The Bayesian applications of this model (e.g., Tsionas, 2001a; Holloway et al., 2005) have apparently encountered less difficulty in estimation of this model.

As explored in section 2.6, the parameters of the underlying distribution of u_i provide a mechanism for introducing heterogeneity into the distribution of inefficiency. The mean of the distribution (or the variance or both) could depend on factors such as industry, location, and capital vintage. One way such factors might be introduced into the model could be to use

$$\mu_i = \mu_0 + \mu_1^T z_i,$$

where z_i is any variables that should appear in this part of the model. As noted, we revisit this possibility further below.

2.4.8 Estimation by COLS method-of-moments estimators

The parameters of the stochastic frontier model can be estimated using the second and third central moments of the OLS residuals, m_2 and m_3. For the half-normal model, the moment equations are

$$m_2 = \left[\frac{\pi - 2}{\pi}\right]\sigma_u^2 + \sigma_v^2,$$

$$m_3 = \sqrt{\frac{2}{\pi}}\left[1 - \left(\frac{4}{\pi}\right)\right]\sigma_u^3.$$

(Note that m_3 is negative, since the offset in ε_i by u_i is negative.) Thus, σ_u and σ_v are easily estimable. Since $E[u_i] = (2/\pi)^{1/2}\sigma_u$, the adjustment of the OLS constant term is $\hat{\alpha} = a + \hat{\sigma}_u\sqrt{2/\pi}$. These MOLS estimators are consistent, but inefficient in comparison to the MLEs. The degree to which they are inefficient remains to be determined, but it is a moot point, since with current software, full MLE is no more difficult than least squares.

Waldman (1982) has pointed out an intriguing quirk in the half-normal model. Normally, there are two roots of the log-likelihood function for the stochastic frontier model: one at the OLS estimates and another at the MLE. In theory, the distribution of the compound disturbance is skewed to the left. But, if the model is badly specified, the OLS residuals can be skewed in the opposite direction. In this instance, the OLS results are the MLEs, and consequently, one must estimate the one-sided terms as 0.0.[46] (Note that if this occurs, the MOLS estimate of σ is undefined.) One might view this as a built-in diagnostic, since the phenomenon is likely to arise in a badly specified model or in an inappropriate application. This "failure"—I use the term advisedly here, since analysts might differ on whether the estimation tools or the analyst has failed—occurs relatively frequently. Coelli's (1995) formulation may be more convenient in this regard (see note 26). He suggests the moment estimators

$$\hat{\sigma}^2 = m_2 + \left(\frac{2}{\pi}\right)\left[\sqrt{\frac{\pi}{2}\left(\frac{\pi}{\pi - 4}\right)}m_{23}\right]^{\frac{2}{3}},$$

$$\hat{\gamma} = \left(\frac{1}{\hat{\sigma}^2}\right)\left[\sqrt{\frac{\pi}{2}\left(\frac{\pi}{\pi - 4}\right)}m_3\right]^{\frac{2}{3}},$$

$$\hat{\alpha} = a + \sqrt{\frac{2\hat{\gamma}\hat{\sigma}^2}{2}}.$$

As before, the "wrong sign" on m_3 can derail estimation of γ, but in this instance, a convenient place to begin is with some small value; Coelli suggests

0.05. As noted above, there is no obvious method-of-moments estimator for μ in Stevenson's truncated-normal model.

The MOLS estimators for the exponential model are based on the moment equations $m_2 = \sigma_v^2 + \sigma_u^2$ and $m_3 = -2\sigma_u^3$. Thus,

$$\hat{\sigma}_u = [-m_3/2]^{\frac{1}{3}}, \hat{\sigma}_v^2 = m_2 - \hat{\sigma}_u^2, \hat{\alpha} = a + \hat{\sigma}_u.$$

For the gamma model, the MOLS estimators are

$$\hat{\sigma}_u = -(m_4 - 3m_2^2)/(3m_3), \hat{P} = -m_3/(2\hat{\sigma}_u^3), \hat{\sigma}_v^2 = m_2 - \hat{P}\hat{\sigma}_u^2, \hat{\alpha} = a + \hat{P}\hat{\sigma}_u.$$

Any of these can be used to obtain a full set of estimates for the stochastic frontier model parameters. They are all consistent. Thereafter, estimates of the efficiency distributions or of the individual coefficients, $-u_i$ or TE_i, can be computed just by adjusting the OLS residuals. There is a question of the *statistical* efficiency of these estimators. One specific result is given in Greene (1980a) for the gamma-distributed, deterministic frontier model, namely, that the ratio of the true variance of the MLE of any of the slope coefficients in the model to its OLS counterpart is $(P-2)/P$. Thus, the greater the asymmetry of the distribution—the gamma density tends to symmetry as P increases—the greater is efficiency gain to using MLE (see Deprins and Simar, 1985, for further results). Of course, efficient estimation of the technical parameters is not necessarily the point of this exercise. Indeed, for many purposes, consistency is all that is desired. As noted, estimation of all of these models is fairly routine with contemporary software. The preceding are likely to be more useful for obtaining starting values for the iterations than as estimators in their own right.

2.4.9 Other specifications for stochastic frontier models

A number of other candidates have been proposed for the parametric forms of the stochastic frontier model. An early study by Lee (1983) proposed a four-parameter Pearson family of distributions for the purpose of testing the distributional assumptions of the model—the Pearson family nests a large number of familiar distributions. The model proved much too cumbersome for general usage, but it does suggest the possibility of alternatives to the familiar paradigm of normality coupled with a limited range of one-sided distributions for u_i. This section surveys a few of the alternative distributions that have been proposed for the stochastic frontier model.

The question of how to model inefficiency in a data set that spans several time periods is a major point in the analysis of panel data. In particular, researchers differ—and the data are inconsistent—on whether it is reasonable to model inefficiency as a time-invariant, firm-specific effect or as an effect that varies freely and randomly over time, or whether some intermediate formulation, in which $u_{i,t}$ (firm i at time t) evolves systematically, is appropriate. This subject is revisited at length in section 2.7. Note at this point, however, a proposal by Tsionas (2003) that could be used to analyze this issue, at least in part. He suggests the dynamic model

$$\ln u_{i,t} | \mathbf{z}_{it}, \gamma, \rho, \omega, u_{i,t-1} \sim N\left[\gamma^T \mathbf{z}_{it} + \rho \ln u_{i,t-1}, \omega^2\right], \quad t = 2, \dots, T,$$

$$\ln u_{i,1} | \mathbf{z}_{i1}, \gamma_1, \omega_1 \sim N[\gamma_1^T \mathbf{z}_{i1}, \omega_1^2],$$

where $\mathbf{z}_{i,t}$ is a vector of exogenous effects (not the inputs). The startup process (initial condition) is allowed to be different from the process governing the evolution of the inefficiency. Tsionas (2003) applies the technique to Bayesian estimation of a cost frontier estimated for a sample of 128 U.S. banks over 12 years. A multiple-output translog function is estimated. The estimated posterior mean of ρ is 0.908, suggesting that, to some approximation, the measured inefficiency in his sample is close to constant over time. Note that this proposal employs a lognormal density for the inefficiency—a specification that has been used quite infrequently (see, e.g., Migon and Medici, 2001; Deprins and Simar, 1989b).

2.4.9.1 Other parametric models

Migon and Medici (2001) also use Bayesian methods to estimate a stochastic frontier model with lognormal inefficiencies. Estimation is straightforward using the MCMC methods they employ. It would be more difficult to replicate this with orthodox classical methods, since forming the density for a normal minus a lognormal is an unsolved problem. The method of Misra and Greene and Misra (2003), shown below, however, which would approach the problem in essentially the same fashion as the Bayesian estimator, could easily be adapted to a lognormal distribution. The normal–lognormal model remains to be explored in this literature. As (possibly) a two-parameter density that resembles the attractive gamma model, I would surmise that this specification offers some interesting potential. Tsionas and Greene (2003) showed how the Bayesian approach outlined above for the normal–gamma model could be adapted to other functional forms. Motivated by the possibility that ordinary outliers in the data might distort the estimated model and ultimately end up expanding the range of variation of u_i in the estimated model, they proposed a Student's t for the symmetric distribution (v_i), that is, a distribution with much thicker tails than the normal. In their discussion of the MCMC procedure, they suggested that formulation of a tractable posterior is the only obstacle to any other distribution. (The half-normal and exponential were demonstrated, as well.) Whether other distributions would provide any benefit, or even substantively change the results, remains to be seen. [An application that considers the lognormal and Weibull distributions in addition to those considered here is Deprins and Simar (1989b).]

    A similar consideration underlies the proposal by Greene and Misra (2003), who essentially followed Tsionas and Greene's (2003) suggestion, in a classical estimator. Recall that the density for the observed data that underlies the log-likelihood is obtained as follows: First, $y_i = \beta^T x_i + v_i - u_i$ and $\varepsilon_i = y_i - \beta^T x_i = v_i - u_i$. A symmetric density is assumed for v_i and a one-sided one for u_i. Then, the unconditional density that enters the likelihood function is

$$f_\varepsilon(\varepsilon_i|\beta,\delta,x_i) = \int_0^\infty f_v(\varepsilon_i + u_i)f_u(u_i)du_i,$$

where δ is any parameters in the model other than α and β, such as σ_u and σ_v in the half-normal and exponential models. The normal–half-normal and normal–exponential models are derived by obtaining a closed form for this integral. Since there is no closed form for the normal–gamma model, the relevant part of the log-likelihood is approximated by simulation. As observed at several pointsabove, the integral above is of the form of an expectation. In principle, it can be accurately approximated by simulation and averaging a number of draws from the appropriate underlying population. In order to apply the principle, the specification requires a distribution for u_i from which a random sample of draws can be obtained, and an explicit specification for the density of v_i. With these in place, a generic formulation of the simulated log-likelihood for the stochastic frontier model would be

$$\log L_S(\alpha,\beta,\delta|\text{data}) = \sum_{i=1}^N \log \frac{1}{Q}\sum_{q=1}^Q f_v[y_i - \alpha - \beta^T x_i + u_i, \delta].$$

This function is then maximized with respect to the underlying parameters. Like the normal–gamma model discussed above, it is smooth and continuous in the parameters. To take a specific example, the following shows an alternative way to estimate the normal–exponential model. The density (PDF) and CDF for the one-sided u_i are

$$f_u(u_i) = (1/\sigma_u)\exp(-u_i/\sigma_u), F(u_i) = 1 - \exp(-u_i/\sigma_u), u_i \geq 0, \sigma_u > 0.$$

Inverting $F(u_i)$ for u_i reveals the strategy for generating random draws on u_i:

$$u_{ir} = -\sigma_u \ln(1 - F_{ir}),$$

where F_{ir} is a random draw from the standard uniform distribution, $U[0,1]$, which one can do with any modern econometrics package. (For simplicity, the draw may simply be F_{ir}, since $1 - F_{ir}$ is also from the $U[0,1]$ population.) The symmetric density is the normal distribution, so the simulated log-likelihood is

$$\text{Ln } L_S(\alpha,\beta,\sigma_v,\sigma_u|\text{data})$$
$$= \sum_{i=1}^N \ln \frac{1}{R}\sum_{r=1}^R \frac{1}{\sigma_v}\phi\left[\frac{y_i - \alpha - \beta^T x_i + (-\sigma_u \log F_{ir})}{\sigma_v}\right]$$

This function and its derivatives are smooth and continuous in the parameters and can be maximized by conventional means (assuming one is able to fix the set of random draws—the same set of R draws must be used each time the function is evaluated). The derivatives of this log-likelihood are as follows: For convenience, let the argument of the normal density be denoted $a_{ir} = y_i - \alpha - \boldsymbol{\beta}^T \mathbf{x}_i - \sigma_u \ln F_{ir}$, so that the bracketed function above is just $\phi(a_{ir}/\sigma_v)$. Let $\boldsymbol{\theta}$ denote the parameter vector $(\alpha, \boldsymbol{\beta}', \sigma_u)'$. Then,

$$\ln L_S(\boldsymbol{\theta}, \sigma_v | \text{data}) = \sum_{i=1}^{N} \ln \frac{1}{R} \sum_{r=1}^{R} \frac{1}{\sigma_v} \phi\left(\frac{a_{ir}}{\sigma_v}\right),$$

$$\frac{\partial \ln L_S(\boldsymbol{\theta}, \sigma_v | \text{data})}{\partial \boldsymbol{\theta}} = \sum_{i=1}^{N} \frac{\frac{1}{R}\sum_{r=1}^{R}\frac{1}{\sigma_v}\left[\left(\frac{a_{ir}}{\sigma_v}\right)\right]\phi\left(\frac{a_{ir}}{\sigma_v}\right)\frac{1}{\sigma_v}\begin{bmatrix} 1 \\ \mathbf{x}_i \\ \ln F_{ir} \end{bmatrix}}{\frac{1}{R}\sum_{r=1}^{R}\frac{1}{\sigma_v}\phi\left(\frac{a_{ir}}{\sigma_v}\right)},$$

$$\frac{\partial \ln L_S(\boldsymbol{\theta}, \sigma_v | \text{data})}{\partial \sigma_v} = \sum_{i=1}^{N} \frac{\frac{1}{R}\sum_{r=1}^{R}\frac{1}{\sigma_v^2}\phi\left(\frac{a_{ir}}{\sigma_v}\right)\left[\left(\frac{a_{ir}}{\sigma_v}\right)^2 - 1\right]}{\frac{1}{R}\sum_{r=1}^{R}\frac{1}{\sigma_v}\phi\left(\frac{a_{ir}}{\sigma_v}\right)},$$

Simultaneous equation of the two gradients to zero produces the maximum simulated likelihood (MSL) estimators. Either the (moderately complicated) Hessian or the BHHH estimator can be used to estimate the asymptotic covariance matrix for the estimator.

In principle, this approach can be used with any pair of densities, $f_v(v_i)$, that has a tractable functional form and $f_u(u_i)$ from which a random sample of draws can be simulated. Greene and Misra (2003) worked out several pairs. Certainly there are others. (I noted the lognormal above, which was not considered by the authors.) There are two real questions yet to be considered in this setting: First, again, does the distribution really matter in terms of the estimates of u_i? (How those are computed remains to be derived. This is revisited below.) Second, in any event, it is unclear how one can choose among the various models. Likelihood ratio tests are inappropriate, because the models are not nested. Vuong's (1989) test for nonnested models probably is appropriate, but it is for pairs of competing models, and there may be more than two here.

Researchers in a number of areas (e.g., Cameron et al., 2004) in their analysis of health care) have suggested the copula method of formalizing bivariate relationships when the marginal distributions are known but the joint distribution remains to be determined. For the stochastic frontier model, the tool suggests a means to consider the possibility of specifying a model in which the inefficiency, u_i, might be correlated with the firm-specific idiosyncratic noise, v_i. The underlying economics may require a bit of investigation, but econometrically, this possibility points toward relaxing yet one more restriction in the stochastic frontier model. Smith (2004) has used the method to analyze (yet again) Christensen and Greene's (1976) electricity generation cost data and the panel data on airlines listed in Greene (1997). Interestingly enough, the copula model applied to the electricity data produce some fairly substantial changes compared to the standard normal–half-normal model. The chi-squared test with one degree of freedom for the copula model against the null of the standard model is 5.32, while the 95% critical value is 3.84. As noted, the economic interpretation of the richer model specification needs to be solidified, but the empirical results suggest an intriguing possibility. This is a nascent literature, so I have no further empirical results to report.

2.4.9.2 Semiparametric models

The stochastic frontier model considered thus far is fully parameterize—the production model is specified in full, and the full distributions of v_i and u_i are known up to the specific values of the parameters, which are estimated using either classical or Bayesian methods. Ongoing research has sought flexible specifications of the technology model and the distributions involved that relax the assumptions of the model. There have been many explorations in the production model and extensions of the distributions. The normal–gamma model, with its richer specification, for example, represents one such model extension. In addition, there have been numerous proposals to move away from specific distributional assumptions. The semiparametric approaches described here retain the essential framework of the stochastic frontier but relax the assumption of a specific distribution for v_i or u_i, or both.

Fan, Li, and Weersink (1996) suggested modifying the production model:

$$y_i = g(x_i) + v_i - u_i,$$

where $g(x_i)$ remains to be specified. Since nearly all applications of the stochastic frontier model employ either the Cobb-Douglas or translog form, a semiparametric specification here represents relaxing one assumption restriction in the model, though it retains the fundamental stochastic (in their case, normal–exponential) specification. Huang and Fu (1999) continued this line of inquiry. In a similar analysis, Koop et al. (1994) specify a "semi-nonparametric" stochastic frontier cost function of the form

$$\ln C_i = H(y_i) + \ln c(w_i) + v_i + u_i,$$

where $H(y)$ is specified semiparametrically, in terms of polynomials in the log of output and $\ln c(w)$ is a Cobb-Douglas or translog function of the input prices.

In a series of studies, Park and Simar (1994), Park et al. (1998), Adams et al. (1999), Sickles et al. (2002), and Sickles (2005) have explored the implications of a variety of distributional assumptions on estimation in the panel-data model

$$y_{it} = \beta^{T} x_{it} + \alpha_i + \varepsilon_{it}.$$

Absent their much more general assumptions, this is a conventional fixed- or random-effects linear regression model. The various extensions involve different assumptions about ε_{it}, the relationships between α_i and x_{it}, and so on. The stochastic frontier aspect of the model is embodied in the use of $\alpha_i - \max_j(\alpha_j)$ in the estimation of inefficiency, in the fashion of the deterministic frontier models discussed above. Instrumental variable, ML, generalized least squares (GLS), and generalized method of moments (GMM) estimation methods all appear in the different treatments. This body of results extends the assumptions behind the deterministic frontier models in a variety of directions but is not directed at the stochastic frontier model. The semiparametric nature of the model relates to the very loose specification of the effects and their relationship to the frontier. Section 2.7 returns to the discussion of panel models.

One way to extend the normal–half-normal stochastic frontier model (or others) with respect to the distribution of v_i is the finite mixture approach suggested by Tsionas and Greene (2003). I return to the methodological aspects of the finite mixture model below; for the moment, let us examine only the model formulation. The frontier model is formulated in terms of J "classes" so that, within a particular class,

$$f_\varepsilon(\varepsilon_i | \text{class} = j) = \frac{2}{\sqrt{2\pi(\sigma_u^2 + \sigma_{vj}^2)}} \left[\Phi\left(\frac{-\varepsilon_i(\sigma_u/\sigma_{vj})}{\sqrt{\sigma_u^2 + \sigma_{vj}^2}} \right) \right] \exp\left(\frac{-\varepsilon_i^2}{2(\sigma_u^2 + \sigma_{vj}^2)} \right),$$

$$\varepsilon_i = y_i - \alpha - \beta^{T} x_i.$$

(Note that the indexation over classes pertains to the variance of the symmetric component of ε_i, $\sigma_{v,j}$.) We thus have a class-specific stochastic frontier model. The unconditional model is a probability weighted mixture over the J classes,

$$f_\varepsilon(\varepsilon_i) = \sum_j \pi_j f_\varepsilon(\varepsilon_i | \text{class} = j), 0 < \pi_j < 1, \sum_j \pi_j = 1.$$

The mixing probabilities are additional parameters to be estimated. The resulting unconditional model preserves the symmetry of the two-sided error component but provides a degree of flexibility that is somewhat greater than the simpler half-normal model. The mixture of normals is, with a finite number of classes, nonnormal.

This model lends itself well to either Bayesian (Tsionas and Greene, 2003) or classical (Orea and Kumbhakar, 2004; Greene, 2004a, 2005; Tsionas and Greene, 2003) estimation methods. The likelihood function is defined over $f_\varepsilon(\varepsilon_i)$ in the usual way and, with the one caveat about the number of classes noted below, is not particularly difficult to maximize.[47] After estimation, a conditional (posterior) estimate of the class that applies to a particular observation can be deduced using Bayes theorem:

$$\text{prob}[\text{class} = j | y_i] = \frac{f(y_i | \text{class} = j)\text{prob}[\text{class} = j]}{\sum_{j=1}^{J} f(y_i | \text{class} = j)\text{prob}[\text{class} = j]} = \hat{\pi}_{j|i}$$

One would then assign an individual observation to the most likely class. Subsequent analysis, for example, efficiency estimation (see section 2.5), would then be based on the respective class for each observation.

Orea and Kumbhakar (2004), Tsionas and Greene (2003), and Greene (2004a, 2005) have extended this model in two directions. First, they allow the entire frontier model, not just the variance of the symmetric error term, to vary across classes. This represents a discrete change in the interpretation of the model. For the case above, the mixture model is essentially a way to generalize the distribution of one of the two error components. For the fully mixed models, we would reinterpret the formulation as representing a latent regime classification. In Greene (2004b), for example, the latent class model is proposed (ultimately with very limited success) as a means of accommodating heterogeneity in the extremely heterogeneous World Health Organization (Evans et al., 2000a, 2000b) data set. The implication of the more general model is that firms are classified into a set of different technologies and efficiency distributions. The specific classification is unknown to the analyst, hence the probabilistic mixing distribution. (This has a distinctly Bayesian flavor to it, as, in fact, the individual firm does reside in a specific class, but the analyst has only a set of priors, or mixing probabilities, to suggest which.) The second extension in the latter papers is to allow heterogeneity in the mixing probabilities:

$$\pi_{ij} = \frac{\exp(\theta_j^{\mathsf{T}} z_i)}{\sum_{j=1}^{J} \exp(\theta_j^{\mathsf{T}} z_i)}, \theta_J = 0$$

The remainder of the model is a class-specific stochastic frontier model

$$f_\varepsilon(\varepsilon_i | \text{class} = j) = \frac{2}{\sigma_j}\phi\left(\frac{\varepsilon_i|j}{\sigma_j}\right)\left[\Phi\left(\frac{-\lambda_j \varepsilon_i|j}{\sigma_j}\right)\right],$$

$$\varepsilon_i|j = y_i - \alpha_j - \beta_j^{\mathsf{T}} x_i$$

This form of the model has all parameters varying by class. By suitable equality restrictions, however, subsets of the coefficients, such as the technology parameters, α and β, can be made generic.

There remains a modeling loose end in this framework. The number of classes has been assumed to be known, but there is no reason to expect this. How to determine the appropriate number of classes is an ongoing problem in this literature. In principle, one could use a likelihood ratio test to test down from a J class model to a $J - 1$ class model. However, the number of degrees of freedom for the test is ambiguous. If the model parameters are the same in two classes, then the number of classes is reduced by one whether or not the two probabilities are similarly restricted. One cannot test "up" from a $J - 1$ class model to a J class model, because if the correct model has J classes, then the $J - 1$ class model estimators will be inconsistent. A number of researchers have produced proposals for handling this problem, many of them involving information criteria such as the Akaike information criterion.

The latent class approach provides a means to build a large amount of cross-firm heterogeneity into the model. As discussed in section 2.6, this is a major, important extension of the model. With a sufficiently large number of classes, one can achieve quite a large amount of generality. As the number of classes grows, the model approximates a full random-parameters model, which is reconsidered in section 2.7.

The recent literature contains a number of studies of semiparametric approaches to frontier modeling. As discussed above, the "semiparametric" aspect of the model means different things in different studies. Sickles et al. (2002) and Sickles (2005) have loosened the assumptions about the "effects" in a deterministic frontier model. Orea, Kumbhakar, Greene, Tsionas, and others have relaxed the assumptions about all the model parameters through a finite mixture approach. Note, finally, two studies, Kopp and Mullahy (1989) and Griffin and Steel (2004), that have retained the essential structure of the stochastic frontier model but specifically focused on the specification of the inefficiency random variable, u_i. Kopp and Mullahy (1989) have derived GMM estimators for the stochastic frontier model that require only that the distribution of v_i be symmetric, that the distribution of u_i be defined over the positive half of the real line, and that moments of u_i and v_i up to order six be finite. This provides a high level of generality, but at the very high cost that the method produces no definable estimate of u_i, which ultimately is the point of the exercise. Under the assumptions made thus far, OLS estimates of the model with an adjusted constant term $(\alpha + E[u_i])$ satisfies the assumptions of the Gauss Markov theorem. Griffin and Steel (2004) explore what one might reluctantly call a "normal–Dirichlet model":

$$y_{it} = \alpha + \beta^{\mathrm{T}} x_{it} + v_{it} - u_i,$$

where the model is all as above specified save for $u_i \sim F$, a "random probability measure generated by a Dirichlet process." A variety of parametric settings are explored, with the finding that the results (estimates of $E[u_i|\text{data}]$—a Bayesian estimator) are fairly strongly dependent on the assumptions. It does emerge that a fully parametric, normal–gamma model (estimated, again, using

MCMC procedures) fairly well resembles the much more general Dirichlet results.

2.4.9.3 Nonparametric approaches

Kumbhakar, Park, Simar, and Tsionas (2005; see also Kumbhakar and Tsionas, 2002) suggested the following nonparametric approach. The global MLE of the parameters of the normal–half-normal model[48] are

$$\left[\hat{\alpha}, \hat{\beta}, \hat{\sigma}, \hat{\lambda}\right]_{\text{MLE}} = \arg\max \ln L(\alpha, \beta, \sigma, \lambda \mid \text{data})$$

$$= \sum_{i=1}^{N} \frac{2}{\sigma} \phi\left(\frac{\varepsilon_i}{\sigma}\right) \left[\Phi\left(\frac{-\varepsilon_i \lambda}{\sigma}\right)\right].$$

Local maximization of the log-likelihood for the nonparametric model involves the following: Choose a multivariate kernel function

$$K(\mathbf{d}) = (2\pi)^{-m/2} |\mathbf{H}|^{-1/2} \exp[-(1/2)\mathbf{d}^{\mathsf{T}} \mathbf{H}^{-1} \mathbf{d}],$$

where $\mathbf{d}$ is a difference vector (defined below), m is the number of parameters in β, $\mathbf{H} = h\mathbf{S}$ where $\mathbf{S}$ is the sample covariance of the variables on the right-hand side, and h is a bandwidth.[49] Then, for a particular value of $\mathbf{x}^*$, the local estimator is defined by

$$\left[\hat{\alpha}, \hat{\beta}, \hat{\sigma}, \hat{\lambda}\right](\mathbf{x}^*) = \arg\max \ln L_K(\alpha, \beta, \sigma, \lambda \mid \text{data})$$

$$= \sum_{i=1}^{N} \frac{2}{\sigma} \phi\left(\frac{\varepsilon_i}{\sigma}\right) \left[\Phi\left(\frac{-\varepsilon_i \lambda}{\sigma}\right)\right] K(\mathbf{x}_i - \mathbf{x}^*).$$

A full vector of parameters is defined for each vector $\mathbf{x}^*$ chosen. The authors suggest four reasons to prefer this approach: (1) There can be no functional form misspecification, since the full-parameter vector is a function of the data at every point. (2) The variances are also functions of $\mathbf{x}$, so the model allows for heteroskedasticity of unknown form. (I return to this issue below.) (3) In their truncation model, the mean of the underlying inefficiency distribution is also a function of $\mathbf{x}$, which represents a considerable generalization of the model. (4) This model generalizes Berger and Humphrey's (1991, 1992) thick frontier. While Berger and Humphrey's approach fits the model to specific quartiles of the data, this model fits the frontier at all points of the sample.

In a series of studies, Berger and Humphrey (e.g., 1991, 1992) analyze what they label the "thick frontier" approach to efficiency estimation. The analysis proceeds by first dividing the sample into classes by size and then within the size classes further subdividing the observations on the basis of average costs. "Best-practice" frontier models are then fit to the lowest quartiles of the size classes using OLS or GLS. Berger and Humphrey (1991) analyze a three-output translog cost function. They argue that this approach combines the logic of the DEA "best practice," data-driven analysis and the appealing feature of the stochastic frontier model that combines both randomness in the frontier (its "thickness") with a formal model of inefficiency. However, the thick frontier approach is somewhat less parameterized than the stochastic frontier while at the same time having more structure than DEA. A number of authors (e.g., Mester, 1994; Wagenvoort and Schure, 2005) have used the thick frontier method to analyze cost inefficiency in the banking industry. Berger and Humphrey (1992) is a panel-data approach that adds exogenous heterogeneity to the basic model. (See section 2.6 for additional material on heterogeneity in efficiency analysis.) To the extent that it isolates inefficiency in the data, this technique is a nonparametric frontier estimator insofar as no distribution is assumed. A thoroughly detailed application of the thick frontier concept is given in Lang and Welzel (1998).

Note, finally, that the entire body of results on DEA can be viewed as a distribution-free, nonparametric approach to frontier estimation and efficiency analysis. Because DEA is treated in great detail in chapter 3, I do not pursue the subject here. Another concise, very readable introduction to the topic is given in Murillo-Zamorano (2004).

2.4.9.4 Conclusion

All of these studies suggest that there is considerable scope for alternatives to the original normal–half-normal model of Aigner et al. All have appeared in applications in the literature. Nonetheless, the normal–half-normal model, along with some of the variants discussed below (e.g., the heteroskedastic model) has provided the most frequent specification for the recent research.

2.5 Stochastic Frontier Cost Functions, Multiple Outputs, and Distance and Profit Functions: Alternatives to the Production Frontier

This section discusses a variety of specifications that model production and (in)efficiency in functional forms that differ from the single-output production function examined up to this point.

2.5.1 Multiple-output production functions

The formal theory of production departs from the transformation function that links the vector of outputs, y, to the vector of inputs, x:

$$T(\mathbf{y}, \mathbf{x}) = 0$$

As it stands, some further assumptions are obviously needed to produce the framework for an empirical model. By assuming homothetic separability, the function may be written in the form

$$A(\mathbf{y}) = f(\mathbf{x})$$

(see Fernandez et al., 2000, for discussion of this assumption). The function $A(\mathbf{y})$ is an output aggregator that links the "aggregate output" to a familiar production function. The assumption is a fairly strong one, but with it in place, we have the platform for an analysis of (in)efficiency along the lines already considered. Fernandez et al. (2000) proposed the multiple-output production model,

$$\left(\sum_{m=1}^{M} \alpha_m^q y_{i,t,m}^q \right)^{1/q} = \boldsymbol{\beta}^{\mathrm{T}} \mathbf{x}_{it} + v_{it} - u_{it}.$$

Inefficiency in this setting reflects the failure of the firm to achieve the maximum aggregate output attainable. Note that the model does not address the economic question of whether the chosen output mix is optimal with respect to the output prices and input costs. That would require a profit function approach. Fernandez et al. (2000) apply the method to a panel of U.S. banks—the 798-bank, 10-year panel analyzed by Berger (1993) and Adams et al. (1999).[50] Fernandez et al. (1999, 2000, 2002, 2005) have extended this model to allow for "bads," that is, undesirable inputs. Their model consists of parallel equations for the "goods" (dairy output of milk and other goods in Dutch dairy farms) and "bads" (nitrogen discharge). The two equations are treated as a Seemingly Unrelated Regressions system and are fit (as is the banking model) using Bayesian MCMC methods. The study of the electric power industry by Atkinson and Dorfman (2005) takes a similar approach, but fits more naturally in section 2.5.4, which examines it in a bit more detail.

2.5.2 Stochastic frontier cost functions

Under a set of regularity conditions (see Shephard, 1953; Nerlove, 1963), an alternative representation of the production technology is the *cost function*,

$$C(y, \mathbf{w}) = \min\{\mathbf{w}^{\mathrm{T}}\mathbf{x} : f(\mathbf{x}) \geq y\},$$

where $\mathbf{w}$ is the vector of exogenously determined input prices. The cost function gives the minimum expenditure needed to produce a given output, y. If a producer is technically inefficient, then its costs of production must exceed the theoretical minimum. It seems natural, then, to consider a frontier cost function as an alternative to the frontier production function model. The interpretation of the inefficiency terms in an empirical model is complicated a bit by the dual approach to estimation, however. Suppose that, on the production side of the model, the representation of a one-sided error term as reflective purely of technical inefficiency is appropriate. The computation is conditional on the inputs chosen, so whether the choice of inputs is itself allocatively efficient is a side issue. On the cost side, however, *any* errors in optimization, technical *or* allocative, must show up as higher costs. As such, a producer that we might assess as operating technically efficiently by a production function measure might still appear inefficient viz-à-viz a cost function.

Similar arguments would apply to a profit function. This does not preclude either formulation, but one should bear in mind the possible ambiguities in interpretation in these alternative models. It might make more sense, then, to relabel the result on the cost side as "cost inefficiency." The strict interpretation of technical inefficiency in the sense of Farrell may be problematic, but it seems counterproductive to let this be a straightjacket. The argument that there is a cost frontier that would apply to any given producer would have no less validity. Deviations from the cost frontier could then be interpreted as the reflection of both technical and allocative inefficiency. At the same time, both inefficiencies have a behavioral interpretation, and whatever effect is carried over to the production side is induced, instead. The same logic would carry over to a profit function. The upshot of this argument is that estimation techniques that seek to decompose cost inefficiency into an allocative and a true Farrell measure of technical inefficiency may neglect to account for the direct influence of output itself on the residual inefficiency once allocative inefficiency is accounted for.

Let us begin by examining the costs of production of a single output conditioned on the actual input choices. That is, neglecting the first-order conditions for optimality of the input choices, we consider the implications for the costs of production of technical inefficiency. For simplicity, we assume constant returns to scale. The production function, $f(\mathbf{x})$, is linearly homogeneous and therefore homothetic. For homothetic production functions,[51]

$$y = F[f(\mathbf{x})],$$

where $F(t)$ is a continuous and monotonically increasing function when t is positive. We have the fundamental result (from Shephard, 1953) that the corresponding cost function is

$$C(y, \mathbf{w}) = F^{-1}(y)c(\mathbf{w}),$$

where $c(\mathbf{w})$ is the unit cost function. For the stochastic frontier production function, then

$$y_i = f(\mathbf{x}_i)\text{TE}_i e^{v_i},$$

so that the cost function is

$$C_i = F^{-1}(y)c(\mathbf{w}_i)\left[\frac{1}{\text{TE}_i}\right]e^{-v_i}.$$

This corresponds to Farrell's (1957) original efficiency measure, that is, the cost savings that would be realized if output were produced efficiently. The theoretical counterpart would be the input-based measure. In logs, then,

$$\ln C_i = \ln F^{-1}(y) + \ln c(w_i) - \ln TE_i - v_i.$$

In terms of our original model, then, the stochastic cost frontier is

$$\ln C_i = \ln F^{-1}(y) + \ln c(w_i) - v_i + u_i,$$

which is what might be expected. The sign on v_i is inconsequential since its mean is zero and the distribution is symmetric (normal).

Now, suppose there are economies of scale in production. For the simplest case, we assume a Cobb-Douglas function with degree of homogeneity γ. The stochastic frontier cost function will be

$$\ln C_i = A' + \beta \ln w_{1i} + (1 - \beta) \ln w_{2i} + \frac{1}{\gamma} \ln y_i + \frac{1}{\gamma}(-v_i) + \frac{1}{\gamma} u_i.$$

Therefore, the composed disturbance on the cost frontier is

$$\varepsilon_i' = \frac{1}{\gamma}(-v_i + u_i).$$

The upshot is that the presence of economies of scale on the production side blurs somewhat the reflection of technical inefficiency on the cost side. The preceding result is general for a production function that exhibits a fixed degree of homogeneity.[52]

Evidently, the simple interpretation of the one-sided error on the cost side as a Farrell measure of inefficiency is inappropriate *unless the measure is redefined in terms of costs, rather than output.* That is, one might choose to make costs, rather than output, the standard against which efficiency is measured. At least in this context, this is nothing more than a matter of interpretation. It is equally clear that by some further manipulation, the estimated inefficiency obtained in the context of a cost function can be translated into a Farrell measure of technical inefficiency, that is, just by multiplying it by γ.

For the simple case above in which the production function is homogeneous, the effect of economies of scale can be removed by rescaling the estimated disturbance. A corresponding adjustment may be possible in more involved models such as the translog model. Suppose that the production function is homothetic, but not homogeneous. For convenience, let

$$G(y_i) = F^{-1}(y_i).$$

Then

$$\ln C_i = \ln c(w_i) + \ln G(y_i).$$

The formulation above is clearly a special case. Unless $\ln G(.)$ is linear in $\ln y_i$, as it is when the production function is homogeneous, the technical inefficiency may be carried over to the cost function in a very complicated manner.[53] The usual assumption that u_i in the stochastic frontier cost function can vary independently of y_i may be problematic.[54]

Any errors in production decisions would have to translate into costs of production higher than the theoretical norm. Likewise, in the context of a profit function, any errors of optimization would necessarily translate into lower profits for the producer. But, at the same time, the stochastic nature of the production frontier would imply that the theoretical minimum cost frontier would also be stochastic. Some recent applications that have been based on cost functions have made this explicit by further decomposing the stochastic term in the cost function to produce

$$\ln C_i = \ln C(y_i, \mathbf{w}_i) + v_i + u_i + A_i,$$

where A_i is strictly attributable to allocative inefficiency (see, e.g., chapter 4 in Kumbhakar and Lovell, 2000).

The preceding describes the production and cost of the firm in long-run "equilibrium." (The concept must be qualified, because it is unclear whether it is appropriate to characterize an inefficient firm as being in equilibrium.) For the short term, in which there are fixed inputs, the variable cost function is

$$\ln C^F = \ln C(y, \mathbf{w}, \mathbf{x}^F).$$

As before, relative to optimal costs, any deviation from optimality must translate into higher costs. Thus, for example, with one output and one fixed input, one might analyze a translog variable cost function

$$\ln C^F = \alpha + \sum_{k=1}^{K} \beta_k \ln w_k + \beta_F \ln F + \beta_y \ln y$$

$$+ \frac{1}{2} \sum_{k=1}^{K} \sum_{l=1}^{K} \gamma_{kl} \ln w_k \ln w_l + \frac{1}{2} \gamma_{FF} \ln^2 F + \frac{1}{2} \gamma_{yy} \ln^2 y.$$

$$+ \sum_{k=1}^{K} \gamma_{kF} \ln w_k \ln F + \sum_{k=1}^{K} \gamma_{ky} \ln w_k \ln y + \gamma_{Fy} \ln F \ln y + v_i + u_i$$

In their analysis of Swiss nursing homes, Farsi and Filippini (2003) specified a cost function with labor and capital treated as variable factors and number of beds treated as a fixed input. The variable cost function provides a useful datum; the shadow cost of a fixed input is $-\partial C^F / \partial x^F$. For the translog variable cost function, this would be

$$\frac{-\partial C^F}{\partial F} = \frac{-F}{C^F} (\beta_F + \gamma_{FF} \ln F + \sum_{k=1}^{K} \gamma_{kF} \ln w_k + \gamma_{Fy} \ln y).$$

2.5.3 Multiple-output cost functions

A significant advantage of analyzing efficiency on the cost side is the ease with which multiple outputs can be accommodated. Consider a transformation function

$$T(\mathbf{y}, \mathbf{x}) = 0,$$

where $\mathbf{y}$ is a vector of M outputs and $\mathbf{x}$ is a vector of K inputs. Assuming that production satisfies the necessary regularity conditions (including monotonicity, smoothness, and quasiconcavity), we may deduce that the cost function is of the form

$$\ln C_i = \ln C(y_1, \dots, y_M, w_1, \dots, w_K),$$

where the cost function is monotonic in outputs, monotonic in each input price, linearly homogeneous in the input prices, and so on. How we proceed from here, and how "inefficiency" enters the specification, depends crucially on the assumptions and will highlight the utility of not allowing the input versus output orientation discussed above to straightjacket the analysis.

Many analyses have proceeded directly to specification of a multiple-output translog cost function

$$\ln C_i = \alpha + \sum_{k=1}^{K} \beta \ln w_{ik} + \frac{1}{2} \sum_{k=1}^{K} \sum_{l=1}^{K} \gamma_{kl} \ln w_{ik} \ln w_{il}$$

$$+ \sum_{m=1}^{M} \delta \ln y_{im} + \frac{1}{2} \sum_{m=1}^{M} \sum_{r=1}^{M} \phi_{mr} \ln y_{im} \ln y_{ir} .$$

$$+ \sum_{m=1}^{M} \sum_{k=1}^{K} \kappa_{mk} \ln y_{im} \ln w_{ik} + v_i + u_i$$

(One could also analyze a multiple-output variable cost function, with one or more fixed factors.) Note that there is no necessary assumption of homotheticity or separability on the production side. Tsionas and Greene (2003) analyze a cost frontier for U.S. banks in which there are five outputs and five inputs. In this formulation, u_i is interpreted as "economic inefficiency." Thus, the source of u_i is either technical or allocative inefficiency, or both.

Analyses of two industries in particular, health care and banking, have yielded a rich crop of applications and development of new methods. Data in the banking industry are of particularly high quality. A few of the innovative studies in banking are as follows:[55]

- Lang and Welzel (1998) fit a translog, five-output, three-input cost function to German banking data. The study develops the thick frontier estimator.

- Ferrier and Lovell (1990) fit a multiple-output cost function to U.S. banking data. Among the innovations in this study were a decomposition of cost inefficiency into technical and allocative components and the inclusion of a large number of "environmental" variables in the cost function.
- Huang and Wang (2004) used the Fourier functional form in conjunction with a translog kernel to study a sample of Taiwanese banks.
- Tsionas and Greene (2003) fit a finite mixture of translog multiple-output cost functions to U.S. banks. Orea and Kumbhakar (2004) fit a similar mixture of translog functions using a panel of Spanish banks.

In each of these cases, the cost functions involved three or five outputs, multiple inputs, and a variety of model specifications. The methodologies span the range of techniques already listed, including both classical and Bayesian methods. The health care industry also provides a natural setting for multiple-output cost frontier analysis. In the banking industry studies, a challenging specification issue is how to identify the inputs and outputs and how to distinguish them—for example, are commercial loans, which produce loan interest income, an input or an output? A reading of the many received studies suggests that researchers have come to some agreement on these questions. In health care, there are difficult issues of identifying what the outputs are and, in some cases, measuring them. For example, the measurement of quality is a recurrent theme in this literature. Another question concerns residents in hospital cost studies—is training of residents an input or an output? Again, there are many questions in the literature, but there does seem to be at least broad agreement. A few studies that illustrate the analyses are as follows:

- Koop et al. (1997) use Bayesian methods to fit translog cost frontiers to a panel of U.S. hospitals. In their study, the outputs are number of discharges, number of inpatient days, number of beds, number of outpatient visits, and a case mix index. They also included a quasi-fixed input, capital in their cost function.
- Rosko (2001) analyzes a panel of U.S. hospitals. The translog cost function includes outputs inpatient discharges and outpatient visits. The mix of cases is also considered in this study but not as an output variable. A variety of panel-data techniques (Battese and Coelli, 1995) and models for heterogeneity in inefficiency are placed in the specification.
- Linna (1998) is similar to Rosko (2001) but also considers nonparametric (DEA) bases of inefficiency.
- Farsi and Filippini's (2003) analysis of Swiss nursing home costs analyzes a single output but includes two indicators of quality: a "dependency" index that reflects the intensity of care received by the facility's patients, and a nursing staff ratio.

2.5.4 Distance functions

The multiple-output cost frontier and the transformation function provide convenient vehicles for analyzing inefficiency in multiple-output contexts. Another approach that has proved useful in numerous empirical studies is based on the distance function. For output vector y and input vector x, Shephard's (1953) *input distance function* is $D_I(y, x) = \max(\lambda : x/\lambda$ is on the isoquant for y). It is clear that $D_I(y, x) \geq 1$ and that the isoquant is the set of x values for which $D_I(y, x) = 1$. The corresponding output distance function would be $D_O(x, y) = \min(\lambda : y/\lambda$ is producible with x). In this instance, $D_O(y, x) \leq 1$. The definitions suggest efficiency measures, as noted earlier. Thus, the input distance suggests the degree to which x exceeds the input requirement for production of y, which we would identify with cost, or "economic" inefficiency. Likewise, the output distance suggests the degree to which output falls short of what can be produced with a given input vector, x, which relates to the technical inefficiency we have examined thus far.

To put these functions in the form of an econometric model, we use the restrictions implied by the underlying theory, namely, that the input distance function is linearly homogeneous in the inputs and the output distance function is linearly homogeneous in the outputs (see Kumbhakar et al., 2004). Thus, we normalize the input distance function on the (arbitrarily chosen) first input, x_1, and the output distance function on y_1 to write

$$x_1 D_I(x_2/x_1, x_3/x_1, \ldots, x_K/x_1, y)\text{TI} = 1,$$

where TI is the technical inefficiency index, $0 \leq \text{TI} \leq 1$. In similar fashion, we can formulate the output distance function,

$$y_1 D_O(x, y_2/y_1, y_3/y_1, \ldots, y_M/y_1)\text{TO} = 1,$$

where TO is the economic inefficiency index, $\text{TO} \geq 1$. This formulation provides a natural framework for a stochastic frontier model. Most applications have used the translog form. Doing likewise, we write

$$0 = \ln x_1 + \ln D_I(x_2/x_1, x_3/x_1, \ldots, x_K/x_1, y) + v + \ln[\exp(-u)],$$

where the deterministic part of the equation is formulated as the production model, v captures the idiosyncratic part of the model as usual, and $u > 0$ produces $\text{TI} = \exp(-u)$. For the output distance function, a similar strategy produces

$$0 = \ln y_1 + \ln D_O(x, y_2/y_1, y_3/y_1, \ldots, y_M/y_1) + v + \ln[\exp(u)].$$

Finally, in order to form a model that is amenable to familiar estimation techniques, we would shift the normalized variable to the left-hand side of the equation. Thus, the input distance stochastic frontier model would appear

$$-\ln x_1 = \ln D_I(x_2/x_1, x_3/x_1, \ldots, x_K/x_1, y) + v - u,$$

and likewise for the output distance equation. Some methodological issues remain. As stated, it would seem that both input and output models would carry some type of simultaneous equations aspect, so that conventional estimators such as OLS would be persistently biased. Coelli (2000) and Cuesta and Orea (2002) consider these issues theoretically. Note that these methodologically oriented examinations come after the leading applications of the distance function technique (e.g., Sickles et al., 2002; Coelli and Perelman, 1996, 1999, 2000; all of which used the translog form as the modeling platform).

The distance function bears close resemblance to other specifications for studying efficiency. Thus, there have been comparisons of inefficiency estimates obtained from estimated distance functions to the counterparts obtained from DEA studies (see Coelli and Perelman, 1999; Sickles et al., 2002). Atkinson, Fare, and Primont (2003) used the concept of the distance function to derive a shadow cost function with which they studied allocative inefficiency. Finally, O'Donnell and Coelli (2005) forced the classical curvature (regulatory) conditions on their estimated distance function. They suggested their method of imposing restrictions on parameters in a Bayesian framework as an alternative to Kleit and Terrell (2001)—they used a Metropolis-Hastings procedure as opposed to Kleit and Terrell's accept/reject iteration.

Atkinson and Dorfman (2005) have extended the distance function method to include both desirable and undesirable outputs in the generation of electricity. The translog input distance function is of the form

$$0 = \gamma_0 + T(\mathbf{y}_g, \mathbf{y}_b, t, \mathbf{x}) + v_{it} - u_{it},$$

where $\mathbf{y}_g$ is a vector of "goods" (residential and commercial/industrial generation), $\mathbf{y}_b$ is a vector of "bads" (sulfur dioxide emissions), t is a time trend, and $\mathbf{x}$ is a vector of inputs (fuel, labor, and capital). $T(\ldots)$ is a full translog function. The underlying theory imposes a large number of linear constraints on the (also large number of) model parameters. In this study, the "bad" is treated as a "technology shifter" (in contrast to Fernandez et al., 2000, who treated nitrogen runoff in dairy farming as an undesirable output). The estimator in this study is an elaborate form of Bayesian method of moments (see Kim, 2002; Zellner and Tobias, 2001).

2.5.5 Profit functions

The methodology described earlier can, in principle, be extended to revenue and profit functions. In terms of the received empirical literature, these two approaches have been less actively pursued than production, cost, and distance functions. Two explanations stand out. First, the estimation of a profit function would require a much greater range of assumptions about producer and market behavior. While production and cost functions are clearly reflective of individual firm optimization behavior, the profit function requires additional assumptions about market structure and price setting. Second, the data demands for profit functions are considerably greater than those for cost and production functions.

A full implementation of a model for a profit frontier would include a production function and the first-order conditions for optimization (see Kumbhakar and Bhattacharyya, 1992; Kumbhakar and Lovell, 2000; Kumbhakar, 2001). For a multiple-output firm/industry, it would also require equations for the optimal mix and levels of the outputs. A full simultaneous equations framework (replete with many nonlinearities) is detailed in Kumbhakar and Lovell (2000; see also chapter 5). The authors also discuss the possibility of a "variable" profit function that takes some inputs as fixed. Again, the underlying assumptions behind such a model require much detail. The profit function framework shares a characteristic with the cost function; profit "inefficiency" would be a mix of both technical and allocative inefficiency. Moreover, there is a third layer that does not enter any of the frameworks considered thus far. For given output prices, any deviation from the optimal mix of outputs must reduce profits. Thus, this model presents yet another application of the "Greene problem" (discussed in greater detail below). Kumbhakar and Lovell (2000, p. 214) list a number of applications of different approaches to profit function estimation. Not surprisingly, because of the ready availability of very high-quality data, several of these studies (e.g., Akhavein et al., 1994; Berger and Mester, 1997; Humphrey and Pulley, 1997; Lozano-Vivas,1997) analyze (in)efficiency in the banking industry.

2.5.6 Output-oriented and input-oriented inefficiency

For output vector **y** and input vector **x**, Shephard's (1953) *input distance function* is $D_I(\mathbf{y},\mathbf{x}) = \max(\lambda : \mathbf{x}/\lambda$ is on the isoquant for $\mathbf{y})$; $D_I(\mathbf{y},\mathbf{x}) \geq 1$. The corresponding output distance function would be $D_O(\mathbf{x},\mathbf{y}) = \min(\theta : \mathbf{y}/\theta$ is producible with $\mathbf{x})$; $D_O(\mathbf{y},\mathbf{x}) \leq 1$. The input distance suggests the degree to which **x** exceeds the input requirement for production of **y**, which we would identify with cost, or "economic" inefficiency. The output distance suggests the degree to which output falls short of what can be produced with a given input vector, **x**, which relates to the technical inefficiency examined thus far. The definitions suggest efficiency measures, as noted above. The translation of these notions into frontier models has produced the familiar modeling platforms for production of a single output. Skipping the obvious algebraic steps, we have the generic stochastic frontier model

$$y_i = f(\mathbf{x}_i)\theta_i \exp(v_i),$$

or

$$\ln y_i = \ln f(\mathbf{x}_i) + v_i + \ln \theta_I,$$

where $\theta_i = \exp(-u_i)$ in our model for output-oriented inefficiency. Taking logs produces our familiar stochastic frontier production model. For input-oriented inefficiency, we have the less commonly used formulation,

$$y_i = f(\lambda_i x_i) \exp(v_i),$$

or

$$\ln y_i = \ln f(\lambda_i x_i) + v_i.$$

In this formulation, the form of inefficiency in the production model is less clear. For example, moving to the usual Cobb-Douglas or translog model leaves a complicated function of $(\ln x_{ki} + \ln \lambda_i)$.

Most of the received applications have measured output-oriented inefficiency on the production side. On the cost side of the production model, the roles of the two measures are reversed. Neglecting v_i for the moment purely for convenience), we have

$$y_i = \theta_i f(x_i) \Leftrightarrow C_i = g(y_i/\theta_i, w_i),$$

so unless y_i enters the cost function (log)linearly, the form that θ_i takes in the cost function will be complicated. In contrast, for input-oriented technical inefficiency, we have

$$y_i = f(\lambda_i x_i) \Leftrightarrow C_i = g(y_i, w_i/\lambda_i).$$

For technologies that satisfy the regularity conditions for the dual relationships to exist, the cost function must be linearly homogeneous in the input prices. Thus, we must have

$$C_i = (1/\lambda_i) g(y_i, w_i).$$

Taking logs here and using the usual interpretation of λ_i produces

$$\ln C_i = \ln g(y_i, w_i) - \ln \lambda_{ii}$$
$$= \ln g(y_i, w_i) + u_i.$$

Thus, we see that familiar applications of stochastic cost frontiers are based on a measure of input inefficiency. [I.e., unless it is assumed that the production function is homogeneous. If so, then $\ln C_i = (1/\gamma) \ln(y_i/\theta_i)c(w_i)$, where γ is the degree of homogeneity (see Christensen and Greene, 1976). In this case, input- and output-oriented inefficiency will be indistinguishable.]

Numerous applications have analyzed the distinction between input- and output-oriented inefficiency. Atkinson and Cornwell (1993), using panel data and a linear fixed-effects (deterministic frontier) model, found (perhaps not surprisingly) that the two assumptions produced different rankings of observations. As they point out, the distinction "matters." In similar kinds of analyses, Kumbhakar et al. (2004) and Alvarez et al. (2004) tested for the presence of the two types of inefficiency. The latter study proceeded more or less on the lines of Atkinson and Cornwell (1993), using a panel-data set on Spanish dairy farms. Orea and Kumbhakar (2004) fit both input- and output-oriented models and a hybrid that included both. They used a Vuong (1989) test was to test for the specification. Kurkalova and Carriquiry (2003) (using a technique suggested by Reinhard, Lovell, and Thijssen, 1999) estimated output-oriented inefficiency measures and then translated them ex post into input-oriented measures. Huang and Wang (2004) have also fit separate cost frontier models for input- and output-oriented inefficiency, in their case using the Fourier flexible form.

The preceding studies have steered around the inherent difficulty of the input orientation on the production side. Consider, in particular, a translog model, where we assume, as other authors have (looking ahead), panel data and time invariance for the inefficiency term. Thus,

$$\ln y_{it} = \alpha + \sum_{k=1}^{K} \beta_k (\ln x_{i,t,k} - u_i)$$

$$+ \frac{1}{2} \sum_{k=1}^{K} \sum_{l=1}^{K} \gamma_{kl} (\ln x_{i,t,k} - u_i)(\ln x_{i,t,l} - u_i) + v_{i,t},$$

where $u_i \geq 0$. Consistent with the received work, we would assume that u_i has a half-normal or exponential (or gamma or lognormal) distribution. As usual, estimation of the parameters is complicated by the presence of the unobserved u_i. Consider the following approach based on MSL suggested by Kumbhakar and Tsionas (2004). (We have stripped their derivation down to its bare essentials here and changed notation a bit.) Note, first, that u_i is the same for all t and for all k, for a given i.

For convenience, write

$$z_{i,t,k}(u_i) = \ln x_{i,t,k} - u_i.$$

Conditioned on u_i, each term in the log-likelihood for y_{it} is the log of the corresponding normal density (for $v_{i,t}$), so

$$\ln L|\mathbf{u} = \sum_{i=1}^{N} \left[-\frac{T_i}{2} \ln 2\pi - \frac{1}{2\sigma^2} \sum_{t=1}^{T_i} \left(\ln y_{it} - T\left[z_{i,t}(u_i)\right]\right)^2 \right].$$

where

$$T\left[z_{i,t}(u_i)\right] = \alpha + \sum_{k=1}^{K} \beta_k z_{i,t,k}(u_i) + \frac{1}{2} \sum_{k=1}^{K} \sum_{l=1}^{K} \gamma_{kl} z_{i,t,k}(u_i) z_{i,t,l}(u_i).$$

The inefficiency term must be integrated out of the log-likelihood before it can be maximized. The unconditional log-likelihood is

$$\ln L = \sum_{i=1}^{N} \int_{u_i} \left[-\frac{T_i}{2} \ln 2\pi - \frac{1}{2\sigma^2} \sum_{t=1}^{T_i} \left(\ln y_{it} - T\left[z_{i,t}(u_i) \right] \right)^2 \right] p(u_i) du_i.$$

The integrals cannot be expressed in closed form, so as it is above, this log-likelihood is not usable. However, for the distributions mentioned (half-normal, exponential), random draws on u_i are easily obtainable. A usable simulated log-likelihood function is

$$\ln L^S = \sum_{i=1}^{N} \frac{1}{R} \sum_{r=1}^{R} \left[-\frac{T_i}{2} \ln 2\pi - \frac{1}{2\sigma^2} \sum_{t=1}^{T_i} \left(\ln y_{it} - T\left[z_{i,t}(u_{i,r}) \right] \right)^2 \right].$$

Maximizing $\ln L^S$ produces estimates of all of the model parameters. [Tsionas (2004) shows how the Fourier transform produces an alternative, possibly simpler and faster algorithm for this optimization.] Ex post, it is useful to obtain an estimate of u_i—this was the purpose of the exercise to begin with. Kumbhakar and Tsionas (2004) suggest a method of approximating $E[u_i|\text{parameters, data}]$. I suggest a different (albeit similar) approach in section 2.7.

There is an element of ambiguity in the model as specified. Which form, input or output, is appropriate for a given setting? Alvarez et al. (2004) suggested that a given firm could be operating in either regime at any time. In their analysis of European railroads, they treated the input and output distance functions as two latent regimes in a finite mixture model. In essence, their model allows the data to sort themselves into the two regimes rather than arbitrarily assuming that all observations obey one or the other at the outset.

2.6 Heterogeneity in Stochastic Frontier Function Models

This section is devoted to the issue of between firm heterogeneity in stochastic frontier modeling. We depart from a "pure" production model,

$$\ln y_{it} = \alpha + \beta^T x_{it} + v_{it} - u_{it},$$

or cost model,

$$\ln C_{it} = C(y_{it}, w_{it}; \beta) + v_{it} + u_{it},$$

in which $v_{it} \sim N[0, \sigma_v^2]$ and u_{it} has some distribution characterized by a constant mean, μ and constant variance, σ_u^2—sometimes both embodied in a single parameter, as in the exponential model. At this departure point, we say that the technology and the inefficiency distributions across individuals and time are homogeneous. They have the same parameters both in the production or cost function and in the inefficiency distribution. Of course, even at this point, that is not quite true, since the "stochastic" part of the *stochastic frontier* model specifically models the production technology as having a firm-specific (and time-specific) shift factor, v_{it}. Thus, at the outset, what we mean by homogeneity in the model is that firms differ only with respect to this random, noisy shift factor. We now wish to incorporate other forms of heterogeneity in the model. This includes, among other features, heteroskedasticity in the random parts of the model and shifts in the technology that are explainable in terms of variables that are neither inputs nor outputs. We begin by defining more precisely what we have in mind by heterogeneity.

2.6.1 Heterogeneity

One important way to categorize heterogeneity is between observable and unobservable heterogeneity. By observable heterogeneity, we mean as reflected in measured variables. This would include specific shift factors that operate on the production or cost function (or elsewhere in the model). For example, in his study of hospital costs, Linna (1998) has an "exogenous" variable reflecting case mix in the cost function. How such variables should enter the model is an important question. (In brainstorming sessions on frontier modeling with my colleagues, we call this "where do we put the z's?") They might shift the production function or the inefficiency distribution (i.e., enter the regression functions) or scale them (i.e., enter in the form of heteroskedasticity), or some combination of both (see Alvarez, Amsler, Orea and Schmidt, 2006, on the "scaling property") All of these possibilities fall in the category of observable heterogeneity (as I see it).

Unobserved heterogeneity, in contrast, enters the model in the form of "effects." This is usually viewed fundamentally as an issue of panel data, though I don't necessarily see it that way. Unobserved heterogeneity might (in principle, perhaps, always) reflect missing variables in the model. When these are not missing factors of production, or their unit prices, they have to be labeled as something different, however. Unobserved heterogeneity enters our model as characteristics, usually time invariant, that may or may not be related to the variables already in the model. We submit that unobserved heterogeneity should be considered as distinct from the unobservable object of most of our study, technical or cost inefficiency. For example, Greene (2004b) analyzes the problem of distinguishing the two in the World Health Organization's (WHO, 2000) vastly heterogeneous panel-data set on world health care attainment that includes 191 countries—virtually all of the world's population. I examine the issue in some detail below.

A related issue is parameter, or technology heterogeneity. Several studies to be discussed below have analyzed models with some type of shifting or cross-firm variation in the structural parameters of the model. Many of these are the sort of "random-parameter" models that are, again, usually associated with modeling in panel-data sets. I digress at this point to pin down a possibly misleading part of the modeling vernacular. In the numerous Bayesian treatments of frontier modeling, the parameters of the model are treated as "random," but the randomness in this context is not what I mean by parameter heterogeneity. In this discussion, what I intend by random parameters [e.g., in Huang (2004) or Orea and Kumbhakar's (2004) latent class model] is random difference across firms or individuals. The "randomness" of the parameters in a Bayesian treatment reflects "uncertainty" of the analyst, not heterogeneity across firms. I suggest the following litmus test: The parameter vector in a "random-parameters model" will contain an observation subscript "i," as in

$$\ln y_{it} = \alpha_i + \boldsymbol{\beta}_i^{\mathrm{T}} \mathbf{x}_{it} + v_{it} - u_{it}.$$

The Bayesian counterpart to this is the "hierarchical model," which adds to the preceding priors that might appear as $\boldsymbol{\beta}_i \sim N[\boldsymbol{\beta}, a\boldsymbol{\Omega}]; \boldsymbol{\beta} \sim N[0, \boldsymbol{\Omega}]$ (see, e.g., Tsionas, 2002; Huang, 2004). Variation in parameters is an important element of many studies. It can also be partly observable, for example, as in Kurkalova and Carriquiry (2003), in which parameters are allowed to vary systematically over time.[56]

A second, very important issue is the distinction between heterogeneity (latent or otherwise) in the production model and heterogeneity in the inefficiency model. These two have quite different implications for modeling and for estimation. Most of the literature on heterogeneity is focused on the latter, although to the extent that omitted heterogeneity in the production or cost model always shows up somewhere else (i.e., in the estimated features of u_{it}), they are not unrelated.

2.6.2 One-step and two-step models

In cases in which heterogeneity is observable, we are sometimes interested in models in which those observables enter in the form of parameterized functions of "exogenous variables." The leading case is in which these variables are believed to affect the distribution of inefficiency. For example, in Greene (2004b), it is suggested that in the provision of health care, per capita income, and the distribution of income are relevant determinants of the efficiency of health care delivery. In such cases, researchers have often analyzed (in)efficiency in two steps. In the first, conventional estimates of inefficiency are obtained without accounting for these exogenous influences (see section 2.8 for estimation of u_i). In the second step, these estimates are regressed or otherwise correlated with the exogenous factors (see, e.g., Greene, 2004b, table 6; Annaert et al., 2001).[57] It is easy to make a convincing argument that not accounting for the exogenous influences at the first step will induce a persistent bias in the estimates that are carried forward into the second. This is analyzed at length in Wang and Schmidt (2002), who argue that this is akin to an omitted variable problem in the linear regression model.

The biases in estimated coefficients will be propagated in subsidiary estimates computed using those coefficients. Caudill and Ford (1993) and Caudill et al. (1995) provide evidence of such first-level biases in estimated technology coefficients that result from neglected heteroskedasticity. Wang and Schmidt (2002) take the analysis another step to consider how this bias affects estimates of "inefficiency."[58] In their model, the neglected heterogeneity "scales" both the mean and variance of the inefficiency distribution. Ultimately, the case made by these authors is that when heterogeneity in the model is parameterized in terms of observables, those features should all appear in the model at the first step. In what follows, I will assume this is the case—the various model extensions noted below all presume "full information" (usually ML) estimation at the first step.

2.6.3 Shifting the production and cost function

I have mentioned numerous applications in which exogenous variables that are not outputs, inputs, or input prices enter the model. Among the examples are time changes that likely reflect technological change [e.g., Berger and Mester (1997), the case mix variables in Linna's (1998) hospital cost study, and exogenous country effects such as form of government and climate in Greene (2004b)]. Little is changed in the model by adding exogenous shifts, environment variables, technical change, and so on, to the production, cost, or distance function, as in

$$\ln y_{it} = f(x_{it}, \beta) + g(z_{it}, \delta) + h(t) + v_{it} - u_{it};$$

however, it must be noted that there is a potential identification issue. The model is obviously indistinguishable from an otherwise "pure" model in which the inefficiency component is $u_{it}^* = g(z_{it}, \delta) + h(t) - u_{it}$. It is up to the model builder to resolve at the outset whether the exogenous factors are part of the technology heterogeneity or whether they are elements of the inefficiency distribution.

The more pernicious identification problem arises in panel-data models in which there is unobservable, time-invariant heterogeneity. A perennial issue in the analysis of efficiency is whether inefficiency is time invariant or varies through time (systematically or haphazardly). I examine several models that relate to this question in this section. In the WHO health care model (Evans et al., 2000a, 2000b), technical inefficiency is deduced from a fixed-effects model (see Schmidt and Sickles, 1984),

$$\ln y_{it} = a_0 + \beta^{T} x_{it} + v_{it} - [\max_{j}(a_j) - a_i].$$

In this application (and others of the same type), any unobserved time-invariant heterogeneity must be captured in the estimated "inefficiency," $[\max_j(a_j) - a_i]$. For the WHO data, this component is potentially enormous, because these are country-level data. A random-effects–style model (see, e.g., Pitt and Lee, 1981; Koop et al., 1997),

$$\ln y_{it} = \alpha + \boldsymbol{\beta}^{\mathrm{T}} \mathbf{x}_{it} + v_{it} - u_i,$$

fares no better—it simply layers on the additional assumption that both inefficiency and heterogeneity are uncorrelated with $\mathbf{x}_{it}$. To accommodate this undesirable feature of both treatments, Greene (2004a, 2004b, 2005) proposes "true" fixed- and random-effects models,

$$\ln y_{it} = a_i + \boldsymbol{\beta}^{\mathrm{T}} \mathbf{x}_{it} + v_{it} - u_{it}$$

and

$$\ln y_{it} = (\alpha + w_i) + \boldsymbol{\beta}^{\mathrm{T}} \mathbf{x}_{it} + v_{it} - u_{it}.^{59}$$

In both cases, the assumptions of the stochastic frontier model are maintained, so the estimators are ML—in the former case by including the dummy variables in the model and in the latter case by MSL. Note that these models substantively change the assumptions about the time-invariant effects. In the prior specifications, the time-invariant term is entirely time-invariant inefficiency, and time-invariant heterogeneity is either assumed away or inadvertently buried in it. In the "true" effects model, all time-invariant effects are treated as unobserved heterogeneity, and the inefficiency component varies freely through time. Doubtless, the "truth" is somewhere between the two extremes. Unfortunately, there is an identification issue that is only resolved through nonsample information (i.e., additional assumptions). Farsi et al. (2003) have studied the impact of the different assumptions in a model of nursing home costs and found, perhaps not surprisingly, that the differences are quite noticeable. Kotzian (2005) extends the notion a bit to full-parameter vector heterogeneity and finds, likewise, that accounting for heterogeneity has substantial impacts on measured inefficiency.

2.6.4 Parameter variation and heterogeneous technologies

In the frontiers context, cross-firm parameter variation would be viewed as heterogeneity in the technology being employed (see Huang, 2004, for discussion). The idea of parameter variability in regression models was proposed by Hildreth and Houck (1968), among others, who applied the idea to linear regression models. The guiding wisdom in many treatments is still provided by the linear model. Textbook treatments of random-parameter models thus often analyze the generalized regression model and methods of "mixing" group-specific least squares estimates—essentially a GLS estimator. Kalirajan and Obwona (1994) is an early application in the frontiers literature. More contemporary treatments have couched parameter variation in terms of parameter heterogeneity, generally in panel-data models. In general, such models, both classical and Bayesian, are handled through likelihood-based and often simulation methods.[60]

When the parameter variation reflects observable heterogeneity, it is straightforward to build it directly in the model. Thus, Kotzian (2005) uses interactions with group-specific dummy variables to accommodate group differences in a model of health care attainment. Kurklova and Carriquiry (2003) do similarly with time variation in a production model for farm production.

A number of recent treatments have modeled technology heterogeneity with less systematic variation. In Orea and Kumbhakar (2004), Greene (2005), and O'Donnell and Griffiths (2004), a latent class specification is suggested to accommodate heterogeneity across firms in the sample. In the first two of these, the formulation captures differences in groups of firms within the sample. O'Donnell and Griffiths (2004), in contrast, use the latent class formulation to capture the effects of different weather "regimes" on rice farming. The latent class model, in general, is a stochastic frontier model,

$$\ln y_{it}|q = f_q(\mathbf{x}_{it}, \boldsymbol{\beta}_q) + v_{it}|q - u_{it}|q,$$

where q indicates the class or regime. Class membership is unknown, so the model proceeds to add the sorting probabilities,

$$\text{prob}[\text{class} = q|\mathbf{z}_i] = p(q|\mathbf{z}_i).$$

Note how exogenous factors may (but need not) enter the class probabilities. O'Donnell and Griffiths (2004) document a Bayesian MCMC method of estimating the model. Greene (2005) and Orea and Kumbhakar (2004) use ML methods instead.

Tsionas (2002) and Huang (2004) proposed a hierarchical Bayesian approach to frontier modeling with heterogeneous technologies. Tsionas's stochastic frontier model [applied to the Christensen and Greene (1976) electricity generation data] is

$$\ln y_{it} = \alpha + \boldsymbol{\beta}_i^T \mathbf{x}_{it} + v_{it} - u_{it},$$

$$f(v_{it}) = N[0, \sigma^2], p(\sigma) = \text{inverted gamma}(s, M) \propto \exp(-s/(2\sigma^2))(\sigma^2)^{-(M+1)/2},$$

$$f(u_{it}) = \theta \exp(-\theta u_{it}), p(\theta) = \text{gamma}(q, N) = \theta^{N-1} \exp(-q\theta)[q^N / \Gamma(N)],$$

$$p(\boldsymbol{\beta}_i) = N[\boldsymbol{\beta}, \boldsymbol{\Omega}], p(\boldsymbol{\beta}) = \text{"flat"} \propto 1, p(\alpha) \propto 1,$$

$$p(\boldsymbol{\Omega}) = \text{inverted Wishart} \propto |\boldsymbol{\Omega}|^{-(K+v+1)/2} \exp(-\text{tr}\boldsymbol{\Omega}^{-1}\mathbf{W}/2).$$

Assumed values for the elements of the priors, s, M, q, N, v, and $\mathbf{W}$ are discussed. The prior for θ is crucial. As Tsionas (2002) notes, $q = -\ln r^*$ is a crucial element in many studies (e.g., Koop et al., 1997). In most of these, the researchers use $r^* = 0.875$, implying a prior median efficiency of 87.5% when $N = 1$ (exponential). Tsionas reports that he used $N = 1$ (exponential prior for θ), but $q = 10^{-6}$, which implies essentially a flat prior for θ over the entire positive half line. For the other parameters, he reports prior values $s = 10^{-6}$ and $M = 1$, so $p(\sigma) \propto 1/\sigma$ (approximately), which is a Jeffrey's (noninformative) prior; $v = 1$, and $\mathbf{W} = 10^{-6}\mathbf{I}$, so $p(\mathbf{\Omega})$ is almost flat also. An MCMC-based Gibbs sampler is described for estimation. The parameter estimates (posterior means) are reasonable, but the estimated posterior mean for θ in the full model is 75.12, implying an inefficiency distribution concentrated almost entirely at zero ("near perfect efficiency"—as he notes, estimated efficiencies are almost uniformly above 0.99). Using the same data, van den Broeck et al. (1994) found values ranging from 0.83 to 0.91 when $r^* = 0.875$ and even lower when $r^* = 0.50$. The difference is attributed to the extension of the model to individual-specific parameters. (The classical MLE of θ is approximately 10, which implies median efficiency of roughly 93%.)

Tsionas (2002) hints at relaxing the exponential distribution assumption for $f(u_{it})$ to allow the more flexible gamma distribution (see Greene, 1993, 2004b), but only suggests how to fit the Erlang form (integer P) of the model for $P = 1$ (as above), 2, and 3. Huang (2004) presents a full extension of the model to the gamma distribution for u_{it},

$$f(u_{it}) = u_{it}^{P-1} \exp(-\theta u_{it})[\theta^P / \Gamma(P)].$$

A second extension allows a subset of the parameters to remain equal across firms—Huang (2004) uses this to force the constant term to be the same for all firms, while the other parameters remain firm specific. The author is (ironically) vague about what prior is used for the parameters of $f(u_{it})$. P is taken to have gamma prior with parameters $(1, 1)$—that is, exponential with mean 1. But, for q in $p(\theta)$, he suggests that he is following van den Broeck et al. (1994) and Tsionas (2002), who use completely different values. A footnote suggests something in the neighborhood of 0.8 is used for $-\ln r^* = q$. Huang's final results do not differ much from Tsionas's. The posterior means for θ and P are 77.433 (Tsionas found 77.12) and 0.9063 (Tsionas forced the latter to equal 1). Huang (2004) likewise finds posterior estimates of mean efficiency that differ only trivially from 0.99. The values that he finds when he assumes homogeneous technologies are more in line with van den Broeck et al. (1994, their figure 2).

These results are not plausible. I surmise that they result from fitting a separate parameter vector to every observation in a cross section, something that cannot be done with classical, MSL procedures. The Gibbs sampler (MCMC) method has no built-in mechanism that will break down when one attempts to do so. (One could trace the Gibbs samples from different starting points in the chain and look for failures to converge. That does not appear to have been done here.) Consider a classical alternative. In Greene (2005), the random-parameters model

$$\ln y_{it} = \alpha_i + \boldsymbol{\beta}_i^T \mathbf{x}_{it} + v_{it} - u_i,$$
$$(\alpha_i, \boldsymbol{\beta}_i) \sim N[(\alpha, \boldsymbol{\beta}), \Sigma],$$

$$v_{it} \sim N[0, \sigma_v^2],$$
$$u_{it} \sim N[0, \sigma_u^2]$$

is estimated by MSL. (An extension is proposed that allows the mean of the normal distribution to include a term Δz_i which produces a two-level model and adds an additional layer of heterogeneity in the model.) As a general rule, the classical estimator of this (any) random-parameters model does not work very well in a cross section. For the same data used in the preceding two studies, the MSL estimates appear quite reasonable, with the exception of the estimate of σ_v, which goes nearly to zero. All of the variation in v_{it} is soaked up by the firm-specific parameters, leaving nothing for the idiosyncratic disturbance. (In contrast, in the hierarchical Bayes model, all the variation in u is absorbed elsewhere in the estimated model.) The estimated efficiency values from this model (discussed further in the next section) are 0.984 (the result of a numerical problem in manipulating the near zero value of σ_v), for every firm in the sample—equally implausible. If the normal–gamma model discussed above, with nonrandom (homogeneous) coefficients, is fit by MSL, the estimated efficiencies from that model (EFFG) produce the kernel density plot shown in figure 2.7. This figure is virtually identical to Huang's (2004) figure 2, which does likewise for the homogeneous technologies model, even including the small second mode near 0.67. To explore the idea suggested above, I divided the sample into 20 size classes and fit the random-parameters model with these 20 groups treated as a panel. The results corresponding to figure 2.7 appear in figure 2.8.

These results are strikingly at odds with the Bayesian estimates. To return to the issue of parameter heterogeneity, note that these are firm-level, not plant-level, data and that most of these firms are fairly large multiplant utilities.

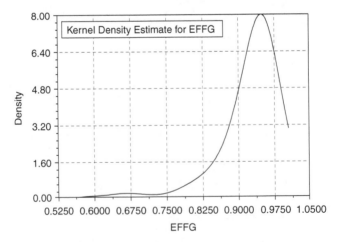

Figure 2.7. Estimated Efficiencies for Electric Power Generation

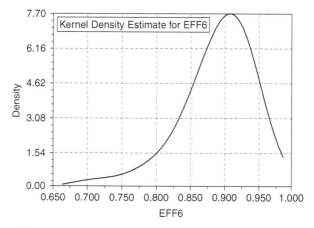

Figure 2.8. Efficiencies for Heterogeneous Technologies Model

The proposition that there are the very large differences in technology across firms suggested by the large parameter variances estimated in the hetero-geneous parameter models seems dubious. The statistical issue of computing individual-specific coefficients in a cross section and the underlying economics suggest that these results need a much closer look.

2.6.5 Location effects on the inefficiency model

Thus far, we have analyzed different approaches to introducing heterogene-ity in the technology into the stochastic frontier while retaining the simple additive homogeneous inefficiency term. Let us now turn attention to models that consider the location and scale of the inefficiency itself. Heterogeneity of the sort examined above is also a natural place to focus the discussion. A central issue in this specification search is how to handle the possibility of time variation in inefficiency in a model for panel data. This is considered in section 2.7.

Kumbhakar's (1993) "production risk model,"

$$\ln y_{it} = \alpha + T(\ln x_{it}, \beta) + g(x_{it}, \delta)\varepsilon_{it},$$

where $g(x_{it}, \delta) = \sum_k \delta_k x_{itk}$ in a translog model (log-quadratic) and $\varepsilon_{it} = \tau_i + \lambda_t + v_{it}$, is similar. In this case, inefficiency is estimated with $g(x_{it}, \hat{\delta})(\hat{\alpha} + \hat{\tau}_i) - \max_j[g(x_{it}, \hat{\delta})(\hat{\alpha} + \hat{\tau}_j)]$.

Whether inefficiency can be appropriately modeled in the preceding fash-ion is the subject of some debate. Forcing a pattern of any sort on all firms in the sample is restrictive. (Of course, it is less so than assuming there is no variation at all.) Another approach to capturing variation in inefficiency is the addition of a nonnegative effect directly to the production function. Deprins and Simar (1989b) suggested $E[u|z_i] = \exp(\delta^T z_i)$, which produces the model

$$\ln y_i = \ln f(x_i, \beta) - \exp(\delta^T z_i) + \varepsilon_I,$$

where $E[\varepsilon_i] = 0$. A formal specification for the distribution of ε completes the model. This approach is somewhat cumbersome analytically, because it loses the essential nature of the nonnegative inefficiency. Kumbhakar, Ghosh, and McGuckin (1991) suggested a similar specification,

$$u_i = \delta^T z_i + \varepsilon_I,$$

with similar shortcomings. Constraining the sign of u_i is difficult in the specifications considered thus far. Kumbhakar et al.'s (1991) solution has been used in many recent applications:

$$u_i = |N[\delta^T z_i, \sigma_u^2]|$$

Reifschneider and Stevenson's (1991) proposal to address the issue is

$$\ln y_i = \alpha + \beta^T x_i - d(\delta, z_i) - u_i^* + v_i,$$

where both $d(\delta, z_i)$ and u_i^* are positive. Specifying $d(\delta, z_i) = \exp(\delta^T z_i)$ and $u_i^* \sim N^+[0, \sigma_u^2]$ satisfies the requirement. This is, of course, similar to Kumbhakar et al.'s (1991) model, but with an additional constraint satisfied. Reifschneider and Stevenson (1991) apply the model with truncated normal, exponential, and Erlang distributions assumed for u_i. Actually, the model is overspecified, since it is not necessary for both $\exp(\delta^T z_i)$ and u_i^* to be positive for $u_i = u_i^* + \exp(\delta^T z_i)$ to be positive. Huang and Liu (1994) complete the specification by formulating the model so that only $u_i^* \geq -\exp(\delta^T z_i)$ is built into the model. This is done by using a truncated normal rather than a half-normal distribution for u_i^*. [In Huang and Liu's formulation, the shift function also includes the levels of the inputs. This has implications for the elasticities as well as some ambiguous implications for whether inefficiency is input or output oriented. Battese and Coelli (1995) propose a specification that is generally similar to that of Huang and Liu (1994).] Since the truncation point enters the log-likelihood function nonlinearly, even for a linear function for $d(\delta, z_i)$, this substantially complicates the estimation. On the other hand, by manipulating the model a bit, we can show that the Huang and Liu model can be obtained from Stevenson's (1980) truncated-normal model just by replacing ε_i with $\varepsilon_i + d(\delta, z_i)$ and v_i with $v_i + d(\delta, z_i)$—Huang and Liu specified $d_i = \delta' z_i$ for a set of variables that need not appear in the production function. The model proposed by Kumbhakar et al. (1991) is, likewise, equivalent to that of Huang and Liu (1994).

A number of other variations on this theme have been suggested. Battese, Rambaldi, and Wan (1994) use

$$y_i = f(x_i, \beta) + d(\delta, z_i)(u_i + v_i).$$

Note the use of an additive as opposed to multiplicative disturbance in this model. Battese et al. were interested specifically in modeling y_i in "natural units" (the authors' term). Technical efficiency in this model, defined as

$$\text{TE}_i = \frac{E[y_i | u_i, \mathbf{x}_i]}{E[y_i | u_i = 0, \mathbf{x}_i]} = 1 - \frac{d_i}{f_i} u_i,$$

clearly depends on d_i. [Note that since y_i is positive, $\text{TE}_i \in (0, 1)$.] Battese et al. present the log-likelihood function for this model with Cobb-Douglas specifications for $f(\cdot)$ and $d(\cdot)$ in an appendix. Estimation is, at least in principle, straightforward, though the use of the additive form of the disturbance probably unnecessarily complicates the function and the maximization process. There is, however, a purpose to doing so; the main subject of the paper is *production risk*, defined for the kth input as

$$\eta_k = \frac{\partial \text{var}[y_i | u_i, \mathbf{x}_i]}{\partial x_{ki}} = 2\beta_k \frac{\text{var}[y_i | u_i, \mathbf{x}_i]}{x_{ki}}$$

for their model.

Last, an intuitively appealing modification of Battese et al.'s (1994) formulation is

$$\ln y_i = f(\mathbf{x}_i, \boldsymbol{\beta}) + v_i - d_i u_i,$$

where, as before, d_i is a nonnegative function and u_i has one of the distributions specified above. Suppose that we assume Stevenson's truncated-normal model for u_i. Then, by using the change of variable formula, it is easy to show that $d_i u_i$ has a truncated normal distribution, as well; when $r_i = d_i u_i$,

$$h(r_i) = \left[\frac{1}{d_i \sigma_u} \right] \frac{\phi[(r_i - d_i \mu)/d_i \sigma_u]}{\Phi[d_i \mu / d_i \sigma_u]}.$$

Therefore, the log-likelihood function and all of the subsequent results needed for estimating the technical efficiency values for the observations can be obtained for this model just by replacing μ with $\mu_i = d_i \mu$ and σ_u with $\sigma_{ui} = d_i \sigma_u$ in Stevenson's model. This implies that the transformed parameters, $\sigma = (\sigma_u^2 + \sigma_v^2)^{1/2}$ and $\lambda = \sigma_u / \sigma_v$, will now be functions of d_i. An application of this model is Caudill and Ford (1993), who use this formulation with $\mu = 0$ and $d_i = [f(x_i, \boldsymbol{\beta})]^\delta$. This adds a single new parameter to the model, δ. Since the authors are interested in the effects of the heteroskedasticity on the parameter estimates, it remains for subsequent researchers to establish how, if at all, this (and, for that matter, any of the aforementioned models) changes the estimates of u_i and TE_i.

2.6.6 Shifting the underlying mean of u_i

The discussion thus far [with the exception of Huang and Liu's (1994) model] has treated the distributions of the stochastic component of the frontier, v_i, and the inefficiency component, u_i, as homogeneous populations, with constant mean and variance and fixed distribution. Heterogeneity in the model arises only in the inputs (and any other control variables) in the production or cost functions. But, there is ample evidence that both of these characteristics can vary widely across firms, as well.

A natural starting point for accommodating heterogeneity in the inefficiency model is in the location of the distribution. Figure 2.9 shows the form of the density for a *truncated-normal* model for three values of $\mu : -0.5, 0.0$ (the half-normal model), and 0.5. Clearly, the value of μ makes a considerable difference in the shape of the distribution. Firm-specific heterogeneity can easily be incorporated into the model as follows:

$$y_i = \boldsymbol{\beta}'\mathbf{x}_i + v_i - u_i,$$
$$v_i \sim N[0, \sigma_v^2],$$
$$u_i = |U_i|,$$

where $U_i \sim N[\mu_i, \sigma_u^2], \mu_i = \mu_0 + \boldsymbol{\mu}_1'\mathbf{z}_i$.

As noted, this is the same as the reduced form of the model proposed by Huang and Liu (1994). The difference is that, here, the heterogeneity is specifically designed as the location parameter in the underlying distribution. One might include in z_i industry-specific effects or other technological attributes. For example, an analysis of production in the airline industry might include load factor (the proportion of seat-miles flown that are also passenger-miles, a number that has often varied around 0.75 in this industry). This brings a relatively minor change in the estimator (in principle), though in practice, the numerical properties of the estimator do change considerably. The modified

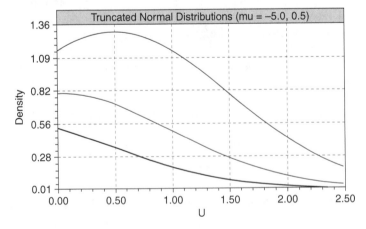

Figure 2.9. Truncated Normal Distributions

log-likelihood is now

$$\text{Ln } L(\alpha, \beta, \sigma, \lambda, \mu^0, \mu_1) = -N \left[\ln \sigma + \frac{1}{2} \ln 2\pi + \ln \Phi(\mu_i/\sigma_u) \right]$$

$$+ \sum_{i=1}^{N} \left[-\frac{1}{2} \left(\frac{\varepsilon_i + \mu_i}{\sigma} \right)^2 + \ln \Phi \left(\frac{\mu_i}{\sigma \lambda} - \frac{\varepsilon_i \lambda}{\sigma} \right) \right],$$

where $\lambda = \sigma_u/\sigma_v$, $\sigma^2 = \sigma_u^2 + \sigma_v^2$ and $\sigma_u = \lambda\sigma/\sqrt{1+\lambda^2}$. The sign of ε_i is reversed in the two appearances for estimation of a cost or output distance frontier. This is a relatively minor modification of the original normal–half-normal, though the interpretation has changed substantively.

2.6.7 Heteroskedasticity

As in other settings, there is no reason to assume that heterogeneity would be limited to the mean of the inefficiency. A model that allows heteroskedasticity in u_i or v_i is a straightforward extension. A convenient generic form would be

$$\text{var}[v_i|h_i] = \sigma_v^2 g_v(h_i, \delta), g_v(h_i, 0) = 1,$$

$$\text{var}[U_i|h_i] = \sigma_u^2 g_u(h_i, \tau), g_u(h_i, 0) = 1$$

(see Reifschneider and Stevenson, 1991; Simar, Lovell, and Eeckhaut, 1994). We have assumed that the same variables appear in both functions, although with suitably placed zeros in the parameter vectors, this can be relaxed. The normalization $g_v(h_i, 0) = 1$ is used to nest the homoskedastic model within the broader one. The two functions are assumed to be strictly continuous and differentiable in their arguments. In applications, linear functions (e.g., $1 + \delta^T h_i$) are likely to be inadequate, because they would allow negative variances. Likewise, a function of the form $\sigma_{ui}^2 = \sigma_u^2(\beta^T x_i)^\delta$ (Caudill and Fort, 1993; Caudill et al., 1995) does not prevent invalid computations.[61] Reifschneider and Stevenson also suggested $\sigma_{ui}^2 = \sigma_u^2 + g_u(h_i, \tau)$, which requires $g_u(h_i, \tau) \geq 0$ and $g_u(h_i, 0) = 0$. A more convenient form is the exponential,

$$g_v(h_i, \delta) = [\exp(\delta^T h_i)]^2 \text{ and } g_u(h_i, \tau) = [\exp(\tau^T h_i)]^2$$

(Hadri, 1999).[62] For estimation, it is necessary to revert to the parameterization that is explicit in the two variances, σ_{vi}^2 and σ_{ui}^2, rather than the form in λ and σ^2, because if either of the underlying variances is heterogeneous, then both of these reduced-form parameters must be heterogeneous, but not in an obvious fashion. The resulting log-likelihood is somewhat cumbersome, but quite manageable computationally. The complication that arises still results from the heterogeneity in the mean:

$$\text{Ln } L(\alpha, \beta, \sigma_u, \sigma_v, \delta, \tau, \mu_0, \mu_1)$$

$$= -\frac{N}{2} \ln 2\pi + \sum_{i=1}^{N} [\ln \sigma_i] + \sum_{i=1}^{N} \ln \Phi \left[\frac{\mu_i}{\sigma_{ui}} \right]$$

$$+ \sum_{i=1}^{N} \left[-\frac{1}{2} \left(\frac{\varepsilon_i + \mu_i}{\sigma_i} \right)^2 + \ln \Phi \left(\frac{\mu_i}{\sigma_i(\sigma_{ui}/\sigma_{vi})} - \frac{\varepsilon_i(\sigma_{ui}/\sigma_{vi})}{\sigma_i} \right) \right]$$

$$\sigma_i = \sqrt{\sigma_v^2[\exp(\delta^T h_i)]^2 + \sigma_u^2[\exp(\tau^T h_i)]^2}$$

$$= \sqrt{\sigma_{vi}^2 + \sigma_{ui}^2}$$

There are numerous applications, including Caudill and Ford (1993), Caudill et al. (1995), Hadri (1999), and Hadri et al. (2003a, 2003b), that specify a model with heteroskedasticity in both error components.

2.6.8 The scaling property

Wang and Schmidt (2002) and Alvarez, Amsler, Orea, and Schmidt (2006) suggest a semiparametric approach to accounting for exogenous influences that they label the "scaling property" proposed by Simar et al. (1994). Thus,

$$u_i = u(\delta, z_i) = h(\delta, z_i) \times u_i^*,$$

where u_i^* is a nonnegative random variable whose distribution does not involve z_i and $h(\delta, z_i)$ is a nonnegative function. [For our purposes, we will also require that $h(\delta, z_i)$ be continuous in δ, though this is not strictly required for the model to be internally consistent.] The extension goes beyond heteroskedasticity, because it implies $E[u_i] = h(\delta, z_i)E[u_i^*]$. Simar et al. (1994) exploit this to develop a nonlinear least squares estimator that does not require a distributional assumption. The likelihood function for the half- or truncated-normal or exponential model is not particularly difficult, however, though it does carry some testable restrictions that relate the mean and variance of the underlying distribution of u_i (for further explorations of the scaling property, see Alvarez, Amsler, Orea, and Schmidt, 2006; see also related results in Bhattacharyya, Kumbhakar, and Bhattacharyya, 1995). Candidates for $h(\delta, z_i)$ are the usual ones, linear, $\delta^T z_i$ and exponential, $\exp(\delta' z_i)$. Simar et al. suggest the truncated normal $N[\mu, \sigma_u^2]^+$ as a convenient specification that carries all of their assumptions. Wang and Schmidt (2002) then provide a lengthy argument why conventional estimators of the production parameters and the JLMS (Jondrow, Lovell, Materov, and Schmidt, 1982) estimates of u_i will be seriously biased. The same arguments apply to estimates of $TE_i = \exp(-u_i)$.

Several parts of the earlier literature predate Wang and Schmidt (2002). Kumbhakar et al. (1991), Huang and Liu (1994), and Battese and Coelli (1995) have all considered normal–truncated-normal models in which $\mu_i = \delta' z_i$. Reifschneider and Stevenson (1991), Caudill and Ford (1993), and Caudill, Ford, and Gropper (1995) suggested different functional forms for the variance, such as $\sigma_{ui} = \sigma_u \times \exp(\delta^T z_i)$. None of these formulations satisfies the scaling property, though a combination does. Let $h(\delta, z_i) = \exp(\delta^T z_i)$ and assume the truncated-normal model. Then it follows that $u_i = |U_i|$, $U_i \sim N\{\mu \times \exp(\delta^T z_i), [\sigma_u \times \exp(\delta^T z_i)]^2\}$. Wang (2002) proposes a model that specifically violates the scaling property, $\sigma_{ui}^2 = \exp(\delta^T z_i)$ and $\mu_i = \delta^T z_i$, to examine nonneutral shifts of the production function. Alvarez, Amsler, Orea and Schmidt (2006) examine the various specifications that are encompassed by this formulation. We note, in all these specifications, the underlying mean of u_i is functionally related to the variance. This is a testable restriction.

The scaling property adds some useful dimensions to the stochastic frontier model. First, it allows firm heterogeneity to show up by shrinking or inflating the inefficiency distribution without changing its basic shape. Second, if $u_i = h(\delta, z_i) \times u_i^*$, then $\partial \ln u_i/\partial z_i = \partial \ln h(\delta, z_i)/\partial z_i$ irrespective of the underlying distribution of u_i^*. Third, in principle, the model parameters can be estimated by nonlinear least squares without a distributional assumption (for discussion, see Alvarez et al., 2006; Kumbhakar and Lovell, 2000). Given the robustness of estimates of u_i explored in the preceding section, we suspect that this is a minor virtue. Moreover, the full model with this assumption built into it is not a major modification of the normal–truncated-normal model already considered, though it does have one built in ambiguity that we now explore. We will allow both u_i and v_i to be exponentially heteroskedastic. The log-likelihood for Wang and Schmidt's (2002) model is then

$$\mathrm{Ln}\, L(\alpha, \beta, \delta, \gamma, \mu^0) = -(N/2)\ln 2\pi - \sum_{i=1}^{N} [\ln \sigma_i + \ln \Phi(\mu_i/\sigma_{ui})]$$

$$+ \sum_{i=1}^{N} \left[-\frac{1}{2}\left(\frac{\varepsilon_i + \mu_i}{\sigma_i}\right)^2 + \ln \Phi\left(\frac{\mu_i}{\sigma_i \lambda_i} - \frac{\varepsilon_i \lambda_i}{\sigma_i}\right) \right]$$

where
$$\mu_i = \mu \exp(\delta^T z_i), \quad \sigma_{ui} = \sigma_u \exp(\delta^T z_i), \quad \sigma_{vi} = \sigma_v \exp(\gamma^T z_i),$$
$\lambda_i = \sigma_{ui}/\sigma_{vi}$, and $\sigma_i = \sqrt{\sigma_{vi}^2 + \sigma_{ui}^2}$.

We allow for σ_{ui} and σ_{vi} to differ by placing zeros in the parameter vectors where needed to allow different variables to appear in the functions. Note that there is a set of equality restrictions built into the model, across μ_i and σ_{ui}. Also, though σ_u and σ_v must be positive [they could be written as $\exp(\delta_0)$ and $\exp(\gamma_0)$ to impose this], μ must be allowed to have either sign.

Wang and Schmidt (2002) provide a Monte Carlo analysis of the biases that result if the scaling property is ignored. The point is well taken. It is also useful, however, to view the scaling property as an alternative specification of the stochastic frontier model that may or may not be consistent with the data (i.e., the underlying population). The assumption is easy to test, because we can simply relax the equality restriction that links the mean and the standard deviation of the distribution. (Note, however, that there remains what is probably a minor restriction in the Wang and Schmidt model, that with or without the scaling property imposed, the specification of the mean does not allow for a linear shift of μ_i independent of z_i; there is no free constant term in the equation for μ_i. For this reason, even with the exponential specification for the variances, the truncation model is usually specified with $\mu_i = \mu_0 + \delta^T z_i$.)

2.7 Panel-Data Models

When producers are observed at several points in time, three shortcomings in the foregoing analysis can be handled explicitly.[63] In the stochastic frontier model, it is necessary to assume that the firm-specific level of inefficiency is uncorrelated with the input levels. This may be unwarranted. Some of the specifications discussed above (e.g., Huang and Liu, 1994) reconstructed the inefficiency term in the model to include functions of x. The assumption of normality for the noise term and half- or truncated normality for the inefficiency, while probably relatively benign, is yet another assumption that one might prefer not to make. A few alternatives are noted in the preceding. Nonetheless, under certain assumptions, more robust panel-data treatments are likely to bring improvements in the estimates. A fundamental question concerns whether inefficiency is properly modeled as fixed over time. The point is moot in a cross section, of course. However, it is very relevant in the analysis of panel data. Intuition should suggest that the longer the panel, the "better" will be the estimator of time-invariant inefficiency in the model, however computed. But, at the same time, the longer the time period of the observation, the less tenable the assumption becomes. This is a perennial issue in this literature, without a simple solution.

In this section, we will detail several models for inefficiency that are amenable to analysis in panel-data sets. Actual computation of estimators of u_i or u_{it} are considered in section 2.8. Treatments of firm and time variation in inefficiency are usefully distinguished in two dimensions. The first, as mentioned, is whether we wish to assume that it is time varying or not. Second, we consider models that make only minimal distributional assumptions about inefficiency ("fixed-effects" models) and models that make specific distributional assumptions such as those made above: half-normal, exponential, and so forth. The former have a virtue of robustness, but this comes at a cost of a downward bias (see Kim and Schmidt, 2000). The latter make possibly restrictive assumptions but bring the benefit of increased precision.

There are N firms and T_i observations on each. (It is customary to assume that T_i is constant across firms, but this is never actually necessary.) If observations on u_{it} and v_{it} are independent over time as well as across individuals, then the panel nature of the data set is irrelevant and the models discussed above will apply to the pooled data set. But, if one is willing to make further assumptions about the nature of the inefficiency, a number of new possibilities arise. We consider several of them here.

2.7.1 Time variation in inefficiency

A large proportion of the research on panel-data applications analyzes (essentially) a deterministic frontier in the context of "fixed-effects" models:

$$\ln y_{it} = \alpha + \beta^\mathsf{T} x_{it} + a_i + v_{it},$$

where a_i is the fixed effect normalized in some way to accommodate the nonzero constant. This regression style model is typically identified with the fixed-effects linear model. If the u_i values are treated as firm-specific constants, the model may be estimated by OLS, as a "fixed-effects" model (using the "within-groups" transformation if the number of firms is too large to accommodate with simple OLS).[64] It is more useful here to think in terms of the specification being distribution free, particularly in view of the Bayesian treatments in which the distinction between "fixed" and "random" effects is ambiguous. Development of this model begins with Schmidt and Sickles (1984), who propose essentially a deterministic frontier treatment of estimated inefficiencies

$$\hat{u}_i = \max_j(\hat{a}_j) - \hat{a}_i.$$

Sickles (2005) presents a wide variety of approaches and interpretations of this model. Note the assumption of time invariance in this treatment. One individual in the sample is fully efficient ($u_i = 0$), and others are compared to it, rather than to an absolute standard.

   This fixed-effects approach has the distinct advantage of dispensing with the assumption that the firm inefficiencies are uncorrelated with the input levels. Moreover, no assumption of normality is needed. Finally, this approach shares the consistency property of the deterministic frontier model in the estimation of u_i. This estimate is consistent in T_i, which may, in practice, be quite small. But, as noted above, this consistency may make no economic sense—the longer the time interval, the less tenable the time invariance assumption.

   An extension suggested by Kumbhakar (1990, 1993) is to add a "time" effect, γ_t, to the fixed-effects model. Strictly in terms of estimation, the statistical properties of $c_t = \hat{\gamma}_t$ depend on N, which is more likely to be amenable to conventional analyses. This can be treated as a fixed- or random-effects model, of course. In either case, it is necessary to compensate for the presence of the time effect in the model. However, since the time effect is the same for all firms in each period, the earlier expression for $\hat{u}_i$ would now define $\hat{u}_{it}$ rather than $\hat{u}_i$. This does relax the assumption of time invariance of the production function, but it does not add to the specification of the inefficiency term in the model. The modification considered next does.

Kumbhakar and Hjalmarsson (1995) also suggested a precursor to Greene's (2004a) true fixed- and random-effects models. They proposed

$$u_{it} = \tau_i + a_{it}$$

where $a_{it} \sim N^+[0, \sigma^2]$. They suggested a two-step estimation procedure that begins with either OLS/dummy variables or feasible GLS and proceeds to a second-step analysis to estimate τ_i. (Greene's estimators are full information MLEs that use only a single step.) Heshmati and Kumbhakar (1994) and Kumbhakar and Heshmati (1995) consider methodological aspects of these models, including how to accommodate technical change.

Cornwell et al. (1990) propose to accommodate systematic variation in inefficiency, by replacing a_i with

$$a_{it} = \alpha_{i0} + \alpha_{i1}t + \alpha_{i2}t^2.$$

Inefficiency is still modeled using $u_{it} = \max(a_{it}) - a_{it}$. With this modified specification, the most efficient firm can change from period to period. Also, since the maximum (or minimum, for a cost frontier) is period specific and need not apply to the same firm in every period, this will interrupt the quadratic relationship between time and the inefficiencies. [Kumbhakar (1990) proposes some modifications of this model and examines the implications of several kinds of restrictions on the parameters.] The signature feature of this formulation is that inefficiency for a given firm evolves systematically over time. Cornwell et al. (1990) analyze the estimation problem in this model at some length (see also Hausman and Taylor, 1981). For large N, this presents a fairly cumbersome problem of estimation (note 65 notwithstanding). But, for data sets of the size in many applications, this enhanced fixed-effects model can comfortably be estimated by simple, unadorned least squares.[65] Alternative approaches are suggested by Kumbhakar (1991a), Kumbhakar and Heshmati (1995), and Kumbhakar and Hjalmarsson (1995). Applications are given by, for example, Cornwell et al. (1990), Schmidt and Sickles (1984), and Gong and Sickles (1989), who apply the preceding to a cost frontier model; and Good, Roller, and Sickles (1993, 1995), Good and Sickles (1995), and Good, Nadiri, Roller, and Sickles (1993), who use various models to analyze the airline industry. Some semiparametric variations on the Cornwell et al. (1990) approach are discussed in Park, Sickles, and Simar (1998) and Park and Simar (1992).

Lee and Schmidt (1993) proposed a less heavily parameterized fixed-effects frontier model,

$$\ln y_{it} = \beta^T x_{it} + a_{it} + v_{it},$$

where $a_{it} = \theta_t a_i$, θ_t is a set of time dummy variable coefficients, and, as before, $\hat{u}_{it} = \max_i (\hat{\theta}_t \hat{a}_i) - \hat{\theta}_t \hat{a}_i$. This differs from the familiar fixed-effects model, $\alpha_{it} = \theta_t + \delta_i$, in two ways. First, the model is nonlinear and requires a more complicated estimator. Second, it allows the unobserved firm effect to vary over time. A benefit is that time-invariant firm effects may now be accommodated. The authors describe both fixed- and random-effects treatments of θ_t.

Numerous similarly motivated specifications have been proposed for the stochastic frontier model

$$\ln y_{it} = \alpha + \boldsymbol{\beta}^T \mathbf{x}_{it} + v_{it} - u_{it}.$$

Two that have proved useful in applications are Kumbhakar's (1990) model,

$$u_{it} = u_i / [1 + \exp(\gamma_1 t + \gamma_2 t^2)],$$

and Battese and Coelli's (1992) formulation (which is the model of choice in many recent applications),

$$u_{it} = u_i \times \exp[-\eta(t - T)].$$

An alternative formulation that allows the variance effect to be nonmonotonic is

$$u_{it} = u_i \times \exp[\eta_1(t - T) + \eta_2(t - T)^2].$$

In all formulations, $u_i = |U_i| \sim N^+[0, \sigma_u^2]$. The Battese and Coelli model has been extended to the truncated-normal model, as well, in Kumbhakar and Orea (2004) and Greene (2004a). Cuesta (2000) also proposed a modification, with firm-specific scale factors, η_i, in the scaling function. The authors present full details on the log-likelihood, its derivatives, and the computation of $E[u|\varepsilon]$ and $E[e^{-u}|\varepsilon]$.

Tsionas (2003) proposed an autoregressive model in which inefficiency evolves via an autoregressive process:

$$\ln u_{it} = \gamma^T z_{it} + \rho \ln u_{i,t-1} + w_{it}$$

(Specific assumptions are also made for the initial value, which would be important here because the typical panel in this setting is very short.) The autoregressive process embodies "new sources of inefficiency." In Tsionas's Bayesian MCMC treatment, the Gibbs sampler is used to draw observations directly from the posterior for u_{it} rather than using the JLMS (Jondrow, Lovell, Materov, and Schmidt, 1982) estimator ex post to estimate firm- and time-specific inefficiency. In an application to U.S. banks, he finds the posterior mean $\rho = 0.91$, which implies that the process is almost static. The implied short- and long-run efficiencies for the whole sample range around 60%.

2.7.2 Distributional assumptions

If the assumption of independence of the inefficiencies and input levels can be maintained, then a random-effects approach brings some benefits in precision.

One advantage of the random-effects model is that it allows time-invariant firm-specific attributes, such as the capital stock of a firm that is not growing, to enter the model. The familiar random-effects regression model is easily adapted to the stochastic frontier model. There are also some interesting variants in the recently received literature. We consider the basic model first.

The relevant log-likelihood for a random-effects model with a half-normal distribution has been derived by Lee and Tyler (1978) and Pitt and Lee (1981) and is discussed further by Battese and Coelli (1988).[66] The truncated-normal model of Stevenson (1980) is adopted here for generality and in order to maintain consistency with Battese and Coelli (1988), who provide a number of interesting results for this model. The half-normal model can be produced simply by restricting μ to equal 0. We also allow the underlying mean to be heterogeneous. Note, as well, that the extension of the model to include multiplicative heteroskedasticity in v_{it} and/or u_{it} is straightforward. I omit this detail in the interest of brevity. The structural model is, then,

$$y_{it} = \alpha + \beta^T x_{it} + v_{it} - u_{it},$$

$$u_i \sim |N[\mu_i, \sigma_u^2]|$$

$$v_{it} \sim N[0, \sigma_v^2].$$

As before, there are T_i observations on the ith firm. Battese and Coelli (1988) and Battese, Coelli, and Colby (1989) have extensively analyzed this model, with Stevenson's extension to the truncated normal distribution for u_i. They also provide the counterpart to the JLMS (Jondrow et al., 1982) estimator of u_i. With our reparameterization, their result is

$$E[u_i|\varepsilon_{i,1}, \varepsilon_{i,2}, \dots, \varepsilon_{i,T_i}] = \mu_i^* + \sigma_{i*} \left[\frac{\phi(\mu_i^*/\sigma_{i*})}{\Phi(-\mu_i^*/\sigma_{i*})} \right],$$

$$\mu_i^* = \gamma_i \mu + (1 - \gamma_i)(-\bar{\varepsilon}_i),$$

$$\varepsilon_{it} = y_{it} - \alpha - \beta^T x_{it},$$

$$\gamma_i = 1/(1 + \lambda T_i),$$

$$\lambda = \sigma_u^2/\sigma_v^2,$$

$$\sigma_{i*}^2 = \gamma_i \sigma_u^2.$$

As $T_i \to \infty$, $\gamma_i \to 0$, and the entire expression collapses to $-\bar{\varepsilon}_i$, which in turn converges to u_i, as might be expected. As Schmidt and Sickles (1984) observe, this be interpreted as the advantage of having observed $u_i N$ times. Taking the mean averages out the noise contained in v_{it}, which only occurs once. It is worth noting that the preceding, perhaps with the simplifying assumption that $\mu = 0$, could be employed after estimation of the random-effects model by GLS, rather than ML. The aforementioned corrections to the moment-based variance estimators would be required, of course. Battese and Coelli (1988,

1992) have also derived the panel-data counterpart to $E[e^{-u_i|\varepsilon_i}]$,

$$E[\exp(-u_i)|\varepsilon_{i1}, \varepsilon_{i2}, \ldots, \varepsilon_{iT_i}] = \left[\frac{\Phi[(\mu_i^*/\sigma_{*i}) - \sigma_{*i}]}{\Phi(\mu_i^*/\sigma_{*i})} \right] \exp[-\mu_{i*} + \tfrac{1}{2}\sigma_{i*}^2].$$

2.7.3 Fixed-effects, random-effects, and Bayesian approaches

An obstacle to the fixed-effects approach is the presence of time-invariant attributes of the firms. If the model is conditioned on firm attributes such as the capital stock, location, or some other characteristics, and if these do not vary over time, then the Least Squares Dummy Variable estimator cannot be computed as shown above. Worse yet, if these effects are simply omitted from the model, then they will reappear in the fixed effects, masquerading as inefficiency (or lack of), when obviously they should be classified otherwise. The question is one of identification. Hausman and Taylor (1981) have discussed conditions for identification of such effects and methods of estimation that might prove useful. However, the economic content of this discussion may be at odds with the algebraic and statistical content. Regardless of how fixed effects enter the model discussed above, they will reappear in the estimates of inefficiency and thereby create some ambiguity in the interpretation of these estimates. As such, alternative treatments, such as the random-effects model, may be preferable.

Consider the base case model,

$$\ln y_{it} = \alpha + \boldsymbol{\beta}^\mathrm{T}\mathbf{x}_{it} + v_{it} - u_i,$$

where either the fixed-effects interpretation described above or the random-effects model described in the next subsection is adopted. The time-invariant element in the model, u_i, is intended to capture all and only the firm-specific inefficiency. If there are time-invariant effects, such as heterogeneity, in the data, they must also appear in u_i whether they belong there or not. [This is exactly the opposite of the argument made by Kumbhakar and Hjalmarsson (1995), who argued that the time-varying v_{it} would inappropriately capture *time-varying* inefficiency.] In analyzing the WHO panel data on 191 countries, Greene (2004b) argued that under either interpretation, u_i would be absorbing a large amount of cross-country heterogeneity that would inappropriately be measured as inefficiency. He proposed a "true" fixed-effects model,

$$\ln y_{it} = \alpha_i + \boldsymbol{\beta}^\mathrm{T}\mathbf{x}_{it} + v_{it} - u_{it},$$

$$v_{it} \sim N[0, \sigma_v^2],$$

$$u_{it} \sim |N[0, \sigma^2]|,$$

which is precisely a normal–half-normal (or truncated-normal or exponential) stochastic frontier model with the firm dummy variables included. This model is a very minor extension of existing models that nonetheless has seen little use. Most panel-data sets in this literature are quite small, so the number of dummy variable coefficients is usually manageable—Greene (2003a, 2004a, 2004b, 2005) shows how to fit the model with large numbers of firms, but in point of fact, in common applications where there are only a few dozen firms or so, this is trivial. The formulation does assume that inefficiency varies randomly across time, however, which is the substantive change in the model. As noted above, the "truth" is probably somewhere between these two strong assumptions. Greene (2005) also considers a "true random-effects" model that modifies the parameterized models in the next section, in this case, a random-parameters (random-constant) model

$$\ln y_{it} = (\alpha + w_i) + \boldsymbol{\beta}^T \mathbf{x}_{it} + v_{it} - u_{it},$$

$$v_{it} \sim N[0, \sigma_v^2],$$

$$u_{it} \sim |N[0, \sigma_u^2]|,$$

$$w_i \sim \text{ with mean 0 and finite variance.}$$

[Note this is the complement to Huang's (2004) model, which contained a homogeneous constant term and heterogeneous slope vectors.] This model is fit by MSL methods. Farsi et al. (2003) examined the relative behavior of these four models in a study of Swiss nursing homes and noted a preference for the true random-effects specification.

The preceding sections have noted a variety of applications of Bayesian methods to estimation of stochastic frontier models. As the next section turns specifically to the estimation of inefficiencies, u_{it}, or efficiency, $\exp(-u_{it})$, note the essential component of the Bayesian approach. Koop, Osiewalski, and Steel (1997; KOS) and numerous references cited there and above lay out this method. For the "fixed-effects" approach,[67] the model is simply a linear regression model with firm dummy variables. The Bayesian inference problem is simply that of the linear model with normal disturbances and $K + N$ regressors. The posterior mean estimator of the slopes and constants are the least squares coefficients and

$$\hat{\alpha}_i = \bar{y}_i - \hat{\boldsymbol{\beta}}^T \bar{\mathbf{x}}_i.$$

Estimation of u_i is done in precisely the same fashion as it classical counterpart:

$$\hat{u}_i = (\max_j \hat{\alpha}_j) - \hat{\alpha}_i$$

(Posterior variances and statistical inference are considered in the next section.) Thus, with noninformative priors, the Bayesian estimators are identical to their classical counterparts (of course). For the "random-effects" approach, u_i values are treated as missing data. The technique of data augmentation is used for estimation. The simplest model specification, based on

KOS (see also Tsionas, 2002), would be

$$\ln y_{it} = \alpha + \beta^T x_{it} + v_{it} - u_i,$$

$$p(v_{it}) = N[0, \sigma^2], p(\sigma) = \text{inverted gamma}(s, M)$$

$$\propto \exp\left[-s/(2\sigma^2)\right] (\sigma^2)^{-(M+1)/2},$$

$$p(u_{it}) = (1/\lambda) \exp(-u_i/\lambda), p(\lambda) \text{ to be determined},$$

$$p(\beta) = \text{"flat"} \propto 1, p(\alpha) \propto 1.$$

The Gibbs sampler for this model is quite simple—see KOS for details. The controversial part is the necessary informative prior density for λ. Kim and Schmidt (2000) describe several alternative approaches.

We note that this formulation has the same two shortcomings as its classical counterpart. The "fixed-effects" form cannot accommodate any time-invariant covariates. Neither the fixed- nor the random-effects form has any provision for unmeasured time-invariant heterogeneity. The true fixed- and random-effects models could also be accommodated in this framework. For the true fixed-effects model,

$$\ln y_{it} = \alpha_i + \beta^T x_{it} + v_{it} - u_{it},$$

$$p(v_{it}) = N[0, \sigma^2], p(\sigma) = \text{inverted gamma}(s, M),$$

$$p(u_{it}) = (1/\lambda) \exp(-u_i/\lambda), p(\lambda) \text{ to be determined},$$

$$p(\beta) = \text{"flat"} \propto 1, p(\alpha_i) \propto 1.$$

This is KOS's random-effects form with a complete set of firm-specific constants and inefficiency both firm and time varying. The joint posterior would involve the $N + K$ regression parameters, σ, λ, and all NT missing values u_{it}. With an ample data set, this is essentially the same as KOS's random-effects model—the dimensionality of the parameter space increases (dramatically so), but the computations are the same. One advantage of this formulation is that the difficult inference problem associated with $\hat{u}_i = (\max_j \hat{\alpha}_j) - \hat{\alpha}_i$ is avoided. For the true random-effects model, we would have

$$\ln y_{it} = \alpha_i + \beta^T x_{it} + v_{it} + w_i - u_{it},$$

$$p(v_{it}) = N[0, \sigma^2], p(\sigma) = \text{inverted gamma}(s, M),$$

$$p(w_i) = N[0, \tau^2], p(\tau) = \text{inverted gamma}(r, T),$$

$$p(u_{it}) = (1/\lambda) \exp(-u_{it}/\lambda), p(\lambda) \text{ to be determined},$$

$$p(\beta) = \propto 1, p(\alpha) \propto 1.$$

Note that w_i is time invariant. Once again, this is the same as KOS's random-effects model. Now, the data augmentation problem is over $N + NT$ dimensions for the values of w_i and u_{it}.

2.8 Estimation of Technical Inefficiency

Arguably, the main purpose of the preceding is to lay the groundwork for estimation of inefficiency, that is, u_i or $\mathrm{TE}_i = \exp(-u_i)$. For example, along with an abundance of DEA applications, regulators in many fields have begun to employ efficiency analyses such as those discussed here to compare and analyze regulated firms and to set policies (see, e.g., the discussion in chapter 1). Bauer et al. (1998) sounded some cautions for regulators who might use the results of the analysis described here in their oversight of financial institutions. Among others, regulators are keenly interested in these techniques. This section describes methods of using the estimated models to estimate technical inefficiency in the stochastic frontier setting.

The core model we have used to reach this point is

$$\ln y_{it} = \alpha + \beta^{\mathrm{T}} \mathbf{x}_{it} + v_{it} - u_{it},$$

where we allow for observations across firms and time. The various model forms, including normal–half-normal, truncation, exponential, and gamma models with heterogeneity of various sorts, panel-data and cross-section treatments, and Bayesian and classical frameworks, have all provided platforms on which the main objective of the estimation is pursued: analysis of inefficiency, u_{it}.

The estimation effort in the preceding sections is all prelude to estimation of the inefficiency term in the equation, u_{it}, or some function of it. Note, before continuing, a variety of obstacles to that objective. Foremost is the fundamental result that the inefficiency component of the model, u_{it}, must be observed indirectly. In the model as stated, the data and estimates provide only estimates of $\varepsilon_{it} = v_{it} - u_{it}$. We will have to devise a strategy for disentangling these, if possible. Second, regardless of how we proceed, we must cope not only with a noisy signal (v_{it} with u_{it}), but we must acknowledge estimation error in our estimate—α and β are not known with certainty. For the "fixed-effects" estimators, estimation of technical inefficiency is only relative. Recall in this setting, the model is

$$\ln y_{it} = \alpha_i + \beta^{\mathrm{T}} \mathbf{x}_{it} + v_{it},$$

and the estimator is $u_i = \max(\alpha_j) - \alpha_i$. Finally, adding to the difficult estimation problem is the complication of devising a method of recognizing a degree of uncertainty in the estimate. A point estimate of u_{it} may be insufficient. It is one thing to suggest that inefficiency is on the order of 10%, but quite another to suggest that one's best guess is from 0 to 35% with a mean of 10%, which conveys considerably less information.

This section details some known results about estimation of technical inefficiency. [Kim and Schmidt (2000) is a useful source for more complete presentation.] I consider both fixed-effects and stochastic frontier estimators, and briefly visit Bayesian as well as the classical estimator. The focus of the discussion is the workhorse of this branch of the literature, Jondrow et al.'s (1982) conditional mean estimator.

2.8.1 Estimators of technical inefficiency in the stochastic frontier model

However the parameters of the model are computed, the residual, $y_{it} - \hat{\boldsymbol{\beta}}^T \mathbf{x}_{it}$ estimates ε_{it}, not u_{it}. The standard estimator of u_{it}, is the conditional mean function, $E[u_{it}|\varepsilon_{it}]$. Recall

$$
\begin{aligned}
f(u_{it}|\varepsilon_i) &= \frac{f(u_{it}, \varepsilon_{it})}{f(\varepsilon_{it})} = \frac{f(u_{it})f(\varepsilon_{it}|u_{it})}{f(\varepsilon_{it})} \\
&= \frac{f_u(u_{it})f_v(\varepsilon_{it} + u_{it})}{\int_0^\infty f_u(u_{it})f_v(\varepsilon_{it} + u_{it})du_{it}}.
\end{aligned}
$$

We will use as the estimator the conditional mean from the conditional distribution,

$$
E(u_{it}|\varepsilon_{it}) = \frac{\int_0^\infty u_{it}f_u(u_{it})f_v(\varepsilon_{it} + u_{it})du_{it}}{\int_0^\infty f_u(u_{it})f_v(\varepsilon_{it} + u_{it})du_{it}}.
$$

In several leading cases, this function has a known form.[68] JLMS (Jondrow, Lovell, Materov, and Schmidt, 1982) present the explicit result for the half-normal model,

$$
E[u_{it}|\varepsilon_{it}] = \left[\frac{\sigma\lambda}{1 + \lambda^2}\right]\left[\tilde{\mu}_{it} + \frac{\phi(\tilde{\mu}_{it})}{\Phi(\tilde{\mu}_{it})}\right], \tilde{\mu}_{it} = \frac{-\lambda\varepsilon_{it}}{\sigma},
$$

where $\phi(.)$ and $\Phi(.)$ are the density and CDF of the standard normal distribution. For the truncated-normal model, the result is obtained by replacing $\tilde{\mu}_{it}$ with $\tilde{\mu}_{it} + \mu\sigma_u^2/\sigma^2$. The corresponding expressions for the exponential and gamma models are

$$
E[u_{it}|\varepsilon_{it}] = z_{it} + \sigma_v\frac{\phi(z_{it}/\sigma_v)}{\Phi(z_{it}/\sigma_v)}, z_{it} = \varepsilon_{it} - \sigma_v^2/\sigma_u
$$

and

$$
E[u_{it}|\varepsilon_{it}] = \frac{q(P, \varepsilon_{it})}{q(P - 1, \varepsilon_{it})},
$$

respectively.[69] Note, for the gamma model, that this must be computed by simulation (see section 2.4.6). The estimator of u_{it} in the random-parameters model (Greene, 2005) is also computed by simulation.

Battese and Coelli (1988) suggested the alternative estimator

$$
E[TE_i|\varepsilon_{it}] = E[\exp(-u_{it})|\varepsilon_{it}].
$$

For the truncated-normal model (which includes the half-normal case), this is

$$E[\exp(-u_{it})|\varepsilon_{it}] = \frac{\Phi[(\mu_{it}^*/\sigma_*) - \sigma_*]}{\Phi[(\mu_{it}^*/\sigma_*)]} \exp\left[-\mu_{it}^* + \frac{1}{2}\sigma_*^2\right],$$

where
$$\mu_{it}^* = \tilde{\mu}_{it} + \mu\sigma_u^2/\sigma^2.$$

Recalling the approximation $u_{it} \approx 1 - \text{TE}_{it}$, Battese and Coelli (1988) observed that the difference between the two estimates reflects the inaccuracy of the approximation $1 - u_{it}$ to $\exp(-u_{it})$. For the JLMS results, Battese and Coelli report the alternative estimate based on the preceding as 8.9% as opposed to 9.6% for the conditional mean. The difference is fairly small in this instance, but many studies report technical efficiency values considerably less than the 90% they reported.

Some additional results that are useful for the practitioner are, first, that estimation of cost inefficiency based on the preceding results can be accomplished simply by changing the sign of ε where it appears in any expression. Second, for analysis of a panel with time-invariant effects, Kim and Schmidt (2000) point out that one need only replace ε with the group mean $\bar{\varepsilon}_i$, and σ_v^2 with σ_v^2/T to obtain the appropriate results. Finally, in all these expressions, the heterogeneous or heteroskedastic models may be imposed simply by employing the firm-specific formulations for μ, σ_u, and/or σ_v. In what follows, I limit attention to a simple model and leave the extensions in these directions to be employed by the practitioner as needed.

2.8.2 Characteristics of the estimator

I digress at this point to note some possible misperceptions in the literature (abetted, alas, by the Greene [1993] survey). The JLMS estimator is unbiased as an estimator of u_{it} only in the sense that it has the same expectation that u_{it} does. It does not estimate u_{it} unbiasedly in the sense that in repeated sampling, the mean of a set of observations on $E[u_{it}|\varepsilon_{it}]$ would equal u_{it}. They would not. First, the notion of repeated sampling is itself inconsistent with the definition, since the estimator is conditioned on a specific set of data. This does not mean that it is conditioned on the data for a particular firm—it is conditioned on a specific y_{it} and x_{it}. To see the logic of this objection, consider that there is nothing inconsistent in doing the analysis on a sample that contains two firms that have identical y_{it} and x_{it}, but different u_{it}. Indeed, that is precisely the point of the stochastic frontier model. Thus, the estimator $E[u_{it}|\varepsilon_{it}]$ is an estimator of the mean of the distribution that produces these two observations with this particular y_{it} and x_{it}. There is nothing in its construction that makes us expect the JLMS estimator to be an *unbiased* estimator of either one of the two hypothetical draws on u_{it}. It is an estimator of the mean of this conditional distribution from which both are drawn. The empirical estimator based on the ML or Bayesian parameter estimates is not unbiased for $E[u_{it}|\varepsilon_{it}]$ either, by the way, since it is a nonlinear function of the parameter estimators.

In general, the empirical estimator of $E[u_{it}|\varepsilon_{it}]$ is a consistent estimator, for the usual reasons. Again, it is conditioned on a particular (y_{it}, x_{it}), so the JLMS estimator is not based on a sample of one at all. The estimator, computed using the MLEs or random draws from the posterior, converges to the true conditional mean function. That is,

$$\text{plim}\left\{\left[\frac{\hat{\sigma}\hat{\lambda}}{1+\hat{\lambda}^2}\right]\left(\hat{\mu}_i + \frac{\varphi(\hat{\mu}_{it})}{\Phi(\hat{\mu}_{it})}\right)\Bigg|\hat{\mu}_{it} = \frac{-\left(y_{it} - \hat{\beta}^T x_{it}\right)\hat{\lambda}}{\hat{\sigma}}\right\} = E[u_{it}|\varepsilon_{it}].$$

The JLMS estimator is not a consistent estimator of u_{it} either, again for the reasons noted above. No amount of data can reveal u_{it} perfectly in the stochastic frontier model. It can in a panel-data model in which it is assumed that u_{it} is time invariant, since then, like any common-effects model, a method-of-moments estimator of the "effect" is consistent in T. But, absent this possibility, the JLMS estimator does not converge to u_{it}. (And, note once again, the idea that u_i would remain the same long enough for asymptotics with respect to T to apply would require some difficult economic justification.) On the other hand, it does converge to something: $E[u_{it}|y_{it}, x_{it}, \beta, \ldots]$. But, again, this is not u_{it}; it is the mean of the distribution from which u_{it} is generated.

The foregoing extends to Bayesian estimation, as well, notwithstanding the reflexive assertion that Bayesian inference is "exact" (while classical inference is inexact) that now fashionably precedes every Bayesian analysis. Indeed, a closer look at the Bayesian estimator of u_{it} in the "standard model" is revealing. In the Gibbs sampling MCMC iterations in the standard, normal–exponential model, we have

$$p(u_{it}|\beta, \sigma_v^2, \sigma_u, y_{it}, x_{it}) = \text{truncated at zero } N\left[\beta^T x_{it} - y_{it} - \sigma_v^2/\sigma_u, \sigma_v^2\right]$$

(see Koop et al., 1995, p. 357). The Gibbs sampler draws observations from this distribution in the cycle. At any particular draw, a close look at this distribution shows that its conditional mean is precisely the JLMS estimator for the exponential distribution, for the specific values of the parameters at that cycle. (It would seem pathological if anything else emerged, since the estimator is, ultimately, the posterior mean in the conditional distribution.) Does this estimator "converge" to something? Ultimately, we hope to sample from the marginal posterior $p(u_{it}|x_{it}, y_{it})$, but clearly at every step on the way, this is going to be computed using draws that employ some model parameters. So, where does this end up? With noninformative priors, the Bayesian posterior means of the parameters are going to converge to the same point that the MLEs converge to. (This is merely the well-known result that, with noninformative priors, the likelihood function must eventually dominate the posterior, and the mode of the likelihood converges to the posterior mean as the sample size grows without bound.) The end result of this argument is that the Bayesian estimators of u_{it} are based on the same estimator as the classical estimator. The former estimates $E[u_{it}|\varepsilon_{it}]$ by sampling from $p(u_{it}|y_{it}, \mathbf{x}_{it}, E[\boldsymbol{\beta}|\text{data}], \text{etc.})$, while the latter computes the function directly using the MLEs. Therefore, the Bayesian estimator, like the classical one, is not a consistent estimator of u_{it}. Nor is it unbiased, again, for the same reasons.

Aside from what are likely to be minor numerical differences, the Bayesian and classical estimators differ in two other respects. [See Kim and Schmidt (2000) and the above study of the gamma model for examples.] The sampling variance of the MLE-based estimator will be larger than its Bayesian counterpart, for the usual reasons. However, this raises another important similarity. The difference in the sampling behavior of the statistics speaks to the behavior of the statistic, not to a difference in the quantity being estimated. That is, we have yet to examine $\text{var}[u_{it}|\varepsilon_{it}]$, which is the same regardless of how we choose to estimate it. Kim and Schmidt (2000) have examined this in detail. I briefly note their results below. A remaining aspect of this comparison, however, concerns how "confidence intervals" for u_{it} are constructed. A natural (at least intuitively appealing) strategy is to use the (admittedly flawed) estimator $E[u_{it}|\varepsilon_{it}]$ and bracket it with two lengths of an estimate of $(\text{var}[u_{it}|\varepsilon_{it}])^{1/2}$. This is essentially what the classical estimators discussed below attempt to do. Indeed, it is becoming customary in both settings to report both the point and variance estimators. But, for the Bayesian estimator, this is a demonstrably suboptimal strategy. Since, for example, for the exponential model, it is known exactly that the posterior density is truncated normal, which is asymmetric, an "HPD interval" containing the usual 95% of the distribution will be less than four standard deviations wide. Bayesian estimators typically include pictures of the posterior density for a few observations. Delineation of the HPD intervals in these densities might be a useful addition to the reported results.

2.8.3 Does the distribution matter?

Many authors have pursued the question in the section title, in cross-section and panel-data sets, across a variety of platforms. Most of the received results suggest the encouraging finding that the estimates of inefficiency are reasonably robust to the model specification. Since all results are application specific, however, the question does not have an analytical answer. In order to continue that thread of discussion, we consider a small example, following along the presentation in Kumbhakar and Lovell (2000). The authors report estimates based on the cost frontier estimated in Greene (1990) using the Christensen and Greene (1976) electricity data (described further below). Kumbhakar and Lovell obtained rank correlations for estimates of inefficiencies from the four distributions examined above that ranged from a low of 0.7467 (exponential and gamma) to a high of 0.9803 (half-normal and truncated normal). The results below based on these same data are considerably stronger. I suspect that at least two reasons lie behind this: First, the results below are based on a full translog model, which is probably a more appropriate functional form—Christensen and Greene (1976) found likewise; second, the simulation-based estimator for the gamma model appears to be a considerably better algorithm than the brute force method used in the above studies. We also fit a production function, rather than a cost function.

The first application (there are several others to follow in later sections) is an extension of Christensen and Greene's (1976) estimates of a translog cost function for U.S. electricity generation in 1970. The sample consists of data on 123 American (fossil-fueled) electric-generating companies. The data set contains the variables described in table 2.1. The authors (and Kumbhakar and Lovell, 2000) used these data to fit a translog cost function in a single output (generation) based on three inputs: capital, labor, and fuel. I obtained physical input figures from the cost, factor shares, and input prices and then used these data to fit a translog production function.

Data on physical units are obtained by computing $x_{k,} = \text{cost} \times \text{share}_k / \text{price}_k$. The translog production function is then

$$\ln y = \alpha + \sum_{k=K,L,F} \beta_k \ln x_k + \sum_{k=K,L,F} \sum_{m=K,L,F} \gamma_{km} \ln x_k \ln x_m + v_i - u_i.$$

Estimates of the parameters of the stochastic frontier functions under various assumptions are shown in table 2.2. (The data are not normalized.) The OLS and method-of-moments estimators for the variance parameters are given in the first column. For brevity, standard errors and indicators of significance are omitted, because at this point the purpose is only to compare the coefficient estimates. Based on the differences in the parameter estimates in table 2.2,

Table 2.1
Descriptive Statistics for Christensen and Greene Electricity Data (123 Observations)

Variable	Mean	Standard Deviation	Minimum	Maximum
Cost	48.467	64.0636	0.1304	282.9401
Output	9501.146	12512.82	4.0	72247.0
Capital price	72.895	9.516264	39.127	92.65
Capital share	0.22776	0.060103	0.0981	0.4571
Labor price	7988.560	1252.83	5063.49	10963.9
Labor share	0.14286	0.0563198	0.0527	0.03291
Fuel price	30.80661	7.928241	9.0	50.4516
Fuel share	0.62783	0.088789	0.02435	0.08136
Capital	0.14397	0.19558	0.000179168	1.28401
Labor	0.074440	0.00098891	0.000004341821	0.00490297
Fuel	1.00465	1.28670	0.002641465	6.9757

Table 2.2
Estimated Stochastic Frontier Production Functions

Parameter	OLS	Half-Normal	Truncated	Exponential	Gamma
α	5.381	6.199	7.137	7.136	7.037
βK	1.364	1.272	1.296	1.299	1.335
βL	−1.403	−1.174	−0.910	−0.911	−0.942
βF	1.327	1.224	0.978	0.976	0.964
γKK	0.479	0.469	0.397	0.394	0.346
γLL	−0.204	−0.170	−0.139	−0.139	−0.148
γFF	0.319	0.316	0.301	0.300	0.276
γKL	0.051	0.041	0.065	0.066	0.084
γKF	−0.581	−0.562	−0.502	−0.500	−0.463
γLF	0.204	0.185	0.133	0.132	0.120
λ	0.218	0.956	15.791	0.806	1.071
σ	0.127	0.144	1.481	0.120	0.133
μ	NA	NA	−29.084	NA	NA
P	NA	NA	NA	NA	0.674
σ_u	0.02714	0.0995	1.477	0.0750	0.097
σ_v	0.1244	0.1041	0.0936	0.0931	0.0906
Ln L	85.996	86.292	88.186	88.209	88.849

it does appear that the functional form matters considerably. However, the estimates of $E[u_i|\varepsilon_i]$ tell a quite different story. Figure 2.10 and tables 2.3 and 2.4 show that the JLMS estimates of u_i are almost identical. The agreement between the exponential and truncated-normal model is striking. Note that the correlation matrix shows both raw correlations among the estimates and rank correlations based on the ranks of the inefficiencies. These results are considerably closer than those found by Kumbhakar and Lovell (2000). The parameter estimates for the truncated-normal model do look extreme. In fact, judging from the estimate of σ^2, the truncated-normal model has considerably altered the results. The estimate of σ is 1.481 compared to 0.144 for the half-normal model, a 10-fold increase. The very large estimate of μ suggests, in turn, that the inefficiency estimates should be drastically affected, but this turns out not to be the case. The argument of the function $E[u|\varepsilon]$ can be written as $[a(-\varepsilon) + (1-a)\mu]$, where $a = \sigma_u^2/\sigma^2$. For these data, a is roughly 0.9945, so, in fact, μ hardly figures into the estimated inefficiencies at all. The kernel density estimate in figure 2.11 based on the estimates of u_i for the truncated-normal model is essentially identical to that obtained for the other three sets of estimates. The estimated residuals, e_i, from the truncation model look essentially the same as for the other distributions, as well. We conclude, based on this example, as noted above, that the estimated inefficiencies seem quite robust to the model specification.

We note, finally, a caution about figure 2.11 (and counterparts in many other studies, such as the nearly identical figure 2 in Huang, 2004): The density

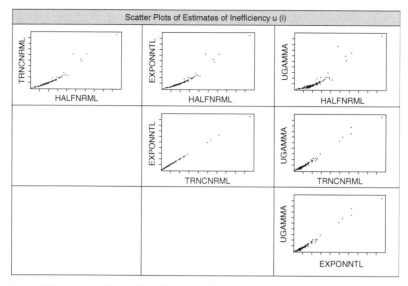

Figure 2.10. Scatter Plots of Inefficiencies from Various Specifications

estimator above shows the distribution of a sample of estimates of $E[u_i|\varepsilon_i]$, not a sample of estimates of u_i. (Huang's figures are correctly identified as such.) The mean of the estimators is correctly suggested by the figure. However, the spread of the distribution of u_i is understated by this figure. In this bivariate distribution, $\text{var}(E[u_i|\varepsilon_i]) = \text{var}[u_i] - E(\text{var}[u_i|\varepsilon_i])$. There

Table 2.3
Descriptive Statistics for Estimates of $E[u_i|\varepsilon_i]$ (123 Observations)

Distribution	Mean	Standard Deviation	Minimum	Maximum
Half-normal	0.07902	0.03246	0.02630	0.27446
Truncated normal	0.07462	0.05936	0.01824	0.47040
Exponential	0.07480	0.06001	0.01810	0.47324
Gamma	0.06530	0.06967	0.01136	0.49552

Table 2.4
Pearson and Spearman Rank Correlations for Estimates of $E[u_i|\varepsilon_i]$[a]

	Half-Normal	Truncated Normal	Exponential	Gamma
Half-normal	1.00000	0.99280	0.99248	0.95540
Truncated normal	0.95291	1.00000	0.99994	0.96864
Exponential	0.95158	0.99998	1.00000	0.96897
Gamma	0.91163	0.98940	0.99019	1.00000

[a] Pearson correlations below diagonal; Spearman rank correlations above diagonal.

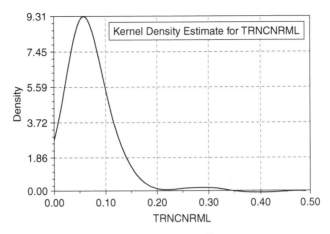

Figure 2.11. Kernel Density Estimator for Mean Efficiency

is no reason to expect the latter term in this expression to be small. We can get a quick suggestion of the extent of this error with a small numerical experiment. We take the normal–half-normal results as the basis. We take the estimates in table 2.2 as if they were the true parameters. Thus, $\sigma_u = 0.0995$, $\sigma_v = 0.1041$, $\sigma = 0.144$, $\lambda = 0.9558$. Derived from these, we have $E[u] = \sigma_u \phi(0)/\Phi(0) = 0.07939$, $\text{var}[u] = \sigma_u^2(\pi - 2)/\pi = 0.003598$, $\text{var}[\varepsilon] = \sigma_v^2 + \text{var}[u] = 0.0144$. Now, using $E[u|\varepsilon] = \text{JLMS}(\varepsilon)$ as given above, a function of ε, we use the delta method to approximate the variance of $E[u|\varepsilon]$. This value based on the results above is 0.008067, so the standard deviation is 0.0284 which is roughly the standard deviation of the data shown in the kernel density estimator above. (This value approximates the 0.03246 in the table.) However, the unconditional standard deviation of u, which is what we actually desire, is the square root of 0.003598, or about 0.05998. The upshot is that, as this example demonstrates, descriptive statistics and kernel density estimators based on the JLMS estimators correctly show the expectation of u but underestimate the variation. Ultimately, a quick indication of the extent is suggested by λ; the smaller is λ, the worse the distortion will be.[70]

2.8.4 Confidence intervals for inefficiency

Horrace and Schmidt (1996, 2000) suggest a useful extension of the JLMS result. Jondrow et al. (1982) have shown that the distribution of $u_i|\varepsilon_i$ is that of an $N[\mu_i^*, \sigma^*]$ random variable, truncated from the left at zero, where $\mu_i^* = -\varepsilon_i \lambda^2/(1 + \lambda^2)$ and $\sigma^* = \sigma\lambda/(1 + \lambda^2)$. This result and standard results for the truncated normal distribution (see, e.g., Greene, 2003a) can be used to obtain the conditional mean and variance of $u_i|\varepsilon_i$. With these in hand, one can construct some of the features of the distribution of $u_i|\varepsilon_i$ or

$E[TE_i|\varepsilon_i] = E[\exp(-u_i)|\varepsilon_i]$. The literature on this subject, including the important contributions of Bera and Sharma (1999) and Kim and Schmidt (2000), refers generally to "confidence intervals" for $u_i|\varepsilon_i$. For reasons that will be clear shortly, we will not use that term—at least not yet, until we have made more precise what we are estimating.

For locating $100(1 - \alpha)\%$ of the conditional distribution of $u_i|\varepsilon_i$, we use the following system of equations:

$$\sigma^2 = \sigma_v^2 + \sigma_u^2$$

$$\lambda = \sigma_u/\sigma_v$$

$$\mu_i^* = -\varepsilon_i\sigma_u^2/\sigma^2 = -\varepsilon_i\lambda^2/(1 + \lambda^2)$$

$$\sigma^* = \sigma_u\sigma_v/\sigma = \sigma\lambda/(1 + \lambda^2)$$

$$LB_i = \mu_i^* + \sigma^*\Phi^{-1}\left[1 - \left(1 - \frac{\alpha}{2}\right)\Phi\left(\mu_i^*/\sigma^*\right)\right]$$

$$UB_i = \mu_i^* + \sigma^*\Phi^{-1}\left[1 - \frac{\alpha}{2}\Phi\left(\mu_i^*/\sigma^*\right)\right]$$

Then, if the elements were the true parameters, the region $[LB_i, UB_i]$ would encompass $100(1 - \alpha)\%$ of the distribution of $u_i|\varepsilon_i$. Although the received papers based on classical methods have labeled this a *confidence interval* for u_i, I emphatically disagree. It is a range that encompasses $100(1 - \alpha)\%$ of the probability in the conditional distribution of $u_i|\varepsilon_i$. The range is based on $E[u_i|\varepsilon_i]$, not u_i itself. This is not a semantic fine point. Once again, note that, in a sample that contains two identical observations in terms of y_i, x_i, they could have quite different u_i, yet this construction produces the same "interval" for both. The interval is "centered" at the estimator of the conditional mean, $E[u_i|\varepsilon_i]$, not the estimator of u_i itself, as a conventional "confidence interval" would be. The distinction is more transparent in a Bayesian context. In drawing the Gibbs sample, the Bayesian estimator is explicitly sampling from, and characterizing the conditional distribution of, $u_i|\varepsilon_i$, not constructing any kind of interval that brackets a particular u_i—that is not possible.[71] For constructing "confidence intervals" for $TE_i|\varepsilon_i$, it is necessary only to compute TE $UB_i = \exp(-LB_i)$ and TE $LB_i = \exp(-UB_i)$.

These limits are conditioned on known values of the parameters, so they ignore any variation in the parameter estimates used to construct them. Thus, we regard this as a minimal width interval.[72]

2.8.5 Fixed-effects estimators

Numerous recent studies have approached efficiency analysis with a fixed-effects model. This frees the analyst from having to layer a distributional assumption on the inefficiency element of the model. The model departs from the usual assumptions,

$$y_{it} = \alpha + \boldsymbol{\beta}^T \mathbf{x}_{it} + v_{it} - u_i.$$

We define $\alpha_i = \alpha - u_i$, then

$$y_{it} = \alpha_i + \boldsymbol{\beta}^T \mathbf{x}_{it} + v_{it},$$

then $u_i = \alpha - \alpha_i$. Estimation proceeds via least squares, Interest in this setting focuses on the relative inefficiencies, which are estimated via

$$\hat{\alpha}_i = \bar{y}_i - \hat{\boldsymbol{\beta}}^T \bar{\mathbf{x}}_i$$

$$= \alpha_i + \bar{v}_i - (\hat{\boldsymbol{\beta}} - \boldsymbol{\beta})^T \bar{\mathbf{x}}_i;$$

$$\hat{\alpha} = \max_j (\hat{\alpha}_j)$$

$$\hat{u}_i = \hat{\alpha} - \hat{\alpha}_i.$$

Technically, efficiency is estimated in the usual fashion via $TE_i = \exp(-u_i)$. By construction, these estimates are relative to the most efficient (at least estimated as such) firm in the sample, whereas the estimates of u_i in the stochastic frontier model are absolute—relative to zero, that is. Horrace and Schmidt (1996, 2000) and Kim and Schmidt (2000) describe methods of computing asymptotic variances and doing statistical inference for these MCB ("multiple comparisons with the best") estimators.

The MCB computations are reasonably complicated. Kim and Schmidt (2000) suggest an alternative bootstrapping procedure (see also Horrace and Richards, 2005). The procedure departs a bit from familiar applications of the bootstrap. The model is fit using the full observed sample as specified above. Bootstrap iterations are constructed by then resampling from the estimated normal distribution of v_{it} and computing the bootstrap sample, $y_{it}^{(b)} = \hat{\alpha}_i + \hat{\boldsymbol{\beta}}^T \mathbf{x}_{it} + \hat{v}_{it}^{(b)}$. The sample of sets of estimates of u_i are used to make inference about the distributions of inefficiency. They also note that these estimators are prone to a downward bias. Kim and Schmidt (2000) propose an adjustment to deal with the bias.

There is a fundamental difference between this approach and the one detailed above for the stochastic frontier model. In this case, the estimator is $\hat{u}_i = \hat{\alpha} - \hat{\alpha}_i$, not $E[u_i|\varepsilon_i]$. There is no "noise" in this estimator. Thus, the "confidence interval" in this setting is for u_i, not for the mean of the distribution that generates u_i. But, it must be borne in mind that the u_i underlying the computations is only relative to the (estimate of the) minimum u_i in the sample.

2.8.6 The Bayesian estimators

Koop et al. (1997) describe procedures for Bayesian estimation of both "fixed-effects" and "random-effects" models for technical inefficiency. We have detailed both of these above. In the fixed-effects approach, they merely add the firm-specific intercepts to the classical normal regression model; the posterior means are the usual within-groups estimators. The posterior distribution is, however, multivariate t, rather than multivariate normal. Since the number of degrees of freedom in any reasonable data set will be sufficiently large to render the posterior essentially normal, it follows that the Bayesian estimators of α_i are the same as the classical ones, as will be the confidence intervals. For the comparisons to the best, $\hat{u}_i = \max_j(\hat{\alpha}_j) - \hat{\alpha}_i$, "exact" inference will be difficult, because the precise distribution will remain complicated even though the marginal posterior is known. However, simple Monte Carlo analysis can be used to reveal characteristics such as the percentiles of the distribution for each $\hat{u}_i$. The authors do note that although a similar analysis can be used for $TE_i = \exp(-\hat{u}_i)$, this estimator will have a built in downward bias. No simple solution is proposed. For the "random-effects," that is, stochastic frontier model, the Gibbs sampler with data augmentation described above is used both for point estimation of $E[u_i|\varepsilon_i]$ and for interval estimation—both mean and variance (and quantiles) of the conditional distribution are computed during the MCMC iterations, so no post estimation processing, other than arranging the sample data, is necessary.

2.8.7 A comparison

Kim and Schmidt (2000) compared the several estimators discussed above in four applications. Consistent with the experiment in section 2.8.3, they found that the different estimators do tell very similar stories. The overall conclusions are that Bayesian and classical estimators of comparable models give comparable results, and by and large, fixed-effects estimators produce greater inefficiency estimates than random effects. Based on the above results and Greene (2004a, 2004b), I would conjecture that at least some of this is due to the role of latent heterogeneity that is not otherwise accommodated in the model. This would be, of course, subject to further investigation.

2.9 Allocative Inefficiency and the Greene Problem

A classic application of the theory of the preceding discussion is the Averch and Johnson (1955) hypothesis that rate-of-return regulation of electric utilities in the United States in the 1950s led to "gold plating" of physical facilities. Utilities were alleged (by economists, at least) to be wasting money on excessively capitalized facilities. This type of inefficiency would clearly fall under what we have labeled "economic inefficiency" and would fall outside the scope of technical inefficiency. *Allocative inefficiency* refers to the extent to which the input choices fail to satisfy the marginal equivalences for cost minimization or profit maximization. The essential element of a complete model would be a cost or profit function with a demand system in which failure to satisfy the optimization conditions for profit maximization or cost minimization, irrespective of what happens on the production side, translates into lower profits or higher costs. The vexing problem, which has come to be known as the "Greene problem" (see the first edition of this survey, Greene, 1993), is the formulation of a complete system in which the demands are derived from the cost function by Shephard's lemma, or a profit function by Hotelling's (1932) lemma, and in which deviations from the optimality conditions in any direction translate to lower profits or higher costs.

Several approaches to measuring allocative inefficiency based on cost functions and demand systems have been suggested. See Greene (1993), for details on some of these early specifications. Lovell and Sickles (1983), for example, analyze a system of output supply and input demand equations. Unfortunately, no method is yet in the mainstream that allows convenient analysis of this type of inefficiency in the context of a fully integrated frontier model. [See Kumbhakar and Tsionas (2004, 2005a) for some significant progress in this direction. Kumbhakar and Lovell (2000, chapter 6) also discuss some of the elements of what would be a complete model.] Some of these models are based on the notion of shadow prices and shadow costs—the nonoptimality of the input choices is taken to reflect "optimality" with respect to the "wrong" or "shadow" prices. Some of the early work in this direction is detailed in the 1993 edition of this survey. A recent study that takes this approach is Atkinson, Fare, and Primont (2003).

Research in this area that would lead to a convenient mainstream methodology remains at an early stage (note the aforementioned), so I leave for the next version of this survey to lay out the details of the emerging research.

2.10 Applications

In order to illustrate the techniques described above, this section presents some limited studies based on several widely traveled data sets. The Christensen and Greene (1976) electricity generation cross-section data have been used by many researchers, particularly those studying Bayesian methods. A small panel-data set from the pre-deregulation U.S. domestic airline industry (admittedly now quite outdated) that was previously used (e.g., in Kumbhakar, 1991a, 1991b) provides a convenient device for illustrating some of the more straightforward fixed- and random-effects techniques.[73] The banking data set used by Kumbhakar and Tsionas (2002) and by Tsionas and Greene (2003) provides a larger, more homogeneous panel that we can use to study some of the more recently proposed panel-data techniques. Finally, WHO (2000) panel-data set on health care attainment has been used by numerous researchers for studying different approaches to efficiency modeling (e.g., Evans et al., 2000a, 2000b; Greene, 2004b; Gravelle et al., 2002a, 2002b; Hollingsworth and Wildman, 2002). For our purposes, these data are a well-focused example of a heterogeneous panel.

As noted in the introduction to this chapter, the body of literature on stochastic frontier estimation is very large and growing rapidly. There have been many methodological innovations in the techniques, some of which have "stuck" and are now in the broad range of tools familiar to practitioners, and others of which have proved less popular. The range of computations in this section is very far from exhaustive. The purpose here is only to illustrate some of the most commonly used methods, not to apply the complete catalogue of the empirical tools that appear in the literature. This section begins with a description of computer programs that are currently used for frontier estimation. Subsequent subsections provide some additional details on the data sets and the series of applications.

As noted above, the applications are based on four well-known data sets. This section provides some additional details on the data. The actual data sets are available from my home page (http://http://www.stern.nyu.edu/~wgreene) in the form of generic *Excel* spreadsheet (.xls) files and *LIMDEP* project (.lpj) files. The *LIMDEP* command sets used to generate the results are also posted so that interested readers can replicate the empirical results.[74] Each of the four applications illustrates some particular aspect or feature of stochastic frontier estimation. We begin with a basic stochastic cost frontier model estimated for U.S. electric power generators.

2.10.1 Computer software

The analysis presented below is carried out using version 8 of *LIMDEP* (Econometric Software, Inc., 2000). Some of the techniques are available in other packages. Of course, least squares and variants thereof can be handled with any econometrics program. Basic panel-data operations for linear regression models (linear fixed- and random-effects estimation) can be carried out with most econometrics packages, such as *SAS* (SAS Institute, Inc., 2005), *TSP* (TSP International, 2005), *RATS* (Estima, 2005), *Stata* (Stata, Inc., 2005), *LIMDEP*, *EViews* (QMS, 2005), or *Gauss* (Aptech Systems, Inc., 2005). Low-level languages such as *Matlab, Gauss, S-plus, Fortran,* and *C++* can be used to carry out most if not all of the computations described here, but contemporary, commercially available software obviates the extensive programming that would be needed for most techniques.[75]

In specific terms, the contemporary software offers essentially the following: *TSP* supports the basic cross-section version of the normal–half-normal stochastic frontier model. The cross-sectional version of the stochastic frontier model is actually quite straightforward and, for example, is easily programmed with *Matlab, Gauss, R,* or *Fortran,* or even with the command languages in *Stata, LIMDEP,* or *TSP.* Coelli's (1996) *Frontier 4.1* also handles a few additional cross-section and panel-data variants of the stochastic frontier model.[76] To date, only two general econometrics programs, Stata and *LIMDEP/NLOGIT*, contain as supported procedures more than the basic stochastic frontier estimator. *Stata* provides estimators for the half- and truncated-normal and exponential models for cross sections (with heteroskedasticity in the distribution of u_i), and panel-data variants for the Battese and Coelli (1992, 1995) specifications. *LIMDEP* and *NLOGIT* include all of these and a variety of additional specifications for heteroskedasticity and heterogeneity for cross sections and numerous additional panel-data specifications for fixed-effects, random-effects, random-parameters, and latent class models.

The preceding are all single-equation methods and estimators. Simultaneous estimation of a cost function and a demand system based on a multivariate normal distribution for all disturbances presents no particular obstacle with modern software (once again, *TSP, LIMDEP, RATS, Gauss*). But, there is no general-purpose program yet available for handling a properly specified system of cost and demand equations that would estimate both technical and allocative inefficiency (i.e., solve the Greene problem). Kumbhakar and Tsionas (2004, 2005a, 2005b, 2005c) used *Gauss* for Bayesian and classical estimation of their technical/allocative inefficiency analysis systems.

There seems to be no general-purpose software for Bayesian estimation of stochastic frontier models. A few authors have offered downloadable code; for example, Griffin and Steel (2004) provide in "zipped" format some *C++* code that users will have to compile on their own computer systems. O'Donnell and Griffiths (2004) offer their *Matlab* code. Other Bayesian estimators appear to have been based on Gauss or Matlab code and the freely distributed *WinBugs* (MRC, 2005) package. As a general proposition, there seem to be a great variety of ad hoc strategies adopted more or less "on the fly" (e.g., Metropolis Hastings algorithms for intractable integrals, experimentation with different priors to see how they affect the results, different strategies for using specified draws from the Markov chain). The lack of a general-purpose program such as *Frontier* seems natural.[77] I did find a reference to "BSFM: a Computer Program for Bayesian Stochastic Frontier Models" by Arickx et al. (1997), but no later reference seems to appear. Since nearly all of the development of Bayesian estimators for stochastic frontier model has occurred after 1997, this is of limited usefulness unless it has been further developed. For better or worse, practitioners who opt for the Bayesian approach to modeling will likely be using their own custom-written computer code.

2.10.2 The stochastic frontier model: electricity generation

The Christensen and Greene (1976) data have been used by many researchers to develop stochastic frontier estimators, both classical and Bayesian. The data are a 1970 cross section of 123 American electric utilities.[78] The main outcome variables are generation (output) in billions of kilowatt hours and total cost (\$million) consisting of total capital, labor, and fuel cost incurred at the generation stage of production. Other variables in the data set are the prices and cost shares for the three inputs. Remaining variables, including logs and squares and products of logs, are derived. The basic data set is described in table 2.1.

2.10.2.1 Cost frontier model specification

The original Christensen and Greene (1976) study was centered on a translog cost function. Many recent applications use the Cobb-Douglas model for the goal function, though the translog function is common, as well. (Variables are provided in the data set for the full translog model for the interested reader.) In order to provide a comparison with numerous other estimates that appear in the recent literature, we will analyze a homothetic, but not homogeneous, version of the cost function, constructed by adding a quadratic term in log output to the Cobb-Douglas cost function:

$$\ln(C/P_F) = \beta_1 + \beta_2 \ln(P_K/P_F) + \beta_3 \ln(P_L/P_F)$$
$$+ \beta_4 \ln y + \beta_5(1/2\ln^2 y) + \varepsilon$$

This is the form used in the Bayesian analyses discussed below and the applications discussed above.

2.10.2.2 Corrected and modified least squares estimators

OLS estimates of the cost function are presented in the first column of table 2.5. Linear homogeneity in prices has been imposed by normalizing cost, P_K and P_L, by the price of fuel, P_F. The functional form conforms to a homothetic but

Table 2.5
Estimated Stochastic Cost Frontiers (Standard Errors in Parentheses)

Variable	Least Squares	Half-Normal	Exponential	Gamma
Constant	−7.294 (0.344)	−7.494 (0.330)	−7.634 (0.327)	−7.652 (0.355)
Ln P_K/P_F	0.0748 (0.0616)	0.0553 (0.0600)	0.0332 (0.0586)	0.0293 (0.0656)
Ln P_L/P_F	0.2608 (0.0681)	0.2606 (0.0655)	0.2701 (0.0632)	0.2727 (0.0678)
Ln y	0.3909 (0.0370)	0.4110 (0.0360)	0.4398 (0.0383)	0.4458 (0.0462)
$1/2 \ln^2 y$	0.0624 (0.00515)	0.0606 (0.00493)	0.0575 (0.00506)	0.0568 (0.00604)
$\lambda = \sigma_u/\sigma_v$	NA	1.373	NA	NA
$\sigma = (\sigma_u^2 + \sigma_v^2)^{1/2}$	0.1439	0.1849	NA	NA
θ	NA	NA	10.263	8.425
P	NA	NA	1.000	0.6702
σ_u (= $1/\theta$ for exp.)	0.1439	0.1494	0.09742	0.09716
σ_v	NA	0.1088	0.1044	0.1060
Log-likelihood	66.4736	66.8650	67.9610	68.1542

not homogeneous production function (see Christensen and Greene, 1976). Economies of scale ES in this model are measured by the scale elasticity:

$$ES = \{1/[\beta_4 + \beta_5 \ln y]\} - 1$$

The estimated coefficients are in line with expectations. The theoretical values for the capital, labor, and fuel coefficients are the factor shares. The sample averages of 0.23, 0.14, and 0.63 are reasonably consistent with the coefficients of 0.07, 0.26, and 0.67. Scale economies range from 100% for the smallest firms to minus 10% for the very largest—the mean is 0.13, which is roughly what was observed in the original study based on a translog model.

The least squares residuals, e_i, provide implied estimates of inefficiencies. Under the assumption of a *deterministic* frontier, we can obtain estimates of u_i by adjusting the intercept of the estimated production or cost function until all residuals (save one that will be zero) have the correct sign. Thus, for the production frontier, $\hat{u}_i = \max_i(e_i) - e_i$ while for a cost frontier, $\hat{u}_i = e_i - \min_i(e_i)$. Under the deterministic frontier interpretation, the mean, $\bar{u}$, and variance, s^2, of the derived estimates of u_i can be used to compute method-of-moments estimators for the underlying parameters. The moment equations and estimates of the various parameters are reported in table 2.6. The sample mean and variance provide conflicting estimates of θ for the exponential distribution. We use a GMM estimator to reconcile them. The sample mean $\bar{u}$ was used as an initial consistent estimator, γ^0, of $E[u] = \gamma = 1/\theta$. [Note that here, $\bar{u} = -\min_i(e_i)$.] The weighting matrix was then $\mathbf{W} = 1/N^2$ times the 2×2 moment matrix for $m_{i1} = (\bar{u}_i - \gamma_0)$ and $m_{i2} = [(\hat{u}_i - \bar{u})^2 - \gamma_0^2]$. We then

Table 2.6
Method of Moments Estimators for Efficiency Distribution for Deterministic Frontier Model Based on OLS Residuals

Estimator	Exponential	Gamma	Half-Normal
	Population Moments		
$E[u_i]$	$1/\theta$	P/θ	$(2/\pi)^{1/2}\sigma_u$
$Var[u_i]$	$1/\theta^2$	P/θ^2	$[(\pi - 2)/\pi]\sigma_u^2$
$E[\exp(-u_i)]$	$[\theta/(1 + \theta)]$	$[\theta/(1 + \theta)]^P$	$2\Phi(-\sigma_u)\exp(\sigma_u^2/2)$
	Implied Estimates[a]		
σ_u	0.3930	0.1415	0.2348
θ	2.544	2.258	NA
P	1.000	1.021	NA
$E[\exp(-u_i)]$	0.7179	0.6424	0.8371
Sample mean efficiency[b]	0.6425	0.6425	0.6425

[a] $\sigma_u = 1/\theta$ for exponential, $\sigma_u = P^{1/2}/\theta$ for gamma.
[b] Sample average of $\exp(-u_i)$.

minimized with respect to γ the quadratic form

$$q = [(\bar{u} - \gamma), (s_u^2 - \gamma^2)]^T \mathbf{W}^{-1}[(\bar{u} - \gamma), (s_u^2 - \gamma^2)].^{79}$$

We use the sample variance to form the estimator for the half-normal frontier. The estimated mean technical efficiency, $E[\exp(-u_i)]$, can be computed using the sample moment or by using the estimated functions of the underlying parameters for the specific model. Overall, the three models produce estimates of mean cost efficiency ranging from 64% to 84%. This is considerably lower than other estimates produced from these data for these models (e.g., see the discussion of the Bayesian estimators below).

Under the assumption of a *stochastic* frontier model, each raw residual e_i is an estimate of

$$y_i - (\alpha - E[u_i]) - \boldsymbol{\beta}^T \mathbf{x}_i = v_i - (u_i - E[u_i]).$$

Moments of the disturbances now involve σ_v^2, as well as the parameters of the distribution of u. The moment equations for the parameters of the distribution of u_i in the models are as follows:

Exponential: $\theta = (-2/m_3)^{1/3}, P = 1.0, \sigma_v = (m_2 - 1/\theta^2)^{1/2}$,
$\quad \alpha = a + 1/\theta$
Gamma: $\theta = -3m_3/(m_4 - 3m_2^2), P = (-1/2)\theta^3 m_3$,
$\quad \sigma_v = (m_2 - P/\theta^2)^{1/2}, \alpha = a + P/\theta$
Half-normal: $\sigma_u = \{m_3/[(2/\pi)^{1/2}(1 - [4/\pi])]\}^{1/3}$,
$\quad \sigma_v = (m_2 - [(\pi - 2)/\pi]\sigma_u^2)^{1/2}, \alpha = a + \sigma_u(2/\pi)^{1/2}$

Counterparts to the results just given for the normal–gamma, normal–exponential, and normal–half-normal models based on the first four central moments (the first is zero) are given in table 2.7. I emphasize that all of these estimators are consistent. They are demonstrably less efficient than the MLEs, but the extent to which this affects the end results remains to be shown. The estimates do seem somewhat erratic—particularly compared to the MLEs given further below. However, the estimates clearly show that allowing for

Table 2.7
Method of Moments Estimates for Stochastic
Frontier Models Based on OLS Residuals

	Exponential	Gamma	Half-Normal
θ	23.62	1.467	NA
P	1.000	0.0002399	NA
σ_u	0.0424	0.0106	0.08864
σ_v	0.1344	0.1406	0.1304
α	−7.256	−7.294	−7.223
$E[\exp(-u)]$	0.9594	0.9999	0.9330

Table 2.8
Descriptive Statistics for JLMS Estimates of $E[u_i|\varepsilon_i]$ Based on
MLEs of Stochastic Frontier Models

Model	Mean	Standard Dev.	Minimum	Maximum
Normal	0.11867	0.060984	0.029822	0.37860
Exponential	0.097438	0.076407	0.022822	0.51387
Gamma	0.081423	0.077979	0.016044	0.52984

the firm-specific stochastic effect v_i considerably reduces the estimated coefficients of inefficiency—the average efficiency rises from about 70% to more than 90%. Clearly, what is estimated to be a considerable amount of random noise in the stochastic frontier model is identified as inefficiency in the deterministic frontier model.

2.10.2.3 MLE of the stochastic cost frontier model

Table 2.5 contains the MLEs of the half-normal, exponential, and gamma stochastic cost frontier models. Though the structural parameters are still fairly variable, the estimated distributions of u_i implied by these estimates are much more stable than the method-of-moments estimators based on OLS. Estimates of the firm-specific inefficiencies, $E[u_i|\varepsilon_i]$, were computed using the JLMS method. Descriptive statistics appear in table 2.8. Figure 2.12 displays the estimated distribution for the efficiency terms from the gamma model.

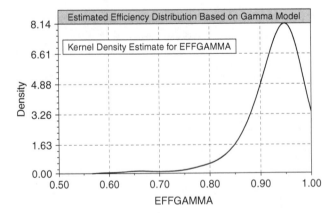

Figure 2.12. Kernel Density Estimate for Estimated Mean Efficiencies Based on Normal–Gamma Stochastic Frontier Model

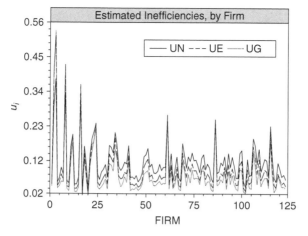

Figure 2.13. Estimates of $E[u_i E_i]$

The three estimates are very similar: The correlations are 0.968 for (normal, exponential), 0.944 for (normal, gamma), and 0.994 for (exponential, gamma). Figure 2.13 shows the three sets of estimates. The observations are sorted by output, so the figure also suggests that the large estimates for u_i mostly correspond to very small outputs, which is to be expected. Finally, figure 2.14 shows the upper and lower confidence bounds for the total efficiency estimates using the Horrace and Schmidt (1996) and Bera and Sharma (1999) procedures described in section 2.8 for the normal–half-normal results.

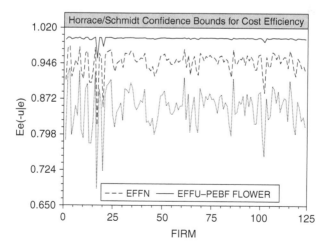

Figure 2.14. Confidence Limits for $E[u_i E_i]$

2.10.2.4 Bayesian and classical estimates of the normal–gamma frontier model

The Aigner-Lovell-Schmidt normal–half-normal model has provided the centerpiece of the stochastic frontier model specification in the large majority of studies. However, the literature contains a long succession of attempts to generalize the model, as discussed above. One of the enduring strands of research, beginning with Greene (1980a) and most recently augmented by Huang (2004), has been the development of the normal–gamma model. The original proposal in Greene (1980) suggested a deterministic frontier model with gamma distributed inefficiencies: $\varepsilon_i = u_i$ and $f(u_i) = [\lambda^P / \Gamma(P)] \exp(-\lambda u_i) u_i^{P-1}$. The deterministic frontier approach in general, and this specification in particular, has since taken a back seat in the evolution of the model. Beckers and Hammond (1987) and Greene (1990) proposed a stochastic frontier form of the gamma model. The normal–gamma model was not successfully implemented in either study. Its title notwithstanding, the complexity of the former seems to have prevented implementation. The latter presented a potentially simpler approach, but numerical difficulties examined closely by van den Broeck at al. (1994) and Ritter and Simar (1997) suggested that the classical MLEs suggested for the model in Greene (1990) were not accurately computed. Bayesian estimators were suggested in van den Broeck et al. (1994, 1995), which demonstrated the feasibility of the Bayesian method. Greene (2003b) has proposed a simulation-based MLE that appears to surmount the numerical problems. Concurrently, Huang's (2004) extension of Tsionas's (2002) and van den Broeck et al.'s (1994) Bayesian estimator brought considerable progress in allowing full variation in the crucial shape parameter in the gamma model.[80]

There have been numerous Bayesian applications of the stochastic frontier model since about 1995 (see, e.g., Koop et al., 1994; Kim and Schmidt, 2000). Owing to the mathematical convenience of the exponential and gamma densities, most of these have relied on the normal–exponential and normal–gamma specification. The theoretical development of the Bayesian approach has often applied the normal–gamma model, and in this strand of the literature, the Christensen and Greene (1976) data used here have provided a convenient common ground. First in the line are van den Broeck et al. (1994) and Koop et al. (1995), who fit the same quadratic model used above. The primary innovation in their study was to propose a data augmentation algorithm that produced posterior estimates of the inefficiency terms, u_i, along with the technology parameters.[81] As has been observed elsewhere (see Koop et al., 1997), estimation of the counterpart of a fixed-effects model in the Bayesian paradigm requires an informative prior. In their case, they equivalently assumed that u_i were drawn from a gamma prior with prior median efficiency $r^* = 0.875$. As shown below, their findings were actually quite similar to those presented here.[82]

Following on van den Broeck et al.'s (1994) model, which assumes the Erlang (integer P) form of the normal–gamma model, Tsionas (2002) shows how the assumptions can be relaxed and the algorithm updated. Unlike Koop et al. (1995), who used importance sampling, Tsionas used a Gibbs sampler to draw observations from the posterior. In addition, his proposed method produces a hierarchical Bayesian estimator (ostensibly suggested for panel data) that yields firm-specific estimates for the technology parameters in the cost function as well as the firm-specific inefficiencies, u_i. It is useful to lay out Tsionas's specification in some detail. The cost model is

$$y_{it} = \alpha + \beta_i^T x_{it} + v_{it} + u_{it},$$

where, initially, $f(u_{it}) = \theta \exp(-\theta u_{it})$. Later, this is extended to the two-parameter gamma model given above. Independent priors for the model are specified: $\alpha, \beta_i \sim N[(a, b), \Omega]$, $i = 1, \dots, N$; $(a, b) \sim N[(0, 0), W]$; $\Omega \sim$ inverted Wishart; $\theta \sim$ two-parameter gamma; $\sigma_v \sim$ inverted gamma. Under his specification, u_{it} values are draws from an exponential population with parameter θ, where the prior mean for θ is, in turn, $q = -\ln r^*$. [Lengthy details on this specification are given in Tsionas's (2002) paper.] The Gibbs sampler for Tsionas's method for exponentially distributed u_{it} ($P = 1$) is as follows:

1. Draw β_i from a conditional normal distribution.
2. Draw σ from a conditional gamma distribution.
3. Draw (a, b) from a conditional normal distribution.
4. Draw Ω from a conditional inverted Wishart distribution.
5. Draw u_{it} from a conditional truncated normal distribution.
6. Draw θ from a conditional gamma distribution.

The samples from the posterior distributions are obtained by cycling through these steps. The slightly more general cases of $P = 2$ and $P = 3$ are also considered. These cases greatly complicate step 5—direct sampling of random draws from the conditional distribution of u_{it} becomes impossible when P is not equal to one. Tsionas proposes a separate algorithm developed in a separate paper (Tsionas, 2000a), whereas Huang (2004) suggests a Metropolis Hastings strategy in his study.

Huang (2004) notes incorrectly that Tsionas allows noninteger values of P in his implementation. Huang, in contrast, does and specifies continuous gamma priors for both θ and P in his model. He goes on to discuss sampling from the posterior distribution of u_{it} under the fully general specification. Thus, arguably, Huang brings full generality to the normal–gamma model. In comparison to Greene's approach, the extension would be the hierarchical Bayes extension of the model to allow separate coefficient vectors *even in a cross section*. Whether this is actually a feasible extension remains for ongoing research to establish. It is worth noting that the Tsionas and Huang methods have established a method of obtaining posterior means and variances (indeed, entire distributions) for 761 parameters, $[(\alpha_i, \boldsymbol{\beta}_i, u_i), i = 1, \ldots, 123]a, b, \boldsymbol{\Omega}, P,$ θ, σ_u) based on a sample that contained 615 values in total on cost, log output and its square, and the logs of the two price ratios.

Table 2.9 displays the sets of estimates of the gamma frontier models obtained by classical MLE methods and the preferred set of Bayesian estimates (posterior means) from each of the three studies. The structural parameter estimates are somewhat similar.[83] The striking aspect of the results is in the estimated inefficiencies. van den Broeck et al.'s estimates are quite close to those here. Tsionas reports an implausible set of estimates that imply that every firm is at least 99.9% efficient. Huang's results for the heterogeneous translog model (firm-specific parameters) are essentially the same as Tsionas's, but those for his homogeneous parameters model are almost identical to those presented here. Indeed, figure 2 in Huang (2004, p. 286) is indistinguishable from figure 2.12, even including the slight second mode around abscissa of 0.67. Moreover, figure 1 in van den Broeck et al. (1994, p. 290) is likewise strikingly similar to figure 2.12 and Huang's figure 2.

With Tsionas (2002), Huang (2004), and Greene (2003b), it does seem that the technological problem of the normal–gamma model has largely been solved. The extension to "random" parameters yielded by the former two in cross-section data does seem overly optimistic. The random-parameters form has been extended to classical "mixed-model" estimation in, for example, Train (2003) and Greene (2003a, 2004b), with attendant "estimators" of the conditional means of individual specific parameter vectors. In both the classical and Bayesian frameworks, it seems at this juncture an interesting to pursue the question of what the implications are of extracting more posterior estimates of parameter distributions than there are numbers in the sample. In

Table 2.9
Estimates of the Normal–Gamma Stochastic Frontier Model (Coefficients or Posterior Means Only)

	Greene		van den Broeck	Tsionas	Huang	
	Exponential	Gamma[a]	Gamma	Gamma	Random	Fixed
Constant	−7.6336	−7.652	−7.479	−7.416	−7.217	−7.4784
$\text{Ln}y$	0.4398	0.4458	0.4276	0.445	0.3668	0.4447
$\text{Ln}^2 y$	0.02875	0.02839	0.0295	0.023	0.0335	0.0284
$\text{Ln}P_L/P_F$	0.2701	0.2727	0.2492	0.247	0.2517	0.2346
$\text{Ln}P_K/P_F$	0.03319	0.02933	0.0449	0.043	0.0695	0.0590
θ	10.263	8.425	11.273	75.12	77.4337	9.9025
P	1.0000	0.6702	1.0000	1.000	0.9063	0.9575
Σ_v	0.1044	0.1060	0.1136	0.0781	0.0374	0.1114
$\text{Ln } L$	67.961	68.154	NA	NA	NA	NA
Mean effect	0.9072	0.9276	0.91	0.999	0.9891	0.9103

[a]Simulations for maximum simulated likelihood are computed using 200 Halton draws.

the end, however, as others have also observed, there appears to be notably little difference between the Bayesian posterior mean and classical MLEs of the stochastic frontier model.

2.10.2.5 Duality between production and cost functions

Christensen and Greene (1976) studied, among other aspects of costs, the appropriate form of the production and cost function. Their specification search ultimately led to a translog cost function that was dual to a nonhomothetic production function. With linear homogeneity in the factor prices imposed, the full cost specification is

$$\ln\left(\frac{C}{PF}\right) = \alpha + \beta_K \ln\left(\frac{PK}{PF}\right) + \beta_L \ln\left(\frac{PL}{PF}\right) + \delta_y \ln y + \delta_{yy}\frac{1}{2}\ln^2 y$$

$$+ \gamma_{KK}\frac{1}{2}\ln^2\left(\frac{PK}{PF}\right) + \gamma_{LL}\frac{1}{2}\ln^2\left(\frac{PL}{PF}\right) + \gamma_{KL}\ln\left(\frac{PK}{PF}\right)\ln\left(\frac{PL}{PF}\right)$$

$$+ \theta_{yK}\ln y \ln\left(\frac{PK}{PF}\right) + \theta_{yL}\ln y \ln\left(\frac{PL}{PF}\right) + v + u.$$

Likelihood ratio tests firmly favored the full translog model over the restricted, homothetic technology that results if the final two terms are omitted. In translating this estimation exercise to the present stochastic frontier exercise, we find that in the nonhomothetic version, the estimate of λ (and with it, any evidence of inefficiency) virtually disappears. With a homothetic function, the estimates of σ_u and σ_v are 0.16826 and 0.09831; thus, u accounts for about 52% of the total variance of $[(\pi - 2)/\pi]\sigma_u^2 + \sigma_v^2$. With the full nonhomothetic form, these fall to 0.0000 and 0.13742, respectively. That is, the nonhomotheticity terms have picked up some of the idiosyncratic variation (in v) and all of the variation in u. Since the previous frontier analyses of these data have all used restricted versions of the cost function, this raises some interesting questions as to what our predecessors have actually found. It does seem reasonable to guess that estimates of inefficiency all equal to zero are themselves implausible as well, so some intriguing possibilities remain for future researchers to sort out.

With the preceding as a backdrop, we recompute the cost function using the homothetic form ($\theta_{yK} = \theta_{yL} = 0$) and recompute the JLMS estimators of cost inefficiency, $E[u|\varepsilon]$. We also compute a translog production frontier, without restricting it to homogeneity. The full unrestricted translog frontier would be

$$\ln y = \alpha_0 + \sum_{j=K,L,F} \beta_j \ln X_j + \frac{1}{2}\sum_{j=K,L,F}\sum_{m=K,L,F} \gamma_{jm} \ln X_j \ln X_m + v - u.$$

(Estimates of the frontier parameters are omitted in the interest of brevity.) We do impose the symmetry restrictions on the second-order terms. (I did not check or impose the second-order monotonicity or quasiconcavity conditions.) As noted above, the relationship between the "inefficiency" in production and that from the cost function is confounded by at least two factors. In the absence of allocative inefficiency, if there are economies of scale, then u_i in the cost function would equal $1/r$ times its counterpart on the production side where r is the degree of homogeneity. The second source of ambiguity is the allocative inefficiency that will enter the cost inefficiency but not the technical (production) inefficiency. Acknowledging this possibility, we compute the JLMS estimates of u_i from both functions. Using the production function parameters, we then compute the implied (local) scale elasticity,

$$ ES = \sum_{j=K,L,F} \frac{\partial \ln y}{\partial \ln X_j} = \sum_{j=K,L,F} \left[\beta_j + \frac{1}{2} \sum_{m=K,L,F} \gamma_{jm} \ln X_m \right]. $$

We then divide each estimated inefficiency from the cost function by this elasticity computed from the production frontier. Figure 2.15 displays the scatter plot of these two sets of inefficiency estimates, which, with the expected variation, are clearly indicating the same "story" about inefficiency in these data. (The correlation between the two sets of estimates is 0.579.) Note that the mean inefficiency on the cost side of 0.124 (oddly close to the standard Bayesian prior value of 0.125) is noticeably larger than its counterpart on the production side of 0.080. It is tempting to attribute the difference to allocative inefficiency, which would not appear on the production side, as well as to a small distortion that results from the effect of economies of scale.

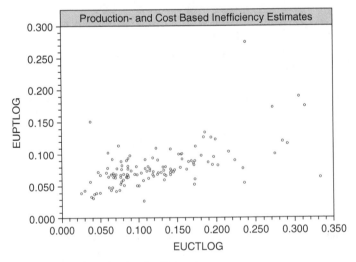

Figure 2.15. Cost and Production Inefficiencies

2.10.3 Time-invariant and time-varying inefficiency: Airlines panel data

These data are from the pre-deregulation days of the U.S. domestic airline industry. The data are an extension of Caves et al. (1980) and Trethaway and Windle (1983). The original raw data set is a balanced panel of 25 firms observed over 15 years (1970–1984). After removing observations because of strikes, mergers, and missing values, the panel becomes an unbalanced one with a total of 256 observations on 25 firms. In a few cases, the time series contain gaps. Some of the models discussed above, notably Battese and Coelli (1992, 1995) and Cornwell et al. (1990), involve functions of time, t, which would have to be computed carefully to ensure the correct treatment of "time"; the gaps must be accounted for in the computations. Also, for firms that are not observed in the first year of the overall data set, when we consider functions of "time" with respect to a baseline, in keeping with the spirit of the stochastic frontier model, this baseline will be for the specific firm, not for the overall sample window. The unbalanced panel has 256 observations with $T_i = 4, 7$, 11, and 13 (one firm each), 12 (two firms) 9, 10, and 14 (three firms), 2 (four firms), and 15 (six firms). We will use these data to estimate frontier models with panel data and time-varying and time-invariant inefficiency.

Production and cost frontiers are fit for a five-input Cobb-Douglas production function: The inputs are labor, fuel, flight equipment, materials, and ground property. Labor is an index of 15 types of employees. Fuel is an index based on total consumption. The remaining variables are types of capital. It might be preferable to aggregate these into a single index, but for present purposes, little would be gained. Output aggregates four types of service: regular passenger service, charter service, mail, and other freight. Costs are also conditioned on two control variables: (log) average stage length, which may capture an economy of scale not reflected directly in the output variable, and load factor, which partly reflects the capital utilization rate. We also condition on the number of points served so as to attempt to capture network effects on costs. The data are described in table 2.10.

2.10.3.1 Cobb-Douglas production frontiers

We first fit a Cobb-Douglas production function. This estimation illustrates a common problem that arises in fitting stochastic frontier models. The least squares residuals are positively skewed—the theory predicts they will be negatively skewed. We are thus unable to compute the usual first-round, method-of-moments estimators of λ and σ to begin the iterations. This finding does not prevent computation of the stochastic frontier model. However, it does necessitate some other strategy for starting the iterations. To force the issue, we simply reverse the sign of the third moment of the OLS residuals and proceed. Consistent with Waldman (1982), however, we then find that the log-likelihood function for the estimated model differs only trivially

Table 2.10
Airlines Data

Variable	Mean	Standard Deviation	Description
FIRM	11.8398438	7.09001883	Firm, $i = 1, \ldots, 25$
OUTPUT	0.628784239	0.591862922	Output, index
COST	1172861.09	1197945.05	Total cost
MTL	0.751572192	0.642973957	Material, quantity
FUEL	0.583878603	0.503828645	Fuel, quantity
EQPT	0.651682905	0.567659248	Equipment, quantity
LABOR	0.595048662	0.508245612	Labor, quantity
PROP	0.656212972	0.692635345	Property, quantity
PM	491733.758	165628.591	Materials price
PF	427637.977	316179.137	Fuel price
PE	266391.048	110114.994	Equipment price
PL	669768.628	269367.140	Labor price
PP	40699.8592	19405.2501	Property price
LOADFCTR	0.526460328	0.120249828	Load factor
STAGE	492.642179	308.399978	Average stage length
POINTS	70.1328125	29.6541823	Number of points served

from the log-likelihood for a linear regression model with no one-sided error term. However, the estimates of σ_u, σ_v, λ, and σ are quite reasonable, as are the remaining parameters and the estimated inefficiencies; indeed, the estimate of λ is statistically significant, suggesting that there is, indeed, evidence of technical inefficiency in the data.[84] The conclusion to be drawn is that, for this data set, and more generally, when the OLS residuals are positively skewed (negatively for a cost frontier), then there is a second maximizer of the log-likelihood, OLS, that may be superior to the stochastic frontier. For our data, the two modes produce roughly equal log-likelihood values. For purposes of the analysis, the finding does suggest that one might want to take a critical look at the model specification and its consistency with the data before proceeding.

The least squares and MLEs of the parameters are given in table 2.11. The Pitt and Lee (1981) random-effects model is also fitted, which assumes that technical inefficiency is fixed through time and still half-normally distributed. The parameter estimates appear in table 2.11. Figure 2.16 shows the relationship between the two sets of estimates of $E[u_i|\varepsilon_i]$. Unfortunately, they are far from consistent. Note the widely different estimates of σ_u: 0.07 in the pooled model and 0.27 in the Pitt and Lee (1981) model. The time-invariant estimates vary widely across firms and are, in general, far larger. The time-varying values actually display relatively little within firm variation—there does not appear to be very much time variation in inefficiency suggested by these results. We might surmise that the time-invariant estimates are actually

Table 2.11
Estimated Cobb-Douglas Production Frontiers (Standard Errors in Parentheses)

Variable	Least Squares	Pooled Frontier	Random Effects
Constant	−1.1124 (0.0102)	−1.0584 (0.0233)	−0.8801 (0.0302)
Ln fuel	0.3828 (0.0712)	0.3835 (0.0704)	0.2110 (0.0951)
Ln materials	0.7192 (0.0773)	0.7167 (0.0765)	0.8170 (0.0666)
Ln equipment	0.2192 (0.0739)	0.2196 (0.0730)	0.3602 (0.120)
Ln labor	−0.4101 (0.0645)	−0.4114 (0.0638)	−0.3166 (0.0770)
Ln property	0.1880 (0.0298)	0.1897 (0.0296)	0.1131 (0.0224)
λ	0.0	0.43515	2.2975
σ	0.1624	0.16933	0.29003
σ_u	0.0	0.06757	0.26593
σ_v	0.1624	0.15527	0.11575
Log-likelihood	105.0588	105.0617	155.3240

dominated by heterogeneity not related to inefficiency. In sum, these results are so inconsistent that, if anything, they suggest a serious specification problem with at least one of the two models. Let us turn to the cost specification to investigate.

2.10.3.2 Stochastic cost frontiers

Estimates of the Cobb-Douglas stochastic frontier cost function are given in table 2.12, with the least squares results for comparison. Cost and the

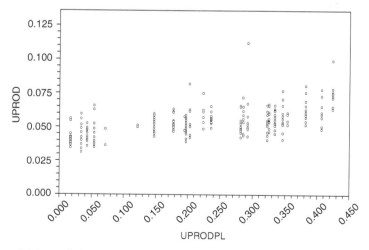

Figure 2.16. Pooled Time-Varying Versus Time-Invariant Inefficiencies

Table 2.12
Estimated Stochastic Cost Frontier Models (Standard Errors in Parentheses)

Variable	Least Squares	Half-Normal	Truncated Normal
Constant	−13.610 (0.0865)	−13.670 (0.0848)	−13.782 (0.145)
$\text{Ln}(P_M/P_P)$	1.953 (0.0754)	1.9598 (0.0726)	1.9556 (0.0666)
$\text{Ln}(P_F/P_P)$	−0.6562 (0.0141)	−0.6601 (0.0139)	−0.6590 (0.01516)
$\text{Ln}(P_L/P_P)$	−0.06088 (0.0533)	−0.07540 (0.0532)	−0.08667 (0.0577)
$\text{Ln}(P_E/P_P)$	−0.1935 (0.0690)	−0.1840 (0.0663)	−0.1652 (0.0546)
Ln y	0.01054 (0.0133)	0.01063 (0.0129)	0.007384 (0.0145)
$1/2 \ln^2 y$	0.009166 (0.00435)	0.008714 (0.00427)	0.007919 (0.00444)
Constant	NA	NA	−0.1372 (0.777)
Load factor	−0.4712 (0.103)	−0.4265 (0.0992)	0.5603 (0.318)
Ln stage length	0.03828 (0.00889)	0.03495 (0.00858)	−0.04397 (0.0437)
Points	0.00007144 (0.000252)	0.00001464 (0.000250)	−0.0002034 (0.000285)
λ	0.0	0.88157	1.05196
σ	0.08915	0.10285	0.09214
σ_u	0.0	0.06801	0.06678
σ_v	0.08915	0.07715	0.06348
Log-likelihood	260.7117	261.1061	261.3801

remaining prices are normalized on the property price. Additional "shift factors" that appear in the cost equation are load factor, the log of stage length, and the number of points served. These three variables affect costs the way we might expect. Note at the outset that three of the price coefficients have the wrong sign, so the model is suspect from this point on. But let us continue for the sake of the example. We compute the JLMS estimates of $E[u_i|\varepsilon_i]$ from the MLEs of the estimated cost frontier. They are essentially uncorrelated ($r = 0.04$) with their counterparts from the production frontier. As noted above, this adds to the impression that there is something amiss with the specification of the model—we suspect the production model. The kernel density estimator for $\exp(-u_i)$ based on the JLMS estimates in figure 2.17 appears reasonable, and at least numerically consistent with the production model. However, like other descriptive statistics, it does mask the very large differences between the individual production and cost estimates. Table 2.12 also presents results for the normal–truncated-normal model in which

$$u_i = |U_i|, E[U_i] = \mu_0 + \mu_1(\text{load factor})_i + \mu_2 \ln(\text{stage length})_i$$
$$+ \mu_3 \text{points}_i$$

That is, these three exogenous influences are now assumed to shift the distribution of inefficiency rather than the cost function itself. Based on the estimates and statistical significance, this model change does not appear to improve it. Surprisingly, the estimated inefficiencies are almost the same.

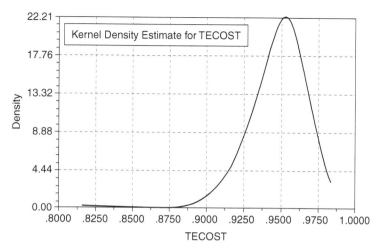

Figure 2.17. Kernel Estimator for $E[\exp(-u_i)]$

Table 2.13
Estimated Stochastic Cost Frontier Models (Standard Errors in Parentheses)

| Variable | Time-Invariant Inefficiency | | Time-Varying Inefficiency | |
	Fixed Effect	Random Effect	Fixed Effect	Random Effect[a]
Constant	NA	−13.548 (0.373)	NA	−13.540 (0.0552)
$\text{Ln}(P_M/P_P)$	1.7741 (0.0869)	2.0037 (0.0763)	1.8970 (0.101)	2.0092 (0.0457)
$\text{Ln}(P_F/P_P)$	−0.5347 (0.0180)	−0.6440 (0.0260)	−0.7115 (0.020)	−0.6417 (0.00962)
$\text{Ln}(P_L/P_P)$	−0.01503 (0.0525)	−0.07291 (0.0952)	−0.04252 (0.0625)	−0.07231 (0.0377)
$\text{Ln}(P_E/P_P)$	−0.2225 (0.0753)	−0.2643 (0.0632)	−0.05125 (0.0898)	−0.2711 (0.0383)
$\text{Ln } y$	−0.1990 (0.0473)	0.01781 (0.0360)	0.03840 (0.0404)	0.01580 (0.00932)
$1/2 \ln^2 y$	−0.009713 (0.00824)	0.0119 (0.00833)	0.008306 (00872)	0.01221 (0.00307)
Load factor	−0.4918 (0.183)	−0.4482 (0.172)	−0.4148 (0.180)	−0.4576 (0.0500)
Ln Stage length	−0.001397 (0.0114)	0.03326 (0.0378)	0.05870 (0.0133)	0.032823 (0.00443)
Points	−0.0006279 (0.0005)	−0.000134 (0.000743)	0.000631 (0.0006)	−0.000119 (0.0002)
λ	0.0	0.58809	0.5243	0.50148
σ	0.07526	0.09668	0.10475	0.08900
σ_u	0.0	0.04901	0.04865	0.03990
σ_v	0.07526	0.08334	0.09278	0.07956
Log-likelihood	317.2061	263.2849	247.2508	262.4393

[a] Estimated standard deviation of w is 0.03306.

2.10.3.3 Panel-data models for costs

Table 2.13 presents estimates of the fixed-effects linear regression and Pitt and Lee random-effects models. The behavior of the latter was discussed above. Figure 2.18 shows the results for the Schmidt and Sickles (1984) calculations

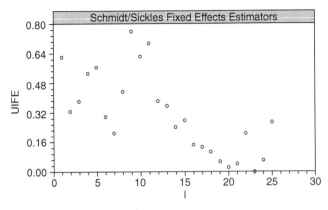

Figure 2.18. Estimated $E[u_i E_i]$ from Fixed-Effects Model

based on the fixed effects. Note, again, that the estimates of u_i are vastly larger for this estimator than for the pooled stochastic frontier cost or production model. We also fit a "true" fixed-effects model with these data, with some surprising results. The model is

$$\ln(C/P_P)_{it} = \sum_k \beta_k \ln(P_k/P_P) + \beta_y \ln y_{it} + \beta_{yy}\left(\frac{1}{2}\ln^2 y_{it}\right) + \gamma_1 (\text{load factor})_{it}$$

$$+ \gamma_2 \ln(\text{stage})_{it} + \gamma_3 \text{points}_{it} + \sum_i \alpha_i d_{it} + v_{it} + u_{it},$$

that is, a stochastic cost frontier model with half-normal inefficiency and with the firm dummy variables. The log-likelihood function has two distinct modes. At one, the values of the parameters are quite reasonable, and the value of the log-likelihood is 247.2508, *compared to 261.1061 for the linear model without the firm dummy variables.* A second maximum of the log-likelihood occurs at the least squares dummy variable estimator—the estimated value of λ is 0.00004226—where the log-likelihood value is 317.2061. We conclude that this model is saturated. While the model that assumes that there is no unobserved heterogeneity and that inefficiency is time invariant (the Pitt and Lee model) creates extreme and apparently distorted values for the inefficiency, this model that assumes that all time-invariant effects are heterogeneity and that inefficiency varies haphazardly over time appears to be overspecified. Finally, to continue this line of inquiry, we fit the "true random-effects model,"

$$\ln(C/P_P)_{it} = (\alpha + w_i) + \sum_k \beta_k \ln(P_k/P_P) + \beta_y \ln y_{it} + \beta_{yy}\left(\frac{1}{2}\ln^2 y_{it}\right)$$

$$+ \gamma_1 (\text{load factor})_{it} + \gamma_2 \ln(\text{stage})_{it} + \gamma_3 \text{points}_{it} + v_{it} + u_{it},$$

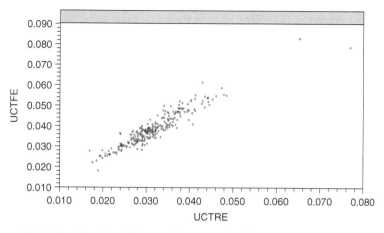

Figure 2.19. True Random-Effects and True Fixed-Effects Estimators

where w_i picks up time-invariant heterogeneity assumed to be uncorrelated with everything else in the model, and $v_{it} + u_{it}$ are the familiar stochastic frontier specification. This model is fit by MSL, using 100 Halton draws for the simulations. Note that this model is an extension of the pooled stochastic frontier model, not the Pitt and Lee model. Figure 2.19 plots the estimated inefficiencies from the two true effects models. The striking agreement is consistent with results found in other studies. In general (see Kim and Schmidt, 2000, for commentary), the differences from one specification to another do not usually hang so much on whether one uses a fixed- or random-effects approach as they do on other aspects of the specification. On the other hand, note also the above findings that distributional assumptions do not appear to be a crucial determinant, either. Nor, it turns out, does the difference between Bayesian and classical treatments often amount to very much. One conclusion that does appear to stand out from the results here, and in Greene (2004a, 2004b, 2005), is that the assumption of time invariance in inefficiency does bring very large effects compared to a model in which inefficiency varies through time.

A final note, the log-likelihood for the true random-effects model is 262.4393, compared to 261.1061 for the pooled model. Chi squared is only 2.666, so we would not reject the hypothesis of the pooled model. The evidence for a panel-data treatment with these data is something less than compelling. As a final indication, we use the Breusch and Pagan (1980) Lagrange multiplier statistic from the simple linear model. The value is only 1.48. As a chi squared with one degree of freedom, this reinforces the above conclusion: For these data, a pooled model is preferable to any panel-data treatment.

2.10.4 Random- and fixed-effects models: data on U.S. banks

Data for this study are taken from the Commercial Bank Holding Company Database maintained by the Chicago Federal Reserve Bank.[85] Data are derived from the Report of Condition and Income (Call Report) for all U.S. commercial banks that report to the Federal Reserve Banks and the Federal Deposit Insurance Corporation. A random sample of 500 banks from a total of more than 5,000 was used. This is a balanced panel of five observations (1996–2000) on each of 500 banks. Observations consist of total costs, C_{it}, five outputs, y_{mit}, and the unit prices, denoted w_{kit}, of five inputs, x_{kit}. The measured variables used to construct the data set used in the analysis are described in table 2.14 (descriptive statistics are omitted for lack of meaning and interest).

The transformed variables contained in the maintained data set and used in the study to follow (the names in the data file) are given in table 2.15. The banking data are used typically to fit multiple-output translog models (see, e.g., Kumbhakar and Tsionas, 2004, 2005a, 2005b). In the interest of maintaining

Table 2.14
Data Used in Cost Frontier Analysis of Banking

Variable	Description
C_{it}	Total cost of transformation of financial and physical resources into loans and investments = the sum of the five cost items described below
y_{1it}	Installment loans to individuals for personal and household expenses
y_{2it}	Real estate loans
y_{3it}	Business loans
y_{4it}	Federal funds sold and securities purchased under agreements to resell
y_{5it}	Other assets
w_{1it}	Price of labor, average wage per employee
w_{2it}	Price of capital = expenses on premises and fixed assets divided by the dollar value of premises and fixed assets
w_{3it}	Price of purchased funds = interest expense on money market deposits plus expense of federal funds purchased and securities sold under agreements to repurchase plus interest expense on demand notes issued by the U.S. Treasury divided by the dollar value of purchased funds
w_{4it}	Price of interest-bearing deposits in total transaction accounts = interest expense on interest-bearing categories of total transaction accounts
w_{5it}	Price of interest-bearing deposits in total nontransaction accounts = interest expense on total deposits minus interest expense on money market deposit accounts divided by the dollar value of interest-bearing deposits in total nontransaction accounts
t	Trend variable; $t = 1, 2, 3, 4, 5$ for years 1996, 1997, 1998, 1999, 2000

Table 2.15
Variables Used in Cost Frontier Analysis of Banking

Variable	Description
C	Log(Cost/w_5)
$y_1, \ldots, y_5$	Logs of outputs
y	Log of sum of all five outputs
$w_1, \ldots, w_4$	Log $(w_1/w_5), \ldots, \log(w_4/w_5)$
$y_{11}, y_{12}, \ldots$	1/2 Squares and cross-products of log output variables
$w_{11}, w_{12}, \ldots$	1/2 Squares and cross-products of log price ratio variables
$w_1 y_1, \ldots, w_4 y_5$	Cross products of log price ratios times log outputs
t_2	$1/2t^2$
$tw_1, \ldots, tw_4$	Cross products of t with log price ratios
$ty_1, \ldots, ty_5$	Cross products of t with log outputs

a simple example for our application, I have combined the outputs into a single scale variable, which is the simple sum of the five outputs. Whether the aggregation would be appropriate given the technology is debatable—it would be testable—but in the interest of keeping the presentation simple, we will maintain the hypothesis. In addition, though these data are detailed and "clean enough" to enable estimation of translog models, we will, again in the interest of simplicity, restrict attention to variants of the (more or less standard) Cobb-Douglas cost function with the additional squared term in log output.

In this application, we will examine some additional panel-data estimators, including fixed-effects, random-effects, random-parameters, and the Battese and Coelli (1992, 1995) model of systematic time variation in inefficiency.

2.10.4.1 Estimating inefficiency and unobserved heterogeneity

The observations in this data set are relatively homogeneous. They do differ substantially with respect to scale. However, the technology of banking is well known and smoothly dispersed, and there is little reason to expect latent heterogeneity to be a major factor. In this application, we will examine the impact of the different specifications for unobserved heterogeneity on estimates of cost inefficiency. Table 2.16 presents estimated parameters for simplest forms of the five common specifications:

$$\ln\left(\frac{C}{w_5}\right) = \alpha + \gamma_y \ln y + \gamma_{yy}\left(\frac{1}{2}\ln^2 y\right) + \sum_{k=1}^{4} \beta_k \ln\left(\frac{w_k}{w_5}\right) + v + u$$

Table 2.16
Estimated Stochastic Cost Frontier Models

	Pooled		Time-Varying Effects		Time-Invariant Effects	
Variable	Half-Normal	Truncated[a]	Random[b]	Fixed	Random	Fixed
Constant	−0.066983	−0.16838	−0.065942	Varies	0.51228	Varies
$\ln y$	0.66914	0.69865	0.66959	0.65829	0.58515	0.58556
$1/2 \ln^2 y$	0.023879	0.021374	0.023835	0.024922	0.030907	0.030743
$\ln w_1/w_5$	0.38815	0.38733	0.38764	0.39766	0.39721	0.38387
$\ln w_2/w_5$	0.020565	0.02010	0.020758	0.016966	0.032037	0.036016
$\ln w_3/w_5$	0.17959	0.17730	0.17995	0.17259	0.17780	0.18758
$\ln w_4/w_5$	0.13479	0.13442	0.13483	0.133419	0.13784	0.13823
λ	1.81064	18.33032	1.82158	1.88219	0.30418	0.0
σ	0.31866	3.07476	0.31796	0.40601	0.23572	0.22750
σ_u	0.27894	3.07019	0.27872	0.35854	0.06860	0.0
σ_v	0.15406	0.16749	0.15301	0.19049	0.22552	0.22750
Log-likelihood	183.9359	207.0714	184.0844	234.4165	136.6902	436.8185

[a] MLE of μ is 60.03185.
[b] MLE of σ_w is 0.01891958.

$$\text{Pooled: } \ln(C/w_5)_{it} = \alpha + \beta^T x_{it} + v_{it} + u_{it}$$

- This model is estimated by ML as discussed above. The JLMS estimator is used to estimate u_{it}.

$$\text{Random Effects: } \ln(C/w_5)_{it} = \alpha + \beta^T x_{it} + v_{it} + u_i$$

- This is the Pitt and Lee (1981) model, also fit by ML. The form of the log-likelihood appears in Pitt and Lee (1981) and Greene (2000). The JLMS estimator is used by replacing ε_{it} with $\bar{\varepsilon}_i$ and σ^2 with σ^2/T (see Kim and Schmidt, 2000).

$$\text{Fixed Effects: } \ln(C/w_5)_{it} = \alpha_0 + \beta^T x_{it} + v_{it} + (\alpha_i - \alpha_0)$$

- This is the Schmidt and Sickles (1984) approach, fit be ordinary (within-groups) OLS, followed by translation of the constants: $u_i = a_i - \min(a_i)$.

$$\text{True Random Effects: } \ln(C/w_5)_{it} = (\alpha + w_i) + \beta^T x_{it} + v_{it} + u_{it}$$

- The model is developed in Greene (2005). The parameters are estimated by MSL. The JLMS estimator is employed by integrating w_i out of $E[u_{it}|\varepsilon_{it}(w_i)]$. That is, ε_{it} is a function of w_i, and then w_i is integrated out of u_{it}.

$$\text{True Fixed Effects: } \ln(C/w_5)_{it} = \alpha_i + \beta^T x_{it} + v_{it} + u_{it}$$

- The model is estimated by brute force ML using the methods described in Greene (2004a). The JLMS estimator is used directly for u_{it}.

Parameter estimates are given table 2.16 to enable comparison of the models. Standard errors are omitted in the interest of brevity.

The estimated parameters are consistent across frameworks but differ surprisingly with respect to the assumption of whether the inefficiency is assumed to be time invariant or not. This finding is consistent with what we have observed elsewhere. In terms of its impact on model estimates, the assumption of time invariance seems to have much greater influence than the difference between fixed and random effects. Note, within the assumption of time-varying inefficiency, that neither the fixed- nor the random-effects model is preferred to the pooled model based on the likelihood ratio statistic. (The likelihood function rises substantially for the fixed-effects model, but with 499 degrees of freedom, the value of 100.96 is far from significant.) The truncation model displays the characteristic erratic behavior. The technology parameters are quite stable, but the truncation model substantially alters the estimated distribution of u_{it}. Superficially, the truncation model appears more reasonable. Figure 2.20 compares the estimated distributions—the upper figure is for $E[u_{it}|\varepsilon_{it}]$ for the half-normal model.

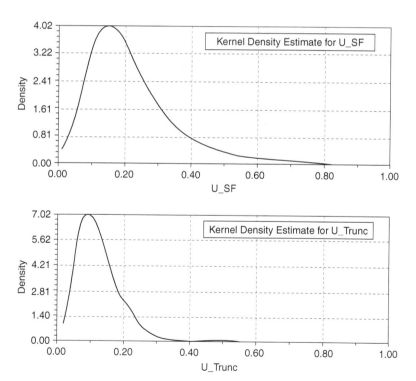

Figure 2.20. Estimated Mean Inefficiencies for Half-Normal (top) and Truncated-Normal (bottom) Models

Table 2.17
Descriptive Statistics for Estimated Inefficiencies

Model	Mean	SD	Skewness	Minimum	Maximum
Pooled	0.220143	0.127907	1.59129	0.0371616	0.795649
True fixed effects	0.255033	0.118152	1.61515	0.0658233	1.02899
True random effects	0.220369	0.130749	1.84823	0.0372414	1.18654
Random effects	0.0546	0.0168001	2.07666	0.0266957	0.165469
Fixed effects	0.291174	0.106474	0.472136	0	0.764483
Truncated normal	0.128167	0.0684533	1.96499	0.0341525	0.54011
Latent class	0.110435	0.082082	2.13809	0.0157056	0.703589
Random parameters	0.199054	0.1217	1.89409	0.0340895	1.08773

Descriptive statistics for the estimates of $E[u_{it}|\varepsilon_{it}]$ (or $E[u_i|\varepsilon_{it}, t = 1, \ldots, T]$ in the case of the time-invariant models) are given in tables 2.17 and 2.18. For the time-invariant cases, consistent with the model, the fixed value of u_i is repeated for the five observations for bank i. Among the notable features of the results are the high correlation between random- and fixed-effects estimates, but the far lower correlations across the two modeling platforms, time-varying and time-invariant effects. This is once again consistent with results observed elsewhere. Finally, scatter plots of the sets of estimates are consistent with what is suggested in tables 2.17 and 2.18. When estimates from one model that assumes u_{it} varies across time are plotted against another, the estimates are essentially the same. However, as observed in Greene (2004a, 2004b), when, for example, the estimates of u_{it} (or the group means) from either true effects model are plotted against (repeated) u_i from the model with time-invariant inefficiency, the plot confirms that the estimates are almost uncorrelated.

2.10.4.2 Parameter heterogeneity

Finally, we consider the two classical methods of allowing for parameter heterogeneity in the model, the random-parameters model and the latent class

Table 2.18
Correlations among Inefficiency Estimates

	Pooled	Truncated	True RE	True FE	Random	Fixed
Pooled	1.00000					
Truncated	0.44376	1.00000				
True FE	0.99567	0.44473	1.00000			
True RE	0.90975	0.10552	0.91713	1.00000		
Random	0.44354	0.99716	0.44570	0.10565	1.00000	
Fixed	0.44675	0.95960	0.44159	0.08743	0.96629	1.00000

FE, fixed effects; RE, random effects.

model, which allows for discrete parameter variation. Both depart from the normal–half-normal stochastic frontier model.

The random-parameters model is

$$y_{it} = \alpha_i + \boldsymbol{\beta}_i^T \mathbf{x}_{it} + v_{it} + u_{it}$$

$$(\alpha_i, \boldsymbol{\beta}_i^T)^T \sim N[(\alpha_0, \boldsymbol{\beta}_0^T)^T, \boldsymbol{\Sigma}].$$

The technology parameters are allowed to vary randomly (normally) across firms. The marginal distributions of the random components, u_{it} and v_{it}, are assumed to be common. The model is estimated by MSL as described in Greene (2004a).[86] It is useful to digress briefly to document the computation of the estimators of $E[u_{it}|\varepsilon_{it}]$. For convenience, let $\boldsymbol{\theta} = (\alpha, \boldsymbol{\beta}^T)^T$ denote the full vector of parameters, so $\boldsymbol{\theta}_i$ is what appears in the model. We can write the random-parameters component of the model as

$$\boldsymbol{\theta}_i = \boldsymbol{\theta} + \mathbf{w}_i,$$

where $\mathbf{w}_i \sim N[0, \boldsymbol{\Sigma}]$.

During estimation, we go a step further, and write $\mathbf{w}_i = \boldsymbol{\Gamma}\mathbf{h}_i$, where $\boldsymbol{\Gamma}\boldsymbol{\Gamma}^T = \boldsymbol{\Sigma}$ and $\mathbf{h}_i \sim N[0, \mathbf{I}]$. Then, the JLMS estimator conditioned on $\mathbf{w}_i$ is

$$\hat{E}[u_{it}|\varepsilon_{it}(\mathbf{w}_i)] = \frac{\lambda\sigma}{1+\lambda^2}\left[\frac{-\varepsilon_{it}(\mathbf{w}_i)\lambda}{\sigma} + \frac{\phi[-\varepsilon_{it}(\mathbf{w}_i)\lambda/\sigma]}{\Phi[-\varepsilon_{it}(\mathbf{w}_i)\lambda/\sigma]}\right],$$

where $\varepsilon_{it}(\mathbf{w}_{ii}) = y_{it} - (\boldsymbol{\theta} + \mathbf{w}_i)^T(1, \mathbf{x}_{it})$.

We now must integrate $\mathbf{w}_i$ out of the expression; the unconditional estimator will be

$$\hat{E}[u_{it}|\text{data}] = E_{\mathbf{w}_i}\hat{E}[u_{it}|\varepsilon_{it}(\mathbf{w}_i)]$$

$$= \int_{\mathbf{w}_i} \frac{\lambda\sigma}{1+\lambda^2}\left[\frac{-\varepsilon_{it}(\mathbf{w}_i)\lambda}{\sigma} + \frac{\phi[-\varepsilon_{it}(\mathbf{w}_i)\lambda/\sigma]}{\Phi[-\varepsilon_{it}(\mathbf{w}_i)\lambda/\sigma]}\right]f(\mathbf{w}_i)d\mathbf{w}_i.$$

(This is essentially the same as the Bayesian posterior mean estimator of the same quantity.) We are conditioning on all the data for this observation, including the dependent variable. Thus, what we have denoted $f(\mathbf{w}_i)$ is actually $f(\mathbf{w}_i|\text{data}_i)$. The simulation-based estimator will condition out the dependent variable (for discussion, see Train, 2003, chapter 10; Greene, 2003a). The integral cannot be computed in closed form, so it is approximated by simulation. The estimator is

$$\hat{E}^S[u_{it}|\text{data}] = \frac{1}{R}\sum_{r=1}^{R}\hat{f}_{ir}\frac{\lambda\sigma}{1+\lambda^2}\left[\frac{-\varepsilon_{it}(\mathbf{w}_{ir})\lambda}{\sigma} + \frac{\phi[-\varepsilon_{it}(\mathbf{w}_{ir})\lambda/\sigma]}{\Phi[-\varepsilon_{it}(\mathbf{w}_{ir})\lambda/\sigma]}\right],$$

where draws from the distribution of $\mathbf{w}_i$ are obtained as $\boldsymbol{\Gamma}\mathbf{h}_i$, where $\mathbf{h}_i$ is a vector of primitive draws from the standard normal distribution and recall

$\Gamma\Gamma^T = \Sigma.$[87] The weights in the summation are

$$\hat{f}_{ir} = \frac{L_{ir}}{\frac{1}{R}\sum_{r=1}^{R} L_{ir}},$$

where L_{ir} is the joint likelihood (not the log) for the T observations for individual (bank) i computed at θ_{ir}, λ, σ. Note that the full set of computations is done ex post based on the MLEs of λ, σ, (α_0, β_0), and Γ. (In implementation, it is convenient to compute this quantity at the same time the simulated log-likelihood is computed, so it does not actually require very much additional computation—at the final iteration, these conditional estimates are present as a byproduct of the computation of the likelihood.)

Estimation of the latent class model is described in section 2.4.9.2. For estimates of $E[u_{it}|\varepsilon_{it}]$, we use the following strategy. [Again, I sketch only the overview. For further details, Greene (2003a, chapter 16) has additional material.] The latent class stochastic frontier model estimates consist of $(\alpha_j, \beta_j, \lambda_j, \sigma_j, \pi_j)$, where j indicates the jth of J classes and π_j is the unconditional (counterpart to "prior") probability of membership in the jth class. The conditional probabilities of class membership for bank i are obtained via Bayes theorem; these equal

$$\pi(j|i) = \frac{\pi_j L(i|j)}{\sum_{j=1}^{J} \pi_j L(i|j)},$$

where $L(i|j)$ is the likelihood (not its log) for bank i, computed at the parameters specific to class j. (These are the counterparts to posterior probabilities in a Bayesian treatment.) Let $E[u_{it}|\varepsilon_{it}, j]$ denote the JLMS estimator of $E[u_{it}|\varepsilon_{it}]$ in specific class j—that is, computed using the parameters of class j. Then, our estimate of $E[u_{it}|\varepsilon_{it}]$ is

$$\hat{E}[u_{it}|\varepsilon_{it}] = \sum_{j=1}^{J} \pi(j|i)\hat{E}[u_{it}|\varepsilon_{it}, j].$$

The computations are done ex post, based on the MLEs of $(\alpha_j, \beta_j, \lambda_j, \sigma_j, \pi_j)$, $j = 1, \ldots, J$. (As in the random-parameters model, this computation is actually done at the same time the log-likelihood is computed, each time it is computed, so that at convergence, the estimated inefficiencies are already computed as a byproduct of the optimization process.)

Table 2.19 contains estimates of the parameters for the pooled stochastic frontier model, a full random-parameters model, and a three-class latent class model. (Three was chosen more or less arbitrarily for this pedagogy. In practice, one would do a more systematic search for the right number of classes.) The full covariance matrix for the random parameters (not shown) is computed using $\Gamma\Lambda\Lambda\Gamma^T$, where Γ is the lower triangular, Cholesky decomposition of the correlation matrix and Λ is the diagonal matrix of standard

Table 2.19
Estimates of Stochastic Frontier Models with Parameter Heterogeneity

| Variable | Pooled | Random Parameters | | Latent Class | | |
		Means	SD	1: π_1=0.2765	2: π_2=0.3656	3: π_3=0.3579
Constant	−0.066983	0.60582	0.94844	0.97366	−1.76168	2.86413
Ln y	0.66914	0.62883	0.08092	0.48163	0.92320	0.49111
$1/2 \ln^2 y$	0.023879	0.027914	0.00763	0.039745	0.0025294	0.040041
$\mathrm{Ln} w_1/wP_5$	0.38815	0.31048	0.06313	0.38237	0.444271	0.067207
$\mathrm{Ln} w_2/w_5$	0.020565	0.025300	0.05939	0.064287	−0.036128	0.026086
$\mathrm{Ln} w_3/w_5$	0.17959	0.14430	0.15692	0.15152	0.22077	−0.00040723
$\mathrm{Ln} w/w_5$	0.13479	0.10129	0.06767	0.143330	0.15303	−0.018279
λ	1.81064	2.27161	0.0	2.23409	1.20080	2.62612
σ	0.31866	0.29715	0.0	0.39960	0.23755	0.25030
σ_u	0.27894	0.27196	0.0	0.36473	0.18255	0.23392
σ_v	0.15406	0.11972	0.0	0.16325	0.15202	0.089073
Log -likelihood	183.9359	249.0411			310.7142	

deviations that are shown in table 2.19. I emphasize that the estimated "standard deviations" (SD) in table 2.19 are not standard errors (one would not divide the means by the standard deviations to compute t ratios). These are the estimates of the standard deviations of the marginal distributions of the parameters distributed across the banks in the sample. The sampling "standard errors" are not shown below. As the results suggest, particularly in the latent class model, there is a fair amount of variation across firms in the frontier model parameters. For the present purposes, the more important question is the impact on the estimated inefficiencies. This is shown in the composite scatter plots in figure 2.21. The two upper figures plot the heterogeneous models against the pooled, base-case stochastic frontier model. The lower panel plots the two random-parameters models. There is, as one might expect, strong similarity across the three sets of estimates. Nonetheless, it is evident that the effects are not negligible. To assess whether the greater generality of the random-parameters approaches are indicated as necessary by the data, we can revert back to a likelihood ratio test. For the random-parameters model, the chi-squared statistic is 130.21 with 28 degrees of freedom (the number of free elements in Σ). The critical value is 41.33, so the hypothesis of homogeneity would be rejected. For the latent class model, the chi-squared statistic is 253.56. The number of degrees of freedom is unclear, since if the parameters are constrained across the three classes, the same model results regardless of the unconditional values of π_j. This suggests that 18 is the appropriate count. If, instead, one must also assume that the three values of π_j equal one-third, then 20 is the appropriate count. In either case, the critical value would be far below the sample statistic. Note, finally, that the framework does not provide an obvious way to choose between continuous and discrete parameter variation.

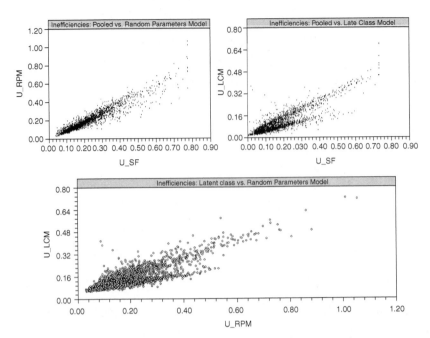

Figure 2.21. Estimated Inefficiencies from Pooled (top) and Random-Parameter (bottom) Models

2.10.5 Heterogeneity in production: WHO data

These data are a country-level panel on health care attainment. The two main variables of interest are "disability-adjusted life expectancy" (DALE) and "composite health attainment" (COMP). The former is a standard variable used to measure health care attainment. The latter is an innovative survey-based measure created by the researchers at WHO. The health attainments are viewed as the outputs of a production (function) process and were modeled in this fashion by WHO (2000) and Greene (2004b). Two input variables are health expenditure (HEXP) and education levels (EDUC). There are a number of other covariates in the data set that I view as shifters of the production function or as influences on the level of inefficiency, but not direct inputs into the production process. The data are measured for five years, 1993–1997. However, only COMP, DALE, HEXP, and EDUC actually vary across the years; the other variables are time invariant, dated 1997. In addition, as discussed by Gravelle et al. (2002a, 2002b), among others, there is relatively little actual time (within country) variation in these data; the within-groups variation for the time-varying variables accounts for less than 2% of the total. This rather limits what can be done in terms of panel-data analysis. However, in spite of this limitation, this data set provides an interesting platform for placing heterogeneity in a stochastic frontier model. [The examples to follow will build on Greene (2004b).] The WHO data are described in table 2.20.

Table 2.20
World Health Organization Data on Health Care Attainment

Variable	Mean	SD	Description
COMP	75.0062726	12.2051123	Composite health care attainment
DALE	58.3082712	12.1442590	Disability-adjusted life expectancy
HEXP	548.214857	694.216237	Health expenditure per capita, PPP units
EDUC	6.31753664	2.73370613	Education, years
WBNUMBER	138.989286	79.8358634	World Bank country number
COUNTRY	97.3421751	54.0810680	Country number omitting internal units
OECD	0.279761905	0.449149577	OECD member country, dummy variable
SMALL	0.373809524	1.20221479	Zero or number if internal state or province
YEAR	1995.21310	1.42464932	Year (1993–1997) (T = year — 1992; Tyy = year dummy variable)
GDPC	8135.10785	7891.20036	Per capita GDP in PPP units
POPDEN	953.119353	2871.84294	Population density per square Kilometer
GINI	0.379477914	0.090206941	Gini coefficient for income distribution
TROPICS	0.463095238	0.498933251	Dummy variable for tropical location
PUBTHE	58.1553571	20.2340835	Proportion of health spending paid by government
GEFF	0.113293978	0.915983955	World bank government effectiveness measure
VOICE	0.192624849	0.952225978	World bank measure of democratization

I have placed these data on my home page (http://http://www.stern.nyu. edu/~wgreene (Publications))for the interested reader who wishes to replicate or extend our results. Some of the variables listed in table 2.20 (e.g., PUBTHE, SMALL) are not used here but are listed as a guide for the reader. These data and the issue they address have been analyzed and discussed widely by researchers at many sites. Greene (2004b) is part of that discussion. I do not replicate any of these studies here. Rather, we will use a subset of the data set (actually, most of it) to examine a few additional models that were not estimated above. Note some features of the data set and analysis: First, the WHO data consist of an unbalanced panel on 191 countries plus a large number of smaller political units (e.g., states of Mexico, Canadian provinces); 140 of the countries were observed in all five years (1993–1997), one (Algeria) was observed in four years, and the remaining units were all observed once, in 1997. Purely for convenience and for purposes of our pedagogy here, we will limit our attention to the balanced panel of the 140 countries observed in all five years. Second, given that the outcome variables in the model (life expectancy and composite health care attainment) are not obviously quantitative measures such as cost or physical output units, the numerical values of efficiency measures (u_{it}) have ambiguous meaning. To accommodate this, the researchers at WHO focused their attention on rankings of efficiency measures, rather than on values. Third, the WHO study was innovative in several respects, notably in its attempt to include many (all) countries, in contrast to above studies that nearly always focused on the 30 member countries of the Organisation for Economic Co-operation (OECD). However, little attention was paid in the WHO studies (Evans et al., 2000a, 2000b) to the distinction between OECD and non-OECD countries in the results, perhaps by design. Greene (2004b) found a striking distinction in the results between the two groups. In short, nearly all of the "action" in the inefficiency distributions pertains to the non-OECD observations. The OECD countries area always clustered near the origin. This is an important angle that might be pursued in further analysis.

The WHO study treated the process of health care provision at the national level as a production process,

$$\text{health}_{it} = f(\text{education}_{it}, \text{expenditure}_{it}).$$

Whether it is reasonable to view the outcome here as an optimization process in which agents maximized the production of "health" while using these two inputs is, of course, debatable. For better or worse, the model employed is

$$\ln \text{health}_{it} = \alpha + \beta_1 \ln \text{HEXP}_{it} + \beta_2 \ln \text{EDUC}_{it} + \beta_3 \ln^2 \text{EDUC}_{it} + v_{it} - u_{it}.$$

Differences among subsequent researchers concerned the functional form, the stochastic specification, and the method of handling the cross heterogeneity. We will explore a few of those issues here, though not with an eye toward commenting on other received analyses. We are interested in two modeling aspects in this section. As noted above, in some applications, notably this one, there are covariates that arguably affect production and/or efficiency. The modeling question raised above is, "where do we put the z's?" That is, how should measured heterogeneity enter the model? Unfortunately, there are numerous choices, and no clearly right answer, as will become obvious presently. The number of possibilities is yet doubled here, as we have two outcome variables to study. Without attempting to resolve the question, I present a handful of model estimates under different formulations to illustrate the techniques. We have no basis on which to prefer any particular one at this juncture. The interested reader may wish to continue the analysis. The second feature we examine, briefly further below, is the extent to which accommodating measured (and unmeasured) heterogeneity affects estimates of inefficiency. It is straightforward to make a case that, under most reasonable specifications, inappropriate treatment of heterogeneity will distort estimates of inefficiency. Whether it will affect rankings of inefficiencies, which were the focus of attention in the WHO study, is, however, unresolved.

2.10.5.1 Accommodating measured heterogeneity

We will define the vectors

$$\mathbf{x}_{it} = \ln \text{HEXP}_{it}, \ln \text{EDUC}_{it}, \ln^2 \text{EDUC}_{it},$$

$$\mathbf{z}_{i,p} = \text{TROPICS}_i, \ln \text{POPDEN}_i,$$

$$\mathbf{z}_{i,e} = \text{GINI}_i, \ln \text{GDPC}_i, \text{GEFF}_i, \text{VOICE}_i, \text{OECD}_i.$$

Note that the latter two are time invariant; only the outputs and inputs are measured in all years. We will condition the production directly on $\mathbf{z}_{i,p}$. The other vector of covariates will enter the efficiency models at various points as shown below. Obviously, other arrangements of the variables are possible. It seems natural that location and population density are less policy related than the other variables and so appear more naturally as shift parameters in the production function. Other assignments might also seem appropriate; the interested reader may wish to experiment—for example, Greene (2004b) also included a time trend in $\mathbf{z}_{i,e}$. Tables 2.21–2.23 present estimates for the following models:

Stochastic Frontier: Normal–Half-Normal (Aigner et al., 1977)

$\ln \text{health}_{it} = \alpha + \boldsymbol{\beta}^T \mathbf{x}_{it} + \boldsymbol{\theta}_p^T \mathbf{z}_{i,p} + \boldsymbol{\theta}_e^T \mathbf{z}_{i,e} + v_{it} - u_{it}$

$v_{it} \sim N[0, \sigma_v^2]$

$u_{it} = |U_{it}|, U_{it} \sim N[0, \sigma_u^2]$

Normal–Truncated Normal (Stevenson, 1980)

$\ln \text{health}_{it} = \alpha + \boldsymbol{\beta}^T \mathbf{x}_{it} + \boldsymbol{\theta}_p^T \mathbf{z}_{i,p} + v_{it} - u_{it}$

$v_{it} \sim N[0, \sigma_v^2]$

$u_{it} = |U_{it}|, U_{it} \sim N[\mu + \boldsymbol{\theta}_e^T \mathbf{z}_{i,e}, \sigma_u^2]$

Heteroskedastic Normal (singly or doubly; Hadri, 1999, and Hadri et al., 2003a,b)

$\ln \text{health}_{it} = \alpha + \boldsymbol{\beta}^T \mathbf{x}_{it} + \boldsymbol{\theta}_p^T \mathbf{z}_{i,p} + v_{it} - u_{it}$

$v_{it} \sim N[0, \sigma_{vi}^2]; \sigma_{vi} = \sigma_v \times \exp(\boldsymbol{\gamma}_{pv}^T \mathbf{z}_{i,e})$

$u_{it} = |U_{it}|, U_{it} \sim N[0, \sigma_{ui}^2]; \sigma_{ui} = \sigma_u \times \exp(\boldsymbol{\gamma}_{pu}^T \mathbf{z}_{i,e})$

Table 2.21
Estimated Heterogeneous Stochastic Frontier Models for lnDALE

Variable	Half-Normal Model			Truncated-Normal Model
Constant	3.50708	3.50885	3.28004	3.90626*
EXP.	0.066364	0.065318	0.019171	0.03532*
EDUC.	0.288112	0.307518	0.277322	0.22911*
EDUC.^{2}	−0.110175	−0.12711	−0.11729	−0.12480*
TROPICS		−0.025347	−0.016577	−0.12480
LnPOPDEN		0.0013475	−0.00028902	0.0014070

	Shift Production Function			Production Function	Mean of U_i
Constant					2.33052*
GINI			−0.21864	−0.090319	1.90648*
LnGDPC			0.072409	−0.0096963	−0.40107*
GEFF			−0.0088535	0.010164	—
				0.0047021	
VOICE			0.012679	0.016304*	—
				0.00092454	
OECD			−0.045681	−0.018195	−2.82321

	Noise and Inefficiency Distributions			
λ	5.72629	5.19739	6.31057	9.92754
σ	0.21063	0.20669	0.20223	0.20818
σ_u	0.21063	0.20297	0.19974	0.20713
σ_v	0.03623	0.03905	0.03165	0.02086
Log-likelihood	501.4585	506.1130	536.9086	859.4868

* Statistically significant at the 95% level.

The truncation and heteroskedasticity models can be combined and permuted. The formulation of the Alvarez et al (2006). scaling model shows one possibility:

Scaling (Alvarez, Amsler, Orea and Schmidt, 2006)

$$\ln \text{health}_{it} = \alpha + \boldsymbol{\beta}^{\mathrm{T}} \mathbf{x}_{it} + \boldsymbol{\theta}_p^{\mathrm{T}} \mathbf{z}_{i,p} + v_{it} - u_{it}$$

$$v_{it} \sim N[0, \sigma_v^2]$$

$$u_{it} = |U_{it}|, \; U_{it} \sim N[\mu_i, \sigma_{ui}^2]; \; \mu_i = \mu \times \exp(\boldsymbol{\gamma}_{pu}^{\mathrm{T}} \mathbf{z}_{i,e}) \sigma_{ui}$$

$$= \sigma_u \times \exp(\boldsymbol{\gamma}_{pu}^{\mathrm{T}} \mathbf{z}_{i,e})$$

Note that the scale factors on the mean and standard deviation of the distribution of u_{it} are identical. This constraint can be relaxed, though if so, the model no longer obeys the scaling property suggested by the authors. Alvarez et al. suggested linear rather than loglinear scale factors. This is potentially problematic since the linear function is not constrained to be positive, and it is not possible to impose the constraint on the optimization procedure. As a final candidate for a platform for the measured heterogeneity, we consider a latent class formulation in which allows both the production and efficiency

Table 2.22
Estimated Heteroskedastic Stochastic Frontier Models

Variable	Half-Normal	Hetero-skedasticity in u	Heteroskedasticity in Both u and v		Heteroskedasticity in u and v; u Time Invariant		Scaling Model; Heterogeneity in $E[U]$, Same Scale for σ_u	
Constant	3.28004	3.67243	3.69419		3.91430		3.64980	
EXP.	0.019171	0.037812	0.04056		0.016895		0.041866	
EDUC.	0.277322	0.34194	0.31867		0.10816		0.32555	
EDUC.^{2}	−0.11729	−0.17715	−0.17415		0.011575		−0.16676	
TROPICS	−0.016577	−0.011027	−0.010097		0.025598		−0.008782	
lnPOPDEN	−0.000289	0.000299	0.00028812		0.003334		−0.000493	
			σ_v	σ_u	σ_v	σ_u	μ	σ_u
Constant		1.78679	−1.23320	1.29694	0.75772	0.68495	−23.1551	2.08169
GINI		9.64724	−3.19744	10.34564	4.28185	7.20613	5.77792	
LnGDPC		−1.13106	−0.64829	−1.10138	−1.0714	−0.63463	−0.65734	
GEFF.		−0.24609	−0.93913	−0.169847	−0.27222	−0.41316	−0.050936	
VOICE		0.14326	0.039271	0.055723	0.58151	0.082344	−0.046971	
OECD		−1.65801	1.562677	−2.09808	−0.27988	0.020814	−1.17259	
		Variance Parameters	Variance Parameters		Variance Parameters		Variance Parameters	
λ	6.31057	4.08669[a]	4.80460[a]		2.11404[a]		15.57378[a]	
σ	0.20223	0.24556[a]	0.25104[a]		0.75772[a]		0.45450[a]	
σ_u	0.19974	0.24467[a]	0.28975[a]		0.68495[b]		0.45382[a]	
σ_v	0.03165	0.05987	0.06218[a]		0.32400[b]		0.024914[a]	
Log-likelihood	536.9086	812.9505	829.5840		1910.944		817.2499	

[a] Computed by averaging the sample estimates of country-specific variances

Table 2.23
Estimated Latent Class Stochastic Frontier Model

Variable	Half-Normal	Class 1	Class 2
Constant	3.28004	3.53884	2.91203
EXP.	0.019171	0.044493	0.025945
EDUC.	0.277322	0.33199	−0.072499
EDUC.	−0.11729	−0.15674	0.12832
TROPICS	−0.016577	−0.001768	−0.0079229
LnPOPDEN	−0.00028902	−0.0033528	0.0058591
GINI	−0.21864	−0.185551	−0.48646
LnGDPC	0.072409	0.016297	0.12076
GEFF.	−0.0088535	0.00056079	0.13722
VOICE	0.012679	0.013583	−0.17573
OECD	−0.045681	−0.022626	0.10688
Class probability	1.00000	0.83916	0.16084
λ	6.31057	1.86032	8.50170
σ	0.20223	0.071261	0.11716
σ_u	0.19974	0.062768	0.116365
σ_v	0.03165	0.033740	0.013687
Log-likelihood	536.9086	1011.858	

heterogeneity to enter the production function, and the efficiency heterogeneity also to enter the class probabilities. The model is

Latent class (Greene, 2004a; Orea and Kumbhakar, 2004)

$$\ln \text{health}_{it}|j = \alpha_j + \boldsymbol{\beta}_j^T \mathbf{x}_{it} + \boldsymbol{\theta}_{p,j}^T \mathbf{z}_{i,p} + \boldsymbol{\theta}_{e,j}^T \mathbf{z}_{i,e} + v_{it} - u_{it}$$
$$v_{it}|j \sim N[0, \sigma_{v,j}^2]$$
$$u_{it}|j = |U_{it}|j|, U_{it}|j \sim N[0, \sigma_{uj}^2]$$
$$\text{Class probability: } \pi_{i,j} = \exp(\tau_{0j} + \boldsymbol{\tau}_j^T \mathbf{z}_{i,e}) / \sum_j \exp(\tau_{0j} + \boldsymbol{\tau}_j^T \mathbf{z}_{i,e})$$

The latent class model can be applied in a cross-section or pooled model. Since we have a panel model, we will fit this as such—the force of the treatment is that the class probabilities apply unchanged to all five observations for each country.

My purpose here is to illustrate computation of the models. The JLMS estimator of $E[u|\varepsilon]$ is computed using all the above results. Since there are so many combinations of the models available, each with its own implied set of estimates, I forgo a secondary analysis of the implied inefficiency estimates, with one exception. An important specification issue for analysts—the subject of this exercise—is the effect of the measured covariates, the "zs," on estimates of $E[u|\varepsilon]$ or $E[\exp(-u)|\varepsilon]$. To pursue this issue, researchers often estimate the generic frontier model without the covariates and then,

Table 2.24
Second-Step Regression of Estimates of $E[u|\varepsilon]$ on Covariates

Variable	Stochastic Frontier Production		Heterogeneous Truncated Normal	
	Estimate	t-Ratio	Estimate	t-Ratio
Constant	0.27632	8.802	0.23059	14.790
Tropics	0.018463	3.431	0.0021116	0.790
LnPOPDEN	−0.0010252	−0.905	−0.00024979	−0.444
GINI	0.15700	5.537	0.056483	4.011
lnGDPC	−0.027559	−7.842	−0.019621	−11.243
GEFF.	0.010052	2.165	0.0039423	1.710
VOICE	−0.0031805	−0.888	−0.0025433	−1.431
OECD	0.035059	4.661	−0.017854	−4.780
R^2	0.2576678		0.5346847	
SE	0.0533936		0.026517	

(handwritten marginalia: closer SE to 0, model has smaller random error component β, fit more useful for prediction)

in a second step, regress the estimated (in)efficiencies on the covariates. Wang and Schmidt (2002) have cautioned against this, arguing that the omission of the covariates at the "first step" is tantamount to the omitted variable problem in ordinary regression. Nonetheless, this procedure is fairly common and, indeed, is routine in the DEA literature. (In fact, the first step of DEA provides no mechanism for including the z values in the model, so this is to be expected.) Table 2.24 shows a second-step analysis of the estimates from the generic model and from the truncated regression model.

Table 2.21 shows the impact of introducing the observed indicators of heterogeneity directly into the production model and into the mean of U_i. The first three columns show the estimation of the half-normal model with progressively more extensive lists of covariates. The base production parameters change relatively little. However, the estimate of σ_u gets progressively smaller, though less than we might have expected. The last set of results shows the normal–truncated-normal model, with the full set of effects both in the production function and in the inefficiency distribution. Intuition might suggest, however incorrectly, that estimation of the model with the variables in both the production function and in $E[U_i]$ would be difficult because of weak identification—a multicollinearity problem, if nothing else. In fact, estimation of the model was routine. For the example, coefficients that were "significant" in this model are indicated by asterisks. Of the 19 parameters estimated in the full model, 12 "t-ratios" were larger than 1.0, and only three were less than 0.5. Figure 2.22 shows the kernel density estimators for the sample of estimates of $E[u_i|\varepsilon_i]$ for the least specified model, at the left, and the most general model, at the right. The x-axes of the two figures are the same. The much tighter distribution of the latter is consistent with expectations about introducing heterogeneity into

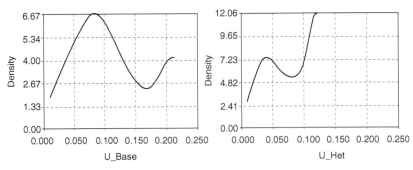

Figure 2.22. Kernel Density Estimates for Inefficiency Distributions

the model. (I have no theory at this point for the bimodality of the two estimates.)

Table 2.22 displays the estimated parameters for models in which the heterogeneity appears in the variances rather than the means. The results do illustrate the computations. It is difficult to frame a prior for whether heterogeneity in the mean of the variance would be the preferred model. That would depend on the application. One interesting outcome is shown in figure 2.23, which plots the estimates of $E[u|\varepsilon]$ for the doubly heteroskedastic model. Though the shape of the distribution is more in line with priors, its range is much larger than that for the preceding model, in which the heterogeneity is in the mean. This may suggest a basis on which to formulate the preferred model. The third set of results displays the Alvarez Amsler, Orea and Schmidt (2006). "scaling model." Again, it is difficult to form priors, but note here that the assumption of the scaling model has the result that nearly all of the variation in ε (and some not found before) is shifted from v to u, compared to the truncation model in table 2.21 and the doubly heteroskedastic model in table 2.22.

The final set of results, in table 2.23, show a two-class latent class model. In the model estimated, the efficiency covariates, $z_{i,e}$, are also determinants of the class probabilities (in the form of a binomial logit model with these as independent variables).

Table 2.24 displays regression results when the JLMS estimates of $E[u|\varepsilon]$ are regressed on the observed indicators of heterogeneity. The estimates computed from the half-normal stochastic frontier model contain only expenditure, education, and its square. In those computed from the normal–truncated-normal model, all variables listed appear in the production function, and the GINI coefficient, lnGDP, and so on, also appear in the mean of the inefficiency distribution. Table 2.24 reveals that the heterogeneity significantly improves the prediction of $E[u|\varepsilon]$. The stochastic frontier results confirm our expectation, that omitted heterogeneity is an important element of the

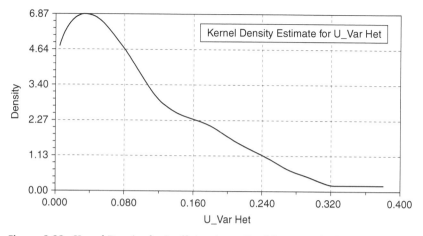

Figure 2.23. Kernel Density for Inefficiencies on Doubly Heteroskedastic Model

measurement of inefficiency in these data. Intuition might suggest something amiss in the normal–truncated-normal results. Since the heterogeneity
is already in the equation, shouldn't it be absent from the residuals? Yes, but
no, because the JLMS estimator of $E[u|e]$ is not the residual; it is explicitly
a function of the data. Thus, there is no surprise in the normal–truncated-
normal results in table 2.24. Note also that the fit of the "regression" is
considerably in the truncated-normal model. The much lower value of s
(0.0265 vs. 0.0534) reflects the purging of these heterogeneity effects from
the estimates of inefficiency. Table 2.24 casts no light on whether the omis-
sion of heterogeneity has significantly impacted the estimates of $E[u|\varepsilon]$,
save for the apparently lower values. Figure 2.24 plots the two sets of estimates against each other.[88] What the figure reveals is that there is much less
correlation between the two than one might hope for—the simple correlation is about 0.7. If we correlate the ranks, instead, the rank correlation
is about 0.65. As a final exercise, we compute the country means of the
estimates and then compute the ranks. The scatter plot of the two sets
of ranks is shown in figure 2.25. The plot is illuminating. It shows, first,
that, in fact, the rankings are crucially dependent on the treatment of heterogeneity. This was the original premise in Greene (2004b). Second, the
nicely arranged line of points at the upper left of the figure consists of
the 30 OECD countries whose high rankings (low estimates) are clearly
evident.

2.10.5.2 The effect of mishandled heterogeneity on inefficiency measurement

The possibility that unmeasured heterogeneity could masquerade as technical
inefficiency has at least an intuitive appeal. To examine the issue, let us compare

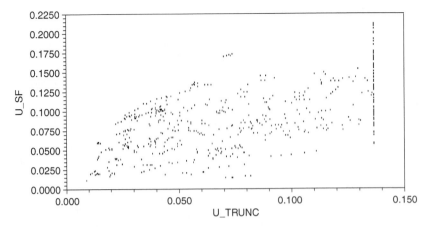

Figure 2.24. Scatter Plot of Estimated Inefficiencies

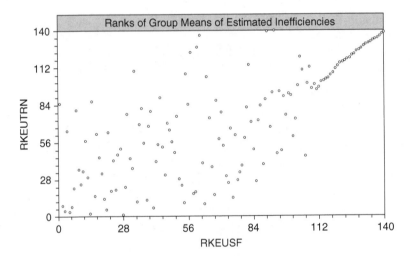

Figure 2.25. Plot of Ranks of Group Means of Inefficiencies

the estimates of $E[u|\varepsilon]$ from a generic, surely underspecified model,

$$\ln \text{health}_{it} = \alpha + \boldsymbol{\beta}^{\mathrm{T}} \mathbf{x}_{it} + v_{it} - u_{it},$$

to several alternatives:

- True random effects: $\ln \text{health}_{it} = (\alpha + w_i) + \boldsymbol{\beta}^{\mathrm{T}} \mathbf{x}_{it} + v_{it} - u_{it}$
- True fixed effects: $\ln \text{health}_{it} = \alpha_i + \boldsymbol{\beta}^{\mathrm{T}} \mathbf{x}_{it} + v_{it} - u_{it}$

• Heterogeneous truncated-normal model

$$\ln \text{health}_{it} = \alpha + \boldsymbol{\beta}^T \mathbf{x}_{it} + \boldsymbol{\theta}_p^T \mathbf{z}_{i,p} + v_{it} - u_{it}$$

$$v_{it} \sim N[0, \sigma_v^2]$$

$$u_{it} = |U_{it}|, U_{it} \sim N[\mu + \boldsymbol{\theta}_e^T \mathbf{z}_{i,e}, \sigma_u^2]$$

In each case, our expectation is that the explicit treatment of heterogeneity (unobserved or measured) should purge the disturbance of this effect. The interesting question is whether the effect being purged would have initially been placed in u_{it} (our conditional mean estimate of it) or in v_{it}. [Note that there is no ambiguity about the outcome in the deterministic frontier methodology analyzed, e.g., in Cornwell et al. (1990) and in Schmidt and Sickles (1984) or in the Pitt and Lee (1981) random-effects model. A demonstration of the effect in these data appears in Greene (2004a, 2004b).]

Table 2.25 gives descriptive statistics for the four sets of estimates of $E[u_{it}|\varepsilon_{it}]$ for both health outcomes. Note, first, that the assumption of the true random-effects model, that the unobserved heterogeneity is uncorrelated with the observed variables, seems extremely unlikely to be correct. The results in table 2.25 seem consistent with this: The estimated inefficiencies are an order of magnitude smaller than the other three. For the others, we see the anticipated effect. The average values are significantly smaller for the models that accommodate heterogeneity (truncation and true fixed effects). The kernel density estimators in figure 2.26 show that the latter distributions are also much tighter. The left pair is for *DALE*; the right is for *COMP*. The upper figure of each pair is the density estimator for the results based on the true fixed-effects estimator. The lower one is the estimator for the base model with no terms for heterogeneity.

Table 2.25
Descriptive statistics for Estimates of $E[u|\varepsilon]$

Model	Mean	SD	Minimum	Maximum
		Ln DALE		
Base	0.11580	0.061660	0.12211	0.21060
True fixed effect	0.077081	0.012237	0.042582	0.17549
True random effect	0.011091	0.0059746	0.0013537	0.074813
Truncation	0.088570	0.043287	0.0094572	0.13648
		Ln COMP		
Base	0.069964	0.034603	0.0075750	0.11065
True fixed effect	0.042728	0.010689	0.018934	0.13264
True random effect	0.0	0.0	0.0	0.0
Truncation	0.038745	0.014894	0.00308415	0.048302

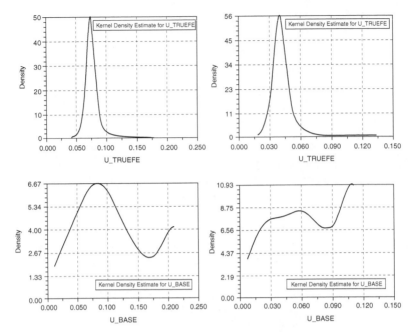

Figure 2.26. Kernel Density Estimators for Estimates of $E[uE]$

2.11 Conclusions

Current practice includes two approaches to efficiency measurement: the programming approach and the econometric approach. The deterministic frontier models presented in section 2.3 represent a hybrid of these two approaches. Although it is difficult to draw general conclusions from a single study, the results of this one concur with the common perception that the main advantage of the econometric approach lies in its ability to shift the deleterious effect of measurement error away from estimates of efficiency. The values produced by the deterministic estimators section 2.10.3 seem not only to be implausibly large, but also to distort the expected relationship between cost and production frontiers.

The stochastic frontier approach has a number of virtues, notably its internal consistency and its ease of implementation. For single-equation, cross-section analysis, with modern computer software, the stochastic frontier model is not appreciably more complex than a linear regression model. The possibility of adding a shift parameter to it, and the numerous interesting ancillary calculations derived by Jondrow et al. (1982) and Battese and Coelli (1992, 1995) suggest that the half-normal model is the most useful formulation. Other variants such as the truncated-normal model with heterogeneity in the mean allow for great flexibility in the modeling tools.

Panel data open up numerous interesting possibilities. Approaches based on regression analysis of the fixed- and random-effects models have the appeal of robustness and the potential for a consistent estimator of inefficiency. The fixed-effects model does carry with it the necessity that the analyst revert back, essentially, to the deterministic frontier model. The random-effects model, on the other hand, has the appeal of the single-equation stochastic frontier. However, as in other settings, the drawback to this approach is that the effects must be assumed to be uncorrelated with the regressors (factors). This is likely to be minor in this context. It is routinely assumed in any event. The impact of the assumption of time invariance of inefficiency seems to be the one large effect of model specification. Consistent with other researchers, we have found in this study that estimates of technical and cost inefficiency are quite robust to distributional assumptions, to the choice of fixed or random effects and to methodology, Bayesian versus classical, but they are quite sensitive to the crucial assumption of time invariance (or the lack thereof).

Notes

1. Some econometric issues that arise in the analysis of primal productions and dual cost functions are discussed in Paris and Caputo (2004).

2. Some current research is directed at blurring this distinction by suggesting a statistical underpinning for DEA. Because DEA is the subject of subsequent chapters in this book, I do not visit the topic here.

3. A more complete listing appears in chapter 1.

4. A second edition of the latter is forthcoming as of this writing.

5. This does not fully solve the problem of zero values in the data, because the appropriate standard errors for the Box-Cox model still require the logarithms of the variables. See Greene (2003a, p. 174).

6. A few other applications do note the idea, including Koop et al. (1994, 1997), Tsionas (2002), and Kumbhakar and Tsionas (2005a). Mention of the "regularity conditions" (to be kept distinct from the regularity conditions for maximum likelihood estimators) is common in the frontier applications, though relatively few actually impose them. It is more common to "check" the conditions after estimation. For example, Farsi and Filippini (2003) estimated a translog cost frontier for Swiss nursing homes and observed ex post that the estimated parameters did not satisfy the concavity conditions in the input prices. This result was attributed to the price-setting mechanism in this market.

7. Førsund et al. (1980, pp. 21–23) argue that economic dogma has essentially painted its proponents into a corner. Every action taken by an economic agent must be efficient, or else it would not have been taken. This takes a bit of artful footwork in some cases.

8. See chapter 1 for a more complete exposition.

9. There is a tendency on the part of many authors in economics to equate an *estimation technique* with a *model*. In few places is this more evident than in the literature on DEA.

10. A crucial assumption that was discussed early in this literature, but is now implicit, is that there is no correlation between x_i and ε_i in the model. Refer to Zellner, Kmenta, and Dreze (1966) for discussion of the proposition that deviations of the observed factor demands x_i from the cost-minimizing or profit-maximizing values could be uncorrelated with the deviation of y_i from its ideal counterpart as specified by the production function. Further discussion and a model specification appear in Sickles and Streitweiser (1992).

11. See Richmond (1974) for the application to this distribution. Afriat (1972) examined TE_i similarly under the assumption of a beta distribution.

12. See Greene (1980a) for discussion.

13. See Greene (1980a) for technical details and Deprins and Simar (1985, 1989b) for some corrections to the derivations.

14. See Christensen and Greene (1976) for discussion. The outer transformation is strictly monotonic, and the inner function is linearly homogeneous.

15. The constrained linear programming solution is not the maximizer of the log-likelihood function.

16. This is an antecedent to the recent DEA literature (e.g., Bankar, 1993, 1997) that has attempted to cast the linear programming approach as the max-imizer of a log-likelihood function. An application, among many, that compares econometric approaches to this linear programming methodology is Ferrier and Lovell (1990).

17. As we can see from the expression for $E[e^{-u_i}]$, when $\theta = 1$, $E[e^{-u_i}]$ is 2^{-P}, which is Richmond's result.

18. For discussion, see Lovell (1993), Ali and Seiford (1993), and chapter 3 of this volume.

19. For extensive commentary on this issue, see Schmidt (1985). Banker and Maindi-ratta (1988) show how DEA gives an upper bound for efficiency. With input price data, one can also use the technique to compute a lower bound.

20. An application that appeared concurrently is Battese and Corra (1977).

21. Recent research has begun to investigate the possibility of correlation across the two components of the composed disturbance. The econometric issues are con-siderable; e.g., identification is a problem. The underlying economics are equally problematic. As of this writing (mid-2007), the returns on this model extension are far from complete, so I eschew further consideration of the possibility.

22. See Schmidt and Lin (1984) for this test and Coelli (1995) for a slightly different form of the test. The statistic appears in a slightly different form in Pagan and Hall (1983).

23. This need not be the case. The skewness of ε_i is entirely due to u_i, and as long as u_i is positive, in fact, the skewness could go in either direction. Nonetheless, in the most common formulations of the stochastic frontier model, involving the normal distribution, the skewness provides an important diagnostic check on the model specification.

24. See Train (2003), Greene (2003a, section 17.8; 2005), and Greene and Misra (2003).

25. The derivation appears in many other sources, e.g., Pitt and Lee (1981), Greene (1990), and Kumbhakar and Lovell (2000).

26. An alternative parameterization that is convenient for some other forms of the model is $\gamma = \sigma_u^2/\sigma^2$. See Battese and Corra (1977), Battese (1992), Coelli (1991), and Greene (2000, chapter 28).

27. The standard statistics, LM, Wald, and LR, are quite well defined, even at $\lambda = 0$, which presents something of a conundrum in this model. There is, in fact, no problem computing a test statistic, but problems of interpretation arise. For related commentary, see Breusch and Pagan (1980). The corresponding argument regarding testing for a one-sided error term would be the same. In this case, the parametric "restriction" would be $\lambda \to +\infty$ or $(1/\lambda) \to 0$, which would be difficult to test formally. More encouraging and useful results are given in Coelli (1995), who shows that the likelihood ratio statistic has a limiting distribution that is a tractable mix of chi-squared variates.

28. The log-likelihood for the normal–half-normal model has two roots, one at OLS with $\lambda = 0$ and one at the MLE with positive λ. In the event noted, the first solution is "superior" to the second.

29. It does create a bit of a dilemma for the practitioner. In itself, the result is an important diagnostic for the model specification. However, it does not carry over to other model formulations and more elaborate extensions. As such, one might choose to proceed despite the warning. Then again, some of the estimators of these elaborate models use the "plain vanilla" ALS frontier estimates as starting values for the iterations. In this case, at least the warning will be heard. I note, for the benefit of the practitioner, that the occurrence of this result is not indicative of a problem with the data or the software—it signals a mismatch between the model and the data. The appropriate conclusion to draw is that the data do not contain evidence of inefficiency. A more encouraging result, however, is that this result is specific to the half-normal model above. Other formulations of the model, or more highly developed specifications, might well reveal the presence of inefficiency. That is, this finding can emerge from several sources.

30. Of course, this assumption is no less restrictive than half-normality.

31. One apparently reliable strategy is based on OLS for the slopes, and the method of moments for the remaining parameters.

32. My literature search returned roughly 35 references in total. Most are described in the various sections to follow, so I eschew a rote listing of them here. I will wait for my next edition of this survey before applying any generic appellation to the nascent Bayesian literature, because at least 16 of those 35 studies were produced by the same four authors. Suffice to say, as of this writing, the Bayesian methodology has made a significant contribution to the larger literature.

33. Other treatments that contain useful entry-level introductory material are Osiewalski and Steel (1998), Kleit and Terrell (2001), Tsionas (2001a), and Kim and Schmidt (2000).

34. Impressions (and assertions) to the contrary notwithstanding, neither Bayesian nor classical procedures estimate u_i, conditionally or otherwise. They estimate the conditional mean function, $E[u_i|\text{data}]$, the mean of the conditional distribution of the population that generated u_i. Section 2.8 revisits this issue.

35. For the production or cost model, Koop and Steel (2001) suggest a refinement to include $p(\beta) \propto$ an indicator function that includes the regularity conditions. [This device is used by Kleit and Terrell (2001).] For example, in a Cobb-Douglas model, we require the elasticities to be positive. As stated, their "indicator function" cannot actually be a "prior" in a flexible functional form, since the regularity conditions are only local and functions of the present data. Given the ambiguity, we will maintain the simpler prior over the technology parameters and leave the question to be resolved elsewhere.

36. Note a point here that appears to have been lost in the received Bayesian applications that frequently cite the shortcomings of the JLMS (Jondrow, Lovell, Materov, and Schmidt, 1982) "estimator" of u_i. The conditional mean being estimated at the data augmentation step of the Gibbs sampler is precisely the same conditional mean function that is computed by the classical estimator using the JLMS results. This is not surprising, of course, since, in fact, conditional means are all that can be estimated in this context under either methodology. I return to this point below.

37. The closed form for a few integer values may be found in Amemiya (1973).

38. However, there is some evidence given by van den Broeck et al. (1994) that Greene's results may have been influenced by some complications in the numerical procedures. Coincidentally, these authors (p. 17) likewise experience considerable difficulty in estimating a nonzero μ in the truncated-normal model.

39. The difficulty lies in accurately computing the moment of the truncated normal distribution [the $q(r, \varepsilon_i)$ function]. An equally complex model that has also not been used empirically is Lee's (1983) four-parameter Pearson family of distributions.

40. The authors obtain some results in this study which suggest that Greene's results were heavily influenced by the method of approximating the integrals $q(r, \varepsilon_i)$. Their results are reasonably strong, though clearly the extension to noninteger P would be useful.

41. Estimation of the posterior mean of u_{it} requires sampling from the truncated normal distribution. Tsionas (2002) suggests acceptance/rejection and a modification thereof for the troublesome tail areas. The inverse probability transformation discussed above would be an improvement.

42. In my literature search, I found, up to mid-2005, roughly 35 applications of Bayesian methods to frontier modeling; five of these, those mentioned above, use the Christensen and Greene (1976; CG) data, and one (Kleit and Terrell, 2001) builds on the principles in CG but uses an updated data set. [The widely circulated "classical" study by Bera and Sharma (1999) also uses these data.] Curiously, Kleit and Terrell (2001) argue that the CG data are outdated (possibly so), but also that the CG data were a "limited sample of fossil fuel electric generators" (p. 524). In fact, the CG 1970 firm-level sample contained within a percent or two the entire universe of privately owned fossil-fueled generators in the United States in 1970, whereas their updated plant-level data set included 78 of the several hundred U.S. generators in 1996. This adds a useful layer to the use of the CG data as an application. While the Bayesian methods limit their inferences to the sample data, classical ("asymptotic") methods attempt to extend the reach of the results to the broader population. But, for these data, in that year, the sample *is* the population. There remains, therefore, some scope for researchers to dig a bit deeper and examine the differences between Bayesian and classical results—small though they usually are. It is also striking that, although one of the oft-touted virtues of the Bayesian methodology is that it enables the researcher to incorporate "prior information," not one of these six studies used a single result from CG or any of the other studies in formulating their "priors" for any of the model parameters or the inefficiency estimates. In the same fashion, several studies (e.g., Tsionas, 2000b; Smith, 2004) have used the airline panel data in Greene (1997), but, again, none of these found useful prior information in any of the predecessors. I note (only) three studies: Tsionas (2001b), in which prior (DEA efficiency) estimates are incorporated in the estimation priors, and Kim and Schmidt (2000) and O'Donnell

and Coelli (2005), which use the classical MLEs for the variance parameters, for the study at hand.

43. Of course, once they are added to commercial software, the issue of difficulty of implementation becomes a moot point.

44. See van den Broeck et al. (1994), Osiewalski and Steel (1998), Koop and Steel (2001), and Tsionas (2001a) for surveys and introductory analyses.

45. This is to be expected given the well-known result that, in the presence of diffuse priors, the Bayesian posterior mean will converge to the mode of the likelihood function—in the absence of prior information, the likelihood function dominates the Bayesian estimator. See Kim and Schmidt (2000) for commentary.

46. The results are extended in Lee (1993), who addresses the issue of inference in the stochastic frontier model at the boundary of the parameter space, $\lambda = 0$.

47. There is a complication in the Bayesian approach to estimation of this model that does not arise in the classical method—the "labeling problem." A Bayesian estimator must actually decide a priori which class is which and make a distinction during estimation. An approach that is sometimes used is to identify as "class 1" the class with the largest prior class probability, and the others similarly. The classical MLE just allows the classes to fall out of the maximization process.

48. The authors analyzed the truncated-normal model and considered a cost frontier model. I have simplified the formulation a bit for purposes of the description, and changed the parameterization slightly, as well.

49. There is a minor ambiguity in Kumbhakar et al. (2005). The authors define m to be the number of parameters in the model, but the definition of the kernel function is only consistent with m equal the number of variables in x_i.

50. Koop (2001) also applied this approach to the output of major league baseball players were the four outputs are singles, doubles and triples, home runs, and walks and the "inputs" are time, team, and league dummy variables—illustrative of the technique, but perhaps of limited policy relevance.

51. See Christensen and Greene (1976).

52. Some additional useful related results appear in Kumbhakar (1991b) and in Kumbhakar and Lovell (2000).

53. Note what would be the utility of the Førsund and Jansen's (1977) input-oriented efficiency formulation, $y_i = F[f(\mathrm{TE}_i x_i)]$. Under this assumption, the cost function would always be of the form $\ln C_i = \ln F^{-1}(y) + \ln c(w_i) - v_i - \ln \mathrm{TE}_i$. See Alvarez, Arias, and Greene (2005) for an analysis along these lines that explicitly accounts for the internal relationships and Alvarez et al. (2004) for an analysis of mixtures of input and output-oriented inefficiency models.

54. The lack of invariance to the units of measurement of output also conflicts with the useful Farrell measure of economic efficiency.

55. As I noted in the preface (section 2.1.5), my apologies to the very large number of researchers whose work is not listed here. For these two industries, there are scores of applications, and in the interest of brevity, I can list only a few of them. Those chosen are only illustrative of these very large literatures.

56. In a remarkably obscure study, Greene (1983) proposed a translog cost model in which all parameters were of the form $\theta_{k,t} = \theta_{k,0} + \theta_{k,1} t$. The Kurkalova and Carriquiry (2003) study does likewise, although with only two periods, their formulation is much simpler. Cornwell et al. (1990) added a quadratic term, $\theta_{k,2} t^2$.

57. This approach has become essentially standard in the DEA literature.

58. It does not follow automatically that biases in the estimates of the parameters of the production or cost function will translate into biases in estimates of inefficiency (though the evidence does suggest it does). In a linear regression model, omitted variable biases in coefficients do not always translate into biases in forecasts. Under some reasonable assumptions, one can, e.g., safely truncate a distributed lag model.

59. These models are anticipated in Kumbhakar and Hjalmarsson (1995), who proposed representing time-varying inefficiency with equivalents to these models. Their proposed estimators do not maintain the stochastic frontier specification, however. Methodological issues are discussed in Heshmati and Kumbhakar (1994) and Kumbhakar and Heshmati (1995).

60. Swamy and Tavlas (2001) label these "first-generation" and "second-generation" methods. In the current literature, one can find a vast library of treatments on "mixed" models, "hierarchical" models, "multilevel" models, and "random-parameters" models, all of which are the same. Applications can be found in every area in the social sciences.

61. Their study demonstrated, as one might guess from the functional form, that ignoring heteroskedasticity of this form would lead to persistent biases in MLEs of the production or cost function parameters.

62. A Monte Carlo study of the properties of this model is Guermat and Hadri (1999). The exponential model with nonmonotonic effects on estimated inefficiency is examined at length in Wang (2002). An application of the doubly heteroskedastic model is Hadri et al. (2003a, 2003b).

63. See Schmidt and Sickles (1984).

64. There seems to be a presumption in some writings that the fixed-effects model when fit to panel data *must* be computed by using the "within" transformation (deviations from group means). In fact, this is merely a means to another end and, with modern software, some of which is quite capable of estimating regressions with hundreds of coefficients (even with desktop computers), may be quite unnecessary. The point is that this ought not to be construed as any sort of model in itself; it is merely a computational device usable for solving a practical problem. Note this is the motivation behind Greene's (2005) "true" fixed-effects model.

65. For example, their model involved 14 basic coefficients and a $[\alpha, \gamma, \delta]_i$ for each of eight firms, a total of 38 coefficients. This is well within the reach of any modern regression package, even on a desktop computer. The point is that there are few practical obstacles to computing estimators for the various frontier models given the current state of computer software.

66. Kumbhakar (1991a) proposes a hybrid of the frontier model and a two-way random-effects model. The disturbance specification is $\varepsilon_{it} = w_i + c_t + v_{it} - u_{it}$ (my notation) in which w_i, c_t, and v_{it} constitute, with normal distributions, a more or less conventional model by Balestra and Nerlove (1968), but u_{it} is the truncation of a normally distributed variable with mean μ_{it} (which may depend on exogenous variables). Thus, the fact that u_{it} is positive embodies the frontier aspect of the model, but the panel nature of the model is carried by w_i and c_t. Once again, this is essentially the same as Greene's (2004a) true random-effects model.

67. In the Bayesian framework, the distinction between fixed and random effects does not have the same interpretation as in the classical framework. As will be evident momentarily, the distinction becomes simply whether the inefficiencies are treated as parameters or as missing data. Estimation is the same either way.

68. Greene and Misra (2003) discuss simulation-based estimation of this quantity for cases in which the precise functional form is not known.

69. For the gamma model, $E[u_{it}^r|\varepsilon_{it}] = q(P + r - 1, \varepsilon_{it})/q(P - 1, \varepsilon_{it})$.

70. I have also investigated experimentally the relationship between the JLMS estimator and the actual inefficiencies when the latter are "known." Not surprisingly, I found that the overall quality of the estimator degrades with smaller λ values, that is, with larger noise components, v. What was a bit surprising was that the JLMS estimator tends systematically to underpredict u when u is small and overpredict it when u is large—again, with improvement as λ increases.

71. There is one other small point that might be considered in either a Bayesian or a classical context. The interval thus constructed is not as short as it might be. In order to encompass $100(1 - \alpha)\%$ of this asymmetric distribution, with the narrowest interval possible, we should find the equivalent of the Bayesian HPD interval. For the truncated normal distribution, we can actually deduce what this is. Suppose we wish to capture 95% of the mass of the distribution. For a density in which more than 2.5% of the untruncated distribution is to the left of zero (and this will be most of the time), the shortest interval will be from zero to the 95th percentile of the truncated normal distribution. By construction, this interval will be shorter than one that puts 2.5% of the mass from zero to L and 2.5% of the mass to the right of U. A simple figure makes this obvious.

72. See Bera and Sharma (1999) and Hjalmarsson, Kumbhakar, and Heshmati (1996). Bera and Sharma also provide the expressions needed for the Battese and Coelli measures, $E[TE_i|\varepsilon_i]$.

73. There have been a number of panel-data analyses of this industry, including Sickles (1987), Sickles, Good, and Johnson (1986), Schmidt and Sickles (1984), Good, Nadiri, Roller, and Sickles (1993), Good, Roller, and Sickles (1993), Good, Roller, and Sickles (1995), Good and Sickles (1995), and Alam and Sickles (1998, 2000), and the references cited therein.

74. Results extracted from other studies, notably the Bayesian estimates reported in section 2.10.2.1, were not replicated here. Researchers who wish to replicate those results should contact the original authors.

75. There are no general-purpose econometric packages that specifically contain MLEs for deterministic frontier models, though there are any number of programs with which the linear and quadratic programming "estimators" can be computed. Likewise, the gamma model with only one-sided residuals can be programmed but presents an exceedingly difficult problem for conventional estimation.

76. A separate package, downloadable at no cost (as is *Frontier 4.2*), distributed by the Center for Efficiency and Productivity Analysis at the University of Queensland in Australia, can be used for DEA (http://http://www.scripting.com/frontier/newReleases/Frontier42.html).

77. The lack of replicability in empirical econometrics has been widely documented and is, ultimately, a major challenge and shortcoming of a large amount of contemporary research (see, e.g., Anderson et al., 2005). Even a cursory reading of the Bayesian applications of stochastic frontier modeling will suggest how difficult it would be to replicate this type of work the way it is currently documented.

78. The original data set contained the 123 observations discussed above and 35 holding company aggregates of some of the firms. My data file contains all 158 observations, but we will be using only the 123 firm-level observations.

79. Using the standard deviation of u_i rather than the mean as the initial estimator of γ to form the weighting matrix led to an implausible value of θ in excess of 6.0.

80. The parameter heterogeneity feature of these two applications takes the model in a different direction. It appears that this feature has induced the peculiar findings with respect to inefficiency, but that is aside from the specification issue.

81. Their conclusion, "This paradigm thus allows direct posterior inference on firm-specific efficiencies, avoiding the much criticized two-step procedure of Jondrow et al. (1982)," overreaches a bit. Subsequent researchers continue to rely comfortably on JLMS and the extensions suggested by Horrace and Schmidt (1996), Bera and Sharma (1999), and Kim and Schmidt (2000). And, as shown above, the Bayesian posterior estimators are essentially the same as the classical JLMS estimator.

82. Kim and Schmidt (2000) found, likewise, that the Bayesian and classical estimators when applied to the same model under the same assumptions tended to produce essentially the same results.

83. It appears that there might have been some small differences in the data used—the "fixed-parameter" estimates reported seem to resemble, but not quite equal, our classical, least squares estimates or our normal–gamma estimates. Because we are interested here only in the methodology, I leave it to subsequent researchers to fine-tune the comparison.

84. If we restrict the sample to only the firms with all 15 years of data, the entire problem vanishes, and there is no problem fitting the stochastic production frontier model. As a general rule, we would not do the specification search in this fashion, so we will not pursue this angle.

85. These data were developed and provided by S. Kumbhakar and E. Tsionas. Their assistance is gratefully acknowledged here.

86. This model as given would be the classical counterpart to a hierarchical Bayes formulation, e.g., in Tsionas (2002). The fixed values of λ and σ would correspond to flat priors, which would lead to the MLEs.

87. In our implementation of this procedure, we do not actually use random draws from the distribution. The terms in the simulation are built up from Halton sequences, which are deterministic. Details on this method of integration appear in Train (2003) and Greene (2003a).

88. The wall of points at the right in the scatter plot is the value produced for relatively extreme observations, where the numerical limit of our ability to compute the standard normal CDF is reached: at about 8.9 standard deviations.

References

Absoft, 2005, *IMSL Libraries, Reference Guide*, http://www.absoft.com/Products/Libraries/imsl.html.

Adams, R., A. Berger, and R. Sickles, 1999, "Semiparametric Approaches to Stochastic Panel Frontiers with Applications in the Banking Industry," *Journal of Business and Economic Statistics*, 17, pp. 349–358.

Afriat, S., 1972, "Efficiency Estimation of Production Functions," *International Economic Review*, 13, pp. 568–598.

Aguilar, R., 1988, "Efficiency in Production: Theory and an Application on Kenyan Smallholders," Ph.D. Dissertation, Department of Economics, University of Göteborg, Sweden.

Aigner, D., T. Amemiya, and D. Poirier, 1976, "On the Estimation of Production Frontiers," *International Economic Review*, 17, pp. 377–396.

Aigner, D., and S. Chu, 1968, "On Estimating the Industry Production Function," *American Economic Review*, 58, pp. 826–839.

Aigner, D., K. Lovell, and P. Schmidt, 1977, "Formulation and Estimation of Stochastic Frontier Production Function Models," *Journal of Econometrics*, 6, pp. 21–37.

Akhavein, J., P. Swamy, and S. Taubman, 1994, "A General Method of Deriving Efficiencies of Banks from a Profit Function," Working Paper No. 94-26, Wharton School, University of Pennsylvania, Philadelphia.

Alam, I., and R. Sickles, 1998, "The Relationship Between Stock Market Returns and Technical Efficiency Innovations: Evidence from the U.S. Airline Industry," *Journal of Productivity Analysis*, 9, pp. 35–51.

Alam, I., and R. Sickles, 2000, "A Time Series Analysis of Deregulatory Dynamics and Technical Efficiency: The Case of the U.S. Airline Industry," *International Economic Review*, 41, pp. 203–218.

Albert, J., and S. Chib, 1993, "Bayesian Analysis of Binary and Polytomous Response Data," *Journal of the American Statistical Association*, 88, pp. 669–679.

Albriktsen, R., and F. Førsund, 1990, "A Productivity Study of the Norwegian Building Industry," *Journal of Productivity Analysis*, 2, pp. 53–66.

Ali, A., and L. Seiford, 1993, "The Mathematical Programming Approach to Efficiency Analysis," in *The Measurement of Productive Efficiency*, H. Fried, K. Lovell, and S. Schmidt, eds. Oxford University Press, New York.

Alvarez, A., C. Amsler, L. Orea, and P. Schmidt, 2006, "Interpreting and Testing the Scaling Property in Models Where Inefficiency Depends on Firm Characteristics," *Journal of Productivity Analysis*, 25, 3, 2006, pp. 201-212.

Alvarez, A., C. Arias, and W. Greene, 2005, "Accounting for Unobservables in Production Models: Management and Inefficiency," Working Paper, Department of Economics, University of Oviedo, Spain.

Alvarez, A., C. Arias, and S. Kumbhakar, 2004, "Additive Versus Interactive Unobservable Individual Effects in the Estimation of Technical Efficiency," Working Paper, Department of Economics, University of Oviedo, Spain.

Amemiya, T., 1973, "Regression Analysis When the Dependent Variable Is Truncated Normal," *Econometrica*, 41, pp. 997–1016.

Anderson, R., W. Greene, B. McCullough, and H. Vinod, 2005, "The Role of Data and Program Archives in the Future of Economic Research," Working Paper 2005-14, Federal Reserve Bank, St. Louis, MO.

Annaert, J., J. van den Broeck, and R. Vennet, 2001, "Determinants of Mutual Fund Performance: A Bayesian Stochastic Frontier Approach," Working Paper 2001/103, University of Gent, Ghent, Belgium.

Aptech Systems, Inc., 2005, *Gauss Reference Guide*, http://http://www.aptech.com, Kent, WA.

Arickx, F., J. Broeckhove, M. Dejonghe, and J. van den Broeck, 1997, "BSFM: A Computer Program for Bayesian Stochastic Frontier Models," *Computational Statistics*, 12, pp. 403–421.

Arrow, K., H. Chenery, B. Minhas, and R. Solow, 1961, "Capital Labor Substitution and Economic Efficiency," *Review of Economics and Statistics*, 45, pp. 225–247.

Atkinson, S., and C. Cornwell, 1993, "Estimation of Technical Efficiency with Panel Data: A Dual Approach," *Journal of Econometrics*, 59, pp. 257–262.

Atkinson, S., and J. Dorfman, 2005, "Bayesian Measurement of Productivity and Efficiency in the Presence of Undesirable Outputs: Crediting Electric Utilities for Reducing Air Pollution," *Journal of Econometrics*, 126, pp. 445–468.

Atkinson, S, R. Fare, and D. Primont, 2003 "Stochastic Estimation of Firm Technology, Inefficiency and Productivity Growth Using Shadow Cost and Distance Functions," *Journal of Econometrics*, 108, pp. 203–226.

Averch, H., and L. Johnson, 1962, "Behavior of the Firm under Regulatory Constraint," *American Economic Review*, 52, pp. 1052–1069.

Balestra, P., and M. Nerlove, 1968, "Pooling Cross Section and Time Series Data in the Estimation of a Dynamic Model: The Demand for Natural Gas," *Econometrica*, 34, pp. 585–612.

Bankar, R., 1993, "Maximum Likelihood, Consistency, and Data Envelopment Analysis," *Management Science*, 39, pp. 1265–1273.

Bankar, R., 1997, "Hypothesis Tests Using Data Envelopment Analysis," *Journal of Productivity Analysis*, 7, pp. 139–159.

Banker, R., and A. Maindiratta, 1988, "Nonparametric Analysis of Technical and Allocative Efficiencies in Production," *Econometrica*, 56, pp. 1315–1332.

Battese, G., 1992, "Frontier Production Functions and Technical Efficiency: A Survey of Empirical Applications in Agricultural Economics," *Agricultural Economics*, 7, pp. 185–208.

Battese, G., and T. Coelli, 1988, "Prediction of Firm-level Technical Efficiencies with a Generalized Frontier Production Function and Panel Data," *Journal of Econometrics*, 38, pp. 387–399.

Battese, G., and T. Coelli, 1992, "Frontier Production Functions, Technical Efficiency and Panel Data: With Application to Paddy Farmers in India," *Journal of Productivity Analysis*, 3, pp. 153–169.

Battese, G., and T. Coelli, 1995, "A Model for Technical Inefficiency Effects in a Stochastic Frontier Production Model for Panel Data," *Empirical Economics*, 20, pp. 325–332.

Battese, G., T. Coelli, and T. Colby, 1989, "Estimation of Frontier Production Functions and the Efficiencies of Indian Farms Using Panel Data from ICRISTAT's Village Level Studies," *Journal of Quantitative Economics*, 5, pp. 327–348.

Battese, G., and G. Corra, 1977, "Estimation of a Production Frontier Model: With Application to the Pastoral Zone of Eastern Australia," *Australian Journal of Agricultural Economics*, 21, pp. 167–179.

Battese, G., A. Rambaldi, and G. Wan, 1997, "A Stochastic Frontier Production Function with Flexible Risk Properties," *Journal of Productivity Analysis*, 8, pp. 269–280.

Bauer, P., 1990, "A Survey of Recent Econometric Developments in Frontier Estimation," *Journal of Econometrics*, 46, pp. 21–39.

Bauer, P., A. Berger, G. Ferrier, and D. Humphrey, 1998, "Consistency Conditions for Regulatory Analysis of Financial Institutions: A Comparison of Frontier Efficiency Methods," *Journal of Economics and Business*, 50, pp. 85–114.

Beckers, D., and C. Hammond, 1987, "A Tractable Likelihood Function for the Normal-Gamma Stochastic Frontier Model," *Economics Letters*, 24, pp. 33–38.

Bera, A., and S. Sharma, 1999, "Estimating Production Uncertainty in Stochastic Frontier Production Function Models," *Journal of Productivity Analysis*, 12, pp. 187–210.

Berger, A., 1993, "Distribution Free Estimates of Efficiency in the U.S. Banking Industry and Tests of the Standard Distributional Assumptions," *Journal of Productivity Analysis*, 4, pp. 261–292.

Berger, A., and D. Humphrey, 1991, "The Dominance of Inefficiencies over Scale and Product Mix Economies in Banking," *Journal of Monetary Economics*, 28, pp. 117–148.

Berger, A., and D. Humphrey, 1992, "Measurement and Efficiency Issues in Commercial Banking," in *National Bureau of Economic Research Studies in Income and Wealth*, Vol. 56, *Output Measurement in the Service Sector*, Z. Griliches, ed., Chicago, University of Chicago Press.

Berger, A., and L. Mester, 1997, "Inside the Black Box: What Explains Differences in Efficiencies of Financial Institutions?" *Journal of Banking and Finance*, 21, pp. 895–947.

Bhattacharyya, A., S. Kumbhakar, and A. Bhattacharyya, 1995, "Ownership Structure and Cost Efficiency: A Study of Publicly Owned Passenger Bus Transportation Companies in India," *Journal of Productivity Analysis*, 6, pp. 47–62.

Bjurek, H., L. Hjalmarsson, and F. Forsund, 1990, "Deterministic Parametric and Nonparametric Estimation of Efficiency in Service Production: A Comparison," *Journal of Econometrics*, 46, pp. 213–227.

Breusch, T., and A. Pagan, 1980, "The LM Test and Its Applications to Model Specification in Econometrics," *Review of Economic Studies*, 47, pp. 239–254.

Cameron, C., T. Li, P. Trivedi, and D. Zimmer, 2004, "Modeling the Differences in Counted Outcomes Using Bivariate Copula Models with Applications to Mismeasured Counts," *Econometrics Journal*, 7, pp. 566–584.

Casella, G., and E. George, 1992, "Explaining the Gibbs Sampler," *American Statistician*, 46, pp. 167–174.

Caudill, S., and Ford, J., 1993, "Biases in Frontier Estimation Due to Heteroskedasticity," *Economics Letters*, 41, pp. 17–20.

Caudill, S., J. Ford, and D. Gropper, 1995, "Frontier Estimation and Firm Specific Inefficiency Measures in the Presence of Heteroscedasticity," *Journal of Business and Economic Statistics*, 13, pp. 105–111.

Caves, D., L. Christensen, and M. Trethaway, 1980, "Flexible Cost Functions for Multiproduct Firms," *Review of Economics and Statistics*, 62, pp. 477–481.

Cazals, C., J. Florens, and L. Simar, 2002, "Nonparametric Frontier Estimation: A Robust Approach," *Journal of Econometrics*, 106, pp. 1–25.

Chakraborty, K., B. Biswas, and W. Lewis, 2001, "Measurement of Technical Efficiency in Public Education: A Stochastic and Nonstochastic Production Function Approach," *Southern Economic Journal*, 67, pp. 889–905.

Chen, T., and D. Tang, 1989, "Comparing Technical Efficiency Between Import Substitution Oriented and Export Oriented Foreign Firms in a Developing Economy," *Journal of Development of Economics*, 26, pp. 277–289.

Christensen, L., and W. Greene, 1976, "Economies of Scale in U.S. Electric Power Generation," *Journal of Political Economy*, 84, pp. 655–676.

Cobb, S., and P. Douglas, 1928, "A Theory of Production," *American Economic Review*, 18, pp. 139–165.

Coelli, T., 1991, "Maximum Likelihood Estimation of Stochastic Frontier Production Functions with Time Varying Technical Efficiency Using the Computer Program Frontier Version 2.0," Department of Economics, University of New England, Armidale, Australia.

Coelli, T., 1995, "Estimators and Hypothesis Tests for a Stochastic Frontier Function: A Monte Carlo Analysis," *Journal of Productivity Analysis*, 6, pp. 247–268.

Coelli, T., 1996, "Frontier Version 4.1: A Computer Program for Stochastic Frontier Production and Cost Function Estimation," Working Paper 96/7, Center for Efficiency and Productivity Analysis, Department of Econometrics, University of New England, Armidale, Australia.

Coelli, T., 2000, "On the Econometric Estimation of the Distance Function Representation of a Production Technology," Working Paper 2000/42, CORE, Catholic University of Louvain, Louvain-la-Neuve, Belgium.

Coelli, T., and S. Perelman, 1996, "Efficiency Measurement, Multiple Output Technologies and Distance Functions: With Application to European Railways," *European Journal of Operational Research*, 117, pp. 326–339.

Coelli, T., and S. Perelman, 1999, "A Comparison of Parametric and Nonparametric Distance Functions: With Application to European Railways," CREPP Discussion Paper 96/25, University of Liège, Belgium.

Coelli, T., and S. Perelman, 2000, "Technical Efficiency of European Railways: A Distance Function Approach," *Applied Economics*, 32, pp. 67–76.

Coelli, T., P. Rao, and G. Battese, 1998, *An Introduction to Efficiency and Productivity Analysis*, Kluwer Academic Publishers, Boston.

Cornwell, C., and P. Schmidt, 1996, "Production Frontiers and Efficiency Measurement," in *The Econometrics of Panel Data: A Handbook of the Theory with Applications*, 2nd rev. ed., L. Matyas and P. Sevestre, eds., Kluwer Academic Publishers, Boston.

Cornwell, C., P. Schmidt, and R. Sickles, 1990, "Production Frontiers with Cross Sectional and Time Series Variation in Efficiency Levels," *Journal of Econometrics*, 46, pp. 185–200.

Cuesta, R., 2000, "A Production Model with Firm Specific Temporal Variation in Technical Efficiency: With Application to Spanish Dairy Farms," *Journal of Productivity Analysis*, 13, pp. 139–158.

Cuesta, R., and L. Orea, 2002, "Mergers and Technical Efficiency in Spanish Savings Banks: A Stochastic Distance Function Approach," *Journal of Banking and Finance*, 26, pp. 2231–2247.

Cummins, J., and H. Zi, 1998, "Comparison of Frontier Efficiency Models: An Application to the U.S. Life Insurance Industry," *Journal of Productivity Analysis*, 10, pp. 131–152.

Dean, J., 1951, *Managerial Economics*, Prentice Hall, Englewood Cliffs, NJ.

Debreu, G., 1951, "The Coefficient of Resource Utilization," *Econometrica*, 19, pp. 273–292.

Deprins, D., and L. Simar, 1985, "A Note on the Asymptotic Relative Efficiency of M.L.E. in a Linear Model with Gamma Disturbances," *Journal of Econometrics*, 27, pp. 383–386.

Deprins, D., and L. Simar, 1989a, "Estimation of Deterministic Frontiers with Exogenous Factors of Inefficiency," *Annals of Economics and Statistics (Paris)*, 14, pp. 117–150.

Deprins, D., and L. Simar, 1989b, "Estimating Technical Inefficiencies with Corrections for Environmental Conditions with an Application to Railway Companies," *Annals of Public and Cooperative Economics*, 60, pp. 81–102.

Econometric Software, Inc., 2000, *LIMDEP, User's Manual*, http://http://www.limdep.com, Plainview, NY.

Estima, 2005, *RATS Reference Guide*, http://http://www.estima.com, Evanston, IL.

Evans, D, A. Tandon, C. Murray, and J. Lauer, 2000a, "The Comparative Efficiency of National Health Systems in Producing Health: An Analysis of 191 Countries," GPE Discussion Paper No. 29, EIP/GPE/EQC, World Health Organization, Geneva.

Evans D, A. Tandon, C. Murray, and J. Lauer, 2000b, "Measuring Overall Health System Performance for 191 Countries," GPE Discussion Paper No. 30, EIP/GPE/EQC, World Health Organization, Geneva.

Fan, Y., Q. Li, and A. Weersink, 1996, "Semiparametric Estimation of Stochastic Production Frontiers," *Journal of Business and Economic Statistics*, 64, pp. 865–890.

Farrell, M., 1957, "The Measurement of Productive Efficiency," *Journal of the Royal Statistical Society A, General*, 120, pp. 253–281.

Farsi, M., and M. Filippini, 2003, "An Empirical Analysis of Cost Efficiency in Non-profit and Public Nursing Homes," Working Paper, Department of Economics, University of Lugano, Switzerland.

Farsi, M., M. Filippini, and M. Kuenzle, 2003, "Unobserved Heterogeneity in Stochastic Cost Frontier Models: A Comparative Analysis," Working Paper 03-11, Department of Economics, University of Lugano, Switzerland.

Fernandez, C., G. Koop, and M. Steel, 1999, "Multiple Output Production with Undesirable Outputs: An Application to Nitrogen Surplus in Agriculture," Working Paper 99-17, Department of Economics, University of Edinburgh, Scotland.

Fernandez, C., G. Koop, and M. Steel, 2000, "A Bayesian Analysis of Multiple Output Production Frontiers," *Journal of Econometrics*, 98, pp. 47–79.

Fernandez, C., G. Koop, and M. Steel, 2002, "Multiple Output Production with Undesirable Outputs: An Application to Nitrogen Surplus in Agriculture," *Journal of the American Statistical Association*, 97, pp. 432–442.

Fernandez, C., G. Koop, and M. Steel, 2005, "Alternative Efficiency Measures for Multiple Output Production," Journal of Econometrics, 126, 2, 2005, pp. 411–444.

Fernandez, C. J. Osiewalski, and M. Steel, 1997, "On the Use of Panel Data in Stochastic Frontier Models with Improper Priors," *Journal of Econometrics*, 79, pp. 169–193.

Ferrier, G., and K. Lovell, 1990, "Measuring Cost Efficiency in Banking: Econometric and Linear Programming Evidence," *Journal of Econometrics*, 46, pp. 229–245.

Førsund, F., 1992, "A Comparison of Parametric and Nonparametric Efficiency Measures: The Case of Norwegian Ferries," *Journal of Productivity Analysis*, 3, pp. 25–44.

Førsund, F., and L. Hjalmarsson, 1974, "On the Measurement of Productive Efficiency," *Swedish Journal of Economics*, 76, pp. 141–154.

Førsund, F., and L. Hjalmarsson, 1979, "Frontier Production Functions and Technical Progress: A Study of General Milk Processing in Swedish Dairy Plants," *Econometrica*, 47, pp. 883–900.

Førsund, F., and E. Jansen, 1977, "On Estimating Average and Best Practice Homothetic Production Functions via Cost Functions," *International Economic Review*, 18, pp. 463–476.

Førsund, F., K. Lovell, and P. Schmidt, 1980, "A Survey of Frontier Production Functions and of Their Relationship to Efficiency Measurement," *Journal of Econometrics*, 13, pp. 5–25.

Gabrielsen, A., 1975, "On Estimating Efficient Production Functions," Working Paper No. A-85, Chr. Michelsen Institute, Department of Humanities and Social Sciences, Bergen, Norway.

Gong, B., and R. Sickles, 1989, "Finite Sample Evidence on the Performance of Stochastic Frontier Models Using Panel Data," *Journal of Productivity Analysis*, 1, pp. 119–261.

Good, D., I. Nadiri, L. Roller, and R. Sickles, 1993, "Efficiency and Productivity Growth Comparisons of European and U.S. Air Carriers: A First Look at the Data," *Journal of Productivity Analysis*, 4, pp. 115–125.

Good, D., L. Roller, and R. Sickles, 1993, "U.S. Airline Deregulation: Implications for European Transport," *Economic Journal*, 103, pp. 1028–1041.

Good, D., L. Roller, and R. Sickles, 1995, "Airline Efficiency Differences Between Europe and the U.S.: Implications for the Pace of E.C. Integration and Domestic Regulation," *European Journal of Operational Research*, 80, pp. 508–518.

Good, D., and Sickles, R., 1995, "East Meets West: A Comparison of the Productive Performance of Eastern European and Western European Air Carriers," Working Paper, Department of Economics, Rice University, Houston, TX.

Gravelle H, R. Jacobs, A. Jones, and A. Street, 2002a, "Comparing the Efficiency of National Health Systems: Econometric Analysis Should Be Handled with Care," Working Paper, Health Economics Unit, University of York, UK.

Gravelle H, R. Jacobs, A. Jones, and A. Street, 2002b, "Comparing the Efficiency of National Health Systems: A Sensitivity Approach," Working Paper, Health Economics Unit, University of York, UK.

Greene, W., 1980a, "Maximum Likelihood Estimation of Econometric Frontier Functions," *Journal of Econometrics*, 13, pp. 27–56.

Greene, W., 1980b, "On the Estimation of a Flexible Frontier Production Model," *Journal of Econometrics*, 3, pp. 101–115.

Greene, W., 1983, "Simultaneous Estimation of Factor Substitution, Economies of Scale, and Non-neutral Technological Change," in *Econometric Analyses of Productive Efficiency*, Dogramaci, A., ed., Nijoff Publishing Co., Dordrecht, The Netherlands.

Greene, W., 1990, "A Gamma Distributed Stochastic Frontier Model," *Journal of Econometrics*, 46, pp. 141–163.

Greene, W., 1993, "The Econometric Approach to Efficiency Analysis," in *The Measurement of Productive Efficiency*, H. Fried, K. Lovell, and S. Schmidt, eds., Oxford University Press, Oxford.

Greene, W., 1997, "Frontier Production Functions," in *Handbook of Applied Econometrics*, Vol. 2, *Microeconomics*, H. Pesaran and P. Schmidt, eds., Oxford University Press, Oxford.

Greene, W., 2000, "LIMDEP Computer Program: Version 8.0," Econometric Software, Plainview, NY.

Greene, W., 2003a, *Econometric Analysis*, 5th ed., Prentice Hall, Upper Saddle River, NJ.

Greene, W., 2003b, "Simulated Likelihood Estimation of the Normal-Gamma Stochastic Frontier Function," *Journal of Productivity Analysis*, 19, pp. 179–190.

Greene, W., 2004a, "Fixed and Random Effects in Stochastic Frontier Models," *Journal of Productivity Analysis*, 23, pp. 7–32.

Greene, W., 2004b, "Distinguishing Between Heterogeneity and Inefficiency: Stochastic Frontier Analysis of the World Health Organization's Panel Data on National Health Care Systems," *Health Economics*, 13, pp. 959–980.

Greene, W., 2005, "Reconsidering Heterogeneity in Panel Data Estimators of the Stochastic Frontier Model," *Journal of Econometrics*, 126, pp. 269–303.

Greene, W., and S. Misra, 2003, "Simulated Maximum Likelihood Estimation of General Stochastic Frontier Regressions," Working Paper, William Simon School of Business, University of Rochester, NY.

Griffin, J., and Steel, M., 2004, "Semiparametric Bayesian Inference for Stochastic Frontier Models," *Journal of Econometrics*, 123, pp. 121–152.

Griffiths, W.E., C. O'Donnell, A. Tan, and R. Cruz, 2000, "Imposing Regularity Conditions on a System of Cost and Cost Share Equations: A Bayesian Approach," *Australian Journal of Agricultural Economics*, 44, pp. 107–127.

Guermat, C., and K. Hadri, 1999, "Heteroscedasticity in Stochastic Frontier Models: A Monte Carlo Analysis," Working Paper, Department of Economics, City University, London, http://http://www.ex.ac.uk/~cguermat/het_mar99.pdf.

Hadri, K., 1999, "Estimation of a Doubly Heteroscedastic Stochastic Frontier Cost Function," *Journal of Business and Economics and Statistics*, 17, pp. 359–363.

Hadri, K., C. Guermat, and J. Whittaker, 2003a, "Estimating Farm Efficiency in the Presence of Double Heteroscedasticity Using Panel Data," *Journal of Applied Economics*, 6, pp. 255–268.

Hadri, K., C. Guermat, and J. Whittaker, 2003b, "Estimation of Technical Inefficiency Effects Using Panel Data and Doubly Heteroscedastic Stochastic Production Frontiers," *Empirical Economics*, 28, pp. 203–222.

Hausman, J., and W. Taylor, 1981, "Panel Data and Unobservable Individual Effects," *Econometrica*, 49, pp. 1377–1398.

Heshmati, A., and S. Kumbhakar, 1994, "Farm Heterogeneity and Technical Efficiency: Some Results from Swedish Dairy Farms," *Journal of Productivity Analysis*, 5, pp. 45–61.

Hicks, J., 1935, The Theory of Monopoly: A Survey," *Econometrica*, 3, pp. 1–20.

Hildebrand, G., and T. Liu, 1965, *Manufacturing Production Functions in the United States*, Cornell University Press, Ithaca, NY.

Hildreth, C., and C. Houck, 1968, "Some Estimators for a Linear Model with Random Coefficients," *Journal of the American Statistical Association*, 63, pp. 584–595.

Hjalmarsson, L., S. Kumbhakar, and A. Heshmati, 1996, "DEA, DFA and SFA: A Comparison," *Journal of Productivity Analysis*, 7, pp. 303–327.

Hollingsworth, J., and B. Wildman, 2002, "The Efficiency of Health Production: Re-estimating the WHO Panel Data Using Parametric and Nonparametric Approaches to Provide Additional Information," *Health Economics*, 11, pp. 1–11.

Holloway, G., D. Tomberlin, and X. Irz, 2005, "Hierarchical Analysis of Production Efficiency in a Coastal Trawl Fishery," in *Simulation Methods in Environmental and Resource Economics*, R. Scarpa and A. Alberini, eds., Springer Publishers, New York, 2005.

Horrace, W., and S. Richards, 2005, "Bootstrapping Efficiency Probabilities in Parametric Stochastic Frontier Models," Working Paper 2005-004, Maxwell School, Syracuse University, Syracuse, NY.

Horrace, W., and P. Schmidt, 1996, "Confidence Statements for Efficiency Estimates from Stochastic Frontier Models," *Journal of Productivity Analysis*, 7, pp. 257–282.

Horrace, W., and P. Schmidt, 2000, "Multiple Comparisons with the Best, with Economic Applications," *Journal of Applied Econometrics*, 15, pp. 1–26.

Hotelling, H., 1932, "Edgeworth's Taxation Paradox and the Nature of Supply and Demand Functions," *Journal of Political Economy*, 40, pp. 577–616.

Huang, C., and T. Fu, 1999, "An Average Derivative Estimator of a Stochastic Frontier," *Journal of Productivity Analysis*, 12, pp. 49–54.

Huang, C., and J. Liu, 1994, "Estimation of a Non-neutral Stochastic Frontier Production Function," *Journal of Productivity Analysis*, 5, pp. 171–180.

Huang, R., 2004, "Estimation of Technical Inefficiencies with Heterogeneous Technologies," *Journal of Productivity Analysis*, 21, pp. 277–296.

Huang, T., and M. Wang, 2004, "Comparisons of Economic Inefficiency Between Output and Input Measures of Technical Inefficiency Using the Fourier Flexible Cost Function," *Journal of Productivity Analysis*, 22, pp. 123–142.

Humphrey, D., and L. Pulley, 1997, 'Banks' Responses to Deregulation: Profits, Technology and Efficiency," *Journal of Money, Credit and Banking*, 29, pp. 73–93.

Hunt, J., Y. Kim, and R. Warren, 1986, "The Effect of Unemployment Duration on Re-employment Earnings: A Gamma Frontier Approach," Working Paper, Department of Economics, University of Georgia, Athens, GA.

Hunt-McCool, J., and R. Warren, 1993, "Earnings Frontiers and Labor Market Efficiency," in *The Measurement of Productive Efficiency*, H. Fried, K. Lovell, and S. Schmidt, eds., Oxford University Press, New York.

Johnston, J. 1959, *Statistical Cost Analysis*, McGraw-Hill, New York.

Jondrow, J., K. Lovell, I. Materov, and P. Schmidt, 1982, "On the Estimation of Technical Inefficiency in the Stochastic Frontier Production Function Model," *Journal of Econometrics*, 19, pp. 233–238.

Kalirajan, K., and M. Obwona, "Frontier Production Function: The Stochastic Coefficients Approach," *Oxford Bulletin of Economics and Statistics*, 56, 1, 1994, pp. 87–96.

Kalirajan, K., and R. Shand, 1999, "Frontier Production Functions and Technical Efficiency Measures," *Journal of Economic Surveys*, 13, pp. 149–172.

Kim, J., 2002, "Limited Information Likelihood and Bayesian Analysis," *Journal of Econometrics*, 107, pp. 175–193.

Kim, Y., and P. Schmidt, 2000, "A Review and Empirical Comparison of Bayesian and Classical Approaches to Inference on Efficiency Levels in Stochastic Frontier Models with Panel Data," *Journal of Productivity Analysis*, 14, pp. 91–98.

Kleit, A., and D. Terrell, 2001, "Measuring Potential Efficiency Gains from Deregulation of Electricity Generation: A Bayesian Approach," *Review of Economics and Statistics*, 83, pp. 523–530.

Klotz, B., R. Madoo, and R. Hansen, 1980, "A Study of High and Low Labor Productivity Establishments in U.S. Manufacturing," in *Studies in Income and Wealth*, Vol. 44, *New Developments in Productivity Measurement and Analysis*, Research Conference on Research in Income and Wealth, J. Kendrick and B. Vaccara, eds., National Bureau of Economic Research, University of Chicago Press, Chicago.

Koop, G., 2001, "Comparing the Performance of Baseball Players: A Multiple Output Approach," Working Paper, University of Glasgow, http://http://www.gla.ac.uk/Acad/PolEcon/Koop.

Koop, G., J. Osiewalski, and M. Steel, 1994, "Bayesian Efficiency Analysis with a Flexible Form: The AIM Cost Function," *Journal of Business and Economic Statistics*, 12, pp. 339–346.

Koop, G., J. Osiewalski, and M. Steel, 1997, "Bayesian Efficiency Analysis Through Individual Effects: Hospital Cost Frontiers," *Journal of Econometrics*, 76, pp. 77–106.

Koop, G., J. Osiewalski, and M. Steel, 1999, "The Components of Output Growth: A Stochastic Frontier Approach," *Oxford Bulletin of Economics and Statistics*, 61, pp. 455–486.

Koop, G., and M. Steel, 2001, "Bayesian Analysis of Stochastic Frontier Models," in *Companion to Theoretical Econometrics*, B. Baltagi, ed., Blackwell Publishers, Oxford, UK.

Koop, G., M. Steel, and J. Osiewalski, 1995, "Posterior Analysis of Stochastic Frontier Models Using Gibbs Sampling," *Computational Statistics*, 10, pp. 353–373.

Kopp, R., and J. Mullahy, 1989, "Moment-Based Estimation and Testing of Stochastic Frontier Models," Discussion Paper No. 89-10, Resources for the Future, Washington, DC.

Kotzian, P., 2005, "Productive Efficiency and Heterogeneity of Health Care Systems: Results of a Measurement for OECD Countries," Working Paper, London School of Economics, London.

Kumbhakar, S., 1989, "Estimation of Technical Efficiency Using Flexible Functional Forms and Panel Data," *Journal of Business and Economic Statistics*, 7, pp. 253–258.

Kumbhakar, S., 1990, "Production Frontiers and Panel Data, and Time Varying Technical Inefficiency," *Journal of Econometrics*, 46, pp. 201–211.

Kumbhakar, S., 1991a, "Estimation of Technical Inefficiency in Panel Data Models with Firm- and Time-Specific Effects," *Economics Letters*, 36, pp. 43–48.

Kumbhakar, S., 1991b, "The Measurement and Decomposition of Cost Inefficiency: The Translog Cost System," *Oxford Economic Papers*, 43, pp. 667–683.

Kumbhakar, S., 1993, "Production Risk, Technical Efficiency, and Panel Data," *Economics Letters*, 41, pp. 11–16.

Kumbhakar, S., 2001, "Estimation of Profit Functions When Profit Is Not Maximum," *American Journal of Agricultural Economics*, 83, pp. 1715–1736.

Kumbhakar, S., and Bhattacharyya, A., 1992, "Price Distortions and Resource Use Efficiency in Indian Agriculture: A Restricted Profit Function Approach," *Review of Economics and Statistics*, 74, pp. 231–239.

Kumbhakar, S., S. Ghosh, and J. McGuckin, 1991, "A Generalized Production Frontier Approach for Estimating Determinants of Inefficiency in U.S. Dairy Farms," *Journal of Business and Economic Statistics*, 9, pp. 279–286.

Kumbhakar, S., and A. Heshmati, 1995, "Efficiency Measurement in Swedish Dairy Farms 1976–1988 Using Rotating Panel Data," *American Journal of Agricultural Economics*, 77, pp. 660–674.

Kumbhakar, S., and L. Hjalmarsson, 1995, "Labor Use Efficiency in Swedish Social Insurance Offices," *Journal of Applied Econometrics*, 10, pp. 33–47.

Kumbhakar, S., G. Karagiannis, and E. Tsionas, 2004, "A Distance Function Approach for Estimating Technical and Allocative Inefficiency," *Indian Economic Review*, 1, pp. 31–54.

Kumbhakar, S., and K. Lovell, 2000, *Stochastic Frontier Analysis*, Cambridge University Press, Cambridge, UK.

Kumbhakar, S., B. Park, L. Simar, and E. Tsionas, 2005, "Nonparametric Stochastic Frontiers: A Local Maximum Likelihood Approach," Working Paper, Department of Economics, State University of New York, Binghamton.

Kumbhakar, S., and E. Tsionas, 2002, "Scale and Efficiency Measurement Using Nonparametric Stochastic Frontier Models," Working Paper, Department of Economics, State University of New York, Binghamton.

Kumbhakar, S., and E. Tsionas, 2004, "Estimation of Technical and Allocative Inefficiency in a Translog Cost System: An Exact Maximum Likelihood Approach," Working Paper, Department of Economics, State University of New York, Binghamton.

Kumbhakar, S., and E. Tsionas, "The Joint Measurement of Technical and Allocative Inefficiency: An Application of Bayesian Inference in Nonlinear Random Effects Models," *Journal of the American Statistical Association*, 100, 2005a, pp. 736–747.

Kumbhakar, S., and E. Tsionas, 2005b, "Estimation of Stochastic Frontier Production Functions with Input-Oriented Technical Efficiency," Working Paper, Department of Economics, State University of New York, Binghamton.

Kumbhakar, S., and E. Tsionas, "Measuring Technical and Allocative Efficiency in the Translog Cost System: A Bayesian Approach," *Journal of Econometrics*, 126, 2005, pp. 355–384.

Kurkalova, L., and A. Carriquiry, 2003, "Input and Output Oriented Technical Efficiency of Ukranian Collective Farms, 1989–1992: Bayesian Analysis of a Stochastic Frontier Production Model," *Journal of Productivity Analysis*, 20, pp. 191–212.

Lang, G., and P. Welzel, 1998, "Technology and Cost Efficiency in Universal Banking: A 'Thick Frontier' Analysis of German Banking Industry," *Journal of Productivity Analysis*, 10, pp. 63–84.

Lee, L., 1983, "A Test for Distributional Assumptions for the Stochastic Frontier Function," *Journal of Econometrics*, 22, pp. 245–267.

Lee, L., 1993, "Asymptotic Distribution of the MLE for a Stochastic Frontier Function with a Singular Information Matrix," *Econometric Theory*, 9, pp. 413–430.

Lee, L., and M. Tyler, 1978, "The Stochastic Frontier Production Function and Average Efficiency," *Journal of Econometrics*, 7, pp. 385–390.

Lee, Y., and Schmidt, P., 1993, "A Production Frontier Model with Flexible Temporal Variation in Technical Efficiency," in *The Measurement of Productive Efficiency*, H. Fried, K. Lovell, and S. Schmidt, eds., Oxford University Press, Oxford, UK.

Leibenstein, H., 1966, "Allocative Efficiency vs. X-Efficiency," *American Economic Review*, 56, pp. 392–415.

Leibenstein, H., 1975, "Aspects of the X-Efficiency Theory of the Firm," *Bell Journal of Economics*, 6, pp. 580–606.

Linna, M., 1998, "Measuring Hospital Cost Efficiency with Panel Data Models," *Health Economics*, 7, pp. 415–427.

Lovell, K., 1993, "Production Frontiers and Productive Efficiency," in *The Measurement of Productive Efficiency*, H. Fried, K. Lovell, and S. Schmidt, eds., Oxford University Press, Oxford, UK.

Lovell, K., and R. Sickles, 1983, "Testing Efficiency Hypotheses in Joint Production: A Parametric Approach," *Review of Economics and Statistics*, 65, pp. 51–58.

Lozano-Vivas, A., 1997, "Profit Efficiency for Spanish Savings Banks," *European Journal of Operational Research*, 98, pp. 381–394.

Martinez-Budria, E., S. Jara-Diaz, and F. Ramos-Real, 2003, "Adopting Productivity Theory to the Quadratic Cost Function: An Application to the Spanish Electric Sector," *Journal of Productivity Analysis*, 20, pp. 213–229.

Meeusen, W., and J. van den Broeck, 1977, "Efficiency Estimation from Cobb-Douglas Production Functions with Composed Error," *International Economic Review*, 18, pp. 435–444.

Mester, L., 1994, "Efficiency of Banks in the Third Federal Reserve District," Working Paper 94-13, Wharton School, University of Pennsylvania, Philadelphia.

Migon, H., and E. Medici, 2001, "Bayesian Hierarchical Models for Stochastic Production Frontier," Working Paper, UFRJ, Brazil.

MRC, 2005, "The BUGS Project," http://http://www.mrc-bsu.cam.ac.uk/bugs/welcome.shtml, Biostatistics Unit, Cambridge University, Cambridge, UK.

Murillo-Zamorano, L., 2004, "Economic Efficiency and Frontier Techniques," *Journal of Economic Surveys*, 18, pp. 33–77.

Murillo-Zamorano, L., and R. Vega-Cervera, 2001, "The Use of Parametric and Nonparametric Frontier Methods to Measure the Productive Efficiency in the Industrial Sector: A Comparative Study," *International Journal of Production Economics*, 69, pp. 265–275.

Nerlove, M., 1963, "Returns to Scale in Electricity Supply," in *Measurement in Economics*, C. Christ et al., eds., Stanford University Press, Stanford, CA.

O'Donnell, J., and T. Coelli, 2005, "A Bayesian Approach to Imposing Curvature on Distance Functions," *Journal of Econometrics*, 126, pp. 493–523.

O'Donnell, C., and W. Griffiths, 2004, "Estimating State Contingent Production Frontiers," Working Paper Number 911, Department of Economics, University of Melbourne.

Orea, C., and S. Kumbhakar, 2004, "Efficiency Measurement Using a Latent Class Stochastic Frontier Model," *Empirical Economics*, 29, pp. 169–184.

Osiewalski, J., and M. Steel, 1998, "Numerical Tools for the Bayesian Analysis of Stochastic Frontier Models," *Journal of Productivity Analysis*, 10, pp. 103–117.

Pagan, A., and A. Hall, 1983, "Diagnostic Tests as Residual Analysis," *Econometric Reviews*, 2, pp. 159–218.

Paris, Q., and M. Caputo, 2004, "Efficient Estimation by the Joint Estimation of All the Primal and Dual Relations," Working Paper, Department of Agricultural and Resource Economics, University of California, Davis.

Park, B., R. Sickles, and L. Simar, 1998, "Stochastic Panel Frontiers: A Semiparametric Approach," *Journal of Econometrics*, 84, pp. 273–301.

Park, B., and L. Simar, 1992, "Efficient Semiparametric Estimation in Stochastic Frontier Models," *Working Paper*, Department of Economics, CORE, Catholic University of Louvain, Louvain-la-Neuve, Belgium.

Park, B., and L. Simar, 1994, "Efficient Semiparametric Estimation in a Stochastic Frontier Model," *Journal of the American Statistical Association*, 89, pp. 929–936.

Pestieau, P., and H. Tulkens, 1993, "Assessing the Performance of Public Sector Activities: Some Recent Evidence from the Productive Efficiency Viewpoint," *Finanz Archiv*, 50, pp. 293–323.

Pitt, M., and L. Lee, 1981, "The Measurement and Sources of Technical Inefficiency in the Indonesian Weaving Industry," *Journal of Development Economics*, 9, pp. 43–64.

QMS, Inc., 2005, *EViews Reference Guide*, http://http://www.eviews.com, Irvine, CA.

Ray, S., and K. Mukherjee, 1995, "Comparing Parametric and Nonparametric Measures of Efficiency: A Reexamination of the Christensen and Greene Data," *Journal of Quantitative Economics*, 11, pp. 155–168.

Reifschnieder, D., and R. Stevenson, 1991, "Systematic Departures from the Frontier: A Framework for the Analysis of Firm Inefficiency," *International Economic Review*, 32, pp. 715–723.

Reinhard, S., K. Lovell, and G. Thijssen, 1999, "Econometric Applications of Technical and Environmental Efficiency: An Application to Dutch Dairy Farms," *American Journal of Agricultural Economics*, 81, pp. 44–60.

Richmond, J., 1974, "Estimating the Efficiency of Production," *International Economic Review*, 15, pp. 515–521.

Ritter, C., and L. Simar, 1997, "Pitfalls of Normal-Gamma Stochastic Frontier Models," *Journal of Productivity Analysis*, 8, pp. 167–182.

Rosko, M., 2001, "Cost Efficiency of US Hospitals: A Stochastic Frontier Approach," *Health Economics*, 10, pp. 539–551.

Salvanes, K., and S. Tjotta, 1998, "A Note on the Importance of Testing for Regularities for Estimated Flexible Functional Forms," *Journal of Productivity Analysis*, 9, pp. 133–143.

Samuelson, P., 1938, *Foundations of Economic Analysis*, Harvard University Press, Cambridge, MA.

SAS Institute, Inc., 2005, *SAS Reference Guide*, http://http://www.sas.com, Cary, NC.

Schmidt, P., 1976, "On the Statistical Estimation of Parametric Frontier Production Functions," *Review of Economics and Statistics*, 58, pp. 238–239.

Schmidt, P., 1985, "Frontier Production Functions," *Econometric Reviews*, 4, pp. 289–328.

Schmidt, P., and T. Lin, 1984, "Simple Tests of Alternative Specifications in Stochastic Frontier Models," *Journal of Econometrics*, 24, pp. 349–361.

Schmidt, P., and R. Sickles, 1984, "Production Frontiers and Panel Data," *Journal of Business and Economic Statistics*, 2, pp. 367–374.

Shephard, R., 1953, *Cost and Production Functions*, Princeton University Press, Princeton, NJ.

Sickles, R., 1987, "Allocative Inefficiency in the Airline Industry: A Case for Deregulation," in *Studies in Productivity Analysis*, Vol. 7, A. Dogramaci, ed., Kluwer-Nijoff, Boston.

Sickles, R., 2005, "Panel Estimators and the Identification of Firm Specific Efficiency Levels in Parametric, Semiparametric and Nonparametric Settings, *Journal of Econometrics*, 126, 2005, pp. 305–324.

Sickles, R., D. Good, and L. Getachew, 2002, "Specification of Distance Functions Using Semi- and Nonparametric Methods with an Application to the Dynamic Performance of Eastern and Western European Air Carriers," *Journal of Productivity Analysis*, 17, pp. 133–156.

Sickles, R., D. Good, and R. Johnson, 1986, "Allocative Distortions and the Regulatory Transition of the Airline Industry," *Journal of Econometrics*, 33, pp. 143–163.

Sickles, R., and M. Streitweiser, 1992, "Technical Inefficiency and Productive Decline in the U.S. Interstate Natural Gas Pipeline Industry under the Natural Gas Policy Act," *Journal of Productivity Analysis*, 3, pp. 119–134.

Simar, L., 1992, "Estimating Efficiencies from Frontier Models with Panel Data: A Comparison of Parametric, Nonparametric, and Semiparametric Methods with Bootstrapping," *Journal of Productivity Analysis*, 3, pp. 167–203.

Simar, L., 1996, "Aspects of Statistical Analysis in DEA-Type Frontier Models," *Journal of Productivity Analysis*, 7, 177–185.

Simar, L., K. Lovell, and P. van den Eeckhaut, 1994, "Stochastic Frontiers Incorporating Exogenous Influences on Efficiency," Discussion Paper No. 9403, Institute of Statistics, Catholic University of Louvain, Louvain-la-Neuve, Belgium.

Simar, L., and P. Wilson, 1998, "Sensitivity Analysis of Efficiency Scores: How to Bootstrap in Nonparametric Frontier Models," *Management Science*, 44, pp. 49–61.

Simar, L., and P. Wilson, 1999, "Of Course We Can Bootstrap DEA Scores! But, Does It Mean Anything?" *Journal of Productivity Analysis*, 11, pp. 67–80.

Smith, M., 2004, "Stochastic Frontier Models with Correlated Error Components," Working Paper, Department of Econometrics and Business Statistics, University of Sydney.

Stata, Inc., 2005, *Stata Reference Guide*, http://http://www.stata.com, College Station, TX.

Stevenson, R., 1980, "Likelihood Functions for Generalized Stochastic Frontier Estimation," *Journal of Econometrics*, 13, pp. 58–66.

Swamy, P., and G. Tavlas, 2001, "Random Coefficient Models," in *Companion to Theoretical Econometrics*, B. Baltagi, ed., Blackwell Publishers, Oxford, UK.

Timmer, P., 1971, "Using a Probabilistic Frontier Production Function to Measure Technical Efficiency," *Journal of Political Economy*, 79, pp. 776–794.

Train, K., 2003, *Discrete Choice Methods with Simulation*, Cambridge University Press, Cambridge, UK.

Trethaway, M., and R. Windle, 1983, "U.S. Airline Cross Section: Sources of Data," Working Paper, Department of Economics, University of Wisconsin, Madison.

Tsionas, E. 2000a, "Combining DEA and Stochastic Frontier Models: An Empirical Bayes Approach," Working Paper, Department of Economics, Athens University of Economics and Business.

Tsionas, E., 2000b, "Full Likelihood Inference in Normal-Gamma Stochastic Frontier Models," *Journal of Productivity Analysis*, 13, pp. 183–206.

Tsionas, E., 2001a, "An Introduction to Efficiency Measurement Using Bayesian Stochastic Frontier Models," *Global Business and Economics Review*, 3, pp. 287–311.

Tsionas, E., 2001b, "Combining DEA and Stochastic Frontier Models: An Empirical Bayes Approach," Working Paper, Department of Economics, Athens University of Business and Economics.

Tsionas, E., 2002, "Stochastic Frontier Models with Random Coefficients," *Journal of Applied Econometrics*, 17, pp. 127–147.

Tsionas, E., 2003, "Inference in Dynamic Stochastic Frontier Models," Working Paper, Department of Economics, Athens University of Economics and Business.

Tsionas, E., 2004, "Maximum Likelihood Estimation of Nonstandard Stochastic Frontiers by the Fourier Transform," Working Paper, Department of Economics, Athens University of Economics and Business.

Tsionas, E., and W. Greene (2003), "Non-Gaussian Stochastic Frontier Models," Working Paper, Department of Economics, Athens University of Economics and Business.

TSP International, 2005, *TSP Reference Guide*, http://http://www.tspintl.com, Palo Alto, CA.

van den Broeck, J., G. Koop, J. Osiewalski, and M. Steel, 1994, "Stochastic Frontier Models: A Bayesian Perspective," *Journal of Econometrics*, 61, pp. 273–303.

Vitaliano, D., 2003, "The Thrift Industry and the Community Reinvestment Act: Assessing the Cost of Social Responsibility," Working Paper No. 0312, Department of Economics, Rensellaer Polytechnic Institute, Troy, NY.

Vuong, Q. 1989, "Likelihood Ratio Tests for Model Selection and Non-nested Hypotheses," *Econometrica* 57, pp. 307–334.

Wagenvoort, R., and P. Schure, 2005, "A Recursive Thick Frontier Approach to Estimating Production Efficiency," Working Paper EWP0503, Department of Economics, University of Victoria, Australia.

Waldman, D., 1982, "A Stationary Point for the Stochastic Frontier Likelihood," *Journal of Econometrics*, 18, pp. 275–279.

Wang, H.-J., 2002, "Heteroscedasticity and Non-monotonic Efficiency Effects of Stochastic Frontier Model," Institute of Economics, Academica Sinica, Taiwan, http://www.sinica.edu.tw/~wanghj/jpa02b.pdf.

Wang, H., and P. Schmidt, 2002, "One Step and Two Step Estimation of the Effects of Exogenous Variables on Technical Efficiency Levels," *Journal of Productivity Analysis*, 18, pp. 129–144.

Weinstein, M., 1964, "The Sum of Values from a Normal and a Truncated Normal Distribution," *Technometrics*, 6, pp. 104–105, 469–470.

WHO, 2000, *The World Health Report, 2000, Health Systems: Improving Performance*, World Health Organization, Geneva.

Winsten, C., 1957, "Discussion on Mr. Farrell's Paper," *Journal of the Royal Statistical Society, Series A, General*, 120, pp. 282–284.

Xue, M., and P. Harker, 1999, "Overcoming the Inherent Dependency of DEA Efficiency Scoring: A Bootstrap Approach," Working Paper, Wharton Financial Institutions Center, University of Pennsylvania, Philadelphia.

Zellner, A., J. Kmenta, and J. Dreze, 1966, "Specification and Estimation of Cobb-Douglas Production Functions," *Econometrica*, 34, pp. 784–795.

Zellner, A., and N. Revankar, 1969, "Generalized Production Functions," *Review of Economic Studies*, 36, pp. 241–250.

Zellner, A., and J. Tobias, 2001, "Further Results on Bayesian Method of Moments Analysis of the Multiple Regression Model," *International Economic Review*, 42, pp. 121–140.

3

Data Envelopment Analysis: The Mathematical Programming Approach to Efficiency Analysis

Emmanuel Thanassoulis, Maria C. S. Portela, and Ozren Despić

3.1 Introduction

This chapter deals with the measurement of efficiency through the nonparametric, mathematical programming-based technique that is best known as data envelopment analysis (DEA), after the developments of Charnes et al. (1978).

Chapter 1 of this book provides a brief introduction to DEA. Chapter 2 discusses the theoretical underpinnings of both parametric and nonparametric efficiency estimation. In the interests of brevity, we use the material in chapters 1 and 2 as our launch pad to explore more fully the theory and application of DEA.

We begin our journey into DEA from the same starting point as the parametric paradigm covered in chapter 2. Specifically (see section 2.2), we begin by defining a producer as an economic agent that takes a set of inputs and transforms them either in form or in location into a set of outputs. In DEA, we refer to the economic agent as a decision-making unit (DMU) to accord with the notion that we are assessing entities that have control over the processes they deploy to convert their inputs into outputs. Thus, we can depict a DMU as in figure 3.1.

The identification of the inputs and the outputs in real-life assessments of DMUs is difficult, but it is of vital significance. The inputs should capture all resources that affect the outputs. The outputs should reflect all relevant outcomes on which we wish to assess the DMUs. Further, any environmental factors that directly affect the transformation of inputs into outputs should also be reflected in the inputs or the outputs.

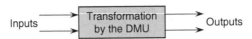

Figure 3.1. A DMU Transforms Inputs into Outputs

We can use DEA to address a large variety of questions about the transformation of inputs into outputs by a DMU. These include but are not limited to such questions as

- The relative efficiency of a DMU (e.g., how far short are its output levels from maximum levels attainable for its input levels?)
- Identification of "suitable" efficient peers for an inefficient DMU to emulate
- Estimates of input–output levels that would render a DMU efficient (i.e., targets for the DMU)
- Measuring and decomposing the change in the productivity of a DMU over time
- Identifying the type of returns to scale holding locally at some efficient DMU
- Measuring scale elasticity locally at some efficient DMU
- Identifying the most productive scale size (MPSS) for a DMU

We cover in this chapter the DEA models that can be used to explore questions such as those listed above and discuss their advantages and limitations.

3.2 Production Possibility Sets

Once the input–output variables are identified for a set of DMUs, in order to assess them by DEA we begin by constructing what is known as the production possibility set (PPS) within which the DMUs operate. The PPS contains all the correspondences of input and output vectors that are feasible in principle even if not actually observed in practice. Once the PPS is known, the location of a DMU within the PPS will provide the answers as to its relative performance, for example, relative efficiency and local returns to scale.

Using the notation introduced in chapters 1 and 2, let us denote the PPS, T, such that

$$T = \left\{ (x, y) \in \Re_{+}^{m+s} \mid x \text{ can produce } y \right\}.$$

The PPS T therefore contains all the feasible in principle correspondences of input levels $x \in \Re_{+}^{m}$ capable of producing output levels $y \in \Re_{+}^{s}$. Note that in defining T we assume nonnegative data $\Re_{+}^{m}, \Re_{+}^{s}, \Re_{+}^{m+s}$. T, often also referred to as production or graph technology, may also be represented from two other perspectives: input or consumption set and production or output set. An input set $L(y)$ is the subset of all input vectors $x \in \Re_{+}^{m}$ yielding at least y, and a production set $P(\mathbf{x})$ is the subset of all output vectors $\mathbf{y} \in \mathfrak{R}_+^s$ that are obtained from $\mathbf{x}$. The input and output sets are therefore defined, respectively, as

$$L(\mathbf{y}) = \{\mathbf{x} \mid (\mathbf{x}, \mathbf{y}) \in T\} \text{ or } L(\mathbf{y}) = \{\mathbf{x} \mid \mathbf{y} \in P(\mathbf{x})\},$$

$$P(\mathbf{x}) = \{\mathbf{y} \mid (\mathbf{x}, \mathbf{y}) \in T\} \text{ or } P(\mathbf{x}) = \{\mathbf{y} \mid \mathbf{x} \in L(\mathbf{y})\}.$$

Thus, a production technology can have alternative and equivalent representations highlighting different aspects of that technology. "The input set models input substitution, and the output set models output substitution. The graph set models both input substitution and output substitution, in addition to modeling input–output transformation" (Färe et al., 1994, p. 27).

A production technology defined by $L(\mathbf{y})$, $P(\mathbf{x})$, or $T(\mathbf{x}, \mathbf{y})$ has some relevant subsets that are useful for efficiency measurement. The characteristics of these correspondences as well as the analysis of these subsets are detailed in Färe et al. (1985). For the present purpose, we are mainly interested in two subsets: the isoquant and the efficient subset.

The input isoquant of $L(\mathbf{y})$, the output isoquant of $P(\mathbf{x})$, and the graph isoquant of $T(\mathbf{x}, \mathbf{y})$ are defined as

$$I(\mathbf{y}) = \{\mathbf{x} \mid \mathbf{x} \in L(\mathbf{y}), \ \lambda\mathbf{x} \notin L(\mathbf{y}), \ \lambda < 1\},$$

$$I(\mathbf{x}) = \{\mathbf{y} \mid \mathbf{y} \in P(\mathbf{x}), \ \theta\mathbf{y} \notin P(\mathbf{x}), \ \theta > 1\}$$

$$I(\mathbf{x}, \mathbf{y}) = \{(\mathbf{x}, \mathbf{y}) \mid (\mathbf{x}, \mathbf{y}) \in T(\mathbf{x}, \mathbf{y}), \ (\lambda\mathbf{x}, \theta\mathbf{y}) \notin T(\mathbf{x}, \mathbf{y}), \ \lambda < 1, \ \theta > 1\}.$$

The efficient subsets of $L(\mathbf{y})$, $P(\mathbf{x})$, and $T(\mathbf{x}, \mathbf{y})$ are defined as

$$
\begin{aligned}
E(\mathbf{y}) &= \{\mathbf{x} \mid \mathbf{x} \in L(\mathbf{y}), \ \mathbf{x}' \le \mathbf{x} \text{ and } \mathbf{x}' \ne \mathbf{x} \ \Rightarrow \ \mathbf{x}' \notin L(\mathbf{y})\} \\
E(\mathbf{x}) &= \{\mathbf{y} \mid \mathbf{y} \in P(\mathbf{x}), \ \mathbf{y}' \ge \mathbf{y} \text{ and } \mathbf{y}' \ne \mathbf{y} \ \Rightarrow \ \mathbf{y}' \notin P(\mathbf{x})\}
\end{aligned},
$$

$$
E(\mathbf{x}, \mathbf{y}) = \left\{ (\mathbf{x}, \mathbf{y}) \ \middle| \
\begin{array}{l}
(\mathbf{x}, \mathbf{y}) \in T(\mathbf{x}, \mathbf{y}), \ (-\mathbf{x}', \mathbf{y}') \ge (-\mathbf{x}, \mathbf{y}) \text{ and} \\
(-\mathbf{x}', \mathbf{y}') \ne (-\mathbf{x}, \mathbf{y}) \ \Rightarrow \ (\mathbf{x}', \mathbf{y}') \notin T(\mathbf{x}, \mathbf{y})
\end{array}
\right\}.
$$

These definitions imply that $I(\mathbf{y}) \supseteq E(\mathbf{y})$ [see Färe et al. (1985) for general conditions under which the two subsets coincide]. The same relationship is valid for the output and graph cases.

Figures 3.2 and 3.3 illustrate the input and output correspondences, respectively, for the typical case of constant returns to scale (CRS) technology. (Later in this chapter we define in more detail various types of returns to scale; suffice it to say at this point that, under CRS and efficient production, scaling of input levels by a certain factor leads to the outputs being scaled by that same factor.) In figure 3.2, the input set $L(\mathbf{y})$ is the space to the right and above the piecewise linear boundary (A'ABCDD'). The input isoquant $I(\mathbf{y})$ is the boundary A'ABCDD'. The efficient subset of the input isoquant $E(\mathbf{y})$ is the part of the isoquant ABC (without the vertical and horizontal extensions).

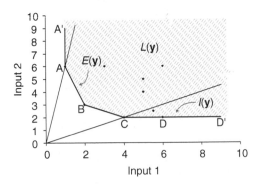

Figure 3.2. Input Space Representation

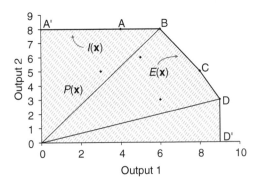

Figure 3.3. Output Space Representation

In figure 3.3, the output set $P(x)$ is the space enclosed by the axes and the piecewise linear boundary A'ABCDD'. The output isoquant $I(x)$ is the boundary A'ABCDD'. The efficient subset of the output isoquant $E(x)$ is the part BCD (without the vertical and horizontal extensions).

The efficient subsets $E(y)$ and $E(x)$ of $L(y)$ and $P(x)$, respectively, in figures 3.2 and 3.3 are efficient in a Pareto-Koopmans sense. Pareto-Koopmans efficiency, or simply Pareto-efficiency, is attained when an increase in any output (or a decrease in any input) requires a decrease in at least another output (or an increase in at least another input; e.g., Lovell, 1993).

The foregoing concepts of PPS, isoquants, and efficient subsets thereof need to be operationalized if we are to measure efficiency and deduce other information on the performance of DMUs. In DEA, the PPS is deduced from observed input–output correspondences by making certain assumptions as to the nature of the PPS. The assumptions can vary, but we begin with the basic assumptions made in Charnes et al. (1978), the seminal paper on DEA.

(i) Convexity:
If $(x, y) \in T$ and $(x', y') \in T$ then $(\lambda(x, y) + (1 - \lambda)(x', y')) \in T$ for any $\lambda \in [0, 1]$

(ii) Monotonicity or strong free disposability of inputs and outputs:
If $(x, y) \in T$ and $x' \geq x$ then $(x', y) \in T$
If $(x, y) \in T$ and $y' \leq y$ then $(x, y') \in T$

(iii) Inclusion of observations:
Each observed DMU $(x_o, y_o) \in T$

(iv) No output can be produced without some input
If $y \geq 0$ and $y \neq 0$ then $(0, y) \notin T$

(v) Constant returns to scale:
If $(x, y) \in T$ then $(\lambda x, \lambda y) \in T$ for any $\lambda \geq 0$

(vi) Minimum extrapolation:
T is the intersection of all sets satisfying (i)–(v)

A PPS $T(x, y)$, satisfying the foregoing assumptions, can be constructed from the observed input–output correspondences at n DMUs as follows:

$$T(x, y) = \left\{ (x, y) \;\middle|\; \sum_{j=1}^{n} \lambda_j y_j \geq y, \; \sum_{j=1}^{n} \lambda_j x_j \leq x, \; \lambda_j \geq 0, \; j = 1, \ldots, n \right\}$$

We conclude this section by outlining how the PPS would change if one or more of the foregoing assumptions were to change.

3.2.1 Dropping the assumption of CRS

As noted above, CRS implies that scaling up or down efficient input–output correspondences is valid. This is a rather restrictive assumption and not always valid in real life. We explore alternative forms of returns to scale in section 3.5. Here we simply illustrate the most relaxed form of returns to scale that we can assume, which is that returns to scale are variable (see Banker et al., 1984). This permits not only constant but also increasing returns to scale (IRS) and decreasing returns to scale (DRS) in the sense that, respectively, outputs rise more than or less than proportionately with inputs.

The piecewise mathematical representation of the PPS under variable returns to scale T^{VRS} is

$$T^{\mathrm{VRS}}(x, y) = \left\{ (x, y) \;\middle|\; \begin{array}{l} \sum_{j=1}^{n} \lambda_j y_j \geq y, \; \sum_{j=1}^{n} \lambda_j x_j \leq x, \\[2mm] \sum_{j=1}^{n} \lambda_j = 1, \; \lambda_j \geq 0, \; j = 1, \ldots, n \end{array} \right\}.$$

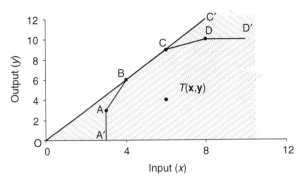

Figure 3.4. Graph Technology Representation

Note that this differs from the PPS under CRS noted above and reproduced below as T^{CRS}:

$$T^{CRS}(x, y) = \left\{ (x, y) \ \middle| \ \sum_{j=1}^{n} \lambda_j y_j \geq y, \sum_{j=1}^{n} \lambda_j x_j \leq x, \ \lambda_j \geq 0, \ j = 1, \ldots, n \right\}$$

In T^{VRS} we have the convexity constraint $\sum \lambda_j = 1$. This constraint is in line with the convexity of the PPS assumed but is invalid under CRS since any feasible and efficient (x, y) correspondence under CRS can be scaled up or down. The difference between the PPS under CRS and that under VRS is illustrated in figure 3.4.

The piecewise linear representation of $T(x, y)$ in figure 3.4 (isoquant: A′ABCDD′ and efficient subset ABCD) satisfies variable returns to scale (VRS). That is, returns to scale are increasing along AB, are constant on BC, and are decreasing along CD. Points along BC have maximum productivity in the sense of output per unit input. In contrast, under CRS the frontier of $T(x, y)$ is OBCC′.

There are also specifications of the PPS that imply other types of returns to scale, such as nonincreasing returns to scale (NIRS) and nondecreasing returns to scale (NDRS). We address such technologies in section 3.5.

3.2.2 Dropping the assumption of convexity of the PPS

All technological sets mentioned hitherto are convex. The convexity of $T(x, y)$ implies that both the input and output sets, $L(y)$ and $P(x)$, are convex, although the converse is not true (see Petersen, 1990).

Convexity is assumed in most economic models of production, but there is some debate in the literature concerning the validity of this assumption. In fact, assuming convexity implies that some return-to-scale characteristics of a production set cannot be modeled. For example, convexity of the PPS excludes the possibility of modeling globally IRS or alternate behaviors of increasing and decreasing returns at different volumes (Bogetoft et al. 2000). In situations where commodities are not continuously divisible, the assumption of convexity also does not apply (Coelli et al., 1998). The main reasons for assuming the convexity of T are, on the one hand, the neoclassical assumption of diminishing marginal rates of substitution and, on the other hand, the fact that convexity is a necessary assumption for establishing the duality between input and output sets and cost and revenue functions (see, e.g., Petersen, 1990; Post, 2001a; Kuosmanen, 2003).

In order to model situations where the convexity of the PPS is not deemed appropriate, some nonconvex production possibilities sets have been developed. The best-known nonconvex technological set that only satisfies free disposability of inputs and outputs is the free disposal hull (FDH), which was first introduced by Deprins et al. (1984). The PPS of this technology is defined in T^{FDH}:

$$
T^{\mathrm{FDH}}(\mathbf{x}, \mathbf{y}) = \left\{ (\mathbf{x}, \mathbf{y}) \left| \begin{array}{l} \sum\limits_{j=1}^{n} \lambda_j \mathbf{y}_j \geq \mathbf{y}, \ \sum\limits_{j=1}^{n} \lambda_j \mathbf{x}_j \leq \mathbf{x}, \\ \sum\limits_{j=1}^{n} \lambda_j = 1, \ \lambda_j \in \{0, 1\}, \ j = 1, \ldots, n \end{array} \right. \right\}
$$

The particularity of a technology defined by T^{FDH} is that it rests only on the assumption of free disposability of inputs and outputs. The nonconvex nature of T^{FDH} is expressed in the binary constraints associated with the λ_j values. Figure 3.5 depicts the PPS under an FDH technology.

An interesting characteristic of T^{FDH} is the fact that the efficient subset of the production frontier is constituted by observed DMUs only, namely, the nondominated DMUs.[1] This makes FDH a useful method to be applied for benchmarking purposes. As pointed out by Bogetoft et al. (2000, p. 2),

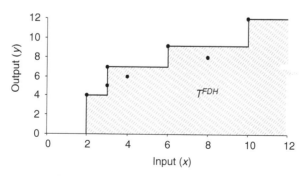

Figure 3.5. FDH Production Possibilities Set

"fictitious production possibilities, generated as convex combinations of those actually observed, are usually less convincing as benchmarks, or reference DMUs, than actually observed production possibilities."

The FDH is among the most used nonconvex technologies (see, e.g., Deprins et al., 1984; Thiery and Tulkens, 1992; Eeckaut et al., 1993; De Borger et al., 1998). Tulkens (1993) introduced a variant of the FDH technology named FRH—free replicability hull. A technology of this type is attained by replacing in T^{FDH} the binary constraints by a constraint imposing that $\lambda_j \in \{0, 1, 2, \ldots\}$. Such a technological set rests on the replicability postulate meaning that the reference set should contain any production unit that is a λ_j-fold replica of the jth observed DMU. The technology in the FRH model is additive, because it is assumed that production plans can be repeated.

A variety of other nonconvex specifications of the technology can be found in the literature. For example, Banker and Maindiratta (1986) replaced the usual convexity postulate by a geometric convexity postulate, in order to allow for increasing marginal products. In practical terms, this means that the VRS boundary is piecewise loglinear rather than piecewise linear. Bogetoft et al. (2000) developed a procedure that permits nonconvex technological sets while keeping input and output sets convex. Other developments on convexity in DEA can be found in Kuosmanen (2001), who replaced the convexity assumption by conditional convexity, and in Agrell et al. (2001), who introduced the convex pairs approach that allows "to work with convexity around one or more observations without assuming convexity across all observations in input space, in output space, or in the full production space." Finally, Podinovski (2005) introduced the concept of selective convexity, useful, among other things, to model nondiscretionary inputs or outputs, as discussed in section 3.8.

3.2.3 Dropping the assumption of strong disposability

Weak disposability of inputs states that if $\mathbf{x} \in L(\mathbf{y})$, then $\beta\mathbf{x} \in L(\mathbf{y})$ for $\beta \geq 1$. (Weak disposability of outputs is defined in an analogous way.) Under weak disposability of inputs, if $\mathbf{x}$ can produce $\mathbf{y}$, then proportional increases in all inputs can yield the production of the same amount of output (Färe and Grosskopf, 2000a). Replacing the assumption of strong disposability of inputs by weak disposability of inputs yields the following production possibilities set (T^{WD}) for the VRS case (see Färe and Grosskopf, 2000a):

$$T^{WD}(\mathbf{x}, \mathbf{y}) = \left\{ (\mathbf{x}, \mathbf{y}) \; \middle| \; \begin{array}{c} \sum_{j=1}^{n} \lambda_j \mathbf{y}_j \geq \mathbf{y}, \;\; \sum_{j=1}^{n} \lambda_j \mathbf{x}_j = \delta\, \mathbf{x}, \;\; \sum_{j=1}^{n} \lambda_j = 1 \\ 0 < \delta \leq 1, \;\; \lambda_j \geq 0, \;\; j = 1, \ldots, n \end{array} \right\}$$

The main difference between the weak- and strong-disposability technological sets is that equalities are assumed above for input equations (since we are

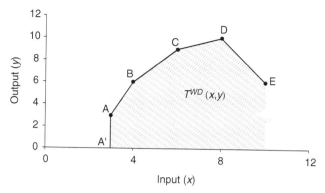

Figure 3.6. Input-Congested Technology

assuming that inputs are weakly disposable while outputs are strongly disposable). Färe and Grosskopf (1998) note that δ in T^{WD} can be set equal to 1 for the case of CRS.

This technological set can be used in situations where increasing (decreasing) inputs may result in a decrease (increase) of outputs [e.g., Cooper et al. (1996) mention miners in an underground mine, whose reduction would improve the amount mined]. This situation is dubbed *input congestion*, and its existence implies that the strong-disposability assumption does not hold and instead weak disposability should be assumed.

A technology that is input congested is represented in figure 3.6. Note that in segment DE of the boundary input, increases are associated with output reductions.

Technologies satisfying weak-disposability assumptions are useful in particular for modeling bad outputs (i.e., byproducts of production processes that are undesirable). We address the issue of badly behaved data in section 3.6, where we come back to congestion.

3.2.4 Final remarks on the axioms of PPS construction

In view of the foregoing variety of alternative assumptions that can be made about the transformation of inputs to outputs, it would be helpful to be able to test the validity of the assumptions made. Unfortunately, this issue has not been much explored in the literature. However, Banker (1993, 1996) has put forward statistical tests that can be used to test the impact of alternative assumptions about the PPS on the efficiencies derived (e.g., see also Post, 2001b). Kuosmanen (1999b), on the other hand, conducted parametric tests of the validity of the convexity assumption using a quadratic regression function.

We conclude the discussion of alternative production possibilities sets in DEA by noting that, apart from altering the foregoing assumptions, it is also possible to add new assumptions that can further alter the production possibilities set. One case in point, frequently used in DEA, is the introduction of value judgments concerning the relative worth (as perceived by the user) of inputs and/or outputs. (E.g., in assessing police forces, it may be acceptable to say that clearing up a violent crime is worth more than clearing up theft from automobiles.) We review the introduction of such value judgments in section 3.7. Suffice it to say at this point that introducing value judgments about the relative worth of inputs and outputs will implicitly transform the PPS.

In summary, we have outlined some possible specifications of the production possibilities set. Traditional specifications assume certain characteristics of the PPS, which being dropped give rise to other PPS (e.g., the FDH PPS when the convexity assumption is dropped, or the weak-disposability PPS when the assumption of strong disposability is dropped). We treat the definition of the technological set independently of the measure of distance used to account for the efficiency of DMUs, since in practice these are two distinct issues in assessing performance.

3.3 Efficiency Measurement

As noted above, once the PPS is specified, the location of a DMU within the PPS contains much of the information we wish about the performance of the DMU. A very first aspect of that performance is a measure of the relative efficiency of the DMU. The relative efficiency of a DMU is intended to capture its distance from the frontier of the PPS. Clearly, this distance in practice need only be calculated for DMUs that are not on the frontier. Fortunately, distance measures can give us information not only on whether a DMU is or is not on the frontier but also on its degree of inefficiency when it is not of the frontier.

There are many measures of efficiency used in DEA models, though the most traditional one is the radial measure of efficiency. We outline the better known measures in this section.

3.3.1 Radial measures of efficiency

Farrell (1957) defined a radial distance function that is the basis of the DEA measures of efficiency. The Farrell measure of efficiency is usually defined either in the input space or in the output space. Figure 3.7 illustrates the Farrell measure of efficiency in input space $L(y)$. The frontier of $L(y)$ is the isoquant labeled $I(y)$.

DMUs A, B, C, and D have technical input efficiency (we define various types of efficiency below) in the Farrell sense of 100%. That is their observed input levels cannot jointly or radially be contracted to lower levels. In contrast, DMUs away from $I(y)$ have efficiency below 100%. Their efficiency is the fraction to which their observed input levels can be radially contracted to reach $I(y)$. For example, DMU G is inefficient because it could produce the

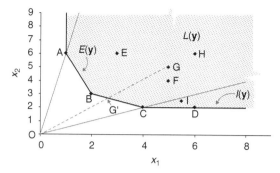

Figure 3.7. Input Efficiency Measurement

same amount of output using lower levels in both of its inputs. The radial distance of this DMU to the input isoquant $I(y)$ is given by $\theta_G^* = OG'/OG$, where OG'/OG is in fact the ratio between the norms of the vector OG' and vector OG ($\|OG'\|/\|OG\|$).

Note that DMU D in figure 3.7, lying on the isoquant, has efficiency of 100% (or 1) but is not Pareto-efficient because it is able to reduce the usage of input x_1 without changing the usage of input x_2. Therefore efficiency of 100% for a DMU does *not* necessarily mean it is Pareto-efficient, but the converse is true.

In the general case, the Farrell measure of efficiency can be computed using linear programming. Consider, for example, DMU_o that has input–output levels (x_o, y_o). Then its technical input efficiency is θ_o^*, the optimal value of θ_o in model (3.1) below. Similarly, the technical output efficiency of DMU_o is $1/\beta_o^*$ where β_o^* is the optimal value of β_o in model (3.2):

$$\text{Min}\left\{\theta_o \left| \begin{array}{l} \displaystyle\sum_{j=1}^{n} \lambda_j y_{rj} - s_r^+ = y_{ro}, \quad r = 1, \ldots, s \\ \displaystyle\sum_{j=1}^{n} \lambda_j x_{ij} + s_i^- = \theta_o x_{io}, \quad i = 1, \ldots, m, \quad \lambda_j \in S \end{array} \right. \right\} \quad (3.1)$$

$$\text{Max}\left\{\beta_o \left| \begin{array}{l} \displaystyle\sum_{j=1}^{n} \lambda_j y_{rj} - s_r^+ = \beta_o y_{ro}, \quad r = 1, \ldots, s \\ \displaystyle\sum_{j=1}^{n} \lambda_j x_{ij} + s_i^- = x_{io}, \quad i = 1, \ldots, m, \quad \lambda_j \in S \end{array} \right. \right\} \quad (3.2)$$

Depending on the specification of the set S in model (3.1) and (3.2), various technological sets can be defined as far as returns to scale are concerned. Originally Charnes et al. (1978) considered only CRS technologies where $S = \{\lambda_j \geq 0\}$. However, other possibilities can be considered, as shown in the previous section (e.g., setting the sum of lambdas equal to 1 for VRS, or lambdas to be binary for FDH). In section 3.5 we state in full the foregoing models for alternative return-to-scale technologies.

As can be gathered from model (3.1), if the optimum value of θ_o is $\theta_o^* < 1$, then DMU_o is not efficient, because the model will have identified another production possibility that secures at least the output vector y_o of DMU_o but using no more than the reduced input vector $\theta_o^* x_o$. Thus, θ_o^* is a measure of the radial input efficiency of DMU_o in that it reflects the proportion to which all of its observed inputs can be reduced pro rata, without detriment to its output levels.

In a similar manner, if the optimum value of β_o in (3.2) is $\beta_o^* > 1$, then DMU_o is not efficient in that the model in (3.2) will have identified another production possibility that secures at least the augmented output vector $\beta_o^* y_o$ using no more than the input vector x_o of DMU_o. Thus, $1/\beta_o^*$ is a measure of the radial output efficiency of DMU_o in that it reflects the largest proportion that any one of its output levels is of the maximum level that output could take given the input vector of DMU_o.

When $\theta_o^* = 1$ or $\beta_o^* = 1$ at the optimal solution to (3.1) or (3.2), respectively, then DMU_o lies on the frontier of the referent production possibilities set and it is deemed to be 100% efficient. That is, all its inputs collectively cannot be reduced pro rata without detriment to its outputs, nor can its outputs be raised pro rata without more inputs. However, DMU_o when 100% efficient in this sense is not necessarily Pareto-efficient because the pro rata improvements to inputs or alternatively to outputs may not be possible but improvements to the individual levels of some inputs or outputs may be possible. Such improvements are captured in the slacks in the input and output constraints of models (3.1) and (3.2). Therefore, models (3.1) and (3.2) do not necessarily identify Pareto-efficiency.

In order to guarantee Pareto-efficiency, models (3.1) or (3.2) can be solved in a first stage, and then in a second-stage model (3.3), maximizing slacks, should also be solved:

$$\text{Max} \left\{ \sum_{i=1}^{m} s_i^- + \sum_{r=1}^{s} s_r^+ \; \middle| \; \begin{array}{l} \displaystyle\sum_{j=1}^{n} \lambda_j y_{rj} - s_r^+ = y_{ro}^*, \quad r = 1, \ldots, s \\[2mm] \displaystyle\sum_{j=1}^{n} \lambda_j x_{ij} + s_i^- = x_{io}^*, \quad i = 1, \ldots, m, \quad \lambda_j \in S \end{array} \right\}$$

$$(3.3)$$

In this model, the input–output levels located on the input or output isoquant (obtained from a radial expansion or contraction of outputs or inputs) are used on the right-hand side of the constraints. If the optimum sum of slacks in (3.3) is zero, then the point (x_o^*, y_o^*) on the isoquant is Pareto-efficient.

As an alternative to this two-stage approach, there is a single-stage formulation that guarantees Pareto-efficiency by subtracting from the objective function in (3.1) or adding to the objective function in (3.2) the sum of slacks multiplied by a very small factor (ε). This single-stage formulation was first proposed by Charnes et al. (1978). It means that, first, preemptive priority is given to the minimization of θ_o, or to the maximization of β_o, and second, the maximization of slacks is sought. Because slacks are multiplied by a very small value (identified by ε), the resulting objective function is in fact virtually equal to the optimal value of θ_o or β_o, respectively. This is what is known as a single-stage approach to arrive at once at the radial efficiency measure and at a Pareto-efficient referent point. It has, however, been pointed out that the single-stage approach may result in computational inaccuracies and erroneous results when the value of ε is specified [see Ali and Seiford (1993), who have analyzed extensively the impact of the choice of ε on DEA results]. This means that in practical applications it is better to use a "two-stage" model to identify, first, the radial efficiency and then to maximize the slacks in the input output constraints of (3.1) or (3.2). [See Chang and Guh (1991), who also discuss the problems around the choice of ε.]

Note that when model (3.1) or (3.2) is used on a PPS specified under CRS, then we have $\theta_o^* = 1/\beta_o^*$, and so the input efficiency of DMU_o equals its output efficiency. This is true only under CRS. Note, however, that whether or not a DMU is classified as boundary will depend on the PPS and not on the orientation in which efficiency is measured. (E.g., under VRS, if a DMU is Pareto-efficient in the input orientation, it will also be so in the output orientation.)

The duals of models (3.1) and (3.2) are shown in (3.4) and (3.5), respectively, for the case where $S = \left\{ \sum \lambda_j = 1 \right\}$:

$$
\mathrm{Max} \left\{ h_o = \sum_{r=1}^{s} u_r y_{ro} + w \;\middle|\; \begin{array}{l} -\sum_{i=1}^{m} v_i x_{ij} + \sum_{r=1}^{s} u_r y_{rj} + w \leq 0, \quad j = 1, \ldots, n \\ \sum_{i=1}^{m} v_i x_{io} = 1, \quad u_r, v_i \geq 0, \quad w \text{ is free} \end{array} \right\}
$$

$$(3.4)$$

$$
\mathrm{Min} \left\{ g_o = \sum_{i=1}^{m} v_i x_{io} + w \;\middle|\; \begin{array}{l} \sum_{i=1}^{m} v_i x_{ij} - \sum_{r=1}^{s} u_r y_{rj} + w \geq 0, \quad j = 1, \ldots, n \\ \sum_{r=1}^{s} u_r y_{ro} = 1, \quad u_r, v_i \geq 0, \quad w \text{ is free} \end{array} \right\}
$$

$$(3.5)$$

The duals in (3.4) and (3.5) are specified for a VRS technology, but a CRS technology can be derived from (3.4) and (3.5) by setting w to zero.

In models (3.4) and (3.5), the variables u_r and v_i represent the weights that DMU_o "assigns" to each one of its inputs and outputs so that its efficiency will be maximized. DMU_o is free to choose these weights, and as such, the efficiency measure will show it in the best possible light.

The models in (3.4) and (3.5) can be presented as linear fractional models in which the objective function is the ratio of the sum of the weighted outputs to the sum of the weighted inputs of DMU_o. The linear fractional form of model (3.4) is reproduced in (3.6).

$$
\text{Max} \left\{ h_o = \frac{\sum\limits_{r=1}^{s} u_r y_{ro} + w}{\sum\limits_{i=1}^{m} v_i x_{io}} \quad \middle| \quad \begin{array}{l} \dfrac{\sum\limits_{r=1}^{s} u_r y_{rj} + w}{\sum\limits_{i=1}^{m} v_i x_{ij}} \leq 1, \\[4pt] j = 1, \ldots, n, \quad u_r, v_i \geq 0, \quad w \text{ is free} \end{array} \right\}
$$

$$(3.6)$$

The equivalence between (3.6) and (3.4) can be readily seen (Charnes and Cooper, 1962) if we note that any optimal set of $(\mathbf{u}, \mathbf{v}, w)$ in (3.6) can be scaled by a constant that will not affect their optimality as the constant cancels in the fractions of (3.6). Model (3.4) simply reflects scaling the optimal values of $(\mathbf{u}, \mathbf{v}, w)$ in (3.6) so that the denominator of the objective function is 1.

In (3.6), the DEA efficiency model maximizes for DMU_o the ratio of the sum of its weighted outputs to the sum of its weighted inputs, subject to the constraint that at no DMU does this ratio exceed some subjective upper bound. The upper bound is simply the maximum value we set for the relative efficiency index, normally 1 or 100. The model in (3.6) allows one to interpret efficiency in the usual "engineering" sense as a ratio of output to input, the inputs and outputs being aggregated through the use of weights.

The interesting feature of model (3.6) is that the weights are not specified a priori but flow out of the solution of the model. So, in fact, this model gives total freedom to DMUs to choose the optimal set of weights that maximize their efficiency. This, in turn, means that DEA is a powerful tool for identifying inefficiency in that if a DMU can choose the weights that show it in the best possible light and even so, other DMUs using this same set of weights appear with higher efficiency, then clearly there is strong evidence of inefficiency at the DMU concerned. By the same token, the efficiency rating of a DMU may be higher than the DMU merits, most notably, the rating may be raised through the use of counterintuitive weights for some of the inputs and outputs. This is one of the reasons behind many developments in the DEA literature, namely, those related with the imposition of weight restrictions, to restrict the flexibility of DMUs in assigning weights to inputs and outputs. In related developments, nonradial measures of efficiency are used, as we show later, to account for all sources of inefficiency.

The duality between models (3.1) and (3.4) and between (3.2) and (3.5) implies that each variable u_r on the multiplier model is linked through duality to s_r^+ in the envelopment model and a similar link exists between each v_i and each s_i^-. In particular, at the optimal solutions to (3.1) and (3.4), the optimal value of u_r equals the reduced cost of s_r^+ or shadow price of the constraint relating to output r in (3.1), and a similar relationship holds between v_i and s_i^-. The same is true for the primal-dual relationships between (3.2) and (3.5). This leads to the complementary slackness conditions such that, for example, when s_r^+ is positive, the existence of slack means that the shadow price of the constraint in (3.1) relating to output r is zero and so u_r is zero in (3.4). Similar statements can be made about s_i^- in (3.1) and v_i in (3.4) and also about models (3.2) and (3.5).

Note, however, that zero weights in the multiplier model do not necessarily lead to nonzero slacks, since some slacks may be basic but equal to zero (degenerate solution). The problem of degenerate solutions in the envelopment model is equivalent to the existence of multiple optimal solutions in the multiplier model. This is, unfortunately, a problem that is often found in DEA models. This problem does not affect the ability of DEA models to identify and quantify inefficiency, but affects the ability of DEA models to find marginal rates of substitution and transformation between inputs and outputs, since the weights identified by DEA multiplier models are not, in general, unique. Nonunique weights mean that several facets may span an efficient corner point.

In practical terms, it is equivalent to solve either the envelopment or the multiplier models, but each of them has special advantages:

- The envelopment model is useful for target-setting purposes and for identifying Pareto-efficiency when a second-stage model is used.
- The multiplier model is useful for finding implied marginal rates of substitution/transformation (with attention to the possible problem of nonunique weights, and zero weights) and for improving the discriminating power of DEA through the imposition of weight restrictions.

We complete our outline of radial measures of efficiency by noting that efficiency measures calculated with respect to an FDH technology require solving an integer linear programming problem. Integer programming problems can be, however, hard to solve and might be very time consuming, especially when the number of DMUs is high. For this reason, Deprins et al. (1984) proposed a method to solve FDH problems, which Tulkens (1993) later called the complete enumeration algorithm. The main principle behind this algorithm is very intuitive. For each DMU, one needs to find the set of DMUs that dominate it. If the set is empty, the DMU is efficient. If it is not, the input-efficiency measure is found by calculating for the dominated DMU ratios between the inputs of a nondominated DMU and the inputs of the dominated DMU. These ratios are calculated for every input, and the maximum is chosen. This is done for every dominating DMU, and the minimum of the resulting values corresponds to the FDH efficiency measure. A similar operation is performed for an output orientation, with the ratios being calculated on outputs.

3.3.2 The notion of targets and their relationship with measures of efficiency

The solution of an envelopment model, such as (3.1) or (3.2), leads to the levels the inputs and outputs of DMU_o need to place it on the boundary of the PPS. Specifically, models (3.1) and (3.2) yield with respect to DMU_o, respectively, the boundary input–output levels $\left(x_o^*, y_o^*\right)$ in (3.7a) and (3.7b):

$$y_{ro}^* = \sum_{j=1}^{n} \lambda_j^* y_{rj} = y_{ro} + s_r^{+*}, \qquad r = 1, \ldots, s$$
$$x_{io}^* = \sum_{j=1}^{n} \lambda_j^* x_{ij} = \theta_o^* x_{io} - s_i^{-*}, \qquad i = 1, \ldots, m$$

$$(3.7a)$$

$$y_{ro}^* = \sum_{j=1}^{n} \lambda_j^* y_{rj} = \beta_o^* y_{ro} + s_r^{+*}, \qquad r = 1, \ldots, s$$
$$x_{io}^* = \sum_{j=1}^{n} \lambda_j^* x_{ij} = x_{io} - s_i^{-*}, \qquad i = 1, \ldots, m$$

$$(3.7b)$$

The input–output levels in (3.7a) and (3.7b) clearly use a linear combination of a set of DMUs located on the efficient part of the boundary. Such DMUs correspond to λ values that are nonzero at the optimal solution to model (3.1) or (3.2), and they are called the *peer units* or *efficient referents* of the DMU_o.

The boundary levels in (3.7a) and (3.7b) may or may not render DMU_o Pareto-efficient. Normally, they are used as a basis for going to Pareto-efficient input–output levels for DMU_o by using them within the second-stage additive model in (3.3), where the slacks are maximized. The input–output levels that would render a DMU efficient[2] are normally referred to as targets. The determination of targets for DMUs is an important theme in DEA, since in many practical applications one is more interested in determining targets that render the DMUs efficient rather than in determining their level of inefficiency. In section 3.9, the target-setting issue is addressed in more detail.

It is interesting to note how targets and efficiency measures are related. The efficiency measure can be seen as the ratio between the norm of a target vector and the norm of the observed vector. Consider, for example, as targets the radial boundary levels $(x^*, y^*) = (\theta^* x, y)$, where the asterisks reflect optimal values in model (3.1). Taking the ratio of the norm of $\theta^* x$ and x, we have $\|\theta^* x\| / \|x\| = \theta^*$, which is, of course, the radial input efficiency of DMU_o. This ratio of norms could, in fact, be used in any circumstance to calculate the distance between a target vector (whatever the method used to find it) and an observed vector, and this could be interpreted as an efficiency score. The only problem with using the ratio of norms in general (i.e., for any type of target, including nonradial targets) is that it is not unit invariant unless the two vectors are collinear (which happens in the case of radial measures). Note that one could normalize the target and observed vectors to make them unit invariant. Such an approach is valid, but results still depend on the normalization procedure used.

3.3.3 Nonradial measures of efficiency

Nonradial measures of efficiency have been developed for various purposes, as will become clear throughout this section. We can define nonradial models as those models that do not preserve the mix within inputs and within outputs in movements toward the frontier. Note that some nonradial models introduced here can become radial models for some specific parameter values, but in general, they are nonradial.

3.3.3.1 The additive model

The additive model was first introduced by Charnes et al. (1985):

$$
\text{Add}_o = \max \left\{ \sum_{i=1}^{m} s_i^- + \sum_{r=1}^{s} s_r^+ \ \middle| \
\begin{aligned}
& \sum_{j=1}^{n} \lambda_j y_{rj} - s_r^+ = y_{ro}, \quad r = 1, \ldots, s, \\
& \sum_{j=1}^{n} \lambda_j x_{ij} + s_i^- = x_{io}, \quad i = 1, \ldots, m, \\
& \lambda_j \in S
\end{aligned}
\right\}
$$

$$(3.8)$$

The objective function of (3.8) is the sum of slacks that is sought to be maximized. Therefore, the additive model does not yield an efficiency measure (at least not one that can be readily interpreted). Nevertheless, the additive model is important in at least two respects: (i) it allows the identification of Pareto-efficient units—those that have a zero sum of slacks in the optimal solution of model (3.8), and (ii) it is among the first nonoriented models introduced in the literature that are important in cases where both inputs and outputs are to be targeted for improvement.

The additive model of Charnes et al. (1985) is one of the most often used nonradial models, since it is very useful for finding Pareto-efficient units. However, using this model to identify target levels for some inefficient DMU may prove problematic since it maximizes the L_1 distance[3] from the DMU to its target point. This means that targets identified by this model are the farthest rather than the closest to the inefficient DMU. There have been attempts in the literature to develop models that try to minimize the distance of a DMU to its targets (e.g., Golany et al., 1993; Frei and Harker, 1999; Portela et al., 2003). These issues are further addressed in section 3.9.

3.3.3.2 Russell measure of efficiency

Oriented efficiency measures reflect the distance of a production unit from the production frontier giving priority either to input contraction or output expansion. In practical situations, however, it may happen that both inputs and outputs (all or some of them only) are controllable and we seek their improvement. Nonoriented measures of efficiency reflect the potential for improvement in desired input and output directions. Nonoriented measures of efficiency are necessarily nonradial distance measures, but nonradial measures may be either oriented or nonoriented.

Nonradial measures of efficiency have, in general, the purpose of assuring that the identified targets lie on the Pareto-efficient subset of the frontier. That is, these models aim at providing a final efficiency score that accounts for all sources of inefficiency (radial, reflected in the radial efficiency score; and nonradial, reflected in slacks). Therefore, the nonradial adjustment reflected in slacks can also be seen as an input or output mix adjustment added to the mix-preserving radial adjustment.

One of the first nonradial efficiency measures is due to Färe and Lovell (1978), who developed the Russell measure of input efficiency. This measure was later generalized for the nonoriented case where both inputs and outputs could change toward the production frontier. The Russell graph measure of technical efficiency (Färe et al., 1985) with reference to a general technology T is

$$\text{Russell}_o = \min \left\{ \frac{\sum_{i=1}^{m} \theta_{io} + \sum_{r=1}^{s} \frac{1}{\beta_{ro}}}{m+s} \,\middle|\, (\theta_{io}x_{io}, \beta_{ro}y_{ro}) \in T, \quad \theta_{io} \leq 1, \quad \beta_{ro} \geq 1 \right\}.$$

$$(3.9)$$

When β_{ro} is not considered, the above objective function reduces to $\sum \theta_{io}/m$, which is the input Russell measure of efficiency as first proposed by Färe and Lovell (1978). The Russell measure can therefore be defined with an input or output orientation or without orientation (as above). In any case, the resulting efficiency measure reflects all the sources of inefficiency. It is equal to 1 only when the assessed DMU is Pareto-efficient. Zieschang (1984) proposed an alternative two-step procedure based on the Russell input measure to account for all sources of inefficiency. In a first step, a Farrell input-oriented efficiency model was solved, and in a second step, the radial targets from this model were used in a Russell input efficiency model to further adjust the radial targets for any existing slacks. The final efficiency score is then the product of the two components of inefficiency (the radial component given by the Farrell efficiency score, and the slacks component given by the Russell measure).

3.3.3.3 Range-adjusted measure of efficiency

There are some variants of the additive model that try to solve two of its problems: the fact that the objective function in the additive model is not unit invariant, and the fact that the additive model does not provide a final efficiency score. One such attempt is that by Cooper et al. (1999), who proposed the range-adjusted measure (RAM) of efficiency.[4] The model for this measure of efficiency modifies the additive model so that slacks in the objective function are normalized by the ranges of the corresponding input–output variables. The model is shown in (3.10):

$$\text{RAM}_o = \min \left\{ 1 - \frac{1}{m+s} \left(\sum_{i=1}^{m} \frac{s_{io}^-}{R_i} + \sum_{r=1}^{s} \frac{s_{ro}^+}{R_r} \right) \mid \left(x_{io} - s_{io}^-, y_{ro} + s_{ro}^+ \right) \in T \right\},$$

$$(3.10)$$

where $R_i = \max_j \{x_{ij}\} - \min_j \{x_{ij}\}$ and $R_r = \max_j \{y_{rj}\} - \min_j \{y_{rj}\}$. Note that in (3.10) the objective function value varies between 0 and 1.

The RAM model as introduced in Cooper et al. (1999) may not be specified correctly when the PPS T is CRS. This is because the RAM measure requires that each ratio between slacks and the corresponding range should be no higher than 1, so that the objective function of (3.10) is bounded by 1. Under CRS, however, it may happen that slacks are greater than the range of the corresponding input–output variable because the PPS of CRS includes scaled input–output values of efficient units.

The RAM measure is very sensitive to the ranges of the input output variables. This, in turn, means that it is very sensitive to both the maximum and minimum input and output values, however unrepresentative these values are of the rest of the range of the input or output variable concerned (for more details on the RAM measure, see also Steinmann and Zweifel, 2001).

3.3.3.4 The slack-based measure of efficiency

The slack-based measure (SBM) of Tone (1993, 2001) is defined as

$$\text{SBM}_o = \min \left\{ \frac{\left(\frac{1}{m} \sum_{i=1}^{m} \frac{x_{io} - s_{io}^-}{x_{io}} \right)}{\left(\frac{1}{s} \sum_{r=1}^{s} \frac{y_{ro} + s_{ro}^+}{y_{ro}} \right)} \mid \left(x_{io} - s_{io}^-, y_{ro} + s_{ro}^+ \right) \in T \right\}. \quad (3.11)$$

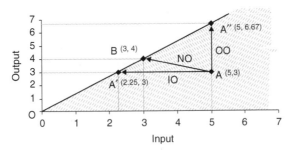

Figure 3.8. Illustration of the SBM Measure on a One-Input One-Output Example (Portela et al. 2003)

The main difference between the RAM and SBM is that the latter multiplies input and output adjustments rather than summing and averaging them. This seems more in line with the spirit of traditional radial efficiency measures. To see this, we can use a simple example from Portela et al. (2003), shown in figure 3.8.

DMU A is an inefficient DMU that is to be projected on the CRS efficient frontier OA′BA″. We consider three alternative projections for this DMU: (i) the output-oriented (OO) projection, which yields for this DMU a radial efficiency score of 45% $(3/6.667)$; (ii) the input-oriented (IO) projection, which yields the same efficiency score (2.25/5); and (iii) the nonoriented (NO) projection that takes DMU A to any point between A′ and A″, for example, to point B. If the nonoriented projection resulted by chance in an oriented target, such as point A′ or A″, then the nonoriented efficiency score should equal the radial efficiency score of 45%. Assuming that a nonoriented model yielded an oriented target A′ for DMU A, the Russell efficiency score would be equal to 72.5% $((0.45 + 1)/2)$, and the RAM would be 31.25% $(1 − 0.5 (2.75/2 + 0/1))$, where ranges have been calculated assuming that the data set was constituted solely by DMUs A and B. None of these measures equals 45% as one would expect. This happens because one is summing contraction of inputs and expansion of outputs rather than multiplying them. If we multiply the input and output adjustments, then the efficiency measure of DMU A (measuring its distance from A′) would be (0.45 × 1) 45%, and so the SBM model would yield a radial efficiency measure.

The multiplication of input contraction and output expansion factors (rather than their summation) has also been used in Brockett et al. (1997a). In their case, however, the authors calculated a measure of efficiency accounting for all sources of inefficiency by first identifying Pareto-efficient targets and then using these targets to compute

$$\left(\sum_{i=1}^{m} \theta_i \times \sum_{r=1}^{s} \frac{1}{\beta_r} \right) \Big/ (m \times s),$$

where θ_i and β_r are required adjustments in all inputs and outputs, respectively, to move from the observed position to a target position[5] (for details, see Portela et al. 2003).

3.3.3.5 The geometric distance function efficiency measure

As noted above, for the single input–output, case it seems logical to multiply input and output changes rather than summing and averaging them in order to express the distance between an observation and the boundary as a measure of efficiency. But for multiple input–output cases, we have the additional problem of deciding how to aggregate the multiple input contraction factors and the multiple output expansion factors before we multiply them. All the above-mentioned measures use the arithmetic average for this purpose. However, the geometric average could also be used, extending the multiplication of factors not only between aggregate input change and output change, but also within inputs and within outputs. The geometric distance function (GDF) proposed by Portela and Thanassoulis (2002, 2005, 2007) is such a type of measure and is defined as

$$
\text{GDF}_o = \min \left\{ \frac{\left(\prod_i \theta_{io} \right)^{1/m}}{\left(\prod_r \beta_{ro} \right)^{1/s}} \;\middle|\; (\theta_{io} x_{io}, \beta_{ro} y_{ro}) \in T, \;\; \theta_{io} \leq 1, \;\; \beta_{ro} \geq 1 \right\}.
$$

(3.12)

The GDF[6] incorporates all the sources of inefficiency since a different expansion and contraction factor is associated with each input and output. Therefore, a GDF efficiency score of 100% occurs only when a DMU is Pareto-efficient.

The GDF is a general measure that reduces to traditional oriented efficiency measures. For example, when all β_r values are set equal to 1 and all θ_i values are set equal to θ, then the GDF reduces to the input-oriented radial efficiency measure. On the other hand, if all θ_i values are set equal to 1 and all β_r values are set equal to β, then the GDF reduces to the output-oriented radial efficiency measure. When all β_r values are set equal to β, all θ_i values are set equal to θ, and β is set equal to $1/\theta$, then the GDF reduces to the hyperbolic distance function where the distance is measured by θ^2 and not θ (see section 3.3.3.6 below).

The multiplicative nature of the GDF means that it can be readily decomposed into scale efficiency, allocative efficiency (to be defined in section 3.4), and other effects. These are detailed in Portela and Thanassoulis (2007) in the context of measuring and decomposing profit efficiency. The issue of profit efficiency measurement is detailed in section 3.4.

3.3.3.6 Hyperbolic and directional efficiency models

The foregoing DEA models had the primary aim of improving performance moving DMUs toward the Pareto-efficient part of the PPS boundary, and therefore providing efficiency measures reflecting both radial and nonradial sources of inefficiency. This last set of models covered here lead to changes both in inputs and outputs to move inefficient production units toward the production frontier, and in that sense, they are nonoriented. However, they do not necessarily project a DMU on the Pareto-efficient subset of the production frontier. Within this class of models, we note the hyperbolic model of Färe et al. (1985) and the directional model of Chambers et al. (1996, 1998).

The hyperbolic efficiency measure of Färe et al. (1985) allows inputs and outputs to change toward the production frontier, but it preserves the mix within inputs and within outputs in this movement. The hyperbolic efficiency measure also assumes that changes in inputs are inversely proportional to changes in outputs as in (3.13).

$$H_o = \min\{\theta_o \mid (\theta_o x_{io}, \theta_o^{-1} y_{ro}) \in T, \quad \theta_o \leq 1\} \tag{3.13}$$

The mix preservation implicit within the hyperbolic model in (3.13) makes it the nonoriented model that is most similar to models that yield radial efficiency measures. However, this mix preservation and the linkage between input contractions and output expansions are strong restrictions that in practice may result in large amounts of input and output slacks not accounted for in the efficiency measure H_o.

The directional distance function introduced by Chambers et al. (1996, 1998) is also a nonoriented measure of efficiency that restricts movements toward the frontier by specifying a priori the direction to be followed (through the specification of a directional vector, $\mathbf{g}$). The directional model is defined as in (3.14).

$$\text{Dir}_o = \max\{\delta_o \mid (x_{io} - \delta_o g_{xi}, y_{ro} + \delta_o g_{yr}) \in T\}, \tag{3.14}$$

where $\mathbf{g} = (\mathbf{g}_x, \mathbf{g}_y)$ is a directional vector chosen a priori. Like the hyperbolic model, the directional model also allows little flexibility in the direction to be followed toward the frontier. This means that an optimal solution to dir_o will potentially result in targets that do not lie on the Pareto-efficient subset of the production frontier, so δ_o cannot account for all the sources of inefficiency. At the same time, however, different specifications of the directional vector can be used, which turns this into a powerful model. Färe and Grosskopf (2000b) specified the directional vector as being equal to the observed inputs or outputs, which made it possible to show the equivalence between the traditional Farrell input or output efficiency measures and the directional model. In fact, if we specify a directional vector $\mathbf{g} = (\mathbf{x}, 0)$, then the directional model would be

$$\text{Dir}_o = \max\{\delta_o \mid (x_{io}(1 - \delta_o), y_{ro}) \in T\}.$$

Replacing $(1 - \delta_o)$ by θ_o reduces dir_o to the Farrell input measure of efficiency. Note that δ_o is not an efficiency but an inefficiency measure.

A suitable specification of the directional vector makes the directional model adequate for modeling undesirable inputs and/or outputs, as shown in Chung et al. (1997). For example, desirable outputs are sought to be increased, whereas undesirable outputs are sought to be decreased. Therefore, by associating a positive direction with the former and a negative direction with the latter, it is possible to model undesirable outputs within the directional model framework. In addition, the directional model can also be used for modeling situations of negative inputs or outputs, as shown in Portela et al. (2004). In section 3.6, we detail DEA models to deal with these two specific situations (negative data and bad inputs or outputs).

3.3.3.7 Other measures of efficiency in brief

There are several other measures of efficiency. We note here in brief a few of them. DEA models that capture all sources of inefficiency can be found in Cherchye and Van Puyenbroeck (2001a), who propose an inverse Färe-Lovell (or Russell) measure of efficiency, and in Cherchye and Van Puyenbroeck (1999), who propose a "proportional slack based efficiency measure" that is calculated as the ratio between the norms of the target vector and observed vector (for the input-oriented case). This measure is then decomposed in the radial Farrell component, and a component that reflects differences in the input mix (or output mix for the output-oriented case) between the radial target and the Pareto-efficient target. (This mix measure is, in fact, the cosine of the angle between the target vector and the observed vector.) Other efficiency measures can be found in Briec (1998), who uses L_p norms to compute efficiency and relate these norms to some known efficiency measures (see also Briec and Lesourd, 1999). Bardhan et al. (1996a, 1996b) also introduce some measures of efficiency dominance (MED) and measures of inefficiency dominance (MID) for the particular setting of FDH technologies where slacks are a more serious problem than in convex sets, when radial models of efficiency are used.

3.3.4 Implied modifications to production possibilities sets through definitions of efficiency measures

So far, we have addressed separately (as far as that was possible) the issues of defining the technological or PPS, on the one hand, and the distance measure used between the boundary of this set and some production unit in order to get a measure of the efficiency of that unit, on the other. We do not leave this topic, however, without noting that the specification of certain requirements on measuring distances to the PPS frontier can implicitly modify the latter. Take, for example, the issue of incorporating all the sources of inefficiency

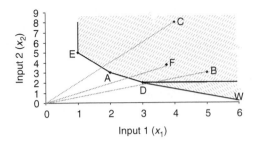

Figure 3.9. Two-Input One-Output Example

into the efficiency measure (e.g., the Russell measure of efficiency). Measures of this type in effect delete the inefficient part of the PPS frontier by implicitly extending the efficient part of the frontier and so modifying it.

To illustrate the point, consider the DMUs in figure 3.9. Let us solve the input-oriented version of model (3.9) in relation to DMU B to derive its Russell measure of efficiency. (The input–output data of the DMUs are tabulated alongside figure 3.9.)

The Russell input efficiency score of DMU B is 63.33%, corresponding to the radial inefficiency that takes the DMU to the flat part of the boundary parallel to the input 1 axis plus the nonradial efficiency that further moves this DMU to DMU D, eliminating the slack in input 1. If one uses the dual (or multiplier) model of the Russell input model, it is easy to see that it corresponds to a model where some restrictions have been added to the weights (see Portela and Thanassoulis, 2006, for details). This, in practice, means that the Russell input measure can be seen as equivalent to a traditional radial efficiency score calculated in relation to a technology where facet DW in figure 3.9 was added to the original efficient frontier, thus enlarging the PPS and eliminating the weakly efficient facet of the original PPS.

Therefore, models that try to account for all sources of inefficiency in the distance measures calculated can be seen as traditional DEA models but set up in relation to a modified PPS (though it is not always easy to identify this new technology). In fact, the issue of reflecting slacks in efficiency scores is closely related to weight restrictions since the problem we are looking at is the same (positive slacks in the envelopment model correspond to zero weights in the multiplier model, and most weight-restricted models aim precisely at avoiding zero weights—though other objectives may motivate the imposition of weight restrictions, as will be clearer in section 3.7).

In summary, in this section we outline several ways through which a distance from the observed point to the frontier of the PPS can be measured. Traditional ways of measuring this distance assume radial expansion/contraction of output/input factors, but there are several reasons why other measures could be preferred for measuring this distance. One such reason is the need to assure projections on the Pareto-efficient frontier that radial traditional models cannot assure. There is now a panoply of nonradial methods in the literature each with its own merits and disadvantages. There are also models that are nonradial mainly because they allow for movements of production units toward the frontier that allow both for changes in input and output levels. Such models do not necessarily assure projections on the Pareto-efficient frontier (e.g., the directional or hyperbolic models), but they are nonradial due to their nonoriented nature. In concluding this section, we show that although we treated the definition of the PPS independently from the measurement of efficiency, the two issues are linked, and in fact the definition of certain measures of efficiency can result in an implicit alteration of the PPS as defined in this section.

3.4 Economic Measures of Efficiency

The efficiency measures defined so far were technical measures of efficiency whose computation does not depend on prices. When price information is available, economic measures of efficiency (cost, revenue, or profit) can be computed and decomposed into allocative and technical components. This topic was already addressed in chapter 1. In this chapter, we focus on the estimation of cost, revenue, and profit efficiency using DEA.

3.4.1 Cost and revenue efficiency measures

Let $w \in \mathfrak{R}_+^m$ be the input price vector and $p \in \mathfrak{R}_+^s$ the output price vector. The cost function is defined by

$$C(y, w) = \min\{wx \mid x \in L(y)\},$$

corresponding to the minimum expenditure required to produce output vector y at input prices w (e.g., Färe et al., 1994). Figure 3.10 illustrates the computation of cost efficiency and its decomposition.

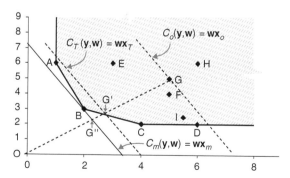

Figure 3.10. Cost Efficiency Measurement

A cost measure of efficiency indicates the extent to which a production unit minimizes the cost of producing a given output vector, given the input prices it faces. In figure 3.10, this measure corresponds, for DMU G, to the ratio of minimum cost to observed cost: $C_m(y, w)/C_o(y, w) = wx_m/wx_o = OG''/OG$. That is, given factor prices, DMU G should be using the input levels at point B and not those currently used. Point B is overall cost efficient because it lies simultaneously on the technological frontier and on the minimum cost line labeled $C_m(y, w)$.

As shown above, the technical efficiency of DMU G is given by OG'/OG. Note that this value is equivalent to the ratio between the cost at the technically efficient point and the observed cost, that is, $C_T(y, w)/C_o(y, w) = wx_T/wx_o = OG'/OG$. For example, a technical efficiency value of 50% means that when inputs decrease by 50%, so that the technical efficient frontier is reached, costs also reduce by 50%.

Assume now that DMU G has eliminated its technical inefficiency by moving to point G'. This point is not cost efficient when compared to point B, which has a lower cost. A movement from point G' to point B implies an adjustment in the mix of inputs of DMU G that further reduces its costs. Note that by keeping the same mix, DMU G' could not reduce further its costs without getting out of the PPS. The adjustment from point G' to a point of minimum cost, B, represents, therefore, gaining allocative (input) efficiency. The allocative (input) efficiency is also called price efficiency, because it measures the extent to which a technically efficient point such as G' falls short of achieving minimum cost because it fails to make the substitutions (or reallocations) involved in moving from G' to B (Cooper et al. 2000a). The allocative efficiency measure can also be expressed in terms of a ratio between the minimum cost at point B and the cost at the technically efficient point G': $C_m(y, w)/C_T(y, w) = wx_m/wx_T$. Note that this cost ratio is equivalent to the quantity ratio OG''/OG'. We can now establish the following relationship:

$$(OG''/OG) = (OG'/OG) \times (OG''/OG'),$$

or

$$\text{Cost efficiency} = \text{technical efficiency} \times \text{allocative efficiency.}$$

It is important to stress that cost efficiency does not have an immediate interpretability in terms of radial input reductions, although the inverse is always true: radial input reductions always have a cost interpretability (e.g., Kerstens and Vanden-Eeckaut, 1995). In fact, if we multiply the input quantities of G by the overall cost efficiency measure, the resulting radial input targets would be located exactly at G'', which is a point outside the PPS and thus nonattainable. This point is therefore used only as a reference to calculate cost efficiency and should not be interpreted as the minimum cost target input levels for DMU G. The minimum cost target input levels for DMU G are at point B.

In the general case, the computation of cost efficiency involves solving the following "minimum cost" model, where the decision variables are λ_j and x_i:

$$
\min_{\lambda_j, x_i} \left\{ C = \sum_{i=1}^{m} w_{io} x_i \; \middle| \; \begin{array}{l} \displaystyle\sum_{j=1}^{n} \lambda_j y_{rj} \geq y_{ro}, \quad r = 1, \ldots, s \\[2ex] \displaystyle\sum_{j=1}^{n} \lambda_j x_{ij} \leq x_i, \quad i = 1, \ldots, m, \;\; \lambda_j \geq 0 \end{array} \right\},
$$

$$(3.15)$$

where w_{io} are the input prices faced by DMU_o. The solution of this model results in optimal input levels x_i yielding minimum cost $C = C_m$. If we denote C_o the total cost of the current input levels of DMU_o, then its cost efficiency is C_m/C_o. Its allocative efficiency can be retrieved residually using the above decomposition of cost efficiency, where technical efficiency can be calculated through a traditional input-oriented DEA model.

Turning now to revenue efficiency, the revenue function is

$$R(\mathbf{x}, \mathbf{p}) = \max\{\mathbf{p}\mathbf{y} \mid \mathbf{y} \in P(\mathbf{x})\},$$

representing the maximum revenue that can be generated from input vector $\mathbf{x}$ at output prices $\mathbf{p}$. Revenue efficiency is calculated in an analogous way to cost efficiency, where the DEA model that determines revenue maximizing output levels is

$$
\max_{\lambda_j, y_r} \left\{ R = \sum_{r=1}^{s} p_{ro} y_r \; \middle| \; \begin{array}{l} \displaystyle\sum_{j=1}^{n} \lambda_j y_{rj} \geq y_r, \quad r = 1, \ldots, s \\[2ex] \displaystyle\sum_{j=1}^{n} \lambda_j x_{ij} \leq x_{io}, \quad i = 1, \ldots, m, \;\; \lambda_j \geq 0 \end{array} \right\},
$$

$$(3.16)$$

where p_{ro} are the output prices faced by DMU_o. The solution of this model results in optimal output levels y_r yielding maximum revenue R_M. If we denote R_o the total value of the current output levels of DMU_o, then its revenue efficiency is R_o/R_M. Allocative (output) efficiency can be calculated as the ratio of revenue efficiency and technical output efficiency, where the latter can be calculated through a traditional output-oriented DEA model.

Cost and revenue efficiencies can be measured in relation to any technology. This means, of course, that technical input or output efficiency should also be calculated in relation to the same technology. In the case of VRS technologies using the results shown in the next section where technical efficiency is decomposed into pure technical efficiency and scale efficiency, we can further decompose cost (or revenue) efficiency as (see Färe et al., 1994)

$$\text{Cost efficiency} = \text{pure technical efficiency} \times \text{scale efficiency}$$
$$\times \text{allocative efficiency.}$$

In the above cost model, inputs are allowed to vary, and outputs are considered fixed. Färe et al. (1994) propose the measurement of input technical and cost efficiency in relation to a "revenue-indirect production technology," where outputs are not completely fixed but can vary within certain ranges defined by a target revenue. In practice, calculating revenue-indirect cost efficiency implies solving a minimum cost model with an additional revenue constraint that states that revenue for the unit being assessed (calculated based on output levels that are decision variables in the revenue-indirect model) should be above a certain level R. For a CRS technology, the revenue-indirect minimum cost is given by

$$\operatorname*{Min}_{\lambda_j, x_i, y_r} \left\{ \text{CI} = \sum_{i=1}^{m} w_{io} x_i \;\middle|\; \begin{array}{ll} \sum_{j=1}^{n} \lambda_j y_{rj} \geq y_r, & r = 1, \ldots, s, \quad \sum_{r=1}^{s} pro y_r \geq R \\ \sum_{j=1}^{n} \lambda_j x_{ij} \leq x_i, & i = 1, \ldots, m, \quad \lambda_j \geq 0 \end{array} \right\}$$

$$(3.17)$$

Price notation in (3.17) is as in (3.15) and (3.16). The ratio between the optimum value of CI and the observed cost $C_o (\text{CI}/C_o)$ is the revenue-indirect cost efficiency. The revenue-indirect input technical efficiency can be calculated (also for CRS) as

$$\operatorname*{Min}_{y_r, \lambda_j, \theta_o} \left\{ \text{TI} = \theta_o \;\middle|\; \begin{array}{ll} \sum_{j=1}^{n} \lambda_j y_{rj} \geq y_r, & r = 1, \ldots, s, \quad \sum_{r=1}^{s} pro y_r \geq R \\ \sum_{j=1}^{n} \lambda_j x_{ij} \leq \theta_o x_{io}, & i = 1, \ldots, m, \quad \lambda_j \geq 0 \end{array} \right\}.$$

$$(3.18)$$

Price notation in (3.18) is as in (3.17). Thus, the revenue-indirect cost efficiency can be decomposed as the product of the revenue-indirect input technical efficiency and revenue-indirect input allocative efficiency. In the case of VRS technologies, the revenue-indirect input technical efficiency can be further decomposed into revenue-indirect pure technical efficiency and revenue-indirect scale efficiency (see Färe et al., 1994, for details).

Camanho and Dyson (2005) applied the revenue-indirect cost efficiency model of Färe et al. (1994) to a sample of bank branches. They, however, related the revenue-indirect cost model to the traditional minimum cost model (3.15) decomposing (for an observed cost C_o): $\text{CI}/C_o = (C_m/C_o) \times (\text{CI}/C_m)$, that is, the indirect revenue cost efficiency equals the product of traditional cost efficiency (C_m/C_o) and another component (CI/C_m) that Camanho and Dyson (2005) called output mix efficiency. This component is related to output mix since the main difference between the revenue-indirect cost model and the traditional cost model is that the former allows for changes in the output levels and output mix so that the target revenue constraint is met.

The cost-indirect output efficiency can be computed as the cost-indirect input efficiency, where in this case the maximum revenue model is further constrained by a cost restriction specifying that the cost of the inputs of the assessed DMU should be lower than a certain amount C [see also Färe et al. (1988), where the cost-indirect technical efficiency model is applied to a sample of school districts].

3.4.2 Profit efficiency measures

The concept of economic efficiency that has perhaps received the least attention in the DEA literature is the concept of profit efficiency (possibly because in the early stages of the DEA literature the method was seen as one for assessing performance of not-for-profit entities). However, in many practical situations DEA is applied in for-profit organizations, such as banks or bank branches, where interest in analyzing profit efficiency is obvious. Profit maximization implies that at least some inputs and some outputs are endogenous (choice) variables (e.g., Kumbhakar, 2001). If all inputs are exogenously fixed, then the maximum profit model reduces to one that seeks maximum revenue. Similarly, if all outputs are exogenous, then maximum profit would result by minimizing cost. If, however, some inputs and some outputs are endogenous, then maximum profit can be attained by suitably changing the relative input and output levels to exploit the available input and output prices. The model needed for determining input and output levels that maximize profit would be a "nonoriented" one, in contrast to the traditional oriented models where either inputs are minimized, holding outputs relatively stable, or the other way round.

Within the DEA framework, the starting point of a profit analysis is the calculation of maximum attainable profit. This can be done using

$$\underset{y_r, x_i, \lambda_j}{\text{Max}} \left\{ \Pi = \sum_{r=1}^{s} p_{ro} y_r - \sum_{i=1}^{m} w_{io} x_i \;\middle|\; \begin{array}{l} \sum_{j=1}^{n} \lambda_j y_{rj} \geq y_r, \quad r = 1, \ldots, s \\ \sum_{j=1}^{n} \lambda_j x_{ij} \leq x_i, \quad i = 1, \ldots, m \\ \sum_{j=1}^{n} \lambda_j = 1, \quad \lambda_j \geq 0 \end{array} \right\}.$$

$$(3.19)$$

This maximum profit model assures profit maximization in the long run because no factors are considered fixed. We also consider here a model where no other constraints apart from technological restrict profit maximization [see Färe et al. (1990), where expenditure constraints were added to the maximum profit model]. The maximum profit model (3.19) assumes VRS since, for a technology exhibiting globally CRS, either the maximum profit level is zero or the solution of the maximum profit model is undefined (see Varian, 1992; Färe et al., 1994).

Profit maximization in relation to a VRS technology implies that perfectly competitive markets are not assumed, since under this assumption all firms have zero profits in the long run. In the maximum profit model in (3.19), the optimum profit, Π^*, may be positive. At the same time, a VRS technology accounts for the differing scales of production units, and therefore, scale efficiency cannot be calculated as a component of overall profit efficiency (unlike the case where cost efficiency or revenue efficiency can be decomposed so that scale efficiency is retrieved). In order to capture scale efficiency, the maximum profit model should be solved under CRS (e.g., Färe et al., 1994). Clearly, a maximum profit point as determined by (3.19) need not be MPSS in the sense of Banker (1984). That is, maximum profit units do not need to be scale efficient (see also Kuosmanen, 1999a).

We illustrate the measurement and decomposition of profit efficiency by means of the technically and profit inefficient DMU A in figure 3.11. DMU A achieves maximum profit when it is projected on the profit frontier (e.g., at A*), where maximum profit equals that of DMU B, a maximum profit unit. If overall profit efficiency is measured by means of a ratio between profit at two points (as happens in the cost and revenue contexts), then the overall profit efficiency of DMU A would be given by the ratio Π/Π^* [see, e.g.,

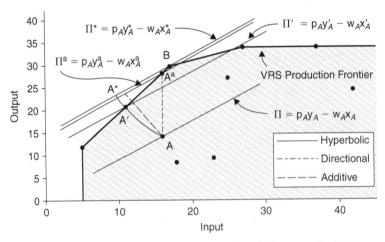

Figure 3.11. Profit Efficiency Measurement (Portela and Thanassoulis, 2007)

Banker and Maindiratta (1988) or Cooper et al. (2000a), which used this ratio-based approach within the DEA framework]. The technical profit efficiency of this DMU could also be calculated by a ratio of profits, namely, as Π/Π', where Π' is the profit at the technically efficient projection A′ of A. The allocative profit efficiency of A (Π'/Π^*) could then be calculated from $\Pi/\Pi^* = (\Pi/\Pi') \times (\Pi'/\Pi^*)$.

The aforementioned ratio-based approach is analogous to what is usually done in cost or revenue settings where ratios of cost or revenue represent efficiency, as shown in the preceding section. In such settings, however, there is no possibility of negative costs or revenues. This is not the case with profits that can be negative. The problem of negative profits was not recognized as such by some authors. For example, Berger and Mester (2000, p. 98) state that "profit efficiency can be negative, since firms can throw away more than 100% of their potential profits." Others, such as Banker and Maindiratta (1988), assume that all production units exhibit positive profit. Finally, some authors have acknowledged this problem and solved it either by using revenue/cost ratios, which can never be negative[7] (see, e.g., Cooper et al., 2000a; Kuosmanen 1999a), or by using differences between profits to avoid negative efficiency measures (e.g., Berger et al., 1993; Coelli et al., 2002).

In our opinion, the ratio of profit levels is not an adequate measure to calculate profit efficiency. This is not only because these ratios can result in negative profit efficiency measures (that are hard to interpret), but also because these ratios do not have a dual interpretation in terms of the required adjustments in inputs and outputs to achieve the maximum profit target. That is, while in a cost setting we can say that reducing all inputs by, say, 50% renders a DMU technically efficient, and this is equivalent to reducing this DMU's costs by 50%, in a profit setting changing inputs and outputs by a certain percentage does not necessarily imply the same percentage change in profit. We return to this issue later.

Rather than using the above ratio-based approach, some authors define overall profit efficiency as being a measure reflecting the required adjustments to the input–output levels of DMU A that moves it to some point A* on the profit frontier. For example, the hyperbolic model of Färe et al. (1985, 1994) defines the technical profit efficiency of DMU A as being θ_A^h defined in the technical efficiency hyperbolic model (3.13) shown in section 3.3. In accordance with this hyperbolic path, the overall profit efficiency (φ_A^h) of DMU A is derived by solving the quadratic equation $\Pi^* = p_A(y_A/\varphi_A^h) - w_A x_A \varphi_A^h$, where Π^* is the maximum profit of A calculated through the maximum profit model (3.19). That is, overall profit efficiency (φ_A^h) represents the amount by which inputs and outputs should be hyperbolically adjusted, so that they are projected on the profit boundary.[8] The overall profit efficiency can then be decomposed as $\varphi_A^h = \theta_A^h \times \gamma_A^h$, where γ_A^h is the allocative profit efficiency.

The directional model of Chambers et al. (1996, 1998) follows a procedure that is similar to that of the hyperbolic model, except that the overall profit efficiency (φ_A^d) would decompose as $\varphi_A^d = \delta_A + \gamma_A^d$, where δ_A represents technical profit efficiency and γ_A^d represents allocative profit efficiency. The measure of profit efficiency is equal to $\varphi_A^d = (\Pi^* - \Pi)/(pg_y + wg_x)$; that is, the profit efficiency is the difference between maximum and observed profit normalized by the value of the directional vector (which can be observed profit if the directional vector equals observed input and output levels). This efficiency measure is also called Nerlovian profit efficiency measure (see Färe and Grosskopf, 2000b). In figure 3.11, both the hyperbolic and directional projections on the technological frontier and on the profit frontier are represented.

The hyperbolic and directional distance function approaches have the problem of possibly calculating overall profit efficiency with reference to infeasible points (outside the PPS), such as A* in figure 3.11. This can also happen in "oriented" cost or revenue settings as we showed with point G'' in figure 3.10, but in those cases projections on infeasible points can be interpreted in terms of ratios of inputs (outputs) between the observed and the infeasible point because such ratios match the ratio of minimum cost (maximum revenue) to that at the observed point. This is no longer so in the nonoriented profit setting. For example, if we assume a hyperbolic path is followed from A to A* in figure 3.11, then the required adjustments in inputs and outputs for DMU A to achieve the profit frontier are given by φ_A^h, as $x_A^*/x_A = y_A/y_A^* = \varphi_A^h$. The profit ratio, on the other hand equals

$$\frac{\Pi}{\Pi^*} = \frac{(p_A y_A - w_A x_A)}{(p_A y_A^* - w_A x_A^*)} = \frac{(p_A y_A - w_A x_A)}{(p_A y_A/\varphi_A^h - w_A x_A \varphi_A^h)},$$

which differs from φ_A^h. (Note that this statement is valid for the directional model, as well.)

The calculation of technical profit efficiency through the hyperbolic and directional models can result in large values for the slacks not accounted for in the final profit efficiency measure. This is an important problem in a context where overall efficiency is being measured because what is not captured by technical efficiency will be incorporated into allocative efficiency, which may therefore be incorrectly estimated.

The additive DEA model can also be used for the purpose of decomposing "profit efficiency" into its components. If the additive model is used for assessing DMU A in figure 3.11, then a technically efficient target (A^a, whose profit is Π^a) and a maximum profit target (B, whose profit is Π^*) are identified. Using these targets, Cooper et al. (1999, 2000a) decomposed the profit lost due to overall profit inefficiency into the profit lost due to technical and allocative inefficiency, that is, $(\Pi^* - \Pi) = (\Pi^a - \Pi) + (\Pi^* - \Pi^a)$. This relationship is not, however, expressed in efficiency terms but in absolute profit values [see Berger et al. (1993) and Coelli et al. (2002), which also used profit differences, though not using the additive model]. The additive model has the advantage of calculating Pareto-efficient targets in the production frontier, and therefore, technical inefficiency contains all possible sources of inefficiency. However, as noted above, the additive model yields technical efficient targets for inefficient DMUs that may be distant from rather than close to the observed DMU. This means that while the hyperbolic and directional models may underestimate technical inefficiency (since they do not account for slacks and these will be reflected in allocative inefficiency), the additive model may overestimate technical inefficiency (since the targets on which technical efficiency is based are the farthest from the observed unit being assessed).[9]

Portela and Thanassoulis (2005, 2007) propose the use of the GDF defined in section 3.3 to measure and decompose profit efficiency. Their approach consists of calculating maximum profit using the model in (3.19) and then using the GDF a posteriori to calculate overall profit efficiency. Using the GDF, and considering an observed point (x, y), a technically efficient point (x', y'), and a profit-maximizing point (x^*, y^*), the following decomposition is possible:

$$\frac{\left(\prod_i \frac{x_i^*}{x_i}\right)^{1/m}}{\left(\prod_r \frac{y_r^*}{y_r}\right)^{1/s}} = \frac{\left(\prod_i \frac{x_i'}{x_i}\right)^{1/m}}{\left(\prod_r \frac{y_r'}{y_r}\right)^{1/s}} \times \frac{\left(\prod_i \frac{x_i^*}{x_i'}\right)^{1/m}}{\left(\prod_r \frac{y_r^*}{y_r'}\right)^{1/s}} \qquad (3.20)$$

That is, overall profit efficiency equals the product of technical profit efficiency and allocative profit efficiency.[10] The allocative profit efficiency reflects movements from a technically efficient point (x', y') to the maximum profit point (x^*, y^*). These movements reflect not only changes in the mix of inputs and outputs that are dictated by factor prices, but also changes in scale size. Interestingly, in a profit setting for the single input–output case, all allocative inefficiency is, in fact, scale inefficiency (see Lovell and Sickles, 1983). The mixture of mix and scale effects in the allocative profit efficiency measure may result in an allocative measure greater than 1 when the GDF decomposition above is used. This is a direct result of the fact that the maximum profit model is specified in relation to a VRS technology, and therefore, maximum profit units can be scale inefficient [see Portela and Thanassoulis (2005), where the authors decompose further the allocative profit efficiency into mix and scale effects].

The GDF approach above to calculate profit efficiency solves the problem of projection to infeasible points and the problem of accounting for slacks in the technical profit efficiency measure. However, the GDF efficiency measure still does not have a dual profit interpretation, while at the same time there is the possibility of overall and allocative profit efficiency measures higher than 1, which are not easily interpreted. For this reason, Portela and Thanassoulis (2007) present an alternative to profit efficiency measurement that the authors called "profitability efficiency." That is, rather than using profit defined as revenue minus cost, the authors used a measure of profitability defined as revenue divided by cost, where each output revenue and each input cost are aggregated through the geometric mean. The resulting profitability ratio, for DMU_o, is defined as

$$\Gamma^o = \frac{\left(\prod_r p_{ro} y_{ro}\right)^{1/s}}{\left(\prod_i w_{io} x_{io}\right)^{1/m}}. \tag{3.21}$$

Using this measure of profitability, its maximum is calculated as

$$\underset{x_i, y_r, \lambda_j}{\text{Max}} \left\{ \frac{\left(\prod_r p_{ro} y_r\right)^{1/s}}{\left(\prod_i w_{io} x_i\right)^{1/m}} \middle| \begin{array}{l} \sum_{j=1}^{n} \lambda_j y_{rj} \geq y_r, \quad r = 1, \ldots, s \\ \sum_{j=1}^{n} \lambda_j x_{ij} \leq x_i, \quad i = 1, \ldots, m \quad \lambda_j \geq 0 \end{array} \right\}. \tag{3.22}$$

Using the targets from this model, it is possible to calculate profitability efficiency as the ratio between observed profitability and maximum profitability, mirroring the usual definition of economic efficiency in the cost and revenue contexts. If we denote maximum profitability resulting from the maximum profitability model (3.22) as Γ^* and observed profitability as Γ^o, then for a CRS technically efficient target $(x_i', y_r') = (x_i \theta_{io}', y_r \beta_{ro}')$, we have

$$\frac{\Gamma^o}{\Gamma^*} = \text{GDF} \times \text{AE} \quad \Leftrightarrow \quad \frac{\Gamma^o}{\Gamma^*} = \frac{\Gamma^o}{\Gamma'} \times \frac{\Gamma'}{\Gamma^*}, \tag{3.23}$$

where Γ' is profitability at a technically efficient point. That is, profitability efficiency equals a GDF measure of technical efficiency multiplied by a measure of allocative efficiency (AE). The GDF measure of technical efficiency can still be decomposed into a pure technical efficiency measure and a scale efficiency component. This decomposition has the advantage of allowing the dual interpretation of profitability efficiency measures in terms of input–output adjustments that none of the other measures allows (see Portela and Thanassoulis, 2007).

In summary, in this section we have outlined the various ways that can be found in the literature to measure cost, revenue, and profit efficiency. We detail especially the profit efficiency measure since the DEA literature is rich in applications that calculate cost or revenue efficiency but poor on applications that calculate profit efficiency. We highlight several difficulties with profit efficiency measures starting with its definition, which varies between being a ratio of maximum to observed profit and a measure of the adjustments required to input and output levels to move a production unit to the profit frontier. We offer some recent developments in the literature that overcome these problems.

3.5 Scale Efficiency and Returns to Scale

3.5.1 The concept of returns to scale

A starting point in coming to grips with the concept of returns to scale is that it relates to average product. We can readily define average product in a single-input/single-output case. For example, let a production unit have input level x and output y. Then its average product is y/x. Returns to scale relate to how, *under efficient operation*, average product would be affected by scale size. If operation is not efficient, then changes in average product as scale size changes can be due both to changes in efficiency, and changes in scale size and it would not be possible to differentiate between the two.

Let us now assume that in the case of a Pareto-efficient unit operating in a single-input/single-output context, with current input x and output y, we scale its input level x by $\alpha \neq 1$, $\alpha \to 1$ to αx. Let the unit remain Pareto-efficient by changing its output level to βy. Its average product has now become $(\beta y/\alpha x) = (\beta/\alpha) \times (y/x)$. Thus, average product has been scaled by the ratio (β/α).

If $(\beta/\alpha) > 1$, the unit's average product has risen since $(\beta/\alpha) \times (y/x) > y/x$. In such a case, we have *local* IRS because the proportional rise in output (β) is larger than the proportional rise of the input by (α). The characterization IRS is local because we considered only a marginal change in the scale of the unit ($\alpha \to 1$). We can readily see by extension of the foregoing that if $(\beta/\alpha) < 1$, we have local DRS, and if $(\beta/\alpha) = 1$, we have CRS locally. This makes clear the practical significance of identifying and exploiting returns to scale at an operating unit. Where the unit is not operating under CRS, in principle, there would be advantage to changing scale size so as to exploit returns to scale. However, this may not always be feasible in practice because scale size may not be under the control of an operating unit.

In the multiple input–output case, the definitions of IRS, CRS, and DRS above in terms of the relationship between the percentage radial changes in input and output levels can be generalized as follows.

Let DMU j be Pareto-efficient and have input levels $\mathbf{x}_j = \{x_{ij}, i = 1, \ldots, m\}$ and output levels $\mathbf{y}_j = \{y_{rj}, \quad r = 1, \ldots, s\}$. Let us scale its input levels to $\alpha \mathbf{x}_j = \{\alpha x_{ij}, \quad i = 1, \ldots, m\}$, where $\alpha > 0$. Let DMU j now with input levels $\alpha \mathbf{x}_j$ be capable in principle of becoming Pareto-efficient with output levels $\beta \mathbf{y}_j = \{\beta y_{rj}, \quad r = 1, \ldots, s\}$. Finally let $\rho = \lim_{\alpha \to 1} ((\beta - 1)/(\alpha - 1))$. Then,

If $\rho > 1$ we have local IRS at $(\mathbf{x}_j, \mathbf{y}_j)$,
If $\rho = 1$ we have local CRS at $(\mathbf{x}_j, \mathbf{y}_j)$, and
If $\rho < 1$ we have local DRS at $(\mathbf{x}_j, \mathbf{y}_j)$.

Note that in scaling input levels by α and output levels by β above, we maintain the input–output mix of DMU j constant. Thus, if local IRS holds at a Pareto-efficient DMU j, then when we expand (contract) its input levels by a small percentage, its output levels will expand (contract) by a larger percentage, assuming the DMU remains Pareto-efficient. Under CRS, the expansion (contraction) of its outputs will be by the same percentage as that of its inputs, while under DRS, its output levels will expand (contract) by a smaller percentage than its inputs, always assuming the DMU remains Pareto-efficient.

3.5.2 Basic DEA models under non-CRS

In constructing the PPS in a DEA framework, we need to first decide what assumptions are most plausible to maintain in terms of the type of returns to scale, characterizing the technology under which the units being assessed operate. At a most basic level, this means deciding whether it is sensible to adopt the notion that CRS or non-CRS (or, as normally known, VRS) holds. The differences between an assessment under CRS and under VRS are illustrated in figure 3.12. It illustrates, for a single input–output case, the CRS and VRS boundaries.

DMU Z is inefficient both under CRS and VRS. The measure of its input technical efficiency calculated in relation to the VRS frontier is $E_{VRS}=OA'/OA$, while the measure of technical efficiency calculated in relation to the CRS frontier is $E_{CRS}=OA''/OA$. The difference arises because under VRS, DMU Z can be compared to virtual DMU Z'', which represents a convex combination of two observed DMUs so that it offers the same scale size as Z on the output. No contraction or expansion of Z'' is permitted. Under CRS, however, we can extrapolate from observed DMUs B and Z' (or some convex combination of theirs), because they offer the largest average product, by raising or lowering their scale size (output) while maintaining their average product (the slope of OBZ') to create the boundary labeled CRS. In this case, we assess the efficiency of Z relative to Z''', which is feasible in principle under CRS as a contraction of either B or Z'. This leads to the derived efficiency rating of Z, $E_{CRS}=OA''/OA$.

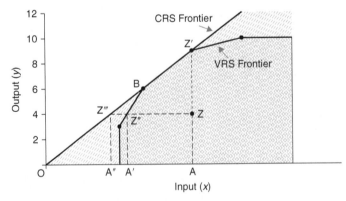

Figure 3.12. Technical and Scale Efficiency Measures

Note that the sole difference between CRS and the VRS boundary is that the latter does not permit extrapolation of scale size from observed DMUs or their convex combination.

The general models for assessing efficiency under CRS and VRS are shown in section 3.3. The input-oriented VRS model for assessing DMU$_o$ is again shown in model (3.24), which shows the single-stage theoretical formulation:

$$
\text{Min} \left\{ \theta_o - \varepsilon \left(\sum_{r=1}^{s} s_r^+ + \sum_{i=1}^{m} s_i^- \right) \; \left| \;
\begin{array}{ll}
\sum_{j=1}^{n} \lambda_j y_{rj} - s_r^+ = y_{ro}, & r = 1, \ldots, s \\
\sum_{j=1}^{n} \lambda_j x_{ij} + s_i^- = \theta_o x_{io}, & i = 1, \ldots . m \\
\sum_{j=1}^{n} \lambda_j = 1, \; \lambda_j \geq 0 &
\end{array}
\right. \right\}
$$

$$(3.24)$$

Model (3.24) differs from the generic model for assessing input efficiency under CRS only in that it includes the convexity constraint $\sum \lambda_j = 1$. This constraint is invalid when the DMUs operate under CRS because contraction or expansion of scale size is permissible under efficient operation. The convexity constraint is, however, necessary under VRS, to prevent any interpolation point constructed from the observed DMUs from being scaled up or down to form a referent point for efficiency measurement.

We refer to θ_o^* yielded by model (3.24) as the pure technical input efficiency of DMU$_o$ because it is the net of any impact of scale size. DMU$_o$ is Pareto-efficient if and only if $\theta_o^* = 1$ and all slacks are equal to zero.

The PPS under VRS is a subset of that under CRS. This can be seen from the fact that model (3.24) incorporates the additional convexity constraint compared to the corresponding model under CRS. (It is also apparent in figure 3.12 that the VRS PPS is a subset of that under CRS.) Thus, the efficiency of a DMU under CRS can never exceed its efficiency under VRS.

We can readily modify the generic model (3.24) for assessing pure technical output efficiency. The VRS output efficiency model is

$$
\text{Max} \left\{ \beta_o + \varepsilon \left(\sum_{r=1}^{s} s_r^+ + \sum_{i=1}^{m} s_i^- \right) \; \left| \;
\begin{array}{ll}
\sum_{j=1}^{n} \lambda_j y_{rj} - s_r^+ = \beta_o y_{ro}, & r = 1, \ldots, s \\
\sum_{j=1}^{n} \lambda_j x_{ij} + s_i^- = x_{io}, & i = 1, \ldots . m \\
\sum_{j=1}^{n} \lambda_j = 1, \; \lambda_j \geq 0 &
\end{array}
\right. \right\} .
$$

$$(3.25)$$

The optimal value β_o^* in (3.25) is the maximum factor by which the output levels of DMU$_o$ can be radially expanded without raising any one of its input levels. Thus, by definition, $1/\beta_o^*$ is a measure of output efficiency of DMU$_o$. We refer to $1/\beta_o^*$ as the *pure* technical output efficiency of DMU$_o$. Similarly to the input-oriented model, a DMU$_o$ is Pareto-efficient if and only if $\beta_o^* = 1$ and all slacks are zero.

The dual models to (3.24) and (3.25) can also be used to assess efficiencies under VRS. Thus, the duals to (3.24) and (3.25) are (3.26) and (3.27), respectively, where w, u_r, and v_i are variables:

$$\text{Max}\left\{ h_o = \sum_{r=1}^{s} u_r y_{ro} + w \left| \begin{array}{l} -\sum_{i=1}^{m} v_i x_{ij} + \sum_{r=1}^{s} u_r y_{rj} + w \leq 0, \quad j = 1,\ldots,n \\ \sum_{i=1}^{m} v_i x_{io} = 1, \quad u_r, v_i \geq \varepsilon, \quad w \text{ is free} \end{array} \right. \right\}$$

$$(3.26)$$

Let the superscript $*$ denote the optimal value of the corresponding variable in (3.26). The pure technical input efficiency of DMU$_o$ as yielded by model (3.26) is h_o^*. DMU$_o$ is Pareto-efficient if and only if $h_o^* = 1$ and all optimal weights u_r and v_i are basic variables (corresponding to the zero slacks in the envelopment model):

$$\text{Min}\left\{ g_o = \sum_{i=1}^{m} v_i x_{io} + w \left| \begin{array}{l} \sum_{i=1}^{m} v_i x_{ij} - \sum_{r=1}^{s} u_r y_{rj} + w \geq 0, \quad j = 1,\ldots,n \\ \sum_{r=1}^{s} u_r y_{ro} = 1, \quad u_r, v_i \geq \varepsilon, \quad w \text{ is free} \end{array} \right. \right\}$$

$$(3.27)$$

The pure technical output efficiency of DMU$_o$ is $1/g_o^*$. DMU$_o$ is Pareto-efficient if and only if $g_o^* = 1$ and all optimal weights are basic variables.

The values of u_r and v_i, in (3.26) and (3.27), when not infinitesimal (or zero), can be used to arrive at marginal rates of substitution between inputs or outputs, or marginal rates of transformation between inputs and outputs. The value of the variable w, which is dual (in linear programming terms) to the convexity constraint in the envelopment models (3.24) and (3.25), as we show later in this chapter, reflects the impact of scale size on the productivity of a DMU. If this variable is zero at an optimal solution, the corresponding model collapses to its CRS equivalent. In such a case, DMU$_o$ lies on or is projected at a point on the Pareto-efficient boundary where locally CRS holds. If the optimal value of w is not zero at any optimal solution to the corresponding model, then its sign, as we show below, indicates the type of returns to scale holding locally where DMU$_o$ lies or is projected on the efficient boundary.

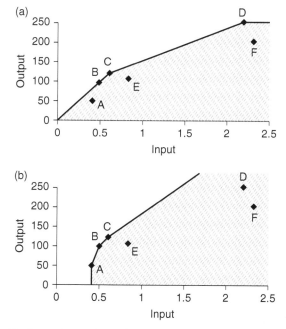

Figure 3.13. Nonincreasing and Nondecreasing Returns to Scale

As we showed in section 3.2, apart from CRS and VRS, we can also model other types of returns to scale in DEA. The NIRS and NDRS technologies are useful for identifying the type of returns to scale that apply locally at the efficient frontier. Figure 3.13 illustrates these two technologies: graph (a) for NIRS and graph (b) for NDRS.

The envelopment models in (3.24) and (3.25) can be readily modified to assess efficiency under NIRS or NDRS. The modifications needed are as follows:

- To assess pure technical input or output efficiency under NIRS, replace the convexity constraint in model (3.24) or (3.25) by the constraint $\sum \lambda_j \leq 1$. This permits scaling efficient input–output combinations pro rata downward but not upward.
- To assess pure technical input (output) efficiency under NDRS replace the convexity constraint in model (3.24) or (3.25) by the constraint $\sum \lambda_j \geq 1$. This permits scaling efficient input–output combinations pro rata upward but not downward.

For a further elaboration on the rationale of these modifications, see Cooper et al. (2000a). We next consider additional return-to-scale issues of interest in a managerial context.

3.5.3 Scale efficiency

Given that, under VRS, scale size affects the average product of a DMU, one important question is to ascertain how far the scale size of a unit is away from "optimal." We define later optimal scale size as "most productive scale size" (MPSS) with reference to a constant mix of inputs and outputs. In a single-input/single-output context, MPSS is offered by the unit(s) offering maximum output to input ratio (i.e., maximum average product). The distance of the scale size of a DMU from MPSS is reflected in its scale efficiency. This measure is defined in either an input or an output orientation as the ratio between technical (i.e., CRS) efficiency and pure technical (i.e., VRS) efficiency, that is,

$$\text{Scale input (output) efficiency of DMU}_o = \frac{\text{CRS efficiency of DMU}_o}{\text{VRS input (output) efficiency of DMU}_o}. \tag{3.28}$$

As we showed above, the technical efficiency of a DMU can never exceed its pure technical efficiency in either orientation. Thus, from the definition of scale efficiency above, we conclude that we always have scale efficiency ≤ 1.

Another way to see scale efficiency is as a measure of the distance between the CRS and VRS boundaries at the scale size of the unit. For example, in figure 3.12, the scale efficiency of DMU Z in the input orientation is OA″/OA′, which equals E_{CRS}/E_{VRS} as defined in (3.28) since we have E_{CRS}=OA″/OA and E_{VRS}=OA′/OA.

The global measure of efficiency (measured in relation to the CRS frontier) is therefore a composite of pure technical efficiency and scale efficiency. With reference to figure 3.12, we have E_{CRS}=OA″/OA = OA′/OA × OA″/OA′, which is equivalent to $E_{CRS} = E_{VRS} \times$ scale efficiency. The larger the divergence between VRS and CRS efficiency ratings, the lower the value of scale efficiency and the more adverse the impact of scale size on productivity.

3.5.4 Identifying local returns to scale

As noted above, if IRS holds at a Pareto-efficient production point, then raising its input levels by a small percentage will lead to an expansion of its output levels by an even larger percentage, assuming the unit remains Pareto-efficient. Thus, knowing the local returns to scale at a DMU is very important for managerial decision making. Obviously, it makes sense for a DMU operating at a point where IRS holds to increase its scale size, if this is under its control, because its additional input requirements may be more than compensated for by a rise in output levels. Similarly, a DMU operating at a point where DRS holds should decrease its scale size. The ideal scale size to operate at is where CRS holds. This scale size, which is input–output mix specific, is what Banker (1984) termed MPSS. We return to the identification of this scale size in the general case after we first look at how we can identify the type of returns to scale holding locally at some point on the efficient boundary.

The issue of identifying the type of returns to scale holding at the locality of a DMU was first addressed by Banker (1984). He used the sum of λ values at the optimal solution to the generic envelopment model under CRS to identify the nature of the returns to scale at the locality of a DMU. However, there could be multiple optimal solutions to that model, and this point was taken up later by Banker and Thrall (1992), on whose work we now draw to state a set of conditions for identifying the nature of returns to scale holding at DMU_o. We can use either envelopment models (3.24) and (3.25), but *without the convexity constraint* in each case, or multiplier DEA models (3.26) and (3.27) to identify the nature of returns to scale holding locally at DMU_o. The conditions are stated here. The relevant proofs are beyond the scope of this chapter and can be found in the original work in Banker and Thrall (1992).

3.5.4.1 Using envelopment DEA models

Consider a set of DMUs ($j = 1, \ldots, n$) operating under VRS and let DMU_o be Pareto-efficient. Solve the input model (3.24) without the convexity constraint with respect to DMU_o, and let the superscript $*$ to a variable denote its optimal value.

Condition 1:

- *If $\sum \lambda_j^* \geq 1$ for all optimal solutions, then DRS holds locally at DMU_o.*
- *If $\sum \lambda_j^* = 1$ for at least one optimal solution, then CRS holds locally at DMU_o.*
- *If $\sum \lambda_j^* \leq 1$ for all optimal solutions, then IRS holds locally at DMU_o.*

For output-oriented models, the nature of returns to scale is identified using the same conditions above except that we solve the output-oriented model (3.25) instead of (3.24), without the convexity constraint.

3.5.4.2 Using multiplier DEA models

Consider a set of DMUs ($j = 1, \ldots, n$) operating under VRS. Solve the input model (3.26) with respect to DMU_o and let DMU_o be Pareto-efficient:

Condition 2:

- If w takes *negative* values in *all* optimal solutions to model (3.26), then locally at DMU_o DRS holds.
- If w takes a *zero* value in *at least one* optimal solution to (3.26), then locally at DMU_o CRS holds.
- If w takes *positive* values in *all* optimal solutions to (3.26), then locally at DMU_o IRS holds.

For output-oriented models, solve model (3.27) with respect to DMU_o and let DMU_o be Pareto-efficient:

- If w takes *negative* values in *all* optimal solutions to model (3.27), then locally at DMU_o IRS holds.
- If w takes a *zero* value in *at least one* optimal solution to (3.27), then locally at DMU_o CRS holds.
- If w takes *positive* values in *all* optimal solutions to (3.27), then locally at DMU_o DRS holds.

One way to test whether these conditions hold (for envelopment models) is as follows. Assume that (3.24) was solved without its convexity constraint and let θ_o^* and λ^* be the optimal values obtained. Solve now one of the following models:

$$
\begin{aligned}
&\text{Min} \sum_{j=1}^{n} \lambda_j' - \varepsilon \left(\sum_{i=1}^{m} s_i^{+'} + \sum_{r=1}^{s} s_r^{-'} \right) &&\text{if } \sum_{j=1}^{n} \lambda_j^* > 1, \text{ or} \\
&\text{Max} \sum_{j=1}^{n} \lambda_j' + \varepsilon \left(\sum_{i=1}^{m} s_i^{+'} + \sum_{r=1}^{s} s_r^{-'} \right) &&\text{if } \sum_{j=1}^{n} \lambda_j^* < 1 \\
&\text{Subject to : } \sum_{j=1}^{n} \lambda_j' y_{rj} - s_r^{+'} = \sum_{j=1}^{n} \lambda_j^* y_{rj}, &&r = 1, \ldots, s \\
&\qquad\qquad\quad \sum_{j=1}^{n} \lambda_j' x_{ij} + s_i^{-'} = \sum_{j=1}^{n} \lambda_j^* x_{ij}, &&i = 1, \ldots, m \\
&\qquad\qquad\quad \lambda_j', s_r^{+'}, s_i^{-'} \geq 0
\end{aligned}
\tag{3.29}
$$

This will reveal whether the sum of λ values is above or below 1 in all optimal solutions or whether it can be 1 at some solutions. Then, the corresponding conclusion can be drawn about the local returns to scale at DMU_o. In a similar manner, models can be set up to maximize w on the constraints of (3.26) or (3.27) after adding a constraint to maintain DMU_o at Pareto-efficiency (see the example below in this section).

Another method that can be applied to characterize returns to scale is that of Färe et al. (1985). Their approach requires three efficiency estimates, respectively, in relation to three technological return-to-scale specifications: CRS, VRS, and NIRS. From the efficiency measures obtained from each of these models, conclusions can be reached concerning returns to scale:

- If the CRS, VRS, and NIRS models yield exactly the same efficiency measure, then the unit lies, or is projected, on a boundary region exhibiting local CRS.
- If the CRS and NIRS efficiency measures are both equal and lower than the VRS efficiency measure, then the unit lies, or is projected, on an IRS region of the boundary.

- If VRS and NIRS efficiency measures are both equal and higher than the CRS efficiency measure, then the unit lies, or is projected, on a DRS region of the boundary.

The Färe et al. (1985) method has the advantage of being unaffected by the existence of multiple optimal solutions. Its main disadvantage seems to be the need to solving three DEA problems (Seiford and Zhu, 1999a).

The foregoing methods provide well-defined return-to-scale classifications only for production units lying on the efficient frontier. For inefficient units, as Banker and Thrall (1992 p. 82) note, "productivity changes due to returns to scale are confounded with productivity changes due to inefficiency elimination," and so return-to-scale characterizations are not possible unless inefficient units are projected on the efficient boundary. However, in that case, the characterization of returns to scale of the inefficient unit would depend on the particular location of the efficient boundary where the unit was projected. Several other references concerning the estimation of returns to scale can be found in the literature. For example, Zhu and Shen (1995) introduce a simple approach that eliminates the need to examining all alternate optima, Färe and Grosskopf (1994) contrast their method to that of Banker and Thrall (1992), and Banker et al. (1996) summarize some methods and prove their equivalence to the method of Färe et al. (1985). Appa and Yue (1999) proposed an interesting procedure to determine unique scale-efficient targets based on the concept of MPSS, which is discussed below. Zhu (2000) extended this approach calculating scale-efficient targets that correspond to either the largest or the smallest MPSS. Two interesting literature reviews on returns to scale are presented by Seiford and Zhu (1999a) and Löthgren and Tambour (1996).

3.5.5 Estimating MPSS for a DMU

It is intuitively obvious that a Pareto-efficient DMU that is not operating under local CRS will gain in productivity if it changes its scale size up to the point where returns to scale become constant. Thus, the *optimal* scale size to operate at is where local CRS holds. Such scale size is known as MPSS. Formally (see Banker and Thrall, 1992, proposition 1), one way to define MPSS is as follows:

Definition 1:

A production possibility is MPSS if and only if it has pure technical and scale efficiency of 1.

Two fairly obvious corollaries of this definition are

Corollary 1:

If a DMU is Pareto-efficient under CRS, it will have MPSS.

Corollary 2:

The average productivity of an input–output mix is maximum at the MPSS for that input–output mix.

In the general multiple input–output case, corollary 2 becomes easier to see if we note the following necessary and sufficient condition for MPSS (Cooper et al., 2000a, model 5.22): Consider n DMUs ($j = 1, \ldots, n$) operating under VRS and using m inputs to secure s outputs. Solve with respect to DMU$_o$ the model:

$$\text{Max} \left\{ \left. \frac{\beta}{\alpha} \; \right| \; \begin{array}{l} \displaystyle\sum_{j=1}^{n} \lambda_j y_{rj} \geq \beta y_{ro}, \quad r = 1, \ldots, s \\[4mm] \displaystyle\sum_{j=1}^{n} \lambda_j x_{ij} \leq \alpha x_{io}, \quad i = 1, \ldots, m, \quad \sum_{j=1}^{n} \lambda_j = 1, \quad \lambda_j, \alpha, \beta \geq 0 \end{array} \right\}$$

$$(3.30)$$

A necessary and sufficient condition for DMU$_o$ to be MPSS is that the optimal objective function value β^*/α^* in (3.30) be 1 and that slacks in all optimal solutions to (3.30) be zero (see Cooper et al., 2000a).

We can view β/α as defined in (3.30) as "average productivity" of an input–output mix in the multiple input–output case since the ratio β/α is of "output" to "input" keeping the input–output mix constant. This ratio is maximum at MPSS.

In the general case, we can identify the Pareto-efficient MPSS for the input–output mix of a DMU as follows: Solve model (3.24) without the convexity constraint with respect to DMU$_o$ and let the superscript $*$ denote a variable's optimal value. Each set of λ values that is consistent with $\theta_o = \theta_o^*$ in (3.24) corresponds to a set of Pareto-efficient MPSS input–output levels

$$\left(x_o^{\text{MPSS}}, y_o^{\text{MPSS}} \right),$$

where

$$x_o^{\text{MPSS}} = \left(x_{io}^{\text{MPSS}}, i = 1, \ldots, m \right), y_o^{\text{MPSS}} = \left(y_{ro}^{\text{MPSS}}, r = 1, \ldots, s \right),$$

and

$$x_{io}^{\text{MPSS}} = \frac{\displaystyle\sum_{j=1}^{n} \lambda_j^* x_{ij}}{\displaystyle\sum_{j=1}^{n} \lambda_j^*}, \quad i = 1, \ldots, m, \qquad y_{ro}^{\text{MPSS}} = \frac{\displaystyle\sum_{j=1}^{n} \lambda_j^* y_{rj}}{\displaystyle\sum_{j=1}^{n} \lambda_j^*}, \quad r = 1, \ldots, s.$$

$$(3.31)$$

For output-oriented models, Pareto-efficient MPSS input–output levels for DMU$_o$ above can be computed using the conditions stated in (3.31) except that we solve the output-oriented envelopment CRS model (3.25) without the convexity constraint, using in the context of (3.31) $\beta_o = \beta_o^*$ instead of $\theta_o = \theta_o^*$.

As it is clear from the foregoing, when there are multiple optimal solutions to (3.24) or (3.25) without the convexity constraint in each case, (3.31)

Table 3.1
Sample Input–Output Data (numerical data from Appa and Yue, 1999)

	DMU 1	DMU 2	DMU 3	DMU 4	DMU 5	DMU 6	DMU 7	DMU 8	DMU 9
Input 1	10	15	35	30	15	60	10	18.75	30
Input 2	15	10	20	25	15	60	10	18.75	27.5
Output	10	10	20	20	10	30	7	15	20

will yield multiple sets of MPSS input–output correspondences. Appa and Yue (1999) have developed a model for estimating what they call "best returns to scale" MPSS input–output levels. These correspond to the smallest or alternatively to the largest scale size that is MPSS. See also Zhu (2000) on this point.

The following numerical example illustrates the identification of returns to scale and an MPSS. Consider the nine DMUs in table 3.1 and assume that they operate an input-to-output transformation process characterized by VRS.

The multiplier generic DEA model for assessing pure technical input efficiency is (3.26). Its instance with respect to DMU 6, for example, can be written as follows:

$$
\begin{aligned}
\text{Max} \quad & 30u + w_1 - w_2 \\
\text{Subject to :} \quad & 60v_1 + 60v_2 = 100 \\
& 10u - 10v_1 - 15v_2 + w_1 - w_2 \le 0 \\
& 10u - 15v_1 - 10v_2 + w_1 - w_2 \le 0 \\
& 20u - 35v_1 - 20v_2 + w_1 - w_2 \le 0 \\
& 20u - 30v_1 - 25v_2 + w_1 - w_2 \le 0 \\
& 10u - 15v_1 - 15v_2 + w_1 - w_2 \le 0 \\
& 30u - 60v_1 - 60v_2 + w_1 - w_2 \le 0 \\
& 7u - 10v_1 - 10v_2 + w_1 - w_2 \le 0 \\
& 15u - 18.75v_1 - 18.75v_2 + w_1 - w_2 \le 0 \\
& 20u - 30v_1 - 27.5v_2 + w_1 - w_2 \le 0 \\
& u, v_1, v_2, w_1, w_2 \ge 0.
\end{aligned}
\tag{3.32}
$$

Note that within model (3.32) we have normalized total virtual input to 100 to reduce the impact of round-off errors and have used the difference of two nonnegative variables ($w_1 - w_2$) to model the free variable w of model (3.26). (We have omitted here the restriction that the input–output weights should be strictly positive so we may identify non-Pareto-efficient units as 100% efficient.)

Part of the optimal solution to model (3.32) is: objective function value = 100, $u = 5.0$, $w_1 = 0.0$, $w_2 = 50.0$, $v_1 = 1.6667$, $v_2 = 0.0$.

Thus, the pure technical input efficiency of DMU 6 is 100(%). Note that the weight attributed to input 2 is zero, but this weight is a basic variable, since the corresponding slack in the dual is zero. This means that there are multiple optimal solutions to the model in (3.32) and that the zero slack for input 2 in the dual means DMU 6 is Pareto-efficient under VRS.

Since DMU 6 is Pareto-efficient, we can identify the nature of local returns to scale at DMU 6 using either a multiplier or an envelopment model. Using first the solution of the multiplier model (3.32), we showed that the w value $(w_1 - w_2)$ was -50. Making recourse to the statement in condition 2, we can conclude that, provided w is negative at all optimal solutions to (3.32), we have locally DRS at DMU 6. This is indeed verified to be the case by maximizing and minimizing in turn $(w_1 - w_2)$ on the constraints of (3.32) after adding the additional constraint $30u + w_1 - w_2 = 100$.

To identify the nature of returns to scale locally, we can alternatively use either the input- or the output-oriented envelopment DEA model under CRS. For example, we can solve the instance of model (3.24), without the convexity constraint, corresponding to DMU 6. The resulting model is

Min $\qquad \theta - 0.001s_1^- - 0.001s_2^- - 0.001s^+$

Subject to :

$10\lambda_1 + 15\lambda_2 + 35\lambda_3 + 30\lambda_4 + 15\lambda_5 + 60\lambda_6 + 10\lambda_7 + 18.75\lambda_8$

$\qquad + 30\lambda_9 + s_1^- - 60\theta = 0$

$15\lambda_1 + 10\lambda_2 + 20\lambda_3 + 25\lambda_4 + 15\lambda_5 + 60\lambda_6 + 10\lambda_7 + 18.75\lambda_8 \qquad (3.33)$

$\qquad + 27.5\lambda_9 + s_2^- - 60\theta = 0$

$10\lambda_1 + 10\lambda_2 + 20\lambda_3 + 20\lambda_4 + 10\lambda_5 + 30\lambda_6 + 7\lambda_7 + 15\lambda_8$

$\qquad + 20\lambda_9 - s^+ = 30$

$\lambda_1, \lambda_2, \lambda_3, \lambda_4, \lambda_5, \lambda_6, \lambda_7, \lambda_8, \lambda_9, s_1^-, s_2^-, s^+ \geq 0.$

The positive values obtained are $\theta_{CRS} = 0.625$ and $\lambda_1 = \lambda_2 = 1.5$. All other variables are zero. In order to use condition 1 to identify the type of returns to scale holding at DMU 6, we need to know if any optimal solution to (3.33) exists in which the λ values sum to 1. We can reformulate (3.33) to minimize the sum of λ values, setting in the constraints of the reformulated model the right-hand side using the optimal λ values above. If the sum of the "new" λ values turns out to be 1 or less, then we will have established that an optimal solution to (3.33) exists in which the λ values sum to 1. In the case of (3.33), the minimum sum of λ values compatible with $\theta = 0.625$ is 2.

Since at all optimal solutions to (3.34) the sum of λ values is greater than 1 using condition 1, we conclude that in the input orientation DMU 6 is operating under DRS.

To identify a set of MPSS levels for DMU 6, we use expression (3.31). One optimal sum of λ values in (3.33) was 3 because the positive λ values were $\lambda_1 = \lambda_2 = 1.5$. This leads, to the following MPSS, based on the expression in (3.31):

Input 1: MPSS level $= (1.5 \times 10 + 1.5 \times 15)/3 = 12.5,$
Input 2: MPSS level $= (1.5 \times 15 + 1.5 \times 10)/3 = 12.5,$
Output: MPSS level $= (1.5 \times 10 + 1.5 \times 10)/3 = 10.$

We have alternative MPSS levels for DMU 6 since we had alternative optimal solutions to (3.33).

3.5.6 Scale elasticity

An issue closely related to returns to scale is that of scale elasticity. This is a measure of the proportionate increase in outputs resulting from an increase in inputs by a given proportion (see Banker and Thrall, 1992; Fukuyama, 2000).

Førsund and Hjalmarsson (2004) have derived the scale efficiency for projections of inefficient points on the boundary of the PPS provided that such projections are in the interior of a full-dimensional efficient facet. [See Olesen and Petersen (1996) on full-dimensional facets in DEA.] For such DMUs, scale elasticity can be computed as follows.

Let the input-oriented VRS model (3.1) be solved with respect to DMU_o, which has input–output levels (x_o, y_o), and let $\theta_o^* < 1$ be the optimal value of θ_o obtained. Let the projection $(\theta_o^* x_o, y_o)$ be on the interior of a full-dimensional efficient facet. Let w^* be the optimal value of w in model (3.4), which is dual to (3.1). Because only full-dimensional efficient facets are being considered, the optimal solution to (3.4) would be unique. The scale elasticity at the point $(\theta_o^* x_o, y_o)$ is

$$\text{Scale elasticity } \left(\theta_o^* x_o, y_o\right) = \frac{\theta^*}{\theta^* - w^*}. \qquad (3.34)$$

In a similar manner, if the output-oriented model under VRS (3.2) is solved with respect to (x_o, y_o), yielding for β_o optimal value β_o^*, and if the projection $(x_o, \beta^* y_o)$ is on the interior of a full-dimensional efficient facet, then the scale elasticity at the point $(x_o, \beta^* y_o)$ is

$$\text{Scale elasticity } \left(x_o, \beta_o^* y_o\right) = 1 - \frac{w^*}{\beta^*}, \qquad (3.35)$$

where w^* is the optimal value of w in model (3.5), which is dual to (3.2).

Scale elasticity greater than 1 would mean that we have local IRS; below 1, local DRS; and 1, CRS.

The expressions in (3.34) and (3.35) are not generally valid for (x_o, y_o) if it turns out to be an efficient point that lies on a vertex and so on several efficient facets. The dual variables in (3.4) and (3.5) in such cases will not be unique. For such points, a range of scale elasticities can be computed. Consider, for example, solving (3.1) under VRS with respect to (x_o, y_o) and let $\theta_o^* = 1$. Let also (3.4), the dual to (3.1) with respect to (x_o, y_o), have multiple optimal solutions, and the minimum and maximum values of w at these solutions are, respectively, w^- and w^+. Then (see Banker and Thrall, 1992), the scale elasticity, ε, ranges $1/(1 - w^-) \leq \varepsilon \leq 1/(1 - w^+)$. The upper and lower bounds on w are calculated by replacing the objective function of model (3.4) by "max w" (for the upper bound) and "min w" (for the lower bound) and adding the constraint $\sum_r u_r y_{ro} + w = 1$. This last constraint imposes that the assessed DMU lies on the production frontier.

Førsund and Hjalmarsson (1979) and Førsund (1996) also provide an analysis of the relationship between scale elasticity and scale efficiency. As shown above, we have $E_{CRS} = E_{VRS}^O \times SE^O$ and $E_{CRS} = E_{VRS}^I \times SE^I$, where the superscripts I and O denote input and output orientation, respectively, and SE denotes scale efficiency. Scale efficiency and scale elasticity can be linked by the "Beam variation equations" (see Førsund and Hjalmarsson, 1979; Førsund, 1996), which state that $\bar{\varepsilon} = (\ln E_{VRS}^O)/(\ln E_{VRS}^I)$, where $\bar{\varepsilon}$ is the average scale elasticity between the two frontier points $(E_{VRS}^I x, y)$ and $(x, y/E_{VRS}^O)$. Necessarily, when $E_{VRS}^O \geq E_{VRS}^I$, we will have average DRS, and when $E_{VRS}^O \leq E_{VRS}^I$, we will have average IRS (see Førsund and Hernaes, 1994). Applying the relationships above between technical efficiency calculated under CRS, VRS, and scale efficiency, the above expression is equivalent to $\bar{\varepsilon} = (\ln E_{CRS} - \ln SE^O)/(\ln E_{CRS} - \ln SE^I)$. In Førsund and Hernaes (1994), these expressions are used to calculate average scale elasticities in DEA. The relationship above is not between scale elasticity and scale efficiency, but between average scale elasticity and scale efficiency. According to Førsund (1996, p. 300), "there are no links between scale efficiency scores and scale elasticity that allow determining the nature of returns to scale from the information on scale efficiency only."

3.5.7 Returns to scale in nonconvex technologies and hybrid CRS and VRS returns to scale

We introduce in brief in this section two departures from the concepts of returns to scale examined so far. The first departure relates to returns to scale under nonconvex production technologies, and the second relates to cases where only subsets of inputs and outputs obey an assumption of CRS while their complements do not.

Let us first consider the case of returns to scale in nonconvex technologies. The concept of returns to scale covered so far relates to local returns to scale in the sense that the relative proportionalities of input and output changes under efficient operation are examined for marginal changes to inputs and outputs. These returns to scale indicate the direction in which a move would lead toward MPSS. For example, under local IRS, increasing scale size would lead to improved productivity and can ultimately lead to MPSS. However, if we drop the assumption of convexity of the PPS, then it is no longer necessarily the case that local returns to scale can indicate the direction in which MPSS can be attained. Podinovski (2004a) develops the concept of global

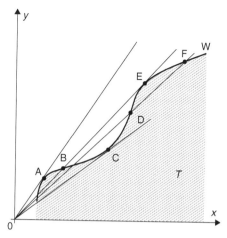

Figure 3.14. The Difference Between Returns to Scale and GRS (Podinovski, 2004a)

returns to scale (GRS) in order to identify where MPSS can be obtained in a nonconvex technology. Figure 3.14 illustrates the difference between local and GRS in identifying the changes needed to attain MPSS when the technology is not convex.

The PPS is labeled T, and the solid line is its boundary. Clearly, the unit at A has the highest ratio of outputs (y) to inputs (x) and hence the highest average productivity. This unit is said to have global CRS. It represents "global" MPSS in this technology. DMUs B, C, D, E, and F are efficient and larger than A, and hence all exhibit global DRS in the sense that they need to reduce their scale of operations to achieve MPSS. However, only some of them exhibit local DRS. More specifically, units on the segment AC and to the right of E where the tangent to the boundary has a positive intercept have local DRS. In contrast, units between C and E such as D where the tangent to the boundary has a negative intercept have local IRS. Finally, units such as A, C, and E exhibit CRS as the tangent to the boundary at these points has zero intercept (to see this use of intercepts in the diagnosis of local returns to scale, see Thanassoulis 2001, p. 143). In convex PPSs, local CRS implies the unit is at MPSS (Banker 1984). This, as illustrated in figure 3.14, does not hold true in nonconvex technologies. The interested reader is referred to Podinovski (2004a) for a fuller discussion of the concept of GRS and its use in identifying MPSS in nonconvex production technologies.

A different departure from the standard notion of a VRS technology while still maintaining the convexity of the PPS is investigated by Podinovski (2004b). The departure is motivated by the fact that, in certain decision contexts, we can maintain CRS between a subset of the inputs and a subset of the outputs and VRS between their complements. For example, in assessing schools, we might use expenditure on staff and prior attainment of pupils (e.g., mean grade on entry) as two inputs and the number of children taught and their mean grade on exit as two outputs. It may be possible to maintain that scaling expenditure on staff by some factor α close to 1 should lead, under efficient operation, to a scaling by the same factor of the number of pupils taught, obeying thus an assumption of CRS. However, it would not be sensible to assume that scaling the mean attainment of pupils on entry by some constant will lead to a scaling by that same constant of mean attainment on exit under efficient operation of the school. In the case of entry and exit attainments, therefore, a VRS assumption would be more suitable. Thus, we have a case of what Podinovski (2004b) calls selective proportionality or hybrid returns to scale (HRS). That is we can maintain the assumption of CRS between some of our inputs and outputs while VRS applies for their complements.

Podinovski (2004b) gives a full description of the HRS technology, including its axiomatic foundations, and develops DEA models for assessing efficiency, deriving targets and efficient peers when HRS holds. These details are beyond the scope of this chapter, and the interested reader is referred to the original source. It is worth noting that Podinovski (2004b) derives CRS and VRS technologies as special cases of the HRS technology. Further, the VRS technology is a subset of the HRS technology, and so efficiencies under HRS are never higher than under VRS. In contrast, neither the CRS nor the HRS technology is necessarily a subset of the other, and so no statement can be made as to whether the CRS or the HRS efficiency will be higher for a given unit.

In summary, in this section we have covered a variety of nonconstant returns to scale. We introduce methods for identifying the types of returns to scale holding at Pareto-efficient points. We note that gains in productivity are possible through changes in scale size and introduce the concept of identifying a MPSS for a unit. We introduce the associated concept of scale efficiency that measures the distance of a unit from MPSS, and the concept of scale elasticity relating to the rate of change of outputs relative to that of inputs. Finally, we make reference to more recent developments on returns to scale when the PPS is not convex, or where some of the input–output variables obey CRS and the rest VRS.

3.6 Beyond Well-Behaved Data

In traditional DEA models, we implicitly assume well-behaved data: data with no errors or random noise, strictly positive data, positive relationships between inputs and outputs, and substitutability within inputs and outputs. Often, data in practice do not satisfy these implicit assumptions. This section outlines some of the problems that can then arise and ways to resolve them. Within this context, we address problems of so-called bad and nonisotonic inputs and outputs, negative or zero data, outliers, and dimensionality issues. We do not, however, cover in this section the related and substantial approaches developed for dealing with random noise in DEA because the main theory in that area, based on bootstrapping methods, is covered in chapter 4 of this book.

3.6.1 Nonisotonic and bad inputs and/or outputs

In DEA, one implicitly assumes that under efficient operation when inputs increase, outputs should also increase. However, in practical applications, this is not always the case. One example is the case of competing establishments in assessing commercial outlets. If they are taken as an input, then when their number rises, the output, which may be revenue generated by an outlet, would be expected to fall, all else being equal. This is an example of a nonisotonic input. A related but different example is that of polluting gases as a byproduct of energy production. They are an output and are isotonic in the sense that they do rise as inputs rise. However, they are an undesirable or bad output in that we wish to minimize polluting gases. Nonisotonic and bad inputs/outputs are two issues that are different, and yet related. Given the contemporary nature of environmental issues, the treatment of bad outputs in efficiency analysis has been receiving much attention in recent literature. We cover here the main approaches to dealing with nonisotonic and bad inputs and outputs.

3.6.1.1 Nonisotonic and bad outputs

We shall refer to nonisotonic or bad outputs as undesirable outputs. The approaches that can be used to deal with undesirable outputs have been detailed in Scheel (2001) and in Dyson et al. (2001). Scheel (2001) classifies these approaches into indirect approaches, which involve some data transformation, and direct approaches, which use the undesirable outputs as they stand.

The indirect approaches to deal with undesirable outputs can be as follows:

(i) Consider undesirable outputs as inputs.
(ii) Subtract the undesirable output from a sufficiently large number to transform it into a desirable output.[11]
(iii) Consider the inverse of the undesirable output as a desirable output.

In order to have an idea about the differences between the above approaches, consider the following illustrative example shown in table 3.2, where good and bad outputs have been normalized by the input to allow for graphical representations. Assuming a CRS technology the efficient frontiers found according to each one of the three approaches above are shown in figures 3.15–3.17.

Clearly, the three approaches would generally yield different results on the performance of units since in every case the units defining the efficient

Table 3.2
Illustrative Example

	Input	Good Output	Undesirable Output	Input	Good Output/ Input	Undesirable Output/ Input
DMU 1	10	50	60	1	5	6
DMU 2	10	200	300	1	20	30
DMU 3	20	500	400	1	25	20
DMU 4	10	100	150	1	10	15
DMU 5	20	600	500	1	30	25
DMU 6	10	120	100	1	12	10

frontier are different. One approach that can be implemented to overcome the problem of undesirable outputs (or, indeed, inputs) is to convert them, when possible, to equivalent variables that are good and/or isotonic. For example, where in an assessment of schools pupils playing truant is an undesirable output, one can use pupils not playing truant as the actual output variable. Another approach is to use negative data when they are meaningful in the context of the assessment and use a DEA model that can handle negative data, as covered below. In contrast, where the data transformation is simply a mathematical device without meaning in the context of the assessment, it should be avoided (see Dyson et al., 2001).

In the VRS case, the first two of the approaches suggested above, namely, treating an undesirable output as input or subtracting it from a large number and treating the result as an output, does not affect the set of DMUs found as Pareto-efficient. To see this, consider the treatment of an undesirable output as

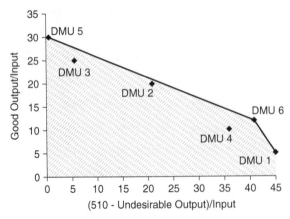

Figure 3.15. CRS Technology When Undesirable Is Treated as Good Output by Subtracting from a Large Number

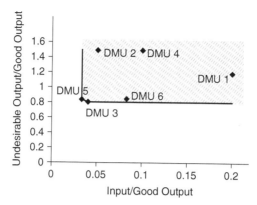

Figure 3.16. CRS Technology When Undesirable Output is Treated as Input

an input [approach (i)] in a standard additive model. The constraint relating to the undesirable output, treated as an input, would be

$$\sum_j \lambda_j y_{rj} = y_{ro} - s_r.$$

If this output was transformed into a good output G through subtracting from some large number K, we would have $G_{rj} = K - y_{rj}$ for the rth output across the DMUs j. Then, the constraint for the transformed output would be

$$\sum_j \lambda_j G_{rj} = G_{ro} + s_r,$$

which is equivalent to the constraint where y_{rj} is treated as an input given that $\sum \lambda_j = 1$. This, in turn, means that the PPS is the same under both

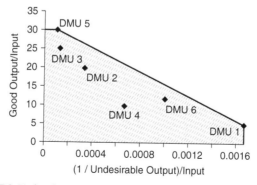

Figure 3.17. CRS Technology When Undesirable is Treated as Good Output by Taking its Inverse

approaches. However, where the DEA model used also yields an efficiency measure, this does not mean that the actual efficiency measure obtained will necessarily be the same under both approaches. That measure depends on the objective function to the DEA model used, which will generally differ under the foregoing two treatments of undesirable outputs. For more details on the use of transformed undesirable outputs, see Seiford and Zhu (2002), who defend the use of this approach to treat undesirable outputs. Note that the additive model does not provide an efficiency measure, and that it is nonoriented and so, irrespective of the transformation of inputs and outputs in the foregoing manner, it identifies the Pareto-efficient units. More care is needed, however, with oriented VRS models because, although the PPS may not change, the efficiency rating obtained can. See Lovell and Pastor (1995) or Cooper et al. (2000b), who demonstrate restricted translation invariance for VRS models. That is translating outputs in an input-oriented model will not affect the efficiency rating but will generally affect efficiencies in an output-oriented model. A similar statement can be made regarding the impact of input translation in oriented VRS models.

A direct approach for dealing with undesirable outputs is that of Färe et al. (1989b), which we outline here. Färe et al. (1989b) deal with undesirable outputs in paper mills by discriminating between desirable and undesirable outputs through differing assumptions on disposability: Desirable outputs are assumed strongly disposable, whereas undesirable outputs are assumed weakly disposable. Thus, when an output is undesirable, for example, a pollutant output, one cannot assume that it is possible to produce less of that output keeping the other outputs and inputs fixed because the pollutant is a byproduct of the production of the remaining outputs. Therefore, the assumption of free disposability of that output is violated and the pollutant output is said to be weakly disposable. In addition to the weak disposability of undesirable outputs, the approach of Färe et al. (1989b) also assumes the condition of null-joint outputs, meaning that the only way to produce zero undesirable outputs is to produce zero desirable outputs, too (see also Färe and Grosskopf, 2004).

Färe et al. (1989b) use a hyperbolic model to deal with undesirable outputs because this model can provide efficiency measures where we can simultaneously permit expansion of desirable outputs and contraction of undesirable outputs. Let us have an output vector subdivided into two vectors $y = (g, b)$, where vector g represents good outputs and vector b represents undesirable outputs. The CRS hyperbolic model proposed by Färe et al. (1989b) for an output-oriented model is

$$\max \left\{ \theta_o \,\middle|\, \sum_j \lambda_j g_{rj} \geq \theta_o g_{ro}, \sum_j \lambda_j b_{rj} = \theta_o^{-1} b_{ro}, \sum_j \lambda_j x_{ij} \leq x_{io} \right\}.$$

$$(3.36)$$

The equality constraint associated with undesirable outputs is because they are not freely disposable. Other models can also be used to confer different treatment between good and bad outputs. See, for example, Chung et al. (1997), who use the nonoriented directional model in (3.37) in this context, where the directional vector is taken equal to the observed levels of inputs and outputs:

$$\text{Max} \left\{ \beta_o \,\middle|\, \begin{array}{l} \sum_j \lambda_j g_{rj} \geq (1 + \beta_o)\, g_{ro}, \;\; \sum_j \lambda_j b_{rj} = (1 - \beta_o)\, b_{ro}, \\[1mm] \sum_j \lambda_j x_{ij} \leq (1 - \beta_o)\, x_{io} \end{array} \right\} \tag{3.37}$$

To illustrate the computation of efficiency scores in the presence of undesirable outputs treated as weakly disposable, consider the illustrative example in table 3.2. Figure 3.18 shows the CRS PPS when weak disposability applies to the undesirable output and strong disposability applies to the desirable output (input is normalized to 1). Note that units are projected onto the frontier by decreasing undesirable outputs and increasing desirable outputs.

Under the usual strong disposability of the undesirable output, the frontier would be constituted only by DMUs 5 and 2 and the corresponding horizontal and vertical extensions to the axis. However, the directional nonoriented model in (3.37) identifies DMUs 1, 4, and 6 as inefficient and DMUs 2, 3, and 5 as efficient. Note that the segment linking DMUs 5 and 2 shows a negative marginal rate of substitution between the bad and the good output; that is, when one of them increases, the other one decreases; in contrast, the segments from the origin to DMU 3 and then to DMU 5 show positive marginal rates of substitution between outputs.

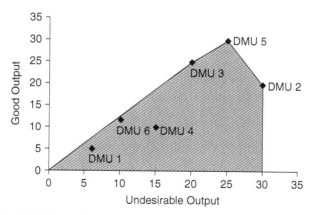

Figure 3.18. CRS PPS under Weak Disposability of the Undesirable Output

Note, in particular, that DMU 2 in figure 3.18 is found Pareto-efficient under the weak-disposability assumption and the use of the model in (3.37). However, as noted by Picazo-Tadeo and Prior (2005), the downward-sloping segment from DMU 5 to DMU 2 allows for the possibility that a DMU "located on the frontier might simultaneously increase production of the good output while reducing production of the bad output," which may be counterintuitive. Picazo-Tadeo and Prior (2005) try to resolve this problem by solving a model without the undesirable outputs so that efficiency from a managerial perspective (unconcerned with environmental issues) is assessed.[12] However, as yet there is no definitive resolution of this issue in the literature.

It should be noted that, when some of the outputs obey weak disposability and the rest strong disposability, one can compute efficiency measures that isolate the impact of the presence of the weakly disposable outputs on performance. This is done by first computing the efficiency of each DMU (E^W) when some outputs are treated as weakly disposable. Then a second efficiency measure (E^S) is computed for each DMU, assuming strong disposability of *all* outputs. The ratio between the two measures (E^S/E^W) (or the difference $E^S - E^W$ if these measures are calculated based on the directional distance model) gives a measure of the impact that the imposition of the weak-disposability assumption had on the estimated efficiency of each DMU. In the case of the ratio above, when it is 1, then strong- and weak-disposability assumptions yield the same results, and therefore production is not affected by the undesirable outputs (this is the case for DMUs 2 and 5 in figure 3.18). If the ratio is different from 1 (which happens for DMU 3 in figure 3.18), then the production process is congested by the undesirable outputs, and its reduction implies a loss in desirable outputs (see Zofio and Prieto, 2001). Therefore, the ratio E^S/E^W "can be converted into a producer-specific measure of potential output loss due to a lack of strong disposability" (Färe et al., 1989b, p. 94). Note that this measure of output loss is equal to a congestion measure that we outline below.

Most empirical applications on environmental efficiency use CRS specifications of the technology. In Scheel (2001) and Färe and Grosskopf (2004), the authors put forward the basis for extending the CRS models to the VRS case. In Zhou et al. (forthcoming), NIRS and VRS models are proposed for measuring the environmental performance of world regions (regarding carbon emissions that are treated as weakly disposable). [See also Picazo-Tadeo and Prior (2005), who put forward VRS models for assessing environmental efficiency.] The directional model applied to the VRS case is

$$\text{Max}\left\{\beta_o \left|\begin{array}{ll} \sum_j \phi\lambda_j g_{rj} \geq (1+\beta_o)g_{ro}, & \sum_j \phi\lambda_j b_{rj} = (1-\beta_o)b_{ro} \\ \sum_j \lambda_j x_{ij} \leq (1-\beta_o)x_{io}, & \sum_j \lambda_j = 1, \quad 0 \leq \phi \leq 1 \end{array}\right.\right\}.$$

(3.38)

The VRS model is similar to the CRS model except for the convexity constraint and for the factor ϕ that permits the scaling down both good and bad outputs. The equality constraints for bad outputs only assure nondisposability of these outputs (Kuosmanen, 2005). In order to also model weak disposability, one needs to introduce this factor ϕ, since under weak disposability of outputs, if a given point $(\mathbf{x}, \mathbf{g}, \mathbf{b}) \in T$, then point $(\mathbf{x}, \phi \mathbf{g}, \phi \mathbf{b}) \in T$ for $0 \le \phi \le 1$.

Kuosmanen (2005) put forward a modification to the treatment of weak disposability under VRS by relaxing the assumption of a uniform scaling of good and bad outputs by ϕ. His formulation, for the case where a directional distance function is being used, is as in (3.39), where λ_j of (3.38) is divided into two components so that $\lambda_j = z_j + u_j$, where $z_j = \phi \lambda_j$ and $u_j = (1 - \phi)\lambda_j$:

$$\text{Max} \left\{ \beta_o \left| \begin{array}{ll} \sum_j z_j g_{rj} \ge (1 + \beta_o)\, g_{ro}, & \sum_j z_j b_{rj} = (1 - \beta_o)\, b_{ro} \\[2mm] \sum_j \left(z_j + u_j \right) x_{ij} \le (1 - \beta_o)\, x_{io}, & \sum_j \left(z_j + u_j \right) = 1, \quad 0 \le \phi \le 1 \end{array} \right. \right\}$$

(3.39)

In (3.39), both outputs are weighted by z_j, that is, the nondisposable part of λ_j, whereas inputs are weighted by the sum of the disposed and the nondisposed components. For CRS, the above model collapses to model (3.37) since in that case u_j is equal to zero and z equals λ.

Note that the assumption that the reduction of bad outputs is costly is not necessarily true in all environments. Coelli T. et al. (2007) propose a method that involves the incorporation of a materials balance equation that handles pollutants within the assessment model. The materials balance equation is then minimized in the same way as a cost function is on a PPS when attempting to isolate the allocative efficiency of a unit (see section 3.4). This produces what the authors call an "environmental efficiency measure," which can then be decomposed into technical and "allocative" components, in a similar manner to the conventional cost efficiency decomposition. The authors demonstrate their approach with the case of phosphorus emission from Belgian pig-finishing farms.

3.6.1.2 Bad or nonisotonic inputs and congestion

The treatment of bad or nonisotonic inputs has not been researched in the DEA literature as much as that of bad outputs. There are some applications where some inputs are not isotonic in that when they rise they can be expected to lead to lower outputs. For example, see Athanassopoulos and Thanassoulis (1995), where competition is a nonisotonic input in assessing retail outlets. However, such inputs are usually transformed numerically to restore isotonicity.

There are bad inputs, however, which are isotonic. One such case is that found in Allen (1999) where waste in a waste-burning power plant is isotonic with the output electric power produced by the waste-burning plant. However,

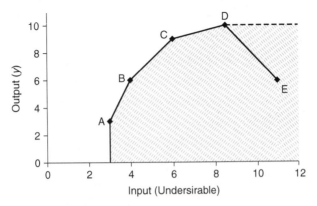

Figure 3.19. Weak Disposability of the Bad Input

one wishes to burn as much waste as possible since this is an undesirable factor, and so one wishes to maximize this input. Using DEA models for weakly disposable inputs is possible in cases of this type since we cannot maintain that it is always possible to burn more waste, keeping other inputs and outputs fixed. (Burning more waste will have the benefit of producing more output.)

In a situation where all outputs are "desirable" and some inputs are undesirable, modeling undesirable inputs through weak disposability would be the same as considering that the technology is input congested. Figure 3.19 is a reproduction of figure 3.6 from section 3.2, where we cover weakly disposable technological sets and assume that the sole input used is undesirable.

Clearly, if one cannot assume that the undesirable input is strongly disposable, then the dashed horizontal line segment from DMU D cannot be part of the technological frontier. Therefore, unit E, using more of the undesirable input, would be considered efficient even if producing less output. Input-congested technologies therefore seem to be useful for modeling undesirable inputs, but more investigation on these issues is desired in the literature since there is a wide body of research dealing with undesirable outputs and virtually no study dealing with undesirable inputs.

As in the case of weakly disposable outputs, so, too, in the case of weakly disposable inputs, the ratio (or difference if directional distance functions are used) of the efficiency computed under strong to that under weak disposability of inputs captures the impact of weakly disposable inputs on the efficiency of a DMU. Such impact is dubbed "congestion" (see also Färe et al., 1985). An alternative approach to this measure of congestion was suggested in Cooper et al. (1996, 2000b, 2001). Their measure of congestion is derived using a two-stage process. In the first stage, the output-oriented VRS model is solved. Then its solution is used in a second-stage model, where input slacks are maximized. The measure of congestion in this case is given for each input as the difference between input slacks in the first stage and second stage.

3.6.2 Zeros in the data

The basic DEA models were initially developed assuming that all data are strictly positive. However, there are situations where some data may be zero or even negative. The treatment of zero data has not received as much attention perhaps as it should. Yet zero data need to be treated with caution in assessments rather than resorting to the convenience of simply replacing zero values with small positive values, as some authors do (see also Thompson et al., 1993, on this point).

Zeros may be the result of a conscious management decision not to use some input or not to produce some output, or they may be the result of missing data that could have been replaced by zeros. One needs to establish first which one of these cases zero data represent and treat them accordingly. According to Kuosmanen (2002), treating an output as zero yields for the DMU exactly the same efficiency score as if it was assessed only with the outputs whose values are greater than zero.

The implications of zeros in outputs differ from those in inputs. We outline briefly each case in turn.

3.6.2.1 Zero outputs

Zero outputs are not a problem in standard efficiency models such as the CRS or VRS model, irrespective of the model orientation. In these models the output constraints are

$$\sum_j \lambda_j y_{rj} \geq \alpha y_{ro},$$

where α is equal to 1 for input-oriented models and is a variable equal to the inverse of the DMU's efficiency measure when the model is output oriented. When an output k of DMU_o being assessed is zero, then the output constraint becomes

$$\sum_j \lambda_j y_{kj} \geq \alpha \times 0.$$

This constraint is always feasible for any peer set within CRS and VRS technologies.

Consider the following illustrative example (figure 3.20) where DMU 1 has a zero value in output 2. DMU 1 is inefficient whether it is assessed in a CRS or VRS technology and whether the model is input or output -oriented. Its CRS efficiency score is 75% (whatever the orientation), its VRS input efficiency is 81.25%, and the VRS output efficiency is 75%.

The main point to note when one uses radial output models to assess units with zero output data is that the radial efficiency score does not have a meaning for the zero output. That is, there is no way one can radially expand a

	Input	Output1	Output 2
DMU 1	10	45	0
DMU 2	5	20	30
DMU 3	10	60	40
DMU 4	5	10	15
DMU 5	12	60	48
DMU 6	6	12	9

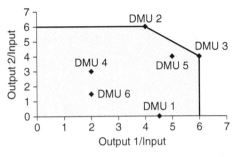

Figure 3.20. Illustrative Example for Zero Output

zero output to a positive output, and therefore, a DMU with a zero output will have radial target levels that maintain the zero value for the specific output. However, that output may still take a positive target value through a positive slack for the output concerned at the optimal solution to the corresponding DEA model. Thus, in figure 3.20, DMU 1 is radially projected in the output 1 axis, so the radial target is zero for output 2. There is, however, inefficiency associated with output 2 identified by a slack for output 2, so that the Pareto-efficient target for DMU 1 is DMU 3.

The existence of positive slacks for DMUs with zero outputs is the dual to zero weights being assigned to the corresponding output, as noted by Kuosmanen (2002). That is, a zero output value forces the DMU to assign a zero weight to that output, and therefore, the resulting radial efficiency measure is the same as one would obtain if the output concerned was not used in the assessment of the DMU at all. Therefore, if one wishes to ignore the output on which the DMU has a zero value, one should use radial efficiency measures that reflect radial expansion of outputs or radial contraction of inputs when these inputs and outputs are different from zero. However, if one wishes to reflect the inefficiency resulting from a DMU not producing one of the outputs, nonradial models should be preferred.

Note that DMU 1 in figure 3.20 could have been Pareto-efficient if the level of output 1 had been 62, for example. This would have given rise to the PPS under CRS, as shown in figure 3.21. With the modified value for output 1, DMU 1 is Pareto-efficient both under VRS and under CRS for both input and output orientations. So zero outputs may be both associated to efficient or inefficient DMUs.

3.6.2.2 Zero inputs

Zero inputs are more problematic in DEA, since at least one unit with a zero input will always be VRS or CRS efficient irrespective of the levels of its remaining inputs or outputs. To see this, note that in the envelopment model

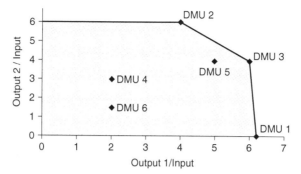

Figure 3.21. DMU 1 with Zero Output is Efficient

the constraint associated with inputs is

$$\sum_j \lambda_j x_{ij} \le \omega x_{ij},$$

where ω is 1 for output-oriented models and corresponds to the efficiency score for input-oriented models. When the DMU being assessed has input k equal to zero the above constraint becomes

$$\sum_j \lambda_j x_{kj} \le \omega \times 0.$$

Whatever the value of ω (i.e., whatever the orientation of the model) for a unit with zero input, the only way to satisfy this constraint is to have

$$\sum_j \lambda_j x_{kj} = 0,$$

meaning that all peers of the DMU being assessed should also have a zero value on input k. Thus, at least one DMU with zero value on input k will be a peer to the DMU assessed and so will be Pareto-efficient irrespective of what values such a peer has on outputs or inputs other than k.

Consider the following example with a single output that illustrates the presence of zero inputs: DMU 1 and DMU 3 have zero level on input 2. DMU 3 is CRS and VRS efficient, but DMU 1 is not CRS efficient. (As shown in figure 3.22, DMU 3 dominates DMU 1.) DMU 1 is, however, VRS efficient since under VRS we cannot find other DMUs that would yield a convex combination of its inputs unless we use DMU 1 itself, which would render it its own peer and thus Pareto-efficient.

Unlike the case of zero outputs, in the case where a zero input is genuinely an input not used rather than missing data, then it is to a unit's advantage to include the input concerned in the assessment. If, however, a zero input

	Input 1	Input 2	Output
DMU 1	10	0	1
DMU 2	5	20	2
DMU 3	20	0	2.5
DMU 4	4	10	2
DMU 5	12	6	1.5
DMU 6	6	3	1.2

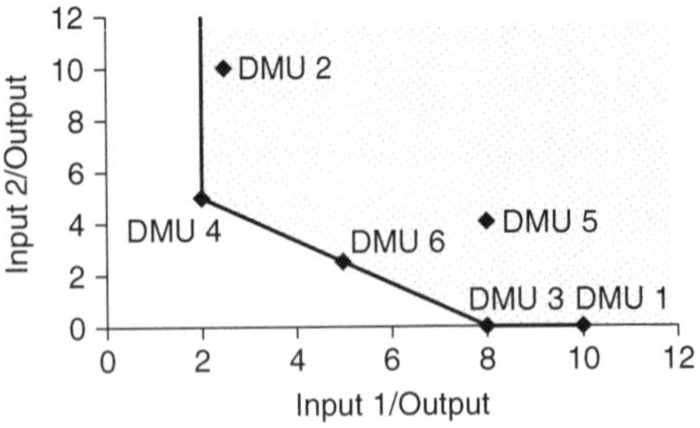

Figure 3.22. Illustrative Example for Zero Inputs

represents missing data, and we wish to ignore the input from the analysis, then we should replace the value of the input by a sufficiently large positive value M as explained in Kuosmanen (2002). This replacement would force the DMU to assign a zero weight to the missing input value, and therefore, the resulting efficiency score would be the same as that obtained when the input is not considered in the analysis at all.

When zero inputs are associated with management choices, then one needs to be aware that they imply the existence of a restricted reference set for the units with zero inputs. This reference set may be restricted in maximum degree (when only one unit has a zero value on a specific input), which implies efficiency of 100%, or in a moderate degree (when more than one DMU has zero values in the same inputs), which implies that these DMUs are only compared among themselves.

The foregoing suggests also that one should question whether production units having zero levels on some input operate the same technology as production units with positive values on that input. Zero inputs mean that the same range, if not quantity, of outputs can be produced without using the resources on which some DMUs have zero level. Thus, the technology may differ between those DMUs that need to use some amount, however small, of a resource and those that do not need to use it at all. If zero data do indicate different technologies, then each DMU should be assessed within its technological comparative group and not across all DMUs. For example, Thompson et al. (1993) refer to a farm example where inputs were the acres of land of type 1, type 2, and type 3. Clearly, many farms have only one type of land, and the zero values for the other two land type inputs were related to different classes of noncomparable DMUs. The relationship between zero data and nominal or ordinal data is therefore an avenue for further investigation that we do not pursue here.

3.6.3 Negative data

Hitherto, negative data have been handled in DEA through data transformations such as adding an arbitrary large positive number to all values so that all negative data are transformed to positive data (see, e.g., Pastor, 1994; Lovell, 1995). When data are transformed a priori, then in principle any DEA model can be applied to the transformed data set. However, one should be aware that such transformations may have implications for the efficiencies obtained (e.g., Seiford and Zhu, 2002) and also on the return-to-scale classifications of DMUs (Thrall, 1996).

There are, however, some models, as noted above, whose solution is invariant to data transformations, which are usually referred to as translation invariant. In the presence of negative data, the most often used model is the VRS additive model of Charnes et al. (1985), which is translation invariant as demonstrated by Ali and Seiford (1990). The additive model is not, however, in its original form, unit invariant (independent of scale of measurement of the variables), though some authors have put forward unit-invariant formulations of the additive DEA model (e.g., Lovell and Pastor, 1995; Pastor, 1996; Thrall, 1996). The main advantage of the additive model is that it can be applied to negative data directly without any need to subjectively transform them. However, the additive model has some drawbacks, as discussed in section 3.3, in particular, the fact that it does not yield an efficiency measure that can be readily interpreted.

Another model that can be applied directly to negative data is the range directional model (RDM) of Portela et al. (2004). The RDM is a directional model as in (3.14), where the directional vector reflects ranges of possible improvement defined for DMU_o as $R_{ro} = \max_j\{y_{rj}\} - y_{ro}$; $r = 1, \ldots, s$ and $R_{io} = x_{io} - \min_j\{x_{ij}\}$; $i = 1, \ldots, m$. These ranges assume implicitly the existence of an ideal point with maximum outputs and minimum inputs. Although there is no evidence that any such ideal production unit (I) can actually exist, the range of possible improvement can be seen as a surrogate for the maximum improvement that DMU_o could in principle achieve on each input and output. The RDM model is

$$RDM_o = \text{Max}\{\beta_o \mid (y_{ro} + \beta_o R_{ro}, x_{io} - \beta_o R_{io}) \in T\} \qquad (3.40)$$

Portela et al. (2004) prove that the RDM model can handle negative data since it is translation and unit invariant (when defined for a VRS technology). Further, the RDM model retains the meaning of radial efficiency measures in the presence of negative data, something that no other model to handle negative data does. To illustrate this, consider the situation depicted in Portela et al. (2004) and reproduced in figure 3.23. U3 is projected on the efficient frontier at point U3* following the direction of the hypothetical ideal point. The efficiency measure $1 - \beta$ of U3 equals the ratio CB/CA, which in turn equals the ratio FE/FD. Note that CB/CA measures the distance between the level of output 1 at the observed point U3 and its target point U3*. FE/FD is interpreted in a similar manner with respect to the level of output 2. This is precisely the definition of output radial technical efficiency.

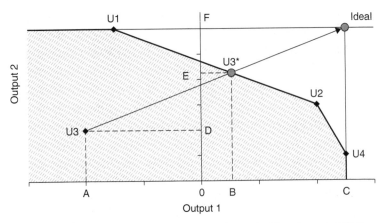

Figure 3.23. RDM in a One-Input Two-Output Example (Portela et al., 2004)

Thus, there is close similarity between the RDM efficiency measure and radial measures of efficiency traditionally used in DEA. The difference lies in the reference point used to measure efficiency. In the RDM case, the reference point is not the origin used in traditional DEA models but rather the ideal point. Note that the origin cannot be used as a reference to measure efficiency radially when some data are negative. In fact, if we rotate figure 3.23 suitably, we can arrive at figure 3.24, in which the ideal point occupies the position of the origin in traditional DEA models.

In figure 3.24, it is easy to see that the efficiency measure yielded by model RDM, $1 - \beta$, is a distance measure between the observed point U3 and the target point U3*, with reference to the ideal point. The smaller this distance, the higher the value of $1 - \beta$ and the more efficient the observed unit will be. To

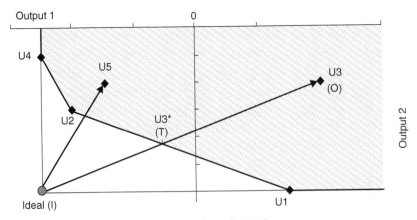

Figure 3.24. Figure 3.23 Inverted (Portela et al., 2004)

see this, note that the direction of improvement followed by inefficient DMUs U3 and U5 in figure 3.24 is defined with reference to the ideal point, a role played by the origin in traditional DEA models. The RDM efficiency measure has the same geometric interpretation as radial measures in DEA provided the ideal point is treated as the origin.

Consider, for example, U3 in figure 3.24 and define two vectors $\mathbf{a} = IT$ and $\mathbf{b} = IO$ that go, respectively, from the ideal (I) to target (T) point and from the ideal to observed (O) point. Then, it is easy to see that the efficiency measure $1 - \beta$ of U3 is given by the ratio between the length of these two vectors, that is by $\|\mathbf{a}\|/\|\mathbf{b}\| = \|IT\|/\|IO\|$, exactly as would be the case under traditional DEA had the point I been the origin.

The similarity of the RDM model with radial measures for handling negative data makes this model suitable for computing Malmquist indexes (see chapter 5 of this volume for details on this topic) when some data are negative (this was done in Portela, 2003).

In Portela et al. (2004) the authors use the RDM model for target-setting purposes. They note that the RDM model specifies a direction toward the production frontier that is biased toward the factors with the largest potential for improvement (and therefore larger ranges of possible improvement). Therefore, the authors propose an alternative model (IRDM), where the inverse of the range is used as the directional vector. This inverse range direction gives priority for improvement in factors where the production unit already performs well (and therefore has a lower range of possible improvement). Such a procedure is appealing when the objective is to find targets that are in principle closer to the observed DMU, but not adequate when the objective is to calculate efficiency scores and rank DMUs based on these. This is because the IRDM model is not unit invariant and the resulting efficiency measures are not comparable among DMUs. This fact, in a sense, shows that the properties of the directional distance function are not independent on the specification of the directional vector, and specifying this vector can have important implications for the efficiency measures obtained.

3.6.4 Outliers

Virtually all information on performance yielded by DEA (e.g., efficiencies, targets, type of returns to scale) is with reference to boundary points. The boundary is typically defined by a small proportion of the units in the assessment set. In view of the critical importance of the boundary that such units define, it is very important that their data, more than that of any other unit, should be reliable. In many instances in practice, however, some of the boundary units are atypical of the comparative set of units, either by virtue of much stronger performance than any other unit and/or by virtue of an atypical mix of inputs and outputs. We may in such cases wish to treat such boundary units in a special way, for example, by not letting them influence the positioning of the boundary either because their data may be unreliable

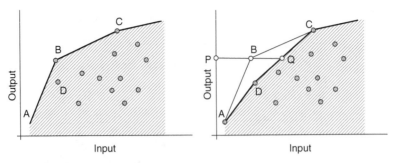

Figure 3.25. Identification of Outliers

and/or because their atypical attainments and/or mix of input–output levels may render them not suitable role models in practice for setting targets for other less well-performing units. We shall refer to such boundary units as *outliers*, borrowing from their counterparts in regression analyses. However, there is an important difference between outliers in regression and as we use the term here. In regression, an "outlier" is an observation that is at a "large distance" from the regression line and that can be in terms of efficiency either for very strong or very weak efficiency. In contrast, under DEA an "outlier" as the term is used here would not be a unit that has weak efficiency.

A number of methods have been proposed to detect outlier observations. Most of these methods apply the superefficiency concept first introduced by Andersen and Petersen (1993). The superefficiency model establishes an efficient frontier based on all units within the assessment set bar the unit being assessed itself. Figure 3.25 demonstrates the concept. The left panel shows the VRS efficient frontier when all assessment units are permitted to be on the boundary, and the right panel shows the case when unit B is being tested for outlier status and so is not permitted to be on the boundary. The boundary does not now include B and becomes ADC.

The "superefficiency" of B is PQ/PB. Clearly, for boundary units in the left panel, the efficiency scores in the right panel will normally be greater than 1, hence the term "superefficiency." The larger the superefficiency of a DMU, the farther it is from the rest of the units in the assessment set. This feature of superefficiencies can be used to identify outliers.

Mathematically, the changes required in basic DEA models to exclude the unit being assessed from the efficient frontier are quite straightforward. Consider the set J_o that includes all the units under analysis except the unit o being assessed. In an envelopment model the terms

$$\sum_{j=1}^{n} \lambda_j y_{rj} \text{ and } \sum_{j=1}^{n} \lambda_j x_{ij}$$

are then modified so that $j \in J_o$. In the dual multiplier model, this corresponds to eliminating the constraint

$$\sum_{i=1}^{m} v_i x_{ij} - \sum_{r=1}^{s} u_r y_{rj} - w \geq 0$$

for $j = o$ (note that $w = 0$ if CRS is assumed). The superefficiency model has been used in the literature for purposes other than the identification of outliers. Some of these are the ranking of efficient units, classification of efficient units into extreme efficient or nonextreme efficient groups, and sensitivity analysis (for details and references on these uses, see Lovell and Rouse, 2003).

Note that, under VRS, the superefficiency model can be infeasible. To see this, consider the example in figure 3.26. If efficient unit F is removed from the reference set and an input-oriented efficiency model is being used, there is no way a reduction (or expansion) in inputs, keeping outputs fixed, can cross the efficient frontier (ODAE) when unit F is not allowed to define that frontier. No input-oriented superefficiency score could therefore be computed for DMU F. However, an output-oriented superefficiency score can still be computed for F. Similarly, for unit D, no output-oriented superefficiency score can be computed, but an input superefficiency can be computed. It is also possible that neither an input nor an output superefficiency score can be computed for certain units. See also Seiford and Zhu (1999b), Zhu (2001), Tone (2002), Lovell and Rouse (2003), and Chen and Sherman (2004) for issues relating to the infeasibility of superefficiency models and ways of trying to solve this problem through nonradial models.

An approach to identify outliers using the superefficiency model was proposed by Thanassoulis (1999) and applied to the school context where the production units considered were pupils. In this approach, a threshold

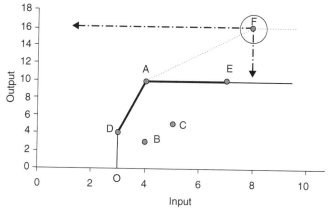

Figure 3.26. Illustrative Example of Infeasible Superefficiency Models

superefficiency is set by the user (e.g., 130%) so that units above that level are deemed superefficient. An algorithm, then, is followed whereby such units are eliminated one at time until either some user-specified percentage (e.g., 10%) of units have been eliminated or some user-specified percentage (e.g., 5%) of units are above a certain efficiency level, such as 90%. Thus, in effect, the algorithm stops further elimination of superefficient units when a prespecifed percentage of the DMUs has been eliminated or there is a certain percentage of the units on or near the efficient boundary as it stands after eliminations of superefficient units so far. The rationale is that in either case the boundary is drawn at a level of performance that a significant percentage of units can attain, and so that is deemed an acceptable benchmark performance in practice.

Another approach for identifying outliers was put forth by Dusansky and Wilson (1994, 1995). They removed efficient units one at a time and recomputed the efficiency scores each time. The efficiency scores resulting after each removal of a unit were averaged and compared with the average efficiency scores of the full sample (see also Wilson, 1995). "Sums of absolute and squared distances in efficiencies across the DMUs were also compared" in order to detect outliers. The criteria under which an observation was deemed an outlier were subjective. No statistical method was used to indicate when changes in average efficiency were statistically significant. The main problem with this approach is that more than one observation can be influential, and a set of influential observations may be determining the shape of the frontier. If one of these is removed, only the shape of the frontier will change, but not its relative position from the other units. Recognizing this problem, Dusansky and Wilson (1994, 1995) also excluded pairs of observations, after which the same type of calculations as above were undertaken.

Wilson (1995) also used the superefficiency model of Andersen and Petersen (1993) to identify outliers, suggesting the elimination of the units presenting higher superefficiency scores in turn. After each elimination, $n - 1$ units were assessed and the number of efficiency scores that changed were counted, and a measure of the "average change in measured efficiency" resulting from deleting the unit was calculated. Counting the number of efficiency scores that changed after a potential influential unit has been deleted can be considered analogous to counting the number of times a unit appears in the peer set of inefficient units. In fact, the more times an efficient unit appears in the peer set of inefficient units, the higher the number of efficiency scores that change when this unit is not allowed to define the efficient boundary. Such a unit can be deemed influential because its presence influences the efficiency scores of a considerable number of units. This influence is not necessarily bad, for example, when the influential unit is relatively close to the bulk of inefficient units.

A further approach to identifying outliers is proposed by Pastor et al. (1999). They compute a measure of the influence of a DMU on the efficiency measures of the remaining DMUs. The method consists of comparing two frontiers: one for the full set of units and another for a reduced set of units where each unit is removed in turn. The procedure evolves as follows:

- Let DMU k be removed from the sample.
- Calculate the efficiency score of each one of the remaining $n - 1$ DMUs and project their inputs and outputs levels onto the frontier.
- Reintroduce DMU k into the set of $n - 1$ "projected" DMUs and run a DEA model with all n units. If DMU k has no influence at all, then all $n - 1$ projected DMUs will have an efficiency score of 1. Otherwise, the efficiencies below 1 will reflect the impact of DMU k on their efficiency rating.

Pastor et al. (1999) propose a statistical test for testing the hypothesis that a given DMU is *influential*. They define the level of influence of a unit as the proportion of the remaining units that reduced their efficiency to less than a certain amount (where the proportion and the efficiency threshold are context dependent). Note that in practice Kolmogorov-Smirnov tests for comparing the frequency distribution of two independent samples could also be used. A similar procedure based on jackknifing was used by Färe et al. (1989a) to detect outliers. However, the technique has been criticized by Ondrich and Ruggiero (2002), who argue that jackknifing is not useful in the detection of outliers and that it cannot deal with multiple outliers.

In summary, a combination of the above methods, and indeed, others (e.g., Fox et al., 2004), can be used to detect outliers or influential observations. (Note that simple methods such as graphical displays of the data can also be useful to detect problems in the data.) No method is perfect, and ultimately all of them are subjective. As stressed in Fox et al. (2004), the detection of outliers and deciding what to do with them are two separate issues. One should always check the data for the possible existence of outliers since these can indicate some errors in data measurement or simply some observations that are atypical (and this should be reported in any analysis). If the outliers are defining the shape of the efficiency frontier and influencing by a large degree the efficiency of the other units, then one can consider an assessment with and without the outliers and compare results. Note that decisions regarding the exclusion of some units is, in most cases, very difficult, if not impossible, to make. The DMUs are, in most cases, also the clients of the efficiency measurement study, and it is hard to say to clients that they were not considered in the assessment and therefore no results are available for them.

More details on outlier detection can be found in chapter 4 of this volume, where, in particular, statistical procedures are put forward to help identifying outliers.

3.6.5 Dimensionality

As outlined in preceding sections of this chapter, DEA allows for a great flexibility in the choice of weights that DMUs assign to each input and output (models that restrict this flexibility are addressed in section 3.7). This implies that the greater the number of input and output variables, the higher the probability that a particular DMU will appear efficient. Therefore, in a DEA analysis, one needs to be careful to have an "interesting" relationship between the number of variables used and the number of DMUs. Dyson et al. (2001) suggest as a "rule of thumb" that the number of DMUs $\geq 2m \times$ s (where m stands for number of inputs and s for number of outputs).

In real applications, one encounters frequently the problem of too many potential variables to be considered in the efficiency assessment and the consequent need to reduce meaningfully the set of variables to actually use. Removal of variables based on correlations should be avoided for the reasons mentioned in Dyson et al. (2001) (in particular, the omission of a highly correlated variable can have a significant impact on the measured efficiency). Other approaches to reduce the dimensionality of the input–output set are the aggregation of inputs and outputs. Aggregating inputs such as various types of staff into a single staff-related variable is very common in the literature (e.g., in banking applications). Another example of aggregation, for example, in agriculture is the aggregation of various types of equipment, such as tractors and harvesters, into an input called "machinery" (see Ray, 2005). On the output side, consideration of such outputs as revenues or costs can also be seen as a way of aggregating various output quantities weighted by their prices. The validity of a specific aggregation procedure can be tested through F-tests, as shown in Ray (2005). This may be particularly useful when various aggregation alternatives are available.

One approach that can also be used for this aggregation is principal component analysis (PCA). PCA can be used to reduce the input and output set to a significant number of principal components that meaningfully aggregate inputs and outputs. DEA can then be run on the principal components rather than on the original variables. This method was used in Adler and Golany (2001) in an application of DEA to the problem of choosing the most appropriate network for an airline. These authors used PCA to aggregate a large number of inputs, whereas the outputs used in the DEA assessment were not aggregated. Adler and Golany (2001) note that a problem related to the use of principal components as inputs or outputs of DEA assessments is that principal components can be negative. Therefore, one of the approaches mentioned above for dealing with negative data needs to be applied when principal components are used for aggregating variables. Prior to the application of Adler and Golany on DEA and PCA, Zhu (1998) had highlighted some advantages of using PCA as a complement to DEA. Zhu created principal components not on the original input–output variables but on ratios of some outputs to some inputs. The linkage initiated in Zhu (1998) between DEA and PCA did not have the aim, however, of reducing the dimensionality of the variable set.[13] Shanmugam and Johnson (2007) advocate the use of PCA on input sets separately from output sets and link DEA and PCA by running a DEA model on the principal components rather than on the original variables (as done in Adler and Golany, 2001). In an interesting application to rank 45 countries with respect to their male and female survival rate for melanoma cancer (taking into account such variables as the latitude of the country, ozone thickness, and ultraviolet rays), Shanmugam and Johnson (2007) reach the conclusion that the two approaches yield statistically significant correlated rankings. The authors also highlight the advantages of using a parametric technique as a complement to DEA, in particular, as far as outlier detection is concerned. That is, PCA has well-established procedures to find influential observations that can be used to identify outliers in DEA.

Problems of dimensionality relate not only to the number of variables to be considered in the assessment, but also to the number of DMUs. Clearly, in circumstances where the number of DMUs is too small, the results yielded by DEA or, indeed, any other technique cannot be very reliable. Whenever possible, the researcher should aim at having as large a set of DMUs as possible. When that is not possible, bootstrapping techniques, referred in detail in chapter 4, can be used to overcome the "curse of dimensionality" (low number of DMUs relative to number of input–output variables) and estimate confidence intervals on the DEA efficiencies.

In summary, the main objective of this section is to alert the reader to a number of problems that may exist in data sets. We describe some methods that can be used to diagnose these problems (e.g., methods for detecting outliers) and methods that can be used to solve these problems, such as not permitting outliers to locate the efficient boundary, models for dealing with negative data or undesirable outputs, and procedures for dealing with zero data or missing values. What is important to bear in mind is that two steps are usually involved here: the diagnosis of the problem and the solution of the problem. The first step is obviously the most important, and it calls attention to the fact that in DEA, as in any other quantitative method, one needs first to understand the data at hand before actually dealing with them.

3.7 Value Judgments in DEA

In the preceding sections, the specification of the production possibilities set and the measures of efficiency presented have not involved any information about any perceived relative worth of inputs or outputs, save for the case of cost and revenue efficiency measures, where external factor prices or, indeed, revenue or cost constraints were involved. However, even away from situations where factor prices are involved, in some cases the analyst may wish to reflect in the DEA assessment some strongly held prior views about the relative worth of inputs and outputs, worth being defined here in a very broad sense. For example, in assessing police forces where the clearing up of violent crimes, of burglary instances, and so on, are outputs, one may legitimately wish to restrict the DEA model to value more highly the clearing up of a violent crime rather than a burglary even if no "price" or more precise information of the relative worth of each type of clear-up is known. Extensive literature now exists about incorporating value judgments of this type in DEA assessments, and this is the subject of this section.

There are various methods that can be used to incorporate value judgments in DEA and to reduce the flexibility of DMUs in choosing their value system, implicit in the weights u_r and v_i in DEA multiplier models such as that in (3.4) or (3.5). In this section (following Thanassoulis et al., 2004), we review two broad types of methods, namely, those that

- Apply restrictions on the DEA weights (weight restrictions)
- Change implicitly the comparative set of DMUs

3.7.1 Weight restrictions

Weight restrictions (WRs) are additional constraints introduced in the DEA multiplier model [see models (3.4) and (3.5) in section 3.3]. These new constraints can be of various types, as shown in table 3.3, where the Greek letters are user-specified constants to reflect value judgments. The restrictions (a_i) to (c_i) in table 3.3 relate to input weights, and (a_o) to (c_o), to output weights. Constraint (d) links input and output weights.

Absolute WRs simply restrict weights to vary within a specific range, without relating the weights with each other. This type of WR was first introduced by Dyson and Thanassoulis (1988) on an application to rates departments. Cook et al. (1991, 1994) also used this type of constraints to evaluate highway maintenance patrols. One of the difficulties associated with absolute WRs is the meaning of the bounds δ_i, τ_i, ρ_r, η_r since, in general, weights are significant only on a relative basis (since ratios of weights incorporate information regarding marginal rates of transformation or substitution between outputs or inputs). This means that, in practice, it is difficult to define bounds for variables whose meaning is unclear. Depending on the context, however, some meaning can be attributed to these bounds [see, e.g., Dyson and Thanassoulis (1988), where output weights are interpreted as the level of input the DEA model allocates per unit of output r, in a single-input/multiple-output setting].

Table 3.3
Types of Weight Restrictions

Absolute WRs			
$\delta_i \leq v_i \leq \tau_i$	(a_i)	$\rho_r \leq u_r \leq \eta_r$	(a_o)
Assurance Regions of Type I (Relative WRs)			
$\kappa_i v_i + \kappa_{i+1} v_{i+1} \leq v_{i+2}$	(b_i)	$\omega_r u_r + \omega_{r+1} u_{r+1} \leq u_{r+2}$	(b_o)
$\alpha_i \leq \frac{v_i}{v_{i+1}} \leq \beta_i$	(c_i)	$\theta_r \leq \frac{u_r}{u_{r+1}} \leq \zeta_r$	(c_o)
Assurance Regions of Type II (Input–Output WRs)			
$\gamma_i v_i \geq u_r$	(d)		

Another difficulty with absolute WRs is the potential infeasibility of DEA models with such restrictions. Podinovski (2001, p. 575) illustrates this fact, also claiming that restricted models "may not identify the maximum relative efficiency of the assessed DMU correctly." In a sense, this means that the DEA weights under absolute WRs may not enable a DMU to appear in the best possible light relative to other DMUs (see also Podinovski, 1999; Podinovski and Athanassopoulos, 1998). Podinovski (2001) proposes the replacement of traditional DEA objective functions (which measure absolute efficiency) by a measure of relative efficiency, thereby removing the possibility of absolute WRs leading to misrepresentations of unit relative efficiencies. Podinovski (2004c) takes analysis and identifies certain types of absolute WRs that do not lead to misrepresentations of unit relative efficiency.

It should be noted that there is a strong interdependence between the bounds on different weights. For example, setting an upper bound on an input weight implicitly imposes a lower bound on the total virtual input, and this in turn has implications for the values the remaining input weights can take. When absolute WRs are used in a DEA model, switching from an input to an output orientation can produce different relative efficiency scores even under CRS. Hence, the bounds need to be set in light of the model orientation used, which will flow out of the context of the DEA application and the degree of exogeneity of the input and the output variables.

Assurance regions of type I (AR-I) link either only input weights [(b_i) and (c_i) in table 3.3] or only output weights [(b_o) and (c_o) in table 3.3] and were first used by Thompson et al. (1986). Use of form (c) is more prevalent in practice, with various applications such as Thompson et al. (1992) to oil/gas producers, Schaffnit et al. (1997) to bank branches, Ray et al. (1998) to the Chinese iron and steel industry, Thanassoulis et al. (1995) to English perinatal care DMUs, and Olesen and Petersen (2002) to hospitals.

ARs are appropriate when there is some price information and one wants to proceed from technical toward economic efficiency measures. When there is a priori information concerning marginal rates of technical substitution (transformation) between inputs (outputs) these are also the suitable WRs to use because they are based on ratios of weights that, as we showed above, reflect these rates. AR-Is have the advantage of providing the same results irrespective of the model orientation as long as a CRS technology is assumed. This is so because, as noted above, WRs of the AR-I type work by changing the PPS and measure efficiency radially in relation to the modified PPS.

In order to illustrate this, here we use the same example as that used in Thanassoulis et al. (2004), considered in table 3.4. In this table, we show the input output levels for nine DMUs, its output prices p_1 and p_2, input price w, and also the solution from the multiplier CRS model. The graphical representation of the CRS frontier against which efficiency was measured is shown in figure 3.27.

Consider the inclusion in the multiplier model of the AR-I constraint: $u_1/u_2 = p_1/p_2$, relating output weights to output prices for each DMU

Table 3.4
Illustrative Example and Results from Multiplier CRS Model
(Output Orientation)

DMU	y_1	y_2	x	p_1	p_2	w	$1/\beta^*$	u_1^*	u_2^*	v^*
A	1	8	2	7	4	5	100.0%	0.040	0.120	0.500
B	4	7	2	2	6	4	100.0%	0.169	0.046	0.500
C	15	10	6	1	5	4	100.0%	0.056	0.015	0.167
D	14	8	8	4	3	6	70.0%	0.071	0	0.179
E	12	16	10	5	3	4	55.4%	0.061	0.017	0.181
F	1	10	5	7	5	6	50.0%	0	0.100	0.400
G	12	24	12	7	3	5	56.0%	0.012	0.036	0.149
H	2	8	3	6	3	2	69.3%	0.038	0.115	0.481
I	3	6	2	5	3	4	84.0%	0.048	0.143	0.595

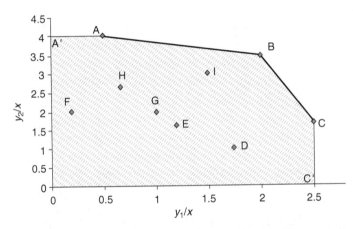

Figure 3.27. Illustrative Example's Graphical Representation (Thanassoulis et al., 2004)

assessed. Adding this constraint to the multiplier model (3.5) implies the addition of a new variable in the envelopment model that reflects trade-offs between the outputs (see Thanassoulis et al., 2004). In addition, we can look at this new constraint as a new facet that was added to the data set. The optimal weights from the multiplier model without the AR-I, when normalized by the input weight, are shown in table 3.5.

When we solve the multiplier model with the AR-I, the optimal solution (with normalized weights) is shown in table 3.6. All efficiency scores have deteriorated with the addition of the AR-I that imposes the ratio between output weights to equal the ratio between output prices. (As we would expect, DEA efficiencies can only deteriorate in the presence of WRs.)

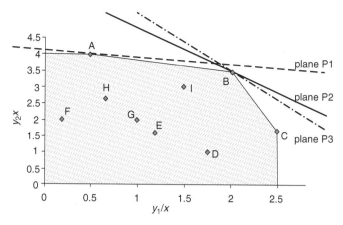

Figure 3.28. Frontier Representation with an AR ($u_1/u_2 = p_1 p_2$)

Table 3.5
Optimal Weights from CRS Radial Model

DMU	A	B	C	D	E	F	G	H	I
u_1^*	0.08	0.3385	0.3385	0.40	0.34	0.00	0.08	0.08	0.08
u_2^*	0.24	0.0923	0.0923	0.00	0.09	0.25	0.24	0.24	0.24
v^*	1	1	1	1	1	1	1	1	1
Face	AB	BC	BC	CC′	BC	A′A	AB	AB	AB
Efficiency	100%	100%	100%	70%	55.4%	50%	56%	69.3%	84%

In practice, all DMUs were assessed in relation to a different hyperplane that passes in most cases through point B. These new hyperplanes are shown in figure 3.28 for DMUs A (plane P3), C (plane P1), and D (plane P2), where each of these DMUs was assessed radially in relation to the corresponding plane, that is, none of those originally existing without the AR-I.

Note that DMU B is the only one that is efficient with the AR-I, but DMU A is used as the referent of DMU C (DMU C is projected on plane P1 that passes through A). This happens because the new hyperplanes are in fact

Table 3.6
Optimal Weights from AR Model ($u_1/u_2 = p_1/p_2$)

DMU	A	B	C	D	E	F	G	H	I
u_1^*	0.25	0.08	0.0488	0.2162	0.2439	0.2222	0.2857	0.2667	0.2439
u_2^*	0.1429	0.24	0.2439	0.1622	0.1463	0.1587	0.1225	0.1333	0.1463
v^*	1	1	1	1	1	1	1	1	1
Efficiency	69.60%	100%	52.90%	54.10%	52.70%	36.20%	53.10%	53.30%	80.50%

equivalent to revenue functions since the coefficients of these hyperplanes are output prices. This means that in fact the efficiency measures resulting from the AR-I model are revenue efficiency scores (equivalent to those given by the ratio between observed revenue and maximum revenue, where the latter is the optimal solution of the maximum revenue model presented in section 3.4). In Thanassoulis et al. (2004), details on proving the equivalence between the AR-I model (which imposes ratios of output weights to equal ratios of prices) and the revenue efficiency are provided, while this same equivalence was proven by Schaffnit et al. (1997) for the case of cost efficiency and an input-oriented AR-I–restricted DEA model.

The relationship between WRs and economic measures of efficiency, when these restrictions convey information on prices, is also linked to the multiple criteria framework called value efficiency analysis (VEA) as described in Halme et al. (1999). In VEA, the decision maker's (DM's) preferences are included in a value function estimated through the knowledge of the DM's most preferred solution. This value function works in a similar way to a revenue or cost function except that it may reveal other preferences than those related with prices (see also Korhonen et al., 2002).

When AR-Is are not as restrictive as the one imposed above, the use of ARs conveying information on prices still represent a movement toward economic measures of efficiency. For example, let us assume that we impose an AR-I stating $1/6 \leq u_1/u_2 \leq 7/3$ for our illustrative example. The assessment of the above 10 DMUs would yield the optimum normalized weights shown in table 3.7.

The new efficient frontier is now WABZ, as shown in figure 3.29, constituted by three facets from which only one (AB) existed before the imposition of the WRs. Since these new facets reflect trade-offs in output prices, the above efficiency measures calculated based on the AR-I model are related to revenue efficiency. In fact, the resulting efficiency scores are higher than the revenue efficiency scores but lower than the technical efficiency scores calculated without the ARs. So we can assume that the resulting efficiency scores calculated under the AR-I model have a component of technical efficiency and a component of revenue efficiency.

Table 3.7
Results from AR Restricted Model ($1/6 \leq u_1/u_2 \leq 7/3$)

DMU	A	B	C	D	E	F	G	H	I
u_1^*	0.0408	0.2857	0.2857	0.2857	0.2857	0.0408	0.08	0.08	0.08
u_2^*	0.2449	0.1225	0.1225	0.1225	0.1225	0.2449	0.24	0.24	0.24
v^*	1	1	1	1	1	1	1	1	1
Face	WA	BZ	BZ	BZ	BZ	WA	AB	AB	AB
Efficiency	100%	100%	91.84%	62.25%	53.88%	49.80%	56%	69.33%	84%

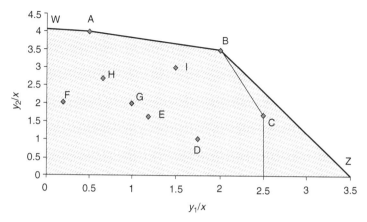

Figure 3.29. Frontier Representation with an AR $1/6 \leq u_1/u_2 \leq 7/3$

Consider now the introduction of a restriction not related with prices but with observable trade-offs on the original PPS, for example, $\min(u_1^*/u_2^*) \leq u_1/u_2 \leq \max(u_1^*/u_2^*)$, where the asterisk means the optimal solution from the unrestricted multiplier CRS model, and maximum and minimum exclude facets with zero weights. This would result in the constraint $0.08/0.24 = 0.333 \leq u_1/u_2 \leq 3.667 = 0.3385/0.0923$, and the AR-I model would generate the results shown in table 3.8 and figure 3.30.

In this case, no new facets were added to the original PPS, but existing facets were extended so that observed trade-offs could be used also by units that were before projected on weakly efficient parts of the frontier. The resulting PPS against which all units are projected is therefore WABCZ. Note that introducing new facets may change the original Pareto-efficient set, and some units may change their efficiency status, though this did not happen in the above example, where existing efficient facets were merely extended to eliminate inefficient parts of the boundary.

The example above shows that AR-Is can be seen as a method that introduces new facets on the frontier (reflecting nonobserved trade-offs) but can also be a means of extending existing facets [see Portela and Thanassoulis (2006), where the authors use ARs to extend facets]. In this sense, ARs can

Table 3.8
Results from the AR-I Restricted Model ($0.333 \leq u_1/u_2 \leq 3.667$)

DMU	A	B	C	D	E	F	G	H	I
u_1^*	0.08	0.3385	0.3385	0.3385	0.3385	0.08	0.08	0.08	0.08
u_2^*	0.24	0.0923	0.0923	0.0923	0.0923	0.24	0.24	0.24	0.24
v^*	1	1	1	1	1	1	1	1	1
Face	AB	BC	BC	BC	BC	AB	AB	AB	AB
Efficiency	100%	100%	100%	68.46%	55.38%	49.6%	56%	69.33%	84%

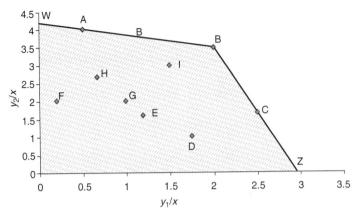

Figure 3.30. Frontier Representation with an AR $(0.333 \leq u_1/u_2 \leq 3.667)$

be "equivalent" to methods that extend facets as the method of Olesen and Petersen (1996; OP) and others like the constrained facet analysis of Bessent et al. (1988) or the controlled envelopment analysis of Lang et al. (1995). Portela and Thanassoulis (2006) show that under certain circumstances the OP method is equivalent to the AR model [and also the cone ratio (CR) model that we will detail later in this section]. This equivalence is, however, restricted to situations of two inputs (used to produce a single output) or two outputs (generated from a single input) since in higher dimensions one cannot extend facets through pairwise comparisons of weights as is done in the AR-I model. Extension of facets needs to consider all rates of input substitution and all rates of output transformation at the same time. We address this issue further below when presenting the CR approach.

Assurance regions type II (AR-II) were introduced by Thompson et al. (1990) and model relationships between input and output weights (the AR-II are also known as linked cone assurance regions, LC-ARs). There are not many practical applications that use AR-IIs since their use is not as straightforward as the use of AR-Is. The problems of AR-IIs relate to "the questions of a single numeraire and absolute profitability," which were left unanswered in Thompson et al. (1990, p. 103). In addition, the authors also refer to infeasibility problems that may be associated with AR-IIs resulting from these being not a CR as AR-Is (Thompson et al., 1995, p. 106).

AR-IIs link input and output weights, and therefore, when the information contained on the AR-IIs relates to price information, they should be related with profit efficiency (where profit is defined in absolute terms as revenues minus costs). Thanassoulis et al. (2004) show that introducing in the multiplier model AR-II constraints results in an efficiency value in the envelopment model that is linked with profit, though the link with profit efficiency is unclear for the reasons pointed out before relating to the problems associated with the definition of profit efficiency.

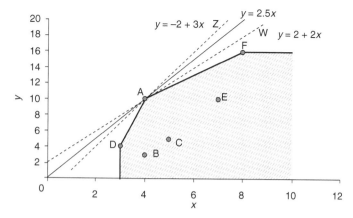

Figure 3.31. Graphical Representation of AR-II (Thanassoulis et al., 2004)

Note that, in the same way as with AR-I constraints, the introduction of AR-II constraints also changes the efficient frontier against which efficiency is measured. Take the example in figure 3.31 of one input (x) one output (y).

With no WRs, the VRS output-oriented multiplier model identifies three possible facets for projection: DA, $y = -14 + 6x$; AF, $y = 4 + 1.5x$; and OA, $y = 2.5x$. (These facets are identified as shown before, i.e. collecting all optimal weights resulting from the multiplier model and reducing them to a number of facets.) Facets DA and AF lie on the VRS frontier, and facet OA corresponds to the CRS frontier that passes through the origin and point A. Note that at DMU A, there are three possible facets that would render this DMU 100% efficient, one of which represents the CRS frontier. The intercepts of the linear segments of the VRS efficient boundary have a return-to-scale interpretation, as shown in section 3.5. A negative intercept implies IRS, a zero intercept CRS and a positive intercept implies DRS. Clearly, the line DA presents IRS, while the line AF presents DRS.

If we now introduce an AR-II in this model stating that $v/u \geq 2$, the segment AF can no longer be on the frontier because it has a rate of transformation between inputs and outputs of 1.5. Therefore, the efficient frontier is DAW, where to the right of point A, it is defined by the line $y = 2 + 2x$. Therefore, DMU F loses its 100% efficiency status. The frontier still has a portion to the left of A with IRS, and a portion to the right of A with DRS, but the latter has changed its magnitude from a rate of input–output transformation of 1.5 to 2. Hence, AR-IIs can also change the scale elasticity of segments on the frontier. In fact, if our AR-II is $v/u \geq 3$, then the new frontier is now defined by DAZ (where AZ is represented by the line $y = -2 + 3x$). Clearly, IRS prevails on the whole new frontier, such that scale elasticity has changed enough to alter the type of returns to scale holding on the efficient boundary.

Consider the assessment of DMU E with input level 7 and output level 10. The unrestricted VRS output model yields for this DMU an efficiency of 10/14.5(68.97%), since its radial target output level on the line AF is 14.5. If we introduce an AR-II with price information stating that $u/v = p/w$, and assume that $p = 6$ and $w = 3$ for DMU E (p is output and w input price), then this AR-II would project DMU E on the line segment AW. The AR-II efficiency score of E would be calculated radially in relation to this new facet and would yield for this DMU an efficiency of 10/16 (62.5%), since the radial output target is now 16. We can look at the new facet against which the efficiency of E is measured as its profit-maximizing frontier, and in this sense, the new efficiency score has something of a technical and also something of an economic efficiency meaning. Note, however, that observed profit at point E is $6 \times 10 - 3 \times 7 = 39$, and profit at its target point on the new facet (AW) is $6 \times 16 - 3 \times 7 = 75$. The ratio between observed profit and target profit is 52% (different from 62.5%). The exact value of 62.5% relates to profit in the following way:

$$62.5\% = \left(\frac{6 \times 16 - 3 \times 7}{6 \times 10} + \frac{3 \times 7}{6 \times 10} \right)^{-1}$$

(for details, see Thanassoulis et al., 2004). This simple example shows that introducing AR-IIs also changes the production frontier against which efficiency is measured. Moreover, when the AR-IIs incorporate price information, there is a link between AR-IIs and profit, but not with profit efficiency (if defined as the ratio between profits, which is a problematic approach, as we have shown in section 3.4). It also shows that returns to scale and WRs are intimately linked because ARs, interpreted as a way of changing the efficient frontier, may affect the return-to-scale characteristics of the frontier. In fact, WRs may be seen as a means of modeling the return-to-scale characteristics of the efficient frontier.

Given the unclear link between AR-II restrictions and profit, Thompson and Thrall (1994) and Thompson et al. (1995) advocate the separate treatment between efficiency and profit analysis. This separate treatment is what Thompson et al. (1995) called "LC-AR profit ratio model" (see also Thompson et al., 1996, 1997). This methodology uses the multiplier model with AR-II restrictions but removes from the model all the constraints of the type (3.41), because they prevent virtual profits from being positive:

$$\frac{\sum\limits_{r=1}^{s} u_r y_{rj}}{\sum\limits_{i=1}^{m} v_i x_{ij}} \leq 1, \qquad j = 1, \ldots, n \qquad (3.41)$$

(Note that the input and output weights of the multiplier model are interpreted by the authors as virtual input and output prices.) Replacing the removed constraints by AR-II restrictions Thompson et al. (1995, 1996) "provide a way to measure absolute profits, both maxima and minima, in contrast to the inability to say anything substantive about profits by use of the DEA CCR ratio (and BCC convex) models" (Thompson et al., 1996, p. 361). The LC-AR profit ratio model relates to profit potential or profit loss depending on whether the objective function is being maximized or minimized.

Applications of AR-IIs are mostly based on the above profit ratio methodology (see also Ray et al., 1998; Taylor et al., 1997), though their use is not very common. An example of the use of AR-IIs can be found in Thanassoulis et al. (1995) in the context of assessing perinatal care units in the United Kingdom. The authors incorporated a constraint in the DEA model forcing the weight on an input (number of babies at risk) to be equal to the weight on an output (number of babies at risk surviving). This is obviously AR-II, where, however, only one input and one output are being linked. Athanassopoulos and Shale (1997) also linked input and output weights in an assessment of U.K. universities, since they realized that some inputs were intrinsically linked to some outputs [e.g., the number of full-time equivalent (FTE) undergraduates (input) is linked with the number of successful leavers (output), and the number of FTE postgraduates (input) is linked with the number of higher degrees awarded (output)]. The relationship between the weights was, however, modeled through virtual weights following the approach of Wong and Beasley (1990), which we address next.

3.7.1.1 Restricting virtual weights

WRs may not only be applied to weights (as shown above for absolute WRs and ARs) but also to *virtual* inputs and outputs. Recall that a virtual output is the product of the output level and the corresponding DEA weight [u_r in model (3.4) or (3.5)]. Virtual inputs are defined in an analogous manner. The main advantage of using restrictions on virtual inputs and outputs is that the latter do not depend on the units of measurement of inputs and outputs (see Thanassoulis et al., 2004) as, depending on orientation, either the sum of virtual inputs or that of virtual outputs is normalized, and the nonnormalized sum of virtual values at the optimal solution to the DEA model (3.4) or (3.5) reflects the efficiency rating of the unit. Thus, virtual inputs or outputs can be readily compared as to their significance for the efficiency rating of a DMU. (In contrast, the weights u_r and v_i should be interpreted carefully, since a larger or smaller weight does not necessarily mean that a high or low importance is attached to a given input or output as the values of the weights depend on the unit of measurement of the corresponding input or output.)

Virtual inputs and outputs can therefore be seen as normalized weights reflecting the extent to which the efficiency rating of a DMU is underscored by a given input or output variable. The first study applying restrictions on virtual inputs/outputs was that of Wong and Beasley (1990). Such restrictions assume the form shown in (3.42), where the proportion of the total virtual output of DMU j accounted for by output r is restricted to lie in the range $[\phi_r, \psi_r]$. A similar restriction can be set on the virtual inputs.

$$\phi_r \leq \frac{u_r y_{rj}}{\sum\limits_{r=1}^{s} u_r y_{rj}} \leq \psi_r \qquad r = 1, \ldots, s \qquad (3.42)$$

The range is normally determined to reflect prior views on the relative "importance" of the individual outputs. The main problem with virtual input and output weights is that constraints such as the above are DMU specific, meaning that the DEA model with such constraints may become computationally expensive if the restriction is to hold for each DMU and for a number of its input–output variables. Wong and Beasley (1990) suggest some modifications for implementing restrictions on virtual values that try to simplify the model. These modifications include adding restrictions only for the DMU being assessed or using constraints for an "average DMU."

Restrictions on the virtual input and/or output weights represent indirectly absolute bounds on the DEA weights of the type shown in (a_i) and (a_o) in table 3.3. Therefore, the incorporation of virtual inputs and/or outputs WRs suffers from the problems of absolute WRs, namely, that restricted models are sensitive to the model orientation and may lead to infeasible solutions. Lins et al. (2007) dealt extensively with the issue of infeasibility of DEA models with restrictions on virtual multipliers. In particular, the authors propose a model to test the feasibility of a solution and a model that adjusts the bounds to guarantee feasible solutions. Pedraja-Chaparro et al. (1997) proposed the introduction of AR type restrictions to virtual inputs/outputs rather than to weights. This model solves the above problems but still suffers from the problem of weights being DMU specific, which can, however, be alleviated by imposing ARs on virtual inputs and outputs only to DMU_o being assessed (on problems with virtual WRs see also Sarrico and Dyson, 2004). On the whole, there are few instances of published DEA applications where restrictions on virtual inputs and/or outputs have been used.

When using WRs, it is important to estimate the appropriate values for the parameters in the restrictions. A number of methods, reviewed in Thanassoulis et al. (2004), have been put forward to aid the estimation of such parameters. These approaches include the use of price information, using the weights from the unbounded DEA model as a reference for establishing WRs, using the weights from the unbounded DEA model of role model DMUs, using expert opinion, or using estimated marginal rates of substitution or transformation as references for establishing WRs. Although most of these procedures have been developed for establishing bounds in specific WR methodologies, in most cases they can be generalized. No method is all-purpose, and different approaches may be appropriate in different contexts.

3.7.2 Changes in the comparative set of DMUs

The approaches to incorporating value judgments in DEA covered so far in this section act directly on the weights (or virtual weights) of the DEA model, which in turn reflect the marginal rates of transformation or substitution that the DEA is permitted to deem acceptable. The marginal rates of substitution or transformation are, however, a feature of the boundary of the PPS and so one can instead act directly on the PPS (rather than implicitly through WRs) in order to reflect user value judgments. Acting directly on the PPS is achieved by artificially altering the input–output data of the DMUs or alternatively adding artificial DMUs to the original set. This section outlines these approaches.

3.7.2.1 Cone ratio

The best-known approach that acts on the data and transforms it is by Charnes et al. (1989) and is called the cone ratio (CR) approach. But Golany (1988a) and Ali et al. (1991) also used data transformations to replace ordinal relationships between weights in DEA.

CRs are a more general approach that includes the special case of ARs, shown above. The CR approach transforms an input–output vector (x, y) into another vector $(x', y') = (Ax, By)$ such that traditional radial models can be used on the transformed data set. The matrixes A and B can be specified in a number of ways, using expert opinion, input and/or output prices, or the set of optimal weights of preferable DMUs found through an unrestricted DEA model (see Brockett et al., 1997b; Charnes et al., 1990; Cooper et al., 2000a).

The choice of the transformation matrix can be such that equivalence between ARs and CRs is assured. To see this, consider the illustrative example in table 3.4 and let us assume that we choose an output transformation matrix (B) using optimal unrestricted DEA weights of the efficient DMUs A, B, and C. The normalized output weights for these DMUs are $(u_1, u_2) = (0.08, 0.24)$, $(0.3385, 0.0923)$, and $(0.3385, 0.0923)$. Since two of these DMUs have the same optimal weights, the resulting transformation matrix B is

$$B = \begin{bmatrix} 0.08 & 0.24 \\ 0.3385 & 0.0923 \end{bmatrix}.$$

Using this matrix to transform original data implies a new output vector equal to

$$Y' = \begin{bmatrix} 0.08 & 0.24 \\ 0.3385 & 0.0923 \end{bmatrix} \times \begin{bmatrix} 1 & 4 & 15 & 14 & 12 & 1 & 12 & 2 & 3 \\ 8 & 7 & 10 & 8 & 16 & 10 & 24 & 8 & 6 \end{bmatrix}$$

$$= \begin{bmatrix} 2 & 2 & 3.6 & 3.04 & 4.8 & 2.48 & 6.72 & 2.08 & 1.68 \\ 1.077 & 2 & 6 & 5.477 & 5.538 & 1.262 & 6.277 & 1.42 & 1.57 \end{bmatrix}.$$

Running a traditional output radial CRS model on the transformed data yields the same results as that shown in table 3.8 containing the results from the AR-restricted model ($0.333 \leq u_1/u_2 \leq 3.667$). The CR approach is therefore in this case exactly equivalent to the AR approach where we restrict the ratio of output weights to vary within maximum and minimum observed values (where facets with zeros are excluded). The equivalence between the CR and AR approaches is shown by Charnes et al. (1990), who note that AR constraints of the form $\mathbf{Du}$ correspond to a CR model where the transformation matrix $\mathbf{B}$ is such that $\mathbf{B}^{\mathrm{T}} = (\mathbf{D}^{\mathrm{T}}\mathbf{D})^{-1}\mathbf{D}^{\mathrm{T}}$. For our illustrative example, D is obtained from the upper and lower limits of the assurance region $0.333 \leq u_1/u_2 \leq 3.667$, so we have

$$\mathbf{D} = \begin{bmatrix} -1 & 3.667 \\ 1 & -0.333 \end{bmatrix} \text{ and}$$

$$\mathbf{Du} = \begin{bmatrix} -1 & 3.667 \\ 1 & -0.333 \end{bmatrix} \times \begin{bmatrix} u_1 \\ u_2 \end{bmatrix} = \begin{cases} -u_1 + 3.667u_2 \geq 0 \\ u_1 - 0.333u_2 \geq 0 \end{cases}.$$

This yields a matrix

$$\mathbf{B}^{\mathrm{T}} = \begin{bmatrix} 0.1 & 1.1 \\ 0.3 & 0.3 \end{bmatrix} \text{ and therefore } \mathbf{B} = \begin{bmatrix} 0.1 & 0.3 \\ 1.1 & 0.3 \end{bmatrix}.$$

This is equivalent to

$$\begin{bmatrix} 0.08 & 0.24 \\ 0.3385 & 0.0923 \end{bmatrix}$$

if we multiply the first line of $\mathbf{B}$ by 0.8 and the second line by 0.30773, which is equivalent to simply rescaling each transformed output, which therefore does not affect the results of the DEA analysis. Therefore, by transforming the data using observed factor trade-offs as deduced from the efficient DMUs, the CR model does not change the status of any efficient unit and works by extending observed facets exactly in the same way as the AR model. Therefore, the CR approach can be equivalent to the AR approach, but it is more general because the AR approach only compares input or output weights pairwise, whereas the transformation matrixes $\mathbf{A}$ and $\mathbf{B}$ can contain all input and all output multipliers.

Note that using optimal weights from efficient DMUs to establish the output transformation matrix ($\mathbf{B}$) in the CR model in fact implies the following computations:

$$\mathbf{Y}' = \begin{bmatrix} u_1^{*F_1} & u_2^{*F_1} \\ u_1^{*F_2} & u_1^{*F_2} \end{bmatrix} \times \begin{bmatrix} y_{1j} \\ y_{2j} \end{bmatrix} = \begin{bmatrix} u_1^{*F_1}y_{1j} + u_2^{*F_1}y_{2j} \\ u_1^{*F_2}y_{1j} + u_2^{*F_2}y_{2j} \end{bmatrix},$$

where $*F_i$ denotes the ith efficient facet of the PPS. This corresponds to computing for each DMU a weighted sum of its outputs using weights of different facets in turn. Take, for example, DMU E in table 3.4, whose observed vector is $(y_1, y_2, x) = (12, 16, 10)$ and target aggregated outputs $(\mathbf{Y'})$ are 4.8 for facet F_1 and 5.538 for facet F_2. As the measure of efficiency in DEA is given by

$$\theta_o = \sum_{r=1}^{s} u_r y_r \bigg/ \sum_{i=1}^{m} v_i x_i,$$

and since we know the facets of the PPS, we can replace the above with

$$\theta = \sum_{r=1}^{s} u_r^* y_r \bigg/ \sum_{i=1}^{m} v_i^* x_i,$$

where we have different optimal values for the weights depending on the PPS facet. Therefore, the efficiency of a DMU under CR is implicitly computed as follows: For different values of θ above, obtained by specifying the weights from different facets, choose the maximum value. Thus, for DMU E the choice would be between 4.8/10 and 5.538/10. The best value is clearly 0.5538, which gives the efficiency score of this unit. (Note that we normalized all the weights by the input weight, and therefore, its optimal value has effectively been set to 1.)

The above example shows that, if we have information regarding the tradeoffs applying at the efficient frontier, we do not need to use DEA to compute efficiency scores since the efficiency score is given generically by

$$\theta^* = \max_{k} \left\{ \frac{\sum_{r=1}^{s} u_r^{*F_k} y_r}{\sum_{i=1}^{m} v_i^{*F_k} x_i} \right\} \quad \text{and by} \quad \theta^* = \max_{k} \left\{ \frac{\sum_{r=1}^{s} u_r^{*F_k} y_r + w^{*F_k}}{\sum_{i=1}^{m} v_i^{*F_k} x_i} \right\}$$

for the CRS case and for the VRS case, respectively. Note that this way of calculating efficiency scores is proposed by Räty (2002), where the author also proposes a procedure for finding the efficient facets of the frontier. Indeed, the main difficulty with this approach is to find the optimal set of weights that define the facets of the efficient frontier. In the above examples, we used the optimal weights resulting from a standard DEA model to define the mathematical expression of the facets that constitute the efficient frontier. This approach works well for lower dimension cases (as is the case for our illustrative example), but for higher dimensions we cannot expect to find the mathematical expressions of the efficient facets through DEA, especially given the problem of multiple optimal solutions. This means that using the CR approach specifying transformation matrices based on the optimal weights assigned by efficient DMUs in an unrestricted model may result in the imposition of arbitrary weights that do not, in fact, correspond to the trade-offs applying at the efficient frontier (see Olesen and Petersen, 2003). In addition, the CR approach specifies input cones and output cones separately. This implies a change in the PPS frontier but does not allow the extension of observed facets since to do this one needs to consider all input and output multipliers on each facet simultaneously [see also Olesen and Petersen (2003), which addresses the issue of separate and linked cones]. If the aim of using CRs is to extend existing facets, one should use a transformation matrix containing the information from input and output optimal weights simultaneously. In this case a matrix W could be specified as

$$
\mathbf{W} = \begin{bmatrix} -v_1^{*F_1} & \cdots & -v_m^{*F_1} & u_1^{*F_1} & \cdots & u_r^{*F_1} \\ \vdots & \ddots & \vdots & \vdots & \ddots & \vdots \\ -v_1^{*F_k} & \cdots & -v_m^{*F_k} & u_1^{*F_k} & \cdots & u_r^{*F_k} \end{bmatrix} = \begin{bmatrix} -\mathbf{A} & \mathbf{B} \end{bmatrix}.
$$

When this matrix is applied to the m observed inputs and the s observed outputs transforms them into k netputs $\mathbf{z} = \mathbf{W} \cdot (\mathbf{X}; \mathbf{Y})$ for each DMU j:

$$
\mathbf{z} = \mathbf{W} \cdot \begin{bmatrix} x_{1j} \\ \vdots \\ x_{mj} \\ y_{1j} \\ \vdots \\ y_{sj} \end{bmatrix} = \begin{bmatrix} -v_1^{*F_1}x_{1j} \ldots - v_m^{*F_1}x_{mj} + u_1^{*F_1}y_{1j} \ldots + u_s^{*F_1}y_{sj} \\ \vdots \\ -v_1^{*F_k}x_{1j} \ldots - v_m^{*Fk}x_{mj} + u_1^{*F_k}y_{1j} \ldots + u_s^{*F_k}y_{sj} \end{bmatrix}
$$

Using these netputs the efficiency score for a DMU could be obtained by solving a DEA model on these netputs, which would take the form of $\min\{ \theta \mid \lambda\mathbf{z} + \theta\mathbf{Ax} \geq \mathbf{By}, \ \lambda \geq 0\}$. The elements of $\mathbf{z}$ are zero when CRS is assumed and equal to w (e.g., see model 3.4 or 3.5) when VRS is assumed. Therefore, the above reduces to choosing the efficiency score θ for each DMU as the maximum value of the weighted outputs to the weighted inputs ($\mathbf{By}/\mathbf{Ax}$) in each facet, as shown above (see Portela and Thanassoulis, 2006, for details).

Data transformations in CRs can be used to extend facets, but also with the purpose of including additional information (e.g., relating to input–output prices) in the model that does not pertain to this aim. In any case, care is needed regarding the use of separate input and output cones or cones that include information relating to the whole facet rather than just a part of it. The main difficulty of using CRs for facet extension purposes is that one needs a good way of identifying the facets. An easy-to-use procedure is the *Qhull* software that is freely available on the Internet.[14] The data required by *Qhull* are the input and output values of the Pareto-efficient units that delineate the efficient frontier. The additive model may be used for identifying these units, and then *Qhull* can be run to provide the facet equations of the efficient frontier. The use of *Qhull* in DEA is detailed in Olesen and Petersen (2003) and was also used in Portela et al. (2003). For details, the reader is referred to Olesen and Petersen (2003), who explain the principles behind the functioning of this software and report some experiments done and the number of full-dimension efficient facets found. They put forth a limit of 25 inputs and outputs and no more than 1,000 Pareto-efficient DMUs. Beyond these dimensions, it would not be possible to find full-dimension efficient facets by *Qhull* or any other of the software mentioned by Olesen and Petersen (2003). Such large numbers of input–output variables and Pareto-efficient units are rarely found, so *Qhull* can handle most real-life problems.

3.7.2.2 Unobserved DMUs

Another way to incorporate value judgments by explicitly changing the production possibilities set is through the addition of unobserved DMUs (UDMUs). The first study to use new DMUs in the reference set was that of Golany and Roll (1994), where "standard" DMUs were introduced in a DEA assessment. Standard DMUs relate to benchmark practices that enlarge the size of the referent set, so that targets for originally efficient DMUs (deemed efficient before standards have been incorporated) can also be imposed. The main difficulty with this approach relates with the establishment of standards. The authors refer to this problem, but no guidelines on how these standards are actually to be generated were provided.

Thanassoulis and Allen (1998) and Allen and Thanassoulis (2004) developed another approach that introduces UDMUs into the reference set. The authors prove the equivalence between this approach and the addition of WRs to the multiplier model.

Consider figure 3.27 of our illustrative example. The mathematical expressions of lines AB and BC are $x = 0.08y_1 + 0.24y_2$ and $x = 0.3385y_1 + 0.0923y_2$, respectively (see table 3.4). Recall that these lines reveal information concerning the relationship between weights, which result in a ratio of weights $u_1/u_2 = 0.333$ for line AB and a ratio of weights $u_1/u_2 = 3.667$ for line BC. This means that when an AR-I restriction $u_1/u_2 \geq 1$ is included in the DEA multiplier model, all the DMUs in the segment AB or those projected on this segment will change their efficiency score because they do not satisfy the marginal rate of transformation implicit in the AR. As we showed above, this implies the assessment of some DMUs in relation to a facet that was not originally observed at the frontier of the PPS. Alternatively, we can see this new facet as being the linear combination of a number of DMUs that were added to the data set. Seeing the introduction of value judgments as the addition of new DMUs can be a powerful method, especially for establishing targets for efficient DMUs in the sense of the standards introduced by Golany and Roll (1994).

Thanassoulis and Allen (1998) have shown that the introduction of an AR-I restriction such as $u_1/u_2 \geq 1$ is equivalent to the addition of a set of DMUs whose input–output levels are equal to the radial targets obtained from the WR model. That is, for our example, the new Pareto-efficient frontier would be constituted by DMUs F′, A′, H′, G′ & I′, B, and C shown in figure 3.32.

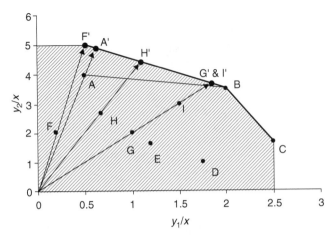

Figure 3.32. Graphical Representation of UDMUs (Thanassoulis et al., 2004)

The ideas illustrated above are developed in Allen and Thanassoulis (2004) into a general-purpose procedure for "improving envelopment" in DEA. The procedure addresses the case where the DMUs operate in a single-input/multioutput CRS context.

The main steps behind the UDMU approach is first identifying Pareto-efficient DMUs and nonenveloped DMUs (DMUs that assign a zero weight to some outputs and are therefore projected on the weakly efficient frontier) and then identifying anchor DMUs (ADMUs) from which UDMUs are constructed. ADMUs are those that delineate the Pareto-efficient part from the Pareto-inefficient part of the frontier (DMUs A and C in figure 3.27). The procedure for identifying ADMUs is based on the superefficiency model of Andersen and Petersen (1993; for details see Thanassoulis and Allen, 1998 or Thanassoulis et al., 2004).

For ADMUs, the approach continues by identifying which outputs to adjust so that suitable UDMUs are constructed. After UDMUs have been added, standard DEA models can be applied to the enlarged data set to obtain efficiency scores. The UDMU approach can determine adjustments in output levels through a mathematical model (see Allen and Thanassoulis, 2004) or through the introduction of the DM's preferences if the DM is able to establish trade-offs between outputs, that is, if the DM can say by how much outputs should increase if a certain output is decreased. Using UDMUs as a means of incorporating value judgments in DEA offers the facility to incorporate local trade-offs between inputs and/or outputs, whereas WRs represent global trade-offs between inputs and/or outputs. Global trade-offs may not hold true, especially in non-CRS technologies where marginal rates of substitution between the factors of production depend on local returns to scale. Another advantage of using UDMUs to incorporate value judgments in DEA is that radial efficiency measures retain their link with targets within the PPS, unlike WRs, as we show below. For a fuller outline of the advantages and drawbacks of using UDMUs to incorporate value judgments in DEA, see Allen and Thanassoulis (2004).

3.7.3 Interpreting results from DEA models with WRs

As we have shown throughout this section, in practice, imposing value judgments on the traditional DEA models implies the transformation of the production frontier. In general, efficiency scores can be seen as radial efficiency scores in relation to the new frontier, [Note, however, that this is only true for ARs, CRs, or the UDMU approach, since for absolute WRs this does not hold (Thanassoulis et al., 2004)], and therefore targets can be calculated on the changed PPS. However, these targets could lie outside the original production possibilities set, meaning that there is no empirical evidence that they can be attained. If, however, trade-offs imposed on the new frontier are deemed acceptable, then one could argue that targets outside the original PPS but based on acceptable trade-offs between factors are, in principle, feasible.

One can, of course, derive targets from restricted DEA models that lie within the original production possibilities set. Such targets are simply those derived in the usual way by using the optimal λ values found in the envelopment model. (I.e., output targets are given by $y_{ro}^* = \sum_{r=1}^s \lambda_j^* y_{rj}$ and input targets are given by $x_{io}^* = \sum_{i=1}^m \lambda_j^* x_{ij}$.) For the CR approach, Brockett et al. (1997b) and Cooper et al. (2000a) take targets resulting from the model used in transformed data (which in some cases will lie in points outside the original PPS frontier) and retransform these targets so that they are meaningful with the original input–output data and lie within the PPS. Targets from restricted models lying on the original PPS frontier will generally be nonradial targets, meaning that these targets imply some changes in the input and/or output mix of the assessed DMU. Moreover, targets derived using WR models lying within the original PPS may also imply the deterioration of some observed input and/or output levels. These features of targets from restricted DEA models are intuitively acceptable. That is, since we now have prior views about the relative worth of inputs and outputs, it is quite acceptable that for a DMU to attain maximum efficiency it may, for example, have to change the mix as well as volumes of its activities. Further, the value judgments incorporated within the model may mean that, by worsening the level of one output, some other output can rise so as to more than compensate for the loss of value due to the worse level on the former output.

As a result of the above, restricted DEA models may also provide DMUs with peers that may offer an input–output mix different from that of the inefficient DMU being assessed. This does not happen in general under unrestricted models, because the peers are those DMUs rated efficient under the weights system of the DMU being assessed. In this sense, peer DMUs and assessed

DMUs have, in general, identical strengths and weaknesses concerning inputs and outputs, meaning that their mix will not be very dissimilar (for details, see Allen et al., 1997; Thanassoulis, 1997). Note that nonradial targets (within the original PPS frontier) may be preferable under restricted models if one is not certain about the trade-offs implicit in the new facets added to the PPS and regard these only as a way of incorporating preferences or value judgments into the assessment. However, if new facets reflect acceptable trade-offs, then there is no reason not to consider targets outside the original PPS as long as the new PPS is seen as a valid one. In this sense, WR models are very similar to some nonradial models introduced in section 3.3 that, as we have shown, also work by changing the original data set against which efficiency is measured radially.

In conclusion to this section, we have outlined several methods that can be used to introduce value judgments in DEA models. We adopt here the perspective of showing the changes implied in the PPS from the imposition of additional constraints. Under this perspective, one can regard WR models as models that add new or extend existing facets to the original frontier. Seeing WR models in this way opens new perspectives for target setting and benchmarking within WR models, since one can allow for projections on the new facets (sometimes outside the original PPS) as long as these represent acceptable trade-offs between inputs and outputs.

3.8 Nondiscretionary Factors

Basic DEA models covered so far in this chapter, when input oriented, implicitly assume that all inputs are discretionary or controllable, and the same implicit assumption holds true for outputs in output-oriented models. However, in many real situations, there can be nondiscretionary or exogenously fixed inputs and/or outputs whatever the orientation of the model, and this should be reflected in the assessments of units.

Nondiscretionary factors can be classified into two types: internal and external. Internal factors are those that, though not controllable, can have trade-offs with other controllable factors (e.g., prior attainment of a child at a school as an input). External factors are those that are noncontrollable but are external to the production process and therefore should not be used in defining the PPS (e.g., population demographics as an input on retailing centers). These two types of nondiscretionary variables are handled in two different ways. Internal variables should feature as input–output variables, but as we show below, the DEA model should be modified so as not to assume that DMUs can make changes to the levels of such variables. In contrast, external nondiscretionary variables should not feature as inputs or outputs. However, they may be used in a post-DEA so-called two-phase assessment, as noted below, to adjust the initial DEA efficiency findings.

We present below three methods to handle nondiscretionary factors using the names coined by Fried et al. (1999): (i) the frontier separation approach,

(ii) the all-in-one approach, and (iii) the two-stage approach. When the nondiscretionary variables are internal, the methods falling in category (ii) are suitable. When the nondiscretionary variables are external, methods in categories (i) and (iii) are suitable.

3.8.1 The Frontier separation approach

The frontier separation approach groups production units according to some criteria (usually categorical) and performs separate efficiency assessments for each one of these groups. The observations in each group are then projected to the efficient boundary of their group, thus, in effect, eliminating artificially managerial inefficiency. An assessment of the pooled projected data is then undertaken in order to isolate any group membership effect on the performance of a unit once its managerial inefficiency has been eliminated as above.

A first application of this approach can be found in Charnes et al. (1981), where schools running under the Follow Through program were compared to those not running under this program. Another example can be found in Portela and Thanassoulis (2001), where the effects of the school and the type of school attended were isolated in assessing pupil attainment.

To illustrate the frontier separation approach, consider figure 3.33, where we assume that there are two types of DMUs, type 1 and type 2 (if DMUs are pupils, then type 1 could be pupils in school 1 and type 2 could be pupils in school 2). Under the frontier separation approach, DMUs belonging to type 1 are assessed within their homogeneous group (consisting only of units of the same type) and DMUs belonging to type 2 are assessed within their own homogeneous group. Thus, DMU A of type 1 in figure 3.33 is assessed in relation to the frontier labeled type 1, and its efficiency relative to B is labeled managerial efficiency, and it is OB/OA. Then A is projected at point B in figure 3.33. This is done for all units of both types in turn. The projected units are then pooled together to arrive at the outer boundary in figure 3.33, which includes the thick solid line. If we now assess point B relative to this boundary of the pooled data, we can isolate the impact of the type to which the DMU belongs on its efficiency. Charnes et al. (1981) called this "program efficiency." Thus, the program efficiency of DMU A is OC/OB.

In the general case, in order to compute program efficiency Charnes et al. (1981) propose replacing the input–output levels of each inefficient DMU by its efficient targets, obtained from the managerial efficiency assessment within its own group, which correct the radial projection illustrated in figure 3.33 for any slacks that there may exist to render it Pareto-efficient. Then, these efficient within-group targets are pooled to a unitary set, and the efficiency of the targets of each unit is assessed within the unitary set. Any inefficiencies identified at this stage are attributable to the policies within which the units operate rather than to their management. This is because the analyst has artificially "eliminated" managerial inefficiencies by adjusting the data of all

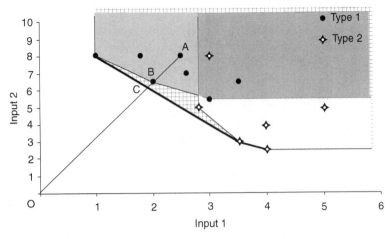

Figure 3.33. Illustration of the Frontier Separation Approach

units to levels efficient within homogeneous groups (for the full technical details of this approach, see Thanassoulis, 2001, chapter 7).

In a variant of the above approach, Portela and Thanassoulis (2001) propose solving for each DMU two DEA models, one within the homogeneous group as above and another within the full set of DMUs. The first model yields the "managerial" or "within-group" efficiency, and the second, the "overall" efficiency of the DMU. Then they apply the decomposition:

Overall efficiency = managerial efficiency × program efficiency.

Thus, we can retrieve program efficiency as the ratio between overall efficiency and within-group efficiency, avoiding the computation of targets within the Charnes et al. approach outlined above. The foregoing decomposition is easily seen in figure 3.33 for DMU A as

Overall efficiency = managerial efficiency × program efficiency.

$$(OC/OA) = (OB/OA) \times (OC/OB)$$

The main difference between the Portela and Thanassoulis (2001) approach and that of Charnes et al. (1981) is that the former compares PPS boundaries while the latter compares only on the efficient parts of those boundaries. Thus, conceptually the Charnes et al. (1981) approach is preferred. However, the Portela and Thanassoulis (2001) approach is slightly less time-consuming because the need to estimate targets and then run models using those targets is eliminated.

Note that the program efficiency in the Portela and Thanassoulis (2001) approach, computed at a DMU, shows the extent to which the frontier of its own group is close to the overall frontier at the input–output mix of the DMU.

This is a program rather than DMU-specific effect. The same comment holds true for the Charnes et al. (1981) approach but with respect to the effect at the mix of inputs–outputs of the targets of the DMU rather than its radial projection to the boundary. If the frontier of homogeneous group 1 envelops that of homogeneous group 2, then the program efficiency of DMUs in group 1 would be always 100%, indicating coincidence between the global frontier and the group 1 frontier. In consequence, the program efficiency of group 2 DMUs would always be less than 100%. This would indicate that group 1 has a more positive impact than does group 2 on the efficiency of DMUs as distinct from that of managers of DMUs. In the more general case, no individual group boundary will envelop in the foregoing manner all others, but rather, there will be a distribution of program efficiency values of 100% or less for the DMUs of each group. Making deductions from these efficiency distributions about program effectiveness requires caution.

Some statistical tests have been used in the literature for comparing program efficiency distributions (e.g., the Mann-Whitney or Kruskal Wallis tests) whose objective is to test the null hypothesis of no difference in efficiency between programs (see, e.g., Brockett and Golany, 1996; Cooper et al., 2000a). However, care is needed with such tests, especially when the sizes of the groups are very different. Indeed, Simpson (2005) showed that the Mann-Whitney test is biased against the smaller programs, and the larger the differences in sample size, the larger the bias. This author proposes a new test that is not sensitive to the size of the groups being compared. Simpson (2007) reviews the methods that have been used to test the existence of program efficiency and concludes that biased results are in general a result of the elimination of managerial inefficiencies [which the Charnes et al. (1981) and the Brockett and Golany (1996) approaches propose] since this process depends on the distribution of efficient DMUs among the programs. The author proposes avoiding this step in testing for differences in program efficiency by assessing units in relation to the pooled frontier and testing whether the inherent hypothesis that programs shared the same frontier is supported by empirical data. This approach is not yet an ideal approach but can yield better results than do existing approaches.

Comparison of different programs can also be made through Malmquist indexes adapted to the situation where different units running under different programs are being compared rather than the same unit in different periods of time. Examples of this type of application can be found in Berg et al. (1993) and Pastor et al. (1997), who compared banks from different countries. First, the banks were assessed in relation to their own country frontier, and later frontiers were compared using Malmquist indices. The Malmquist indices used by these authors make use of an average (or weighted average) DMU (bank) that is used for interfrontier comparisons.

Camanho and Dyson (2006), on the other, hand have proposed the use of Malmquist indices to compare group boundaries without the need to specify any average DMU. Instead, information regarding all DMUs is used in the Malmquist index computation. Thus, let D_{jA}^A be the distance function of DMU j belonging to technology A and assessed in relation to technology A, and D_{jA}^B the distance function of the same unit assessed in relation to technology B. Then, the Malmquist index proposed by Camanho and Dyson (2006) aggregates the various efficiency measures obtained for each DMU j through a geometric average, taking the following form for comparing two groups A and B of DMUs:

$$
I^{AB} = \left(\frac{\left(\prod_{j=1}^{N_A} D_{jA}^A \right)^{1/N_A}}{\left(\prod_{j=1}^{N_B} D_{jB}^A \right)^{1/N_B}} \times \frac{\left(\prod_{j=1}^{N_A} D_{jA}^B \right)^{1/N_A}}{\left(\prod_{j=1}^{N_B} D_{jB}^B \right)^{1/N_B}} \right)^{1/2}
$$

$$
= \frac{\left(\prod_{j=1}^{N_A} D_{jA}^A \right)^{1/N_A}}{\left(\prod_{j=1}^{N_B} D_{jB}^B \right)^{1/N_B}} \times \left(\frac{\left(\prod_{j=1}^{N_A} D_{jA}^B \right)^{1/N_A}}{\left(\prod_{j=1}^{N_A} D_{jA}^A \right)^{1/N_A}} \times \frac{\left(\prod_{j=1}^{N_B} D_{jB}^B \right)^{1/N_B}}{\left(\prod_{j=1}^{N_B} D_{jB}^A \right)^{1/N_B}} \right)^{1/2}
$$

(3.43)

As can be seen in (3.43), this index can be decomposed in the usual way in two components. The ratio of geometric averages

$$
\left(\prod_{j=1}^{N_A} D_{jA}^A \right)^{1/N_A} \Big/ \left(\prod_{j=1}^{N_B} D_{jB}^B \right)^{1/N_B}
$$

compares the efficiency spread of DMUs within their own frontier. The closer DMUs in group B are to their own frontier relative to that of DMUs in group A the larger the ratio. The square root expression multiplying the foregoing ratio of geometric averages measures the distance between the frontiers of groups A and B. The information derived from the Malmquist type index in (3.43) for comparing groups of DMUs can therefore provide more information than the traditional techniques where program efficiency is computed and then aggregated in some way to give an idea regarding how programs/policies compare among themselves. Note that the above index can be used for comparing more than two groups, as explained in Camanho and Dyson (2006).

The frontier separation approach is appropriate for dealing with nondiscretionary factors (e.g., the type of school or the location type of a bank branch) that are qualitative or categorical variables. In this sense, the approach developed by Banker and Morey (1986a) for dealing with categorical variables can also be included under frontier separation methods. This approach consists of introducing a set of dummy variables concerning the categorical factor so that units belonging to a given group can be compared only with units in less favorable groups than the unit being assessed. In this sense, we can visualize a set of frontiers that are building up. That is, each new frontier includes all the members from the other, less favorable, groups. DMUs in the least favorable group (e.g., category 1) are only compared with units in the same group, but units in category 2 are compared with DMUs in categories 1 and 2, and so on (see also Charnes et al. 1994, pp. 51–54). This procedure can, according to Banker and Morey (1986a), also be used when nondiscretionary factors are continuous variables, because any continuous variable can be transformed to a categorical variable. Some improvements in the Banker and Morey (1986a) approach can be found in Kamakura (1988) and Rousseau and Semple (1993).

There are at least two disadvantages in the frontier separation approach. First, it may imply the various categories to be ordered hierarchically, which is not always natural (Førsund, 2001). Second, when there are several criteria, the homogeneous groups of DMUs may be very small. Because the power of discrimination of DEA depends on the number of DMUs relative to the number of input–output variables considered in the assessment, the smaller the group, the lower the discrimination on performance between production units achieved by DEA. Staat (1999) (and Simpson, 2005) refers also to the problem associated with differing sample sizes across groups (see also Zhang and Bartels, 1998, on this subject) and to the problem of comparability between the resulting efficiency scores. Indeed, when production units are grouped according to some criteria, only efficiency rankings inside the same group can be meaningfully compared.

3.8.2 The all-in-one approach

When the nondiscretionary factors are continuous variables, such as mean income in the demographic area of the DMU or entry levels of pupils in a school, the all-in-one approach may be suitable. This is particularly so when one concludes that the nondiscretionary variables are internal to the production process and should be allowed to define the PPS. Note that, in this case, one should be aware that input-oriented DEA models implicitly treat outputs as nondiscretionary and that output-oriented DEA models implicitly treat inputs as nondiscretionary or noncontrollable. In view of this, we need special DEA models to cope with cases where one wants to focus on input reductions but some inputs are noncontrollable, or in contexts where one wants to focus on output expansions but some outputs are noncontrollable.

The best-known procedure within this general approach is that developed by Banker and Morey (1986b). The proposed DEA model, in its envelopment VRS form, consists of associating the expansion (contraction) factor of the DEA model solved only with discretionary outputs (inputs), and maximizing the sum of the slacks associated only with the discretionary factors. The resulting *first phase* VRS DEA model for an input-oriented model, where D is the set of discretionary inputs and ND is the set of nondiscretionary inputs, is

$$
\text{Min} \left\{ \theta_o \;\middle|\;
\begin{array}{ll}
\sum_{j=1}^{n} \lambda_j y_{rj} \geq y_{ro}, \quad r = 1, \ldots, s, & \sum_{j=1}^{n} \lambda_j x_{ij} \leq \theta_o x_{io}, \quad i \in D \\
\sum_{j=1}^{n} \lambda_j x_{ij} \leq x_{io}, \quad i \in \text{ND}, & \sum_{j=1}^{n} \lambda_j = 1, \quad \lambda_j \geq 0
\end{array}
\right\}.
$$

(3.44)

For CRS technologies the method proposed by Banker and Morey (1986b) changes the traditional CRS model as shown in (3.45) for the input-oriented case:

$$
\text{Min} \left\{ \theta_o \;\middle|\;
\begin{array}{ll}
\sum_{j=1}^{n} \lambda_j y_{rj} \geq y_{ro}, \quad r = 1, \ldots, s, & \sum_{j=1}^{n} \lambda_j x_{ij} \leq \theta_o x_{io}, \quad i \in D \\
\sum_{j=1}^{n} \lambda_j x_{ij} \leq \sum_{j=1}^{n} \lambda_j x_{io}, \quad i \in \text{ND}, & \lambda_j \geq 0
\end{array}
\right\}.
$$

(3.45)

Note that the constraint associated with nondiscretionary inputs in (3.45) means that the nondiscretionary inputs are not scaled up or down within the referent DMU but are merely restricted not to exceed the nondiscretionary input level, because we have

$$
\left(\sum_{j=1}^{n} \lambda_j x_{ij} \middle/ \sum_{j=1}^{n} \lambda_j \right) \leq x_{io}, \quad \forall i \in \text{ND}.
$$

This is intuitively correct as the DMU cannot change the level of nondiscretionary variables to exploit returns to scale.[15]

Some criticisms of the Banker and Morey (1986b) model can be found in Ruggiero (1996, 1998), where the author advocates that the Banker and Morey (1986b) model does not properly restrict the reference set. According to (Ruggiero, 1998), the imposition of convexity on the nondiscretionary factors "leads to improper restriction of the PPS and distorted efficiency measurement" (p. 463). Another criticism of the Banker and Morey (1986b) model concerns the fact that targets may be constructed from any set of units (which is a direct result of assuming convexity for all factors, including the nondiscretionary factors). That is, a DMU in a "medium" environment may have as peers units in a "good" environment and DMUs in a "bad" environment. One way to avoid this is to consider in the reference set only DMUs with environmental conditions that are the same or worse than those of the DMU being assessed. This is the approach proposed by Ruggiero (1996). [See also Staat (1999), which we detail later in this section.]

Muñiz (2002) also criticizes the Banker and Morey (1986b) approach, pointing out that the resulting frontier is exactly the same as it would be if the nondiscretionary factors were considered controllable. As a result, the environmental conditions have no influence on the efficiency status of production units, and only those that are inefficient are actually penalized by the consideration of some factors as being nondiscretionary. Note, however, that this criticism is valid only for the VRS production technology and not for the CRS technology. In addition, behind this criticism is a comparison between including nondiscretionary factors as controllable or noncontrollable in a DEA model. However, choosing between the alternatives of including or not including the nondiscretionary variables when defining the PPS their inclusion can only improve the efficiency scores of units, and therefore considering nondiscretionary variables in the construction of the PPS favors DMUs (particularly in bad environments where the value of the nondiscretionary variables, when used as inputs, is lower; see Lozano-Vivas et al., 2002).

In order to explore the foregoing issues, consider the illustrative example in figure 3.34 (from Vaz, 2006), where input 1 is discretionary and input 2 is nondiscretionary (we assume that a higher value for this input is associated with more favorable environmental conditions). The CRS representation of the technology, where both inputs are normalized by the output is also shown. The results from the traditional CRS and VRS models where no factors are considered nondiscretionary and the results from the Banker and Morey (1986b) models where input 2 is considered nondiscretionary, are shown in table 3.9.

Note that, for the VRS case, all DMUs that were initially Pareto-efficient are also so in the Banker and Morey (1986b) model. Two DMUs, F and H, were initially weakly efficient (in the discretionary input) in relation to E and C, respectively, as can be easily seen in the raw data shown in figure 3.34. That is why their efficiency dropped from 100% to 75% when input 2 was considered nondiscretionary. By maintaining the convexity assumption for the nondiscretionary inputs, the Banker and Morey (1986b) VRS model implies no change in the Pareto-efficient frontier, and the efficiency scores of the inefficient units deteriorate in this model, which considers inputs as nondiscretionary (as claimed in Muñiz, 2002). For the CRS case, however,

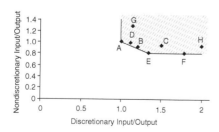

DMU	x_1(D)	x_2(ND)	y
A	8	8	8
B	6	4.6	5
C	3	1.9	2
D	10	9	9
E	6	3.6	4.5
F	8	3.6	4.5
G	8	9	7
H	4	1.9	2

Figure 3.34. Illustrative Example (Vaz, 2006)

Table 3.9
Results for Illustrative Example

	All Discretionary		Considering x_2ND	
	CRS	VRS	CRS	VRS
A	100.00%	100.00%	100.00%	100.00%
B	97.56%	98.92%	93.31%	98.02%
C	86.49%	100.00%	100.00%	100.00%
D	96.00%	100.00%	90.00%	100.00%
E	100.00%	100.00%	89.73%	100.00%
F	100.00%	100.00%	67.30%	75.00%
G	87.50%	89.58%	87.50%	89.58%
H	84.21%	100.00%	75.00%	75.00%

this is not so, since the efficient frontier in fact changes with some DMUs, changing from inefficient to efficient (e.g., C), and others lose their efficiency status (e.g., E) due to the consideration of input 2 as nondiscretionary. The changes in the frontier can be seen graphically in figure 3.35 if for each DMU we consider a new variable (given by the difference $x_{2j} - x_{2o}$). Therefore, for DMUs C and E, for example, the CRS efficiency frontiers when input 2 is taken as nondiscretionary are as in figure 3.35.

The DMUs defining the new frontier are always the same for all assessments, where DMUs A and C are shaping that frontier, but values of the new variable ($x_{2j} - x_{2o}$) are different for each DMU. There are also possibly some negative values for the new variable, but these should not pose any serious problems to the assessment since the radial contraction factor is not linked with the new variable. Note that DMUs being assessed always have the value of the new variable ($x_{ij} - x_{io}$) equal to zero. Therefore, the peer units of the assessed DMU can present the nondiscretionary factor either above (and the new variable positive) or below (and the new variable negative) its observed levels.

Note that the efficiency measures resulting from the Banker and Morey (1986b) approach are not radial measures. For example, assessing DMU E

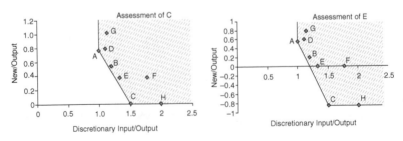

Figure 3.35. Frontiers for Assessing DMU C and E

in figure 3.35 implies a horizontal movement from this DMU level of discretionary input–output (6/4.5) to the discretionary input level of the linear combination of DMUs A and C (A consuming more of the nondiscretionary input and therefore with $x_{2A} - x_{2E}$ greater than zero, and C consuming less of the nondiscretionary input and therefore with $x_{2C} - x_{2E}$ lower than zero).[16]

In summary, the Banker and Morey (1986b) approach changes the CRS frontier to account for the fact that the nondiscretionary variable is not scalable but does not change the VRS frontier. This means, for the VRS case, that convexity and free disposability assumptions apply equally to the discretionary and nondiscretionary factors. This may be a reasonable assumption in cases where the nondiscretionary input factor is, for example, attainment level of pupils at the beginning of a stage of education, or may be a wrong assumption if the nondiscretionary input factor is the total population served by a retail store. Therefore, the above criticisms to the Banker and Morey approach result, in general, from a misapplication to the method in situations where it should not have been applied rather than to intrinsic problems of the method. Note that Golany and Roll (1993) extended the work of Banker and Morey (1986b) by addressing the question of simultaneous nondiscretionary inputs and outputs and also partially nondiscretionary factors.

3.8.3 The two-stage approach

A different approach to handle nondiscretionary factors was introduced by Ray (1988) and further developed in Ray (1991). According to this approach, nondiscretionary or environmental factors should not be included in a DEA assessment. A DEA assessment should include only controllable factors, and then in a second phase, a regression model should be used to estimate the part of efficiency that is explained by uncontrollable factors. The difference between the efficiency score estimated through the regression model and the efficiency score obtained from the DEA analysis is interpreted by Ray (1991, p. 1627) as the extent of managerial inefficiency not caused by external factors. That is, inefficiency is calculated as the shortfall of the DEA efficiency score from the estimated efficiency score and not from 1. As pointed out by Ruggiero (1998), this approach requires the specification of a functional form to the regression model, meaning that a misspecification may distort the results (see also McCarty and Yaisawarng, 1993).

One problem of the two-stage approach relates to the possible correlation between the input–output factors used to calculate the DEA efficiency scores and the independent variables used in the regression model (see Grosskopf, 1996). Another problem is the dependency problem. That is, the DEA efficiency scores are dependent on each other, which "violates a basic assumption required by regression analysis: the assumption of independence within the sample" (Xue and Harker, 1999, p. 3).

Note that two-stage models have been "improved" since Ray (1991) to consider in the second-stage tobit models[17] rather than traditional regression models to account for the fact that the dependent variable (the efficiency score) is bounded between 0 and 1.[18] The use of tobit models cannot resolve, however, the dependency problem mentioned above, and therefore, they are, according to Simar and Wilson (2007), invalid. The reader can find further details on this issue in chapter 4 of this book, where bootstrapping techniques are used on the second-stage analysis.

3.8.4 Other approaches for dealing with nondiscretionary variables

Apart from the methods mentioned hitherto to deal with nondiscretionary factors, there are other alternatives that have been proposed in the literature. In order to circumvent the problems of the Banker and Morey (1986b) VRS model, Ruggiero (1996) proposes solving a DEA model restricting the reference set for each DMU being evaluated to DMUs presenting only more disadvantaged conditions in terms of the nondiscretionary factor. This is equivalent to what Banker and Morey (1986a) proposed for dealing with categorical variables and reduces to a model of the following form (input-oriented and VRS technology):

$$
\min \left\{ \theta_o \,\middle|\,
\begin{array}{l}
\displaystyle\sum_{j=1}^{n} \lambda_j y_{rj} \geq y_{ro}, \quad r = 1,\dots,s, \quad \sum_{j=1}^{n} \lambda_j x_{ij} \leq \theta_o x_{io}, \quad i \in D \\[2mm]
\text{for } \lambda_j > 0, \quad x_{ij} \leq x_{io}, \quad i \in ND, \quad \displaystyle\sum_{j=1}^{n} \lambda_j = 1, \quad \lambda_j \geq 0
\end{array}
\right\}
$$

(3.46)

This model in practice does not impose the convexity assumption on the nondiscretionary inputs, and therefore, the resulting frontier is completely different from the types of frontiers we show in section 3.2. In fact, the production technology in this case exhibits what Podinovski (2005) has called selective convexity (a case where convexity is not imposed on all inputs and outputs), which mixes the traditional VRS technologies with FDH technologies.

We can look at the above model also as one that assesses the efficiency of each production unit in relation to a traditional VRS frontier (defined based on discretionary variables only), where this frontier changes depending on the DMU being assessed (since for each DMU the referents are only those presenting worst or equal environmental conditions). To see this, consider table 3.10, which shows the results of Ruggiero's model applied to our illustrative example, and figure 3.36, which shows the different VRS frontiers against which efficiency was measured. Note that the nondiscretionary factor cannot be part of the axis in figure 3.36 since it is not defining the efficient frontier. The nondiscretionary factor is simply implying different frontiers for each DMU being assessed.

Table 3.10
Results from Model (3.46) Applied to the Illustrative Example

	CRS		VRS	
DMU	Efficiency	Peers	Efficiency	Peers
A	100.0%	$\lambda_A = 1$	100.0%	$\lambda_A = 1$
B	100.0%	$\lambda_B = 1$	100.0%	$\lambda_B = 1$
C	100.0%	$\lambda_C = 1$	100.0%	$\lambda_C = 1$
D	90.0%	$\lambda_A = 1.125$	100.0%	$\lambda_D = 1$
E	100.0%	$\lambda_E = 1$	100.0%	$\lambda_E = 1$
F	75.0%	$\lambda_E = 1$	75.0%	$\lambda_E = 1$
G	87.5%	$\lambda_A = 0.875$	89.6%	$\lambda_A = 0.83, \lambda_C = 0.17$
H	75.0%	$\lambda_C = 1$	75.0%	$\lambda_C = 1$

The Ruggiero model implicitly models nondiscretionary variables as external to the production process, since the different frontiers are defined only on discretionary factors. For the VRS case, the only difference between this approach and the Banker and Morey (1986b) approach for our illustrative example is the consideration of DMU B as efficient. This happens because this DMU (lying on frontier 3 in figure 3.36) is now compared with a restricted group of DMUs exhibiting the same or worse environmental conditions (C, E, F, and H), while before DMU A, having better environmental conditions, was one of the peers of DMU B. Note that classifying unit B as efficient may be a wrong classification if the nondiscretionary variable should define the PPS, but it may be the right classification if the environmental variables should not define the PPS. To see this, compare DMU B to DMU E. DMU E input and outputs are $(y, x, ND) = (4.5, 6, 3.6)$ and DMU B inputs and outputs are $(y, x, ND) = (5, 6, 4.6)$. So DMU E, in a worse environment, uses the same amount of discretionary input to produce almost the same amount of output as the DMU in the more favorable environment. Note that if DMU B and

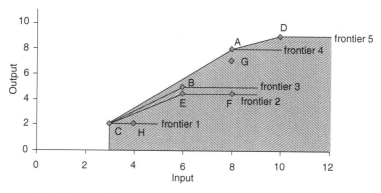

Figure 3.36. Different VRS Frontiers in Ruggerio's Model for Different DMUs

E had exactly the same amount of output (they would be the same point in figure 3.36), DMU B would still be classified as efficient (though in this case we would have a multiple solution—that where the peer unit for B would be itself and another where the peer would be unit E). This would be intuitively correct if we cannot estimate the impact of the ND factor on efficiency and therefore cannot say that unit B having a better environment should produce more output or use less input, but would be wrong if the ND variable should be defining the PPS since in this case unit B would be inefficient in relation to E.

For the CRS case, there are larger differences, since in the Banker and Morey (1986b) approach only DMUs A and C were efficient, while under the Ruggiero (1996) approach DMUs A, B, C, and E are CRS efficient. DMUs B and E become CRS efficient under the Ruggiero approach due to the smaller reference sets against which they are compared that allowed these two DMUs to be ranked fully efficient.

Note that as the number of nondiscretionary factors increases, the probability of a unit being rated efficient in model (3.46) also increases. In addition, with multiple nondiscretionary variables, the model of Ruggiero (1996) ignores possible trade-offs between these variables (see Muñiz et al., 2006). Recognizing these problems, Ruggiero (1998) proposed to change the above model, linking it with the approach of Ray (1991), where nondiscretionary factors are considered in a weighted "index" that assigns different importance to the various factors according to the results of a regression analysis. The aggregate environmental variable resulting from this approach is $z = \sum_i \beta_i z_i$, where β_i values are the regression coefficients and z_i values are the nondiscretionary variables. This model uses the regression only to calculate the weights to assign to the environmental factors and not to calculate an adjusted measure of efficiency. This means, according to Ruggiero (1998), that no distributional assumptions are made regarding efficiency. The final model that incorporates through z the effect of multiple environmental factors is given by

$$\text{Min} \left\{ \theta_o \;\middle|\; \begin{array}{l} \sum\limits_{j=1}^{n} \lambda_j y_{rj} \geq y_{ro}, \quad r = 1, ..., s, \quad \sum\limits_{j=1}^{n} \lambda_j x_{ij} \leq \theta_o x_{io}, \quad i \in D \\ \lambda_j = 0, \;\; \text{if } z_j \geq z_o, \quad \sum\limits_{j=1}^{n} \lambda_j = 1, \;\; \lambda_j \geq 0 \end{array} \right\}.$$

$$(3.47)$$

Another multistage model introduced by Fried et al. (1999) deals with environmental factors in four stages. The first phase consists of solving a basic DEA model (input-oriented) without environmental factors. In a second-stage m regression equations are estimated for each input, where the dependent variable is, in each equation, the total amount of input slack (radial plus nonradial slack) and the independent variables are environmental. In a third phase, the actual input levels are adjusted by a factor that equals the difference between the maximum predicted slack minus the predicted slack value. In a final stage, these adjusted values are included in a basic DEA model whose results take environmental factors into account. According to Fried et al. (1999), this procedure has the advantage of accounting for all sources of inefficiency as it regresses slacks (through a tobit model) on environmental factors instead of radial efficiency scores. In addition, it also has the advantage of not requiring a prespecification of environmental factors as inputs or outputs [which is required, e.g., in an all-in-one approach; see also Fried et al. (2002) and Muñiz (2002), which propose some changes to the Fried et al. (1999) approach]. The approach of Fried et al. (1999) outlined above assumes input-oriented models. In principle, this approach would also be valid for output-oriented models or even nonoriented models with required adjustments.

In summary, there are several approaches in the literature for dealing with nondiscretionary variables, but this is definitely an area where there is not much consensus among researchers. The largely unresolved issue is how to identify nondiscretionary variables that can be deemed internal and therefore taken on board when constructing the PPS, as opposed to being deemed external and therefore taken on board after the assessment using the PPS. Once this identification is made, there are still a variety of proposals, as we showed, regarding how to deal with internal or external nondiscretionary variables. See also chapter 4 of this book for more details on the issue of nondiscretionary variables (section 4.6). Every method has its own advantages and drawbacks depending on the features of the situation in which it is applied.

3.9 Target Setting and Benchmarking

One of the key outcomes in an efficiency assessment is the identification of targets and efficient peers. In practical applications, nonspecialists find the identification of efficient peers especially useful for gaining an intuitive feeling for the comparative efficiency results yielded by DEA. This is done by a straightforward comparison of the inefficient DMU with its peers. Setting the target input and/or output levels that would render an inefficient DMU efficient is closely connected with benchmarking, which can be defined as the process of comparing the performance of one unit against that of "best practice" units. Within the DEA framework, where the "best practice" units define the frontier of the PPS T, benchmarking is equivalently defined as the process of comparing the performance of a DMU to the frontier of T. Since in the very nature of the DEA mechanism is a comparison of observed producers to each other, it seems logical to expect that DEA is particularly suitable for target settings and benchmarking.

In using DEA for benchmarking, important issues need to be considered from both the theoretical and, even more so, the practical perspective. In section 3.3, we briefly touch upon the target levels derived from some traditional DEA models. There, we recognize the problem that radial projections of DMUs to the boundary of the PPS may not necessarily be Pareto-efficient and state that one of the main reasons for specifying various nonradial measures of efficiency is in fact to ensure that the identified targets lie on the

Pareto-efficient subset of the frontier. From a practical perspective, targets, even when Pareto-efficient, still may not be suitable. Management may find them not in line with its own preferences, unrealistic, or even unattainable due to some external conditions. In this section, we present DEA models that address practical issues of this kind.

Nonradial DEA models, as discussed in section 3.3, are the main instruments for resolving theoretical issues surrounding target setting and benchmarking. The material covered in the preceding section, where we discuss nondiscretionary variables, also need to be taken into account if we want the resulting targets to be achievable in practice. In addition, to make the resulting targets also realistic and in line with the DMU's own ideas of the preferred improvement paths, it will be necessary to revisit subjectivity once again. Thus, besides the issue of incorporating value judgments into DEA models, covered in section 3.7, setting sound targets and realistic benchmarking is another reason for incorporating user preference information in DEA models. Most of the research with respect to identifying targets and benchmarking in DEA has revolved around flexible and interactive preference modeling. We say more about the advances in the area later in this section. Right now, we first address some of the basic concepts when identifying efficient targets and peers within some of the classical DEA models.

3.9.1 Radial targets and efficient peers

Finding efficient targets and reference units using radial DEA models is briefly discussed in section 3.3. Here, we give a more detailed exposition covering also the most important practical aspects of the results obtained. To explain the main principles, we also limit ourselves to the most representative radial model introduced by Charnes et al. (1978). In the beginning of section 3.3, we introduce the two generalized forms of this model (3.1) and (3.2), which correspond to the envelopment form of the input- and output-oriented CRS model respectively. For the sake of convenience, here we give a single-stage theoretical formulation of an input-oriented CCR model in its envelopment and in its multiplier form:

$$\text{Min} \left\{ \theta_o - \varepsilon \left(\sum_{r=1}^{s} s_r^+ + \sum_{i=1}^{m} s_i^- \right) \left| \begin{array}{l} \sum_{j=1}^{n} \lambda_j x_{ij} + s_i^- = \theta_o x_{io}, \quad i = 1,\ldots.m, \\[2mm] \sum_{j=1}^{n} \lambda_j y_{rj} - s_r^+ = y_{ro}, \quad r = 1,\ldots,s, \\[2mm] \lambda_j, s_r^+, s_i^- \geq 0 \end{array} \right. \right\}$$

$$(3.48)$$

$$\text{Max} \left\{ h_o = \sum_{r=1}^{s} u_r y_{ro} \quad \middle| \quad \begin{array}{l} -\sum_{i=1}^{m} v_i x_{ij} + \sum_{r=1}^{s} u_r y_{rj} \leq 0, \quad j = 1, \ldots n \\[2mm] \sum_{i=1}^{m} v_i x_{ij} = 1, \quad\quad u_r, v_i \geq \varepsilon \end{array} \right\}$$

$$(3.49)$$

Irrespective of whether we use input- or output-oriented DEA models, information about targets and efficient peers can be directly obtained from the envelopment form of the DEA models, such as the one shown in (3.48).

3.9.1.1 Radial targets

Consider the solution of model (3.48) to assess the technical input efficiency of DMU_o. Using the superscript * to denote the optimal values of variables in that model, a set of efficient input–output levels (x_{io}^t, y_{ro}^t) is

$$x_{io}^t = \sum_{j=1}^{n} \lambda_j^* x_{ij} = \theta_o^* x_{io} - s_i^{-*} \quad\quad i = 1, \ldots, m$$

$$y_{ro}^t = \sum_{j=1}^{n} \lambda_j^* y_{rj} = y_{ro} + s_r^{+*} \quad\quad r = 1, \ldots, s. \tag{3.50}$$

Mathematically, the input–output levels (x_{io}^t, y_{ro}^t) defined in (3.50) are the coordinates of the point on the efficient frontier used as a benchmark for evaluating DMU_o. A practical interpretation of (x_{io}^t, y_{ro}^t) is that it constitutes a virtual DMU whose performance DMU_o should, in principle, be capable of attaining. The proof that the input–output levels in (3.50) would render DMU_o Pareto-efficient can be found in Cooper et al. (2000a). These levels are often referred to as a projection point of DMU_o on the efficient boundary or simply as targets for DMU_o.

When a DMU is Pareto-inefficient, the input–output levels in (3.50) can be used as the basis for setting its targets so that it can improve its performance. There are generally infinite input–output level combinations that would render any given DMU Pareto-efficient. The specific combination in (3.50) corresponds to giving preemptive priority to the radial contraction of the input levels of DMU_o without lowering any one of its output levels. This means that the targets in (3.50) preserve in large measure the *mix* of inputs and outputs of DMU_o, though if any slack values are positive, the mix of the target input–output levels differs from that of DMU_o. The preservation of the input–output mix in target setting has some advantages. The mix typically reflects a combination of operating choices (e.g., the relative levels of labor and automation) and uncontrollable factors (e.g., the types of crime dealt with by a police force). Setting inefficient DMU targets that preserve in large measure their own mix of inputs and outputs makes it easier for the DMU to accept them and attempt to attain them. This is because the targets will reflect in large measure the DMU's own operating priorities, history, and environment. By the same token, however, by their very nature, the targets in (3.50) will not be suitable in contexts where the aim is to encourage certain inefficient DMUs to alter operating priorities and/or move to new environments. In these circumstances, we are more interested in identifying more appropriate nonradial target levels, which are considered further below.

The efficient target levels from the output maximizing DEA model, such as that shown in model (3.25), are obtained in a similar way. The model identifies with respect to DMU$_o$ a set of Pareto-efficient input–output levels (x_{io}^t, y_{ro}^t) where

$$x_{io}^t = \sum_{j=1}^{n} \lambda_j^* x_{ij} = x_{io} - s_i^{-*} \qquad i = 1, \ldots, m,$$

$$y_{ro}^t = \sum_{j=1}^{n} \lambda_j^* y_{rj} = \beta_o^* y_{ro} + s_r^{+*} \qquad r = 1, \ldots, s. \tag{3.51}$$

The key difference between the target levels in (3.50) and (3.51) is that those in (3.51) are arrived at by giving preemptive priority to the radial expansion of the output levels of DMU$_o$ without raising any one of its input levels. When radial expansion of outputs is complete, the targets exploit further reductions in individual input and/or rises in individual output levels that are feasible at the radially expanded output levels. Such individual input savings and/or output augmentations are reflected in the slack values s_i^{-*} and s_r^{+*}.

Clearly, the targets in (3.50) would be more suitable in cases where in the short-term input levels are controllable while output levels are not. The targets in (3.51) are more suitable when the opposite is the case. Often, in practice, some of the inputs and some of the outputs are controllable while others are not. For those cases, specially adapted DEA models have been developed, most of which were discussed in section 3.8. Here, we simply note that if we use, say, the targets in (3.50) in a case where outputs are uncontrollable, any output augmentations indicated in the targets can still be meaningful. Take, for example, water distribution, where inputs may be various types of expenditure while the outputs may include the length of main used, an uncontrollable output (at least in the short term). Then, any augmentation to the length of main within the targets in (3.50) can be interpreted as saying that even if length of main were to increase (e.g., through extensions to new housing estates) to the level indicated in the targets, the radially contracted input (expenditure level) should still be sufficient.

3.9.1.2 Efficient peers

We can readily identify the efficient peers to a DMU whether we use envelopment or a multiplier DEA model. The two models bring to the fore different aspects of the significance of a peer. Let us first consider the envelopment model (3.48). Using * again to denote the optimal values of the corresponding variables in that model, the efficient peers or efficient referents to DMU_o are those DMUs that correspond to positive λ values.

We can see the practical significance of the efficient peers now if we look again at the targets in (3.50), which model (3.48) yields for DMU_o. It is clear that the target level for DMU_o on a given input is a linear combination of the levels of that input at its efficient peers. The same is true of the target level on each output for DMU_o. Further, it is easy to deduce from (3.48) that the efficiency rating θ_o^* of DMU_o is the maximum of the ratios x_{io}^t/x_{io} $(i = 1, \ldots, m)$. Thus, the target input–output levels of DMU_o and its efficiency rating are exclusively dependent on the observed input–output levels of its efficient peers and on no other DMUs. Recall that different priorities on input–output improvements (and, indeed, other DEA models covered in section 3.8) will lead generally to different efficient peers.

Consider now using one of the multiplier DEA models, say (3.49), to assess DMU_o. Its efficient peers are the DMUs corresponding to constraints that are binding at its optimal solution. These are, of course, the same efficient peers as would be identified had model (3.48) been used to assess DMU_o instead. This can be shown to be true by recourse to the duality between models (3.48) and (3.49), covered in most textbooks on linear programming.

One of the features of the DEA weights is that they represent imputed input–output values that are DMU specific, chosen to maximize the efficiency rating of DMU_o. Thus, the optimal DEA weights of model (3.49) favor the mix of input–output levels of DMU_o, and since they render its peers efficient, the latter must have similar mixes of input–output levels to DMU_o. Here, the term "mix of input–output levels" refers to the ratios of the input–output levels of a DMU to each other. Thus, the efficient peers have a mix of input–output levels that are "similar" (if not identical) to that of DMU_o but at more efficient absolute levels. That is, its efficient peers generally will have lower input relative to output levels than does DMU_o.

In sum, the features of efficient peers we have identified make them very useful in practice as role models that DMU_o can emulate so that it may improve its performance. They are efficient, and given that they have a mix of input–output levels similar to that of DMU_o, they are likely to operate in similar environments and/or to favor similar operating practices to DMU_o.

3.9.1.3 Benchmarking reports

Due to the importance of the benchmarking results from a practical perspective, presenting the relevant findings to the managers and the units assessed deserves special attention. In fact, most of the traditional DEA-based efficiency reports are largely based on the results concerning target settings and efficient peer identification. As described in Thanassoulis (2001), the information most readily obtainable from a DEA analysis is the following:

(i) A measure of the efficiency of the DMU
(ii) Where the DMU is Pareto-efficient: getting a view on the scope for the DMU to be a role model for other DMUs
(iii) Where the DMU is Pareto-inefficient: identifying efficient DMUs whose operating practices it may attempt to emulate to improve its performance, and estimating target input–output levels that the DMU should in principle be capable of attaining under efficient operation

Clearly, besides the efficiency score, target settings and peer identification are largely the purpose of the DEA analysis. In practical applications, nonspecialists find the identification of efficient peers especially useful for gaining an intuitive feeling for the comparative efficiency results yielded by DEA. To facilitate this understanding, the relevant results should be presented in a highly informative yet in a clear and succinct way. Typically, various types of graphs, bar charts, and well-designed tables are utilized for this purpose.

Figure 3.37 illustrates a graphical manner for presenting a report for some inefficient DMU. To put it into the context, the report relates to the input-oriented DEA model of the central administrative services (CAS) of higher education institutions in the United Kingdom. CAS staff cost is the only input, and the four outputs are O1 = total income from students; O2 = nonadministrative staff cost; O3 = income from consultancy and other services, labeled "technology transfer"; and O4 = research income (QR). A particular university I-14 is found to be inefficient, and its efficient peers were identified to be I-15, I-17, and I-9. I-14 is hence compared with each of these peers in turn through the corresponding radar charts and tables showing normalized input–output levels in figure 3.37. The last radar chart and the table beneath it compare I-14 with its efficiency target as defined through a linear combination of its three efficient peers. Such a linear combination provides the target levels for I-14 that would render it efficient.

To read the radar charts, let us examine the upper right one comparing I-14 with I-15. The shaded area reflecting I-15 indicates that its input is less than half that of I-14, which stands at the level 10. Yet on two of the outputs, O1 and O4, I-15 performs better than I-14, and it comes close to attaining the performance of I-14 on output O3. Only in output O2 does I-14 perform better than I-15, but this is clearly not enough to compensate for its weaker performance elsewhere compared to I-15. On balance, this suggests that I-15 performs better than I-14. The remaining radar plots can be read in a similar way.

3.9.2 Theoretical extensions to target settings and benchmarking

To focus on benchmark selection in relation to efficiency measurement is a relatively recent project (Hougaard and Tvede, 2002). DEA-related research was and perhaps still is mainly oriented toward devising sound, more flexible,

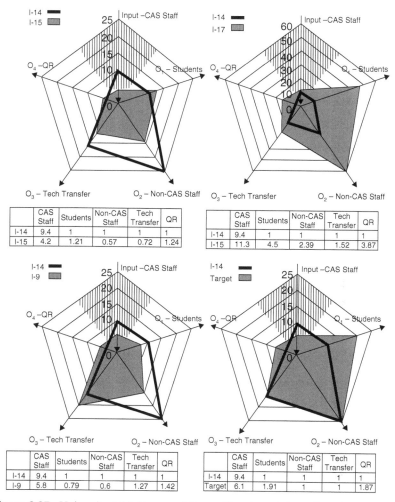

Figure 3.37. University I-14: Peers and Target (Benchmark Spend) with Respect to CAS Staff

and more appropriate mathematical models that could aptly identify the best performers in a variety of settings. In fact, the material covered so far in this chapter has been almost exclusively focused in this direction. From the benchmarking process perspective, setting appropriate targets and benchmarking goals, after the best performers are identified, is quite a natural next step. However, using DEA to focus on this step does reverse its basic philosophical orientation—from its standard ex post evaluation stance to become an ex ante planning tool.

Even though it is not the main research direction in DEA, the research on setting targets and benchmarking using DEA is reasonably rich, and as such, it greatly contributes to making the DEA a viable tool for supporting a benchmarking process. The ability of DEA to suggest to the DMUs meaningful ways to improve their current practices makes it also a well-rounded performance management tool. Performance measurement and interpretations of such measurements are some of the key components of the performance management system, where the DEA can be well utilized. Still, a complete performance management system should also include the instruments to encourage appropriate organizational responses to performance information. From the DEA perspective, this response stage is closely related to the appropriate identification of targets and setting meaningful benchmarking goals. It has been recognized that this behavioral aspect of performance management is the weakest link not only for DEA but also for any other performance management tool (Smith and Godard, 2002). Gaining on its maturity, however, DEA-based research is slowly shifting its attention toward these later stages of performance management.

In this section, we first explore some theoretical advances in DEA, where more appropriate projections of an inefficient DMU onto the efficient frontier are being sought. A common denominator for the models presented in this section is their attempt to make the analytical results more sound and ready to apply in practice without any further ado. Different theoretical extensions to create better DEA models for target setting were inspired by different issues, the most common of which we use to categorize different models into the corresponding subsections in the text below. Target-setting models that are utilizing various types of information that can be obtained from the experts (DMs) are presented further below.

3.9.2.1 Closest targets

As discussed above, the basic DEA models yield targets such as those in (3.50) and (3.51), which we have labeled "radial targets" because they are derived though giving preemptive priority to the conservation of the input or output mix of the DMU concerned, depending on model orientation. A weakness of radial models is the perceived arbitrariness in imposing targets preserving the mix within inputs or within outputs, when the operating unit's objective might often be the desire to change that mix (Chambers and Mitchell, 2001). To set more realistic targets for inefficient DMUs, we need to consider some nonradial and even nonoriented models. In fact, we need to address the questions of what variables are discretionary, in what time frame, and what are the preferences over improvements to those variables before devising a DEA model that yields targets in line with those preferences. We outline here one set of models that attempt to derive targets that are the "closest" in some sense to the current operating levels of a unit while also being Pareto-efficient.

The logic behind closest targets rests on the assumption that such targets will require less effort from an inefficient unit to attain them than would be needed to attain other targets. The idea of finding closest targets and corresponding peers has appeared in the literature associated both with oriented models (e.g., Coelli, 1998; Cherchye and Van Puyenbroeck, 2001b) and with nonoriented models (e.g., Frei and Harker, 1999; Golany et al., 1993; Portela et al., 2003).

Frei and Harker (1999) considered more meaningful projections onto the efficiency frontier and developed a method that allows an inefficient DMU to benchmark against those efficient DMUs that are more similar to itself in terms of input and output absolute values. This is done by finding the shortest projection to the frontier. However, the method suffers from not being invariant with respect to the scale of the units used for the inputs or outputs. In González and Álvarez (2001), this problem is solved by using input-specific contractions to find the shortest path to the frontier. This information then can be used to find the most similar efficient DMU—seen as the most relevant benchmark for the DMU analyzed.

Portela et al. (2003) have explored the issue of closest target for the most general case of nonoriented DEA models. In the context of nonradial and nonoriented efficiency measurement, they have developed a procedure for identifying the closest targets in convex as well as in FDH technologies. The method can be seen as equivalent to a minimization of the sum of slacks from an inefficient unit to the efficient part of the PPS boundary. This requires first the identification of all efficient facets of the PPS that can be accomplished by procedures such as the *Qhull* (Olesen and Petersen, 2003). The information on facets is then used to ensure projections on efficient parts of the PPS, since these projections could lie inside the PPS in a slacks minimization model. The model used yields not only targets but also a measure of efficiency. The details of the procedure are beyond the scope of this chapter and can be found in Portela et al. (2003).

3.9.2.2 Axiomatic approach to benchmarking

The benchmarking process in general is an important and, at the same time, a rather sensitive issue in management practices. For this reason, some authors suggest that benchmarking and target selection should follow an axiomatic approach, where a number of general selection principles specified in advance will in some way ensure a consistent and transparent benchmarking procedure. Hence, the emphasis in these approaches is to identify the minimal set of principles (axioms) that are acceptable for a large class of problems, while at the same time, these very principles either will uniquely determine the benchmark (or the target) for an observed unit or will narrow down the possible selection to a small number of alternatives.

As noted above, while the standard DEA projection (radial projection) seems to be a reasonable proxy for similarity, it is easy to imagine a situation in which two firms sharing the same input mix may be quite different. Along these lines, Bogetoft and Hougaard (1999) note that in DEA models the choice of direction in which to look for improvements should reflect production potentials. By stressing only proportional variations in inputs (or outputs), DEA thus ignores important aspects of the technology. It was then shown that the selection of classical radial DEA targets is uniquely specified by the following three axioms: weak efficiency (requiring the target to belong to the isoquant of the PPS), invariance to linear transformation, and strong symmetry axiom (requiring the inputs of the target to be used in equal amounts if the inputs of the unit projected are also used in equal amounts). To rectify the situation, the authors propose and argue for a different set of axioms: strict efficiency (requiring the target to belong to the efficient frontier), invariance to affine transformation, and symmetry with respect to the ideal point (commonly defined as the point whose coordinates are the maximum values of the corresponding projections of the weak dominance set of the DMU being considered). The symmetry axiom requires the inputs of the target to be used in equal amounts if the inputs of both the projected unit and its corresponding ideal point are used in equal amounts. It is then shown that these three axioms are satisfied only when the improvement direction is the line passing through the DMU and its corresponding ideal point. This line is called the diagonal of the DMU in the axiomatization approach suggested by Hougaard and Tvede (2002), described next.

An approach applied to benchmark selection, developed by Hougaard and Tvede (2002), uses two main axioms: one on strict efficiency and a second one on comprehensive monotonicity. In support of the first axiom, the authors argue that only efficient benchmarks make sense to be used as role models since "if for some reason inefficient benchmark units are preferred, the production technology seems to be misspecified" (p. 222). This statement certainly stands to reason. However, it is hard even to imagine a model that, in practice, is not misspecified to some extent, especially in omitting potential inputs or outputs. Perhaps it would be more natural to consider the degrees of model misspecification. Reasonably well-specified models (or models with a low degree of misspecification) may still be very useful in practice for benchmarking, while the applicability of the strict efficiency axiom may be questionable. Bogetoft and Hougaard (2003) in their work on rational inefficiencies (inefficiencies as the result of a rational choice made by the DMU to draw utility from maintaining some degree of inefficiency) also note that model misspecification may be the main cause for the existence of rational inefficiencies. As we discuss further below, some researchers offer even more arguments why targets need not lie on the efficient part of the PPS.

The second axiom, comprehensive monotonicity, is somewhat more complex and involves the concept of reference production plan. The reference production plan of the DMU is defined as the maximal element in the intersection of the FDH of the weak dominance set of the DMU considered and its diagonal. The comprehensive monotonicity axiom requires that the benchmark of an inefficient DMU k must weakly dominate the benchmark of any DMU r with efficient reference point and common diagonal whenever the weak dominance set of the DMU r is included in the FDH of the weak dominance set of the DMU k.

Using the above two axioms, Hougaard and Tvede (2002) then show that, for a very broad class of production technologies (including nonconvex, Cobb-Douglas, and Leontief technologies), the set of feasible benchmarks is reduced to the efficient DMUs dominating the reference DMU. By adding two additional axioms, one on affine invariance and one on comprehensive independence of irrelevant production plans, they further reduce the set of feasible targets. For further details and proofs, the interested reader can consult Hougaard and Tvede (2002), where a brief discussion on the issue of the axiomatization of benchmarking is also given.

3.9.2.3 Restricted targets

In section 3.8, we discuss various models for dealing with environmental or nondiscretionary variables. The models considered there are the same ones we would use for setting targets and identifying appropriate benchmarks when some of the inputs and/or some of the outputs are exogenously fixed from the perspective of management.

Besides the models featuring nondiscretionary variables, in some applications our target selection can also be restricted by the type of variables used in the model. One example is the presence of categorical variables, which was also covered under the frontier separation approach of section 3.8, and which can only be used to group units. Another example that we will cover here is the case when some variables (inputs and/or outputs) are restricted to take only integer values. In general, the computed efficient targets will not respect integer requirements (unless the FDH technology is assumed where the targets coincide with one of the existing DMUs), in which case it is necessary to develop appropriate target-setting models that will ensure integer target values for integer components.

What is the best way to deal with integer-valued components largely depends on the importance or the value of one unit of each such component. If one unit of an integer variable is insignificant in comparison to the overall average values the variable normally takes, then the error in using the targets obtained through one of the standard DEA models and subsequently rounding off any fractional values is usually acceptable for setting the target. Whether such a target is suboptimal (inside the PPS) or infeasible (outside of the PPS) will be of little practical significance. However, when one unit of an integer component is of significant importance, then we need to model its integer restriction.

Lozano and Villa (2006) suggest using a classical mixed integer linear programming DEA model (3.52) to deal with integer components represented by I' (integer-valued inputs) and R' (integer-valued outputs):

$$
\text{Min} \left\{ \theta_o - \varepsilon \left(\sum_{i=1}^{m} s_i^- + \sum_{r=1}^{s} s_r^+ \right) \left|
\begin{array}{l}
\sum_{j=1}^{n} \lambda_j y_{rj} = y_r, \quad y_r = y_{ro} + s_r^+, \\[2mm]
s_r^+, y_r \geq 0, \quad \forall r \\[2mm]
\sum_{j=1}^{n} \lambda_j x_{ij} = x_i, \quad x_i = \theta_o x_{io} - s_i^-, \\[2mm]
s_i^-, x_i \geq 0, \quad \forall i \\[2mm]
\lambda_j \geq 0, \quad x_i = \text{integer } \forall i \in I', \\[2mm]
y_r = \text{integer } \forall r \in R'
\end{array} \right. \right\}
$$

$$(3.52)$$

Through the integer restrictions, integer targets are assured by the above model. At the same time, the model yields efficiency scores that are always between the efficiency scores produced by the CRS and the FDH efficiency models. Hence, even though the FDH model also yields integer targets, the targets identified by the model in (3.52) will, in general, require larger reduction in inputs than the targets selected by the FDH model.

3.9.2.4 Scale-efficient targets

The models specifically designed to identify scale-efficient targets are largely covered in section 3.5. Theoretical developments with respect to the MPSS target models are those given by Banker (1984), Appa and Yue (1999), and Zhu (2000)—all discussed in section 3.5. In the line with Appa and Yue (1999) and Zhu (2000), Camanho and Dyson (1999) also developed the scale efficiency targets corresponding to the largest and the smallest MPSS, which they use in an assessment of Portuguese bank branches. The smallest MPSS targets were selected for branches with IRS, and the largest MPSS targets, for branches found to be operating under DRS. The whole study focuses on the effort to identify meaningful targets for inefficient branches and to ensure that target recommendations do not have a paralyzing effect to the units under evaluation. This goes along with the good practices of performance management where efficiency measurement is not the final product but where encouraging appropriate organizational response is seen as an integral part of the process.

Obtaining more sensible performance targets that are well accepted by the units evaluated is probably one of the main motivating factors of benchmarking and target-setting models that allow for the preferences to be directly incorporated within the model. These models are discussed next.

3.9.3 Preference target setting and benchmarking

As suggested above, DEA based benchmarking, although simple and sound, may not make the best selection of peers and targets from the perspective of a DMU being analyzed. This is because a DMU's policies, preferences, and external restrictions were not part of the DEA model. We discuss in section 3.7 how the DEA model can be extended to incorporate some types of preferences by imposing restrictions on the weights in models (3.4) and (3.5). However, these restrictions are applied globally to all DMUs, and again, they do not have to agree with the unique conditions within which each DMU operates. As a matter of fact, introducing WRs in a DEA model may contribute to the inappropriateness of the selected benchmarks (Post and Spronk, 1999).

To present the wealth of the material developed in this area, we follow a somewhat arbitrary classification borrowed from the multiobjective linear programming (MOLP) classification scheme: We split the preference target models into (i) models that allow for a priori preference specifications, (ii) interactive preference models, and (iii) models for a posteriori preference specifications. This classification of the models is based on the actual stage in the evaluation process when the DM's preferences are introduced in the model. However, the reader should bear in mind that many of the models can be utilized in more than one way, allowing for different timing of preference specifications, but it is either their primary purpose or their mathematical structure that led us to classify them under different classes.

3.9.3.1 Models with a priori preference specifications

Some of the first models with preference structure were developed by Thanassoulis and Dyson (1992). The rationale behind these models is not only to allow for nonradial projection on the frontier but also to allow the DMU to articulate its preferences a priori. One of the models proposed by the authors estimates potential improvements to input–output levels given a preference structure over such improvements. The model also allows for the specification of the subsets R' of outputs $R(R' \subseteq R)$ and the subset I' of inputs $I(I' \subseteq I)$ whose levels the DMU under evaluation wishes to improve. The mathematical formulation of this model is

$$\max \left\{ \sum_{r \in R'} u_r \tau_r - \sum_{i \in I'} v_i \sigma_i \; \left| \; \begin{array}{l} \sum_{j=1}^{n} \lambda_j y_{rj} = \begin{cases} \tau_r y_{ro}, & \tau_r \geq 1, \quad \forall r \in R' \\ y_{ro} + s_r^+, & s_r^+ \geq 0, \quad \forall r \notin R' \end{cases} \\ \sum_{j=1}^{n} \lambda_j x_{ij} = \begin{cases} \sigma_i x_{io}, & \sigma_i \leq 1, \quad \forall i \in I' \\ x_{io} - s_i^-, & s_i^- \geq 0, \quad \forall i \notin I' \end{cases} \\ \lambda_j \geq 0, \quad \forall j \end{array} \right. \right\}. \tag{3.53}$$

The parameters u_r and v_i are user-supplied weights through which the relative desirability of improving, respectively, the level of output r and input i is modeled. These weights are assumed to be nonnegative, with at least one of them being positive. After specifying the subsets R' and I' and supplying the weights u_r and v_i, model (3.53) finds the optimal values for the factors τ_r and σ_i, which represent the proportions by which the output r is increased and input i decreased, respectively. A relatively efficient DMU will have the optimal values for all τ_r and σ_i equal to 1. In the case of an inefficient DMU, its efficient targets are

$$y_{ro}^t = \begin{cases} \tau_r^* y_{ro}, & r \in R' \\ y_{ro} + s_r^{+*}, & r \notin R' \end{cases} \quad \text{and} \quad x_{io}^t = \begin{cases} \sigma_i^* x_{io}, & r \in R' \\ x_{io} - s_i^{-*}, & r \notin R' \end{cases},$$

where * denotes the optimum value of the corresponding variable.

As suggested by the title of this subsection, the weights reflecting the DM's preferences need to be specified a priori. However, using sensitivity analysis, it is always possible to let DMs vary the weights initially supplied and in that way arrive at acceptable targets and corresponding efficient peers for each DMU.

In addition to the above model, Thanassoulis and Dyson (1992) also developed the model, which estimates targets for a DMU on the basis of ideal target input–output levels the DMU may be able to specify. Since these levels may be neither feasible nor efficient, a two-stage process is followed whereby first a set of feasible input–output levels is obtained, and then in the second stage, this set used to obtain efficient targets. For the details of this two-stage process, the reader is referred to the original publication. Let us simply note here that the advantage of this two-stage process (besides perhaps being an easier articulation of preferences in certain contexts) is the ability of this model to identify targets anywhere on the efficient part of the PPS, including points where some of the inputs of the DMU concerned may increase while some of its outputs may decrease. The models developed by Thanassoulis and Dyson (1992) were applied in the assessment of the units providing perinatal care in England (Thanassoulis et al., 1995). While the models did not yield measures of relative efficiency, they were generally providing good targets and greatly facilitated the effort of the units to incorporate relevant information on desired changes to input–output levels into the model.

Somewhat similar in structure to model (3.53) is the model in (3.54) proposed by Zhu (1996):

$$\text{Max} \left\{ \sum_{r=1}^{s} u_r \tau_r - \sum_{i=1}^{m} v_i \sigma_i \middle| \begin{array}{ll} \sum_{j=1}^{n} \lambda_j y_{rj} = \tau_r y_{ro} + s_r^+, & r = 1, \ldots s \\ \sum_{j=1}^{n} \lambda_j x_{ij} = \sigma_i x_{io} - s_i^-, & i = 1, \ldots m \\ \sum_{r=1}^{s} u_r - \sum_{i=1}^{m} v_i = 1, & \lambda_j, s_i^-, s_r^+, u_r, v_i \geq 0, \end{array} \right\}$$

$$(3.54)$$

Preference information required by model (3.54) is the same as required by model (3.53). Note that the normalization constraint in the last line of model (3.54) does not necessarily require extra information from the DM since any set of preference weights u_r and v_i supplied can be easily normalized before running the model.

While in many aspects (3.53) and (3.54) are similar models, (3.54) does relax the restrictions on the factors τ_r and σ_i imposed in (3.53). These factors are unbounded in model (3.54), which effectively allows a DMU to be projected to a reference point that is not from its weak dominance subset of the PPS. Efficient output–input targets in (3.54) are given by $y_{ro}^t = \tau_r^* y_{ro}$, $r = 1, \ldots, s$ and $x_{io}^t = \sigma_i^* x_{io}$, $i = 1, \ldots, m$, respectively.

There are many proposed models for preference benchmarking that build upon or extend the models proposed by Thanassoulis and Dyson (1992). An interesting extension is found in the work of Athanassopoulos et al. (1999), where an enhanced version of the model in (3.53) is developed and used for setting targets to electricity-generating plants. In their work, the authors clearly demonstrate that mathematical feasibility of a projection is not equivalent to feasibility in practice. The suggested model with preference structure, named DESA (data envelopment scenario analysis), is

$$\text{Max} \left\{ \sum_{r=1}^{s} u_r \tau_r - \sum_{i=1}^{m} v_i \sigma_i \left| \begin{array}{ll} \sum_{j=1}^{n} \lambda_j y_{rj} = \tau_r y_{ro}, & r = 1, \ldots s \\ \sum_{j=1}^{n} \lambda_j x_{ij} = \sigma_i x_{io}, & i = 1, \ldots m \\ \sigma_i x_{io} \geq K_i, & i \in I_k \\ \tau_r y_{ro} \leq K_r, & r \in R_k, \quad \lambda_j, \sigma_i, \tau_r \geq 0, \end{array} \right. \right\}.$$

$$(3.55)$$

Once again, we can observe parameters similar to the ones used in model (3.53). This time, however, we have additional parameters K_i and K_r, which allow the DMU to set bounds for the estimated targets of input i and output r. These bounds are imposed only to the subset of inputs and outputs, denoted by I_k and R_k. Notation otherwise in (3.55) is as in (3.53). Other authors proposing limits on targets include Cooper et al. (2000a).

Letting the DM specify the bounds on the estimated targets in this policy-making scenario model is particularly useful when modeling has to preserve some restrictions associated with the definitions of the inputs and outputs, for example, the capacity of a stadium or where crimes cleared by police cannot exceed those reported to the police. Besides this extra feature, the model in (3.55) is highly flexible in terms of modeling many additional restrictions that may be helpful to DMs in specifying their preferences. For example, with some additional constraints, it is possible to link the targets of certain input and output variables.

In presenting models (3.53), (3.54), and (3.55), we have shown only their CRS versions. It should be noted, however, that they are all applicable to the VRS technology by adding the convexity constraint.

There are many other models that could be placed within this class of preference targeting models. For example, Sowlati and Paradi (2004) utilize bank managements' knowledge rather than preferences to obtain feasible disturbances of the observed inputs and outputs of the efficient bank branches. This information helps them to create artificial DMUs that define a "practical frontier," which is in turn used to set efficiency targets not only for inefficient units but also for empirically efficient ones.

Bala and Cook (2003) also use bank branch consultant/expert judgments as to what makes good and poor performance of branches. This time, however, such judgments are used to quantify the functional relationship that best captures the expert's mental model for performance, which ultimately helps in better specification of the model and therefore contributes to a much better acceptance of the benchmarking results by the inefficient branches.

Lozano and Villa (2005) offer yet another interesting approach on how to use managers' judgments in order to specify more acceptable targets. They were motivated by unrealistic targets observed in many practical applications of DEA, where improvements in the range of 20% to 30% are not uncommon. They argue that setting targets that are so far away from the DMU's observed values can have a counterproductive or paralyzing effect. To avoid this, they propose a model that can determine a sequence of targets gradually diverging from the DMU's original position toward an efficient point on the frontier. Setting intermediate target levels is considered to be a much more acceptable practice from the perspective of the units assessed. In their model, the managers' judgment is used to specify acceptable relative amounts of input reductions and output augmentations in each step. An interesting property of their model is that the final target never requires more (proportional) changes in inputs and outputs than the one-step approach.

3.9.3.2 Interactive preference target setting

The stream of research that can be classified as interactive preference target setting is centered on combining DEA with interactive decision-making procedures from multiple criteria decision-making theory (e.g., Golany, 1988b; Belton and Vickers 1993; Post and Spronk, 1999). The models developed are focused on assisting a decision maker in a benchmark selection procedure; that is, the focus of attention is the transition from the analytical results to making decisions based on those results in an interactive fashion.

The research on benchmark selection that combines DEA with multiple criteria decision-making theory perhaps starts with Golany (1988b). The author proposes an interactive decision-making procedure combining DEA and MOLP, which allows the DM to select a most preferred alternative from a set of different DEA efficient points. Belton and Vickers (1993) use a multiattribute value function in combination with DEA to build a visual inter-active decision support system. While the main focus of their work is to make the DEA procedure more transparent and amenable to visual representation, the byproduct is also a possibility of visual comparison that forms the basis for establishing performance targets. An important aspect of this approach is that it increases the understanding of DEA by nontechnical users, thus enabling them to feel more in control of the investigation rather than having to place their trust completely in an analyst.

An argument used in favor of interactive decision-making processes is that the DM may become more involved in the solution of the problem. This is shown by Post and Spronk (1999), where they develop an interac-tive DEA (IDEA) model for performance benchmarking. Their approach in selecting performance benchmarks is more flexible than the former two since

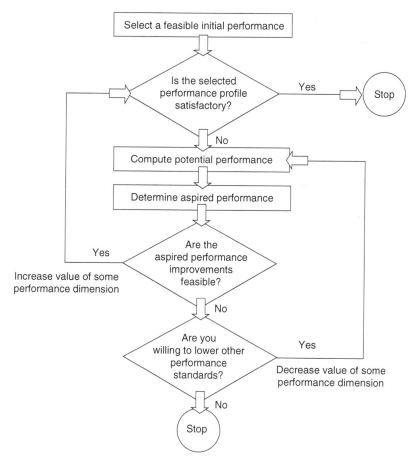

Figure 3.38. Flow Chart of the IDEA Performance Benchmarking Procedure (Post and Spronk, 1999)

it considers both production frontier units and the interior units (the units not on the frontier). This is a very useful feature when the DM wishes to intentionally include internal slacks, because of organizational and psychological considerations, which are excluded from the original model formulation. Figure 3.38, reproduced from Post and Spronk (1999), describes their IDEA procedure.

In the first step of IDEA, the current input–output levels of the DMU evaluated are usually taken as a feasible initial performance. The second step is computation, for each input and output variable separately, of the maximum performance improvement that is feasible without deterioration in any other performance dimension. These potential performance improvements are not feasible simultaneously. In the third step, the DM adjusts the selected performance profile by sequentially specifying aspired input–output levels. The interactive process ends when the DM selects performance benchmarks that are both feasible and desirable.

A number of different approaches for identifying meaningful targets are based on the use of MOLP and progressive articulation of preferences. Joro (1998), for example, suggests a reference point approach:

$$
\text{Max} \left\{ \omega + \varepsilon \left(s_r^+ + s_i^- \right) \middle|
\begin{array}{l}
\displaystyle\sum_{j=1}^{n} \lambda_j y_{rj} - s_r^+ = q_r + u_r \omega, \quad r = 1, \ldots, s, \\[4mm]
\displaystyle\sum_{j=1}^{n} \lambda_j x_{ij} + s_i^- = p_i - v_i \omega, \quad i = 1, \ldots, m, \\[4mm]
\lambda_j, s_r^+, s_i^- \geq 0
\end{array}
\right\}
$$

(3.56)

In (3.56), q_r and p_i are preference parameters, and they are, respectively, interpreted as aspiration levels for outputs and aspiration levels for inputs. In addition to the aspiration levels q_r and p_i, preference information is incorporated through the weighting parameters for inputs and outputs: u_r and v_i, the ones that were also utilized in models (3.53)–(3.55). Two different sets of preference parameters make possible scanning the efficient frontier in two different ways: either by fixing the aspiration levels and changing the weighting parameters, or the other way around, which is computationally more effective.

The reference point approach, as suggested by Joro (1998), besides having the ability to fully scan part of the efficient frontier weakly dominating the selected DMU, does not qualify as a truly interactive preference targeting procedure. Nevertheless, by replacing aspiration levels q_r and p_i, respectively, with $q_r + t_r d_r$ and $p_i + t_i d_i$, the reference point approach is transformed into what is known as reference direction formulation (Korhonen and Laakso, 1986). Dynamic extension of the reference direction approach, known as Pareto race, developed by Korhonen and Wallenius (1988), and its software implementation provide the user with the ability to search the targets in a truly interactive fashion.

Another important MOLP approach for interactive preference target setting is based on the concept of VEA (Halme et al., 1999). The basic premise of this approach is to locate the DM's most preferred solution. For a brief review of VEA, the reader is referred to section 3.7.1, where the main concepts are described within the framework of DEA WRs, and, of course, to the authors original publication.

3.9.3.3 Models with a posteriori preference specifications

Preference target-setting models in this class are, in general, any target-setting models that find two or more different target points and let the DMU express its preference after some plausible targets have been identified. Some of these models are, however, directly related to the target models presented in (3.53) and (3.54). These models are developed by Lins et al. (2004) with the purpose of overcoming the major drawback of the models in (3.53) and (3.54). Namely, the models as designed by Thanassoulis and Dyson (1992) and Zhu (1996) are difficult to use when there is no guidance to help us select the most appropriate weights. As noted above, in such situations, the only way to gain some knowledge about the weight mixes leading to meaningful solutions is sensitivity analysis. To alleviate this problem, Lins et al. (2004) suggest the use of a multiple objective ratio optimization (MORO) model:

$$
\begin{aligned}
\max \tau_1, \dots, \tau_s \\
\min \sigma_1, \dots, \sigma_m
\end{aligned}
\left|
\begin{aligned}
& \sum_{j=1}^{n} \lambda_j y_{rj} = \tau_r y_{ro}, \quad r = 1, \dots s \\
& \sum_{j=1}^{n} \lambda_j x_{ij} = \sigma_i x_{io}, \quad i = 1, \dots m, \quad \lambda_j, \sigma_i, \tau_r \geq 0
\end{aligned}
\right.
$$

$$(3.57)$$

Using an appropriate MOLP software, such as *ADBASE* (see Steuer, 1995), we can identify all the extreme efficient solutions to (3.57). A compromise solution can then be reached by the DMU trading off the attainments of inputs–outputs at the solutions identified (see Lins et al., 2004). This leads to a final set of optimal values $\tau_1^*, \dots, \tau_s^*, \sigma_1^*, \dots \sigma_s^*$ and $\lambda_1^*, \dots, \lambda_n^*$. The corresponding targets are then computed as $y_{ro}^t = \tau_r^* y_{ro}$, $r = 1, \dots, s$ and $x_{io}^t = \sigma_i^* x_{io}$, $i = 1, \dots, m$.

Another model proposed in Lins et al. (2004), MORO with dominance (MORO-D), is in fact the restriction of the model in (3.57) to account for the constraints ensuring that the targets selected weakly dominate the observed DMU. The additional constraints are as in model (3.53), namely, $\tau_r \geq 1$ and $\sigma_i \leq 1$. What is demonstrated by Lins et al. (2004) is that the MORO-D and MORO models identify the same targets as the preference structure models

(3.53) and (3.54). The advantage of MORO and MORO-D models is that the same nondominated solutions are obtained a priori without the need to specify any preferences before solving the models. The authors observe that the models (3.53) and (3.54), on the other hand, can be considered as weighted-sum a priori preference aggregation MOLP models.

In addition to the MORO and MORO-D models, Lins et al. (2004) also develop interactive multiple objective target optimization (MOTO), which is enabling an interactive approach (Pareto race) in the target selection process. The MOTO model differs from MORO in the specification of its objective functions—instead of parameters τ_r and σ_i used in the MORO model, the MOTO model uses the products between these parameters and corresponding observed input and output values. As such, the MOTO model is able to explore nonextreme efficient solutions in addition to the extreme ones.

In Quariguasi Frota Neto and Angulo-Meza (2007), the traditional radial projection models, the preference structure models (3.53) and (3.54), and the multiobjective models MORO and MORO-D are compared in the case study of the Rio de Janeiro odontological public health system. Some of the objectives of their study were to compare the applicability of the three target models in the presence of exogenous and integer variables and to identify the main advantages and drawbacks of each approach. Their findings indicate that multiobjective models are able to select the targets that the preference structure models were not able to identify in spite of the mathematical equivalency between the two approaches. Radial projection models, on the other hand, were found to be completely useless within these particular settings. On the negative side, the MOLP models were not always able to project an observed DMU in the most preferred point on the frontier. Also, with the increasing number of DMUs, computer processing time was becoming an important consideration.

Another study with a similar objective to compare the MOLP approaches with radial projections in DEA was performed by Korhonen et al. (2003). Their findings are that radial projection (taken as the representative model for the value-free techniques) not allowing any flexibility to a DM to choose a target for an observed inefficient unit undermines the significance of a target unit in practice. In particular, Korhonen et al. (2003) found that, in the situations where the time frame is an important consideration, the radial projections are way too restrictive and the reference points selected are a poor approximation for the most preferred targets. They conclude their investigation by recommending the use of the MOLP-based procedures whenever a DMU has control over some inputs or outputs.

Several studies do not use MOLP-based procedures for setting the targets but nevertheless can be classified as the target models with a posteriori preference specifications. Typically, these are the models that, for various reasons (usually application led), opt to derive two or more different projection points, which are then presented to the DMU either to make the final choice or to try to create a compromise solution based on the targets offered and postoptimality analysis. Examples from the literature include Thanassoulis (1996) and Portela et al. (2004).

3.9.4 Hybrid and other approaches to target setting

The target-setting models discussed so far in this section cover the majority of research in this aspect of DEA. However, there are some additional target-setting models that do not easily fit within these broad target-setting approaches. We describe here some of the better known alternative approaches for target models.

We begin with what we could term as *hybrid* target-setting models. They are hybrid in the sense that they combine DEA with some other technique to identify meaningful targets. (This was also the case with DEA and MOLP discussed above but that approach is more widely researched than the methods described here.) Some examples of methodologies used in combination with DEA are statistical tests to estimate the distribution of output targets (Gstach, 2005) and the use of simulation to combine the observed practices to create even more efficient operating practices (Greasley, 2005). Both approaches are suitable for setting targets even for the units that are identified by DEA as efficient. Therefore, they represent a value-free alternative to the model by Sowlati and Paradi (2004) noted above.

Another hybrid method for target setting is that by Doyle and Green (1994). They applied a clustering algorithm to the correlation matrix formed by computing correlation coefficients between a pair of columns corresponding to the cross-efficiency values of two DMUs. (The cross-efficiency values for some DMU A are calculated by applying the optimal DEA weights of all DMUs in turn to the input and output values of DMU A.) The correlation coefficient between the cross-efficiency vectors of DMUs A and B reflects how similarly the two DMUs are appraised by the rest of the DMUs. Clustering DMUs based on this type of similarity is then used to identify benchmarks within the same cluster. This approach was applied by Lu and Lo (2007) in the context of regional sustainable development in China.

Another frequently used approach to enrich and improve the benchmarking process is to create a two-dimensional performance matrix. The general idea is to evaluate performances of DMUs along two different performance dimensions and then use a two-dimensional scatter plot to visualize the relative performance of the DMUs with respect to a pair of performance indicators. Visual representation of this kind can be utilized to perform a simple visual clustering of DMUs into four performance quadrants. This technique is very simple yet very effective way to cluster DMUs, which in turn can help us to better identify viable practices and set more appropriate benchmarks for inefficient units. The most common performance matrix used is the efficiency–profitability matrix, examples of which can be found in Athanassopoulos and Thanassoulis (1995) and Sarrico and Dyson (2000). It is also possible to evaluate performance of DMUs along more than two performance dimensions. In this case, the performance matrices can be created for each pair of performance dimensions. This approach is illustrated in section 3.10.

A notable development in the DEA-based benchmarking is also observed within the context of centralized planning and resource allocation. These models conceptually differ from those discussed so far since the main focus here is to distribute resources in an optimal way from the perspective of a central authority. The targets in this case refer to the global targets for the total consumption of each input and the total production of each output. Examples of DEA models developed for this type of benchmarking can be found in Athanassopoulos (1995, 1998) and Lozano et al. (2004).

Some of the recent developments in DEA-based benchmarking include the approaches that particularly stress the individual learning and decision-making perspective. One approach is the development of a highly interactive Internet-based benchmarking environment. The other approach relates to the use of artificial intelligence (AI) to automatically derive simple yet sufficiently accurate natural language rules that fully describe various efficiency levels of the PPS defined by a given data set. In the remaining text, we give some more details on these two novel developments and their use in DEA-based benchmarking.

An Internet-based benchmarking environment has been developed by Bogetoft and Nielsen (2005). Another Internet-based benchmarking approach has already been commercially implemented for warehouse operations (http://www.isye.gatech.edu/ideas/).

Bogetoft and Nielsen (2005) demonstrate how Internet-based benchmarking using DEA can be a very attractive tool for DMUs wishing to improve their current practices and to learn from their peers. Using the application located on the World Wide Web, any DMU has an instant access to make a self-evaluation of its current practices relative to a number of other similar DMUs. While this kind of benchmarking is certainly an attractive proposition, many issues remain to be explored in order to generalize the concept and make it usable for the variety of possible settings. In terms of nonparametric-based benchmarking, the authors describe only a specific case study involving Danish commercial and savings banks, where the PPS is assumed to be convex and a VRS technology is assumed. Benchmarks are then calculated using a directional distance function, effectively allowing the DMU to search the frontier interactively by changing its preferred directions. This process also allows the DMU to evaluate its performance with adjusted levels of inputs and outputs that may reflect the DMU's perception of what would be the attainable input and output levels in future. In other words, the DMUs are given the possibility to explore alternative improvement strategies. For each different scenario, the Web-based application not only finds the corresponding efficiency scores but also identifies the efficient peer(s) that are closest to the input and output levels given for evaluation.

DMUs using this kind of service can obtain some very useful information, yet the process of choosing their optimal target toward being efficient lacks in one dimension: While DMUs may have a pretty good idea about their specific conditions and, in this respect, what output or input target levels would be easier to achieve, the information about what changes are the most beneficial in terms of efficiency improvement is not easily obtainable. The only way to do this using the existing design of the Internet-based benchmarking methodology is to evaluate a large number of different alternatives. With a relatively large number of inputs and outputs, even this approach could not give any significant insight.

The use of Internet benchmarking is still in the very early stages, and so far we have seen only a few modest steps in this direction. However, with the increasing number of business applications relying on the Internet, it is expected that this particular area of research will increase in importance. While still in its early development, the main research questions tend to be related to the implementation, user friendliness, and anonymity issues—all the areas that are quite outside the usual scope of DEA. Successfully addressing these issues will certainly open up some new research questions directly related to the DEA methodologies and techniques, particularly those relating to interactive, dynamic use of DEA-based benchmarking.

An important contribution to the advances in Internet-based benchmarking may come from the efforts to exploit some of the AI tools applied to DEA problems. Linguistic analysis of efficiency (LAE) developed by Despić (2003) is one such example. The main idea behind LAE is to translate the DEA mechanism into a set of natural language rules directly relating ranges of input–output values with the various discrete levels of efficiency ratings. AI techniques are utilized to automatically learn, select, and keep the most relevant rules describing different regions of efficiency within the PPS defined by a given data set.

By characterizing the PPS through natural language rules, LAE allows any DM, including those not familiar with DEA, to clearly visualize the position of a DMU in the production space, the reasons for the DMU having a particular efficiency score, and the most promising paths toward improving its efficiency. Any inefficient unit is then able to easily identify what performance indicators are important to take care of in order to reach higher efficiency levels (e.g., by comparing current output to input ratios with the ratio levels that LAE rules suggest are necessary to move to some higher level of efficiency). In essence, LAE provides the units under assessment with a clear map of the most promising paths in improving their performance, which in turn can be easily contrasted with their most preferred (or feasible) directions.

In addition to the benefits that come from a rule-based characterization of the PPS, many other AI techniques, such as supervised and unsupervised clustering or neural networks, are well positioned to significantly contribute to the further development of Internet (or intranet)-based benchmarking. Such approaches are not yet developed enough and represent future research directions.

To conclude this section, let us single out three important observations on target setting using DEA. The first is that DEA may be very useful in providing a valid starting point for specifying performance targets because it focuses on observed operating practice. Second, there are a variety of DEA models to enable a user to steer the process toward identifying targets in line with user preferences and/or restrictions. Third, there is a strong argument for the simplified interactive procedures since it increases the understanding of the efficiency evaluation procedure by nontechnical users and therefore facilitates organizational learning.

3.10 Sample Applications

In this section, we present some sample applications of DEA in various fields. Applications of DEA are too numerous to present exhaustively, so our aim here is to illustrate the application of DEA highlighting the issues arising in setting up such assessments, the information derived, and the caveats in using the information. Clearly, every application of DEA raises a unique set of issues relating to its particular context. However, some general points can be made at the outset regarding applying DEA:

- The choices of inputs and outputs are some of the most important decisions in a DEA analysis because the results will depend critically on these choices. Note that, depending on the aspect of the performance of a set of units that is to be assessed, different input–output variables may apply. For example, in assessing retail outlets on their ability to attract customers, one may use the size of its local market as an input to set against customers attracted as an output. However, in assessing the same outlets on their efficiency in serving customers, one may use the cost of running the outlet as an input variable to set against volume of customers served. Thus, we can have different perspectives of efficiency that allow for a multidimensional analysis of the performance of units.
- Most DEA studies are based on single-period, cross-sectional analyses. However, one is usually interested in assessing performance over time. This is covered to some extent by the use of panel data in the framework of Malmquist indices, but they, too, are based on comparing two time periods at a time. More is needed in reflecting performance over continuous time that underlies the life of real DMUs.
- Software is available to handle most of the models mentioned in this chapter. Therefore, in most applications, more attention is needed in formulating the input–output set and obtaining the necessary data and then interpreting the results, rather than actually solving the DEA models per se. In all the applications covered here, the software used was *Warwick* software, updated now as *DEAsoft*-V1,[19] except for the application on bank branches, where *GAMS*[20] and *EMS*[21] were used. For a recent review on the software available for solving DEA models, see

Barr (2004). Note that *DEAsoft-V1* is not mentioned in Barr's review since it is more recent software. It has some facilities not included in other software, such as the possibility of calculating Malmquist indexes and bootstrapping.

3.10.1 Education

The sample application that we present here regards an analysis of schools from a local education authority (LEA) in England as detailed in Thanassoulis and Dunstan (1994). Applications of DEA in the education field are many and can be applied to the context of comparing schools (e.g., Lovell et al., 1994; Mancebón and Bandrés, 1999; Bradley et al., 2001; Mizala et al., 2002), pupils (e.g., Portela and Thanassoulis, 2001; Thanassoulis, 1999), school districts (e.g., Grosskopf et al., 1997; Banker et al., 2004; Primont and Domazlicky, 2006), and higher education (e.g., Johnes and Johnes, 1995; Athanassopoulos and Shale, 1997; Warning, 2004).

3.10.1.1 Input–output variables

The application focused on outcomes of pupils 16 years of age and data from 14 schools of the LEA was used. The inputs and outputs used in the school assessment are displayed in figure 3.39. The measured inputs and outputs refer to an individual cohort of pupils at each school. The outputs reflect the achievements of the cohort on exit from a stage of education, and the inputs reflect the academic attainment of that same cohort some five years earlier, on entry to that stage of education and the family background of the cohort.

The choice of the input variables drew from a body of research concluding that some of the best predictors of examination results on exit from education at age 16 in the United Kingdom are provided by verbal reasoning scores of pupils on intake to secondary education, "social disadvantage" as reflected by whether or not the pupil qualifies for free school meals, and parental occupation. The input variable mean verbal reasoning score per pupil on entry is thus intended to reflect the potential for academic attainment by the pupils at the school. The second input variable, percentage of pupils not receiving free school meals, was intended to account for the parental background of

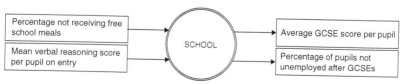

Figure 3.39. Inputs and Outputs Used in the School Assessment

pupils, in particular, to reflect social advantage. There were no data on parental occupations of pupils at each school.

On the output side, "average GCSE score per pupil" is intended to reflect the academic attainment on exit of the cohort on which the school is being assessed. Note that the GCSE (general certificate of secondary education) in the United Kingdom is the qualification open to pupils at the end of their compulsory education, normally at age 16. The certificate gives for each subject taken a grade from A to G (at the time, A was the top grade), with an unclassified "grade U" for those not attaining the bottom grade G. Mean score per pupil was computed by weighting pupil GCSE grades with weights conventionally used in the United Kingdom for this purpose (Thanassoulis and Dunstan 1994).

The second output, "percentage of pupils not unemployed after GCSEs," is used to reflect the achievement of schools in finding placements for their pupils upon completion of their studies. The authors note that while they would expect that academic achievement and placement to be highly correlated in view of the fact that placement includes progression of pupils to further studies, it was nevertheless felt that securing placements for pupils is a separate outcome from schools. The outcome reflects a school's provision of career counseling and generally developing the social skills and attitudes necessary for progression to employment or further education. Should the pupils from schools face differing employment prospects due to the general economic condition in their area, then that needs to be reflected in the model. This was not felt to be the case in this study in view of the fact that the schools were within the same geographical economic area.

The above input and output variables were adjusted in Thanassoulis and Dunstan (1994) so that a CRS model could be used to aid discrimination in view of the low number of schools to be assessed.

3.10.1.2 Benchmark schools and peers

One of the important results presented by the authors to the LEA was the peers for each inefficient school identified by the DEA model. These were to be seen as role models that the less well-performing schools could emulate. Further, the authors estimated attainment targets for the inefficient schools using both the standard DEA model and models where preferences for improvement (Thanassoulis and Dyson 1992) have been introduced.

To illustrate the type of results obtained in Thanassoulis and Dunstan (1994), take, for example, school Sc9010 that was found to have relative efficiency of 72.74%. One of its efficient peer schools was Sc912. Contrasting the performance of Sc9010 with that of Sc912 (see table 3.11), we see that both schools have pupils of similar verbal reasoning score upon entry, which is the main predictor of pupil academic attainment on exit. School Sc912, compared to Sc9010, has some 14 percentage points advantage on the percentage of pupils not taking free school meals. However, on exit, pupils at Sc912 attain far better GCSE scores, having an average nearly 54% higher than that of pupils at

Table 3.11
Efficient Peer Schools for Sc9010

Inputs and Outputs[a]	Sc9010 Actual	Sc912 Actual	Sc9010 Targets
− Non-FSM	67.29	81.28	67.29
− VR	45.00	47.4	45.00
+ Mean GCSE	40.50	62.26	55.67
+ Placements	17.34	31.35	25.35

FSM, free school meals; VR, Verbal reasoning.
[a]Prefix–for Inputs, + for Outputs.

Sc9010. Further, at Sc912, nearly twice the percentage of pupils of Sc9010 proceed to placements on exit. This is enough evidence to offer intuitive support to the DEA finding that Sc9010 does not do as well as Sc912.

Contrasting inefficient schools with their peers in this way can help reinforce the case that the inefficient school needs to improve performance. Sc912 may well prove a useful role model for Sc9010, since the two schools recruit pupils of similar academic ability.

The targets for Sc9010 can be seen in the last column of table 3.11. These targets indicate that for the mean verbal reasoning score of its pupils and given that about 67% of them do not receive free school meals, Sc9010 ought to offer a mean GCSE score of 55.67 and place some 25% of its pupils on leaving school.

3.10.1.3 Preference target setting

Targets such as those in table 3.11 do not reflect any emphasis on improving specific educational outcomes at a school. They merely indicate the maximum radial improvement feasible to *all* outcomes at a school. In order to introduce preferences over target improvements, the DEA models developed in Thanassoulis and Dyson (1992) were used. The results from this approach for one school (Sc8914) are illustrated in table 3.12 for the case where it was desired

Table 3.12
Targets for School Sc8914

Inputs and Outputs	Actual Values	Targets under Equal Priority to Both Outputs	Targets When only Mean GCSE Score is Given Priority to Improve
− Non-FSM	76.50	76.50	76.50
− VR	50.10	48.60	50.10
+ Mean GCSE	44.01	54.55	62.48
+ Placements	24.71	30.63	28.93

See table 3.12 notes for details.

to estimate targets in which the improvement of the mean GCSE score is to be given preemptive priority.

Thus, if school Sc8914 wishes to give equal emphasis to the improvement of its two output levels, then it should aim to raise by some 24% its output levels to attain relative efficiency. In contrast, if the school wishes to give priority to the improvement of its academic results over placements, then it should be capable of raising its mean GCSE score by some 42% and its placements by some 17% in order to become relatively efficient. Thus, the targets yielded by the priority targets model offer a trade-off so that a larger improvement in academic results is expected at the expense of a lower proportion of pupils placed on leaving school.

In table 3.12, the solution of the models reveals that when preemptive priority is given to maximizing mean GCSE score, school Sc8914 cannot afford to admit pupils of mean verbal reasoning score lower than 50.1 offered by its current intake if it is to achieve its targets. In contrast, when equal priority is given to raising academic results and placements, the school can, in principle, achieve its targets even if pupils admitted offered the slightly lower mean verbal reasoning score of 48.6 rather than the current 50.1.

Particularly valuable is the fact that the priority targets model yields efficient peers that are in line with its preferences over improvements to its outputs. Table 3.13 shows two of the efficient peers for school Sc8914, Sc9111 when equal priority is given to the outputs to improve, and Sc912 when GCSE score on exit is given preemptive priority to improve.

Both peers recruit weaker pupils on entry than Sc8914, with similar percentages qualifying for free school meals in all three cases. Both peers dominate Sc8914 on exit attainment, showing clearly that Sc8914 is not as efficient. More to the point in this case, however, is that peer school Sc912 offers much better academic results than does peer school Sc9111. This makes peer school Sc912 more suitable than peer school Sc9111 for school Sc8914 to emulate when it wishes to improve its mean GCSE score above all else.

Table 3.13
Efficient Peers for School Sc8914

Inputs and Outputs	Actual Values	Equal Priority to Both Outputs	Only Mean GCSE Score is Given Priority to Improve
School	Sc 8914	Sc9111	Sc912
− Non-FSM	76.50	74.42	81.30
− Verbal reasoning	50.10	39.88	47.41
+ Mean GCSE	44.01	46.66	62.26
+ Placements	24.71	30.74	31.35

For details, see table 3.12 note.

3.10.2 Banking

Applications of DEA in banking have focused on two different units of analysis: banks and bank branches [see Berger and Humphrey (1997), for a literature review on banking applications]. The issues posed for each level of analysis are not necessarily the same, though they are related.

Because banks and bank branches are complex units of analysis, it is almost impossible to analyze their efficiency without focusing on specific aspects of their operations. Two of the perspectives most often used with respect to banks and bank branches are the production perspective and the intermediation perspective (see Colwell and Davis, 1992, for details). The *production approach* takes the perspective of operations that go on in a bank or bank branch. These are seen as production units that use a set of resources, such as staff, computer terminals, and space, to produce a set of services such as transactions on various types of accounts, loan provision, and insurance. In this sense, banks are seen as service providers, where the emphasis is on operational activities rather than on market oriented financial activities.[22] The *intermediation approach* looks at banks or bank branches as intermediaries—collectors of funds that are intermediated into loans and other income-generating assets. Under this approach, the bank is seen as borrowing funds at some price and selling them at a higher price. In this sense, the bank earns some revenues that are the outputs of the efficiency assessment. It also incurs some costs, which are considered the inputs of the assessment.[23]

We present here a sample application of DEA to bank branches, carried out by Portela and Thanassoulis (2007). In this application, 57 Portuguese bank branches of a bank (the client of the study) were analyzed using data covering a period of 18 months. The objective was to assess bank branches with respect to three main objectives of the bank:

- To foster an effective use of new distribution channels so that branch personnel can use their time on value-added activities (mostly related to selling rather than to banking transactions);
- To increase sales and the customer base of the branch, while serving the clients that visit the branch with high service-quality levels;
- To manage the product mix in a way that generates high profitability, without reducing service quality associated with any product.

3.10.2.1 Input–output variables

Different input–output variables were appropriate for each one of the foregoing objectives. For the first objective, a *transactional* efficiency measure was developed, for the second an *operational* efficiency measure was developed, and for the third objective a *profit* efficiency measure was used. We present here only the operational and profit efficiency assessments, where the variables used were as shown in figures 3.40 and 3.41.

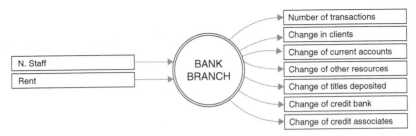

Figure 3.40. Variables Used in Operational Efficiency Assessment

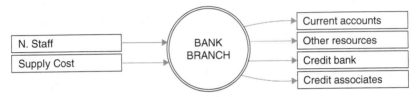

Figure 3.41. Variables Used in Profit Efficiency Assessment

In the *operational efficiency* assessment, the inputs used reflect the main resource of bank branches, staff, and its location, which is reflected in the rent, that is, whether or not the branch actually rents its space. Obviously, other data would have been important in this assessment, such as inputs relating to the market potential in the locality of the branch, since this is a factor affecting its ability to attract customers, but no such data were available. The outputs are intended to reflect the main operational objectives of bank branches: (i) to increase the customer base (reflected in the output change in number of clients), (ii) to increase sales of the various products the branch has to offer (reflected in outputs 2 to 6),[24] and (iii) to serve clients (reflected in the output number of general transactions). It would have been better in place of outputs 2–6 to use the values of products sold had they been available. The use of change values from month $t - 1$ to month t resulted in some outputs being negative. This presents issues with the basic DEA models, and therefore the RDM model presented in section 3.6 was used to calculate operational efficiencies. The RDM model used was output-oriented but the output "number of transactions" was treated as nondiscretionary in line with the approach of Banker and Morey (1986b). Number of transactions was nondiscretionary because the bank simply wished to carry out transactions as of necessity but not to seek to increase their number.

For the *profit efficiency* assessment, the input–output variables used are consistent with the intermediation approach noted above. Thus, on the input side we have the cost of the intermediated funds and the manpower carrying out the intermediation, while on the output side we have sources of revenue. The variables used here, again, were constrained by data availability. In particular, the authors would have liked to have also included additional income streams, most notably noninterest revenue. This is increasingly important since competitive pressures have led bank branches to create other sources of revenues through commissions and fees. However, such data were not available.

The variables in figure 3.41 were used to compute two types of efficiency: *technical* and *overall profit* efficiency. The profit efficiency required the use of input–output prices. For staff, average salaries were used as price. For the outputs, prices were net interest rates, meaning that when outputs were multiplied by prices, the result was net interest revenue (interest revenue – interest cost) rather than simply interest revenue. We present below some of the results from this application. Fuller results, including the decomposition of the overall profit efficiency into technical and allocative components, can be found in Portela and Thanassoulis (2005).

3.10.2.2 Efficiency results

Monthly efficiency results were produced for each input–output set and for a total of 57 bank branches. To provide a picture of the performance of bank branches jointly in any two objectives, the authors used graphs of the type depicted in figure 3.42, which reports the average over time results on technical (not overall) profit and operational efficiency. Technical profit efficiency was computed using the input–output variables in figure 3.41 without recourse to input–output prices.

Bank branches with good performance in both profit and operational terms can be classified as "stars," and they represent benchmarks to be emulated by inefficient branches. Such branches are clearly identified in the top panel of figure 3.42, extracted from the lower panel. Problematic branches are those that have low operational and low profit (LOLP) technical efficiency, situated in the southwest quartile of figure 3.42. Special attention should be paid to these branches, and action is needed to diagnose their problems and to improve their performance.

Bank branches with good profit efficiency and low operational efficiency (figure 3.42, southeast quartile) do not exist in our data set.[25] This is in line with intuition, since branches with low operating efficiency (i.e., showing a poor performance in selling and attracting new customers) are not likely to be efficient in generating profits. The correlation coefficient between average profit and average operational efficiency is 0.3. This is not a very high correlation coefficient, but it is statistically significant at the 5% level.

A more detailed analysis of star branches and problematic branches in figure 3.42 can be undertaken by analyzing differences in their input–output levels. In the radar graphs shown in figure 3.43, we can compare the operational and technical profit efficiency average input–output levels of star branches with those of LOLP branches. (See also section 3.9 for the more general use of such graphs for comparing inefficient units and their peers.)

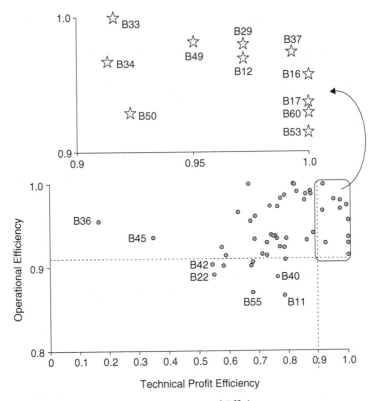

Figure 3.42. Technical Profit Versus Operational Efficiency

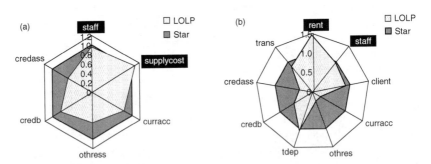

Figure 3.43. Star Versus Branches Using Profit Efficiency Variables (a) and Operational Efficiency Variables (b)

In graph (a), we can see that LOLP branches use, on average, about the same staff and supply costs as star branches, to produce much less of all the outputs considered in the profit assessment. Differences are even more marked in graph (b) for the case of the inputs and outputs used to measure operational efficiency. This means that in order to improve the operational efficiency of bank branches, particular emphasis should be placed on improving growth of current accounts, other resources, and credit associates. In terms of titles deposited and client growth, these branches perform, on average, similarly to star branches, and therefore these areas do not give particular cause for concern.

3.10.2.3 DEA results versus perception of bank managers

The study reported in Portela and Thanassoulis (2007) was performed in close consultation with bank managers who wanted to test the consistency between their views on the performance of bank branches and the results obtained through the DEA assessment. There was general agreement between managerial views and the DEA results on the performance of the bank branches in all dimensions. There was, however, more agreement on the identification of the worst performers rather than on best performers. This is perhaps as we might expect given that DEA by nature makes a stronger identification of weak performers, while efficient units may appear so through an odd combination of input–output levels and lack of similar comparators. As far as best performers were concerned, there was less agreement. In some cases, the best-performing branches by DEA were located in small rural towns, and managers did not expect these bank branches to be best performers. This mainly arises because the business volume at these branches is not very high, and therefore this type of bank branch is not seen as contributing much to the profits of the bank as a whole. DEA, however, through the rent input variable, controls for location and so even a less profitable branch could be doing well enough given its location, an allowance that cannot be made when looking at absolute profit figures.

3.10.3 Regulation

In this section, we outline the use of DEA in the regulation of water companies in England and Wales during their 1994 periodic review by the regulator.

The privatization of publicly owned assets and, in particular, utility companies such as those supplying water, energy, and telecommunications grew apace from the 1980s on in the United Kingdom and, indeed, elsewhere in the world, based on a premise that private ownership would bring in better management and more efficiency, with consequent benefits for the consumer. However, the privatized utilities still maintained a de facto monopoly in many instances, which necessitated setting up regulatory regimes to oversee the functioning of privatized companies in tandem with the privatizations concerned. Regulation regimes are intended to protect the public from the monopolistic powers enjoyed by the respective privatized companies while also ensuring their long-term survival. In the case of English and Welsh water companies privatized in 1989, the regulator is the Office of Water Services (OFWAT).

OFWAT conducts every five years a review of the water companies under its remit. One of the questions addressed in such reviews is what scope is there for efficiency savings and productivity growth in each water company so that it can be taken into account in setting a limit to the prices the company can charge for its services until the next periodic review. DEA is one of the methods used to address this question, and this section outlines the use of DEA by OFWAT in the lead-up to its 1994 review of English and Welsh water companies. Fuller details can be found in Thanassoulis (2000a, 2000b, 2002). [For other efficiency assessment applications in regulation in the United Kingdom, see *Utilities Policy*, volume 13, special issue 4 (2005).] Other applications of DEA to water companies can be found in Aida et al. (1998), Tupper and Resende (2004), and Anwandter and Ozuna (2002).

3.10.3.1 Unit of assessment

Water companies are entities too complex to constitute a unit of assessment. Some of them serve millions of customers. For example, Severn Trent Water serves a population of 8.3 million in England and Wales, operates over 1000 sewage treatment works, and generates gross annual revenues of approximately US$2 billion, employing on average 5,000 people in 2000. At the time of the first periodic review by OFWAT (1994) (and still so at the time of this writing), some 10 companies delivered clean water and processed sewage. Such companies are referred to here as water and sewage companies (WASCs). A further 22 companies had only clean water functions, and these are referred to here as water-only companies (WoCs). (Since 1994, WoCs have shrunk in number due to mergers and takeovers.) Thus, there were relatively few observations on a cross-sectional basis to estimate a cost model. This combination of limited observations and the multitude of variables needed to reflect the functioning of a water company means that there would be serious loss of discriminatory power on efficiency if the company were to be the unit of analysis. To overcome this problem, OFWAT assesses companies at the function level. Moreover, in the case of two functions, sewerage and sewage treatment (see figure 3.44), the unit of assessment is below the function level.

Figure 3.44 shows the two-level decomposition of companies for the purposes of defining units of assessment for estimating the scope for efficiency savings. As shown in figure 3.44, the clean water service is broken down to three functions:

- *Water distribution*, relating to conveying the water from exit from treatment to customers;
- *Resources and treatment*, relating to extracting and treating water to make it suitable for distribution to customers;
- *Business activities*, relating to headquarter management, scientific services, and so forth.

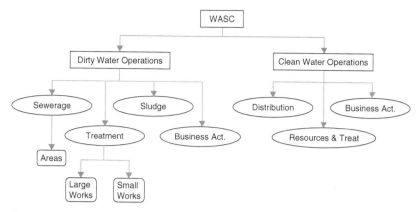

Figure 3.44. Grouping Water Company Operations into Functions (Thanassoulis, 2000b)

Sewage removal is subdivided into four functions:

- *Sewerage*, relating to conveying sewage to treatment works
- Sewage treatment
- *Sludge treatment and disposal*, following sewage treatment
- *Business activities*, defined as for clean water services but relating to dirty water activities

Two of the sewage removal functions are further subdivided into self-contained units, as shown in figure 3.44. Sewerage is divided into geographical areas so that the 10 companies return data for a total of 61 units of assessment, each relating to sewerage services within a specified geographical area. Finally, sewage treatment is subdivided into a large number of self-contained units or works, grouped separately for modeling purposes into "large" and "small" sewage treatment works.

Once assessments are carried out at function or subfunction level, the estimated efficient cost levels are aggregated to the company level. This reveals the scope for efficiency savings at the company level, which is then input to OFWAT's decision process for setting the price limits for the company concerned until the next periodic review.

Assessment at the function level has its advantages in reducing the complexities of the units being assessed. However, it also presents certain problems that must be borne in mind, which we briefly outline here:

- *Functions need to be self-contained*: To assess at the function level, we need to assume that the input–output variables of each function are self-contained in the sense that the input variables we use with respect to a function affect the output variables of that function and only those. Further, the output variables of the function concerned should not be affected by any factors other than those reflected in the input set. In practice, such self-containment of the input–output variables of the functions and subfunctions specified in figure 3.44 is not complete.

- *Non-CRS at the company level can bias the results*: There may be economies of scale at the water company level that cannot be captured by modeling at the function level. This is essentially another form of absence of full self-containment of the functions being modeled. Put another way, the PPS at function or subfunction level may be conditional on the scale size of the parent company. This dependence can make subunits that belong to companies of different scale size not comparable within a DEA framework, where it is implicitly assumed that the units in the comparative set have equal potential to attain output levels from given input levels.

- *Apportioned expenditure*: There is expenditure that relates to more than one function or subfunction. For example, in the case of sewerage districts indirect expenditure known as "general and support expenditure" was not identifiable at the district level and was apportioned in proportion to direct expenditure to the sewerage districts. Where trade-offs between direct and apportioned indirect expenditure exist, the assessment of performance can be biased if a unit is apportioned higher expenditure than it made use of.

Notwithstanding the foregoing difficulties with decomposing water companies for assessment of performance, there are also certain advantages beyond the motivating one of creating more discriminatory models through reducing the number of input–output variables needed at the function level. In particular, the following advantages are worth mentioning:

- Carrying out assessments at the function level makes it possible to identify the functions in which a complex entity such as a water company is efficient and the functions where it has scope to improve its performance. This is more valuable from at least the managerial if not the regulatory perspective than simply identifying an aggregate measure of the scope for improvement at the company level. However, companies need to be mindful of possible biased results on efficiencies at the function level because of possible trade-offs between functions. For example, a company may treat sewage more cheaply at the expense of raising the costs of sludge treatment. Thus, while a company may be cost efficient in one function, this may be at the expense of another function.

- Assessment by function can in some circumstances make it possible to compare units operating in totally different industries as long as the units carry out the same function. For example, laying pipes is a function carried out by a variety of network companies (water, gas, telecommunications), and if this is defined as the unit of assessment, the units across a variety of industries can be compared, taking care to compare like with like. This can enhance the scope of identifying genuinely good practice on a function to be found in whichever industry carries out that function.

3.10.3.2 Input–output variables

The DEA assessments were carried out independently of parallel assessments of efficiency carried out by OFWAT using a variant of corrected ordinary least squares (COLS) regression (see Stewart, 1993). However, OFWAT passed on information to the DEA analysis regarding potential input–output variables that had been derived by OFWAT from a combination of experience in the water industry and regression-based analyses. The DEA analyses then proceeded to select input–output variables from those that regression and industry experience had suggested as candidates. The choice, of course, was also influenced by the variables for which data existed.

For illustrative purposes, we summarize here the arrival at a final set of input–output variables used in assessing the water distribution function by DEA. Fuller details can be found in Thanassoulis (2000a). As far as input variables are concerned generally in assessments carried out for regulatory purposes, and especially in the case of water companies, only one input is used, that of expenditure for the function being assessed. This is understandable given that the primary aim of the regulator is to estimate the scope for cost savings possible through efficiency improvements so that they can be passed on to consumers. Thus, expenditure on water distribution by each company was used as the sole input.

Table 3.14 shows three sets of candidate output variables. The choice of each set was based on those variables being seen as sensible alternatives from the industry perspective in capturing the main expenditure drivers in water distribution. Regression analyses were also used to support the choice of potential sets of output variables. "Properties" reflects the number of connections served by a company, "length of main" reflects their geographical dispersion, and "WDELA" stands for water delivered. The outputs collectively

Table 3.14
Three Potential Output Sets for Assessing
DEA Efficiencies in Water Distribution

1.	Properties, Length of main, and WDELA
2.	Properties and Length of main
3.	Length of main and WDELA

explained in large measure variations in OPEX on water distribution across companies.

Companies were assessed using each output set in turn to see whether there was any material difference in the findings for any companies depending on output set used. WoCs were not permitted as referent units throughout for practical reasons. (It is possible that OFWAT's motivation for this was that the industry would need to accept the efficiency findings and that using role models that account but for a small percentage of the industry would not help in that endeavor.) The bulk of the companies (some 25 out of 32 at the time) changed very little in efficiency rank: no more than two places in the three assessments. A further four changed rank by only three to five places, which again, is not substantial.

Only three companies changed efficiency rank substantially across the output sets in table 3.14. Two of them changed rank by 16 and 9 places, respectively, and were relatively more efficient when water delivered replaced properties as an output. Closer inspection showed this was because they delivered an unusually large amount of water to businesses rather than to residential customers. In contrast, a third company changed rank by 11 places for the worse when water delivered was used instead of properties served. The company had by far the lowest proportion of water delivered to businesses across the sector. Water to businesses is delivered in large volumes per client and therefore should reflect lower expenditure than the same volume of water delivered to households. Thus, the output set {length, properties} should give the more accurate reflection of company cost efficiency among the output sets in table 3.14. A further investigation was made by adding to these two outputs, in turn, bursts and two components reflecting separately water delivered to businesses and water delivered to households. "Bursts" relates to incidents of bursts of water mains. Bursts were used as a proxy for the condition of the mains. Thus, though in the long run they would be treated as an "undesirable" output, at the time of the assessment, only five years after privatization, bursts reflected bad inherited rather than badly managed mains and so were treated as a normal output. The results for splitting water to that for businesses and that for households were very similar to those where water delivered in aggregate had been used. Finally, only one company changed efficiency rank substantially when bursts were added as an output. That company had by far the largest number of bursts per kilometer of main. Its data were deemed atypical, and bursts were excluded as a potential output variable.

Following the above investigations, it was concluded that ranks for the bulk of the companies do not change much on efficiency whichever output set is used. Moreover, for the small number of companies where ranks do change substantially, it is because of unusual quantities of water delivered to businesses rather than to residential customers. To treat such companies fairly, it was decided to use {properties, length of main, WDELA} as the output variables. Thus, irrespective of the mix of water delivered to properties, the company would be assessed fairly.

3.10.3.3 Use made by OFWAT of the DEA assessment results

Following the identification of the input–output variables, input-oriented efficiencies were computed. These were assessed under CRS or VRS, depending on the type of model ultimately adopted following the OLS analyses that OFWAT had previously undertaken for the function concerned. The potential savings SAV_o in operating expense $OPEX_o$ at company o were then $SAV_o = (1 - \theta_o^*)$ $OPEX_o$, where θ_o^* is the DEA input efficiency using OPEX as the sole input.

Assessments by DEA were carried out for three functions: water distribution (Thanassoulis, 2000a), sewerage (Thanassoulis, 2002), and water resources and treatment, the stage the water goes through before being distributed. The precise use of the results from the DEA assessments is confidential to OFWAT. However, from published accounts, the DEA estimates of efficient cost levels in distribution and in resources and treatment

> were added to overall average [clean] water business activities costs and the result divided by the actual distribution, treatment and business costs to give an overall [DEA-based] efficiency ratio [of clean water operations]. In most cases the results [on company efficiency on clean water operations] were similar to those of the regressions. If they were significantly better, the Director [of OFWAT] moved the company up one band [on efficiency in clean water]. (OFWAT, 1995, p. 414)

Thus, the DEA results were used by OFWAT in conjunction with the COLS regression results to arrive at a ranking of companies on efficiency. Once the ranks on efficiency were obtained, OFWAT took further company-specific factors into account before arriving at the final price determinations.

While a direct link between the DEA applications and the final OFWAT price determinations of 1994 is difficult to establish, their potential impact is very high in monetary terms. The clean water industry cost the public in England and Wales in 1993–1994 and at prices of that time about US\$4 billion. The price determinations were to last for up to 10 years, potentially affecting costs on the order of US\$40 billion at 1993–1994 prices. Thus, even minor differences in the final price determinations attributable to the DEA analyses could have had a very substantial financial impact both for the public and for the companies.

3.10.4 Retail

Applications of DEA in retail are few if we exclude banking efficiency analysis. In this section, we focus on an application to pubs of a brewery as detailed in Athanassopoulos and Thanassoulis (1995). Pubs in the United Kingdom are outlets where clients can have either drinks only or a meal with drinks, as in a restaurant. Other applications of DEA in retail include that of Barros and Alves (2004), who used Malmquist indexes to assess a Portuguese multimarket retail chain; Keh and Chu (2003), who analyzed grocery stores in the United States; Donthu and Yoo (1998), who analyzed 24 outlets of a fast food restaurant chain; and Grewal et al. (1999), who analyzed the efficiency of 59 retail outlets of a Fortune 500 retailing and manufacturing firm.

Retail is in general a private-sector activity that is guided by profitability. Profitability alone, however, may not be adequate to compare units since the different environments in which units operate may affect their profit. Athanassopoulos and Thanassoulis (1995) analyzed pub performance using two complementary measures of performance: market efficiency, defined as the ability of a unit to generate revenue given its resources and environment, and cost efficiency, defined as the ability of a unit to control costs for its revenue level.

3.10.4.1 Input–output variables

The input and output variables used by Athanassopoulos and Thanassoulis (1995) to assess market efficiency are shown in figure 3.45. Note that in referring to this application we report only on results from the market, rather than the cost efficiency assessment.

The single output turnover reflects the share a pub secures of the local market of beer sales. Consumption of beer in the catchment area reflects the size of the market in which the pub operates. The bar area of the pub reflects its capacity to accommodate customers, and we would expect that the larger the bar area, the larger the turnover, all else being equal. Finally, the number of pubs and clubs in the catchment area reflects the competition faced by each pub. Athanassopoulos and Thanassoulis (1995) detail the definition of the catchment area and justify the use of the inverse of the number of competing pubs as the input variable because competition negatively affects the sales in a pub. (See also section 3.6 for the more general debate about the treatment of such variables in DEA.)

Two groups of pubs, 60 in total, were assessed. The first group, numbering 18, consisted of so-called "local" pubs that benefited little from passing trade. This group is referred to as NPT (no passing trade). The second group benefited from passing trade and is referred to as PT. It could be argued that the two sets of pubs are not comparable and should be assessed separately. However, from the company's perspective, it was important to identify the best pubs

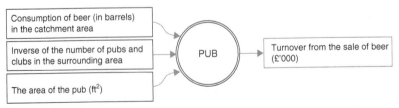

Figure 3.45. Input-Output Variables to Assess the Market Efficiency of Pubs

across the two categories rather than in each category, because the company can choose in the medium and longer term whether pubs should be oriented toward passing trade or not.

3.10.4.2 Benchmarks and peers

Results from the assessment in Athanassopoulos and Thanassoulis (1995) included the identification of benchmark pubs. DEA efficient pubs are obviously the best candidates for benchmarking. However, pubs may be DEA efficient due to lack of comparators rather than truly efficient performance. In order to handle this issue, the authors selected as benchmarks those of the market-efficient pubs that were frequently cited as efficient peers to inefficient pubs and were influential in estimating target turnover for such pubs. The aggregation of the contributions of an efficient pub to the target turnover of all inefficient pubs was taken as a measure of its influence in estimating target turnover for inefficient pubs. The more influential a pub is in estimating target turnover and the more frequently it is cited as a peer, the more confident we are of its good performance. Adopting the foregoing criteria of frequency of peer citing and influence on target turnover, the authors identified a number of pubs as benchmarks (those marked with an asterisk) on the market efficiency assessment shown in table 3.15.

Table 3.15
Profitability, Contribution, and Frequency of Comparator Pubs (Athanassopoulos and Thanassoulis, 1995)

Pub	Profitability (%)	Contribution (%)	Frequency
NPT Pubs			
A17*	8.1	40	9
A16*	12.7	22	4
A18*	6.9	16	6
A15*	13.8	11	6
A14	6.7	2	2
Total		100	
PT Pubs			
B36*	12.5	37	24
B41*	11.7	21	16
B38*	10.3	10	15
B35*	13.6	10	6
B39*	8.0	9	14
B42*	12.0	9	12
B40	12.6	4	6
B37	7.7	0	0
Total		100	

Benchmark pubs covered a wide range of profitability (gross profit to turnover), suggesting that pubs that fully exploit their market potential (therefore showing high market efficiency) are not necessarily always profitable. They may be using a large staff and other resource base to sustain the turnover, leading to low profitability. It is interesting to look at pub A17 in table 3.15. It has high market efficiency but low profitability. This suggests it has poor control over its operating costs, or the market in which it operates yields a low turnover even though the pub is exploiting in comparison to other pubs the full potential of its market. The pub may still offer good operating practice for other pubs to emulate in attracting customers.

3.10.4.3 Market efficiency versus profitability

The separation of the market efficiency component of profitability makes it possible to gain a better insight into the performance of a pub so that we can see whether it is a good benchmark for high efficiency in market exploitation, in controlling operating costs, or in both. We can see this by means of an "efficiency profitability matrix," as depicted in figure 3.46, which shows an illustrative scatter diagram on profitability and market efficiency. Each of the two axes is split into two ranges of values, one range containing "high" and the other "low" values. The cut-off point between the ranges of low and high levels is subjective, and clearly there is some gray area. Pubs with high profitability and market efficiency levels are plotted in the area labeled "stars." Pubs with high profitability but low market efficiency are plotted in the area labeled "sleepers" because they "sleep," so to speak, on the market potential they could exploit. In contrast, pubs with high market efficiency but low profitability are

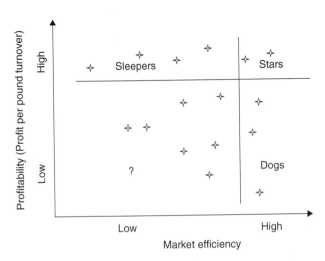

Figure 3.46. Market Efficiency Versus Profitability

plotted in the area labeled "dogs" because they work hard on their market potential but this does not translate to high profits. Finally, pubs with low market efficiency and profitability are plotted in the area labeled "?"

Athanassopoulos and Thanassoulis (1995) found that not all pubs with high profitability had high market efficiency. The picture was even more marked when one viewed pubs with high market efficiency. Only some of them had high profitability. Clearly, judging long-term prospects of pubs on profitability alone would run the risk of overlooking pubs good in maximizing revenue given the market in which they operated.

3.10.4.4 Managerial and programmatic efficiency

The market efficiency of a pub reflects the competence of local management, but it also reflects the location and type of pub (NPT or PT)—decisions that were made by higher echelons of management. Athanassopoulos and Thanassoulis (1995) decomposed the market efficiency of each pub into a component attributable to local and a component attributable to higher echelons of management. Market efficiency was therefore decomposed into managerial efficiency and programmatic efficiency following the approach of Charnes et al. (1981), explained in detail in section 3.8.

The average market efficiencies of pubs after managerial inefficiencies were eliminated were 86% and 99.4% for NPT and PT pubs, respectively. The standard deviation of the market efficiencies of NPT pubs was 12.4 percentage points, while that of PT pubs was only 1.3 percentage points (see Athanassopoulos and Thanassoulis, 1995). Thus, PT pubs were consistently more efficient than NPT pubs, once local managerial inefficiencies were controlled for. Clearly, findings as to which type of outlet is more successful as distinct from the competence of those running the outlet has important implications for decisions regarding the longer term acquisition and divestment of pubs. However, as noted in section 3.8, we must beware of bias in comparisons of this kind, especially where, as here, the two groups of units being compared differ significantly in size (see also section 3.8 on this point).

3.10.5 Police

This account is drawn from an application of DEA to data on police forces in England and Wales. A fuller account can be found in Thanassoulis (1995). Recent DEA applications on police forces can also be found in Drake and Simper (2005) on the U.K. police forces, Sun (2002) on Taiwan police forces, and Barros (2006) on Portuguese police forces.

The application reported in Thanassoulis (1995) and summarized here was carried out on behalf of the Audit Commission of the United Kingdom. The Audit Commission is an independent body that undertakes studies of public services with a view to making recommendations for improving their economic, efficient, and effective delivery. A study of this kind into "crime

Figure 3.47. Input and Output Variables in Police Assessments

management" by police was undertaken by the Audit Commission in 1992–1993, and the application reported here was commissioned in the context of that study. Crime management includes a raft of police activities, notably, strategies to prevent crime and investigation once it has occurred. However, the bulk of police effort is applied to investigation, and the assessment reported here focuses on this aspect of police work.

The assessment covered 41 out of a total of 43 police forces in England and Wales. It excluded the London Metropolitan and the City of London police forces. These two forces were not deemed comparable to other forces because of their special duties, such as the provision of diplomatic protection, which are not generally found at forces outside London.

3.10.5.1 Input–output variables

The aim of the assessment was to identify the efficiency of each force in clearing up crimes. There is a large variety of crimes, ranging from multiple murders to vandalism. It was necessary to use a small number of categories of crime so that only a few variables would be needed to reflect police activities. The need to use very few variables was dictated by the limited number of assessment units at our disposal. The Audit Commission had decided to group crimes by "seriousness" and "complexity of detection." This had resulted in the following three types of crime: (i) violent, (ii) burglary, and (iii) other.

It was agreed that these three crime categories were sufficient to convey an overview of the seriousness and complexity of crime found, and they were retained for the purposes of the assessment by DEA, as well. Using the foregoing crime categories, the variables in figure 3.47 were defined for assessing the performance of police forces.

Manpower was taken as of the end of the year of assessment. A crime was deemed cleared up if it had resulted in a summons or charge or a caution, if no further action was deemed appropriate, or if it was deemed to have been "taken into consideration" with some other cleared-up offense. Capital data reflecting computers, cars, and so on, were ignored. The police were at the time funded using a "standard spending assessment" formula that allocated "nonlabor" costs in proportion to manpower costs. Thus, the level of "officers" reflects also capital budgets.

3.10.5.2 The initial DEA assessment

The assessment was run using CRS and an output orientation. The output orientation is consistent with the notion that reported crime levels are largely outside the control of the police and that efficient operation should, at least in the short term, result in higher clear-ups rather than lower reported crime level. The assessment maintained CRS in converting crimes to clear-ups. While this is a relatively strong assumption, it is nevertheless plausible that as crimes and manpower rise by some percentage, so should clear-ups under efficient operation.

The efficiencies obtained ranged from 65% to 100% with median efficiency 88%. The efficiency ratings were not the only information of interest at this stage. There was a desire to understand better the basis of the efficiency rating of each force and to strengthen the intuitive support for the results obtained. We now outline the steps taken in these directions.

Some 13 forces had an efficiency rating of 100%. Because DEA, by design, shows a force in the best possible light relative to other forces, there was a desire to test whether the top efficiencies derived would stand further scrutiny. In this respect, efficient forces were put through two additional tests, examining, first, their virtual inputs and outputs, and second, how frequently each force had been used as an efficient peer for other forces.

The virtual output, say, on violent crime clear-ups, is the product of the level of such clear-ups and the optimal weight on this output in model (3.5) in section 3.3. Virtual inputs and outputs reveal (e.g., see section 3.7 on WR) the variables underpinning the efficiency rating of a force, though as noted, typically there are multiple weighting structures that can render a force 100% efficient. The problem of multiple optimal sets of DEA weights was resolved by using DEA software (e.g., *PIM DEASoft-V1*, http://www.deasoftware.co.uk), which automatically identifies an optimal weighting structure that *maximizes the minimum* virtual input or output of each force. Although this does not fully identify the sets of all alternative optimal weighting structures when they exist, it does convey information as to whether all variables can take "significant" virtual values without detriment to the efficiency rating of a force.

Inspection of the virtual inputs and outputs of the efficient forces led to the identification of two groups of forces. The first group contained eight forces that had minimum virtual inputs or outputs of 10% or more. The second group had five forces that had at least one virtual input or output below 10%. The threshold of 10% here for virtual values is subjective. Forces in the first group were deemed to offer more acceptable performance in that there was no prior indication (in the form of a low minimum virtual value) that some input or output variable plays a very minor role in the efficiency rating of the force.

An inspection was next made of how frequently each efficient force was used as a comparator or "efficient peer" for inefficient forces. Only four forces were used most frequently as efficient peers. These forces were also in the first group of forces above, and so out of the 13 initial efficient forces, only four were identified at this point as candidate "good" forces that may act as role model for other forces.

3.10.5.3 Further exploratory DEA assessments

The initial results were useful in giving an overall view of the performance of forces. The identification of efficient peers that can be used as benchmarks in assessing the performance of inefficient forces was thought especially valuable. However, it was also felt that the assessment needed to be strengthened in a number of ways to make the results more acceptable. In particular, it was felt that clearing up a violent crime was more valuable than clearing up a burglary, itself more valuable than clearing up an "other" crime because the latter largely related to theft (of cars and other property) and vandalism. Yet efficiency ratings of many forces were based on output weights whose magnitudes ran counter to these intuitive relative values. In order to address this concern, the assessment was rerun imposing restrictions on the output weights. However, while the need for WRs was broadly accepted, it was difficult to reach a consensus on the precise restrictions to use. For illustrative purposes and in order to assess the likely impact of WRs on earlier unrestricted efficiency ratings, a value system was adopted that had a commonsense credibility:

> Weight on one violent crime clear-up $\geq$ 10× weight on one burglary clear-up;
> Weight on one burglary clear-up $\geq$ 2× weight on one "other" crime clear-up.

This value system ensures that output weights are more in line with intuitive feeling on the relative importance of outputs, though it cannot be claimed that it reflects in any way broadly accepted relative crime clear-up values by society.

The value system imposed generally did not have a very substantial impact on the efficiency ratings of forces except in a few cases where efficiency dropped by more than 10 percentage points. The WRs had a more dramatic effect on the number of forces that could be deemed to be 100% efficient. The number dropped from the initial 13 to only 3 efficient forces. Of these three efficient forces, only one had been in the four forces identified previously as good performers. This may appear surprising at first since the four forces initially identified as good performers have virtual values of at least 10% on all inputs and outputs. This, however, does not necessarily ensure that they observed the relative worth imposed above for each type of clear-up. Nevertheless, the remaining three of the four forces initially identified as good performers are still so after the imposition of the DEA WRs showing efficiencies less than 100% but greater than 90%. Thus, the conclusion was reached that a total of six forces, namely the initial four plus the two additional forces of the three efficient under the WRs were retained as role models where good practice may be identified for dissemination to other forces.

3.10.5.4 Efficient peers

One valuable aspect of the assessment of force performance by DEA was the identification of efficient peer forces for each inefficient force. The performance of the inefficient force could be contrasted with that of its efficient peers to shed light on its weaknesses. There was, however, uneasiness about the comparability between some of the inefficient forces and their efficient peers. It was felt, for example, that the more economically and socially deprived an area is, the harder it is to solve crimes for reasons such as many suspects having no fixed address and the general public being uncooperative with the police. This meant that an inefficient force covering relatively deprived areas could not really be compared with those of its efficient peers that did not cover similarly deprived areas.

The Audit Commission had divided forces into "families" using a number of socioeconomic and settlement pattern indicators so that a consensus existed that forces in each family cover similar policing environments. Thus, an inefficient force could be contrasted with efficient peers from its own family. Where an inefficient force did have peers from its own family, and this was so for the majority of forces, it was contrasted to peers from within rather than outside its family, even if they were not its DEA peers. All families had at least one efficient force, and no inefficient force had more than one peer from its own family.

Inefficient forces were contrasted with peer or otherwise efficient forces from their own family by means of ratios as illustrated in table 3.16. The ratios were constructed from the input–output variables used in the DEA assessment, as follows: Clear-up rate is the ratio between each type of crime clear-up and the total number of crimes of each type, violent, burglaries, and other. Clear-ups per officer is the ratio of clear-ups (of each type of crime) and the number of officers in the force. The forces were listed by family in the manner illustrated in table 3.17 for family A. The tables were divided in sections by comparator efficient force. Section (a) relates to efficient force A1. The section is divided into part (i), containing the inefficient forces for which force A1 is a DEA peer, and part (ii), containing the inefficient forces to be compared to force A1 because they had no DEA peer from family A.

Table 3.16
Ratios Constructed for Clear-Up rate and Clear-Ups per officer

Variable		Clear-Up Rate	Variable		Clear-Ups per Officer
VILCLPR	=	Violent crime	VILCLPO	=	Violent crime
BURCLPR	=	Burglaries	BURGCLPO	=	Burglaries
OTHCLPR	=	"Other" crime	OTHCLPO	=	"Other" crime

Force A1 has better ratio values than any of the inefficient forces listed. Only in the three cases highlighted under burglary clear-ups per officer (BURGCLPO) does force A1 perform somewhat worse than the inefficient forces concerned. It can be held out as a role model for the inefficient forces, the problem of comparability having been resolved because all forces come from the same family. It is noteworthy that despite force A1 not being a DEA peer of the forces in part (ii), it nevertheless proves a useful comparator for them in the sense of showing their performance to be deficient. This is not necessarily coincidental. DEA selects peers for an inefficient force that largely match its input–output mix. However, there will generally be many other forces with input–output mixes not matching closely that of the inefficient force but that nevertheless outperform it on many input–output ratios.

The creation of tables such as table 3.17 made it possible to discuss the DEA identifications of weaker and stronger forces on performance without recourse to the technical detail of DEA but by merely focusing on ratios. Ratios precede DEA as instruments of performance assessment, and many find them easier to use. The strength of DEA over conventional ratio analysis

Table 3.17
Family A (Thanassoulis, 1995)

FORCE	VILCLPR	BURCLPR	OTHCLPR	VILCLPO	BURGCLPO	OTHCLPO
Section (a)—Force A1						
Force A1	1.03[a]	0.22	0.35	2.50	1.62	9.21
Part (i)—Force A1 Is a DEA Peer						
A2	0.61	0.10	0.16	1.54	1.25	6.15
A3	0.79	0.18	0.24	2.04	1.87	8.66
A4	0.88	0.17	0.30	1.53	1.49	7.48
A5	0.78	0.12	0.19	1.43	1.32	6.88
A6	0.72	0.13	0.17	1.37	1.20	6.19
A7	0.76	0.11	0.18	1.03	0.77	4.04
A8	0.76	0.14	0.17	1.08	1.47	4.83
A9	0.68	0.08	0.17	1.63	0.89	6.26
Part (ii)—Force A1 Is the Efficient Comparator but Not a DEA Pees						
A10	0.75	0.18	0.22	1.20	1.55	5.88
A11	0.73	0.14	0.22	1.42	1.45	7.55
A12	0.86	0.19	0.27	1.23	1.26	6.86
A13	0.73	0.19	0.19	1.80	2.27	6.98
A14	0.74	0.18	0.21	1.65	1.98	8.45
A15	0.68	0.11	0.17	1.14	1.05	6.96

[a]Note that here clear-ups of crime from previous years can make the percentage cleared in any one year above 100%.

lies in that it simultaneously accounts for all input and output variables rather than one output-to-input ratio at a time, which could lead to misleading conclusions.

3.10.5.5 Decomposing police efficiency

The input–output variables used in the assessment so far permit the measurement of the overall performance of a force in terms of its clear-up levels relative to its crime and manpower levels. It is, however, possible to assess the performance of a force in specific areas. Two such areas are the force's resource efficiency given the volume of crime it has to deal with and its efficiency in securing clear-ups given its crime levels.

Forces were assessed on their resource efficiency given the volume of crime they face using as input the number of officers and all the outputs in figure 3.47. The efficiencies obtained with this input–output set were referred to as "manpower efficiencies." These efficiencies can reveal the extent to which a force may be underresourced for the crime level it faces. The second assessment was carried out using all inputs in figure 3.47 except officers and the full set of outputs.[26] The efficiencies obtained with this set of input–output variables are referred to as "clear-up efficiencies." The clear-up efficiencies differ from the overall efficiencies obtained in the initial assessment in that they do not take account of the manpower level of a force. They merely reflect the proportions of crime cleared and leave open the question as to whether good clear-up rates can be attributed to excessive use of manpower and/or to more effective use of manpower. Forces efficient in manpower terms that also secure good clear-up levels given their crime levels are not underresourced. However, those that are efficient in manpower terms but do not clear up satisfactory proportions of their crimes may be underresourced. The issues of clearing up crime and potential underresourcing of forces were addressed by using a graph similar to the efficiency–profitability matrix in figure 3.46. The manpower and clear-up efficiencies give a two-dimensional view of the performance of each force. A good force should offer a high clear-up and a high manpower efficiency. Such a force would be achieving the highest clear-up levels found anywhere for its crime levels, while also having the lowest manpower level for its crime levels. Forces were divided into four quadrants, and conclusions were drawn about areas where police forces needed to improve in the manner illustrated in figure 3.46.

Looking at all the forces, the correlation coefficient between clear-up and manpower efficiencies is –0.231, which is significant at the 10% level. Thus, there is weak negative association between the two efficiencies, indicating only a weak tendency for relatively high staffing levels (i.e., low manpower efficiencies) to go with good clear-up rates (i.e., high clear-up efficiencies). This is intuitively acceptable in that it indicates that raising staffing levels would lead to more crimes being cleared.

In this section, we have summarized a number of DEA applications in different fields: education, banking, regulation, retail, and police. This chapter would be double in length if we tried to include here other relevant fields of application of DEA (e.g., health, electricity, insurance, municipal services, transports, telecommunications). Chapter 1 (table 1.1) presents an enormous list of applications of DEA to various fields that the reader can consult for reference. Our aim in this section was simply to illustrate the kinds of issues that arise in each context (and these depend to a large extent on the context) and also the types of results that can be provided by DEA that have managerial relevance and utility.

3.11 Conclusion

In this chapter, we have covered the programming method of DEA for measuring comparative efficiency. Since the seminal paper of Charnes et al. (1978), which spawned DEA, the field has grown exponentially in terms of methodological developments and applications, numbering at the time of this writing more than 3,000 papers, books, and monographs by more than 1,600 authors worldwide (see Emrouznejad et al., forthcoming). We hope we have distilled in this chapter enough of this vast literature to:

- give readers an introduction to the fundamental concepts of DEA;
- familiarize them with some of the latest thinking on key aspects of DEA such as target setting, incorporating value judgments in DEA assessments, scale effects on productivity, outlier detection, dealing with exogenous factors, and badly behaved data; and
- illustrate some applications of DEA.

This should enable the reader to carry out assessments of performance in many practical contexts, especially in view of readily available software in the area such as noted in section 3.10. Moreover, the grounding within the chapter should also enable the researcher or practitioner in the area to explore more readily the field for aspects of theory and application of DEA not covered here, such as dynamic DEA, where assessment addresses the presence of capital assets that affect performance over long periods of time (e.g., see Emrouznejad and Thanassoulis, 2005), or the various aspects of assessing productivity change over time using Malmquist indices covered in chapter 5 of this book.

DEA comfortably models the most general multiple input–output production contexts and avoids the need to specify a function between them or to make assumptions about inefficiency distribution of production units. This makes it a powerful tool at the hands of those wishing to analyze issues of comparative efficiency and productivity. Moreover, DEA is increasingly proving of value well outside the "production" context. For example, witness the use of DEA in multicriteria decision making such as choosing the location for a facility or choosing among competing products. Ultimately, DEA is a flexible tool that has been used and no doubt will continue to be used in a large variety of contexts. In this chapter, we have outlined the major issues related to the measurement of efficiency through nonparametric methods.

Notes

1. A production unit is nondominated if there is no other unit that when compared to it presents lower or equal inputs and higher or equal outputs.

2. We use the word "efficient" in a broad sense here, since we are referring to Pareto-efficiency, radial efficiency, or any other type of efficiency that we can arrive at in the context of defining target levels, as will be clear in section 3.9. Note, however, that, in general, targets are associated with the concept of Pareto-efficiency since usually one wishes to arrive at targets that are Pareto-efficient.

3. The L_p distance (or p-norm distance) between points A and B is given by

$$\left(\sum_{i=1}^{n} |A_i - B_i|^p \right)^{\frac{1}{p}} ,$$

where p is set to 1 for the one-norm distance or Manhattan distance, to 2 for the two-norm Euclidean distance, and to infinity for Chebyshev distance.

4. There are also some other unit-invariant versions of the additive model. See, e.g., Charnes et al. (1985), Green et al. (1997), and Lovell and Pastor (1995).

5. This measure of efficiency is very similar to the SBM measure of Tone (1993, 2001) when we note that the SBM measure of Tone can also be written as

$$\frac{\sum_{i=1}^{m} \theta_i}{m} \times \frac{s}{\sum_{r=1}^{s} \beta_r}$$

(slacks are replaced by multiplying factors).

6. Färe et al. (2002) also introduced a measure of efficiency (the multiplicative Russell measure) that corresponds to the input-oriented version of the GDF in (3.12).

7. Under this approach, the profit efficiency of unit A (see figure 3.11) would be defined as a ratio of revenue to cost, such that

$$\frac{p_A y_A / w_A x_A}{p_A y_A^{**} / w_A x_A^{**}},$$

where the double asterisk is the optimal solution of

$$\max \left\{ \frac{p_A y}{w_A x} \ \Big| \ (x, y) \in T \right\}$$

(for details, see Cooper et al., 2000a).

8. When the technology satisfies CRS, maximum profit is assumed to be zero and the quadratic equation solution reduces to

$$\varphi_A^h = \sqrt{\frac{p_A y_A}{w_A x_A}}$$

(for details, see Fare et al, 1985, 1994).

9. Chavas and Cox (1999) also address the issue of closest technical efficient targets in a model where they measure and decompose profit efficiency. The model of Chavas and Cox (1999) calculates the technical profit efficiency of unit A as δ_A defined in

$$\min \left\{ \delta_o \mid \left(\delta_o^{1-\alpha} x_{io}, \delta_o^{-\alpha} y_{ro} \right) \in T \right\}.$$

Chavas and Cox (1999) also propose the calculation of allocative profit and overall profit efficiency and introduce some concepts relating to scale efficiency in a profit context.

10. Note that in this framework any DEA model can be used to calculate technically efficient targets, and then the GDF can be used a posteriori to reflect the adjustments between the observed point and its targets.

11. Note that this approach can be seen as equivalent to one where undesirable outputs are treated as negative and negative data were transformed into positive. Alternatively, one can use negative outputs if the model to be used can handle this type of data (see next section).

12. Note that Färe et al. (1996) also proposed solving models with and without environmental variables and used the two measures to derive a measure of environmental efficiency of fossil-fuel–fired electric utilities.

13. The Zhu (1998) approach has been improved by Premachandra (2001) and criticized by Shanmugam and Johnson (2007). The latter authors point out that ratios of variables as those used by Zhu (1998) are not distributed accordingly to the multivariate Gaussian distribution, violating, therefore, one of the required assumptions to apply PCA.

14. Available at http://www.qhull.org.

15. Note that the constraint associated to nondiscretionary inputs can also be expressed as

$$\sum_{j=1}^{n} \lambda_j \left(x_{ij} - x_{io} \right) \leq 0,$$

meaning that it imposes convexity not to the nondiscretionary inputs, but to a new variable reflecting the difference between the nondiscretionary level of input i of referent units and DMU$_o$ being assessed.

16. In figure 3.35 point A is $(1, 0.55)$ and point C has coordinates $(1.5, -0.85)$. The linear segment AC is therefore given by New$/y = 3.35 - 2.8 x_1 /y$. Therefore for a level of the new variable of 0 for DMU E the target point on the line segment AC is 1.196429, and therefore the efficiency of DMU E is given by the ratio between the target and the observed value of x_1/y, i.e., $1.196429/1.33333 = 89.73\%$.

17. See Simar and Wilson (2007) for an exhaustive list of articles that have used tobit second-stage models.

18. Note that tobit second-stage models can be used not necessarily to adjust efficiency scores calculated in relation to discretionary factors (in the spirit of Ray, 1991) but rather to explain differences in efficiency between production units.

19. Available at http://www.deasoftware.co.uk.

20. Available at http://www.gams.com/contrib/gamsdea/dea.htm.

21. Available at http://www.wiso.uni-dortmund.de/lsfg/or/scheel/doordea.htm.

22. For examples of studies using the production approach, see Sherman and Gold (1985), Athanassopoulos (1997), Vassiloglou and Giokas (1990), Drake and Howcroft (1994), Schaffnit et al. (1997), and Camanho and Dyson (1999, 2005) for bank branch studies and Ferrier and Lovell (1990), Berger et al. (1987), and Berg et al. (1991) for bank studies.

23. For examples of studies using the intermediation approach, see Berger and Mester (2000), Berger et al. (1987), Berger and Humphrey (1991), Aly et al. (1990), and Barr et al. (1993) for bank studies and Berger et al. (1997), Athanassopoulos (1997), and Camanho and Dyson (2005) for bank branch studies.

24. Some of these outputs deserve some explanations. Other resources include term deposit accounts, emigrant accounts, investment funds, savings insurance, and so on, and credit is divided into two types: credit by the bank, which includes consumer credit, card credit, and overdrafts; and credit by associates, which includes factoring and leasing, which is provided by associate companies inside the same financial group.

25. Even though the cut-off point used to separate good and poor operational efficiency is arbitrary, it is clear that branches with lower operational efficiency values tend to also have low technical profit efficiency values.

26. It should be noted that in this assessment we have essentially self-contained output-to-input ratios in the sense that some ratios are meaningful (e.g., violent crimes cleared to violent crimes reported) whereas others are not (e.g., violent crimes cleared to burglaries reported). Recent literature in DEA focuses on ratios of outputs to inputs as the basis of assessment of performance. This has a number of advantages, including the ability to ignore within the DEA assessment ratios that may not be particularly meaningful. For the use of ratios in this way in DEA, see Despić et al. (2007) and Salerian and Chan (2005).

Bibliography

Adler, N., and Golany, B. (2001) Evaluation of deregulated airline networks using data envelopment analysis combined with principal component analysis with an application to Western Europe, *European Journal of Operational Research 132*, 260–273.

Agrell, P.J., Bogetoft, P., Brock, M., and Tind, J. (2001) Efficiency evaluation with convex pairs, Paper presented at the 7th European Workshop on Efficiency and Productivity Analysis, Oviedo, Spain, 25–29 September 2001.

Aida, K., Cooper, W.W., Pastor, J.T., and Sueyoshi, T. (1998) Evaluating water supply services in JAPAN with RAM: A range-adjusted measure of inefficiency, *Omega 26/2*, 207–232.

Ali, A.I., and Seiford, L.M. (1990) Translation invariance in data envelopment analysis, *Operations Research Letters 9*, 403–405.

Ali, A.I., Cook, W.D., and Seiford, L.M. (1991) Strict vs. weak ordinal relations for multipliers in data envelopment analysis, *Management Science 37*, 733–738.

Ali, A.I., and Seiford, LM (1993) Computational accuracy and infinitesimals in data envelopment analysis, *INFOR 31/4*, 290–297.

Allen, K. (1999) DEA in the ecological context—an overview. In Westermann, G. (Ed.), *Data Envelopment Analysis in the Service Sector*, Gabler, Wiesbaden, 203–235.

Allen, R., Athanassopoulos, A., Dyson, R.G., and Thanassoulis, E. (1997) Weights restrictions and value judgments in data envelopment analysis: Evolution, development and future directions, *Annals of Operations Research 73*, 13–34.

Allen, R., and Thanassoulis, E. (2004) Improving envelopment in data envelopment analysis, *European Journal of Operational research 154/2*, 363–379.

Aly, H.Y., Grabowski, R., Pasurka, C., and Rangan, N. (1990) Technical, scale, and allocative efficiencies in U.S. banking: An empirical investigation, *Review of Economics and Statistics 72*, 211–218.

Andersen, P., and Petersen, N. (1993) A procedure for ranking efficient units in data envelopment analysis, *Management Science 39/10*, 1261–1264.

Anwandter, L., and Ozuna, T., Jr. (2002) Can public sector reforms improve the efficiency of public water utilities? *Environmental and Development Economics 7*, 687–700.

Appa, G., and Yue, M. (1999) On setting scale efficient targets in DEA, *Journal of the Operational Research Society 50/1*, 60–69.

Athanassopoulos, A.D., and Thanassoulis, E. (1995) Separating market efficiency from profitability and its implications for planning, *Journal of the Operational Research Society 46/1*, 20–34.

Athanassopoulos, A.D. (1995) Goal programming and data envelopment analysis (GoDEA) for target-based multi-level planning: Allocating central grants to the Greek local authorities, *European Journal of Operational Research 87*, 535–550.

Athanassopoulos, A.D. (1997) Service quality and operating efficiency synergies for management control in the provision of financial services: Evidence from Greek bank branches, *European Journal of Operational Research 98*, 300–313.

Athanassopoulos, A.D., and Shale, E. (1997) Assessing the comparative efficiency of higher education institutions in the UK by means of data envelopment analysis, *Education Economics 5/2*, 117–134.

Athanassopoulos, D. (1998) Decision support for target-based resource allocation of public services in multiunit and multilevel systems, *Management Science 1998 44/2*, 173–187.

Athanassopoulos, A.D., Lambroukos, N., and Seiford, L. (1999) Data envelopment scenario analysis for setting targets to electricity generating plants, *European Journal of Operational Research 115*, 413–428.

Bala, K., and Cook, W.D. (2003) Performance measurement with classification information: An enhanced additive DEA model, *Omega, The International Journal of Management Science 31*, 439–450

Banker, R.D., Charnes, A., and Cooper, W.W. (1984) Some models for estimating technical and scale inefficiencies in Data Envelopment Analysis, *Management Science 30*, 1078–1092.

Banker, R.D. (1984) Estimating most productive scale size using data envelopment analysis, *European Journal of Operational Research 17*, 35–44.

Banker, R.D., and Morey, R.C. (1986a) The use of Categorical variables in Data envelopment analysis, *Management Science 32/12*, 1613–1627.

Banker, R.D., and Morey, R.C. (1986b) Efficiency analysis for exogenously fixed inputs and outputs, *Operations Research 34/4*, 513–520.

Banker, R.D., and Maindiratta, A. (1986) Piecewise log-linear estimation of efficient production surfaces, *Management Science 32/1*, 126–135.

Banker, R.D., and Maindiratta, A. (1988) Nonparametric Analysis of technical and allocative efficiencies in production, *Econometrica 56/6*, 1315–1332.

Banker, R.D., and Thrall, R.M. (1992) Estimation of returns to scale using data envelopment analysis, European *Journal of Operational Research 62*, 74–84

Banker, R.D. (1993) Maximum likelihood, consistency and data envelopment analysis: A statistical foundation, *Management Science 39/10*, 1265–1273.

Banker, R.D., Chang, H., and Cooper, W.W. (1996) Equivalence and implementation of alternative methods for determining returns to scale in data envelopment analysis, *European Journal of Operational Research 89*, 473–481.

Banker, R.D. (1996) Hypothesis tests using data envelopment analysis, *Journal of Productivity Analysis 7*, 139–159.

Banker, R.D., Janakiraman, S., and Natarajan, R. (2004) Analysis of trends in technical and allocative efficiency: An application to Texas public school districts, *European Journal of Operational Research 154/2*, 477–491.

Bardhan, I., Bowlin, W.F., Cooper, W.W., and Sueyoshi, T. (1996a) Models and Measures for efficiency dominance in DEA. Part I: Additive Models and MED measures, *Journal of the Operations Research Society of Japan 39/3*, 322–332.

Bardhan, I., Bowlin, W.F., Cooper, W.W., and Sueyoshi, T. (1996b) Models and Measures for efficiency dominance in DEA. Part II: free disposal hull (FDH) and Russell measure (RM) approaches, *Journal of the Operations Research Society of Japan 39/3*, 333–344.

Barr, R.D., Seiford, L.M., and Siems, T.F. (1993) An envelopment-analysis approach to measuring the managerial efficiency of banks, *Annals of Operations Research 45*, 1–9.

Barr, R.D. (2004) DEA software tools and technology, in Cooper, W.W., Seiford, L.M., and Zhu, J. (Eds.), *Handbook on Data Envelopment Analysis*, Kluwer Academic Publishers, 539–566.

Barros, C.P., and Alves, C. (2004) An empirical analysis of productivity growth in a Portuguese retail chain using Malmquist productivity index, *Journal of Retailing and Consumer Services 11*, 269–278.

Barros, C.P. (2006) Productivity growth in the Lisbon police force, *Public Organization Review 6*, 21–35.

Belton, V., and Vickers SP. (1993) Desmystifying DEA—a visual interactive approach based on multicriteria analysis, *Journal of the Operational Research Society 44/9*, 883–896.

Berg, A.S., Førsund, F.R., and Jansen, E.S. (1991) Technical efficiency of Norwegian banks: The non-parametric approach to efficiency measurement, *Journal of Productivity Analysis 2/2*, 127–142.

Berg, S.A., Førsund, F.R., Hjalmarsson, L., and Suominen, M. (1993) Banking efficiency in the Nordic countries, *Journal of Banking and Finance 17*, 371–388.

Berger, A.N., Hanweck, G.A., and Humphrey, D.B. (1987) Competitive viability in banking: Scale, scope and product mix economies, *Journal of Monetary Economics 20*, 501–520.

Berger, A.N., and Humphrey, D.B. (1991) The dominance of inefficiencies over scale and product mix economies and banking, *Journal of Monetary Economics 28*, 117–148.

Berger, A.N., Hancock, D., and Humphrey, D.B. (1993) Bank efficiency derived from the profit function, *Journal of Banking and Finance 17*, 314–347.

Berger, A.N., and Humphrey D.B. (1997) Efficiency of Financial Institutions: International Survey and Directions for Future Research, *European Journal of Operational Research 98*, 175–212.

Berger, A.N., Leusner, J.H., and Mingo, J.J. (1997) The efficiency of bank branches *Journal of Monetary Economics 40/1*, 141–162.

Berger, A.N., and Mester, L.J. (2000) Inside the black box; what explains differences in the efficiencies of financial institutions? in Harker, P.T., and Zenios, S.A. (Eds.), *Performance of Financial Institutions: Efficiency, Innovation and Regulation*, Cambridge University Press, 93–150.

Bessent, A., Bessent, W., Elam, J., and Clark, T. (1988) Efficiency frontier determination by constrained facet analysis, *Journal of the Operational Research Society 36/5*, 785–796.

Bogetoft, P., Tama, J.M., and Tind, J. (2000) Convex input and output projections of Nonconvex production possibility sets, *Management Science 46*, 858–869.

Bogetoft, P., and Hougaard, J.L. (1999) Efficiency evaluation based on potential non-proportional improvements, *Journal of Productivity Analysis 12*, 233–247.

Bogetoft, P., and Hougaard, J.L. (2003) Rational inefficiencies, *Journal of Productivity Analysis 20*, 243–271.

Bogetoft, P., and Nielsen, K. (2005) Internet based benchmarking, *Group Decision and Negotiation 14*, 195–215.

Bradley, S., Johnes, G., and Millington, J. (2001) The effect of competition on the efficiency of secondary schools in England, *European Journal of Operational Research 135*, 545–568.

Briec, W. (1998) Hölder distance function and measurement of technical efficiency, *Journal of Productivity Analysis 11/2*, 111–131.

Briec, W., and Lesourd, J.B. (1999) Metric distance function and profit: Some duality results, *Journal of Optimization Theory and Applications 101*, 15–33.

Brockett, P.L., Rousseau, J.J., Wang, Y., and Zhow, L. (1997a) Implementation of DEA Models Using GAMS, Research Report 765, University of Texas, Austin.

Brockett, P.L., Charnes, A., Cooper, W.W., Huang, Z.M., and Sun, D.B. (1997b) Data transformations in DEA cone ratio envelopment approaches for monitoring bank performances, *European Journal of Operational Research 98*, 250–268.

Brockett, P.L., and Golany, B. (1996) Using rank statistics for determining programmatic efficiency differences in data envelopment analysis, *Management Science 42/3*, 466–472.

Camanho, A.S., and Dyson, R.G. (1999) Efficiency, size, benchmarks and targets for bank branches: an application of data envelopment analysis, *Journal of the Operational Research Society 50/9*, 903–915.

Camanho, A.S., and Dyson, R.G. (2005) Cost efficiency, production and value-added models in the analysis of bank branch performance, *Journal of the Operational Research Society 56*, 483–494.

Camanho, A.S., and Dyson, R.G. (2006) Data envelopment analysis and Malmquist indices for measuring group performance, *Journal of Productivity Analysis 26/1*, 35–49.

Chambers, R.G., and Chung, Y., and Färe, R. (1996) Benefit and distance functions, *Journal of Economic Theory 70*, 407–419.

Chambers, R.G., and Chung, Y., and Färe, R. (1998) Profit, directional distance functions, and Nerlovian efficiency, *Journal of Optimization Theory and Applications 98/2*, 351–364.

Chambers, R.G., and Mitchell, T. (2001) Homotheticity and non-radial changes, *Journal of Productivity Analysis 15/1*, 31–39.

Chang, K.-P., and Guh, Y.-Y. (1991) Linear production functions and the data envelopment analysis, *European Journal of Operational Research 52*, 215–223.

Charnes, A., and Cooper, W.W. (1962) Programming with linear fractional functionals, *Naval Logistics Research Quarterly 9*(3,4), 181–185.

Charnes, A., Cooper, W.W., and Rhodes, E. (1978) Measuring efficiency of decision making units, *European Journal of Operational Research 2*, 429–444.

Charnes, A., Cooper, W.W., and Rhodes, E. (1981) Evaluating program and managerial efficiency: an application of data envelopment analysis to program follow through, *Management Science 27/6*, 668–697.

Charnes, A., Cooper, W.W., Golany, B., Seiford, L., and Stutz, J. (1985) Foundations of data envelopment analysis for Pareto-Koopmans efficient empirical production functions, *Journal of Econometrics 30*, 91–107.

Charnes, A., Cooper, W.W., Wei, Q.L., and Huang, Z.M. (1989) Cone ratio data envelopment analysis and multi-objective programming, *International Journal of Systems Science 20/7*, 1099–1118.

Charnes, A., Cooper, W.W., Huang, Z.M., and Sun, D.B. (1990) Polyhedral cone-ratio DEA models with an illustrative application to large industrial banks, *Journal of Econometrics 46*, 73–91.

Charnes, A., Cooper, W.W., Lewin, A.Y., and Seiford, L.W. (1994) *Data Envelopment Analysis: Theory, Methodology and Applications*, Kluwer Academic Publishers, Dordrecht.

Chavas, J.P., and Cox, T.L. (1999) A Generalized distance function and the analysis of production efficiency, *Southern Economic Journal 66/2*, 294–348.

Chen, Y., and Sherman, H.D. (2004) The benefits of non-radial vs non-radial super-efficiency DEA: An application to burden-sharing amongst NATO member nations, *Socio-Economic Planning Sciences 38*, 307–320.

Cherchye, L., and Van Puyenbroeck, T. (1999) Learning from Input-output mixes in DEA: A proportional measure for slack-based efficient projections, *Managerial and Decision Economics 20*, 151–161.

Cherchye, L., and Van Puyenbroeck, T. (2001a) Product mixes as objects of choice in non-parametric efficiency measurement, *European Journal of Operational Research 132/2*, 287–295.

Cherchye, L., and Van Puyenbroeck, T. (2001b) A comment on multi-stage DEA methodology, *Operations Research Letters 28*, 93–98.

Chung, Y.H., Färe, R., and Grosskopf, S. (1997) Productivity and undesirable outputs: A directional distance function approach, *Journal of Environmental Management 51/3*, 229–240.

Coelli, T., Rao, D.S.P., and Battese, G.E. (1998) *An Introduction to Efficiency and Productivity Analysis*, Kluwer Academic Publishers, Boston.

Coelli, T. (1998) A multi-stage methodology for the solution of orientated DEA models, *Operations Research Letters 23*, 143–149.

Coelli, T., Grifell-Tatjé, E., and Perelman, S. (2002) Capacity utilization and profitability: A decomposition of short run profit efficiency, *International Journal of Production Economics 79*, 261–278.

Coelli, T., Lauwers, L., and Van Huylenbroeck, G., (2007) Environmental efficiency measurement and the materials balance condition, *Journal of Productivity Analysis* 28, 3–12.

Colwell, R.J., and Davis, E.P. (1992) Output and productivity in banking, *Scandinavian Journal of Economics* 94, 111–129.

Cook, W.D., Kazakov, A., Roll, Y., and Seiford, L.M. (1991) A data envelopment analysis approach to measuring efficiency: Case analysis of highway maintenance patrols, *The Journal of Socio-economics* 20/1, 83–103.

Cook, W.D., Kazakov, A., Roll, Y. (1994) On the measurement and monitoring of relative efficiency of Highway maintenance patrols, in Charnes, A., Cooper, W.W., Lewin, A.Y., and Seiford, L.M. (Eds.), *Data Envelopment Analysis, Theory, Methodology and Applications*, Kluwer Academic Publishers, 195–210.

Cooper, W.W., Thompson, R.G., and Thrall, R.M. (1996) Introduction: Extensions and new developments in DEA, *Annals of Operations Research* 66, 3–45.

Cooper, W.W., Park, K.S., and Pastor, J.T. (1999) RAM: A range measure of inefficiency for use with additive models, and relations to other models and measures in DEA, *Journal of Productivity Analysis* 11, 5–42.

Cooper, W.W., Seiford, L.M., and Tone, K. (2000a) *Data Envelopment Analysis: A comprehensive text with models, applications, references and DEA-Solver software*, Kluwer Academic Publishers.

Cooper, W.W., Seiford, L.M., and Zhu, J. (2000b) A unified additive model approach for evaluating inefficiency and congestion with associated measures in DEA, *Socio-economic Planning Sciences* 34, 1–25.

Cooper, W.W., Gu, B., and Li, S. (2001) Comparisons and evaluations of alternative approaches to the treatment of congestion in DEA, *European Journal of Operational Research* 132, 62–74.

De Borger, B., Ferrier, G.D., and Kerstens, K. (1998) The choice of a technical efficiency measure on the free disposal hull reference technology: A comparison using US banking data, *European Journal of Operational Research* 105, 427–446.

Deprins, D., Simar, L., and Tulkens, H. (1984) Measuring labour efficiency in post-offices, in Marchand, M., Pestieau, P., and Tulkens, H. (Eds.), *The performance of Public Enterprises: Concepts and Measurement*, Elsevier Science Publishers, B.V., 243–267.

Despić, O. (2003) Linguistic Analysis of Efficiency using Fuzzy System Theory and Data Envelopment Analysis, PhD Thesis, University of Toronto, Toronto.

Despić, O., Despić, M., and Paradi, J. (2007) DEA-R: ratio-based comparative efficiency model, its mathematical relation to DEA and its use in applications, *Journal of Productivity Analysis* 28, 33–44.

Donthu, N., and Yoo, B. (1998) Retail productivity assessment using data envelopment analysis, *Journal of Retailing* 74/1, 89–105.

Doyle, J., and Green, R. (1994) Efficiency and Cross-Efficiency in DEA: Derivations, meanings and uses, *Journal of Operational Research Society* 45/5, 567–578.

Drake, L.M., and Simper, R. (2005) Police efficiency in offences cleared: An analysis of English "basic command units," *International Review of Law and Economics* 25, 186–208.

Drake, L., and Howcroft, B. (1994) Relative Efficiency in the Branch Network of a UK Bank: An Empirical Study, *Omega, The International Journal of Management Science* 22/1, 83–90.

Dusansky, R., and Wilson, P.W. (1994) Technical Efficiency in the decentralized care of the developmentally disabled, *Review of Economics and Statistics 76*, 340–345.

Dusansky, R., and Wilson, P.W. (1995) On the relative efficiency of alternative models of producing a public sector output: The case of the developmentally disabled, *European Journal of Operational Research 80*, 608–618.

Dyson, R.G., and Thanassoulis, E. (1988) Reducing weight flexibility in data envelopment analysis, *Journal of the Operational Research Society 39/6*, 563–576.

Dyson, R., Allen, R., Camanho, A.S., Podinovski, V.V., Sarrico, C.S., and Shale, E.A. (2001) Pitfalls and protocols in DEA, *European Journal of Operational Research 132/2*, 245–259.

Eeckaut, P.V., Tulkens, H., and Jamar, M.-A. (1993) Cost efficiency in Belgium Municipalities, in Fried, H.O., Lovell, C.A.K., and Schmidt, S.S. (Eds.), *The measurement of productive efficiency: Techniques and applications*, Oxford University Press, 300–334.

Emrouznejad, A., and Thanassoulis, E. (2005) A mathematical model for dynamic efficiency using data envelopment analysis, *Applied Mathematics and Computation 160/2*, 363–378.

Emrouznejad, A., Tavares, G., and Parker, B. (2007). A bibliography of data envelopment analysis (1978–2003), *to appear in Socio-Economic Planning Sciences.*

Färe, R., and Lovell, C.A.K. (1978) Measuring the technical efficiency of production, *Journal of Economic Theory 19/1*, 150–162.

Färe, R., Grosskopf, S., and Lovell, C.A.K. (1985) *The measurement of efficiency of production*, Kluwer-Nijhoff Publishing, Boston.

Färe, R., Grosskopf, S., and Lovell, C.A.K. (1988) An indirect approach to the evaluation of producer performance, *Journal of Public Economics 37/1*, 71–89.

Färe, R., Grosskopf, S., and Weber, W.L. (1989a) Measuring school district performance, *Public Finance Quarterly 17/4*, 409–428.

Färe, R., Grosskopf, S., Lovell, C.A.K., and Pasurka, C. (1989b) Multilateral productivity comparisons when some outputs are undesirable: A nonparametric approach, *Review of Economics and Statistics 71*, 90–98.

Färe, R., Grosskopf, S., and Lee, H. (1990) A nonparametric approach to expenditure constrained profit maximization, *American Journal of Agricultural Economics 12/3*, 574–581.

Färe, R., Grosskopf, S., and Lovell, C.A.K. (1994) *Production frontiers*, Cambridge University Press.

Färe, R., and Grosskopf, S. (1994) Estimation of returns to scale using data envelopment analysis: A comment, *European Journal of Operational Research 79*, 379–382.

Färe, R., Grosskopf, S., and Tyteca, D. (1996) An activity analysis model of the environmental performance of firms—application to fossil-fuel-fired electric utilities, *Ecological Economics 18*, 161–175.

Färe, R., and Grosskopf, S. (1998) Congestion: A note, *Socio-economic Planning Sciences 32/1*, 21–23.

Färe, R., and Grosskopf, S. (2000a) Slacks and congestion: A comment, *Socio-economic Planning Sciences 34*, 27–33.

Färe, R., and Grosskopf, S. (2000b) Theory and application of directional distance functions, *Journal of Productivity Analysis 13/2*, 93–103.

Färe, R., Grosskopf, S., and Zelenyuk, V. (2002) Finding Common ground: Efficiency indices, Paper presented at the North American productivity Workshop, Schenectady, N.Y. (Also forthcoming in a book in honor of R.R. Russell, published by Springer-Verlag)

Färe, R., and Grosskopf, S. (2004) *New directions: Efficiency and productivity*, Kluwer Academic Publishers.

Farrell, M.J. (1957) The measurement of productive efficiency, *Journal of the Royal Statistical Society, Series A, general 120/Part 3*, 253–281.

Ferrier, G.D., and Lovell, C.A.K. (1990) Measuring cost efficiency in banking: Econometric and linear programming evidence, *Journal of Econometrics 46*, 229–245.

Førsund, F.R., and Hjalmarsson, L. (1979) Generalised Farrell measures of efficiency: An application to milk processing in Swedish dairy plants, *Economic Journal 89*, 294–315.

Førsund, F.R., and Hernaes, E. (1994) A comparative analysis of ferry transport in Norway, in Charnes, A., Cooper, W.W., Lewin, A.Y., and Seiford, L.W. (Eds.), *Data envelopment analysis, theory, methodology and applications*, Kluwer Academic Publishers, 285–311.

Førsund, F.R. (1996) On the calculation of the scale elasticity in DEA models, *Journal of Productivity Analysis 7*, 283–302.

Førsund, F.R. (2001) Categorical Variables in DEA, International Centre for Economic Research Working Paper, 06-2007.

Førsund, F.R., and Hjalmarsson, L. (2004) Calculating scale elasticity in DEA models, *Journal of Operational Research Society 55*, 1023–1038.

Fox, K.J., Hill, R.J., and Diewert, W.E. (2004) Identifying outliers in multi-output models, *Journal of Productivity Analysis 22*, 1–2, 73–94.

Frei, F.X., and Harker, P.T. (1999) Projections onto efficient frontiers: Theoretical and computational extensions to DEA, *Journal of Productivity Analysis 11/3*, 275–300.

Fried, H.O., Schmidt, S.S., and Yaisawarng, S. (1999) Incorporating the operational environment into a nonparametric measure of technical efficiency, *Journal of Productivity Analysis 12*, 249–267.

Fried, H.O., Lovell, C.A.K., Schmidt, S.S., and Yaisawarng, S. (2002) Accounting for environmental effects and statistical noise in data envelopment analysis, *Journal of Productivity Analysis 17*, 157–174.

Fukuyama, H. (2000) Returns to scale and scale elasticity in data envelopment analysis *European Journal of Operational Research 125/1*, 93–112.

Golany, B. (1988a) A note on including ordinal relations among multipliers in data envelopment analysis, *Management Science 34*, 1029–1033.

Golany, B. (1988b) An interactive MOLP procedure for the extension of DEA to effectiveness analysis, *Journal of the Operational Research Society 39/8*, 725–734.

Golany, B., Phillips, F.Y., and Rousseau, J.J. (1993) Models for improved effectiveness based on DEA efficiency results, *IIE Transactions 25/6*, 2–10.

Golany, B., and Roll, Y. (1993) Some extensions of techniques to handle non-discretionary factors in data envelopment analysis, *Journal of Productivity Analysis 4*, 419–432.

Golany, B., and Roll, Y. (1994) Incorporating standards in DEA, in Charnes, A., Cooper, W.W., Lewin, A.Y., and Seiford, L.W. (Eds.), *Data envelopment analysis: theory, methodology and applications*, Kluwer Academic Publishers, 393–422.

González, E., and Álvarez, A. (2001) From efficiency measurement to efficiency improvement: The choice of a relevant benchmark, *European Journal of Operational Research 133*, 512–520

Greasley, A. (2005) Using DEA and simulation in guiding operating units to improved performance, *Journal of the Operational Research Society 56*, 727–731.

Green, R.H., Cook, W., and Doyle, J. (1997) A note on the additive data envelopment analysis model, *Journal of the Operational Research Society 48*, 446–448.

Grewal, D., Levy, M., Mehrotra, A., and Sharma, A. (1999) Planning merchandising decisions to account for regional and product assortment differences, *Journal of Retailing 75/3*, 405–424.

Grosskopf, S. (1996) Statistical inference and nonparametric efficiency: A selective survey, *Journal of Productivity Analysis 7*, 161–176.

Grosskopf, S., Hayes, K., Taylor, L., and Weber, W. (1997) Budget constrained frontier measures of fiscal equity and efficiency in schooling, *The Review of Economics and Statistics 79/2*, 116–124.

Gstach, D. (2005) Estimating output targets to evaluate output-specific efficiencies: A statistical framework, *European Journal of Operational Research 161*, 564–578.

Halme, M., Joro, T., Korhonen, P., Salo, S., and Wallenius, J. (1999) A value efficiency approach to incorporating preference information in data envelopment analysis, *Management Science 45/1*, 103–115.

Hougaard, J.L., and Tvede, M. (2002) Benchmark selection: An axiomatic approach, *European Journal of Operational Research 137*, 218–228.

Johnes. J., and Johnes, G. (1995) Research funding and performance in UK university departments of economics: A frontier analysis, *Economics of Education Review 14/3*, 301–314.

Joro, T. (1998) Models for identifying target units in data envelopment analysis: Comparison and extension, Interim Report IR-98-055, International Institute for Applied Systems Analysis.

Kamakura, W.A. (1988) A note on the use of categorical variables in data envelopment analysis, *Management Science 34/10*, 1273–1276.

Keh, H.T., and Chu, S. (2003) Retail Productivity and scale economies at the firm level: A DEA approach, *Omega, The International Journal of Management Science 31*, 75–82.

Kerstens, K., and Vanden-Eeckaut, P. (1995) Technical Efficiency measures on DEA and FDH: A reconsideration of the axiomatic literature, CORE discussion paper 9513, Center for Operations Research and Econometrics, Universite Catholique de Louvain.

Korhonen, P., and Laakso, J. (1986) A visual interactive method for solving the multiple criteria problem, *European Journal of the Operational Research 24*, 277–287.

Korhonen, P., and Wallenius, J. (1988) A Pareto Race, *Naval Research Logistics 35*, 615–623.

Korhonen, P., Soismaa, M., and Siljamäki, A. (2002) On the use of value efficiency analysis and some further developments, *Journal of Productivity Analysis 17*, 49–65.

Korhonen, P., Stenfors, S., Syrjanen, M. (2003) Multiple objective approach as an alternative to radial projection in DEA, *Journal of Productivity Analysis 20/3*, 305–321.

Kumbhakar, S.C. (2001) Estimation of profit functions when profit is not maximum, *American Journal of Agricultural Economics 83/1*, 1–19.

Kuosmanen, T. (1999a) Some remarks on scale efficiency and returns to scale in DEA, Helsinki School of Economics and Business Administration.

Kuosmanen, T. (1999b) Data envelopment analysis of non-convex technology: With empirical evidence from the batting technology of Finnish Super-League Pesis Players, Working Paper 224, Helsinki School of Economics and Business Administration.

Kuosmanen, T. (2001) DEA with efficiency classification preserving conditional convexity, *European Journal of Operational Research 132/2*, 326–342.

Kuosmanen, T. (2002) Modeling blank data entries in data envelopment analysis, EconWPA working paper No. 0210001 (Econometrics), Available online at: http://ideas.repec.org/p/wpa/wuwpem/0210001.html.

Kuosmanen, T. (2003) Duality theory of non-convex technologies, *Journal of Productivity Analysis 20*, 273–304.

Kuosmanen, T. (2005) Weak disposability in nonparametric production analysis with undesirable outputs, *American Journal of Agricultural Economics 87/4*, 1077–1082.

Lang, P., Yolalan, O.R., and Kettani, O. (1995) Controlled envelopment by face extension in DEA, *Journal of Operational Research Society 46/4*, 473–491.

Lins, M.P.E., Angulo-Meza, L., and Moreira da Silva, A.C. (2004) A multi-objective approach to determine alternative targets in data envelopment analysis, *Journal of the Operational Research Society 55*, 1090–1101.

Lins, M.P.E., Lovell, C.A.K., and Silva, A.C.M. (2007) Avoiding infeasibility in DEA models with weight restrictions, *European Journal of Operational Research 181*, 956–966.

Lovell, C.A.K., and Sickles, R.C. (1983) Testing efficiency hypothesis in joint production: A parametric approach, *Review of Economics and Statistics 65/1*, 51–58.

Lovell, C.A.K. (1993) Production Frontiers and productive efficiency, in Fried, H.O., Lovell, C.A.K., and Schmidt, S.S. (Eds.), *The measurement of productive efficiency: Techniques and applications*, Oxford University Press, 3–67.

Lovell, C.A.K., Walters, L.C., and Wood, L.L. (1994) Stratified models of education production using modified DEA and regression analysis, in Charnes, A., Cooper, W.W., Lewin, A.Y., and Seiford, L.W. (Eds.), *Data envelopment analysis, theory, methodology and applications*, Kluwer Academic Publishers.

Lovell, C.A.K. (1995) Measuring the macroeconomic performance of the Taiwanese economy, *International Journal of Production Economics 39*, 165–178.

Lovell, C.A.K., and Pastor, J. (1995) Units invariant and translation invariant DEA models, *Operations Research Letters 18*, 147–151.

Lovell, C.A.K., and Rouse, A.P.B. (2003) Equivalent standard DEA models to provide super-efficiency scores, *Journal of the Operational Research Society 54*, 101–108.

Lozano, S., Villa, G., and Adenso-Díaz, B. (2004) Centralised target setting for regional recycling operations using DEA, *Omega, The International Journal of Management Science 32*, 101–110.

Lozano, S., and Villa, G. (2005) Determining a sequence of targets in DEA, *Journal of the Operational Research Society 56*, 1439–1447.

Lozano, S., and Villa, G. (2006) Data envelopment analysis of integer-valued inputs and outputs, *Computers and Operations Research 33*, 3004–3014.

Lozano-Vivas, A., Pastor, J.T., and Pastor, J.M. (2002) An efficiency comparison of European banking systems operating under different environmental conditions, *Journal of Productivity Analysis 18/1*, 59–77.

Löthgren, M., and Tambour, M. (1996) Alternative approaches to estimate returns to scale in DEA-models, Working Paper Series in Economics and Finance no. 90, Stockholm School of Economics.

Lu, W.-M., and Lo, S.-F. (2007) A benchmark-learning roadmap for regional sustainable development in China, *Journal of the Operational Research Society 58*, 841–849.

Mancebón, M.-J., and Bandrés, E. (1999) Efficiency evaluation in secondary schools: The key role of model specification and ex post analysis of results, *Education Economics 7/2*, 131–152.

McCarty, T.A., and Yaisawarng, S. (1993) Technical efficiency in New Jersey School districts, in Fried, H.O., Lovell, C.A.K., and Schmidt, S.S. (Eds.), *The measurement of productive efficiency: Techniques and applications*, Oxford University Press, 271–287.

Mizala, A., Romaguera, P., and Farren, D. (2002) The technical efficiency of schools in Chile, *Applied Economics 34*, 1533–1552.

Muñiz, M.A. (2002) Separating managerial inefficiency and external conditions in data envelopment analysis, *European Journal of Operational Research 143*, 625–643.

Muñiz, M., Paradi, J. Ruggiero, J., and Yang, Z. (2006) Evaluating alternative DEA models used to control for non-discretionary inputs, *Computers and Operations Research 33*, 1173–1183.

OFWAT. (1994) 1993–94 report on the cost of water delivered and sewage collected, Office of Water Services, Birmingham, UK.

OFWAT. (1995) South West Water Services Ltd, Her Majesty's Stationery Office.

Olesen, O.B., and Petersen, N.C. (1996) Indicators of ill-conditioned data sets and model misspecification in data envelopment analysis: An extended facet approach, *Management Science 42/2*, 205–219.

Olesen, O.B., and Petersen, N.C. (2002) The use of data envelopment analysis with probabilistic assurance regions for measuring hospital efficiency, *Journal of Productivity Analysis 17*, 83–109.

Olesen, O.B., and Petersen, N.C. (2003) Identification and use of efficient faces and facets in DEA, *Journal of Productivity Analysis 20/3*, 323–360.

Ondrich, J., and Ruggiero, J. (2002) Outlier detection in data envelopment analysis: An analysis of jackknifing, *Journal of the Operational Research Society 53/3*, 342–346.

Pastor, J.T. (1994) How to discount environmental effects in DEA: An application to bank branches, Working Paper No. 011/94, Depto Estadistica *e* Investigacion Operativa, Universidad de Alicante, Spain.

Pastor, J.T. (1996) Translation invariance in data envelopment analysis: A generalisation, *Annals of Operations Research 66*, 93–102.

Pastor, J.M., Pérez, F., and Quesada, J. (1997) Efficiency analysis in banking firms: An international comparison, *European Journal of Operational Research 98/2*, 395–407.

Pastor, J.T., Ruiz, J.L., and Sirvent, I. (1999) A statistical test for detecting influential observations in DEA, *European Journal of Operational Research 115*, 542–554.

Pedraja-Chaparro, F., Salinas-Jimenez, J., and Smith, P. (1997) On the role of weight restrictions in data envelopment analysis, *Journal of Productivity Analysis 8*, 215–230.

Petersen, N.C. (1990) Data envelopment analysis on a relaxed set of assumptions, *Management Science 36/3*, 305–314.

Picazo-Tadeo, A.J., and Prior, D. (2005) Efficiency and environmental regulation: A 'complex situation', Universitat Autònoma de Barcelona, Documents de Treball núm 05/2.

Podinovski, V.V. (1999) Side effects of absolute weight bounds in DEA models, *European Journal of Operational Research 115/3*, 583–595.

Podinovski, V.V. (2001) DEA models for the explicit maximisation of relative efficiency, *European Journal of Operational Research 131*, 572–586.

Podinovski, V.V. (2004a) Efficiency and global scale characteristics on the "no free lunch" assumption only. *Journal of Productivity Analysis 22*, 227–257.

Podinovski, V.V. (2004b) Bridging the gap between the constant and variable returns-to-scale models: Selective proportionality in data envelopment, analysis, *Journal of the Operational Research Society 55*, 265-276.

Podinovski, V.V. (2004c) Suitability and redundancy of non-homogeneous weight restrictions for measuring the relative efficiency in DEA, *European Journal of Operational Research 154/2*, 380–395.

Podinovski, V.V. (2005) Selective convexity in DEA models, *European Journal of Operational Research 161*, 552–563

Podinovski, V.V., and Athanassopoulos, A.D. (1998) Assessing the relative efficiency of decision making units using DEA models with weights restrictions, *Journal of the Operational Research Society 49/5*, 500–508.

Portela, M.C.A.S., and Thanassoulis, E. (2001) Decomposing school and school type efficiency, *European Journal of Operational Research 132/2*, 114–130.

Portela, M.C.A.S., and Thanassoulis, E. (2002) Profit efficiency in DEA, Aston Business School Research Paper RP 0206, University of Aston, Aston Triangle, Birmingham, UK.

Portela, M.C.A.S. (2003) New insights on measuring bank branches efficiency through DEA: Transactional, operational, and profit assessments, Ph.D. Thesis, Aston Business School, Aston University, Birmingham, UK.

Portela, M.C.A.S., Borges, P.C., and Thanassoulis, E. (2003) Finding closest targets in non-oriented DEA models: The case of convex and non-convex technologies, *Journal of Productivity Analysis 19/2–3*, 251–269.

Portela, M.C.A.S., Thanassoulis, E., and Simpson, G.P.M. (2004) Negative data in DEA: A directional distance approach applied to bank branches, *Journal of the Operational Research Society 55*, 1111–1121.

Portela, M.C.A.S., and Thanassoulis, E. (2005) Profitability of a sample of Portuguese bank branches and its decomposition into technical and allocative components, *European Journal of Operational Research 162/3*, 850–866.

Portela, M.C.A.S., and Thanassoulis, E. (2007) Developing a decomposable measure of profit efficiency using DEA, *Journal of the Operational Research Society 58*, 481–490.

Portela, M.C.A.S., and Thanassoulis, E. (2006) Zero weights and non-zero slacks: Different solutions to the same problem, *Annals of Operational Research 145/1*, 129–147.

Portela, M.C.A.S., and Thanassoulis, E. (2007) Comparative efficiency analysis of Portuguese bank branches, *European Journal of Operational Research 177*, 1275–1278.

Post, T., and Spronk, J. (1999) Performance benchmarking using interactive data envelopment analysis, *European Journal of Operational Research 115*, 472–487.

Post, T. (2001a) Estimating non-convex production sets—imposing convex input sets and output sets in data envelopment analysis, *European Journal of Operational Research 131/1*, 132–142.

Post, T. (2001b) Transconcave data envelopment analysis, *European Journal of Operational Research 132/2*, 374–389.

Premachandra, I.M. (2001) A note on DEA vs principal component analysis: An improvement to Joe Zhu's approach, *European Journal of Operational Research 132*, 553–560.

Primont, D.F., and Domazlicky, B. (2006) Student achievement and efficiency in Missouri schools and the No Child left Behind Act, *Economics of Education Review 25*, 77–90.

Quariguasi Frota Neto, J.Q., and Angulo-Meza, L. (2007) Alternative targets for data envelopment analysis through multi-objective linear programming: Rio de Janeiro odontological public health system case study, *Journal of the Operational Research Society 58*, 865–873.

Räty, T. (2002) Efficient facet based efficiency index: A variable returns to scale specification, *Journal of Productivity Analysis 17*, 65–82.

Ray, S.C. (1988) Data envelopment analysis, Nondiscretionary inputs and efficiency: An alternative interpretation, *Socio-Economic Planning Sciences 22/4*, 167–176.

Ray, S.C. (1991) Resource-Use Efficiency in Public Schools: A Study of Connecticut Data, *Management Science 37/12*, 1620–1628.

Ray, S.C., Seiford, L.M., and Zhu, J. (1998) Market Entity behavior of Chinese state-owned enterprises, *Omega, The International Journal of Management Science 26/2*, 263–278.

Ray, S.C. (2005) Input aggregation in models of data envelopment analysis: A statistical test with an application to Indian manufacturing, University of Connecticut, Department of Economics Working Paper Series, WP 2005–54.

Rousseau, J.J., and Semple, J.H. (1993) Notes: Categorical Outputs in Data Envelopment Analysis, *Management Science 39/3*, 384–386.

Ruggiero, J. (1996) On the measurement of technical efficiency in the public sector, *European Journal of Operational Research 90*, 553–565.

Ruggiero, J. (1998) Non-discretionary inputs in data envelopment analysis, *European Journal of Operational Research 111/3*, 461–469.

Salerian, J., and Chan, C. (2005) Restricting Multiple-Output Multiple-Input DEA Models by Disaggregating the Output–Input Vector, *Journal of Productivity Analysis 24*, 5–29.

Sarrico, C.S., and Dyson, R.G. (2000) Using DEA for Planning in UK Universities—An Institutional Perspective, *Journal of the Operational Research Society 51/7*, 789–800.

Sarrico, C.S., and Dyson, R.G. (2004) Restricting virtual weights in data envelopment analysis. *European Journal of Operational Research 159*, 17–34.

Schaffnit, C., Rosen, D., and Paradi, J.C. (1997) Best practice analysis of bank branches: An application of DEA in a large Canadian bank, *European Journal of Operational Research 98*, 269–289.

Scheel, H. (2001) Undesirable outputs in efficiency valuations, *European Journal of Operational Research 132/2*, 400–410.

Seiford, L.M., and Zhu, J. (1999a) An investigation of returns to scale in data envelopment analysis, *Omega, The International Journal of Management Science 27*, 1–11.

Seiford, L.M., and Zhu, J. (1999b) Infeasibility of Super-efficiency data envelopment analysis models, *INFOR 37/2*, 174–187.

Seiford, L.M., and Zhu, J. (2002) Modeling undesirable factors in efficiency evaluation, *European Journal of Operational Research 142*, 16–20.

Shanmugam, R., and Johnson, C. (2007) At a crossroad of data envelopment and principal component analyses, *Omega, The International Journal of Management Science 35*, 351–364.

Sherman, H.D., and Gold, F. (1985) Bank Branch Operating Efficiency: Evaluation with DEA, *Journal of Banking and Finance 9/2*, 297–315.

Simar, L., and Wilson, P.W. (2007) Estimation and inference in two-stage, semi parametric models of production processes, *Journal of Econometrics* 136, 31–64.

Simpson, G. (2005) Programmatic efficiency comparisons between unequally sized groups of DMUs in DEA, *Journal of the Operational Research Society* 56, 1431–1438.

Simpson, G. (2007) A cautionary note on methods of comparing programmatic efficiency between two or more groups of DMUs in Data Envelopment Analysis, *Journal of productivity Analysis.*, 28, 141–147.

Smith, P.C., and Goddard, M. (2002) Performance Management and Operational Research: A marriage made in heaven? *Journal of the Operational Research Society* 53/3, 247–255.

Sowlati, *T* and Paradi, J. (2004) Establishing the "practical frontier" in data envelopment analysis, *Omega, The International Journal of Management Science 32*, 261–272.

Staat, M. (1999) Treating non-discretionary variables one way or the other: Implications for efficiency scores and their interpretation. In Westermann, G., ed., *Data Envelopment Analysis in the Service Sector*, Gabler Edition Wissenschaft, 23–49.

Steinmann, L., and Zweifel, P. (2001) The Range Adjusted Measure (RAM) in DEA: Comment, *Journal of Productivity Analysis 15/2*, 139–144.

Steuer, R. (1995) *Manual for the ADBASE Multiple Objective Programming Package*, The University of Georgia, Athens, G.A., USA.

Stewart, M. (1993) Modelling water costs 1992–3, OFWAT Research Paper No. 2, Office of Water Services, Birmingham, UK.

Sun, S. (2002) Measuring the relative efficiency of police precincts using data envelopment analysis, *Socio-Economic Planning Sciences 36*, 51–71.

Taylor, W.M., Thompson, R.G., Thrall, R.M., and Dharmapala, P.S. (1997) DEA/AR efficiency and profitability of Mexican banks. A total income model, *European Journal of Operational Research 98*, 346–363.

Thanassoulis, E., and Dyson, R.G. (1992) Estimating preferred input-output levels using data envelopment analysis, *European Journal of Operational Research 56*, 80–97.

Thanassoulis, E., and Dunstan, P. (1994) Guiding Schools to Improved Performance Using Data Envelopment Analysis: An Illustration with Data from a Local Education Authority, *Journal of Operational Research Society 45/11*, 1247–1262.

Thanassoulis, E. (1995) Assessing police forces in England and Wales using data envelopment analysis, *European Journal of Operational Research 87*, 641–657 *(EURO 20th anniversary issue of the journal)*.

Thanassoulis, E., Boussofiane, A., and Dyson, R.G. (1995) Exploring output quality targets in the provision of perinatal care in England using data envelopment analysis, *European Journal of Operational Research 80*, 588–607.

Thanassoulis, E. (1996) Altering the Bias in Differential School Effectiveness Using Data Envelopment Analysis, *Journal of the Operational Research Society 47/7*, 882–894.

Thanassoulis, E. (1997) Duality in Data Envelopment Analysis under Constant Returns to Scale, *IMA Journal of Mathematics Applied in Business and Industry 8/3*, 253–266.

Thanassoulis, E., and Allen, R. (1998) Simulating weights restrictions in data envelopment analysis by means of unobserved DMUs, *Management Science 44/4*, 586–594.

Thanassoulis, E. (1999) Setting achievement targets for school children, *Education Economics* 7/2, 101–119.

Thanassoulis, E. (2000a) The Use of Data Envelopment Analysis in the Regulation of UK Water Utilities: Water Distribution, *European Journal of Operational Research* 126/2, 436–453.

Thanassoulis, E. (2000b) DEA and its Use in the Regulation of Water Companies, *European Journal of Operational Research* 127/1, 1–13.

Thanassoulis, E. (2001) *Introduction to the theory and application of Data Envelopment analysis: A foundation text with integrated software.* Kluwer Academic Publishers.

Thanassoulis, E. (2002) Comparative Performance Measurement in Regulation: The Case of English and Welsh Sewerage Services, *Journal of the Operational Research Society* 53/3, 292–302.

Thanassoulis, E., Portela, M.C.A.S., and Allen, R. (2004) Incorporating Value Judgments in DEA. In Cooper, Seiford and Zhu editors, *Handbook on Data Envelopment Analysis*, Kluwer Academic publishers, 99–138.

Thompson, R.G., Singleton, F.D., Jr., Thrall, R.M., and Smith, B.A. (1986) Comparative site evaluations for locating a high-energy physics lab in Texas, *Interfaces 16*, 35–49.

Thompson, R.G., Langemeier, L.N., Lee, C., Lee, E., and Thrall, R.M. (1990) The role of multiplier bounds in efficiency analysis with application to Kansas farming, *Journal of Econometrics 46*, 93–108.

Thompson, R.G., Lee, E., and Thrall, R.M. (1992) DEA/AR-efficiency of U.S. independent oil/gas producers over time, *Computers and Operations Research 19/5*, 377–391.

Thompson, R.G., Dharmapala, P.S., and Thrall, R.M. (1993) Importance for DEA of zeros in data, multipliers and solutions, *Journal of Productivity Analysis 4/4*, 379–390.

Thompson, R.G., and Thrall, R.M. (1994) Polyhedral assurance regions with linked constraints. In Cooper, W.W., and Whinston, A.B., eds., *New Directions in Computational Economics*, Kluwer Academic Publishers, 121–133.

Thompson, R.G., Dharmapala, P.S., and Thrall, R.M. (1995) Linked-cone DEA profit ratios and technical efficiency with application to Illinois Coal mines, *International Journal of Production Economics 39*, 99–115.

Thompson, R.G., Dharmapala, PS,. Rothenberg, L.J., and Thrall, R.M. (1996) DEA/AR efficiency and profitability of 14 major oil companies in US exploration and production, *Computers and Operations Research 23/4*, 357–373.

Thompson, R.G., Brinkmann, E.J., Dharmapala, P.S., Gonzalez-Lima, M.D., and Thrall, R.M. (1997) DEA/AR profit ratios and sensitivity of 100 large, U.S. banks, *European Journal of Operational Research 98*, 213–229.

Thiry, B., and Tulkens, H. (1992) Allowing for technical inefficiency in parametric estimation of production functions for urban transit firms, *Journal of Productivity Analysis 3*, 45–65.

Thrall, R.M. (1996) The lack of invariance of optimal dual solutions under translation, *Annals of Operations Research 66*, 103–108.

Tone, K. (1993) An e-free DEA and a new measure of efficiency, *Journal of the Operations Research Society of Japan 36/3*, 167–174.

Tone, K. (2001) A slacks-based measure of efficiency in data envelopment analysis, *European Journal of Operational Research 130*, 498–509.

Tone, K. (2002) A slacks-based measure of super-efficiency in data envelopment analysis, *European Journal of Operational Research 143/1*, 32–41.

Tulkens, H. (1993) On FDH efficiency analysis: Some methodological issues and applications to retail banking, courts and urban transit, *Journal of Productivity Analysis 4*, 183–210.

Tupper, H.C., and Resende, M. (2004) Efficiency and regulatory issues in the Brazilian water and sewage sector: An empirical study, *Utilities Policy 12*, 29–40.

Varian, H.R. (1992) *Microeconomic analysis*, W.W. Norton and Company, 3rd edition.

Vassiloglou, M., Giokas, D. (1990) A Study of the Relative Efficiency of bank Branches: An Application of Data Envelopment Analysis, *Journal of Operational Research Society 41*, 591–597.

Vaz, C.B. (2006) Desenvolvimento de um sistema de avaliação e melhoria de desempenho no sector do retalho [in Portuguese]. PhD Thesis, Faculdade de Engenharia da Universidade do Porto.

Warning, S. (2004) Performance differences in German Higher Education: Empirical analysis of strategic groups, *Review of Industrial Organization 24*, 393–408.

Wilson, P.W. (1995) Detecting Influential Observations in Data Envelopment Analysis, *Journal of Productivity Analysis 6*, 27–45.

Wong, Y-H. B., and Beasley, J.E. (1990) Restricting weight flexibility in data envelopment analysis, *Journal of Operational Research Society 41/9*, 829–835.

Xue, M., and Harker, P.T. (1999) Overcoming the inherent dependency of DEA efficiency scores: A bootstrap approach, Working paper 99–17 Wharton Financial Institutions Center.

Zhang, Y., and Bartels, R. (1998) The effect of sample size on the mean efficiency in DEA with an application to electric distribution in Australia, Sweden and New Zealand, *Journal of Productivity Analysis 9*, 187–204.

Zhou, P., Ang, B.W., and Poh, K.L. (forthcoming) Measuring environmental performance under different environmental DEA technologies, *to appear in Energy Economics*. (Available online)

Zhu, J., and Shen, Z. (1995) A discussion of testing DMUs returns to scale, *European Journal of Operational Research 81*, 590–596.

Zhu, J. (1996) Data Envelopment Analysis with preference structure, *Journal of the Operational Research Society 47/1*, 136–150.

Zhu, J. (1998) Data envelopment analysis vs principal component analysis: Na illustrative study of economic performance of Chinese cities, *European Journal of Operational Research 111*, 50–61.

Zhu, J. (2000) Setting scale efficient targets in DEA via returns to scale estimation method, *Journal of the Operational Research Society 51/3*, 376–378.

Zhu, J. (2001) Super-efficiency and DEA sensitivity analysis, *European Journal of Operational Research 129*, 443–455.

Zieschang, K.D. (1984) An Extended Farrell Technical Efficiency Measure, *Journal of Economic Theory 33*, 387–396.

Zofio, J.L., and Prieto, A.M. (2001) Environmental efficiency and regulatory standards: The case of CO_2 emissions from OECD industries, *Resource and Energy Economics 23*, 63–83.

4

Statistical Inference in Nonparametric Frontier Models: Recent Developments and Perspectives

Léopold Simar and Paul W. Wilson

4.1 Frontier Analysis and the Statistical Paradigm

4.1.1 The Frontier Model: Economic Theory

As discussed in chapter 1, the economic theory underlying efficiency analysis dates to the work of Koopmans (1951), Debreu (1951), and Farrell (1957), who made the first attempt at empirical estimation of efficiencies for a set of observed production units. In this section, the basic concepts and notation used in this chapter are introduced. The production process is constrained by the production set Ψ, which is the set of physically attainable points (x, y); that is,

$$\Psi = \{(x, y) \in \mathscr{R}_+^{N+M} \mid x \text{ can produce } y\}, \tag{4.1}$$

where $x \in \mathscr{R}_+^N$ is the input vector and $y \in \mathscr{R}_+^M$ is the output vector.

For purposes of efficiency measurement, the upper boundary of Ψ is of interest. The efficient boundary (frontier) of Ψ is the locus of optimal production plans (e.g., minimal achievable input level for a given output, or maximal achievable output given the level of the inputs). The boundary of Ψ,

$$\partial\Psi = \{(x, y) \in \Psi \mid (\theta x, y) \notin \Psi, \ \forall 0 < \theta < 1, \ (x, \lambda y) \notin \Psi, \ \forall \lambda > 1\}, \tag{4.2}$$

is sometimes referred to as the *technology frontier* or the *production frontier* and is given by the intersection of Ψ and the closure of its complement. Firms that are technically inefficient operate at points in the interior of Ψ, while those that are technically efficient operate somewhere along the technology defined by $\partial\Psi$.

It is often useful to describe the production set Ψ by its sections. For instance, the input requirement set is defined for all $y \in \mathcal{R}_+^M$ by

$$X(y) = \{x \in \mathcal{R}_+^N \mid (x, y) \in \Psi\}. \tag{4.3}$$

The (input-oriented) efficiency boundary $\partial X(y)$ is defined for a given $y \in \mathcal{R}_+^M$ by

$$\partial X(y) = \{x \mid x \in X(y), \theta x \notin X(y), \forall 0 < \theta < 1\}. \tag{4.4}$$

Finally, the Debreu-Farrell input measure of efficiency for a given point (x, y) is given by

$$\theta(x, y) = \inf\{\theta \mid \theta x \in X(y)\}$$
$$= \inf\{\theta \mid (\theta x, y) \in \Psi\}. \tag{4.5}$$

Given an output level y and an input mix (a direction) given by the vector x, the efficient level of input is determined by

$$x^\partial(y) = \theta(x, y)x, \tag{4.6}$$

which is the projection of (x, y) onto the efficient boundary $\partial\Psi$, along the ray x and orthogonal to vector y. Hence $\theta(x, y)$ is the proportionate reduction of inputs a unit located at (x, y) could undertake to become technically efficient. By construction, for all $(x, y) \in \Psi, \theta(x, y) \leq 1$, and (x, y) is efficient if and only if $\theta(x, y) = 1$. This measure is the reciprocal of the Shephard (1970) input distance function.

The efficient boundary of Ψ can also be described in terms of output efficiency scores. The production set Ψ is characterized by output feasibility sets defined for all $x \in \mathcal{R}_+^N$ as

$$Y(x) = \{y \in \mathcal{R}_+^M \mid (x, y) \in \Psi\}. \tag{4.7}$$

Then, the (output-oriented) efficiency boundary $\partial Y(x)$ is defined for a given $x \in \mathcal{R}_+^N$ as

$$\partial Y(x) = \{y \mid y \in Y(x), \lambda y \notin Y(x), \forall \lambda > 1\}, \tag{4.8}$$

and the Debreu-Farrell output measure of efficiency for a production unit located at $(x, y) \in \mathcal{R}_+^{N+M}$ is

$$\lambda(x, y) = \sup\{\lambda \mid (x, \lambda y) \in \Psi\}. \tag{4.9}$$

Analogous to the input-oriented case described above, $\lambda(x, y)$ is the proportionate, feasible increase in outputs for a unit located (x, y) that would achieve technical efficiency. By construction, for all $(x, y) \in \Psi, \lambda(x, y) \geq 1$,

and (x, y) is technically efficient if and only if $\lambda(x, y) = 1$. The output efficiency measure $\lambda(x, y)$ is the reciprocal of the Shephard (1970) output distance
function. The efficient level of output, for the input level x and for the direction
of the output vector determined by y is given by

$$y^{\partial}(x) = \lambda(x, y)y. \tag{4.10}$$

Thus, the efficient boundary of Ψ can be described in either of two ways: in
terms of the input direction or in terms of the output direction. In other words,
the unit at (x, y) in the interior of Ψ can achieve technical efficiency either (i)
by moving from (x, y) to $(x^{\partial}(y), y)$, or (ii) by moving from (x, y) to $(x, y^{\partial}(x))$.
Note, however, that there is only one well-defined efficient boundary of Ψ.

A variety of assumptions on Ψ are found in the literature (e.g., free disposability, convexity, etc.; see Shephard, 1970, for examples). The assumptions
about Ψ determine the appropriate estimator that should be used to estimate
$\partial\Psi, \theta(x, y)$, or $\lambda(x, y)$. This issue is discussed below in detail.

4.1.2 The statistical paradigm

In any interesting application, the attainable set Ψ as well as $X(y)$, $\partial X(y)$,
$Y(x)$, and $\partial Y(x)$ are unknown. Consequently, the efficiency scores $\theta(x, y)$ and
$\lambda(x, y)$ of a particular unit operating at input–output levels are also unknown.

Typically, the only information available to the analyst is a sample

$$\mathcal{X}_n = \{(x_i, y_i), \ i = 1, \dots, n\} \tag{4.11}$$

of observations on input and output levels for a set of production units engaged
in the activity of interest.[1] The statistical paradigm poses the following question that must be answered: What can be learned by observing $\mathcal{X}_n$? In other
words, how can the information in $\mathcal{X}_n$ be used to estimate $\theta(x, y)$ and $\lambda(x, y)$,
or Ψ and hence $X(y)$, $\partial X(y)$, $Y(x)$, and $\partial Y(x)$?

Answering these questions involves much more than writing a linear program and throwing the data in $\mathcal{X}_n$ into a computer to compute a solution to
the linear program. Indeed, one could ask, What is learned from an estimate
of $\theta(x, y)$ or $\lambda(x, y)$ (i.e., numbers computed from $\mathcal{X}_n$ by solving a linear program)? The answer is clear: *almost nothing*. One might learn, for example, that
unit A uses less input quantities while producing greater output quantities
than unit B, but little else can be learned from estimates of $\theta(x, y)$ and $\lambda(x, y)$
alone.

Before anything can be learned about $\theta(x, y)$ or $\lambda(x, y)$, or, by extension,
about Ψ and its various characterizations, one must use methods of statistical
analysis to understand the properties of whatever estimators have been used to
obtain estimates of the things of interest.[2] This raises the following questions:

- Is the estimator *consistent?*
- Is the estimator *biased?*

- If the estimator is biased, does the bias disappear as the sample size tends toward infinity?
- If the estimator is biased, can the bias be corrected, and at what cost?
- Can confidence intervals for the values of interest be estimated?
- Can interesting hypotheses about the production process be tested, and if so, how?

Notions of statistical consistency, and so forth, are discussed in section 4.2.5.

Before these questions can be answered, indeed, before it can be known what is estimated, a statistical model must be defined. Statistical models consist of two parts: (i) a probability model, which in the present case includes assumptions on the production set Ψ and the distribution of input–output vectors (x, y) over Ψ; and (ii) a sampling process. The statistical model describes the process that yields the data in the sample $\mathcal{X}_n$, and is sometimes called the data-generating process (DGP).

In cases where a group of productive units are observed at the same point in time, that is, where cross-sectional data are observed, it is convenient and often reasonable to assume the sampling process involves independent draws from the probability distribution defined in the DGP's probability model. With regard to the probability model, one must attempt reasonable assumptions. Of course, there are trade-offs here: The assumptions on the probability model must be strong enough to permit estimation using estimators that have desirable properties, and to allow those properties to be deduced, yet not so strong as to impose conditions on the DGP that do not reflect reality. The goal should be, in all cases, to make flexible, minimal assumptions in order to let the data reveal as much as possible about the underlying DGP, rather than making strong, untested assumptions that have potential to influence results of estimation and inference in perhaps large and misleading ways. The assumptions defining the statistical model are of crucial importance, since any inference that might be made will typically be valid only if the assumptions are in fact *true*.

The above considerations apply equally to the parametric approach described in chapter 2 as well as to the nonparametric approaches to estimation discussed in this chapter. It is useful to imagine a spectrum of estimation approaches, ranging from fully parametric (most restrictive) to fully nonparametric (least restrictive). Fully parametric estimation strategies necessarily involve stronger assumptions on the probability model, which is completely specified in terms of a specific probability distribution function, structural equations, and so on. Semiparametric strategies are less restrictive; in these approaches, some (but not all) features of the probability model are left unspecified (e.g., in a regression setting, one might specify parametric forms for some, but not all, of the moments of a distribution function in the probability model). Fully nonparametric approaches assume no parametric forms for any features of the probability model. Instead, only (relatively) mild assumptions on broad features of the probability distribution are made, usually involving assumptions of various types of continuity, degrees of smoothness, and so on.

With nonparametric approaches to efficiency estimation, no specific analytical function describing the frontier is assumed. In addition, (too) restrictive assumptions on the stochastic part of the model, describing the probabilistic behavior of the observations in the sample with respect to the efficient boundary of Ψ, are also avoided.

The most general nonparametric approach would assume that observations (x_i, y_i) on input–output vectors are drawn randomly, independently from a *population* of firms whose input–output vectors are distributed on the attainable set Ψ according to some unknown probability law described by a probability density function $f(x, y)$ or the corresponding distribution function $F(x, y) = \text{prob}(X \leq x, Y \leq y)$. This chapter focuses on *deterministic* frontier models where all observations are assumed to be technically attainable. Formally,

$$\text{prob}((x_i, y_i) \in \Psi) = 1. \tag{4.12}$$

The most popular nonparametric estimators are based on the idea of estimating the attainable set Ψ by the smallest set $\widehat{\Psi}$ within some class of sets that envelop the observed data. Depending on assumptions made on Ψ, this idea leads to the free disposal hull (FDH) estimator of Deprins et al. (1984), which relies only on an assumption of free disposability, and the data envelopment analysis (DEA) estimators that incorporate additional assumptions. Farrell (1957) was the first to use a DEA estimator in an empirical application, but the idea remained obscure until it was popularized by Charnes et al. (1978) and Banker et al. (1984). Charnes et al. (1978) estimated Ψ by the convex cone of the FDH estimator of Ψ, thus imposing constant returns to scale, while Banker et al. (1984) used the convex hull of the FDH estimator of Ψ, thereby allowing for variable returns to scale.

Among deterministic frontier models, the primary advantage of nonparametric models and estimators lies in their great flexibility (as opposed to parametric, deterministic frontier models). In addition, the nonparametric estimators are easy to compute, and today most of their statistical properties are well established. As is discussed below, inference is available using bootstrap methods.

The main drawbacks of deterministic frontier models—both nonparametric and parametric models—is that they are very sensitive to outliers and extreme values, and that noisy data are not allowed. As discussed in section 4.8.1, a fully nonparametric approach when noise is introduced into the DGP leads to identification problems. Some alternative approaches are described later.

It should be noted that allowing for noise in frontier models presents difficult problems, even in a fully parametric framework where one can rely on the assumed parametric structure. In fully parametric models where the DGP involves a one-sided error process reflecting inefficiency and a two-sided error process reflecting statistical noise, numerical identification of the statistical model's features is sometimes highly problematic even with large (but finite) samples (see Ritter and Simar, 1997, for examples).

Apart from the issue of numerical identification, fully parametric, stochastic frontier models present other difficulties. Efficiency estimates in these models are based on residual terms that are unidentified. Researchers instead base efficiency estimates on an expectation, conditional on a composite residual; estimating an *expected inefficiency* is rather different from estimating *actual* inefficiency. An additional problem arises from the fact that, even if the fully parametric, stochastic frontier model is correctly specified, there is typically a nontrivial probability of drawing samples with the "wrong" skewness (e.g., when estimating cost functions, one would expect composite residuals with right-skewness, but it is certainly possible to draw finite samples with left-skewness—the probability of doing so depends on the sample size and the mean of the composite errors). Since there are apparently no published studies, and also apparently no working papers in circulation, where researchers report composite residuals with the "wrong" skewness when fully parametric, stochastic frontier models are estimated, it appears that estimates are sometimes, perhaps often, conditioned (i) on either drawing observations until the desired skewness is obtained or (ii) on model specifications that result in the desired skewness. This raises formidable questions for inference.

The remainder of this chapter is organized as follows. Section 4.2 presents in a unified notation the basic assumptions needed to define the DGP and show how the nonparametric estimators (FDH and DEA) can be described easily in this framework. Section 4.2.4 shows how the Debreu-Farrell concepts of efficiency can be formalized in an intuitive probabilistic framework. All the available statistical properties of FDH/DEA estimators are then summarized and the basic ideas for performing consistent inference using bootstrap methods are described. Section 4.3 discusses bootstrap methods for inference based on DEA and FDH estimates. Section 4.3.7 illustrates how the bootstrap can be used to solve relevant testing issues: comparison of groups of firms, testing returns to scale, and testing restrictions (specification tests).

Section 4.4 discusses two ways FDH estimators can be improved, using bias corrections and interpolation. As noted above, the envelopment estimators are very sensitive to outliers and extreme values; section 4.5 proposes a way for defining robust nonparametric estimators of the frontier, based on a concept of "partial frontiers" (order-m frontiers or order-α quantile frontiers). These robust estimators are particularly easy to compute and are useful for detecting outliers.

An important issue in efficiency analysis is the explanation of the observed inefficiency. Often, researchers seek to explain (in)efficiency in terms of some environmental factors. Section 4.6 surveys the most recent techniques allowing investigation of the effects of these external factors on efficiency. Parametric and nonparametric methods have often been viewed as presenting paradoxes in the literature. In section 4.7, the two approaches are reconciled with each other, and a nonparametric method is shown to be particularly useful even if in the end a parametric model is desired. This mixed "semiparametric" approach seems to outperform the usual parametric approaches based on regression ideas. Section 4.8 concludes with a discussion of still-important, open issues and questions for future research.

4.2 The Nonparametric Envelopment Estimators

4.2.1 The data-generating process

They assumptions listed below are adapted from Kneip et al. (1998, 2003) and Park et al. (2000). These assumptions define a statistical model (i.e., a DGP), are very flexible, and seem quite reasonable in many practical situations. The first assumption reflects the deterministic frontier model defined in (4.12). In addition, for the sake of simplicity, the standard independence hypothesis is assumed, meaning that the observed firms are considered as being drawn randomly and independently from a population of firms.

Assumption 4.2.1.

The sample observations (x_i, y_i) in $\mathcal{X}_n$ are realizations of identically, independently distributed (iid) random variables (X, Y) with probability density function $f(x, y)$, which has support over $\Psi \subset \mathcal{R}_+^{N+M}$, the production set as defined in (4.1); that is, $\text{prob}[(X, Y) \in \Psi] = 1$.

The next assumption is a regularity condition sufficient for proving the consistency of all the nonparametric estimators described in this chapter. It says that the probability of observing firms in any open neighborhood of the frontier is strictly positive—quite a reasonable property since microeconomic theory indicates that, with competitive input and output markets, firms that are inefficient will, in the long run, be driven from the market:

Assumption 4.2.2.

The density $f(x, y)$ is strictly positive on the boundary $\partial\Psi$ of the production set Ψ and is continuous in any direction toward the interior of Ψ.

The next assumptions regarding Ψ are standard in microeconomic theory of the firm (see, e.g., Shephard, 1970 and Färe, 1988:

Assumption 4.2.3.

All production requires use of some inputs: $(x, y) \notin \Psi$ if $x = 0$ and $y \geq 0$, $y \neq 0$.

Assumption 4.2.4.

Both inputs and outputs are freely disposable: if $(x, y) \in \Psi$, then for any (x', y') such that $x' \geq x$ and $y' \leq y$, $(x', y') \in \Psi$.

Assumption 4.2.3 means that there are no "free lunches." The disposability assumption is sometimes called "strong disposability" and is equivalent to an assumption of monotonicity of the technology. This property also characterizes the technical possibility of wasting resources (i.e., the possibility of producing less with more resources).

Assumption 4.2.5.

Ψ is convex: if $(x_1, y_1), (x_2, y_2) \in \Psi$, then $(x, y) \in \Psi$ for $(x, y) = \alpha(x_1, y_1) + (1 - \alpha)(x_2, y_2)$, for all $\alpha \in [0, 1]$.

This convexity assumption may be really questionable in many situations. Several recent studies focus on the convexity assumption in frontier models (e.g., Bogetoft, 1996; Bogetoft et al., 2000; Briec et al., 2004). Assumption 4.2.5 is relaxed at various points below.

Assumption 4.2.6.

Ψ is closed.

Closedness of the attainable set Ψ is a technical condition, avoiding mathematical problems for infinite production plans.

Finally, in order to prove consistency of the estimators, the production frontier must be sufficiently smooth:

Assumption 4.2.7.

For all (x, y) in the interior of Ψ, the functions $\theta(x, y)$ and $\lambda(x, y)$ are differentiable in both their arguments.

The characterization of smoothness in assumption 4.2.1 is stronger than required for the consistency of the nonparametric estimators. Kneip et al. (1998) require only Lipschitz continuity of the efficiency scores, which is implied by the simpler but stronger requirement presented here. However, derivation of limiting distributions of the nonparametric estimators has been obtained only with the stronger assumption made here.

4.2.2 The FDH estimator

The FDH estimator was first proposed by Deprins et al. (1984) and is discussed in chapter 1. It relies only on the free disposability assumption in assumption 4.2.4 and does not require assumption 4.2.5. The Deprins et al. estimator $\widehat{\Psi}_{\text{FDH}}$ of the attainable set Ψ is simply the FDH of the observed sample $\mathcal{X}_n$

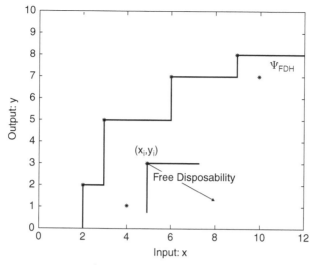

Figure 4.1. FDH Estimator $\widehat{\Psi}_{\text{FDH}}$ of the Production Set Ψ

given by

$$
\begin{aligned}
\widehat{\Psi}_{\text{FDH}} &= \left\{ (x, y) \in \mathscr{R}_+^{N+M} \mid y \leq y_i, \ x \geq x_i, \ (x_i, y_i) \in \mathcal{X}_n \right\} \\
&= \bigcup_{(x_i, y_i) \in \mathcal{X}_n} \left\{ (x, y) \in \mathscr{R}_+^{p+q} \mid y \leq y_i, \ x \geq x_i \right\}
\end{aligned}
\tag{4.13}
$$

and is the union of all the southeast orthants with vertices (x_i, y_i). Figure 4.1 illustrates the idea when $N = M = 1$.

A nonparametric estimator of the input efficiency for a given point (x, y) is obtained by replacing the true production set Ψ in the definition of $\theta(x, y)$ given by (4.5) with the estimator $\widehat{\Psi}_{\text{FDH}}$, yielding

$$
\widehat{\theta}_{\text{FDH}}(x, y) = \inf\{\theta \mid (\theta x, y) \in \widehat{\Psi}_{\text{FDH}}\}.
\tag{4.14}
$$

Estimates can be computed in two steps: first, identify the set D of observed points dominating (x, y):

$$
D(x, y) = \{i \mid (x_i, y_i) \in \mathcal{X}_n, \ x_i \leq x, \ y_i \geq y\};
$$

then, $\widehat{\theta}(x, y)$ is computed simply by evaluating

$$
\widehat{\theta}_{\text{FDH}}(x, y) = \min_{i \in D(x,y)} \ \max_{j=1,\dots,N} \left(\frac{x_i^j}{x^j} \right),
\tag{4.15}
$$

where for a vector a, a^j denotes the jth element of a. The estimator in (4.15) can be computed quickly and easily, since it involves only simple sorting algorithms.

An estimate of the efficient levels of inputs for a given output levels y and a given input direction determined by the input vector x is obtained by

$$\widehat{x}^{\partial}(y) = \widehat{\theta}_{\text{FDH}}(x, y)x. \tag{4.16}$$

By construction, $\widehat{\mathbf{\Psi}}_{\text{FDH}} \subseteq \mathbf{\Psi}$, and so $\widehat{\partial X(y)}$ is an upward-biased estimator of $\partial X(y)$. Therefore, for the efficiency scores, $\widehat{\theta}_{\text{FDH}}(x, y)$ is an upward-biased estimator of $\theta(x, y)$; that is, $\widehat{\theta}_{\text{FDH}}(x, y) \geq \theta(x, y)$.

Things work similarly in the output orientation. The FDH estimator of $\lambda(x, y)$ is defined by

$$\widehat{\lambda}_{\text{FDH}}(x, y) = \sup\{\lambda \mid (x, \lambda y) \in \widehat{\mathbf{\Psi}}_{\text{FDH}}\}. \tag{4.17}$$

This is computed quickly and easily by evaluating

$$\widehat{\lambda}_{\text{FDH}}(x, y) = \max_{i \in D(x,y)} \quad \min_{j=1,\dots,M} \left(\frac{y_i^j}{y^j}\right). \tag{4.18}$$

Efficient output levels for given input levels x and given an output mix (direction) described by the vector y are estimated by

$$\widehat{y}^{\partial}(x) = \widehat{\lambda}_{\text{FDH}}(x, y)y. \tag{4.19}$$

By construction, $\widehat{\lambda}_{\text{FDH}}(x, y)$ is an downward-biased estimator of $\lambda(x, y)$; for all $(x, y) \in \mathbf{\Psi}$, $\widehat{\lambda}_{\text{FDH}}(x, y) \leq \lambda(x, y)$.

4.2.3 The DEA estimators

Although DEA estimators were first used by Farrell (1957) to measure technical efficiency for a set of observed firms, the idea did not gain wide acceptance until Charnes et al. (1978) appeared 21 years later. Charnes et al. used the convex cone (rather than the convex hull) of $\widehat{\mathbf{\Psi}}_{\text{FDH}}$ to estimate $\mathbf{\Psi}$, which would be appropriate if returns to scale are everywhere constant. Later, Banker et al. (1984) used the convex hull of $\widehat{\mathbf{\Psi}}_{\text{FDH}}$ to estimate $\mathbf{\Psi}$, thus allowing variable returns to scale. Here, "DEA" refers to both of these approaches, as well as others that involve using linear programs to define a convex set enveloping the FDH estimator $\widehat{\mathbf{\Psi}}_{\text{FDH}}$.

The most general DEA estimator of the attainable set Ψ is simply the convex hull of the FDH estimator; that is,

$$\widehat{\Psi}_{VRS} = \left\{ (x,y) \in \mathscr{R}^{N+M} \mid y \le \sum_{i=1}^{n} \gamma_i y_i; \; x \ge \sum_{i=1}^{n} \gamma_i x_i \text{ for } (\gamma_1, \ldots, \gamma_n) \right.$$

$$\left. \text{such that } \sum_{i=1}^{n} \gamma_i = 1; \; \gamma_i \ge 0, i = 1, \ldots, n \right\}. \quad (4.20)$$

Alternatively, the conical hull of the FDH estimator, used by Charnes et al. (1978), is obtained by dropping the constraint in (4.20) requiring the γ values to sum to 1:

$$\widehat{\Psi}_{CRS} = \left\{ (x,y) \in \mathscr{R}^{N+M} \mid y \le \sum_{i=1}^{n} \gamma_i y_i; \; x \ge \sum_{i=1}^{n} \gamma_i x_i \text{ for } (\gamma_1, \ldots, \gamma_n) \right.$$

$$\left. \text{such that } \gamma_i \ge 0, i = 1, \ldots, n \right\}. \quad (4.21)$$

Other estimators can be defined by modifying the constraint on the sum of the γ values in (4.20). For example, the estimator

$$\widehat{\Psi}_{NIRS} = \left\{ (x,y) \in \mathscr{R}^{N+M} \mid y \le \sum_{i=1}^{n} \gamma_i y_i; \; x \ge \sum_{i=1}^{n} \gamma_i x_i \text{ for } (\gamma_1, \ldots, \gamma_n) \right.$$

$$\left. \text{such that } \sum_{i=1}^{n} \gamma_i \le 1; \; \gamma_i \ge 0, i = 1, \ldots, n \right\} \quad (4.22)$$

incorporates an assumption of nonincreasing returns to scale (NIRS). In other words, returns to scale along the boundary of $\widehat{\Psi}_{NIRS}$ are either constant or decreasing, but not increasing. By contrast, returns to scale along the boundary of $\widehat{\Psi}_{VRS}$ are either increasing, constant, or decreasing, while returns to scale along the boundary of $\widehat{\Psi}_{CRS}$ are constant everywhere.

Figure 4.2 illustrates the DEA estimator $\widehat{\Psi}_{VRS}$ for the case of one input and one output ($N = M = 1$).

As with the FDH estimators, DEA estimators of the efficiency scores $\theta(x,y)$ and $\lambda(x,y)$ defined in (4.5) and (4.9) can be obtained by replacing the true, but unknown, production set Ψ with one of the estimators $\widehat{\Psi}_{VRS}$, $\widehat{\Psi}_{CRS}$, or $\widehat{\Psi}_{NIRS}$. For example, in the input orientation, with varying returns to scale, using $\widehat{\Psi}_{VRS}$ to replace Ψ in (4.5) leads to the estimator

$$\widehat{\theta}_{VRS}(x,y) = \inf\{\theta \mid (\theta x, y) \in \widehat{\Psi}_{VRS}\}. \quad (4.23)$$

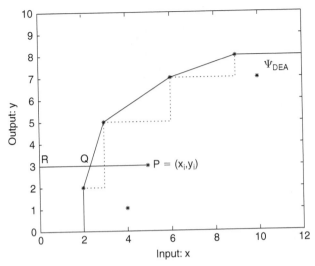

Figure 4.2. DEA Estimator $\widehat{\Psi}_{VRS}$ of the Production Set Ψ

As a practical matter, $\widehat{\theta}_{VRS}(x, y)$ can be computed by solving the linear program

$$\widehat{\theta}_{VRS}(x, y) = \min \left\{ \theta > 0 \mid y \leq \sum_{i=1}^{n} \gamma_i y_i; \ \theta x \geq \sum_{i=1}^{n} \gamma_i x_i \text{ for } (\gamma_1, \dots, \gamma_n) \right.$$

$$\left. \text{such that } \sum_{i=1}^{n} \gamma_i = 1; \ \gamma_i \geq 0, \ i = 1, \dots, n \right\}. \quad (4.24)$$

Today, a number of algorithms exist to solve linear programs such as the one in (4.24), and so in principle, solutions are obtained easily. However, the computational burden represented by (4.24) is typically greater than that posed by the FDH estimators.

These ideas extend naturally to the output orientation. For example, replacing Ψ with $\widehat{\Psi}_{VRS}$ in (4.9) yields

$$\widehat{\lambda}_{VRS}(x, y) = \sup\{\lambda \mid (x, \lambda y) \in \widehat{\Psi}_{VRS}\}, \quad (4.25)$$

which can be computed by solving the linear program

$$\widehat{\lambda}_{VRS}(x, y) = \sup \left\{ \lambda \mid \lambda y \leq \sum_{i=1}^{n} \gamma_i y_i; \ x \geq \sum_{i=1}^{n} \gamma_i x_i \text{ for } (\gamma_1, \dots, \gamma_n) \right.$$

$$\left. \text{such that } \sum_{i=1}^{n} \gamma_i = 1; \ \gamma_i \geq 0, \ i = 1, \dots, n \right\}. \quad (4.26)$$

In the input orientation, the technically efficient level of inputs, for a given level of outputs y, is estimated by $(\widehat{\theta}_{VRS}(x, y)x, y)$. Similarly, in the output orientation the technically efficient level of outputs for a given level of inputs x is estimated by $(x, \widehat{\lambda}_{VRS}(x, y)y)$.

All of the FDH and DEA estimators are biased by construction since $\widehat{\Psi}_{FDH} \subseteq \widehat{\Psi}_{VRS} \subseteq \Psi$. Moreover, $\widehat{\Psi}_{VRS} \subseteq \widehat{\Psi}_{NIRS} \subseteq \widehat{\Psi}_{CRS}$. If the technology $\partial\Psi$ exhibits constant returns to scale everywhere, then $\widehat{\Psi}_{CRS} \subseteq \Psi$; otherwise, $\widehat{\Psi}_{CRS}$ will not be a statistically consistent estimator of Ψ (of course, if Ψ is not convex, then $\widehat{\Psi}_{VRS}$ will also be inconsistent). These relations further imply that $\widehat{\theta}_{FDH}(x, y) \geq \widehat{\theta}_{VRS}(x, y) \geq \theta(x, y)$ and $\widehat{\theta}_{VRS}(x, y) \geq \widehat{\theta}_{NIRS}(x, y) \geq \widehat{\theta}_{CRS}(x, y)$. Alternatively, in the output orientation, $\widehat{\lambda}_{FDH}(x, y) \leq \widehat{\lambda}_{VRS}(x, y) \leq \lambda(x, y)$ and $\widehat{\lambda}_{VRS}(x, y) \leq \widehat{\lambda}_{NIRS}(x, y) \leq \widehat{\lambda}_{CRS}(x, y)$.

4.2.4 An alternative probabilistic formulation of the DGP

The presentation of the DGP in section 4.2.1 is traditional. However, it is also possible to present the DGP in a way that allows a probabilistic interpretation of the Debreu-Farrell efficiency scores, providing a new way of describing the nonparametric FDH estimators. This new formulation will be useful for introducing extensions of the FDH and DEA estimators described above. The presentation here follows that of Daraio and Simar (2005), who extend the ideas of Cazals et al. (2002).

The stochastic part of the DGP introduced in section 4.2.1 through the probability density function $f(x, y)$ (or the corresponding distribution function $F(x, y)$) is completely characterized by the following probability function:

$$H_{XY}(x, y) = \text{prob}(X \leq x, Y \geq y) \tag{4.27}$$

Note that this is not a standard distribution function, since the cumulative form is used for the inputs x and the survival form is used for the outputs y. The function has a nice interpretation and interesting properties:

- $H_{XY}(x, y)$ gives the probability that a unit operating at input–output levels (x, y) is *dominated,* that is, that another unit produces at least as much output while using no more of any input than the unit operating at (x, y).
- $H_{XY}(x, y)$ is monotone nondecreasing in x and monotone nonincreasing in y.
- The support of the distribution function $H_{XY}(\cdot, \cdot)$ is the attainable set Ψ; that is,

$$H_{XY}(x, y) = 0 \; \forall (x, y) \notin \Psi. \tag{4.28}$$

The joint probability $H_{XY}(x,y)$ can be decomposed using Bayes's rule by writing

$$H_{XY}(x,y) = \underbrace{\text{prob}(X \leq x | Y \geq y)}_{=F_{X|Y}(x|y)} \underbrace{\text{prob}(Y \geq y)}_{=S_Y(y)} \qquad (4.29)$$

$$= \underbrace{\text{prob}(Y \geq y | X \leq x)}_{=S_{Y|X}(y|x)} \underbrace{\text{prob}(X \leq x)}_{=F_X(x)}, \qquad (4.30)$$

where $S_Y(y) = \text{prob}(Y \geq y)$ denotes the survivor function of Y, $S_{Y|X}(y|x) = \text{prob}(Y \geq y \mid X \leq x)$ denotes the conditional survivor function of Y, and the conditional distribution and survivor functions are assumed to exist whenever used (i.e., when needed, $S_Y(y) > 0$ and $F_X(x) > 0$). Since the support of the joint distribution is the attainable set, boundaries of Ψ can be defined in terms of the conditional distributions defined above by (4.29) and (4.30). This allows definition of some new concepts of efficiency.

For the input-oriented case, assuming $S_Y(y) > 0$, define

$$\widetilde{\theta}(x,y) = \inf\{\theta \mid F_{X|Y}(\theta x|y) > 0\} = \inf\{\theta \mid H_{XY}(\theta x, y) > 0\}. \qquad (4.31)$$

Similarly, for the output-oriented case, assuming $F_X(x) > 0$, define

$$\widetilde{\lambda}(x,y) = \sup\{\lambda \mid S_{Y|X}(\lambda y|x) > 0\} = \sup\{\lambda \mid H_{XY}(x, \lambda y) > 0\}. \qquad (4.32)$$

The input efficiency score $\widetilde{\theta}(x,y)$ may be interpreted as the proportionate reduction of inputs (holding output levels fixed) required for a unit operating at $(x,y) \in \Psi$ to achieve zero probability of being dominated. Analogously, the output efficiency score $\widetilde{\lambda}(x,y)$ gives the proportionate increase in outputs required for the same unit to have zero probability of being dominated, holding input levels fixed. Note that in a multivariate framework, the radial nature of the Debreu-Farrell measures is preserved.

From the properties of the distribution function $H_{XY}(x,y)$, it is clear that the new efficiency scores defined in (4.31) and (4.32) have some interesting (and reasonable) properties. In particular,

- $\widetilde{\theta}(x,y)$ is monotone nonincreasing with x and monotone nondecreasing with y.
- $\widetilde{\lambda}(x,y)$ is monotone nondecreasing with x and monotone nonincreasing with y.

Most important, if Ψ is free disposal (an assumption that will be maintained throughout this chapter), it is trivial to show that

$$\widetilde{\theta}(x,y) \equiv \theta(x,y) \quad \text{and} \quad \widetilde{\lambda}(x,y) \equiv \lambda(x,y).$$

Therefore, under the assumption of free disposability of inputs and outputs, the probabilistic formulation presented here leads to a new representation of the traditional Debreu-Farrell efficiency scores.

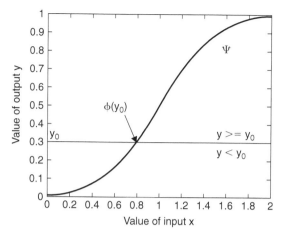

Figure 4.3. Input-Oriented Frontier Function $\phi(y)$ for the Bivariate Case $(N = M = 1)$

For a given y, the efficient frontier of Ψ can be characterized as noted above by $x^{\partial}(y)$ defined in (4.6). If x is univariate, $x^{\partial}(y)$ determines a frontier function $\phi(y)$ as a function of y, where

$$\phi(y) = \inf\{x | F_X(x|y) > 0\} \quad \forall y \in \mathcal{R}_+^M \tag{4.33}$$

(this was called a factor requirements set in chapter 1). This function is illustrated in figure 4.3. The intersection of the horizontal line at output level y_0 and the curve representing $\phi(y)$ gives the minimum input level $\phi(y_0)$ than can produce output level y_0. Similarly, working in the output direction, a production function is obtained if y is univariate.

Nonparametric estimators of the efficiency scores $\widetilde{\theta}(x, y)$ and $\widetilde{\lambda}(x, y)$ (hence, also of $\theta(x, y)$ and $\lambda(x, y)$ can be obtained using the same plug-in approach that was used to define DEA estimators. In the present case, this amounts to substituting the empirical distribution $\widehat{H}_{XY,n}(x, y)$ for $H_{XY}(x, y)$ in (4.31) and (4.32). This empirical analog of $H_{XY}(x, y)$ is given by

$$\widehat{H}_{XY,n}(x, y) = \frac{1}{n}\sum_{i=1}^{n} \mathscr{I}(x_i \leq x, y_i \geq y), \tag{4.34}$$

where $\mathscr{I}(\cdot)$ is the indicator function $[\mathscr{I}(A) = 1$ if A is true; otherwise, $\mathscr{I}(A) = 0]$. So, at any point (x, y), $\widehat{H}_{XY,n}(x, y)$ is the proportion of sample points in $\mathcal{X}_n$ with values $x_i \leq x$ and $y_i \geq y$; that is, $\widehat{H}_{XY,n}(x, y)$ gives the proportion of points in the sample $\mathcal{X}_n$ dominating (x, y).

Now the nonparametric estimators can be defined. In the input-oriented case,

$$\widehat{\theta}_n(x, y) = \inf\{\theta \mid \widehat{F}_{X|Y,n}(\theta x|y) > 0\}, \tag{4.35}$$

where $\widehat{F}_{X|Y,n}(x|y)$ is the empirical conditional distribution function:

$$\widehat{F}_{X|Y,n}(x|y) = \frac{\widehat{H}_{XY,n}(x, y)}{\widehat{H}_{XY,n}(\infty, y)} \tag{4.36}$$

For the output-oriented case,

$$\widehat{\lambda}_n(x, y) = \sup\{\lambda \mid \widehat{S}_{Y|X,n}(\lambda y|x) > 0\}, \tag{4.37}$$

where $\widehat{S}_{Y|X,n}(y|x)$ is the empirical conditional survival function:

$$\widehat{S}_{Y|X,n}(y|x) = \frac{\widehat{H}_{XY,n}(x, y)}{\widehat{H}_{XY,n}(x, 0)} \tag{4.38}$$

It is easy to show that these estimators coincide with the FDH estimators of the Debreu-Farrell efficiency scores. Indeed,

$$\widehat{\theta}_n(x, y) = \min_{i|Y_i \geq y} \max_{j=1,\ldots,p} x_i^j/x^j \equiv \widehat{\theta}_{\text{FDH}}(x, y), \tag{4.39}$$

and

$$\widehat{\lambda}_n(x, y) = \max_{i|X_i \leq x} \min_{j=1,\ldots,q} y_i^j/y^j \equiv \widehat{\lambda}_{\text{FDH}}(x, y). \tag{4.40}$$

Here, the FDH estimators are presented as intuitive, empirical versions of the Debreu-Farrell efficiency scores, without explicit reference to the FDH of the observed cloud of points.

The presentation in this section is certainly appealing for the FDH estimators since they appear as the most natural nonparametric estimator of the Debreu-Farrell efficiency scores by using the plug-in principle.

The probabilistic, plug-in presentation in this section is very useful for providing extensions of the FDH estimators later in this chapter. In section 4.4.1, a useful bias-corrected FDH estimator is derived. Then in section 4.5, definitions are given for some robust nonparametric estimators, and section 4.6.2 shows how this framework can be used to investigate the effect of environmental variables on the production process.

4.2.5 Properties of FDH/DEA estimators

It is necessary to investigate the statistical properties of any estimator before it can be known what, if anything, the estimator may be able to reveal about the underlying quantity that one wishes to estimate. An understanding of the properties of an estimator is necessary in order to make inference. Above, the FDH and DEA estimators were shown to be biased. Here, we consider whether, and to what extent, these estimators can reveal useful information about efficiency, and under what conditions. Simar and Wilson (2000a) surveyed the statistical properties of FDH and DEA estimators, but more recent results have been obtained.

4.2.5.1 Stochastic convergence and rates of convergence

Perhaps the most fundamental property that an estimator should possess is that of *consistency*. Loosely speaking, if an estimator $\widehat{\beta}_n$ of an unknown parameter β is consistent, then the estimator converges (in some sense) to β as the sample size n increases toward infinity (a subscript n is often attached to notation for estimators to remind the reader that one can think of an infinite sequence of estimators, each based on a different sample size). In other words, if an estimator is consistent, then more data should be helpful—quite a sensible property. If an estimator is inconsistent, then in general even an infinite amount of data would offer no particular hope or guarantee of getting "close" to the true value that one wishes to estimate. It is this sense in which consistency is the *most fundamental* property that an estimator might have; if an estimator is not consistent, there is no reason to consider what other properties the estimator might have, nor is there typically be any reason to use such an estimator.

To be more precise, first consider the notion of convergence in probability, denoted $\widehat{\beta}_n \xrightarrow{p} \beta$. Convergence in probability occurs whenever

$$\lim_{n\to\infty} \text{prob}(|\widehat{\beta}_n - \beta| < \varepsilon) = 1 \qquad \text{for any } \varepsilon > 0.$$

An estimator that converges in probability (to the quantity of interest) is said to be weakly consistent; other types of consistency can also be defined (e.g., see Serfling, 1980). Convergence in probability means that, for any arbitrarily small (but strictly positive) ε, the probability of obtaining an estimate different from β by more than ε in either direction tends to 0 as $n \to \infty$.

Note that consistency does not mean that it is impossible to obtain an estimate very different from β using a consistent estimator with a very large sample size. Rather, consistency is an asymptotic property; it describes only what happens in the limit. Although consistency is a fundamental property, it is also a minimal property in this sense. Depending on the rate, or speed, with which $\widehat{\beta}_n$ converges to β, a particular sample size may or may not offer much hope of obtaining an accurate, useful estimate.

In nonparametric statistics, it is often difficult to prove convergence of an estimator and to obtain its rate of convergence. Often, convergence and its rate are expressed in terms of the stochastic order of the error of estimation. The weakest notion of the stochastic order is related to the notion of "bounded in probability." A sequence of random variables A_n is said to be bounded in probability if there exists B_ε and n_ε such that for all $n > n_\varepsilon$ and $\varepsilon > 0$, $\text{prob}(A_n > B_\varepsilon) < \varepsilon$; such cases are denoted by writing $A_n = O_p(1)$. This means that when n is large, the random variable A_n is bounded, with probability tending to one. The notation $A_n = O_p(n^{-\alpha})$, where $\alpha > 0$, denotes that the sequence $A_n/n^{-\alpha} = n^\alpha A_n$ is $O_p(1)$. In this case, A_n is said to converge to a small quantity of order $n^{-\alpha}$. With some abuse of language, one can say also that A_n converges at the rate n^α because even multiplied by n^α (which can be rather large if n is large and if α is not too small), the sequence $n^\alpha A_n$ remains bounded in probability. Consequently, if α is small (near zero), the rate of convergence is very slow, because $n^{-\alpha}$ is not so small even when n is large.

This type of convergence is weaker than convergence in probability. If $\widehat{A}_n$ converges in probability at the rate n^α ($\alpha > 0$), then $A_n/n^{-\alpha} = n^\alpha A_n \xrightarrow{p} 0$, which can be denoted by writing $A_n = o_p(n^{-\alpha})$ or $n^\alpha A_n = o_p(1)$ (this is sometimes called "big-O, little-o" notation). Writing $A_n = O_p(n^{-\alpha})$ means that $n^\alpha A_n$ remains bounded when $n \to \infty$, but writing $A_n = o_p(n^{-\alpha})$ means that $n^\alpha A_n \xrightarrow{p} 0$ when $n \to \infty$.

In terms of the convergence of an estimator $\widehat{\beta}_n$ of β, writing $\widehat{\beta}_n - \beta = o_p(n^{-\alpha})$ means that $\widehat{\beta}_n$ converges in probability at rate n^α. Writing $\widehat{\beta}_n - \beta = O_p(n^{-\alpha})$ implies the weaker form of convergence, but the rate is still said to be n^α. Standard, parametric estimation problems usually yield estimators that converge in probability at the rate $\sqrt{n}$ (corresponding to $\alpha = 1/2$) and are said to be root-n consistent in such cases; this provides a familiar benchmark to which the rates of convergence of other, nonparametric estimators can be compared.

In all cases, the value of α plays a crucial role by indicating the "stochastic order" of the error of estimation. Since in many nonparametric problems α will be small (i.e., smaller than 1/2), it is illuminating to look at table 4.1 where the values of $n^{-\alpha}$ are displayed for some values of n and of α. Table 4.1 illustrates that as α diminishes, the sample size n must increase exponentially to maintain the same order of estimation error. For example, to achieve the same order of estimation error that one attains with $n = 10$ when $\alpha = 1$, one needs $n = 100$ observations when $\alpha = 1/2$, $n = 1,000$ observations when $\alpha = 1/3$, and $n = 10,000$ observations when $\alpha = 1/4$.

Parametric estimators, such as those described in chapter 2, typically achieve a convergence rate of $n^{-1/2}$, while many nonparametric estimators achieve only a (sometimes far) slower rate of convergence. The trade-offs are clear: Parametric estimators offer fast convergence, and hence it is possible to obtain meaningful estimates with smaller amounts of data than would be required by nonparametric estimators with slower convergence rates. But this is valid only if the parametric model that is estimated accurately reflects the true DGP; if not, there is specification error, calling into question consistency (and perhaps other properties) of the parametric estimators. By contrast, the nonparametric estimators discussed in this chapter largely avoid the risk of

Table 4.1
Values of the Order $n^{-\alpha}$ for Various n and α

$n \setminus \alpha$	$1 = 2/2$	$2/3$	$2/4$	$2/5$	$2/6$	$2/7$	$2/8$	$2/9$	$2/10$
10	0.1000	0.2154	0.3162	0.3981	0.4642	0.5179	0.5623	0.5995	0.6310
50	0.0200	0.0737	0.1414	0.2091	0.2714	0.3270	0.3761	0.4192	0.4573
100	0.0100	0.0464	0.1000	0.1585	0.2154	0.2683	0.3162	0.3594	0.3981
500	0.0020	0.0159	0.0447	0.0833	0.1260	0.1694	0.2115	0.2513	0.2885
1,000	0.0010	0.0100	0.0316	0.0631	0.1000	0.1389	0.1778	0.2154	0.2512
5,000	0.0002	0.0034	0.0141	0.0331	0.0585	0.0877	0.1189	0.1507	0.1821
10,000	0.0001	0.0022	0.0100	0.0251	0.0464	0.0720	0.1000	0.1292	0.1585

specification error, but (in some, but not all cases) at the cost of slower convergence rates and hence larger data requirements. What might constitute a "large sample" varies, depending on the stochastic order of the estimation error for the estimator that one chooses. Unfortunately, as we show below, many published applications of DEA estimators have used far fewer data than what might reasonably be required to obtain statistically meaningful results.

In an effort to simplify notation, the subscript n on the estimators in subsequent sections will be omitted.

4.2.5.2 Consistency of DEA/FDH estimators

This section summarizes the consistency results for the nonparametric envelopment estimators under the assumptions 4.2.1 through 4.2.7 given above. For the DEA estimators, convexity of Ψ (assumption 4.2.5) is needed, but for the FDH case, the results are valid with or without this assumption

Research on consistency and rates of convergence of efficiency estimators first examined the simpler cases where either inputs or outputs were unidimensional. For $N = 1$ and $M \geq 1$, Banker (1993) showed consistency of the input efficiency estimator $\widehat{\theta}_{VRS}$ for convex Ψ but obtained no information on the rate of convergence.

The first systematic analysis of the convergence properties of the envelopment estimators ($\widehat{\Psi}_{FDH}$ and $\widehat{\Psi}_{VRS}$) appeared in Korostelev et al. (1995a, 1995b). For for the case $N = 1$ and $M \geq 1$, they found that when Ψ satisfies free disposability, but not convexity,

$$d_\Delta(\widehat{\Psi}_{FDH}, \Psi) = O_p(n^{-\frac{1}{M+1}}), \tag{4.41}$$

and when Ψ satisfies both free disposability and convexity,

$$d_\Delta(\widehat{\Psi}_{VRS}, \Psi) = O_p(n^{-\frac{2}{M+2}}), \tag{4.42}$$

where $d_\Delta(\cdot, \cdot)$ is the Lebesgue measure (giving the volume) of the difference between the two sets.

The rates of convergence for $\widehat{\Psi}_{FDH}$ and $\widehat{\Psi}_{VRS}$ are not very different; however, for all $M \geq 1$, $n^{-1/(M+1)} > n^{-2/(M+2)}$. Moreover, the difference is larger for small values of M as revealed by table 4.1. Hence, incorporation of the convexity assumption into the estimator of Ψ (as done by $\widehat{\Psi}_{VRS}$) improves the rate of convergence. But, as noted above, if the true set is nonconvex, the DEA estimator is not consistent and hence does not converge, whereas the FDH estimator converges regardless of whether Ψ is convex. The rates of convergence depend on the dimensionality of the problem, that is, on the number of outputs M (when $N = 1$). This is yet another manifestation of the "curse of dimensionality" shared by most nonparametric approaches in statistics and econometrics; additional discussion on this issue is given below.

Despite the curse of dimensionality, Korostelev et al. (1995a, 1995b) show that the FDH and DEA estimators share some optimality properties. In particular, under free disposability (but not convexity), $\widehat{\Psi}_{FDH}$ is the most efficient estimator of Ψ (in terms of the minimax risk over the set of estimators sharing the free disposability assumption, where the loss function is d_Δ). Where Ψ is both free disposal and convex, $\widehat{\Psi}_{VRS}$ becomes the most efficient estimator over the class of all the estimators sharing the free disposal and the convexity assumption. These are quite important results and suggest the inherent quality of the envelopment estimators, even if imprecise in small samples where M large.

The full multivariate case, where both N and M are greater than one, was investigated later; results were established in terms of the efficiency scores themselves. Kneip et al. (1998) obtained results for DEA estimators, and Park et al. (2000) obtained results for FDH estimators. To summarize,

$$\widehat{\theta}_{FDH}(x, y) - \theta(x, y) = O_p(n^{-\frac{1}{N+M}}),\qquad(4.43)$$

and

$$\widehat{\theta}_{VRS}(x, y) - \theta(x, y) = O_p(n^{-\frac{2}{N+M+1}}).\qquad(4.44)$$

The rates obtained above when $N = 1$ are a special case of the results here. The curse of dimensionality acts symmetrically in both input and output spaces; that is, the curse of dimensionality is exacerbated, to the same degree, regardless of whether N or M is increased. The same rates of convergence can be derived for the output-oriented efficiency scores.

The convergence rate for $\widehat{\theta}_{VRS}(x, y)$ is slightly faster than for $\widehat{\theta}_{FDH}(x, y)$, provided assumption 4.2.1 is satisfied; otherwise, $\widehat{\theta}_{VRS}(x, y)$ is inconsistent. The faster convergence rate for the DEA estimator is due to the fact that $\widehat{\Psi}_{FDH} \subseteq \widehat{\Psi}_{DEA} \subseteq \widehat{\Psi}$. To date, the convergence rate for $\widehat{\theta}_{CRS}(x, y)$ has not been established, but we can imagine that its convergence rate would be faster than the rate achieved by $\widehat{\theta}_{CRS}(x, y)$ if $\partial\Psi$ displays globally constant returns to scale for similar reasons.

4.2.5.3 Curse of dimensionality: Parametric versus nonparametric inference

Returning to table 4.1, it is clear that if $M + N$ increases, a much larger sample size is needed to reach the precision obtained in the simplest case where $M = N = 1$, where the parametric rate $n^{1/2}$ is obtained by the FDH estimator, or where an even better rate $n^{2/3}$ is obtained by the DEA estimator. When $M + N$ is large, unless a very large quantity of data is available, the resulting imprecision will manifest in the form of large bias, large variance, and very wide confidence intervals.

This has been confirmed in Monte Carlo experiments. In fact, as the number of outputs is increased, the number of observations must increase at an exponential rate to maintain a given mean square error with the nonparametric estimators of Ψ. General statements on the number of observations required to achieve a given level of mean square error are not possible, since the exact convergence of the nonparametric estimators depends on unknown constants related to the features of the unobserved Ψ. Nonetheless, for estimation purposes, it is always true that more data are better than fewer data (recall that this is a consequence of consistency). In the case of nonparametric estimators such as $\widehat{\Psi}_{FDH}$ and $\widehat{\Psi}_{VRS}$, this statement is more than doubly true—it is exponentially true! To illustrate this fact, from table 4.1 it can be seen that, ceteras paribus, inference with $n = 10,000$ observations when the number of inputs and outputs is above or equal to 9 is less accurate than with $n = 10$ observations with one input and one output! In fact, with $N + M = 9$, one would need not 10,000 observations, but $10 \times 10,000 = 100,000$ observations to achieve the same estimation error as with $n = 10$ observations when $N = M = 1$. A number of applied papers using relatively small numbers of observations with many dimensions have appeared in the literature, but we hope that no more will appear.

The curse of dimensionality results from the fact that, as a given set of n observations are projected in an increasing number of orthogonal directions, the Euclidean distance between the observations necessarily must increase. Moreover, for a given sample size, increasing the number of dimensions will result in more observations lying on the boundaries of the estimators $\widehat{\Psi}_{FDH}$ and $\widehat{\Psi}_{VRS}$. The FDH estimator is particularly affected by this problem. The DEA estimator is also affected, often to a lesser degree due to its incorporation of the convexity assumption (recall that $\widehat{\Psi}_{VRS}$ is merely the convex hull of $\widehat{\Psi}_{FDH}$; consequently, fewer points will lie on the boundary of $\widehat{\Psi}_{VRS}$ than on the boundary of $\widehat{\Psi}_{FDH}$). Wheelock and Wilson (2003) and Wilson (2004) have found cases where all or nearly all observations in samples of several thousand observations lie on the boundary of $\widehat{\Psi}_{FDH}$, while relatively few observations lie on the boundary of $\widehat{\Psi}_{VRS}$. Both papers argue that the FDH estimator should be used as a diagnostic to check whether it might be reasonable to employ the DEA estimator in a given application; large numbers of observations falling on the boundary of $\widehat{\Psi}_{FDH}$ may indicate problems due to the curse of dimensionality.

Parametric estimators suffer little from this phenomenon in the sense that their rate of convergence typically does not depend on dimensionality of the problem. The parametric structure incorporates information from all of the observations in a sample, regardless of the dimensionality of Ψ. This also explains why parametric estimators are usually (but not always) more efficient in a statistical sense than their nonparametric counterparts—the parametric estimators extract more information from the data, assuming, of course, that the parametric assumptions that have been made are correct. This is frequently a *big* assumption.

Additional insight is provided by comparing parametric maximum likelihood estimators and nonparametric FDH and DEA estimators. Parametric maximum likelihood estimation is the most frequently used parametric estimation method. Under some regularity conditions that do not involve dimensionality of the problem at hand (see, e.g., Spanos 1999), maximum likelihood estimators are root-n consistent. Maximum likelihood estimation involves maximizing a likelihood function in which each observation is weighted equally. Hence, maximum likelihood estimators are *global* estimators, as opposed to FDH and DEA estimators, which are *local* estimators. With FDH or DEA estimators of the frontier, only observations near the point where the frontier is being estimated contribute to the estimate at that point; faraway observations contribute little or nothing to estimation at the point of interest.

It remains true, however, that when data are projected in an increasing number of orthogonal directions, Euclidean distance between the observations necessarily increases. This is problematic for FDH and DEA estimators, because it means that increasing dimensionality results in fewer nearby observations that can impart information about the frontier at a particular point of interest. But increasing distance between observations means also that parametric, maximum likelihood estimators are combining information, and weighting it equally, from observations that are increasingly far apart (with increasing dimensionality). Hence, increasing dimensionality means that the researcher must rely increasingly on the parametric assumptions of the model. Again, these are often big assumptions and should be tested, though often they are not.

The points made here go to the heart of the trade-off between nonparametric and parametric estimators. Parametric estimators incur the risk of misspecification which typically results in inconsistency, but are almost always statistically more efficient than nonparametric estimators if properly specified. Nonparametric estimators avoid the risk of misspecification, but usually involve more noise than parametric estimators. Lunch is not free, and the world is full of trade-offs, which creates employment opportunities for economists and statisticians.

4.2.5.4 Asymptotic sampling distributions

As discussed above, consistency is an essential property for any estimator. However, consistency is a minimal theoretical property. The preceding discussion indicates that DEA or FDH efficiency estimators converge as the sample size increases (although at perhaps a slow rate), but by themselves, these results have little practical use other than to confirm that the DEA or FDH estimators are *possibly* reasonable to use for efficiency estimation.

For empirical applications, more is needed—in particular, the applied researcher must have some knowledge of the sampling distributions in order to make inferences about the true levels of efficiency or inefficiency (e.g., correction for the bias and construction of confidence intervals). This is particularly important in situations where point estimates of efficiency might be highly variable due to the curse of dimensionality or other problems. In the nonparametric framework of FDH and DEA, as is often the case, only asymptotic results are available. For FDH estimators, a rather general result is available, but for DEA estimators, useful results have been obtained only for the case of one input and one output ($M = N = 1$). A general result is also available, but it is of little practical use.

FDH with N, M $\geq$ 1. Park et al. (2000) obtained a well-known limiting distribution for the error of estimation for this case:

$$n^{\frac{1}{N+M}} \left[\widehat{\theta}_{\mathrm{FDH}}(x,y) - \theta(x,y) \right] \xrightarrow{d} \mathrm{Weibull}(\mu_{x,y}, N + M), \qquad (4.45)$$

where $\mu_{x,y}$ is a constant depending on the DGP. The constant is proportional to the probability of observing a firm dominating a point on the ray x, in a neighborhood of the frontier point $x^{\partial}(y)$. This constant $\mu_{x,y}$ is larger (smaller) as the density $f(x,y)$ provides more (less) mass in the neighborhood of the frontier point. The bias and standard deviation of the FDH estimator are of the order $n^{-1/(N+M)}$ and are proportional to $\mu_{x,y}^{-1/(N+M)}$. Also, the ratio of the mean to the standard deviation of $\widehat{\theta}_{\mathrm{FDH}}(x,y) - \theta(x,y)$ does not depend on $\mu_{x,y}$ or on n and increases as the dimensionality $M + N$ increases. Thus, the curse of dimensionality here is twofold: Not only does the rate of convergence worsen with increasing dimensionality, but also bias worsens. These results suggest a strong need for a bias-corrected version of the FDH estimator; such an improvement is proposed later in this chapter.

Park et al. (2000) propose a consistent estimator of $\mu_{x,y}$ in order to obtain a bias-corrected estimator and asymptotic confidence intervals. However, Monte Carlo studies indicate that the noise introduced by estimating $\mu_{x,y}$ reduces the quality of inference when $N + M$ is large with moderate sample sizes (e.g., $n \leq 1,000$ with $M + N \geq 5$). Here again, the bootstrap might provide a useful alternative, but some smoothing of the FDH estimator might even be more appropriate than it is in the case of the bootstrap with DEA estimators (Jeong and Simar, 2006). This point is briefly discussed in sections 4.3.6 and 4.4.2.

DEA with M = N = 1. In this case, the efficient boundary can be represented by a function, and Gijbels et al. (1999) obtain the asymptotic result

$$n^{2/3} \left(\widehat{\theta}_{VRS}(x, y) - \theta(x, y) \right) \xrightarrow{d} Q_1(\cdot), \qquad (4.46)$$

as well as an analytical form for the limiting distribution $Q_1(\cdot)$. The limiting distribution is a regular distribution function known up to some constants. These constants depend on features of the DGP involving the curvature of the frontier and the magnitude of the density $f(x, y)$ at the true frontier point $(\theta(x, y)x, y)$. Expressions for the asymptotic bias and variance are also provided. As expected for the DEA estimator, the bias is of the order $n^{-2/3}$ and is larger for greater curvature of the true frontier (DEA is a piecewise linear estimator, so increasing curvature of the true frontier makes estimation more difficult) and decreases when the density at the true frontier point increases (large density at $[\theta(x, y)x, y]$ implies greater chances of observing observations near the point of interest that can impart useful information; recall again that DEA is a local estimator). The variance of the DEA estimator behaves similarly. It appears also that, in most cases, the bias will be much larger than the variance.

Using simple estimators of the two constants in $Q_1(\cdot)$, Gijbels et al. provide a bias-corrected estimator and a procedure for building confidence intervals for $\theta(x, y)$. Monte Carlo experiments indicate that, even for moderate sample size ($n = 100$), the procedure works reasonably well.

Although the results of Gijbels et al. (1999) are limited to the case where $N = M = 1$, their use extends beyond this simple case. The results provide insight for inference by identifying which features of the DGP affect the quality of inference making. One would expect that in a more general multivariate setting, the same features should play similar roles, but perhaps in a more complicated fashion.

DEA with N, M ≥ 1. Deriving analytical results for DEA estimators in multivariate settings is necessarily more difficult, and consequently, the results are less satisfying. Kneip et al. (2003) have obtained an important key result, namely,

$$n^{\frac{2}{N+M+1}} \left(\frac{\widehat{\theta}_{VRS}(x, y)}{\theta(x, y)} - 1 \right) \xrightarrow{d} Q_2(\cdot), \qquad (4.47)$$

where $Q_2(\cdot)$ is a regular distribution function known up to some constants. However, in this case, no closed analytical from for $Q_2(\cdot)$ is available, and hence the result is of little practical use for inference. In particular, the moments and the quantiles of $Q_2(\cdot)$ are not available, so neither bias correction nor confidence intervals can be provided easily using only the result in (4.47). Rather, the importance of this result lies in the fact that it is needed for proving the consistency of the bootstrap approximation (see below). The bootstrap remains the only practical tool for inference here.

To summarize, where limiting distributions are available and tractable, one can estimate the bias of FDH or DEA estimators and build confidence intervals. However, additional noise is introduced by estimating unknown constants appearing in the limiting distributions. Hence, the bootstrap remains an attractive alternative and is, to date, the only practical way of making inference in the multivariate DEA case.

4.3 Bootstrapping DEA and FDH Efficiency Scores

The bootstrap provides an attractive alternative to the theoretical results discussed in the preceding section. The essence of the bootstrap idea (Efron, 1979, 1982; Efron and Tibshirani, 1993) is to approximate the sampling distributions of interest by simulating, or mimicking, the DGP. The first use of the bootstrap in frontier models dates to Simar (1992). Its use for nonparametric envelopment estimators was developed by Simar and Wilson (1998, 2000a). Theoretical properties of the bootstrap with DEA estimators is provided in Kneip et al. (2003), and for FDH estimators in Jeong and Simar (2006).

The presentation below is in terms of the input-oriented case, but it can easily be translated to the output-oriented case. The bootstrap is intended to provide approximations of the sampling distributions of $\widehat{\theta}(x, y) - \theta(x, y)$ or $\widehat{\theta}(x, y)/\theta(x, y)$, which may be used as an alternative to the asymptotic results described above.

4.3.1 General principles

The presentation in this section follows Simar and Wilson (2000a). The original data $\mathcal{X}_n$ are generated from the DGP, which is completely characterized by knowledge of $\boldsymbol{\Psi}$ and of the probability density function $f(x, y)$. Let $\mathcal{P}$ denote the DGP. Then $\mathcal{P} = P[\boldsymbol{\Psi}, f(\cdot, \cdot)]$. Let $\widehat{\mathcal{P}}(\mathcal{X}_n)$ be a consistent estimator of the DGP $\mathcal{P}$, where

$$\widehat{\mathcal{P}}(\mathcal{X}_n) = P\left(\widehat{\boldsymbol{\Psi}}, \widehat{f}(\cdot, \cdot)\right). \tag{4.48}$$

In the *true world*, $\mathcal{P}$, $\boldsymbol{\Psi}$, and $\theta(x, y)$ are unknown ((x, y) is a given, fixed point of interest). Only the data $\mathcal{X}_n$ are observed, and these must be used to construct estimates of $\mathcal{P}$, $\boldsymbol{\Psi}$, and $\theta_{VRS}(x, y)$.

Now consider a virtual, simulated world, that is, the bootstrap world. This bootstrap world is analogous to the true world, but in the bootstrap world, estimates $\widehat{\mathcal{P}}$, $\widehat{\boldsymbol{\Psi}}$, and $\widehat{\theta}_{VRS}(x, y)$ take the place of $\mathcal{P}$, $\boldsymbol{\Psi}$, and $\theta(x, y)$ in the true world. In other words, in the true world $\mathcal{P}$ is the true DGP, while $\widehat{\mathcal{P}}$ is an estimate of $\mathcal{P}$, but in the bootstrap world, $\widehat{\mathcal{P}}$ is the true DGP. In the bootstrap world, a new data set $\mathcal{X}_n^* = \{(x_i^*, y_i^*), \ i = 1, \ldots, n\}$ can be drawn from $\widehat{\mathcal{P}}$, since $\widehat{\mathcal{P}}$ is a known estimate. Within the bootstrap world, $\widehat{\Psi}$ is the true attainable set, and the union of the free disposal and the convex hulls of $\mathcal{X}_n^*$ gives an estimator of $\widehat{\Psi}$, namely,

$$\widehat{\Psi}^* = \widehat{\Psi}(\mathcal{X}_n^*) = \left[(x, y) \in \mathscr{R}^{N+M} \,\middle|\, y \leq \sum_{i=1}^{n} \gamma_i y_i^*, \; x \geq \sum_{i=1}^{n} \gamma_i x_i^* \right.$$
$$\left. \sum_{i=1}^{n} \gamma_i = 1, \; \gamma_i \geq 0 \; \forall i = 1, \ldots, n \right]. \tag{4.49}$$

For the fixed point (x, y), an estimator of $\widehat{\theta}_{VRS}(x, y)$ is provided by

$$\widehat{\theta}_{VRS}^*(x, y) = \inf\{\theta \mid (\theta x, y) \in \widehat{\Psi}^*\} \tag{4.50}$$

[recall that in the bootstrap world, $\widehat{\theta}_{VRS}(x, y)$ is the quantity estimated, analogous to $\theta(x, y)$ in the true world]. The estimator $\widehat{\theta}_{VRS}^*(x, y)$ may be computed by solving the linear program

$$\widehat{\theta}_{VRS}^*(x, y) = \min \left\{ \theta > 0 \,\middle|\, y \leq \sum_{i=1}^{n} \gamma_i y_i^*, \; \theta x \geq \sum_{i=1}^{n} \gamma_i x_i^*, \right.$$
$$\left. \sum_{i=1}^{n} \gamma_i = 1, \; \gamma_i \geq 0 \; \forall i = 1, \ldots, n \right\}. \tag{4.51}$$

The *key relation* here is that *within the true world*, $\widehat{\theta}_{VRS}(x, y)$ is an estimator of $\theta(x, y)$, based on the sample $\mathcal{X}_n$ generated from $\mathcal{P}$, whereas *in the bootstrap world*, $\widehat{\theta}_{VRS}^*(x, y)$ is an estimator of $\widehat{\theta}_{VRS}(x, y)$, based on the pseudosample $\mathcal{X}_n^*$ generated from $\widehat{\mathcal{P}}(\mathcal{X}_n)$. If the bootstrap is *consistent*, then

$$\left(\widehat{\theta}_{VRS}^*(x, y) - \widehat{\theta}_{VRS}(x, y) \right) \mid \widehat{\mathcal{P}}(\mathcal{X}_n) \overset{\text{approx.}}{\sim} \left(\widehat{\theta}_{VRS}(x, y) - \theta(x, y) \right) \mid \mathcal{P}, \tag{4.52}$$

or equivalently,

$$\frac{\widehat{\theta}_{VRS}^*(x, y)}{\widehat{\theta}_{VRS}(x, y)} \middle| \widehat{\mathcal{P}}(\mathcal{X}_n) \overset{\text{approx.}}{\sim} \frac{\widehat{\theta}_{VRS}(x, y)}{\theta(x, y)} \middle| \mathcal{P}. \tag{4.53}$$

Within the bootstrap world and conditional on the observed data $\mathcal{X}_n$, the sampling distribution of $\widehat{\theta}_{VRS}^*(x, y)$ is (in principle) completely known since $\widehat{\mathcal{P}}(\mathcal{X}_n)$ is known. However, in practice, it is impossible to compute this analytically. Hence Monte Carlo simulations are necessary to approximate the left-hand sides of (4.52) or (4.53).

Using $\widehat{\mathcal{P}}(\mathcal{X}_n)$ to generate B samples $\mathcal{X}_{n_b}^*$ of size n, $b = 1, \ldots, B$ and applying the original estimator to these pseudosamples yields a set of B pseudoestimates $\widehat{\theta}_{VRS,b}^*(x, y)$, $b = 1, \ldots, B$. The empirical distribution of these bootstrap values gives a Monte Carlo approximation of the sampling distribution of $\widehat{\theta}^*_{VRS}(x,y)$, conditional on $\widehat{\mathcal{P}}(\mathcal{X}_n)$, that is, the left-hand side of (4.52) [or of (4.53) if the ratio formulation is used]. The quality of the approximation relies in part on the value of B: By the law of large numbers, when $B \to \infty$, the error of this approximation due to the bootstrap resampling (i.e., drawing from $\widehat{\mathcal{P}}$) tends to zero. The practical choice of B is limited by the speed of one's computer; for confidence intervals, values of 2,000 or more may be needed to give a reasonable approximation.

The issue of computational constraints continues to diminish in importance as computing technology advances. For many problems, however, a single desktop system may be sufficient. Given the independence of each of the B replications in the Monte Carlo approximation, the bootstrap algorithm is easily adaptable to parallel computing environments or by using a series of networked personal computers; the price of these machines continues to decline while processor speeds increase.

The bootstrap is an asymptotic procedure, as indicated by the conditioning on the left-hand-side of (4.52) or of (4.53). Thus, the quality of the bootstrap approximation depends on both the number of replications B and and the sample size n. When the bootstrap is consistent, the approximation becomes exact as $B \to \infty$ and $n \to \infty$.

4.3.2 Bootstrap confidence intervals

The procedure described in Simar and Wilson (1998) for constructing the confidence intervals depends on using bootstrap estimates of bias to correct for the bias of the DEA estimators; in addition, the procedure described there requires using these bias estimates to shift obtained bootstrap distributions appropriately. Use of bias estimates introduces additional noise into the procedure.

Simar and Wilson (1999c) propose an improved procedure outlined below which automatically corrects for bias without explicit use of a noisy bias estimator. The procedure is presented below in terms of the difference $\widehat{\theta}_{VRS}(x,y) - \theta(x,y)$; in Kneip et al. (2003), the procedure is adapted to the ratio $\widehat{\theta}_{VRS}(x,y)/\theta(x,y)$.

For practical purposes, it is advantageous to parameterize the input efficiency scores in term of the Shephard (1970) input distance function

$$\delta(x,y) \equiv \frac{1}{\theta(x,y)}. \tag{4.54}$$

The corresponding estimator (allowing for variable returns to scale) is defined by

$$\widehat{\delta}_{VRS}(x,y) \equiv \frac{1}{\widehat{\theta}_{VRS}(x,y)}. \tag{4.55}$$

In some cases, failure to reparameterize the problem may result in estimated lower bounds for confidence intervals that are negative; this results because of the boundary at zero. With the reparameterization, only the boundary at one need be considered.

If the distribution of $(\widehat{\delta}_{VRS}(x, y) - \delta(x, y))$ were known, then it would be trivial to find values $c_{\alpha/2}$ and $c_{1-\alpha/2}$ such that

$$\text{prob}\left(c_{\alpha/2} \leq \widehat{\delta}_{VRS}(x, y) - \delta(x, y) \leq c_{1-\alpha/2}\right) = 1 - \alpha, \tag{4.56}$$

where c_a denotes the ath-quantile of the sampling distribution of $(\widehat{\delta}_{VRS}(x, y) - \delta(x, y))$. Note that $c_a \geq 0$ for all $a \in [0, 1]$. Then,

$$\widehat{\delta}_{VRS}(x, y) - c_{1-\alpha/2} \leq \delta(x, y) \leq \widehat{\delta}_{VRS}(x, y) - c_{\alpha/2} \tag{4.57}$$

would give a $(1 - \alpha) \times 100\%$ confidence interval for $\delta(x, y)$, and hence

$$\frac{1}{\widehat{\delta}_{VRS}(x, y) - c_{\alpha/2}} \leq \theta(x, y) \leq \frac{1}{\widehat{\delta}_{VRS}(x, y) - c_{1-\alpha/2}} \tag{4.58}$$

would give a $(1 - \alpha) \times 100\%$ confidence interval for $\theta(x, y)$, due to the reciprocal relation in (4.54).

Of course, the quantiles c_a are unknown, but from the empirical bootstrap distribution of the pseudoestimates $\widehat{\delta}^*_{VRS,b}$, $b = 1, \ldots, B$, estimates of c_a can be found for any value of $a \in [0, 1]$. For example, if $\widehat{c}_a$ is the ath sample quantile of the empirical distribution of $[\widehat{\delta}^*_{VRS,b}(x, y) - \widehat{\delta}_{VRS}(x, y)]$, $b = 1, \ldots, B$, then

$$\text{prob}\left(\widehat{c}_{\alpha/2} \leq \widehat{\delta}^*_{VRS}(x, y) - \widehat{\delta}_{VRS}(x, y) \leq \widehat{c}_{1-\alpha/2} \mid \widehat{P}(\mathcal{X}_n)\right) = 1 - \alpha. \tag{4.59}$$

In practice, finding $\widehat{c}_{\alpha/2}$ and $\widehat{c}_{1-\alpha/2}$ involves sorting the values $(\widehat{\delta}^*_{VRS,b}(x, y) - \widehat{\delta}_{VRS}(x, y))$, $b = 1, \ldots, B$ in increasing order, and then deleting $(\frac{\alpha}{2} \times 100)$-percent of the elements at either end of the sorted list. Then, set $\widehat{c}_{\alpha/2}$ and $\widehat{c}_{1-\alpha/2}$ equal to the endpoints of the truncated, sorted array. The bootstrap approximation of (4.56) is then

$$\text{prob}\left(\widehat{c}_{\alpha/2} \leq \widehat{\delta}_{VRS}(x, y) - \delta(x, y) \leq \widehat{c}_{1-\alpha/2}\right) \approx 1 - \alpha, \tag{4.60}$$

and the estimated $(1 - \alpha) \times 100\%$ confidence interval for $\delta(x, y)$ is

$$\widehat{\delta}_{VRS}(x, y) - \widehat{c}_{1-\alpha/2} \leq \delta(x, y) \leq \widehat{\delta}_{VRS}(x, y) - \widehat{c}_{\alpha/2}, \tag{4.61}$$

or

$$\frac{1}{\widehat{\delta}_{VRS}(x, y) - \widehat{c}_{\alpha/2}} \leq \theta(x, y) \leq \frac{1}{\widehat{\delta}_{VRS}(x, y) - \widehat{c}_{1-\alpha/2}}. \tag{4.62}$$

Since $0 \leq \widehat{c}_{\alpha/2} \leq \widehat{c}_{1-\alpha/2}$, the estimated confidence interval will include the original estimate $\widehat{\delta}_{VRS}(x, y)$ on its upper boundary only if $\widehat{c}_{\alpha/2} = 0$. This may seem strange until one recalls that the boundary of support of $f(x, y)$ is being estimated; under the assumptions, distance from (x, y) to the frontier can be *no less than* the distance indicated by $\widehat{\delta}_{VRS}(x, y)$, but is likely more.

The procedure outlined here can be used for any point $(x, y) \in \mathscr{R}_+^{N+M}$ for which $\widehat{\theta}_{VRS}(x, y)$ exists. Typically, the applied researcher is interested in the efficiency scores of the observed units themselves; in this case, the above procedure can be repeated n times, with (x, y) taking values (x_i, y_i), $i = 1, \ldots, n$, producing a set of n confidence intervals of the form (4.62) for each firm in the sample. Alternatively, in cases where the computational burden is large due to large numbers of observations, one might select a few representative firms, or perhaps a small number of hypothetical firms. For example, rather than reporting results for several thousand firms, one might report results for a few hypothetical firms represented by the means (or medians) of input and output levels for observed firms in quintiles or deciles determined by size or some other feature of the observed firms.

4.3.3 Bootstrap bias corrections

DEA (and FDH) estimators were shown above to be biased, by construction. By definition,

$$\text{bias}\left(\widehat{\theta}_{VRS}(x, y)\right) \equiv E\left(\widehat{\theta}_{VRS}(x, y)\right) - \theta(x, y). \tag{4.63}$$

The bootstrap bias estimate for the original estimator $\widehat{\theta}_{VRS}(x, y)$ is the empirical analog of (4.63):

$$\widehat{\text{bias}}_B\left(\widehat{\theta}_{VRS}(x, y)\right) = B^{-1} \sum_{b=1}^{B} \widehat{\theta}^*_{VRS,b}(x, y) - \widehat{\theta}_{VRS}(x, y). \tag{4.64}$$

It is tempting to construct a bias-corrected estimator of $\theta(x, y)$ by computing

$$\widehat{\widehat{\theta}}_{VRS}(x, y) = \widehat{\theta}_{VRS}(x, y) - \widehat{\text{bias}}_B\left(\widehat{\theta}_{VRS}(x, y)\right)$$

$$= 2\widehat{\theta}_{VRS}(x, y) - B^{-1} \sum_{b=1}^{B} \widehat{\theta}^*_{VRS,b}(x, y). \tag{4.65}$$

It is well known (e.g., see Efron and Tibshirani, 1993), however, that this bias correction introduces additional noise; the mean square error of $\widehat{\widehat{\theta}}_{VRS}(x, y)$ may be greater than the mean square error of $\widehat{\theta}_{VRS}(x, y)$. The sample variance of the bootstrap values $\widehat{\theta}^*_{VRS,b}(x, y)$,

$$\widehat{\sigma}^2 = B^{-1} \sum_{b=1}^{B} \left[\widehat{\theta}^*_{VRS,b}(x, y) - B^{-1} \sum_{b=1}^{B} \widehat{\theta}^*_{VRS,b}(x, y) \right]^2, \tag{4.66}$$

provides an estimate of the variance of $\widehat{\theta}_{VRS}(x, y)$. Hence, the variance of the bias-corrected estimator: $\widehat{\widehat{\theta}}_{VRS}(x, y)$ is approximately $4\widehat{\sigma}^2$, ignoring any correlation between $\widehat{\theta}_{VRS}(x, y)$ and the summation term in the second line of (4.65). Therefore, the bias correction should not be used unless $4\widehat{\sigma}^2$ is well less than $\left[\widehat{\text{bias}}_B\left(\widehat{\theta}_{VRS}(x, y)\right)\right]^2$; otherwise, $\widehat{\widehat{\theta}}_{VRS}(x, y)$ is likely to have mean square erro larger than the mean square error of $\widehat{\theta}_{VRS}(x, y)$. A useful rule of thumb is to avoid the bias correction in (4.65) unless

$$\frac{\left|\widehat{\text{bias}}_B\left(\widehat{\theta}_{VRS}(x, y)\right)\right|}{\widehat{\sigma}} > \frac{1}{\sqrt{3}}. \tag{4.67}$$

Alternatively, Efron and Tibshirani (1993) propose a less conservative rule, suggesting that the bias correction be avoided unless

$$\frac{\left|\widehat{\text{bias}}_B\left(\widehat{\theta}_{VRS}(x, y)\right)\right|}{\widehat{\sigma}} > \frac{1}{4}. \tag{4.68}$$

4.3.4 Bootstrapping DEA in action

The remaining question concerns how a bootstrap sample $\mathcal{X}_n^*$ from the consistent estimator of $\mathcal{P}$ might be simulated. The standard, and simplest, nonparametric bootstrap technique, called the "naive" bootstrap, consists of drawing pseudoobservation (x_i^*, y_i^*), $i = 1, \ldots, n$ independently, uniformly, and with replacement from the set $\mathcal{X}_n$ of original observations. Unfortunately, however, this naive bootstrap is inconsistent in the context of boundary estimation. In other words, even if $B \rightarrow \infty$ and $n \rightarrow \infty$, the Monte Carlo empirical distribution of the $\widehat{\theta}_{VRS,b}^*(x, y)$ will not approximate the sampling distribution of $\widehat{\theta}_{VRS}(x, y)$.

The bootstrap literature contains numerous univariate examples of this problem; see Bickel and Freedman (1981) and Efron and Tibshirani (1993) for examples. Simar and Wilson (1999a, 1999b) discuss this issue in the context of multivariate frontier estimation. As illustrated below, the problem comes from the fact that in the naive bootstrap, the efficient facet determining the value of $\widehat{\theta}_{VRS}(x, y)$, appears too often, and with a fixed probability, in the pseudosamples $\mathcal{X}_n^*$. This fixed probability does not depend on the real DGP (other than the number N of inputs and the number M of outputs) and does not vanish, even when $n \rightarrow \infty$.

There are two solutions to this problem: either subsampling techniques (drawing pseudosamples of size $m = n^\kappa$, where $\kappa < 1$) or smoothing techniques (where a smooth estimate of the joint density $f(x, y)$ is employed to simulate $\mathcal{X}_n^*$). Kneip et al. (2003) analyze the properties of these techniques for strictly convex sets Ψ and in both approaches prove that the bootstrap provides consistent approximation of the sampling distribution of $\widehat{\theta}_{VRS}(x, y) - \theta(x, y)$

[or of the ratio $\widehat{\theta}_{VRS}(x, y)/\theta(x, y)$, if preferred]. The ideas are summarized below, again for the input-oriented case; the procedure can easily be translated for the out-put oriented case.

4.3.4.1 Subsampling DEA scores

Of the two solutions mentioned above, this one is easiest to implement since it is similar to the naive bootstrap except that pseudosamples of size $m = n^\kappa$ for some $\kappa \in (0, 1)$ $(0 < \kappa < 1)$ are drawn. For bootstrap replications $b = 1, \dots, B$, let $\mathcal{X}^*_{n_{m,b}}$ denote a random subsample of size m drawn from $\mathcal{X}_n$. Let $\widehat{\theta}_{VRS,m,b}(x, y)$ denote the DEA efficiency estimate for the fixed point (x, y) computed using the reference sample $\mathcal{X}^*_{n_{m,b}}$. Kneip et al. (2003) prove that the Monte Carlo empirical distribution of $m^{2/(N+M+1)}(\widehat{\theta}_{VRS,m,b}(x, y) - \widehat{\theta}_{VRS}(x, y))$ given $\mathcal{X}_n$ approximates the exact sampling distribution of $n^{2/(N+M+1)}(\widehat{\theta}_{VRS}(x, y) - \theta(x, y))$ as $B \to \infty$.

Using this approach, a bootstrap bias estimate of the DEA estimator is obtained by computing

$$\widehat{\mathrm{bias}}_B\left(\widehat{\theta}_{VRS}(x, y)\right) = \left(\frac{m}{n}\right)^{\frac{2}{(N+M+1)}}$$

$$\times \left[\frac{1}{B} \sum_{b=1}^{B} \widehat{\theta}^*_{VRS,m,b}(x, y) - \widehat{\theta}_{VRS}(x, y) \right], \quad (4.69)$$

and a bias-corrected estimator of the DEA efficiency score is given by

$$\widehat{\widehat{\theta}}_{VRS}(x, y) = \widehat{\theta}_{VRS}(x, y) - \widehat{\mathrm{bias}}_B\left(\widehat{\theta}_{VRS}(x, y)\right). \quad (4.70)$$

Note that (4.69) differs from (4.64) by inclusion of the factor $(m/n)^{2/(N+M+1)}$, which is necessary to correct for the effects of different sample sizes in the true world and bootstrap world.

Following the same arguments as in section 4.3.2, but again adjusting for different sample sizes in the true and bootstrap worlds, the following $(1 - \alpha) \times 100\%$ bootstrap confidence interval is obtained for $\theta(x, y)$:

$$\frac{1}{\widehat{\delta}_{VRS}(x, y) - \eta c^*_{1-\alpha/2}} \le \theta(x, y) \le \frac{1}{\widehat{\delta}_{VRS}(x, y) - \eta c^*_{\alpha/2}}, \quad (4.71)$$

where $\eta = (m/n)^{2/(N+M+1)}$ and c^*_a is the ath empirical quantile of $(\widehat{\delta}_{VRS,m,b}(x, y) - \widehat{\delta}_{VRS}(x, y))$, $b = 1, \dots, B$.

In practice, with finite samples, some subsamples $\mathcal{X}^*_{n_{m,b}}$ may yield no feasible solutions for the linear program used to compute $\widehat{\delta}^*_{VRS,m,b}(x, y)$. This will occur more frequently when y is large compared to the original output values y_i in $\mathcal{X}_n$. In fact, this problem arises if $y \not\ge \max\{y_j|(x_j, y_j) \in \mathcal{X}^*_{n_{m,b}}\}$.[3]

In such cases, one could add the point of interest (x, y) to the drawn subsample $\mathcal{X}^*_{n_{m,b}}$, resulting in $\widehat{\delta}^*_{VRS,m,b}(x, y) = 1$. This will solve the numerical difficulties, and does not affect the asymptotic properties of the bootstrap since under the assumptions of the DGP, for all $(x, y) \in \Psi$, the probability of this event tends to zero. As shown in Kneip et al. (2003), any value of $\kappa < 1$ produces a consistent bootstrap, but in finite sample the choice of κ seems to be critical. More work is needed on this problem.

4.3.4.2 Smoothing techniques

As an alternative to the subsampling version of the bootstrap method, pseudo-samples can be drawn from a smooth, nonparametric estimate of the unknown density $f(x, y)$. The problem is complicated by the fact that the support of this density, Ψ, is unknown. There are possibly several ways of addressing this problem, but the procedures proposed by Simar and Wilson (1998, 2000b) are straightforward and less complicated than other methods that might be used.

A number of nonparametric density estimators are available. Histogram estimators (see Scott, 1992, for discussion) are easy to apply and do not suffer degenerate behavior near support boundaries, but are not smooth. The lack of smoothness can be eliminated while preserving the nondegenerate behavior near support boundaries by using local polynomial regression methods to smooth a histogram estimate of a density as proposed by Cheng et al. (1997). However, it is difficult to simulate draws from such a density estimate. Kernel estimators are perhaps the most commonly used nonparametric density estimators; these provide smooth density estimates, and it is easy to take draws from a kernel density estimate. However, in their standard form and with finite samples, kernel density estimators are severely biased near boundaries of support; the existence of support boundaries also affects their rates of convergence. Fortunately, several methods exist for repairing these problems near support boundaries; here, a reflection method similar to the idea of Schuster (1985) is used.[4]

In univariate density estimation problems, the reflection method is very simple; one simply reflects the n observations around a known boundary, estimates the density of the original and reflected data ($2n$ observations), and then truncates this density estimate at the boundary point. In the present context, however, the method is more complicated due to three factors:

(i) the problem involves multiple $(N + M)$ dimensions,
(ii) the boundary of support, $\partial \Psi$, is unknown, and
(iii) the boundary is nonlinear.

These problems can be solved by exploiting the radial nature of the efficiencies $\theta(x, y)$ and $\lambda(x, y)$.

The third problem listed in the previous paragraph can be dealt with by transforming the problem from Cartesian coordinates to spherical coordinates, which are a combination of Cartesian and polar coordinates. In the input orientation, the Cartesian coordinates for the input space are transformed to polar coordinates, while in the output orientation, the Cartesian coordinates for the output space would be transformed to polar coordinates. The method is illustrated here for the input orientation; once again, it is easy to adapt the method to the output orientation.

For the input orientation, the Cartesian coordinates (x, y) are transformed to (ω, η, y), where (ω, η) are the polar coordinates of x in $\mathscr{R}_+^N$. The modulus $\omega = \omega(x) \in \mathscr{R}_+^1$ of x is given by the square root of the sum of the squared elements of x, and the jth element of the corresponding angle $\eta = \eta(x) \in [0, \frac{\pi}{2}]^{N-1}$ of x is given by $\arctan(x^{j+1}/x^1)$ for $x^1 \neq 0$; if $x^1 = 0$, then all elements of $\eta(x)$ equal $\pi/2$.

The DGP is completely determined by $f(x, y)$, and hence is also completely determined by the density $f(\omega, \eta, y)$ after transforming from Cartesian coordinates to spherical coordinates. In order to generate sample points in the spherical coordinate representation, the density $f(\omega, \eta, y)$ can be decomposed (using Bayes's rule) to obtain

$$f(\omega, \eta, y) = f(\omega \mid \eta, y) f(\eta \mid y) f(y), \qquad (4.72)$$

where each of conditional densities are assumed to be well defined. For a given (y, η), the corresponding frontier point $x^\partial(y)$ is defined by (4.6); this point has modulus

$$\omega(x^\partial(y)) = \inf\{\omega \in \mathscr{R}^+ \mid f(\omega \mid y, \eta) > 0\}. \qquad (4.73)$$

Assumption 4.2.2 implies that for all y and η, $f(\omega(x^\partial(y)) \mid y, \eta) > 0$.

From the definition of the input efficiency score,

$$0 \leq \theta(x, y) = \frac{\omega(x^\partial(y))}{\omega(x)} \leq 1. \qquad (4.74)$$

The density $f(\omega \mid y, \eta)$ on $[\omega(x^\partial(y)), \infty]$ induces a density $f(\theta \mid y, \eta)$ on $[0, 1]$. This decomposition of the DGP is illustrated in figure 4.4: The DGP generates an output level, according to the marginal $f(y)$; then, conditional on y, $f(\eta \mid y)$ generates an input mix in the input-requirement set $X(y)$; finally, the observation P is randomly generated inside Ψ, from the frontier point, along the ray defined by η and according to $f(\theta \mid \eta, y)$, the conditional density of the efficiency θ on $[0, 1]$.

Once again, for practical purposes, it is easier to parameterize the input efficiency scores in terms of the Shephard (1970) input distance function as in (4.54) and (4.55). Working in terms of $\delta(x, y)$ and $\widehat{\delta}_{VRS}(x, y)$ has the advantage that $\delta(x, y) \geq 1$ for all $(x, y) \in \Psi$; consequently, when simulating the bootstrap values, there will be only one boundary condition for δ to deal

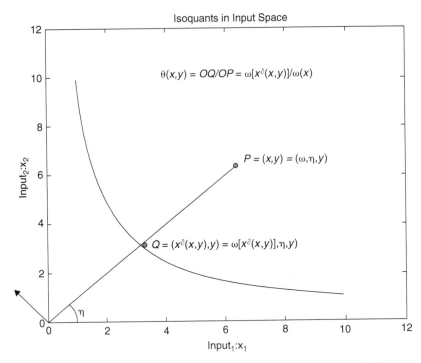

Figure 4.4. Polar Coordinates in the Input Space for a Particular Section $X(y)$

with, not two as is the case of θ (in the output orientation, efficiency scores $\lambda(x, y)$ are greater than one for all $(x, y) \in \Psi$, so the reciprocal transformation is not needed). Using (4.54), (4.74) can be rewritten as

$$\delta(x, y) = \frac{\omega(x)}{\omega(x^\partial(y))} \geq 1. \tag{4.75}$$

Here, the density $f(\omega \mid y, \eta)$ on $[\omega(x^\partial(y)), \infty)$ induces a density $f(\delta \mid y, \eta)$ on $[1, \infty)$.

The idea of the smooth bootstrap in this general, multivariate framework is to generate sample points $(\delta_i^*, \eta_i^*, y_i^*)$, $i = 1, \ldots, n$ from a smooth estimate of the density $f(\delta, \eta, y)$. To accomplish this, first the original data $(x_i, y_i) \in \mathcal{X}_n$ are transformed to polar coordinates (δ_i, η_i, y_i). Since the true frontier is unknown, δ_i is unknown, but δ_i can be replaced by its consistent DEA estimator $\widehat{\delta_i} = \widehat{\delta}_{VRS}(x_i, y_i)$. Estimation of the density is then based on the sample values $(\widehat{\delta_i}, \eta_i, y_i)$, $i = 1, \ldots, n$. Kernel smoothing techniques can be used, along with the reflection method to account for the boundary conditions (see Silverman, 1986). This step involves the choice of a smoothing parameter, that is, the bandwidth (this issue is discussed below). Then, as a final step, the simulated observations $(\delta_i^*, \eta_i^*, y_i^*)$ must be transformed back to Cartesian coordinates (x_i^*, y_i^*), $i = 1, \ldots, n$. This yields a bootstrap sample $\mathcal{X}_n^*$.

The last step requires several steps, including solution of an additional linear program:

(i) Let $\tilde{x}$ be any point in the x-space on the ray with angle η_i^* (e.g., take $\tilde{x}_1 = 1$ and $\tilde{x}_{j+1} = \tan(\eta_{ij}^*)$ for $j = 1, \ldots, N - 1$; here the subscripts on $\tilde{x}$ denote individual elements of the vector $\tilde{x}$).

(ii) For the point $(\tilde{x}, y_i^*)$, compute the DEA estimator $\widehat{\delta}_{VRS}(\tilde{x}, y_i^*)$ using the reference set $\mathcal{X}_n$.

(iii) An estimator of the input-efficient level of inputs, given the output y_i^* and the direction given by the input vector $\tilde{x}_i$, is given by adapting (4.6) to the bootstrap world:

$$\widehat{x}^{\partial *}(y_i^*) = \frac{\tilde{x}}{\widehat{\delta}_{VRS}(\tilde{x}, y_i^*)}$$

(iv) Compute

$$x_i^* = \delta_i^* \widehat{x}^{\partial *}(y_i^*)$$

to obtain the Cartesian coordinates x_i^*.

In the procedure above, the main difficulty lies in estimating $f(\delta, \eta, y)$ because of the bound on δ. Simar and Wilson (2000b) reflected the points $(\widehat{\delta}_i, \eta_i, y_i)$ about the boundary characterized by the values $\widehat{\delta}_i = 1$; that is, Simar and Wilson add points $(2 - \delta_i, \eta_i, y_i)$, $i = 1, \ldots, n$ to the original observations in $\mathcal{X}_n$. This was also proposed by Kneip et al. (2003), where, in addition, the values $\widehat{\delta}_i$ are adjusted to smooth the DEA estimator of Ψ. These procedures are not easy to implement. So far, there seems to be no simple way to avoid the considerable complexity required in such a general framework.

4.3.4.3 The Homogeneous smoothed bootstrap

The bootstrap procedure described above can be substantially simplified if one is willing to make additional assumptions on the DGP. In particular, assume that the distribution of efficiency is homogeneous over the input–output space (this is analogous to an assumption of homoskedasticity in linear regression problems). In other words, assume that

$$f(\delta \mid \eta, y) = f(\delta). \tag{4.76}$$

This may be a reasonable assumption in many practical situations. Wilson (2003) surveys tests for independence that may be used to check where data might satisfy the assumption in (4.76).

Adoption of the homogeneity assumption in (4.76) makes the problem similar to the bootstrap one would use in homoskedastic regression models (see Bickel and Freedman, 1981), that is, where the bootstrap is based on the residuals. In the present context, the residuals correspond to the distances $\widehat{\delta}_i = \widehat{\delta}_{VRS}(x_i, y_i)$, $i = 1, \ldots, n$, and so the problem becomes essentially univariate, avoiding the complexity of estimating a multivariate density for $(\widehat{\delta}_i, \eta_i, y_i)$. The idea is create a bootstrap sample by projecting each observation (x_i, y_i) onto the estimated frontier and then projecting this point away from the frontier randomly, resulting in points $(\delta_i^* x_i / \widehat{\delta}_i, y)$, where δ_i^* is a draw from a smooth estimate of the marginal density $f(\delta)$ obtained from the sample of estimates $\widehat{\delta}_1, \ldots, \widehat{\delta}_n$. Hence, standard, univariate kernel density estimation, combined with the reflection method, can be used.

The steps are summarized as follows:

(i) Let $\widehat{f}(\delta)$ be a smooth estimate obtained from the observed $\{\widehat{\delta}_i \mid i = 1, \ldots, n\}$, and draw a bootstrap sample $(\delta_i^*, \ i = 1, \ldots, n)$ from this density estimate.

(ii) Define the bootstrap sample $\mathcal{X}_n^* = \{(x_i^*, y_i); \ i = 1, \ldots, n\}$, where

$$x_i^* = \delta_i^* \widehat{x}^{\partial}(y_i) = \frac{\delta_i^*}{\widehat{\delta}_i} x_i.$$

The idea is illustrated in figure 4.5, where the circles are the original observations (x_i, y_i), and the asterisks are the pseudoobservations (x_i^*, y_i). For the point $P = (x, y)$, $\delta(x, y) = |OP|/|OQ|$, $\widehat{\delta}(x, y) = |OP|/|OQ_{VRS}|$, and $\widehat{\delta}^*(x, y) = |OP|/|OQ_{VRS}^*|$. The hope is that $\widehat{\delta}^*(x, y) - \widehat{\delta}(x, y) \sim \widehat{\delta}(x, y) - \delta(x, y)$.

It is easy to understand why a naive bootstrap technique, where the δ_i^* are drawn identically, uniformly, and with replacement from the set

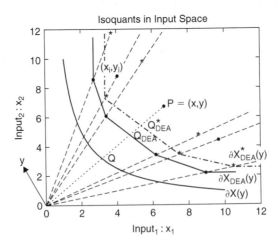

Figure 4.5. The Bootstrap Idea

$\{\widehat{\delta}_i \mid i = 1, \ldots, n\}$, would be inconsistent. As observed by Simar and Wilson (1999a), this would yield

$$\text{prob}(\widehat{\delta}^*(x, y) = \widehat{\delta}(x, y) \mid \mathcal{X}_n) = 1 - (1 - n^{-1})^n > 0,$$

with

$$\lim_{n \to \infty} \text{prob}\left(\widehat{\delta}^*(x, y) = \widehat{\delta}(x, y) \mid \mathcal{X}_n\right) = 1 - e^{-1} \approx 0.632. \tag{4.77}$$

The naive bootstrap is inconsistent since there is absolutely no reason to believe that this probability should equal approximately 0.632, independently of any features of the DGP. In fact, if $f(\delta)$ is continuous over $\delta \in [1, \infty)$, the probability in (4.77) should be zero, since in this case

$$\text{prob}(\widehat{\delta}(x, y) = \delta(x, y)) = 0.$$

Even if the true probability density function $f(\delta)$ had a mass at the boundary, there is no reason to believe this mass would be equal to 0.632.

The problem with the naive bootstrap arises from the fact that a continuous density $f(\delta)$ is approximated by a discrete density putting a mass $1/n$ at each observed $\widehat{\delta}$. The problem is avoided by estimating $f(\delta)$ by using a smooth kernel estimator $\widehat{f}_h(\delta)$ while accounting for the boundary condition $\delta \geq 1$, that is, by using a nonparametric kernel estimator with the reflection method. A description of how the procedure works follows.

4.3.5 Practical considerations for the bootstrap

4.3.5.1 Estimation of $f(\delta)$

The standard kernel density estimator of a density $f(\delta)$ evaluated at an arbitrary point δ is given by

$$\widehat{f}_h(\delta) = (nh)^{-1} \sum_{i=1}^n K\left(\frac{\delta - \widehat{\delta}_i}{h}\right), \tag{4.78}$$

where h is a smoothing parameter, or bandwidth, and $K(\cdot)$ is a kernel function satisfying $K(t) = K(-t)$, $\int_{-\infty}^{\infty} K(t)\, dt = 1$, and $\int_{-\infty}^{\infty} tK(t)\, dt = 0$. Any symmetric probability density function with mean zero satisfies these conditions. If a probability density function is used for $K(\cdot)$, then $\widehat{f}_h(\delta)$ can be viewed as the average of n different densities K centered on the observed points $\widehat{\delta}_i$, with h playing the role of a scaling parameter. The bandwidth h is used as a tuning parameter to control the dispersion of the n densities.

Two choices must be made in order to implement kernel density estimation: a kernel function and the bandwidth. The standard normal (Gaussian) probability density function is frequently used, although the Epanechnikov kernel given by

$$K(t) = \frac{3}{4}(1 - t)^2 \mathscr{I}(|t| \leq 1) \qquad (4.79)$$

is optimal in the sense of minimizing asymptotic mean integrated square error (AMISE).[5]

The choice of kernel function is of relatively minor importance; the choice of bandwidth has a far greater effect on the quality of the resulting estimator in terms of AMISE. A sensible choice of h is determined, in part, by the following considerations:

- As h is becomes small, fewer observations—only those closest to the point δ where the density is estimated—influence the estimate $\widehat{f_h}(\delta)$;
- As h is increased, increasing numbers of faraway observations play a role in determining $\widehat{f_h}(\delta)$;
- If $h \rightarrow 0$, the density will degenerate into the empirical density function, which is discrete with mass $1/n$ at each observed point $\widehat{\delta_i}$—this case results in the naive bootstrap, with no smoothing;
- If $h \rightarrow \infty$, the density will degenerate to a flat horizontal line.

The choice of bandwidth h used with kernel density estimators presents a fundamental trade-off between bias and variance. If h is chosen too small, the resulting density estimate will have high variance but low bias; if h is chosen too large, the density estimate will have low variance but high bias. Optimal choices of h are usually defined in terms of an approximation of AMISE.

The standard kernel density estimator in (4.78) does not take into account the boundary condition $\delta \geq 1$ and can be shown to be biased and inconsistent near the boundary. The reflection method, described by Silverman (1986) and others, provides a simple way to overcome this difficulty. To implement the method, reflect each point $\widehat{\delta_i} \geq 1$ around unity, yielding $2 - \widehat{\delta_i} \leq 1, i = 1, \ldots, n$. Next, use the standard kernel density estimator in (4.78) to estimate the density of the resulting $2n$ points; denote this estimate $\widehat{g_h}(t)$, where

$$\widehat{g_h}(t) = (2nh)^{-1} \sum_{i=1}^{n} \left[K\left(\frac{t - \widehat{\delta_i}}{h}\right) + K\left(\frac{t - (2 - \widehat{\delta_i})}{h}\right) \right]. \qquad (4.80)$$

Then define

$$\widehat{f_h}(t) = \begin{cases} 2\widehat{g_h}(t) & \forall t \geq 1, \\ 0 & \text{otherwise.} \end{cases} \qquad (4.81)$$

A method is given below for making random draws of the δ_i^*s from $\widehat{f_h}(\cdot)$; this does not require computation of the density estimate. Only a value for the selected bandwidth h is needed. The bandwidth should be chosen sensibly, and several data-driven approaches exist for selecting a bandwidth. Although one might try several values of the bandwidth parameter as a check on robustness, this potentially would be computationally burdensome. Experience has shown that the resulting inference is not very sensitive to the choice of h, at least within broad ranges around the values returned by the data-driven algorithms. These are discussed next.

4.3.5.2 Practical bandwidth selection

Statistical theory reveals that under mild regularity conditions on the true density f and on the kernel function K, and for a "good" choice of $h = O(n^{-1/5})$, $\widehat{f}_h(t) \to f(t)$ as $n \to \infty$ and $\widehat{f}_h(t)$ is asymptotically normally distributed. In theory, optimal values of h can be found by deriving the AMISE of $\widehat{f}_h(t)$, which depends upon the true density $f(t)$ and the kernel function $K(\cdot)$, and then minimizing this with respect to h. Silverman (1986) provides an optimal value for h in cases where $f(t)$ is a normal density function and $K(\cdot)$ is standard normal; this is referred to as the "normal reference rule," and the corresponding value of the optimal value of h is

$$h_{NR} = 1.06 \widehat{\sigma} n^{-1/5}, \qquad (4.82)$$

where $\widehat{\sigma}$ is the sample standard deviation of the observations used to estimate the density. A more robust choice (with respect to the assumption of normality for $f(t)$) is given by (again, assuming the kernel function is standard normal)

$$h_R = 1.06 \min\left(\widehat{\sigma}, \ \widehat{R}/1.34\right) n^{-1/5}, \qquad (4.83)$$

where $\widehat{R}$ is the interquartile range.

In efficiency applications, the density of the efficiency scores is likely to be far from normal, although the density of the reflected data is necessarily symmetric. However, this density may have moments very different from a normal distribution and may have more than one mode. Consequently, data-driven methods for choosing h are preferred to simple, ad hoc reference rules such as the ones discussed in the preceding paragraph. One approach is to minimize an estimate of either mean-integrated square error (MISE) or its asymptotic version (AMISE); these approaches are called unbiased and biased cross-validation, respectively (see Scott, 1992). The least-squares cross-validation method described by Silverman (1986) is a form of unbiased cross-validation; this method was adapted to the DEA context by Simar and Wilson (2002).

In the DEA framework, the set of estimates $\{\widehat{\delta}_i\}$ contain some number of spurious values equal to 1. This provides spurious mass (greater than $1/n$) at the boundary value 1 in the discrete density to be smoothed. These spurious values can be eliminated for purposes of selecting a bandwidth; they are merely an artifact of the nature of the DEA estimator of Ψ. Suppose $m < n$ values $\widehat{\delta}_i > 1$ remain after deleting observations where the DEA efficiency estimate equals 1. Then after reflecting these, there are $2m$ observations. MISE of the kernel density estimator is given by

$$MISE_{\widehat{g}}(h) = E\left[\int_{-\infty}^{\infty} [\widehat{g}_h(\delta) - g(\delta)]^2 \, d\delta \right].$$ (4.84)

This is estimated by the least-squares cross-validation function

$$CV(h) = \int_{-\infty}^{\infty} \widehat{g}_h^2(\delta) \, d\delta - \frac{1}{2m} \sum_{i=1}^{2m} \widehat{g}_{h,(i)}^2(\widetilde{\delta}_i),$$ (4.85)

where $\widehat{g}_{h,(i)}$ is the leave-one-out estimator of $g(\delta)$ based on the original observations (the m values $\widehat{\delta}_j \neq 1$), except $\widehat{\delta}_i$, with bandwidth h. Let h_{cv} be the minimizer of (4.85). This must be adjusted by computing

$$h_{CV} = h_{cv} 2^{1/5} \left(\frac{m}{n} \right)^{1/5} \left(\frac{s_n}{s_{2m}} \right),$$ (4.86)

where s_n is the sample standard deviation of the original n values $\widehat{\delta}_i$ and s_{2m} is the sample standard deviation of the $2m$ reflected observations, to adjust for (i) the fact that the reflected data contain twice the number of actual observations, (ii) the difference in the number of observations used, m, and the number of observations in the sample, n, and (iii) the difference in variances between the original data and the reflected data.

As an example, DEA output efficiency estimates $\widehat{\lambda}_1, \ldots, \widehat{\lambda}_{70}$ were computed for each of the 70 observations in the program follow-through (PFT) data used by Charnes et al. (1981) to analyze an experimental education program administered in U.S. schools. Here, the $\widehat{\lambda}_i$ plays the same role as the $\widehat{\delta}_i$ above. Using the $m = 43$ observations where $\widehat{\lambda}_i > 1$ to minimize the cross-validation function in (4.85) yields $h_{cv} = 0.04344$, or $h_{CV} = 0.03999$ after applying the correction in (4.86). Figure 4.6 displays a histogram estimator of the complete set of 70 efficiency estimates $\widehat{\lambda}_i$, and figure 4.7 shows the smooth kernel density estimate obtained using a Gaussian kernel with bandwidth $h = h_{CV}$ as well as an estimated, parametric, half-normal density (shown by the dashed line in figure 4.7). Necessarily, sharp features in the histogram estimate are smoothed away by the kernel estimate, which is the point of the exercise. The kernel density estimate in figure 4.7 places less mass near unity and more mass farther from unity than does the parametric estimate.[6]

4.3.5.3 Generating the δ^*s

Generating samples $\delta_1^*, \ldots, \delta_n^*$ from $\widehat{f}_h(\delta)$ is very simple and does not require that the kernel density estimate be computed. Rather, only the bandwidth and kernel function are needed. Let

$$\mathcal{D}_{2n} = \{\widehat{\delta}_1, \ldots, \widehat{\delta}_n, (2 - \widehat{\delta}_1), \ldots, (2 - \widehat{\delta}_n)\}.$$ (4.87)

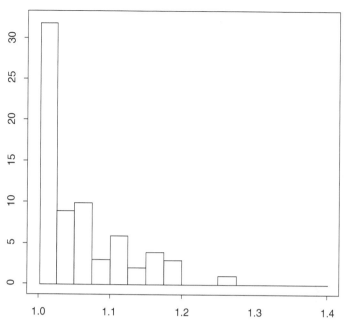

Figure 4.6. Histogram Estimate for 70 Output Efficiency Scores (data from Charnes et al., 1981)

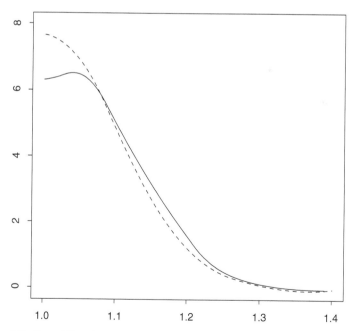

Figure 4.7. Kernel Density Estimate (solid curve) and Half-Normal Density Estimate (dashed curve) for 70 Output Efficiency Scores (data from Charnes et al., 1981)

Then let $\beta_1^*,\ldots,\beta_n^*$ be a naive bootstrap sample from $\mathcal{D}_{2n}$, obtained by drawing n times, independently, uniformly, and with replacement from the $2n$ elements of $\mathcal{D}_{2n}$. Next, perturb these draws by setting $\beta_i^{**} = \beta_i^* + h_{CV}\varepsilon_i^*$ for each $i = 1,\ldots,n$, where ε_i^* represents independent draws from the probability density function used as the kernel function $K(\cdot)$.

It is straightforward to show that the β_i^{**} are a random sample of size n from $\widehat{g}_h(\delta)$ given in (4.80) (e.g., Silverman, 1986; Efron and Tibshirani, 1993). As is typical with kernel estimation techniques, however, with finite samples these draws will not have the same mean and variance as the elements of $\mathcal{D}_{2n}$. This can be corrected by computing

$$\beta_i^{***} = \overline{\beta^*} + \frac{\beta_i^{**} - \overline{\beta^*}}{(1 + h_{CV}^2\sigma_K^2\sigma_\beta^{-2})^{1/2}},\qquad(4.88)$$

where $\overline{\beta^*} = n^{-1}\sum_{i=1}^n \beta_i^*$ is the sample mean of the β_i^*, $\sigma_\beta^2 = n^{-1}\sum_{i=1}^n(\beta_i^* - \overline{\beta^*})^2$ is the sample variance of the β_i^*, and σ_K^2 is the variance of the probability density function used for the kernel function. Finally, the draws among the β_i^{***} that are less than unity must be reflected as in (4.81) by computing

$$\delta_i^* = \begin{cases} 2 - \beta_i^{***} & \forall \beta_i^{***} < 1, \\ \beta_i^{***} & \text{otherwise.} \end{cases}\qquad(4.89)$$

4.3.5.4 The homogeneous bootstrap algorithm

The homogeneous bootstrap algorithm for obtaining a set of bootstrap estimates $\{\widehat{\delta}_b^*(x,y) \mid b = 1,\ldots,B\}$ for a given fixed point (x,y) is summarized by the following steps:

1. From the original data set $\mathcal{X}_n$, compute $\widehat{\delta}_i = \widehat{\delta}(x_i,y_i)\ \forall\ i = 1,\ldots,n$.
2. Select a value for h using one of the methods described above.
3. Generate $\beta_1^*,\ldots,\beta_n^*$ by drawing with replacement from the set $\mathcal{D}_{2n}$ defined in (4.87).
4. Draw $\varepsilon_i^*, i = 1,\ldots,n$ independently from the kernel function $K(\cdot)$ and compute $\beta_i^{**} = \beta_i^* + h_{CV}\varepsilon_i^*$ for each $i = 1,\ldots,n$.
5. For each $i = 1,\ldots,n$, compute β_i^{***} as in (4.88) and then compute δ_i^* as in (4.89).
6. Define the bootstrap sample $\mathcal{X}_n^* = \{(x_i^*,y_i) \mid i = 1,\ldots,n\}$, where $x_i^* = \delta_i^*\widehat{x}^\partial(y_i) = \delta_i^*\widehat{\delta}_i^{-1}x_i$.
7. Compute the DEA efficiency estimate $\widehat{\delta}^*(x,y)$ for the fixed point (x,y), using the reference set $\mathcal{X}_n^*$.
8. Repeat steps 3–7 B times to obtain a set of bootstrap estimates $\{\widehat{\delta}_b^*(x,y) \mid b = 1,\ldots,B\}$.

The computations in the above algorithm can be performed for any point (x, y) of interest. For example, in many applications, when n is not too large, it is interesting to compute bias and/or confidence intervals for each of the $\delta_i = \delta(x_i, y_i)$. In this case, in step 7 one would compute the DEA efficiency estimates $\widehat{\delta}^*(x_i, y_i)$ for each point using the reference set $\mathcal{X}_n^*$. Then there will be, in step 8, n sets of bootstrap estimates $\{\widehat{\delta}_b^*(x_i, y_i) \mid b = 1, \ldots, B\}$, for each $i = 1, \ldots, n$. In this case, $(1 + n * B)$ linear programs must be solved, where B should be greater than, say, 2,000.

4.3.5.5 Examples

Mouchart and Simar (2002) examined technical efficiency of European air traffic controllers. Data were available for 37 units operating in the year 2000 and included four output variables (total flight hours controlled, number of air movements controlled, number of sectors controlled, and sum of sector hours worked) and two input variables (the number of air controllers, measured in full-time equivalents (FTEs), and the total number of hours worked by air controllers). Due to the small number of observations and the high degree of correlation among both the inputs and the outputs, inputs were aggregated into a single measure representing, in a rough sense, the labor force of each unit. Outputs were also aggregated into a single measure representing the level of the activity (see Mouchart and Simar, 2002, for details). The analysis that was performed using data for one input and one output ($N = M = 1$) provides a convenient example for illustrating the ideas discussed above.

Figure 4.8 shows the resulting two-dimensional, aggregated data on air traffic controllers, along with the corresponding DEA estimates of the frontier assuming either constant (CRS) or variable (VRS) returns to scale. Mouchart and Simar (2002) used an input orientation, since the output is not under the control of the air controllers. Four units—7, 9, 26, and 33—lie on the VRS estimate of the frontier, and the CRS model seems to be rejected by the data (a formal test, as suggested in section 4.3.7, rejects the null CRS hypothesis at the 0.05 level).

Bootstrap samples were generated as described above for the "homogeneous" bootstrap, using a bandwidth selected by minimizing the cross-validation function (4.85), yielding $h_{cv} = 0.4735$, or $h_{CV} = 0.3369$ after making the correction for sample size in (4.86). A histogram showing the original values of the Shepard (1970) input-distance function estimates is shown in figure 4.9; the kernel density estimate (4.81), obtained using bandwidth $h_{CV} = 0.3369$, is plotted in figure 4.10, along with a parametric, half-normal density (estimated by the maximum likelihood method) shown by the dashed curve. As in figure 4.7, the parametric estimate in figure 4.10 places more mass near unity, and less mass away from unity, than does the kernel density estimator.

Table 4.2 displays results of the homogeneous bootstrap described above, giving the original efficiency estimates as well as the bias-corrected estimates.

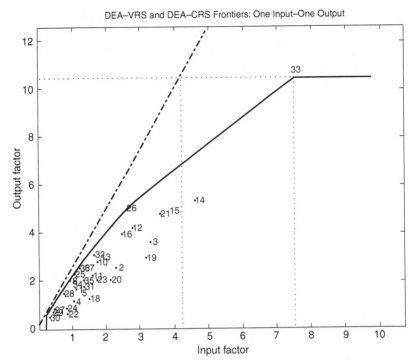

Figure 4.8. DEA Estimators VRS (solid) and CRS (dash-dot) for Air Controllers Data

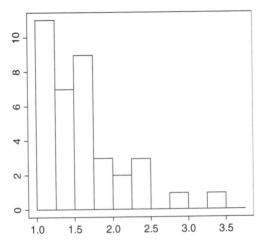

Figure 4.9. Histogram Estimate for 37 (Inverse) Input Efficiency Scores, Air Controller Data

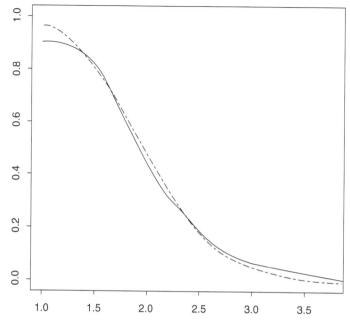

Figure 4.10. Kernel Density Estimate (solid curve) and Parametric, Half-Normal Density Estimate (dashed curve) for 37 (inverse) Input Efficiency Scores, Air-Controller Data

Since the bias is large relative to the variance in every case, the bias-corrected estimates are preferred to the original estimates. Table 4.2 also shows bootstrap estimates of 95% confidence intervals. Note that the widest interval corresponds to observation 33, which is the most remote observation in figure 4.8. Figure 4.8 shows that there are simply no other observations near 33 that would help estimate the frontier in this region.

The original efficiency estimates lie outside the estimated confidence intervals in the last two columns of table 4.2 in every instance. This is due to the bias in the original estimates, and the fact that the confidence interval estimates correct for this bias. Note also that the estimated confidence interval for observation 33 does not include the corresponding bias-corrected efficiency estimates. This is because the bias corrections are made in terms of the original efficiency estimates, while reciprocals are used to construct the confidence interval estimates. This anomaly can be avoided by applying the bias correction to the $\widehat{\delta}_i$ and then taking the inverse of this bias-corrected measure, instead of applying the bias correction directly to the input-oriented Farrell efficiency scores. On the other hand, when bias corrections are made as outlined above, results such as that for observation 33 may be indicative of outliers.

Table 4.2
Bootstrap Results: Input Efficiency Scores with VRS Model ($B = 2000$)

Units	Efficiency Scores (VRS)	Bias Corrected	Bias	Standard Error	Lower Bound	Upper Bound
1	0.6458	0.6105	0.0353	0.0247	0.5799	0.6397
2	0.4862	0.4467	0.0395	0.0235	0.4254	0.4807
3	0.5333	0.4822	0.0511	0.0361	0.4495	0.5250
4	0.4694	0.4378	0.0317	0.0208	0.4155	0.4628
5	0.5340	0.5046	0.0294	0.0205	0.4796	0.5287
6	0.7174	0.6774	0.0400	0.0279	0.6440	0.7104
7	1.0000	0.9171	0.0829	0.0483	0.8739	0.9871
8	0.9367	0.8823	0.0544	0.0386	0.8376	0.9297
9	1.0000	0.7447	0.2553	0.1463	0.7423	0.9578
10	0.7249	0.6691	0.0558	0.0342	0.6351	0.7136
11	0.6137	0.5725	0.0412	0.0265	0.5437	0.6075
12	0.7594	0.6663	0.0931	0.0676	0.6175	0.7463
13	0.7658	0.7065	0.0593	0.0385	0.6679	0.7555
14	0.6286	0.4861	0.1425	0.0925	0.4699	0.6080
15	0.6633	0.5456	0.1177	0.0813	0.5147	0.6481
16	0.7937	0.7067	0.0869	0.0632	0.6561	0.7806
17	0.6573	0.5246	0.1326	0.1003	0.4941	0.6489
18	0.3554	0.3332	0.0221	0.0148	0.3171	0.3513
19	0.4344	0.4009	0.0334	0.0216	0.3789	0.4285
20	0.4213	0.3957	0.0256	0.0176	0.3757	0.4175
21	0.6838	0.5735	0.1103	0.0789	0.5360	0.6713
22	0.3029	0.2526	0.0504	0.0339	0.2372	0.2958
23	0.5219	0.4908	0.0311	0.0217	0.4659	0.5176
24	0.4355	0.3944	0.0410	0.0287	0.3685	0.4289
25	0.9376	0.8716	0.0660	0.0413	0.8292	0.9267
26	1.0000	0.8000	0.2000	0.1298	0.7646	0.9649
27	0.6592	0.5857	0.0735	0.0523	0.5443	0.6487
28	0.8472	0.8001	0.0470	0.0328	0.7606	0.8390
29	0.6439	0.5504	0.0935	0.0659	0.5133	0.6327
30	0.6832	0.5330	0.1503	0.1024	0.5115	0.6697
31	0.5750	0.5431	0.0319	0.0225	0.5157	0.5699
32	0.8725	0.8034	0.0692	0.0450	0.7604	0.8599
33	1.0000	0.4079	0.5921	0.4855	0.6228	0.9511
34	0.8197	0.7735	0.0462	0.0329	0.7342	0.8133
35	0.6632	0.6244	0.0388	0.0274	0.5926	0.6580
36	0.9253	0.8496	0.0758	0.0448	0.8093	0.9151
37	0.8309	0.7642	0.0667	0.0399	0.7278	0.8212

As a second example, consider again the program follow-through (PFT) data used by Charnes et al. (1981) in an analysis of an experimental education program administered in U.S. schools. Charnes et al. list data for 49 schools that implemented PFT, and 21 schools that did not, for a total of 70 observations.

Each observation consists of five input variables describing characteristics of the school:

  (i) Education level of students' mothers (percentage of high school graduates among the mothers)
  (ii) Highest occupation of a family member (according a prearranged rating scale)
  (iii) Parental visit to school index (number of visits to the school)
  (iv) Parent counseling index (time spent with child on school-related topics)
  (v) Number of teachers in the school

In addition, the observations include three output variables obtained from results of standardized tests:

  (i) Total reading score (Metropolitan Achievement Test [MAT])
  (ii) Total mathematics score (MAT),
  (iii) Coopersmith Self-Esteem Inventory (measure of self-esteem)

PFT was designed to improve students' performance in each of the areas measured by the output variables. Consequently, the (Farrell) output-oriented efficiency measures are used. Least-squares cross-validation using the original efficiency estimates yielded a bandwidth (after adjusting for sample size) $h_{CV} = 0.03999$ when (4.85) was minimized. Estimation results are shown in table 4.3. Observations 1–49 correspond to the PFT schools, whereas observations 50–70 correspond to the remaining 21 non-PFT schools. The bootstrap estimates were produced using $B = 2,000$ bootstrap replications.

   The results in table 4.3 indicate substantial bias. Since the bias estimates are large relative to the standard error estimates, the bias-corrected efficiency estimates are preferred to the original estimates. With the bias correction, none of the resulting efficiency estimates equals one. Despite the fact that the sample size is rather small in this high-dimensional problem, the confidence intervals are of moderate length. The length is, as expected, often larger for the units that were on the original DEA frontier (indicated by original efficiency estimates equal to one).

   Comparing the two groups of schools, the means of efficiency scores across the two groups are not very different: The 49 PFT schools have mean DEA estimated efficiency equal to 1.0589, while the non-PFT schools have mean DEA estimated efficiency equal to 1.0384. In terms of the bias-corrected efficiency estimates, the PFT and non-PFT schools have mean efficiency estimates 1.0950 and 1.0750, respectively. Hence, no substantial differences are observed between the two groups of schools in terms of estimated technical efficiency, although the question of whether the apparent small differences are statistically significant remains. (A formal test of this question is discussed in section 4.3.7.)

Table 4.3
Efficiencies for Charnes et al. (1981) Data ($B = 2000$)

Units	Efficiency Scores (VRS)	Bias Corrected	$\widehat{\text{bias}}$ Bound	$\hat{\sigma}$	Lower Bound	Upper Bound
1	1.0323	1.0661	−0.0338	0.0232	1.0361	1.1109
2	1.1094	1.1390	−0.0296	0.0158	1.1138	1.1657
3	1.0685	1.0992	−0.0307	0.0189	1.0732	1.1332
4	1.1074	1.1264	−0.0190	0.0099	1.1114	1.1434
5	1.0000	1.0552	−0.0552	0.0456	1.0039	1.1479
6	1.1051	1.1362	−0.0311	0.0162	1.1096	1.1625
7	1.1192	1.1399	−0.0207	0.0097	1.1234	1.1551
8	1.1042	1.1379	−0.0337	0.0244	1.1081	1.1872
9	1.1608	1.1857	−0.0249	0.0129	1.1648	1.2071
10	1.0545	1.0880	−0.0335	0.0223	1.0588	1.1286
11	1.0000	1.0464	−0.0464	0.0301	1.0039	1.0981
12	1.0000	1.0456	−0.0456	0.0285	1.0036	1.0936
13	1.1561	1.1745	−0.0184	0.0085	1.1612	1.1889
14	1.0155	1.0459	−0.0304	0.0183	1.0197	1.0791
15	1.0000	1.0541	−0.0541	0.0452	1.0036	1.1465
16	1.0521	1.0809	−0.0288	0.0205	1.0562	1.1208
17	1.0000	1.0565	−0.0565	0.0465	1.0033	1.1467
18	1.0000	1.0421	−0.0421	0.0253	1.0035	1.0832
19	1.0492	1.0771	−0.0279	0.0165	1.0540	1.1075
20	1.0000	1.0535	−0.0535	0.0420	1.0043	1.1388
21	1.0000	1.0496	−0.0496	0.0379	1.0032	1.1169
22	1.0000	1.0315	−0.0315	0.0159	1.0037	1.0552
23	1.0253	1.0468	−0.0215	0.0129	1.0291	1.0709
24	1.0000	1.0537	−0.0537	0.0403	1.0041	1.1285
25	1.0215	1.0381	−0.0167	0.0070	1.0255	1.0496
26	1.0602	1.0803	−0.0201	0.0100	1.0642	1.0972
27	1.0000	1.0485	−0.0485	0.0312	1.0040	1.0995
28	1.0125	1.0390	−0.0265	0.0151	1.0163	1.0650
29	1.1797	1.2128	−0.0331	0.0207	1.1840	1.2527
30	1.1174	1.1418	−0.0244	0.0122	1.1212	1.1626
31	1.1929	1.2157	−0.0228	0.0106	1.1971	1.2330
32	1.0000	1.0558	−0.0558	0.0453	1.0042	1.1497
33	1.0493	1.0732	−0.0239	0.0137	1.0536	1.0979
34	1.1609	1.1845	−0.0236	0.0134	1.1650	1.2094
35	1.0000	1.0411	−0.0411	0.0258	1.0043	1.0875
36	1.2686	1.2984	−0.0299	0.0146	1.2744	1.3227
37	1.1919	1.2229	−0.0310	0.0160	1.1963	1.2482
38	1.0000	1.0540	−0.0540	0.0448	1.0039	1.1446
39	1.0671	1.1010	−0.0339	0.0220	1.0709	1.1427
40	1.0530	1.0788	−0.0259	0.0160	1.0570	1.1080
41	1.0489	1.0627	−0.0138	0.0065	1.0526	1.0742
42	1.0553	1.0856	−0.0303	0.0190	1.0589	1.1214

(Continued)

Units	Efficiency Scores (VRS)	Bias Corrected	$\widehat{\text{bias}}$ Bound	$\hat{\sigma}$	Lower Bound	Upper Bound
43	1.1563	1.1873	−0.0310	0.0196	1.1610	1.2240
44	1.0000	1.0547	−0.0547	0.0461	1.0033	1.1470
45	1.0000	1.0404	−0.0404	0.0280	1.0043	1.0945
46	1.0937	1.1152	−0.0214	0.0118	1.0976	1.1365
47	1.0000	1.0536	−0.0536	0.0400	1.0041	1.1282
48	1.0000	1.0556	−0.0556	0.0448	1.0042	1.1447
49	1.0000	1.0483	−0.0483	0.0331	1.0038	1.1020
50	1.0436	1.0725	−0.0288	0.0217	1.0461	1.1140
51	1.0872	1.1105	−0.0233	0.0126	1.0915	1.1336
52	1.0000	1.0539	−0.0539	0.0430	1.0037	1.1418
53	1.1465	1.1715	−0.0250	0.0121	1.1509	1.1916
54	1.0000	1.0551	−0.0551	0.0437	1.0043	1.1440
55	1.0007	1.0320	−0.0313	0.0195	1.0049	1.0679
56	1.0000	1.0511	−0.0511	0.0395	1.0036	1.1241
57	1.0776	1.1082	−0.0306	0.0224	1.0808	1.1527
58	1.0000	1.0570	−0.0570	0.0473	1.0038	1.1535
59	1.0000	1.0540	−0.0540	0.0445	1.0042	1.1447
60	1.0196	1.0393	−0.0197	0.0092	1.0231	1.0540
61	1.1344	1.1655	−0.0310	0.0225	1.1389	1.2140
62	1.0000	1.0557	−0.0557	0.0452	1.0041	1.1473
63	1.0383	1.0624	−0.0241	0.0125	1.0430	1.0854
64	1.0738	1.0925	−0.0188	0.0091	1.0781	1.1079
65	1.0270	1.0522	−0.0252	0.0132	1.0310	1.0756
66	1.0675	1.0824	−0.0150	0.0068	1.0717	1.0936
67	1.0554	1.0753	−0.0199	0.0098	1.0586	1.0916
68	1.0000	1.0543	−0.0543	0.0424	1.0041	1.1357
69	1.0000	1.0586	−0.0586	0.0483	1.0038	1.1545
70	1.0366	1.0557	−0.0191	0.0092	1.0401	1.0712

Both the example with the air controller data and the PFT data suggest two points. First, the estimated confidence intervals in tables 4.2 and 4.3 are typically less wide than those estimated in parametric, stochastic frontier models in chapter 2. This is because there is no noise in the models that have been estimated here, and lack of noise translates into more certainty about underlying efficiencies.

The second point is that the confidence interval estimates provide a partial ordering of observations in the two data sets in terms of efficiency. The ordering is partial to the extent that estimated confidence intervals overlap. Andersen and Petersen (1993) suggested a leave-one-out (LOO) version of the DEA estimator that allows one to rank ostensibly efficient observations (i.e., those with a conventional DEA efficiency estimate equal to one); this idea has been used in a number of applied papers. As remarked in section 4.6.1, it is not clear what the LOO estimator estimates; in any case, the method of Andersen and Petersen does not rely on inference. The confidence interval estimates in tables 4.2 and 4.3 reveal that, at least for the air controller data and the PFT data, there is a great deal of overlap among confidence intervals estimated for observations with an initial efficiency estimate equal to one.

4.3.6 Bootstrapping FDH efficiency scores

Since the asymptotic distribution of the FDH estimator is available in a closed form, even in a multivariate setup, the bootstrap might be seen as less important for making inferences with FDH estimators than with DEA estimators. However, as noted in section 4.2.5, the limiting distribution depends on an unknown parameter $\mu_{x,y}$ which can be consistently estimated (see Park et al., 2000), but the estimation introduces additional noise that may decrease the precision of inference in finite samples. Nonparametric estimation of this parameter depends also on a smoothing parameter that may be difficult to choose.

It is clear that a naive bootstrap will also be inconsistent here as in the case of DEA estimators, for largely the same reasons. In addition, FDH estimators present a further difficulty for bootstrap methods. The number of FDH efficiency scores equal to one will necessarily be larger than in the case of DEA estimators, increasing the spurious mass at one in the empirical distribution of $\widehat{\theta}_{\mathrm{FDH}}(x_i, y_i)$, $i = 1, \ldots, n$ relative to the DEA case. Jeong and Simar (2006) show that a bootstrap based on subsampling (with or without replacement) of size $m = [n^\kappa]$, where $0 < \kappa < 1$ provides a consistent approximation of the sampling distribution of $\widehat{\theta}_{\mathrm{FDH}}(x, y) - \theta(x, y)$ (or of $\widehat{\theta}_{\mathrm{FDH}}(x, y)/\theta(x, y)$ if the ratio is preferred).

The procedure is exactly the same as the one described in section 4.3.4 for subsampling of DEA scores, except that here, for each subsample, the FDH estimator is used in place of the DEA estimator. As before, let $\mathcal{X}^*_{n_{m,b}}$ denote a random subsample of size $m < n$ drawn from $\mathcal{X}_n$, $b = 1, \ldots, B$ and let $\widehat{\theta}^*_{\mathrm{FDH},m,b}(x, y)$ denote the FDH efficiency score of the fixed point (x, y) computed with this reference sample $\mathcal{X}^*_{n_{m,b}}$. The set of bootstrap estimates $\widehat{\theta}^*_{\mathrm{FDH},m,b}(x, y)$, $b = 1, \ldots, B$ permits construction of bias-corrected FDH scores and estimation of confidence intervals for θ, analogous to the above discussion for the DEA case.

One might doubt the usefulness of the bootstrap in small samples. Monte Carlo experiments described in Jeong and Simar (2006) indicate that the subsampling method works somewhat well for bias correction. For the experiments described there, where $n = 100$ and $M = N = 2$, with an optimal choice of $\kappa = 0.65$ (with respect to the mean square error criterion), bias is reduced by a factor of 15 along with a reduction of mean square error by a factor of 2.4. Other choices of κ between 0.5 and 1.00 also give substantial improvements for the bias and for the mean square error. Similar results were observed with larger sample sizes and for larger dimensionality (i.e., greater numbers of inputs and outputs). These small Monte Carlo experiments indicate that the results are rather robust with respect to the choice of κ, and hence the precise choice of κ does not appear to crucial, although optimal values perform better than other values.

By contrast, for confidence intervals, the coverages obtained in the Monte Carlo experiments of Jeong and Simar (2006) perform poorly in terms of coverages, except when the sample size is very large (much larger than, e.g., 1,000 observations). This is primarily due to the nature of the FDH estimator rather than that of subsampling. The value of the FDH estimate is completely determined by only one point among the FDH-efficient units in the data. So, in this case, the approximate discrete distribution obtained through subsampling tends to give too much probability mass on this one point. Therefore, the approximation of the sampling distribution will have very poor accuracy, particularly in the tail, when the sample size is too small. For the bias correction, this poor accuracy is less crucial due to the averaging used in estimating the bias of the FDH estimator. This argues in favor of improving the performances of the FDH estimators by using some smoothing; such an approach is described in section 4.4.2.

4.3.7 Extensions of the bootstrap ideas

The bootstrap ideas developed above can be applied and extended to several other interesting and important research questions. Two extensions are briefly discussed here: (i) the problem of testing hypotheses, which might be useful for choosing among various model specifications discussed in chapter 2, and (ii) the problem of making inference on Malmquist indices and their components in various decompositions that are discussed in chapter 5.

4.3.7.1 Hypothesis testing

In addition to bias estimation and correction, and estimation of confidence intervals, the bootstrap can also be very useful for testing various hypotheses about efficiency or features of the DGP.

In hypothesis testing, the bootstrap can be used either to estimate the p-value of a null hypothesis or to build a critical region. Often, the implementation of the bootstrap makes it easy to evaluate p-values; a null hypothesis H_0 is rejected at the desired level when the p-value is too small, that is, lower than the desired level.

Two issues must be considered in any testing problem where the bootstrap is used. First, as for any testing procedure, an appropriate statistic that is able to discriminate between the null and the alternative hypotheses must be chosen. Any such statistic will be a function of the data; denote it by $\tau(\mathcal{X}_n)$. Recall that the data result from a random process (i.e., the DGP); hence, $\tau(\mathcal{X}_n)$ is a random variable. In many cases, $\tau(\mathcal{X}_n)$ will be bounded on the left, often at zero; the idea is to determine whether the realized value $\tau(\mathcal{X}_n)$ (i.e., the value computed from the sample observations) is large enough to cast sufficient doubt on the null hypothesis that it can be rejected. In such cases, the p-value is defined by

$$p\text{-value} = \text{prob}(\tau(\mathcal{X}_n) \geq \tau_{\text{obs}} \mid H_0), \tag{4.90}$$

where τ_{obs} is the realized value of the test statistic obtained from the observed sample. This probability can be estimated by bootstrap methods.

Let $\mathcal{X}_{n_b}{}^*$ denote a random sample obtained by an appropriate bootstrap algorithm using the original data $\mathcal{X}_n$. Then, the sampling distribution of the random variable $\tau(\mathcal{X}_n)$ can be approximated by the empirical Monte Carlo distribution of $\tau(\mathcal{X}_{n_b}^*)$, $b = 1, \ldots, B$. In particular, the p-value is estimated by

$$\widehat{p}\text{-value} = \text{prob}(\tau(\mathcal{X}_n{}^*) \geq \tau_{\text{obs}} \mid \mathcal{X}_n, H_0). \tag{4.91}$$

In practice, the estimated p-value is computed using the empirical version of (4.91), namely,

$$\widehat{p}\text{-value} = \frac{\{\#\tau(\mathcal{X}_{n_b}^*) \geq \tau_{\text{obs}} \mid b = 1, \ldots, B\}}{B}. \tag{4.92}$$

It is important to note that the probabilities in (4.91)–(4.92) are conditional on H_0. This means that the random samples $\mathcal{X}_{n_b}^*$ must be generated appropriately under the conditions specified by the null hypothesis.

As an example, recall that in the case of the Charnes et al. (1981) data on PFT and non-PFT schools, the mean of DEA (output) efficiency estimates for the $n_1 = 49$ PFT schools was 1.0589, while the mean of DEA (output) efficiency estimates for the $n_2 = 21$ non-PFT schools was 1.0384. Suppose that the two groups have access to the same technology, and so they operate within the same attainable set Ψ. Further suppose that under the null hypothesis the two groups have the same DGP, and hence the mean efficiencies for the two groups are equal. Denote these means by $E(\lambda_1)$ and $E(\lambda_2)$, and consider a test of the null hypothesis

$$H_0 \; : \; E(\lambda_1) = E(\lambda_2) \tag{4.93}$$

against the alternative hypothesis

$$H_1 \; : \; E(\lambda_1) > E(\lambda_2). \tag{4.94}$$

Let $\mathcal{X}_{n_1}$ denote the sample of n_1 units from group 1 (PFT schools), and let $\mathcal{X}_{n_2}$ denote the sample of n_2 units from group 2 (non-PFT schools). The full sample of size $n = n_1 + n_2$ is denoted by $\mathcal{X}_n = \mathcal{X}_{n_1} \cup \mathcal{X}_{n_2}$. A reasonable test statistic would be

$$\tau(\mathcal{X}_n) = \frac{n_1^{-1}\sum_{\{i|(x_i,y_i)\in\mathcal{X}_{n1}\}}\widehat{\lambda}(x_i,y_i)}{n_2^{-1}\sum_{\{i|(x_i,y_i)\in\mathcal{X}_{n2}\}}\widehat{\lambda}(x_i,y_i)}, \qquad (4.95)$$

where $\widehat{\lambda}(x_i,y_i)$ is the output-oriented DEA efficiency estimator of the unit (x_i,y_i) computed using the full sample $\mathcal{X}_n$ as the reference set (since the two groups face the same attainable set, $\mathbf{\Psi}$). When the null is true, then by construction, $\tau(\mathcal{X}_n)$ will be "close" to 1. On the other hand, when the alternative hypothesis is true, $\tau(\mathcal{X}_n)$ will be "far" from (larger than) one. Hence, the p-value for this test has the form given in (4.90), and the null hypothesis should be rejected if the realized, observed value of $\tau(\mathcal{X}_n)$, τ_{obs}, is too large. The bootstrap can be used to determine how large τ_{obs} must be to be "too large."

To implement the bootstrap, the pseudosamples $\mathcal{X}_{n_b}^*$ must be generated as if the null hypothesis is true; in the output orientation, the following steps can performed:

1. From the original data set $\mathcal{X}_n$, compute $\widehat{\lambda}_i = \widehat{\lambda}(x_i,y_i)\ \forall\ i=1,\dots,n$.
2. Select a value for h using one of the methods described above.
3. Generate $\beta_1^*,\dots,\beta_n^*$ by drawing with replacement from the set

$$\{\widehat{\lambda}_1,\dots,\widehat{\lambda}_n, (2-\widehat{\lambda}_1), \dots, (2-\widehat{\lambda}_n)\}. \qquad (4.96)$$

4. Draw $\varepsilon_i^*, i=1,\dots,n$ independently from the kernel function $K(\cdot)$ and compute $\beta_i^{**} = \beta_i^* + h\varepsilon_i^*$ for each $i=1,\dots,n$.
5. For each $i=1,\dots,n$, compute β_i^{***} as in (4.88) and then compute λ_i^* as in (4.89).
6. Define the bootstrap sample $\mathcal{X}_n^* = \{(x_i^*,y_i) \mid i=1,\dots,n\}$, where $x_i^* = \lambda_i^*\widehat{x}^\partial(y_i) = \lambda_i^*\widehat{\lambda}_i^{-1}x_i$.
7. Compute the DEA efficiency estimates $\widehat{\lambda}^*(x_i,y_i)$ for each of the original sample observations (x_i,y_i), using the reference set $\mathcal{X}_n^*$, to obtain a set of bootstrap estimates $\{\widehat{\lambda}^*(x_i,y_i) \mid i=1,\dots,n\}$.
8. Use the set of bootstrap values from step 7 to compute

$$\widehat{\tau}_b^* = \frac{n_1^{-1}\sum_{\{i|(x_i,y_i)\in\mathcal{X}_{n1}\}}\widehat{\lambda}^*(x_i,y_i)}{n_2^{-1}\sum_{\{i|(x_i,y_i)\in\mathcal{X}_{n2}\}}\widehat{\lambda}^*(x_i,y_i)}.$$

9. Repeat steps 3–8 B times to obtain a set of bootstrap estimates $\{\widehat{\tau}_b^* \mid b=1,\dots,B\}$.

The p-value is approximated by

$$\widehat{p} = \frac{\#\{\widehat{\tau}_b^*) > \tau_{\text{obs}}\}}{B} = \frac{\sum_{b=1}^B \mathscr{I}(\tau_b^* > T_{\text{obs}})}{B}, \qquad (4.97)$$

where $\mathscr{I}(\cdot)$ is the indicator function.

Implementing the above algorithm using the Charnes et al. (1981) data with $B = 2,000$ replications yielded an estimated p-value $\hat{p} = 0.5220$. Consequently, the null hypothesis cannot be reasonably rejected; the mean efficiencies of PFT and non-PFT schools are not significantly different at any meaningful level.

Of course, many other test statistics (mean or median of the ratios, Kolmogoroff-Smirnoff distance, etc., ...) could be used to test the equality of means. One should also realize that testing whether means are equivalent is different from testing whether the distributions of efficiency among two groups are the same; many different distributions can be found that have the same means.

The bootstrap procedure can be adapted to many other testing problems. Simar and Zelenyuk (2006b) adapt the procedure to consider aggregation issues; this involves computation of weighted averages in each group in an appropriate way. Simar and Zelenyuk (2006a) propose a test of the equality of the densities of the efficiency of each group. For this test, a statistic based on mean squared ($\mathcal{L}_2$) distance between nonparametric estimators of densities of the DEA efficiency scores for the two groups is used. Monte Carlo experiments have shown that a simple bootstrap test provides a testing procedure with appropriate nominal size and with very good power properties.

Simar and Wilson (2002) adapt the testing procedure described above to the problem of testing returns to scale. They investigate the properties of the test through intensive Monte Carlo experiments. Their Monte Carlo experiments indicate that the bootstrap test procedure has reasonable size properties and good power properties. It has also been shown in Monte Carlo experiments (e.g., Kittelsen, 1997; Simar and Wilson, 2002) that other approaches proposed in the literature not based on the bootstrap idea, but rather on dubious distributional assumptions or uncertain approximations (e.g., Banker, 1996), have serious drawbacks in terms of the accuracy of the size of the test, as well as in term of the power.

Simar and Wilson (2001) provide a bootstrap test procedure for testing restrictions in frontier models. Their methods can be used to test the relevance of particular inputs or outputs (analogous to t-tests or F-tests in linear regression) and to test additivity of inputs or of outputs, which is important for possible dimension reduction through aggregation.

4.3.7.2 Inference on Malmquist indices

When panel data are available, Malmquist indices are sometimes estimated to examine changes in productivity over time. Various decompositions of Malmquist indices have been proposed that allow productivity change to be divided among changes in efficiency, technology, and so on. All of these measures involve ratios of distance functions. For each measure, a value of 1 indicates no change between the two periods considered, while values greater than or less than 1 indicate some change (either improvement or a worsening, depending on the particular definition that is used). Thus, it is interesting to test the null hypothesis of no change versus a two-sided alternative hypothesis of change, or perhaps a one-sided alternative hypothesis of change in a particular direction (i.e., either worsening or improvement, but not both).

Bootstrap procedures for tests of these types, using panel data, are given in Simar and Wilson (1999c). The idea there is similar to the ideas discussed above, with the added complication that observations on the same unit may be correlated across time periods. This affects how bootstrap pseudodata must be generated; failure to account for autocorrelations in the data will result in a bootstrap that does not replicate the DGP, yielding uncertain and perhaps inconsistent results. Simar and Wilson (1999c) deal with this problem by extending the smooth bootstrap discussed above by estimating, and drawing from, the joint density of inputs and outputs over the two time periods under consideration. This allows estimation of confidence intervals for Malmquist indices and the various component indices obtained from the decompositions that have been proposed in the literature.

4.4 Improving the FDH estimator

This section briefly discusses some recent improvements of the FDH estimator. The first estimator is based on the idea of correcting for bias while avoiding the bootstrap. The second approach defines a new nonparametric envelopment estimator for possibly nonconvex production sets; this estimator is a smooth (linearized) version of the FDH estimator.

4.4.1 Bias-corrected FDH

By construction, the FDH estimator is highly biased. Badin and Simar (2004) proposed a simple way to derive a bias-corrected version of the FDH estimator. Recall from the probabilistic formulation of the production process developed in section 4.2.4 that, under the free disposability assumption, the Debreu-Farrell input efficiency scores at (x, y) can be defined as $\theta(x, y) = \inf\{\theta \mid F_{X|Y}(\theta x|y) > 0\}$, where $F_{X|Y}(x|y) = \text{prob}(X \leq x \mid Y \geq y)$. The FDH estimator is the empirical analog of this, obtained by replacing $F_{X|Y}$ with its nonparametric estimator $F_{X|Y,n}$, yielding $\widehat{\theta}_{\text{FDH}}(x, y) = \inf\{\theta \mid \widehat{F}_{X|Y,n}(\theta x|y) > 0\}$.

Since $\widehat{\theta}_{\text{FDH}}(x, y)$ is characterized only by the conditional $\widehat{F}_{X|Y,n}$, the population mean of $\widehat{\theta}_{\text{FDH}}(x, y)$ can be computed with respect to the population distribution $F_{X|Y}$. It can be shown that the conditional sampling distribution of $\widehat{\theta}_{\text{FDH}}(x, y)$, given that $Y \geq y$, is

$$\text{prob}(\widehat{\theta}_{\text{FDH}}(x, y) \leq u \mid Y \geq y) = 1 - [1 - F_{X|Y}(ux|y)]^{n_y},$$

where n_y is the number of observations (x_i, y_i) such that $y_i \geq y$. Some further algebra leads to

$$E(\widehat{\theta}_{FDH}(x, y) \mid Y \geq y) = \theta(x, y) + \int_{\theta(x,y)}^{\infty} [1 - F_{X|Y}(ux|y)]^{n_y} \, du. \quad (4.98)$$

The last term in (4.98) gives an expression for the bias of the FDH estimator. Although this expression depends on unknowns $(\theta(x, y)$ and $F_{X|Y}(\cdot|y))$, the bias can be estimated by replacing the unknowns with their empirical counterparts, that is, by replacing $F_{X|Y}(\cdot|y)$ with $\widehat{F}_{X|Y,n}(\cdot|y)$ and replacing $\theta(x, y)$ with $\widehat{\theta}_{FDH}(x, y)$.

This suggests a bias-corrected FDH estimator of θ defined by

$$\widehat{\theta}_{bcFDH}(x, y) = \widehat{\theta}_{FDH}(x, y) - \int_{\widehat{\theta}_{FDH}(x,y)}^{\infty} [1 - \widehat{F}_{X|Y,n}(ux|y)]^{n_y} \, du. \quad (4.99)$$

The integral in (4.99) can be computed easily and rapidly using numerical methods. The computation is much faster than the bias correction computed by the bootstrap. In addition, there are no smoothing parameters to specify here; when the subsampling bootstrap described in section 4.3.6 is used, one must choose the subsample size. The method here is thus an attractive alternative to the bootstrap bias correction method.

The theoretical properties of the bias-corrected FDH estimator are investigated in Badin and Simar (2004). To summarize, the bias-corrected FDH estimator and the ordinary FDH estimator share the same the same asymptotic distribution. Without a formal proof, it can be seen here that the bias correction must vanish as n increases since the integral in (4.99) goes to zero as $n \to \infty$. In finite samples, however, which is the case in any real application, the gain in terms of reductions in bias and mean square error may be considerable.

Monte Carlo experiments reported in Badin and Simar (2004) suggest that, in finite samples, the bias-corrected FDH estimator behaves well when compared to the FDH estimator. The Monte Carlo experiments confirm that, as expected, the bias is reduced (by a factor 1.46 to 1.36 when the sample size grows from $n = 50$ to 800 for the case $M = N = 1$). More important, mean square error is also found to decrease with the bias-corrected estimator (by a factor 2.12 to 1.8 in the same scenario). Of course, when the sample size n is larger, the gain is less dramatic, but still worthwhile. Badin and Simar observe similar behavior for problems involving greater dimensionality.

4.4.2 Linearly interpolated FDH

In addition to the curse of dimensionality shared by most of the nonparametric techniques, the nonsmoothness of the FDH estimator makes its use very difficult for statistical inference in finite samples. Although in principle the bootstrap provides a method for making inference (recall that the subsampling bootstrap provides a consistent approximation of the sampling distribution of FDH estimators), simulation studies in Jeong and Simar (2006) indicate that the subsampling bootstrap is not a good idea for estimating confidence intervals for reasons discussed in section 4.3.6.

Since under the assumptions in section 4.2.1 the true frontier is continuous, one might hope to improve the performance of the FDH estimator by smoothing its corresponding frontier. This is the idea of the linearized (LFDH) estimator introduced by Jeong and Simar (2006), who show that, indeed, the LFDH estimator outperforms the FDH estimator while still allowing for a nonconvex production set Ψ.

Linear interpolation is perhaps the simplest way to smooth the FDH frontier. The idea is to interpolate the vertices of the free disposal hull of a given data set to obtain a smoothed version of the FDH frontier estimate. In a two-dimensional framework ($N = M = 1$), this would be easy to accomplish, by drawing a polygonal line smoothing the staircase-shaped estimate of the production frontier shown in figure 4.1. But in a multidimensional scenario, it is not straightforward to identify the points that must be interpolated.

Jeong and Simar (2006) propose an algorithm to identify the points to be interpolated for the LFDH estimator. To illustrate, consider estimation of $\theta(x, y)$ (or of $\lambda(x, y)$, in the output-oriented case) for a given fixed point of interest, (x, y). The method is summarized by the following steps:

1. Identify the vertices of the FDH of the observations $\mathcal{X}_n$.
2. Move the vertices to a convex surface along the direction parallel to x (or parallel to y for the output-oriented case).
3. Compute the convex hull of the relocated points.
4. Identify the vertices defining the facet that intersects the ray θx (or λy for the output-oriented case).
5. Interpolate the points identified in step 4.

Steps 2–3 seem rather difficult when both input and output variables are multidimensional, but using tools closely related to Delaunay triangulation (or tessellation) in computational geometry (e.g., Brown, 1979), Jeong and Simar (2006) propose an algorithm. The idea of the tessellation is illustrated in figure 4.11 in the two-dimensional case (one input, one output), where the asterisks are observations and the article is the point (x, y). The FDH-efficient points are moved parallel to θx to the points denoted the plus symbols (step 2). The dot-dashed line is the convex hull of these points (step 3). The two FDH-efficient points indicated by the circled stars are identified as the facet (here, a line) intersecting θx (step 4). These are the two points to be interpolated. In this two-dimensional, input-oriented illustration, these two points define the two consecutive edges of the staircase-shaped estimate of the production frontier that surround the given value of y (see figure 4.11).

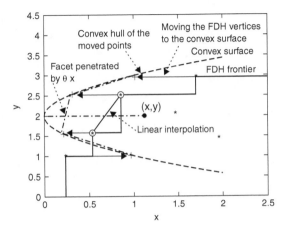

Figure 4.11. Tessellation Idea

More generally, let $\mathcal{I}_{x,y}$ denote the set of vertices identified in step 4. Then, the LFDH estimator $\tilde{\theta}(x, y)$ is given by

$$\widehat{\theta}_{\text{LFDH}}(x, y) = \min\left\{\theta > 0 \mid \theta x \geq \sum_{i\in\mathcal{I}_{x,y}} \gamma_i x_i, y \leq \sum_{i\in\mathcal{I}_{x,y}} \gamma_i y_i\right.$$

$$\text{for some } \gamma_i \geq 0, i \in \mathcal{I}_{x,y}$$

$$\left.\text{such that } \sum_{i\in\mathcal{I}_{x,y}} \gamma_i = 1\right\}. \tag{4.100}$$

The LFDH estimator coincides with the DEA estimator with reference set consisting of the points $\{(x_i, y_i) \mid i \in \mathcal{I}_{x,y}\}$. The LFDH estimator also satisfies the free disposability assumption. The corresponding LFDH estimator of the attainable set Ψ is given by

$$\widehat{\Psi}_{\text{LFDH}} = \left\{(x, y) \in \mathcal{R}_+^{N+M} \mid x \geq \widehat{\theta}_{\text{LFDH}}(u, v)u, \ y \leq v,\right.$$

$$\left.\text{for some } (u, v) \in \widehat{\Psi}_{\text{FDH}}\right\}. \tag{4.101}$$

The asymptotic distribution of $n^{1/(N+M)}(\widehat{\theta}_{\text{LFDH}}(x, y) - \theta(x, y))$ is the same as the non-degenerate limiting distribution of a random variable ζ_n that can be easily simulated. In other words, the asymptotic distribution of $n^{1/(N+M)}(\widehat{\theta}_{\text{LFDH}}(x, y) - \theta(x, y))$ can be simulated by taking a large number of random draws of ζ_n; this provides a route to inference making. By estimating the mean or quantiles of ζ_n, a bias-corrected estimator can be constructed or confidence intervals for $\theta(x, y)$ of any desired level can be estimated (see Jeong and Simar, 2006, for details).

The Monte Carlo experiments described in Jeong and Simar (2006) indicate that the LFDH estimator outperforms the FDH estimator in terms of both bias (bias is reduced by a factor more than 2) and mean square error (which is reduced by a factor of the order 4), for sample sizes $n = 100$ or 400 and when $N = M = 2$ or when $N = 4$ and $M = 1$.

The LFDH estimator involves a greater computational burden than the FDH, since it requires solution of two linear programs: one for solving the problem in step 3 above, and one (of limited size) for solving (4.100).

4.5 Robust Nonparametric Frontier Estimators

All the nonparametric envelopment estimators of frontiers are particularly sensitive to extreme observations, or outliers. These extreme points may disproportionately, and perhaps misleadingly, influence the evaluation of the performance of other firms. This drawback also plagues parametric frontier estimators when deterministic frontier models are considered. One approach to this problem would be to identify any outliers in the data, and then perhaps delete them if they result from corrupted data. A number of techniques exist for finding outliers in frontier settings (e.g., Wilson, 1993, 1995; Simar, 2003; Porembski et al., 2005). Alternatively, one can use robust estimators that have been recently developed, which also offer other advantages.

Cazals et al. (2002), Daraio and Simar (2005), Aragon et al. (2005), and Daouia and Simar (2005, 2007) have developed robust alternatives to the traditional FDH and DEA estimators. These new estimators involve the concept of a "partial" frontier, as opposed to the traditional idea of a "full" frontier that envelops all the data. The new ideas replace the goals of estimating the absolute lowest (uppermost) technically achievable level of input (output) for a given level of output (input) with the idea of estimating something "close" to these quantities.

As such, the partial frontiers considered in this section are "less extreme" than the full frontier. Since estimation of partial frontiers avoids many of the statistical problems inherent in estimating a full frontier, partial frontiers provide a more useful benchmark against which firms can be compared. Natural nonparametric estimators of these partial frontiers are proposed that are very easy and fast to compute.

Two families of partial frontiers have been proposed: (i) order-m frontiers, where m can be viewed as a trimming parameter, and (ii) order-α quantile frontiers, analogous to traditional quantile functions but adapted to the frontier problem. It turns out that the resulting nonparametric estimators have much better properties than the usual nonparametric (DEA or FDH) frontier estimators; the new estimators do not suffer from the curse of dimensionality, and the standard parametric $\sqrt{n}$ rate of convergence is achieved along with asymptotic normality.

Another interesting feature is that both estimators of these partial frontiers are also consistent estimators of the full frontier, by allowing the order of the frontier (m or α) to grow (at an appropriate rate) with increasing sample size (although for practical applications, where sample size is typically fixed, this theoretical result may be of limited use). These new estimators of the full frontier share the same asymptotic properties as FDH estimators. But, in finite samples, the new estimators do not envelop all the data, so are much more robust with respect to outliers and extreme values in the sample than the usual FDH or DEA estimators. As a side benefit, these "partial-order" frontiers and their estimators provide very useful tools for detecting outliers (e.g., Simar, 2003). The basic ideas are based on the probabilistic formulation of a production process as developed in section 4.2.4.

4.5.1 Order-m frontiers

The discussion in this section is presented in terms of the input orientation, but as before, the concepts adapt easily to the output orientation. For clarification, a summary of concepts for the output orientation is given at the end of this section.

4.5.1.1 Definition and basic ideas

Recall that in section 4.2.4 the production process was modeled in terms of the probability distribution function $H_{XY}(x, y) = \text{prob}(X \leq x, Y \geq y)$. For the input orientation, the full frontier and the resulting Debreu-Farrell efficiency scores are characterized by properties of the conditional distribution $F_{X|Y}(x|y) = \text{prob}(X \leq x \mid Y \geq y)$ that describes the behavior of firms that produce at least level y of output. In terms of the input efficiency score,

$$\theta(x, y) = \inf\{\theta \mid F_{X|Y}(\theta x|y) > 0\}, \qquad (4.102)$$

assuming free disposability; see (4.31).

The full frontier can be viewed as the lower radial boundary of $F_{X|Y}(x|y)$, or as the *minimum achievable* lower boundary of inputs for *all* possible firms producing at least level y of output. This is a rather extreme and absolute (theoretical) concept: It gives the full minimum achievable level of input over all production plans that are technically feasible. An alternative benchmark is obtained by defining the *expected* minimum input achieved by any m firms chosen randomly from the population and producing at least output level y, For finite values of m, this will be shown shortly to provide a potentially more useful benchmark for comparing firms in terms of their efficiencies than the frontier $\partial\Psi$. It will also be apparent that if m goes to infinity, the problem becomes identical to FDH estimation of the full frontier $\partial\Psi$.

To make things more precise, suppose an output level y is given. Consider m identically, independently distributed (iid) random variables X_i,

$i = 1, \ldots, m$ drawn from the conditional N-variate distribution function $F_X(\cdot \mid y)$, and define the set

$$\Psi_m(y) = \{(x', y') \in \mathcal{R}_+^{N+M} \mid x' \geq X_i, \ y' \geq y, \ i = 1, \ldots, m\}. \qquad (4.103)$$

This random set is the FDH of m firms that produce at least the level y of output. Then, for any x and the given y, the Debreu-Farrell input efficiency score relative to the set $\Psi_m(y)$ is

$$\widetilde{\theta}_m(x, y) = \inf\{\theta \mid (\theta x, y) \in \Psi_m(y)\}. \qquad (4.104)$$

The set $\Psi_m(y)$ is random, since it depends on the random variables X_i with (conditional) distribution function $F_X(\cdot \mid y)$. Hence, the efficiency score $\widetilde{\theta}_m(x, y)$ is also random. For a given realization of the m values X_i, a realization of $\widetilde{\theta}_m(x, y)$ is obtained by computing

$$\widetilde{\theta}_m(x, y) = \min_{i=1,\ldots,m} \left\{ \max_{j=1,\ldots,p} \left(\frac{X_i^j}{x^j} \right) \right\}. \qquad (4.105)$$

The order-m input efficiency score is defined as follows:

Definition 4.5.1

For all y such that $S_Y(y) = \mathrm{prob}(Y \geq y) > 0$, the (expected) order-$m$ input efficiency measure, the order-m input efficiency score is given by

$$\theta_m(x, y) \equiv E(\widetilde{\theta}_m(x, y) \mid Y \geq y), \qquad (4.106)$$

The order-m input efficiency score benchmarks a unit operating at (x, y) against the expected minimum input among m peers randomly drawn from the population of units producing at least y. This efficiency measure, in turn, defines an order-m input-efficient frontier. For any $(x, y) \in \Psi$, the expected minimum level of inputs of order-m for a unit producing output level y and for an input mix determined by the vector x is given by

$$x_m^{\partial}(y) = \theta_m(x, y) \, x. \qquad (4.107)$$

For comparison, recall that the full frontier $\partial\Psi$ is defined (at output level y) by $x^{\partial}(y) = \theta(x, y) \, x$ in (4.6).

If x is univariate, this new, order-m input frontier can be described by an input function of order-m:

$$x_m^{\partial}(y) = \phi_m(y) = E\left[\min(X^1, \ldots, X^m) \mid Y \geq y\right]$$

$$= \int_0^{\infty} [1 - F_X(x \mid y)]^m \, dx. \qquad (4.108)$$

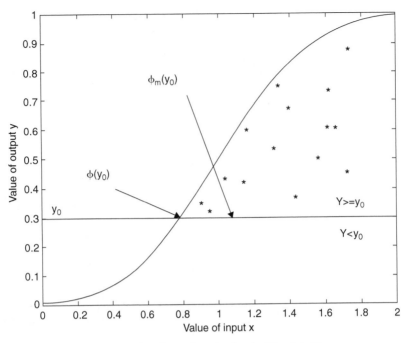

Figure 4.12. Input-Oriented Order-m Frontier for the Bivariate Case

The concept is illustrated in figure 4.12, which resembles figure 4.3. Figure 4.12 shows the input-oriented order-m frontier for a particular value y_0 in the bivariate case. For this (or for any other) y_0, $\phi_m(y_0) = E[\min(X^1, \ldots, X^m) \mid Y \geq y_0]$. The asterisks represent m draws $X^1, \ldots, X^m$ for $Y \geq y_0$. For finite m, the order-m frontier function is under (to the right of) the full frontier function $\phi(y)$ as defined in (4.33) and shown by the upward-sloping curve in figure 4.12.

As a matter of fact, the order-m efficiency score has an explicit expression that depends only on the distribution $F_X(x \mid y)$. It can be proved that

$$\theta_m(x, y) = \int_0^\infty (1 - F_X(ux \mid y))^m \, du$$

$$= \theta(x, y) + \int_{\theta(x,y)}^\infty (1 - F_X(ux \mid y))^m \, du. \qquad (4.109)$$

Note that the integral is univariate, even in a full multivariate setting where $(N, M) \geq 1$. As expected, as $m \to \infty$, the order-m frontier tends to the full frontier. From (4.109), it is obvious that

$$\lim_{m \to \infty} \theta_m(x, y) = \theta(x, y) \qquad (4.110)$$

since the integrand in (4.109) is less or equal to 1.

4.5.1.2 Nonparametric estimators

We show above that for the full frontier approach, the probabilistic formulation in section 4.2.4 allows the plug-in principle to be used to provide an appealing, alternative characterization of FDH estimators.

Following the same ideas here, an intuitive, nonparametric estimator of $\theta_m(x, y)$ is obtained by plugging the empirical version of $F_X(x \mid y)$ into (4.109) to obtain

$$\widehat{\theta}_{m,n}(x, y) = \widehat{E}(\tilde{\theta}_m(x, y) \mid Y \geq y)$$

$$= \int_0^\infty (1 - \widehat{F}_{X,n}(ux \mid y))^m \, du,$$

$$= \widehat{\theta}_{\mathrm{FDH}}(x, y) + \int_{\widehat{\theta}_{\mathrm{FDH}}(x,y)}^\infty (1 - \widehat{F}_{X,n}(ux \mid y))^m \, du. \qquad (4.111)$$

This estimator involves the computation of a univariate integral that is easy to solve using numerical methods. Even for large values of N, M, and m, the estimator is very fast to compute because the integral remains one dimensional. When $N = 1$, an explicit analytical solution is available (see Cazals et al., 2002). For the full multivariate setting, Daraio and Simar (2005) propose a Monte Carlo algorithm for approximating the expectation in (4.111), thereby avoiding the need for numerical integration. However, for large values of m, computing the integral in (4.111) is faster.

Analogous to (4.107), for a firm operating at $(x, y) \in \Psi$, an estimate of its expected minimum input level of order-m is

$$\widehat{x}_m^\partial(y) = \widehat{\theta}_{m,n}(x, y) \, x. \qquad (4.112)$$

Just as (4.107) can be evaluated over the range of possible output levels y to trace out the *expected minimum input frontier* of order m, denoted $\partial \Psi_m^{\mathrm{in}}$, (4.112) can also be evaluated for the possible values of y to trace out an estimate $\widehat{\partial \Psi}_m^{\mathrm{in}}$ of $\partial \Psi_m^{\mathrm{in}}$.

By construction, the estimator $\widehat{\partial \Psi}_m^{\mathrm{in}}$ with finite m does not envelop all the observations in the sample $\mathcal{X}_n$. Consequently, the estimator is less sensitive than either the FDH or DEA frontier estimators to extreme points or outliers. Again, the estimator $\widehat{\partial \Psi}_m^{\mathrm{in}}$ shares the same property as its population counterpart, $\partial \Psi_m^{\text{in}}$: As m increases, for a fixed sample size n, $\widehat{\partial \Psi}_m^{\text{in}}$ converges to the usual FDH estimator of $\partial \Psi$, while $\partial \Psi_m^{\text{in}}$ converges to $\partial \Psi$; that is,

$$\widehat{\theta}_{m,n}(x,y) \to \widehat{\theta}_{\text{FDH}}(x,y), \text{ as } m \to \infty. \tag{4.113}$$

The proof is trivial.

4.5.1.3 Statistical properties

The estimators described above in section 4.5.1.2 possess some interesting properties that are unusual among nonparametric estimators. First, for any fixed value of m, $\widehat{\theta}_{m,n}(x,y)$ converges to $\theta_m(x,y)$ at the rate $\sqrt{n}$, and its asymptotic distribution is normal; that is,

$$\sqrt{n}\left[\widehat{\theta}_{m,n}(x,y) - \theta_m(x,y)\right] \xrightarrow{d} \mathcal{N}(0, \sigma_{\text{in}}^2(x,y)), \tag{4.114}$$

where the variance for $\sigma_{\text{in}}^2(x,y)$ depends on $F_X(x \mid y)$ (see Cazals et al., 2002, for details). This variance can be estimated consistently using the plug-in principle, where $F_X(\cdot \mid y)$ is replaced by its empirical analog $\widehat{F}_{X,n}(\cdot \mid y)$ in the expression for $\sigma_{\text{in}}^2(x,y)$ given by Cazals et al. Alternatively, this variance can be estimated using a naive bootstrap, where pseudosamples are obtained by drawing from the empirical distribution of the observations in $\mathcal{X}_n$. The naive bootstrap can be used (provided m is finite) since the boundaries of support for $f(x,y)$ are not estimated; that is, both $\partial \Psi_m^{\text{in}}$ and $\widehat{\partial \Psi}_m^{\text{in}}$ lie in the interior of Ψ, away from $\partial \Psi$. Estimates of confidence intervals can also be obtained easily using a naive bootstrap approach.

Since $\theta_m(x,y) \to \theta(x,y)$ as $m \to \infty$, one might be tempted to use $\widehat{\theta}_{m,n}(x,y)$ as an estimator of $\theta(x,y)$ itself, by using large values of m. Cazals et al. (2002) show that if $m = m(n) \to \infty$ as $n \to \infty$ (with m increasing at an appropriate rate),

$$n^{\frac{1}{p+q}}\left[\widehat{\theta}_{m,n}(x,y) - \theta(x,y)\right] \xrightarrow{d} \text{Weibull}(\mu_{x,y}, N+M), \tag{4.115}$$

where the parameter of the Weibull is the same as in section 4.2.5. Hence, if $n \to \infty$ and $m = m(n) \to \infty$, $\widehat{\theta}_{m,n}(x,y)$ shares the same properties as the FDH estimator. In finite samples, however, the order-m estimator will be more robust with respect to outliers and extreme values since it does not envelop all the (extreme) observations in the sample.

This latter property gives another appealing feature of the order-m estimators. In practice, the choice of a particular value of m should be guided by this robustness property. Since the estimator involves little computational burden, it can be computed for several values of m (e.g., $m = 25, 50, 100, 150, 200, \ldots$). For each value of m, one can observe the percentage of observations in the sample that lie outside the resulting order-m frontier estimate [such observations are indicated by a value $\widehat{\theta}_{m,n}(x_i, y_i) > 1$]. This percentage will decrease as m increases; as described below, this property can also be used to detect outliers. The final value of m can be chosen in terms of the desired level of robustness; for example, one might choose a value for m that results in approximately 5% of the observations in $\mathcal{X}_n$ lying outside $\widehat{\partial \Psi}_m^{in}$. Experience has shown that, in many applications, qualitative conclusions are little affected by particular choices of m, provided the values of m are somewhat less than the sample size, n.

4.5.1.4 Summary for the output-oriented case

For an output-oriented analysis, suppose an input level x in the interior of the support of X is given, and consider m iid random variables Y_i, $i = 1, \ldots, m$ drawn from the conditional M-variate distribution function $F_Y(y \mid x) = \text{prob}(Y \leq y \mid X \leq x)$. Analogous to (4.103), define the random set

$$\Psi_m(x) = \{(x', y) \in \mathcal{R}_+^{N+M} \mid x' \leq x, Y_i \leq y, i = 1, \ldots, m\}. \qquad (4.116)$$

Then, for any y, define

$$\widetilde{\lambda}_m(x, y) = \sup\{\lambda \mid (x, \lambda y) \in \Psi_m(x)\}$$

$$= \max_{i=1,\ldots,m} \left\{ \min_{j=1,\ldots,p} \left(\frac{Y_i^j}{y^j} \right) \right\}. \qquad (4.117)$$

The order-m output efficiency measure is defined as follows:

Definition 4.5.2.

For any $y \in \mathcal{R}_+^M$, the (expected) order-m output efficiency measure, denoted by $\lambda_m(x, y)$, is defined for all x in the interior of the support of X by

$$\lambda_m(x, y) \equiv E(\widetilde{\lambda}_m(x, y) \mid X \leq x), \qquad (4.118)$$

where the expectation is assumed to exist.

Analogous to (4.109) and (4.110),

$$\lambda_m(x, y) = \int_0^\infty \left[1 - (1 - S_Y(uy \mid x))^m \right] du$$

$$= \lambda(x, y) - \int_0^{\lambda(x,y)} (1 - S_Y(uy \mid x))^m \, du, \qquad (4.119)$$

and

$$\lim_{m \to \infty} \lambda_m(x, y) = \lambda(x, y). \qquad (4.120)$$

A nonparametric estimator of $\lambda_m(x, y)$ is given by

$$\widehat{\lambda}_m(x, y) = \int_0^\infty \left[1 - [1 - \widehat{S}_{Y,n}(uy \mid x)]^m \right] du$$

$$= \widehat{\lambda}_n(x, y) - \int_0^{\widehat{\lambda}_n(x,y)} (1 - \widehat{S}_{Y,n}(uy \mid x))^m \, du. \qquad (4.121)$$

This estimator shares properties analogous to those of the input-oriented estimator. In particular, the output-oriented estimator also achieves $\sqrt{n}$-consistency and asymptotic normality; that is,

$$\sqrt{n} \left[\widehat{\lambda}_{m,n}(x, y) - \lambda_m(x, y) \right] \xrightarrow{d} \mathcal{N}(0, \sigma_{\text{out}}^2(x, y)). \qquad (4.122)$$

In addition, as $m \to \infty$, $\lambda_m(x, y) \to \lambda(x, y)$ and $\widehat{\lambda}_{m,n}(x, y) \to \widehat{\lambda}_{\text{FDH}}(x, y)$. Analogous to (4.115), if $m = m(n) \to \infty$ at an appropriate rate as $n \to \infty$,

$$n^{\frac{1}{p+q}} \left[\widehat{\lambda}_{m,n}(x, y) - \lambda(x, y) \right] \xrightarrow{d} \text{Weibull}(\mu_{x,y}, N + M) \text{ as } n \to \infty. \qquad (4.123)$$

As $m = m(n) \to \infty$, the estimator $\widehat{\lambda}_{m,n}(x, y)$ shares the same properties as the FDH estimator. But, in finite samples, it will be more robust to outliers and extreme values since it will not envelop all the observations in the sample.

4.5.1.5 Examples

To illustrate the order-m estimators, consider a simple example where $N = M = 1$ and the upper boundary of the production set Ψ is described by

$$y = g(x) = (2x - x^2)^{1/2}. \qquad (4.124)$$

Suppose interest lies in the fixed point $(x_0, y_0) = (0.5, 0.5)$, and that observations result from independent draws from the probability density function $f(x, y)$ with support over the production set Ψ. Suppose also that the joint probability density of inputs and outputs, $f(x, y)$, is uniform over Ψ; hence,

$$f(x, y) = \begin{cases} \frac{4}{\pi} & \forall x \in [0, 1], \ y \in [0, g(x)], \\ 0 & \text{otherwise.} \end{cases} \qquad (4.125)$$

Given (4.124) and (4.125), the true order-m frontiers can be recovered. For the input-orientation, $F_{X|Y}(x \mid Y \geq y) = \text{prob}(X \leq x \mid Y \geq y)$ is needed. From the joint density given in (4.125), the marginal density of y is given by

$$f(y) = \int_{1-\sqrt{1-y^2}}^{1} f(x, y)\, dx$$

$$= 4\pi^{-1}(1 - y^2)^{1/2},\qquad\qquad (4.126)$$

and hence the marginal distribution function of y is

$$F(y) = \text{prob}(Y \le y)$$

$$= \begin{cases} 1 & \forall Y > 1, \\ 4\pi^{-1}\left[\frac{1}{2}y(1 - y^2)^{1/2} + \frac{1}{2}\sin^{-1}(y)\right] & \times \forall Y \in [0, 1], \\ 0 & \text{otherwise.} \end{cases} \qquad (4.127)$$

Conditional on $Y \ge y$, the joint density of (X, Y) is

$$f(x, y \mid Y \ge y) = \left[1 - F(y)\right]^{-1} f(x, y);$$

integrating with respect to Y gives the conditional density of X:

$$f(x \mid Y \ge y) = \left[1 - F(y)\right]^{-1} \int_{y}^{(2x-x^2)^{1/2}} 4\pi^{-1}\, du$$

$$= \left[1 - F(y)\right]^{-1} 4\pi^{-1}\left[(2x - x^2)^{1/2} - y\right] \qquad (4.128)$$

for all $x \in \left[1 - \sqrt{1 - y_0^2}, 1\right]$. Integrating in (4.128) with respect to x gives the conditional distribution function for x,

$$F_{X\mid Y}(x \mid Y \ge y) = \text{prob}(X \le x \mid Y \ge y)$$

$$= \left[1 - F(y)\right]^{-1} 4\pi^{-1} \int_{1-\sqrt{1-y^2}}^{x} \left[(2u - u^2)^{1/2} - y\right] du$$

$$\times \forall x \in [1 - \sqrt{1 - y^2}, 1]$$

$$
= \begin{cases}
1 & \forall x > 1; \\
\begin{aligned}
& \left[1 - F(y)\right]^{-1} 4\pi^{-1} \\
& \times \left[\frac{x-1}{2}(2x - x^2)^{1/2}\right. \\
& + \frac{1}{2}\sin^{-1}(x - 1) - yx \\
& - \frac{1}{2}y(1 - y^2)^{1/2} \\
& \left. - \frac{1}{2}\sin^{-1}(-\sqrt{1 - y^2}) + y\right] & \forall x \in \mathcal{A}, \\
\end{aligned} \\
0 & \text{otherwise,}
\end{cases}
$$

$$(4.129)$$

where $\mathcal{A}$ represents the interval $\left[1 - \sqrt{1 - y^2}, \ 1\right]$.

Recall that for the univariate case, the (true) expected input order-m frontier is given by (4.108). Since $F_{X|Y}(x \mid Y \geq y)$ is given above by (4.129), $\partial x_m(y_0)$ can be computed for a variety of values of y_0 to trace out the expected input order-m frontier. This has been done in figure 4.13, where the solid curve shows the boundary $\partial\Psi$ of the production set Ψ, and the dashed curve gives the *true* expected input order-m frontier (for $m = 50$).

Of course, the *true* order-m frontiers are not observed and must be estimated from data. Figure 4.14 shows 20 observations represented by open circles; these were drawn from the uniform density over Ψ defined in (4.125). The solid circle at $(0.5, 0.5)$ represents the point of interest; note that this point does not correspond to one of the sample observations, although it could be chosen to do so if desired. The vertical dotted line in figure 4.14 shows the minimum input level among the six observations with output level greater than 0.5, the output level of the point of interest. These six observations have coordinates $(0.9, 0.97)$, $(0.43, 0.72)$, $(0.73, 0.81)$, $(0.34, 0.65)$, $(0.43, 0.63)$, and $(0.54, 0.7)$. But what is the *expected* minimum input level among draws of size m, conditional on $Y \geq 0.5$?

Now suppose three draws of size $m = 2$ are taken from among the six points with output level greater than 0.5. Suppose, by chance, the first draw selects $(0.9, 0.97)$ and $(0.54, 0.7)$, the second draw selects $(0.9, 0.97)$ and $(0.34, 0.65)$, and the third draw selects $(0.9, 0.97)$ and $(0.34, 0.65)$ again. Then the minimum input levels on each of the three draws are 0.54, 0.34, and 0.34. Their mean is $(0.54 + 0.34 + 0.34)/3 = 0.41$; this is an *estimate* of the expected minimum input level of order $m = 2$ for $y_0 = 0.5$. This is shown by the "x" on the horizontal dashed line passing through the solid circle in figure 4.14.

It is also possible to compute expected maximum output levels of order-m. The *true* expected order-m output frontier for the two-dimensional problem here is

$$
\partial y_m(x) = \int_0^x 1 - \left[F_{Y|X}(y \mid x)\right]^m \, dy \quad \forall x \in [0, 1]. \tag{4.130}
$$

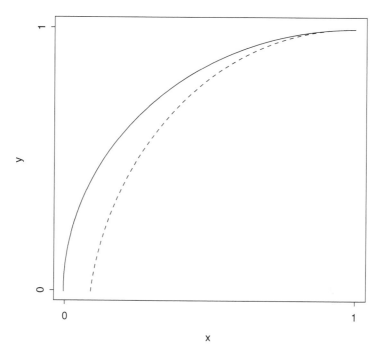

Figure 4.13. True Input Order-m Frontier ($m = 50$)

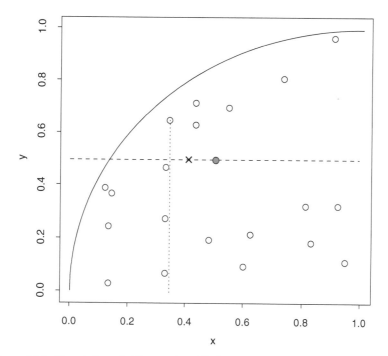

Figure 4.14. Twenty Sample Observations Circles

To derive the conditional distribution $F_{Y|X}(y \mid x)$, note that the marginal density of x is given by

$$f(x) = \int_0^{g(x)} f(x, y)\, dy$$

$$= \frac{4}{\pi}(2x - x^2)^{1/2} \qquad (4.131)$$

and the marginal distribution function of x is

$$F_X(x) = \text{prob}(X \le x)$$

$$= \begin{cases} 1 & \forall x > 1, \\ 4\pi^{-1}\left[\frac{x-1}{2}(2x - x^2)^{1/2} \right. \\ \left. +\frac{1}{2}\sin^{-1}(x_0 - 1) + \frac{\pi}{4}\right] & \forall x \in [0, 1], \\ 0 & \forall x < 0. \end{cases} \qquad (4.132)$$

The joint density of x and y, given $X \le x$, is then $f(x, y \mid X \le x) = F_X(x)^{-1} f(x, y) \; \forall y \in [0, g(x)]$, $X \le x$, and therefore the marginal density of y given $X \le x$, is

$$f(y \mid X \le x) = F_X(x)^{-1} \int_{1-\sqrt{1-y^2}}^{x} f(u, y)\, du$$

$$= F_X(x)^{-1} 4\pi^{-1}\left[x - 1 + (1 - y^2)^{1/2}\right]$$

$$\forall y \in [0, g(x_0)]. \qquad (4.133)$$

Then,

$$F_{Y|X}(y \mid X \le x) = \text{prob}(Y \le y \mid X \le x)$$

$$= \begin{cases} 1 & \forall y > g(x), \\ F_X(x)^{-1} 4\pi^{-1}\Big\{(x-1)y \\ \quad +\frac{1}{2}\big[y(1 - y^2)^{1/2} \\ \quad + \sin^{-1}(y)\big]\Big\} & \forall y \in [0, g(x)], \\ 0 & \forall y < 0. \end{cases} \qquad (4.134)$$

Using the expression for $F_{Y|X}(y \mid x)$ given by (4.134), $\partial y_m(x)$ can be computed for variety of values of x to trace out the expected order-m output frontier. This has been done in figure 4.15, where the solid curve shows the boundary $\partial\Psi$ of the production set Ψ, and the dashed curve depicts the true expected order-m output frontier (for $m = 50$).

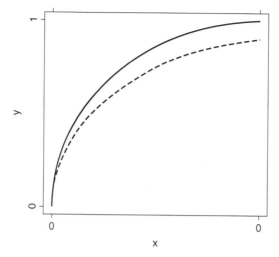

Figure 4.15. True Output Order-m Frontier ($m = 50$)

4.5.2 Order-α quantile frontiers

As noted in the preceding section, the quantity m in order-m frontier estimation serves as a trimming parameter that determines the percentage of points that will lie above the order-m frontier. The idea underlying order-α quantile frontiers is to reverse this causation and choose the proportion of the data lying above the frontier directly.

Quantile estimation in regression contexts is an old idea. In the case of linear (or nonlinear) parametric regression where $y = g(x \mid \beta) + \varepsilon$, instead of minimizing the sum of squared errors to estimate parameters, one can minimize the sum of absolute values of the errors to obtain a least-absolute deviation (LAD) estimator of β; the estimated regression equation is then interpreted as an estimate of the median, or 50% quantile function, conditional on the regressors in x. More generally, Koenker and Bassett (1978) proposed minimizing (with respect to parameters)

$$\sum_{i|y_i \geq g(x_i|\beta)} \alpha|y_i - g(x_i \mid \beta)| + \sum_{i|y_i < g(x_i|\beta)} (1-\alpha)|y_i - g(x_i \mid \beta)| \quad (4.135)$$

to estimate the $\alpha \times 100\%$ quantile function (again, conditional on x). In the case of production relationships, the Koenker and Bassett (1978) approach presents two new problems: (i) the conditional quantile function must be specified parametrically, a priori, with the risk of misspecification; and (ii) it is apparently not possible to constrain estimates of the conditional quantile function to be monotonic in multivariate settings, suggesting a loss of statistical efficiency at a minimum, and perhaps worse problems for interpretation of any estimates that are obtained.

In the framework of production frontiers, using the probabilistic formulation of the DGP developed in section 4.2.4, is it straightforward to adapt the order-m ideas to order-α quantile estimation. These ideas were developed for the univariate case by Aragon et al. (2005) and extended to the multivariate setting by Daouia and Simar (2007). For purposes of illustration, the ideas are described below in terms of the input orientation.

4.5.2.1 Definition and basic ideas

As discussed above, using order-m partial frontiers, a unit operating at (x, y) is benchmarked against the expected minimum input among m peers drawn randomly from the population of units producing output levels of at least y. By contrast, order-α quantile frontiers benchmark the unit at (x, y) against the input level not exceeded by $(1 - \alpha) \times 100\%$ of firms among the population of units producing output levels of at least y.

Definition 4.5.3.

For all y such that $S_Y(y) > 0$ and for $\alpha \in (0, 1]$, the α-quantile input efficiency score for the unit operating at $(x, y) \in \Psi$ is defined by

$$\theta_\alpha(x, y) = \inf\{\theta \mid F_{X|Y}(\theta x \mid y) > 1 - \alpha\}. \tag{4.136}$$

This concept can be interpreted as follows. First, suppose that $\theta_\alpha(x, y) = 1$; then the unit is the said to be input efficient at the level $\alpha \times 100\%$ since it is dominated by firms producing more than y with a probability of $1 - \alpha$. Then, more generally, if $\theta_\alpha(x, y)(<, >)1$, the firm at (x, y) can (reduce, increase) its input usage to $\theta_\alpha(x, y)x$ to become input efficient at the level $\alpha \times 100\%$. The quantity $\theta_\alpha(x, y)$ is called the "input efficiency at level $\alpha \times 100\%$."

The idea of the order-α conditional quantile is illustrated in figure 4.16 for the case of univariate x. Figure 4.16 the plots the conditional distribution function $F(x \mid Y \geq y_0)$, which equals zero at $x = \phi(y_0)$, defining the full input frontier for a unit producing output level y_0. The $(1 - \alpha)$ quantile input frontier is given by $x = \phi_\alpha(y_0)$. For a unit operating at levels (x_0, y_0), its α-quantile input efficiency is given by $\theta_\alpha(x_0, y_0) = \phi_\alpha(y_0)/x_0$, whereas its Farrell input efficiency score is given as usual by $\theta(x_0, y_0) = \phi(y_0)/x_0$.

It is clear from the definition that if $\alpha = 1$, the full frontier $\partial\Psi$ is recovered; in this case, $\theta_1(x, y) \equiv \theta(x, y)$ is the Debreu-Farrell input measure of efficiency. In fact, it can be proved that the convergence of $\theta_\alpha(x, y)$ to $\theta(x, y)$ when $\alpha \to 1$ is monotone; that is,

$$\lim_{\alpha \to 1} \searrow \theta_\alpha(x, y) = \theta(x, y), \tag{4.137}$$

where "$\searrow$" denotes monotone convergence from above.

The concept of efficiency of order-α allows definition of the corresponding efficient frontier at the level $\alpha \times 100\%$. This production frontier is called

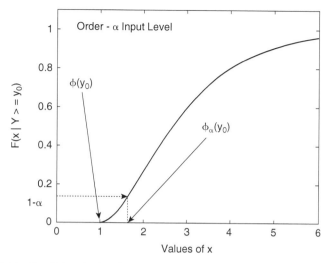

Figure 4.16. Conditional Distribution Function $F(x \mid Y \geq y_0)$ and the Order-α quantile

the α-quantile efficient frontier. It may be defined as the efficient input at the level $\alpha \times 100\%$ for a given level of output y, and for an input mix given by an input vector x:

$$x_\alpha^\partial(y) = \theta_\alpha(x, y)\, x \qquad (4.138)$$

By definition, a unit operating at the point $(x_\alpha^\partial(y), y) \in \Psi$ has a probability $H_{XY}(x_\alpha^\partial(y), y) = (1 - \alpha)S_Y(y) \leq 1 - \alpha$ of being dominated. Analogous to $\partial\Psi_m^{in}$, $x_\alpha^\partial(y)$ can be evaluated for all possible y to trace out an order-α input frontier, denoted $\partial\Psi_\alpha^{in}$.

The order-α efficiency concept comes with an important existence property. It can be proved that if $F_{X|Y}$ is continuous and monotone increasing in x, then, for all (x, y) in the interior of Ψ, there exists an $\alpha \in (0, 1]$ such that $\theta_\alpha(x, y) = 1$, where $\alpha = 1 - F_{X|Y}(x|y)$. In other words, any point (x, y) in the interior of Ψ belongs to some α-quantile input efficient frontier. Therefore, the value $\alpha = \alpha(x, y)$ such that $(x, y) \in \partial\Psi_\alpha^{in}$ (i.e., the value of α that defines an order-α frontier containing (x, y)) can be used as a new measure of input efficiency. Order-m frontiers do not have an analogous property, due to the discrete, integer-valued parameter m.

4.5.2.2 Nonparametric estimator

Here again, the plug-in principle can be used to obtain an intuitive, nonparametric estimator of $\theta_\alpha(x, y)$ replacing $F_{X|Y}(\cdot \mid \cdot)$ in (4.136) with its empirical counterpart to obtain

$$\widehat{\theta}_{\alpha,n}(x, y) = \inf\{\theta \mid \widehat{F}_{X|Y,n}(\theta x|y) > 1 - \alpha\}. \tag{4.139}$$

Computation of this estimator is very fast. An explicit analytical formula is available for the case $N = 1$ (see Aragon et al., 2005), and a simple algorithm for the multivariate case is given in Daouia and Simar (2007).

As for the estimator of the order-m efficiencies, this estimator does not envelop all the observed data in $\mathcal{X}_n$ when $\alpha < 1$. Hence, it is less sensitive to extreme points and to outliers than the traditional FDH and DEA estimators. This estimator also shares the same property as the corresponding population concept; that is, for a fixed sample size n, as $\alpha \to 1$, the order-α estimator converges to the usual FDH estimator of the full frontier. It is easy to prove that

$$\widehat{\theta}_{\alpha,n}(x, y) \searrow \widehat{\theta}_{FDH}(x, y) \text{ as } \alpha \to 1. \tag{4.140}$$

4.5.2.3 Statistical properties

Not surprisingly, the statistical properties of the order-α quantile estimators are very similar to those of the order-m estimators. In particular,

$$\sqrt{n}\left[\widehat{\theta}_{\alpha,n}(x, y) - \theta_\alpha(x, y)\right] \xrightarrow{d} \mathcal{N}(0, \sigma_\alpha^2(x, y)). \tag{4.141}$$

An expression is available for the variance term $\sigma_\alpha^2(x, y)$ (see Daouia and Simar, 2007, for details). Hence, the nonparametric order-α efficiency estimator is $\sqrt{n}$-consistent with an asymptotic normal distribution.

In addition, analogous to the order-m estimators, when $\alpha = \alpha(n) \to 1$ at an appropriate rate as $n \to \infty$,

$$n^{\frac{1}{N+M}}\left[\widehat{\theta}_{\alpha(n),n}(x, y) - \theta(x, y)\right] \xrightarrow{d} \text{Weibull}(\mu_{x,y}, N + M). \tag{4.142}$$

Hence, $\widehat{\theta}_{\alpha(n),n}(x, y)$ shares the same asymptotic property as the FDH estimator but, since the corresponding frontier does not envelop all the observed data points, $\widehat{\theta}_{\alpha(n),n}(x, y)$ is more robust to outliers in finite sample than is the FDH estimator.

4.5.2.4 Summary for the output-oriented case

For the output-oriented case, the order-α efficiency measure can be defined as follows:

Definition 4.5.4.

For all x such that $F_X(x) > 0$ and for $\alpha \in (0, 1]$, the α-quantile output efficiency score for the unit operating at $(x, y) \in \Psi$ is defined as

$$\lambda_\alpha(x, y) = \sup\{\lambda \mid S_{Y|X}(\lambda y \mid x) > 1 - \alpha\}. \tag{4.143}$$

If $\lambda_\alpha(x, y)(<, >)1$, then the output-oriented measure gives the proportionate (reduction, increase) in outputs needed to move a unit operating at $(x, y) \in \Psi$ in the output direction so that it is dominated by firms using less input (than the level x) with probability $1 - \alpha$.

Analogous to the input-oriented order-α efficiency measure, $\lambda_\alpha(x, y)$ converges monotonically to the Debreu-Farrell output efficiency measure; that is,

$$\lim_{\alpha \to 1} \nearrow \lambda_\alpha(x, y) = \lambda(x, y) \tag{4.144}$$

where "$\nearrow$" denotes monotonic convergence from below. Moreover, for all $(x, y) \in \Psi$, $(x, y) \notin \partial\Psi$, there exists an $\alpha \in (0, 1]$ such that $\lambda_\alpha(x, y) = 1$, where $\alpha = 1 - S_{Y|X}(y \mid x)$.

A nonparametric estimator of $\lambda_\alpha(x, y)$ is obtained by substituting the empirical counterpart of $S_{Y|X,n}(\cdot \mid \cdot)$ into (4.143) to obtain

$$\widehat{\lambda}_{\alpha,n}(x, y) = \sup\left\{\lambda \mid \widehat{S}_{Y|X,n}(\lambda y \mid x) > 1 - \alpha\right\}; \tag{4.145}$$

recall that $\widehat{S}_{Y|X,n}$ was defined in section 4.2.4. This estimator also has $\sqrt{n}$-convergence and asymptotic normality,

$$\sqrt{n}(\widehat{\lambda}_{\alpha,n}(x, y) - \lambda_\alpha(x, y)) \xrightarrow{d} N(0, \sigma_{\text{out}}^2(x, y)), \quad \text{as } n \to \infty, \tag{4.146}$$

and converges to the FDH estimator as $\alpha \to 1$:

$$\lim_{\alpha \to 1} \nearrow \widehat{\lambda}_{\alpha,n}(x, y) = \widehat{\lambda}_{\text{FDH}}(x, y) \tag{4.147}$$

Finally, $\widehat{\lambda}_{\alpha,n}(x, y)$ provides a robust estimator of the full-frontier efficiency scores: as $\alpha = \alpha(n) \to 1$ at an appropriate rate as $n \to \infty$,

$$n^{\frac{1}{N+M}} \left[\widehat{\lambda}_{\alpha(n),n}(x, y) - \lambda(x, y)\right] \xrightarrow{d} \text{Weibull}(\mu_{x,y}, N + M). \tag{4.148}$$

4.5.2.5 An example

Table 4.4 gives input-oriented FDH, α-quantile, and order-m efficiency estimates for the 37 European air traffic controllers introduced in section 4.3.5. The second column gives the number n_d of observations that dominate each observation. The third column gives the FDH efficiency estimate, while the next three columns give the α-quantile estimates for $\alpha = 0.90, 0.95$, and 0.99. The last three columns give the order-m estimates for $m = 10, 20$, and 150.

The results illustrate that, for the α-quantile estimator, increasing α toward unity moves the α-quantile efficiency estimates toward the FDH efficiency

Table 4.4
FDH, Order-α, and Order-m Efficiency Estimates for European Air Controllers

Observation	n_d	$\hat{\theta}_n$	$\hat{\theta}_{0.90,n}$	$\hat{\theta}_{0.95,n}$	$\hat{\theta}_{0.99,n}$	$\hat{\theta}_{10,n}$	$\hat{\theta}_{20,n}$	$\hat{\theta}_{150,n}$
1	4	0.8433	0.9645	0.9163	0.8433	0.9430	0.8887	0.8435
2	4	0.5941	0.7188	0.5941	0.5941	0.6737	0.6248	0.5941
3	3	0.7484	0.7484	0.7484	0.7484	0.7645	0.7517	0.7484
4	4	0.7261	0.9003	0.8481	0.7261	0.8879	0.8133	0.7268
5	6	0.7571	0.8658	0.8226	0.7571	0.8466	0.7996	0.7573
6	1	0.8561	1.0616	1.0000	0.8561	1.0453	0.9532	0.8568
7	0	1.0000	1.0889	1.0000	1.0000	1.1297	1.0392	1.0000
8	0	1.0000	1.1806	1.1436	1.0000	1.1630	1.0709	1.0001
9	0	1.0000	3.3728	1.9091	1.0000	2.5316	1.8318	1.0118
10	1	0.9453	1.0000	0.9453	0.9453	0.9979	0.9572	0.9453
11	4	0.6738	0.6956	0.6738	0.6738	0.7372	0.6903	0.6738
12	1	0.9419	0.9419	0.9419	0.9419	0.9564	0.9435	0.9419
13	1	0.9067	0.9067	0.9067	0.9067	0.9802	0.9222	0.9067
14	0	1.0000	1.0000	1.0000	1.0000	1.0006	1.0000	1.0000
15	1	0.6848	0.6848	0.6848	0.6848	0.7027	0.6858	0.6848
16	0	1.0000	1.0000	1.0000	1.0000	1.0163	1.0028	1.0000
17	2	0.6573	1.2548	0.9620	0.6573	1.3411	0.9627	0.6623
18	12	0.5025	0.6231	0.5870	0.5025	0.6170	0.5618	0.5030
19	5	0.5220	0.5757	0.5220	0.5220	0.5728	0.5337	0.5220
20	8	0.4951	0.5111	0.4951	0.4951	0.5463	0.5089	0.4951
21	1	0.7315	0.7315	0.7315	0.7315	0.7608	0.7346	0.7315
22	4	0.4969	0.9610	0.5631	0.4969	0.7928	0.6468	0.4977
23	6	0.6224	0.6425	0.6425	0.6224	0.6914	0.6417	0.6224
24	1	0.9134	1.1326	1.0000	0.9134	1.0780	0.9925	0.9141
25	0	1.0000	1.0323	1.0000	1.0000	1.0907	1.0217	1.0000
26	0	1.0000	1.0000	1.0000	1.0000	1.0130	1.0002	1.0000
27	0	1.0000	1.8207	1.5588	1.0000	1.6113	1.3676	1.0048
28	0	1.0000	1.3472	1.2399	1.0000	1.2650	1.1456	1.0008
29	0	1.0000	1.9341	1.1333	1.0000	1.6073	1.2972	1.0014
30	1	0.6832	1.4783	1.0000	0.6832	1.5329	1.0860	0.6879
31	7	0.6792	0.7767	0.7379	0.6792	0.7662	0.7157	0.6793
32	0	1.0000	1.0000	1.0000	1.0000	1.1614	1.0473	1.0000
33	0	1.0000	1.0000	1.0000	1.0000	1.0000	1.0000	1.0000
34	1	0.9204	1.0526	1.0000	0.9204	1.0355	0.9670	0.9205
35	3	0.8043	0.9041	0.8303	0.8043	0.8857	0.8291	0.8043
36	0	1.0000	1.1375	1.0000	1.0000	1.1455	1.0494	1.0000
37	0	1.0000	1.2100	1.0000	1.0000	1.1245	1.0454	1.0000
mean	2.2	0.8299	1.0610	0.9227	0.8299	1.0274	0.9224	0.8308

estimate. Similarly, for the order-m estimator, increasing m yields estimates increasingly close to the FDH efficiency estimate. Recall from figure 4.8 that observation 33 lies in a remote part of the sample space. Consequently, in table 4.4, this observation yields an efficiency estimate equal to one for each of the values of α and m that were considered. Put simply, since there are no other observations near unit 33, the sample contains no information that would allow us to gauge the efficiency of this unit. In terms of the discussion in chapter 1, this unit may represent "best practice," but this does not mean that it lies on the boundary of the production set.

4.5.3 Outlier detection

The traditional nonparametric, deterministic FDH and DEA frontier estimators are appealing because they rely on only a few mild assumptions. Their history in applied use is now long. Moreover, they estimate the full frontier $\partial \Psi$, rather than the partial frontiers described above. This feature, however, is a double-edged sword: By construction, FDH and DEA estimators are highly sensitive to extreme values and to outliers.

Outliers are atypical observations. Some outliers are the result of recording or measurement errors and should be corrected (if possible) or deleted from the data. Outliers might also appear in a given sample if, inadvertently, observations are drawn from different DGPs. If data are viewed as having come from a probability distribution, then it is quite possible to observe points with low probability. One would not expect to observe many such points given their low probability, and hence they appear as outliers. Cook and Weisberg (1982) observe that outliers of this type may lead to the recognition of important phenomena that might otherwise have gone unnoticed; in some cases, such outliers may be the most interesting part of the data.

Since FDH and DEA estimators continue to be used, outlier detection is of vital importance. In simple, bivariate scenarios where $N = M = 1$, one could merely look at a scatter plot to find any outliers that might exist. Unfortunately, in higher dimensions, detecting outliers is much more difficult. Although there is a large literature in statistics and econometrics on outlier detection, most methods that have been proposed were designed for the problem of conditional mean estimation and do not take aspects of frontier models into account (see Wilson, 1993, for discussion). In the frontier setting, the most worrisome outliers are those that have undue influence on the estimated efficiencies of other observations. Many of the standard methods for outlier detection are also very computer intensive in multivariate settings.

A relatively small number of outlier-detection methods have been proposed specifically for the context of frontier estimation. It is unlikely that a single method will be able to find all outliers in all instances when the number of dimensions is large. Consequently, many have argued that several methods should be employed on a given data set. All outlier-detection methods should be viewed as diagnostic tools; the goal is to first identify a small set of observations for further scrutiny (for further discussion, see Wilson, 1993; Olesen et al., 1996, Simar, 2007).

Wilson (1995) proposed a procedure similar to jackknife estimation, wherein observations are deleted one at a time, with efficiency for the remaining $(n - 1)$ observations reestimated with each deletion to gauge the influence of each observation on the estimated efficiencies of other observations in the sample. The process is then repeated, deleting pairs of observations, then repeated again while deleting triplets, and so forth, in order to uncover *masking* effects. Masking occurs when two (or more) outliers lie close to each other; removing only one of these will not reveal undue influence, which can be discovered only if the entire *group* of nearby outliers is removed. Although effective, the number of linear program solutions that must be obtained to implement the Wilson (1995) procedure if pairs, triplets, and so on, are deleted grows combinatorially with sample size. The procedure becomes very costly in terms of required computational time as the sample size becomes large and, consequently, is not practical for use with samples larger than a few hundred observations.

Wilson (1993) proposed another method employing an influence function based on the geometric volume spanned by the sample observations and the sensitivity of this volume with respect to deletions of singletons, pairs, triplets and so forth, from the sample. Some notation is required to explain the method. For a value ξ computed from a set of observations indexed by $S = \{1, \ldots, n\}$, let $D_L^{(\ell)}(\xi)$ denote the value computed similarly from observations with indices $S - L$, where $L \subset S$ and L contains ℓ elements, $\ell < n$. Let $\bar{D}_L^{(\ell)}(\xi)$ denote the value computed similarly from observations only in L; for example, $D_L^{(\ell)}(\xi) = \bar{D}_{S-L}^{(\ell)}(\xi)$. For any matrix $\mathbf{A}$ of full column rank, let $D^{(\ell)}(|\mathbf{A}|)$ denote the determinant of the matrix $D^{(\ell)}(\mathbf{A})$.

Let X be an $(N \times n)$ matrix of observations on n input vectors, and Y be an $(M \times n)$ matrix of observations on the corresponding output vectors. Then add a row of ones to X by defining the $((N+1) \times n)$ matrix $\mathbf{Z} = \begin{bmatrix} 1 & X' \end{bmatrix}'$. Define the $((N + M + 1) \times n)$ partitioned matrix $\mathbf{Z}^* = \begin{bmatrix} \mathbf{Z}' & \mathbf{Y}' \end{bmatrix}'$. For the case of M outputs, $M \geq 1$, $|\mathbf{Z}^* \mathbf{Z}^{*\prime}| = |\mathbf{ZZ}'| \cdot |\mathbf{YY}' - \mathbf{YZ}'B|$ with $B = (\mathbf{ZZ}')^{-1}\mathbf{ZY}'$. For $j, k = 1, \ldots, M$, $Y_j Y_k' - Y_j Z' b_k = Y_j (Y_k' - Z' b_k) = Y_j e_k' = Y_j M_Z Y_k' = Y_j M_Z' M_Z Y_k' = e_j e_k'$, where M_Z is the idempotent matrix $(I - Z'(ZZ')^{-1}Z)$ and e_j, e_k are ordinary least squares (OLS) residuals from the regressions of Y_j', Y_k' on Z'. Then, $|\mathbf{Z}^* \mathbf{Z}^{*\prime}| = |\mathbf{ZZ}'| \times |\mathbf{YY}' - \mathbf{YZ}'B| = |\mathbf{ZZ}'| \times |\mathbf{\Omega}|$, where $\mathbf{\Omega} = [e_j e_k']$, $j, k = 1, \ldots, q$. The statistic

$$R_L^{(\ell)}(\mathbf{Z}^*) = D_L^{(\ell)}\left(|\mathbf{Z}'\mathbf{Z}|\right)|\mathbf{Z}'\mathbf{Z}|^{-1}\left[D_L^{(\ell)}(|\mathbf{\Omega}|)\right]|\mathbf{\Omega}|^{-1} \tag{4.149}$$

represents the proportion of the geometric volume in $(N + M + 1)$ space spanned by a subset of the data obtained by deleting the ℓ observations with indices in the set L, relative to the volume spanned by the entire set of n observations.

Wilson (1993) discusses a statistical procedure for deriving significance levels for the statistic defined in (4.149), and also describes a graphical analysis where log-ratios $\log\left[R_L^{(\ell)}(\mathbf{Z}^*)/R_{\min}^{(\ell)}\right]$, where $R_{\min}^{(\ell)} = \min_L\left\{R_L^{(\ell)}(\mathbf{Z}^{*\prime})\right\}$, are plotted as a function of ℓ, the number of observations deleted. This method is implemented in the *FEAR* software package described by Wilson (2007). [See Wilson (1993) for further details and empirical examples].

Simar (2007) proposed an outlier detection strategy using the ideas of partial frontiers developed in the preceding sections. If a sample observation remains outside the order-m frontier as m increases or, alternatively, outside the order-α frontier as α increases, then such an observation may be an outlier. The procedure is implemented by first computing, for each sample observation (x_i, y_i), $i = 1, \ldots, n$, the leave-one-out order-m efficiencies $\widehat{\theta}_{m,n}^{(i)}(x_i, y_i)$ for several values of m, for example, $m \in \{10, 25, 50, 75, 00, 150, \ldots\}$, where $\widehat{\theta}_{m,n}^{(i)}(x_i, y_i)$ denotes the order-m efficiency estimate for the ith observation computed after deleting the ith observation. Next, the percentage of points lying outside the order-m frontier [identified by values $\widehat{\theta}_{m,n}^{(i)}(x_i, y_i) > 1$ in the input orientation, or $\widehat{\lambda}_{m,n}^{(i)}(x_i, y_i) < 1$ in the output orientation] can be plotted as a function of m; the resulting points can be connected by line segments to form a piecewise-linear relationship that is necessarily downward sloping due to the properties of the order-m estimator. If there are no outliers in the data set, the plotted relationship should be nearly linear. If the graph shows an elbow effect (i.e., a sharp bend, with large negative slope becoming much less negative at a particular value of m), firms remaining outside the order-m frontier for the value of m where the sharp bend occurs are likely outliers and should be carefully scrutinized for data errors, and so on. The analysis can be performed using both input- and output-oriented perspectives to detect potential outliers in both directions.

This method requires that threshold values be chosen for deciding when the values $\widehat{\theta}_{m,n}^{(i)}(x_i, y_i)$ or $\widehat{\lambda}_{m,n}^{(i)}(x_i, y_i)$ are significantly greater or less than one. Ideally, these threshold values should be computed from the asymptotic standard deviations of the estimators. However, to make the procedure simple and easy to compute, Simar (2007) suggests producing several diagnostic plots as described above using percentages of points with $\widehat{\theta}_{m,n}^{(i)}(x_i, y_i) > 1 + \zeta$ or $\widehat{\lambda}_{m,n}^{(i)}(x_i, y_i) > 1 - \zeta$ with several small, arbitrary values of ζ; for example, $\zeta \in \{0, 0.05, 0.10, 0.15, 0.20, \ldots\}$.

Although the method proposed by Simar (2007) does not explicitly address the possibility of masking among outliers, if only a small number of outliers lie close to each other, the robustness properties of the order-m estimator makes it likely that these will be detected. Once an initial set of outliers has been identified, the analysis could be repeated after deleting the initial set of outliers. The method is implemented in the *FEAR* package (Wilson, 2007); in addition, Matlab code for the procedure and several examples are provided in Simar (2007).

4.6 Explaining Efficiencies

For many years, researchers have sought to explain differences in estimated efficiencies across firms. Often, researchers have in mind a set of environmental factors that might be related to efficiency differences; these factors might reflect differences in ownership type or structure, regulatory constraints, business environment, competition, and so on, among the firms under analysis. Typically, such factors are viewed as possibly affecting the production process, but not under the control of firms' managers. Understanding how such factors might be related to efficiency is important for determining how firms' performances might be improved. In addition, from a public policy perspective, understanding these relationships is important for assessing the costs of regulation.

One approach (e.g., Coelli et al., 1998) is to augment the model introduced in section 4.1.1 by treating the (continuous) environmental factors z as free disposal inputs or outputs that contribute to defining the attainable set $\Psi \subset \mathcal{R}_+^N \times \mathcal{R}_+^M \times \mathcal{R}^R$, and to modify the efficiency scores defined in (4.5) and (4.9) to reflect the view that the environmental variables are beyond managers' control. For example, the analog of (4.5) would be

$$\theta(x, y \mid z) = \inf\{\theta \mid (\theta x, y, z) \in \Psi\}. \tag{4.150}$$

The FDH and DEA estimators of Ψ in this case would be defined as before after adding the variables z and treating them as either inputs or outputs (if z is a vector of variables, some elements of z might be treated as inputs, while others might be treated as outputs).

There are at least two drawbacks to this approach. First, one must decide a priori what the role of z is; in other words, do the variables contained in z contribute to, or hinder, production of quantities y? Second, free disposability is assumed when FDH or DEA estimators are used; in addition, convexity of Ψ is also assumed when DEA estimators are employed. For many environmental variables, it is difficult to find arguments for why these assumptions might be appropriate.

When discrete, categorical factors are considered (e.g., for-profit vs. nonprofit organizations, private vs. public ownership, etc.), the categorical variables effectively divide producers into different groups. If there are R binary, discrete categorical variables, then there are potentially 2^R different groups represented among the n sample observations. In this case, it is straightforward to adapt the bootstrap methods described in section 4.3.7 for testing hypothesis about differences in average efficiency, and so forth, across groups to make comparisons among the 2^R implied groups of firms. One might test, for example, whether the various groups face the same technology, or whether the distributions of efficiencies are the same across groups if they do face the same technology.

When the environmental variables z are continuous, observations are not grouped into a small number of categories. In this section, two approaches for investigating the effects of continuous environmental variables on efficiency are discussed. The first is based on a two-stage approach that has been widely used in the literature but too often with dubious specifications and invalid inference. The second approach was recently proposed by Daraio and Simar (2005) and involves an extension of the techniques in section 4.5.1 for estimating partial frontiers.

4.6.1 Two-stage regression approach

A plethora of papers have employed a two-stage approach wherein nonparametric, DEA efficiency estimates are regressed on continuous environmental variables in a parametric, second-stage analysis. The idea is widespread: The Internet search engine Google.com reported approximately 1,500 results using the key words "dea," "two-stage," and "efficiency" on January 27, 2005, while the key words "dea" and "tobit" yielded approximately 825 results; in addition, Simar and Wilson (2007) cite 47 published papers that use this approach.

Apparently, *none* of the papers written to date that have regressed DEA or FDH efficiency estimates in a second-stage model, with the exception of Simar and Wilson (2007), defines a DGP that would make a second-stage regression sensible. In addition, to our knowledge, inference on the parameters of the second-stage regressions is invalid in these papers.

Simar and Wilson (2007) define a DGP that provides a rational basis for regressing efficiency estimates in a second-stage analysis. In addition, they suggest bootstrap procedures to provide valid inference in the second-stage regression, as well as to increase the efficiency of estimation there. Monte Carlo experiments confirm the improvements.

4.6.1.1 A DGP with environmental variables

The basic DGPs defined in section 4.2.1 must be modified to incorporate the role of environmental variables Z that may influence the production process. Here, $X \in \mathcal{R}_+^N$, $Y \in \mathcal{R}_+^M$, and $Z \in \mathcal{R}^R$ (the elements of Z may be continuous or discrete). A sample $\mathcal{S}_n = \{(x_i, y_i, z_i)\}_{i=1}^n$ is observed but, of course, Ψ remains unknown. Replace assumption 4.2.1 with the following assumption:

Assumption 4.6.1.

The sample observations (x_i, y_i, z_i) in $\mathcal{S}_n$ are iid realizations of random variables (X, Y, Z) with probability density function $f(x, y, z)$, which has support $\Psi \times \mathcal{R}^R$, where Ψ is the production set as defined in (4.1) with $\text{prob}((X, Y) \in \Psi) = 1$.

Note that assumption 4.6.1.1 introduces a separability condition between the production space for inputs inputs and outputs, Ψ, and the space of the environmental variables. In other words, the variables Z do not influence the shape or boundary of Ψ; they lie in a space apart from Ψ. This is a rather restrictive assumption, but this is implicit (but not stated) in all the two-stage regression approaches that exist to date. The alternative approach described in section 4.6.2 avoids this assumption. Of course, in any interesting case, Z is not independent with respect to (X, Y); that is, $f(x, y \mid z) \neq f(x, y)$. However, Z may influence efficiency.

For purposes of illustration, the presentation that follows is in terms of the output orientation. We make the presentation here in the output-oriented case, where for some point $(x, y) \in \mathscr{R}_+^{M+N}$, the goal is to estimate the Debreu-Farrell output measure of efficiency $\lambda = \lambda(x, y)$ defined in (4.9). Recall that for all $(x, y) \in \Psi, \lambda(x, y) \geq 1$.

The following assumption makes explicit the mechanism by which the environmental variables influence efficiency:

Assumption 4.6.2.

The conditioning in $f(\lambda_i \mid z_i)$ operates through the following mechanism:

$$\lambda_i = \lambda(x_i, y_i) = \beta' z_i + \varepsilon_i \geq 1 \qquad (4.151)$$

where β is a vector of parameters, and ε_i is a continuous iid random variable, independent of z_i.

The inequality in (4.151) results in a truncated linear regression model. Of course, other specifications are possible in assumption 4.6.1.1; the model could be made nonlinear or semi- or nonparametric. To make the second stage fully parametric, as has been done in all examples known to the authors, a distributional assumption is required for the error term in (4.151). A normality assumption is adopted here, but other assumptions are also possible:

Assumption 4.6.3.

The error term ε_i in (4.151) is distributed $N(0, \sigma_\varepsilon^2)$ with left-truncation at $1 - \beta' z_i$ for each i.

Assumptions 4.6.1–4.6.3 complement assumptions 4.2.2–4.2.7 from section 4.2.1 to define a DGP that allows environmental variables to influence firms' efficiencies, thus providing a rationale for the two-stage approach. The separability condition 4.6.1 is the most severe among the new assumptions; this assumption creates the need for the second-stage regression. The other new assumptions merely define how the second-stage model should be estimated, and thus could be modified at little cost.

4.6.1.2 Typical two-stage approaches

Let $\widehat{\lambda}_i$, $i = 1, \ldots, n$ denote estimates of the Debreu-Farrell output efficiency measure for observations in S_n; these estimates are based on estimates of $\widehat{\Psi}$ of Ψ and could be obtained from DEA, FDH, LFDH, or perhaps other estimators. Most of the two-stage studies that have appeared in the literature have regressed the $\widehat{\lambda}_i$ on the z_i using censored (tobit) regression. A number have argued that censored regression techniques are appropriate due to the mass of estimates $\widehat{\lambda}_i$ equal to one. This is nonsense.

Under the DGP defined by assumptions 4.2.2–4.2.7 and 4.6.1–4.6.3, the model to be estimated in the second stage, (4.151), involves a truncated, rather than censored, error term. Of course, one might drop assumption 4.2.2 and instead assume that $f(x, y)$ has a mass along the frontier $\partial \Psi$, but none of the two-stage papers has made such an assumption. In addition, if one were to adopt such an assumption, tobit regression would still be inappropriate unless one also assumed that the process governing whether $\lambda_i = 1$ or $\lambda_i > 1$ depends on the same $\beta' z_i$ that determines the magnitude of λ_i when $\lambda_i > 1$; otherwise, one should estimate a generalized censored regression model in the second stage (see the appendix in Simar and Wilson, 2003, for details). Moreover, if one were to assume that $f(x, y)$ possesses a mass along the frontier $\partial \Psi$, there are likely more efficient methods of estimation for the first stage than FDH or DEA, which do not incorporate such information.

A few of the existing two-stage papers have used OLS in the second-stage regression after transforming the bounded estimates of efficiency using log, logistic, or log-normal transformations, and in some cases adding or subtracting an arbitrary constant to avoid division by zero or taking the log of zero. Still others have used in the first-stage estimation a leave-one-out estimator of efficiency originally suggested by Andersen and Petersen (1993). Unfortunately, however, it is difficult to give a statistical interpretation to this estimator, even if the second-stage regressions are ignored. Still others have regressed ratios of efficiency estimates, Malmquist indices, or differences in efficiency estimates in the second stage; these have avoided boundary problems but have still not provided a coherent description of a DGP that would make such regressions sensible.

Even if the true, truncated normal regression model in (4.151) were estimated a second stage using the method of maximum likelihood to obtain maximum likelihood estimators (MLEs) of β and σ, the usual, conventional method of inference (based on the Cramér-Rao theorem and involving variance estimates obtained from the inverse of the negative Hessian of the log-likelihood function) is flawed.

The problems arise from the fact that the dependent variable λ_i in (4.151) is unobserved and must be replaced by an estimate $\widehat{\lambda}_i$, yielding

$$\widehat{\lambda}_i \approx z_i \beta + \varepsilon_i \geq 1. \tag{4.152}$$

Unfortunately, however,

- $\widehat{\lambda}_i$ is a biased estimator of λ_i;
- the $\widehat{\lambda}_i$ are serially correlated, in a complicated, unknown way; and
- since x_i and y_i are correlated with z_i, the error term ε_i is correlated with z_i.

The correlation among the $\widehat{\lambda}_i$ values arises for much the same reason that estimated residuals in linear regression problems are correlated, even if the true residuals are not. In the regression case, perturbing a single observation will affect the slope of the estimated regression line, and hence affect the estimated residuals for all observations. Also in the regression case, this phenomenon disappears quickly as the sample size n increases (see Maddala, 1988, pp. 409–411 for discussion). Similarly, in the DEA case, perturbing an observation on the estimated frontier (or any other observation, if it is perturbed enough, and in the right direction) will cause the estimated frontier to shift, thereby affecting estimated efficiencies for some, perhaps all, of the other observations.

Both the correlation among the ε_i values as well as the correlation between ε_i and z_i disappear asymptotically, although only at the same slow rate with which $\widehat{\lambda}_i$ converges and not at the usual $\sqrt{n}$-rate achieved by MLEs in standard parametric truncated regression models. Hence, MLEs for β and σ are consistent. Conventional inference, however, is based on a second-order Taylor approximation; the slow rate with which the serial correlation among the $\widehat{\lambda}_i$ disappears means that higher order terms cannot be disregarded, and hence conventional inference will be invalid in this setting.

In addition, the fact that $\widehat{\lambda}_i$ is a biased estimator of λ_i suggests that MLEs of the parameters in (4.151) may also be biased and perhaps inefficient in a statistical sense, since the MLEs are nonlinear due to the truncation. These problems might be mitigated by constructing bias-corrected estimates

$$\widehat{\widehat{\lambda}}_i = \widehat{\lambda}_i - \widehat{\text{bias}}(\widehat{\lambda}_i)$$

and using these to replace λ_i in (4.151), yielding

$$\widehat{\widehat{\lambda}}_i \approx z_i \beta + \varepsilon_i \geq 1, \tag{4.153}$$

and then estimating this model in the second stage instead of estimating (4.152).

The bootstrap methods described in section 4.3.3 can be used to construct the bias-corrected estimator $\widehat{\widehat{\lambda}}_i$. A second, parametric bootstrap can then be used to obtain valid confidence interval estimates for the parameters in the second-stage regression. The entire procedure, developed in Simar and Wilson (2007), consists of the following steps:

1. Using the original data $\mathcal{S}$, compute $\widehat{\lambda}_i = \widehat{\lambda}(x_i, y_i)$, $i = 1, \ldots, n$, by DEA.
2. Compute MLEs $\widehat{\beta}$ and $\widehat{\sigma}_\varepsilon$ from the (left normal) truncated regression of $\widehat{\lambda}_i$ on z_i (use only estimates $\widehat{\lambda}_i > 1$ in this step).

3. Loop over the next four steps (3.1–3.4) L_1 times to obtain
$\mathcal{B}_i = \{\widehat{\lambda}^*_{ib}\}^{L_1}_{b=1}, i = 1, \ldots, n$:
   3.1. For $i = 1, \ldots, n$, draw ε^*_i from $N(0, \widehat{\sigma}_\varepsilon)$ with left truncation at $(1 - \widehat{\beta}' z_i)$.
   3.2. Compute $\lambda^*_i = \widehat{\beta}' z_i + \varepsilon^*_i, i = 1, \ldots, n$.
   3.3. Set $x^*_i = x_i, \; y^*_i = y_i \widehat{\lambda}_i / \lambda^*_i$ for all $i = 1, \ldots, n$.
   3.4. Compute $\widehat{\lambda}^*_i = \lambda(x_i, y_i \mid \widehat{\Psi}^*), i = 1, \ldots, n$, where $\widehat{\Psi}^*$ is obtained by replacing (x_i, y_i) by (x^*_i, y^*_i).

4. Compute the bias-corrected estimator $\widehat{\widehat{\lambda}}_i$ using the bootstrap estimates in $\mathcal{B}_i$ and the original estimate $\widehat{\lambda}_i$.

5. Estimate (by maximum likelihood) the truncated regression of $\widehat{\widehat{\lambda}}_i$ on z_i, yielding $(\widehat{\widehat{\beta}}, \widehat{\widehat{\sigma}})$.

6. Loop over the next three steps (6.1–6.3) L_2 times to obtain a set of bootstrap estimates $\mathcal{C} = \{(\widehat{\widehat{\beta}}^*, \widehat{\widehat{\sigma}}^*_\varepsilon)_b\}^{L_2}_{b=1}$:
   6.1 For $i = 1, \ldots, n$, draw ε^{**}_i from $N(0, \widehat{\widehat{\sigma}})$ with left truncation at $(1 - \widehat{\widehat{\beta}}' z_i)$.
   6.2. Compute $\lambda^{**}_i = \widehat{\widehat{\beta}}' z_i + \varepsilon^{**}_i, i = 1, \ldots, n$.
   6.3. Estimate (by maximum likelihood) the truncated regression of λ^{**}_i on z_i, yielding estimates $(\widehat{\widehat{\beta}}^*, \widehat{\widehat{\sigma}}^*)$.

7. Use the bootstrap values in $\mathcal{C}$ and the original estimates $\widehat{\widehat{\beta}}, \widehat{\widehat{\sigma}}$ to construct estimated confidence intervals for β and σ_ε.

Note that in a truncated-normal regression model, with left truncation at 1, the probability of observations on the left-hand side variable equal to one is zero. Hence, in step 2 of the algorithm above, only the estimates from step 1 that are strictly greater than 1 are used to obtain estimates of the parameters of the truncated regression model; for purposes of the truncated regression, the estimates from step 1 equal to one are spurious. These parameter estimates obtained in step 2 are then used in steps 3–4 to produce n pseudovalues $\widehat{\widehat{\lambda}}_i$ that are used in step 5.

Monte Carlo experiments reported in Simar and Wilson (2007) indicate that existing two-stage methods using tobit result in catastrophe both for estimation as well as inference. The experiments also suggest that the double bootstrap described above performs very well, in terms of both coverage for estimated confidence intervals and root mean square error.

4.6.2 Conditional Efficiency Measures

Daraio and Simar (2005) extend the ideas of Cazals et al. (2002) by proposing an intuitive way to introduce environmental factors into the production process, by defining a conditional efficiency measure. The approach requires neither an a priori assumption on the effect of Z on efficiency as in existing one-stage approaches, nor a separability condition as required by the two-stage approach. The approach follows from the probabilistic formulation of the production process described in section 4.2.4 that was used for defining the partial frontiers of section 4.5.

Recall that the production process is characterized by a joint probability measure of (X, Y) on $\mathcal{R}_+^N \times \mathcal{R}_+^M$ generating observations $\{(x_i, y_i)\}$, $i = 1, \ldots, n$, where the support of (X, Y) is the attainable set Ψ. Recall also that under the free-disposability assumption, the input-oriented Debreu-Farrell efficiency measure can be defined in terms of the conditional distribution function where $F_{X|Y}(x \mid y) = \text{prob}(X \leq x \mid Y \geq y)$ as in (4.31) (and that the output-oriented Debreu-Farrell efficiency measure can be defined analogously as in (4.32)). The corresponding FDH estimator can be defined in terms of the empirical analog of (4.31), as was done in (4.35) and (4.37).

Environmental variables can be introduced by conditioning on $Z = z$ and considering the joint distribution of (X, Y) conditioned on $Z = z$. A conditional measure of efficiency for a firm operating at the levels $(x, y) \in \Psi$ under the environmental conditions implied by $Z = z$ may be defined by

$$\theta(x, y \mid z) = \inf\{\theta \mid F_{X|Y}(\theta x \mid y, z) > 0\}, \qquad (4.154)$$

where $F_{X|Y}(x \mid y, z) = \text{prob}(X \leq x \mid Y \geq y, Z = z)$. The conditioning is on both $Y \geq y$ and $Z = z$; there are no a priori assumptions on Z (e.g., Z acting as a free disposal input, or as an undesired, freely disposable output).

A nonparametric estimator of this conditional efficiency measure is obtained by plugging a nonparametric estimator of $F_{X|Y}(x|y, z)$ into (4.154). Due to the conditioning on $Z = z$, this requires some smoothing of z, which is accomplished by adding a kernel-type estimator to the empirical distribution function to obtain

$$\widehat{F}_{X,n}(x \mid y, z) = \frac{\sum_{i=1}^n \mathscr{I}(x_i \leq x, \ y_i \geq y) K\left(\frac{z - z_i}{h}\right)}{\sum_{i=1}^n \mathscr{I}(y_i \geq y) K\left(\frac{z - z_i}{h}\right)}, \qquad (4.155)$$

where $K(\cdot)$ is a kernel function and h is a bandwidth of appropriate size.

The *conditional* FDH efficiency measure is now defined as

$$\widehat{\theta}_n(x, y \mid z) = \inf\{\theta \mid \widehat{F}_{X|Y,n}(\theta x \mid y, z) > 0\}. \qquad (4.156)$$

Details for computing this estimator, and in particular for choosing the bandwidth, are given in Daraio and Simar (2005). As observed there, for kernels with unbounded support (e.g., the Gaussian kernel), $\widehat{\theta}_n(x, y \mid z) \equiv \widehat{\theta}_{\text{FDH}}(x, y)$; hence, only kernels such as the Epanechnikov kernel in (4.79) that have compact support (e.g., $K(u) = 0 \ \forall u \notin [0, 1]$) can be used. When the kernel function has compact support, the estimator $\widehat{\theta}_n(x, y \mid z)$ can be written as

$$\widehat{\theta}_n(x, y \mid z) = \min_{\{i \mid y_i \geq y, \; |z_i - z| \leq h\}} \left(\max_{j=1,\dots,N} \frac{x_i^j}{x^j} \right). \qquad (4.157)$$

This estimator provides a tool for investigating the effect of a particular factor Z on the production process by comparing $\widehat{\theta}_n(x, y \mid z)$ with $\widehat{\theta}_{\mathrm{FDH}}(x, y)$. Daraio and Simar (2005) propose regressing the ratios $\widehat{\theta}_n(x, y \mid z)/\widehat{\theta}_{\mathrm{FDH}}(x, y)$ nonparametrically on the observed z values (e.g., using a Nadarya-Watson or local linear estimator); if the resulting regression curve is increasing, Z is detrimental (unfavorable) to efficiency, and if the regression curve is decreasing, Z is conducive (favorable) to efficiency.

Indeed, if Z is unfavorable, the environmental variable acts as an "extra," *undesired* output requiring the use of more inputs in production activity, and hence Z has an adverse effect on the production process. By construction, $\widehat{\theta}_n(x, y \mid z)$ is always larger than $\widehat{\theta}_{\mathrm{FDH}}(x, y)$, but if Z is unfavorable, $\widehat{\theta}_n(x, y \mid z)$ will be much larger than $\widehat{\theta}_{\mathrm{FDH}}(x, y)$ for large values of Z than for small values of Z. Hence, if Z is unfavorable, the ratios $\widehat{\theta}_n(x, y \mid z)/\widehat{\theta}_{\mathrm{FDH}}(x, y)$ will, on average, increase with Z.

On the other hand, if Z is favorable to the production process, then the environmental variable plays the role of a "substitutive" input in the production process, providing an opportunity to conserve input quantities x while producing y. In this case, Z has a positive effect on the production process, and the ratios $\widehat{\theta}_n(x, y \mid z)/\widehat{\theta}_{\mathrm{FDH}}(x, y)$ will, on average, decrease when Z increases.

Conceivably, one might discover situations where the ratios are, on average, increasing with z for some range of values of z, neutral for another range, and then perhaps decreasing for still another range of values of z. Because the method is fully nonparametric, it is flexible enough to detect various possibilities. Daraio and Simar (2005) illustrate the method with simulated data, confirming the method's usefulness and its ability to detect the true effect of Z on the production process.

Of course, the ideas here easily adapt to the output-oriented case. Daraio and Simar (2005) have adapted the method to the robust order-m efficiency scores, and Daraio and Simar (2007) have extended the idea to convex technologies, introducing conditional DEA efficiency scores along the same lines as the conditional FDH scores discussed here.

4.7 Parametric Approximations of Nonparametric Frontier

4.7.1 Parametric versus nonparametric models

Nonparametric estimators are very appealing because they rely on only a small number of (typically) innocuous assumptions; no particular shape for the attainable set and its frontier must be assumed, nor must one make any particular distributional assumptions for the distribution of (X, Y) on the production set Ψ. Their great flexibility makes these models attractive, but the flexibility comes with a cost. It is more difficult to interpret the estimators in terms of the sensitivity of the production of the output to particular inputs, or to infer the shape of production function, elasticities, and so on, than is the case with parametric approaches. Also, even if inference is available, it is frequently more difficult to implement than with typical parametric models. Finally, when using full frontier estimators (DEA or FDH), the curse of dimensionality makes life difficult. On the other hand, a parametric form for the production function allows easier, perhaps richer, economic interpretation and is often easier to estimate. But the parametric specification must be a reasonable approximation of the underlying true model.[7]

In parametric approaches, a parametric family of functions must be defined. Here, to illustrate, a parametric family of production functions is defined on $\mathscr{R}_+^N$:

$$\{\varphi(\cdot \mid \theta) \mid \theta \in \Theta \subseteq \mathscr{R}^k\}, \tag{4.158}$$

where the production frontier $\varphi(\cdot; \theta)$ can be written as a fully specified analytical function depending on a finite number k of parameters θ.[8] Then, the parametric model can be written as

$$Y = \varphi(X \mid \theta) - U, \tag{4.159}$$

where $U \geq 0$, with probability one, and the random variables (X, Y) have joint probability distribution function $F(x, y)$. As in all cases, the goal is to to estimate this model from a random sample of observations, $\mathcal{X}_n = \{(x_i, y_i) \mid i = 1, \ldots, n\}$.

The basic parametric approaches for deterministic models for production (or cost) functions date to the work of Aigner and Chu (1968), who proposed mathematical programs to define what are sometimes called "mathematical programming" frontier estimators. Aigner and Chu (1968) proposed estimating the model, in the linear case where $\varphi(x \mid \theta) = \alpha + \beta' x$, by solving either the constrained linear program

$$\min_{\alpha, \beta} \sum_{i=1}^{n} |y_i - \alpha - \beta' x_i| \tag{4.160}$$

$$\text{s.t. } y_i \leq \alpha + \beta' x_i, \ i = 1, \ldots, n$$

or the constrained quadratic program

$$\min_{\alpha, \beta} \sum_{i=1}^{n} (y_i - \alpha - \beta' x_i)^2 \tag{4.161}$$

$$\text{s.t. } y_i \leq \alpha + \beta' x_i, \ i = 1, \ldots, n.$$

Their method is interesting since it does not imply any distributional assumptions, but apparently no statistical properties have been developed (so far) for the estimators of θ. Consequently, no inference (even asymptotically) is available. Without first establishing consistency of the estimator of θ, even a bootstrap procedure would be questionable. In addition, the method of Aigner and Chu suffers from the problem that observations far from the frontier will have much more weight in the objective function (especially in the quadratic case) than observations near the frontier. Apart from the lack of intuition for this feature, the estimator is not robust with respect to outliers that may lie far from the frontier into the interior of Ψ, in addition to outliers in the other direction that also plague FDH and DEA estimators.

Another set of approaches based on the work of Greene (1980) has been developed in the econometric literature. These consist of "regression-type" frontier estimators, using either least-squares methods adapted to the frontier setting (shifted and modified OLS) or maximum likelihood methods. In certain situations, shifting the regression function is very sensible. For example, if U is independent of X, then from (4.159),

$$E(Y \mid X = x) = \varphi(x \mid \theta) - E(U \mid X = x). \qquad (4.162)$$

So, estimating the conditional mean $E(Y \mid X = x)$ by regressing Y on X and then adding an estimate (i.e., shifting) $E(U \mid X = x)$ should produce a reasonable estimate of the frontier function $\varphi(x \mid \theta)$. Greene (1980) proposes a shifted OLS procedure to estimate (4.159) in the linear case where $\theta = (\alpha, \beta)$. The idea is to estimate the slope β by OLS and then shift the resulting estimated hyperplane upward so that all the residuals are negative. This defines the estimator of α that under Greene's conditions (independence between U and X) is proved to be consistent.

When specifying a parametric family of distributions for U, independent of X, Greene also proposes a modified OLS and an MLE of (α, β): The modified OLS corrects the OLS estimator of α by taking the particular conditions on the first moments of U into account, derived from the chosen family of distribution functions, to estimate the shift $E(U)$. Greene shows that, for a gamma distribution of U, the MLE shares its traditional sampling properties, if the shape parameter of the gamma distribution is large enough, to avoid unknown boundary problems.

The usefulness of this approach is limited by the strong restrictions on the distribution of (X, U) (e.g., independence between U and X) for all the proposed estimators (or at least $E(U|X = x) = \mu$ for shifted OLS) and restrictions on the shape of $f(u)$ when the corrected OLS and/or the MLE estimators are used. The required independence between X and U is especially problematic. Since $U \geq 0$, if the variance of U depends on X, which is quite likely in any application, then necessarily the mean of U must also depend on X; for any one-sided distribution, there is necessarily a direct link between the first and second moments.

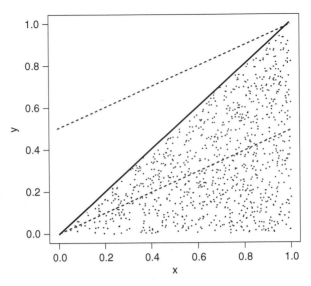

Figure 4.17. Shifted OLS Estimate of the Frontier

To make the point more clearly, suppose Ψ is the unit triangle with vertices at $(0,0), (1,0)$, and $(1,1)$, and suppose $f(x,y)$ is uniform over Ψ. Then, simple algebra reveals that $f(Y \mid X) = X^{-1} \; \forall \; X \in [0,1]$ and $Y \in [0,X]$, and $E(Y \mid X) = \frac{1}{2}X$. Estimating the implied regression model

$$y_i = \beta x_i + v_i \qquad (4.163)$$

by OLS and then taking $\widehat{\beta} + \max(\widehat{v}_1, \ldots, \widehat{v}_n)$ as an estimate of the frontier function (which has slope equal to one and contains $(0,0)$ and $(1,1)$ results in something silly. This is illustrated in figure 4.17, where 1,000 observations from the DGP described above are plotted, along with a solid line showing the boundary of Ψ and dashed lines indicating the conditional mean estimate obtained with OLS and the frontier estimate resulting from shifting the conditional mean regression estimate by $\max(\widehat{v}_1, \ldots, \widehat{v}_n)$. The problem is that the errors in (4.163) are heteroskedastic (it is easy to show that $\text{Var}(v \mid x) = x^2/12$), and due to the one-sided nature of the errors when the model is written in terms of a frontier model as in (4.159), x and v are not independent. Any estimation procedure will capture the shape of the middle of the cloud of data points but is not a natural approach in the context of frontier estimation; it would be better to capture the shape of the boundary of the observed cloud of points.

To avoid this problem, Thiry and Tulkens (1992) and Simar (1992) proposed a two-stage approach, using nonparametric techniques in a first step to reach the boundary, and then fitting a parametric model on the nonparametric estimated frontier. However, inference in the second stage as proposed by

Thiry and Tulkens was incorrect (due to the nonstandard fit in the second step, using an FDH estimator of the frontier). Simar (1992) proposed a bootstrap approach, but with no theoretical justification.

Recently, Florens and Simar (2005) provided the full theory for this two-stage estimation procedure, extending the idea with the use of robust nonparametric frontier estimation in the first step. The main feature of the approach is that it does not require strong assumptions on the DGP (as in the regression-type approach), nor are distributional assumptions needed. In a certain sense, this approach reconciles the parametric and nonparametric methods, since the latter method allows one to improve the former method. These ideas are summarized below.

4.7.2 Formalization of the problem and two-stage procedure

Consider the probabilistic formulation of the production process $(X, Y) \in \Psi \subset \mathcal{R}_+^N \times \mathcal{R}_+^1$ with distribution function $F(x, y)$. As shown in section 4.2.4, under free disposability, the production frontier is characterized (in the output direction) by the upper boundary of the support of $F_{Y|X}(y \mid x) = \mathrm{prob}(Y \le y \mid X \le x)$:

$$\varphi(x) = \sup\{y \mid F_{Y|X}(y \mid x) < 1\}. \tag{4.164}$$

The order-m frontier was defined in section 4.5.1 by

$$\varphi_m(x) = E\left[\max(Y^1, \ldots, Y^m) \mid X \le x\right]$$

$$= \int_0^\infty (1 - [F_{Y|X}(y \mid x)]^m) dy, \tag{4.165}$$

where the random variables $Y^1, \ldots, Y^m$ are generated from $F_{Y|X}(y|x)$. The corresponding nonparametric estimators are, for the full frontier,

$$\widehat{\varphi}_n(x) = \max_{i \mid x_i \le x} (y_i) \tag{4.166}$$

and, for the order-m frontier,

$$\widehat{\varphi}_{m,n}(x) = \int_0^\infty \left(1 - \left[\widehat{F}_{c,n}(y \mid x)\right]^m\right) dy. \tag{4.167}$$

Now consider a parametric family of functions defined on $\mathcal{R}_+^N$, $\{\varphi(\cdot \mid \theta) \mid \theta \in \Theta\}$. For simplicity, consider linear models where $\varphi(x \mid \theta) = g(x)\theta$, where $g(x) = [g_1(x) \ldots g_k(x)]$, θ is a $(k \times 1)$ matrix of parameters, and the k functions $g_j(\cdot)$ are known.

The goal is to estimate the value of $\theta \in \mathcal{R}^k$ corresponding to the "best" (in the sense of minimum mean integrated square difference [MISD]) parametric approximation of the frontier function. This defines the concept of pseudotrue values, which are the values of the parameters θ that give the "best" parametric approximation of the true (but unknown) production frontier (either the order-m frontier $\varphi_m(x)$ or full efficient frontier $\varphi(x)$).

For the order-m frontier, the pseudotrue value of θ is defined as

$$\theta^m = \arg\min_{\theta} \left[\sum_{i=1}^{n} (\varphi_m(x_i) - \varphi(x_i \mid \theta))^2 \right]. \tag{4.168}$$

For the full frontier $\partial\Psi$, the pseudotrue value of θ is defined as

$$\theta = \arg\min_{\theta} \left[\sum_{i=1}^{n} [\varphi(x_i) - \varphi(x_i \mid \theta)]^2 \right]. \tag{4.169}$$

Note that the definitions in (4.168) and (4.169) are in terms of sums of squared differences. By the theory of Riemann integration, these approximate MISD. Other measures of the discrepancies are also possible (see Florens and Simar, 2005, for examples). Of course, if the parametric model is the "true" model, (either for the frontier or for the order-m frontier), then the pseudotrue values of θ are equivalent to the true values of θ.

The corresponding two-stage semiparametric estimators are defined by

$$\widehat{\theta}_n^m = \arg\min_{\theta} \left[\sum_{i=1}^{n} (\widehat{\varphi}_{m,n}(x_i) - \varphi(x_i; \theta))^2 \right] \tag{4.170}$$

and

$$\widehat{\theta}_n = \arg\min_{\theta} \left[\sum_{i=1}^{n} (\widehat{\varphi}_n(x_i) - \varphi(x_i; \theta))^2 \right]. \tag{4.171}$$

These are obtained by replacing the unknown functions in (4.168) and (4.169) with their corresponding nonparametric estimators.

The statistical properties of these estimators are described in Florens and Simar (2005). For the case of the order-m frontier, strong consistency is obtained as $\sqrt{n}$-convergence and asymptotic normality; that is, $\widehat{\theta}_n^m \xrightarrow{a.s.} \theta^m$ and

$$\sqrt{n} \left(\widehat{\theta}_n^m - \theta^m \right) \xrightarrow{d} \mathcal{N}(0, A\Sigma A), \tag{4.172}$$

where $A = \left(E[g(x)g'(x)] \right)^{-1}$ and Σ is defined in Florens and Simar (2005). In applications, a bootstrap approximation can be used to estimate the asymptotic variance. In the case of the full frontier, the only result obtained to date is (weak) consistency of $\widehat{\theta}_n$; that is, $\left(\widehat{\theta}_n - \theta \right) \xrightarrow{p} 0$.

As shown in preceding sections of this chapter, estimating the full frontier $\partial\Psi$ is necessarily a much harder problem than estimating an order-m frontier.

The approach outlined here can also be adapted to parametric approximations of order-α quantile frontiers.

4.7.2.1 Some examples

We illustrate the approach with the air controllers data (see section 4.3.5), which allows a bivariate representation. We consider here as potential model for the frontiers (full frontiers and order-m frontiers) a log-linear model:

$$\ln y_i = \alpha + \beta \ln x_i \qquad (4.173)$$

Depending on the value of m, the values for the estimates of the log-linear model are displayed in table 4.5, where we also give the estimates obtained by the shifted OLS technique (Greene, 1980). The estimates in table 4.5 show that the shifted OLS frontier is different from the order-m frontiers (in particular, for the intercept) and how the estimation of the parametric approximations are stable with respect to m. The results are also displayed in figure 4.18, where the two top panels correspond to $m = 25$ (left) and $m = 50$ (right) and the two bottom panels correspond to $m = 100$ (left) and FDH (i.e., $m \to \infty$; right). In each panel, solid curves give the order-m frontier and its linear approximation, while the dot-dashed line shows the shifted OLS fit. Here again, the advantage of the order-m frontiers is demonstrated: They are less sensitive to extreme points, even if $m \to \infty$.

The bootstrap 95% confidence intervals for the parameters, in the case of $m = 100$, turn out to be (we used a bootstrap approximation of the variance in (4.172) with $B = 1000$ Monte Carlo replications)

$$\alpha \in [0.4490, 0.6399],$$

$$\beta \in [0.7839, 0.9949].$$

These confidence intervals are not symmetric about the estimates of α and β shown in table 4.5 for $m = 100$, reflecting the fact that the distributions of bootstrap values used to obtain the confidence interval estimates are asymmetric.

Table 4.5
Estimates of Parametric Approximations of
Order-m Frontiers

Method	α	β
Shifted-OLS	0.8238	0.8833
Order-m ($m = 25$)	0.5676	0.8347
Order-m ($m = 50$)	0.5825	0.8627
Order-m ($m = 100$)	0.5877	0.8786
FDH ($m = \infty$)	0.5886	0.8838

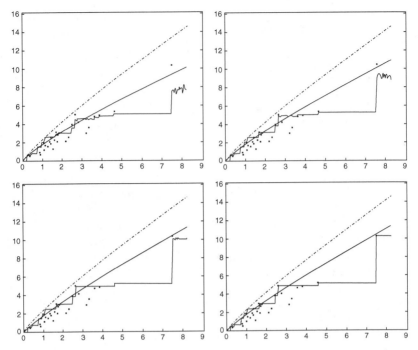

Figure 4.18. Order-m, Linearly Approximated Order-m, and Shifted OLS Fits for Air Controller Data

4.8 Open Issues and Conclusions

A number of open issues and problems remain to be addressed in future research.

4.8.1 Allowing for noise in DEA/FDH

Allowing for noise in nonparametric frontier models is perhaps one of the most challenging issues is production analysis. The problem is hard because, without some restrictions, the model is not identified (this is true even in the simplest univariate frontier problem; see Hall and Simar, 2002, for discussion). Using envelopment estimators when there is noise in the data will lead to inconsistent estimation. However, Hall and Simar show that when the noise is not to large (in terms of noise to signal ratio), the usual boundary estimates (based on minimal, or maximal, order statistics) can be used to obtain reasonable estimators of the boundary. These ideas have been developed for the multivariate setting in Simar (2007), where stochastic versions of

FDH and DEA estimators are developed for situations where the noise is of moderate size.

Still, more general approaches are desired. Kumbhakar et al. (2007) suggest an approach for nonparametric stochastic frontier model using local maximum likelihood methods. The idea is to start with a global model in the spirit of Aigner et al. (1977) and then, by localization, generate a much more flexible model approximating a much wider class of models than the global model.

Another nonparametric method for stochastic frontier models in the case of a panel of data has been proposed by Kneip and Simar (1996). In their approach, identification comes from repeated observations of the same firms over time. The drawback is the need of a large numbers of time periods for getting sensible results, and the implicit assumption that inefficiency does not change over time. The latter assumption likely to be problematic in many economic applications.

4.8.2 Inference with DEA/FDH estimators

Tools for statistical inference are available. But here, too, improvements are needed. For instance, other (than bootstrap) approximations of the limiting distributions of DEA estimators that would be easy to simulate and would ease the task of bias correction and estimation of confidence intervals are desired, along the lines of what has been obtained for FDH estimators. Some initial progress in this direction has been made by Jeong (2004).

With regard to the bootstrap, subsampling offers the easiest way of implementing inference using bootstrap methods. The remaining issue, however, is to develop an easy, reliable way of determining the optimal subsample sizes. The smoothed bootstrap proposed Kneip et al. (2003) for the heterogeneous case is difficult to implement; additional work is also needed to develop algorithms that are easier to use in applied work.

4.8.3 Results for cases of constant returns to scale

As noted in section 4.2.5, statistical properties of the constant returns-to-scale versions of the DEA estimators, $\widehat{\theta}_{CRS}(x, y)$ and $\widehat{\lambda}_{CRS}(x, y)$, have not yet been derived. There are, to date, no proofs of consistency for these estimators, nor have either their convergence rates or sampling distributions been derived. Provided $\partial \Psi$ displays globally constant returns to scale, it is difficult to doubt that the CRS versions of the DEA estimators are consistent, but a formal proof would be nice. Their limiting distributions are required to establish consistency of any bootstrap that might be used for inference with these estimators; even with this result, some work would be required to establish consistency of a bootstrap, since the proofs in Kneip et al. (2003) do not extend easily to the CRS case.

4.8.4 Tools for dimension reduction

Several tools are used in nonparametric regression to reduce dimensionality in an effort to mitigate the curse of dimensionality. For example, one can transform the exogenous data to principal components space and examine eigenvalues to see whether some of the dimensions in principal components space are nearly redundant (due to multicollinearity in the original data space, which is common in economic applications) and might reasonably be deleted. This approach was employed by Wheelock and Wilson (2001) and Wilson and Carey (2004) to estimate cost functions for banks and hospitals. Other approaches have been suggested by Härdle (1990) and Scott (1992).

In multidimensional settings where DEA estimators are used, however, the estimators' radial nature precludes many of the transformation techniques that might be used in regression problem. For example, the estimators lose their independence from units of measurement if the data are transformed to principal components space.

Simar and Wilson (2001) provided bootstrap tests for aggregation possibilities among inputs and outputs in the DEA setting. These test hypotheses about the underlying structure of the true frontier $\partial\Psi$; if satisfied, inputs or outputs can be aggregated, resulting in a reduction of dimensionality, which leads to faster convergence rates, and hence less estimation noise for a given sample size. Given the cost incurred by the curse of dimensionality, more work on dimension reduction is needed.

4.8.5 Final conclusions

Statistical inference in now available for nonparametric frontier models, even if not always easy to implement. Increasing availability of software packages such as the new *FEAR* package (Wilson, 2007) implementing bootstrap methods for inference in frontier models will encourage wider use; already, there is little excuse for not making inferences properly in frontier applications.

The new concepts of order-m and order-α partial frontiers are very appealing. They are robust with respect to outliers, are very easy to compute, and avoid the curse of dimensionality shared by most of the nonparametric techniques in statistics. In addition, they provide another tool for detecting outliers in deterministic frontier models.

A DGP has been provided that rationalizes two-stage approaches, where efficiencies are estimated (using FDH or DEA estimators) in a first stage, and then the efficiency estimates are regressed on environmental variables in a second stage. In addition, it is now understood how inferences regarding the second-stage regression parameters must be made. In addition, using the probabilistic formulation of the production process introduced in section 4.2.4, tools have been developed to investigate the impact of environmental factors on the production process while making fewer assumptions than required in the two-stage approach.

The fact that the issues discussed in sections 4.8.1–4.8.4 remain (to date) unsolved is good news for theoreticians, if not for practitioners.

Acknowledgments

Research support from the "Inter-university Attraction Pole," Phase V (no. P5/24) sponsored by the Belgian government (Belgian Science Policy) is gratefully acknowledged.

All discussion papers from Institut de Statistique, Catholique Université Louvain, are available at http://stat1ux.stat.ucl.ac.be/ISpub/ISdp.html. Wilson (2007) is available at http://www.clemson.edu/economics/faculty/wilson.

Notes

1. In order to simplify notation, a random sample is denoted by the lowercase letters (x_i, y_i) and not, as in standard textbooks, by the uppercase (X_i, Y_i). The context will determine whether (x_i, y_i) are random variables or their realized, observed values, which are real numbers.

2. Note that an *estimator* is a random variable, while an *estimate* is a realization of an estimator (random variable). An estimator can take perhaps infinitely many values with different probabilities, while an estimate is merely a known, nonrandom value.

3. The expression $a \gtreqqless b$ indicates that the elements of a are weakly greater than the corresponding elements of b, with at least one element of a strictly greater than the corresponding element of b.

4. One could also use asymmetric boundary kernels, which change shape as one approaches the boundary of support; see Scott (1992) for examples. This would introduce additional complications, however, and the choice of methods is of second-order importance for the bootstrap procedures described here.

5. See Scott (1992) for details.

6. Both estimates in figure 4.7 were obtained after omitting efficiency estimates equal to unity. Noting that assumption 4.2.2 implies that the marginal distribution of efficiency scores does not contain a mass at one, it is clear that the collection of efficiency estimates equal to one is a spurious artifact of DEA estimators. The half-normal density was estimated by the maximum likelihood method.

7. One of the most commonly used parametric models, the translog cost function, is trivially rejected by various data; see Wheelock and Wilson (2001) and Wilson and Carey (2004), for examples.

8. One could also specify a family of cost, profit, revenue, or other functions.

References

Aigner, D.J. and S.F. Chu (1968), On estimating the industry production function, *American Economic Review* 58, 826–839.
Aigner, D., C.A.K. Lovell, and P. Schmidt (1977), Formulation and estimation of stochastic frontier production function models, *Journal of Econometrics* 6, 21–37.

Andersen, P., and N.C. Petersen (1993), A procedure for ranking efficient units in data envelopment analysis, *Management Science* 39, 1261–1264.

Aragon, Y., A. Daouia, and C. Thomas-Agnan (2005), Nonparametric frontier estimation: A conditional quantile-based approach, *Econometric Theory* 21, 358–389.

Badin, L., and L. Simar (2004), A bias corrected nonparametric envelopment estimator of frontiers, Discussion Paper 0406, Institut de Statistique, Université Catholique de Louvain, Louvain-la-Neuve, Belgium.

Banker, R.D. (1993), Maximum likelihood, consistency and data envelopment analysis: A statistical foundation, *Management Science* 39, 1265–1273.

Banker, R.D. (1996), Hypothesis tests using data envelopment analysis, *Journal of Productivity Analysis* 7, 139–159.

Banker, R.D., A. Charnes, and W.W. Cooper (1984), Some models for estimating technical and scale inefficiencies in data envelopment analysis, *Management Science* 30, 1078–1092.

Bickel, P.J., and D.A. Freedman (1981), Some asymptotic theory for the bootstrap, *Annals of Statistics* 9, 1196–1217.

Bogetoft, P. (1996), DEA on relaxed convexity assumptions, *Management Science* 42, 457–465.

Bogetoft, P., J.M. Tama, and J. Tind (2000), Convex input and output projections of nonconvex production possibility sets, *Management Science* 46, 858–869.

Briec, W., K. Kerstens, and P. Van den Eeckaut (2004), Non-convex technologies and cost functions: Definitions, duality and nonparametric tests of convexity, *Journal of Economics* 81, 155–192.

Brown, D.F. (1979), Voronoi diagrams from convex hulls, *Information Processing Letters* 9, 223–228.

Cazals, C., J.P. Florens, and L. Simar (2002), Nonparametric frontier estimation: A robust approach, *Journal of Econometrics* 106, 1–25.

Charnes, A., W.W. Cooper, and E. Rhodes (1978), Measuring the inefficiency of decision making units, *European Journal of Operational Research* 2, 429–444.

Charnes, A., W.W. Cooper, and E. Rhodes (1981), Evaluating program and managerial efficiency: An application of data envelopment analysis to program follow through, *Management Science* 27, 668–697.

Cheng, M.Y., J. Fan, and J.S. Marron (1997), On automatic boundary corrections, *Annals of Statistics* 25, 1691–1708.

Cook, R.D., and Weisberg, S. (1982), *Residuals and Influence in Regression*, New York: Chapman and Hall.

Coelli, T., D.S.P. Rao, and G.E. Battese (1998), *An Introduction to Efficiency and Productivity Analysis*, Boston: Kluwer.

Daouia, A., and L. Simar (2005), Robust nonparametric estimators of monotone boundaries, *Journal of Multivariate Analysis*, 96, 311–331.

Daouia, A., and L. Simar (2007), Nonparametric efficiency analysis: A multivariate conditional quantile approach, *Journal of Econometrics*, in press.

Daraio, C., and L. Simar (2005), Introducing environmental variables in nonparametric frontier models: A probabilistic approach, *Journal of Productivity Analysis* 24, 93–121.

Daraio, C., and L. Simar (2007), Conditional nonparametric frontier models for convex and non convex technologies: a unifying approach, *Journal of Productivity Analysis*, forthcoming.

Debreu, G. (1951), The coefficient of resource utilization, *Econometrica* 19(3), 273–292.

Deprins, D., L. Simar, and H. Tulkens (1984), Measuring labor inefficiency in post offices, in *The Performance of Public Enterprises: Concepts and measurements*, ed. M. Marchand, P. Pestieau, and H. Tulkens, Amsterdam: North-Holland, 243–267.

Efron, B. (1979), Bootstrap methods: another look at the jackknife, *Annals of Statistics* 7, 1–16.

Efron, B. (1982), *The Jackknife, the Bootstrap and Other Resampling Plans*, CBMS-NSF Regional Conference Series in Applied Mathematics, no. 38, Philadelphia: Society for Industrial and Applied Mathematics.

Efron, B., and R.J. Tibshirani (1993), *An Introduction to the Bootstrap*, London: Chapman and Hall.

Färe, R. (1988), *Fundamentals of Production Theory*, Berlin: Springer-Verlag.

Farrell, M.J. (1957), The measurement of productive efficiency, *Journal of the Royal Statistical Society, Series A*, 120, 253–281.

Florens, J.P., and L. Simar (2005), Parametric approximations of nonparametric frontier, *Journal of Econometrics* 124, 91–116.

Gijbels, I., E. Mammen, B.U. Park, and L. Simar (1999), On estimation of monotone and concave frontier functions, *Journal of the American Statistical Association* 94, 220–228.

Greene, W.H. (1980), Maximum likelihood estimation of econometric frontier, *Journal of Econometrics* 13, 27–56.

Härdle, W. (1990), *Applied Nonparametric Regression*, Cambridge: Cambridge University Press.

Hall, P., and L. Simar (2002), Estimating a changepoint, boundary or frontier in the presence of observation error, *Journal of the American Statistical Association* 97, 523–534.

Jeong, S.O. (2004), Asymptotic distribution of DEA efficiency scores, *Journal of the Korean Statistical Society*, 33, 449–458.

Jeong, S.O., and L. Simar (2006), Linearly interpolated FDH efficiency score for nonconvex frontiers, *Journal of Multivariate Analysis* 97, 2141–2161.

Kittelsen, S.A.C. (1997), Monte Carlo simulations of DEA efficiency measures and hypothesis tests, Unpublished Working Paper, SNF Oslo, Oslo, Norway.

Kneip, A., B.U. Park, and L. Simar (1998), A note on the convergence of nonparametric DEA estimators for production efficiency scores, *Econometric Theory* 14, 783–793.

Kneip, A., and L. Simar (1996), A general framework for frontier estimation with panel data, *Journal of Productivity Analysis* 7, 187–212.

Kneip, A., L. Simar, and P.W. Wilson (2003), Asymptotics for DEA estimators in non-parametric frontier models, Discussion Paper no. 0317, Institut de Statistique, Université Catholique de Louvain, Louvain-la-Neuve, Belgium.

Koenker, R., and G. Bassett (1978), Regression quantiles, *Econometrica* 46, 33–50.

Koopmans, T.C. (1951), An analysis of production as an efficient combination of activities, in *Activity Analysis of Production and Allocation*, ed. T.C. Koopmans, Cowles Commission for Research in Economics, Monograph 13, New York: John-Wiley and Sons.

Korostelev, A., L. Simar, and A.B. Tsybakov (1995a), Efficient estimation of monotone boundaries, *Annals of Statistics* 23, 476–489.

Korostelev, A., L. Simar, and A.B. Tsybakov (1995b), On estimation of monotone and convex boundaries, *Publications de l'Institut de Statistique de l'Université de Paris* *39*, (1), 3–18.

Kumbhakar, S.C., B.U. Park, L. Simar, and E.G. Tsionas (2007), Nonparametric stochastic frontiers: A local likelihood approach, *Journal of Econometrics* 137(1), 1–27.

Maddala, G.S. (1988), *Introduction to Econometrics*, New York: Macmillan.

Mouchart, M., and L. Simar (2002), Efficiency analysis of air controllers: First insights, Consulting Report no. 0202, Institut de Statistique, Université Catholique de Louvain, Belgium.

Olesen, O.B., N.C. Petersen, and C.A.K. Lovell (1996), Summary of the workshop discussion, *Journal of Productivity Analysis* 7, 341–345.

Park, B., L. Simar, and C. Weiner (2000), The FDH estimator for productivity efficiency scores: Asymptotic properties, *Econometric Theory* 16, 855–877.

Porembski, M., K. Breitenstein, and P. Alpar (2005), Visualizing efficiency and reference relations in data envelopment analysis with an application to the branches of a German Bank, *Journal of Productivity Analysis*, 23, 203–221.

Ritter, C., and L. Simar (1997), Pitfalls of normal-gamma stochastic frontier models, *Journal of Productivity Analysis* 8, 167–182.

Schuster, E.F. (1985), Incorporating support constraints into nonparametric estimators of densities, *Communications in Statistics: Theory and Methods* 14, 1123–1136.

Scott, D.W. (1992), *Multivariate Density Estimation: Theory, Practice, and Visualization*, New York: John Wiley and Sons.

Serfling, R.J. (1980), *Approximation Theorems of Mathematical Statistics*, New York: John Wiley and Sons.

Shephard, R.W. (1970), *Theory of Cost and Production Function*, Princeton, NJ: Princeton University Press.

Silverman, B.W. (1986), *Density Estimation for Statistics and Data Analysis*, London: Chapman and Hall.

Simar, L. (1992), Estimating efficiencies from frontier models with panel data: A comparison of parametric, non-parametric and semi-parametric methods with bootstrapping, *Journal of Productivity Analysis* 3, 167–203.

Simar, L. (2003), Detecting outliers in frontiers models: A simple approach, *Journal of Productivity Analysis* 20, 391–424.

Simar, L. (2007), How to Improve the Performances of DEA/FDH Estimators in the Presence of Noise? *Journal of Productivity Analysis*, forthcoming.

Simar, L., and P.W. Wilson (1998), Sensitivity analysis of efficiency scores: How to bootstrap in nonparametric frontier models, *Management Science* 44, 49–61.

Simar, L., and P.W. Wilson (1999a), Some problems with the Ferrier/Hirschberg bootstrap idea, *Journal of Productivity Analysis* 11, 67–80.

Simar, L., and P.W. Wilson (1999b), Of course we can bootstrap DEA scores! But does it mean anything? Logic trumps wishful thinking, *Journal of Productivity Analysis* 11, 93–97.

Simar, L., and P.W. Wilson (1999c), Estimating and bootstrapping Malmquist indices, *European Journal of Operational Research* 115, 459–471.

Simar, L., and P.W. Wilson (2000a), Statistical inference in nonparametric frontier models: The state of the art, *Journal of Productivity Analysis* 13, 49–78.

Simar, L., and P.W. Wilson (2000b), A general methodology for bootstrapping in nonparametric frontier models, *Journal of Applied Statistics* 27, 779–802.

Simar L., and P.W. Wilson (2001), Testing restrictions in nonparametric frontier models, *Communications in Statistics: Simulation and Computation* 30, 161–186.

Simar L., and P.W. Wilson (2002), Nonparametric tests of return to scale, *European Journal of Operational Research* 139, 115–132.

Simar, L., and P.W. Wilson (2007), Estimation and inference in two-stage, semi-parametric models of production processes, *Journal of Econometrics* 136, 31–64.

Simar, L., and V. Zelenyuk (2006a), On testing equality of two distribution functions of efficiency score estimated via DEA, *Econometric Reviews*, 25(4), 497–522.

Simar, L., and V. Zelenyuk (2006b), Statistical inference for aggregates of Farrell-type efficiencies, *Journal of Applied Econometrics*, forthcoming.

Spanos, A. (1999), *Probability Theory and Statistical Inference: Econometric Modeling with Observational Data*, Cambridge: Cambridge University Press.

Thiry, B., and H. Tulkens (1992), Allowing for technical efficiency in parametric estimates of production functions: With an application to urban transit firms, *Journal of Productivity Analysis* 3, 41–65.

Wheelock, D.C., and P.W. Wilson (2001), New evidence on returns to scale and product mix among U.S. commercial banks, *Journal of Monetary Economics* 47, 653–674.

Wheelock, D.C., and P.W. Wilson (2003), Robust nonparametric estimation of efficiency and technical change in U.S. commercial banking, Unpublished Working Paper, Department of Economics, Clemson University, Clemson, SC.

Wilson, P.W. (1993), Detecting outliers in deterministic nonparametric frontier models with multiple outputs, *Journal of Business and Economic Statistics* 11, 319–323.

Wilson, P.W. (1995), Detecting influential observations in data envelopment analysis, *Journal of Productivity Analysis* 6, 27–45.

Wilson, P.W. (2003), Testing independence in models of productive efficiency, *Journal of Productivity Analysis* 20, 361–390.

Wilson, P.W. (2004), A preliminary non-parametric analysis of public education and health expenditures developing countries, Unpublished Working Paper, Department of Economics, Clemson University, Clemson, SC.

Wilson, P.W. (2007), FEAR: A software package for frontier efficiency analysis with R, *Socio-Economics Planning Sciences*, forthcoming.

Wilson, P.W., and K. Carey (2004), Nonparametric analysis of returns to scale and product mix among U.S. hospitals, *Journal of Applied Econometrics* 19, 505–524.

5

Efficiency and Productivity: Malmquist and More

Rolf Färe, Shawna Grosskopf, and Dimitri Margaritis

Introduction

Productivity is the subject of this chapter. This notion is one of the most intuitive and familiar measures of performance at all levels—from the individual worker or firm up to a measure of national economic performance. It is a key economic indicator, believed to be a critical driver or factor in accounting for economic growth and prosperity, as well as firm profitability. In this chapter, we provide a link between the efficiency issues raised in chapters 1–3 of this volume and the traditional measures we have of productivity and productivity growth. One of the key insights this link provides is the identification of the contributions of innovation (technical change or shifts in the frontier of technology) and diffusion and learning (catching up or efficiency change) to productivity growth.

We all have an intuitive idea of what we mean by productivity; one simple version would be how much we get out of the resources we have. Here, we start with thinking of productivity as the ratio of output y (what we produce) over input x (the resources we use):

$$\text{Productivity} = y/x \tag{5.1}$$

Labor productivity is a simple and familiar example, where output might be approximated by gross domestic product (GDP) at the national level with input measured in terms of total labor hours employed in a given time period. Labor productivity, a measure of single-factor productivity, is the working horse of statistical agencies around the world. What we focus on here is a broader measure of productivity that includes all of the products and services produced and accounts for all of the resources—not just labor—used to produce these goods and services. This is referred to as multifactor productivity or total factor productivity (TFP).

TFP is thus the ratio of all of outputs produced over all of the inputs employed to produce them—essentially, a generalized notion of the average product in (5.1) familiar from your introductory economics textbook. The first hurdle in estimating TFP is thus finding a way to aggregate outputs and inputs. As it turns out, economic theory provides us with a number of different ways of doing this. The traditional productivity indexes—think of Paasche, Laspeyres, Fisher, and Törnqvist—all use price information to allow us to add up the apples and oranges we produce from labor, land, and capital services, for example. Essentially, we are using revenues to approximate total outputs and costs to approximate total inputs. The indexes named above provide alternative "parametric" formulas for this approximation.

An alternative approach, which is our focus here, is to use economic aggregators based directly on technology and input and output quantities, maintaining a closer link to our definition of productivity above. A simple example when we have only one output is the production function—it aggregates multiple inputs and relates them to output. Generalizing to the case in which we also have multiple outputs and inputs requires a close relative of the production function, namely, the distance function. As its name suggests, it tells us about distance, namely, from some observed input–output combination to the frontier of technology. For our purposes, distance functions are extremely useful not only in terms of aggregation—because we do not need price information—but also because they are natural performance or efficiency measures themselves. Moreover, they are connected to costs, revenues, and profits through what is known as *duality theory*. This duality provides a natural link to and rationalization for the traditional productivity indexes. These indexes use price information to aggregate and provide an approximation of the information we obtain from the distance functions. These dual relationships are spelled out in some detail in section 5.1.

Figure 5.1 provides an intuitive illustration of distance functions for the single input and output case. Suppose the frontier of technology is described by the curve bounding the set of all feasible inputs and outputs, which is our technology T. Suppose we are interested in the observation labeled "a," which uses x^a units of input to produce y^a units of output. Clearly, this combination is not the best we could do given technology; with inputs x^a we should be able to produce more output, that is, y^*. Bundle (x^a, y^*) "dominates" (x^a, y^a), since it would provide a firm, for example, with more revenue at the same cost as bundle (x^a, y^a). The Shephard output distance function mimics this idea by increasing output as much as is technically feasible, given input, by the line segment emanating from point "a" northward to the boundary in the figure. One could also imagine thinking about dominance in terms of minimizing input usage for a given output. That is the intuition behind the Shephard input

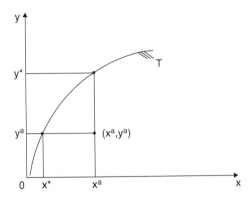

Figure 5.1. Technology and Distance Functions

distance function, indicated by the line segment from (x^a, y^a) to (x^*, y^a) in the figure. Clearly, we could produce output y^a at lower cost if input usage is reduced to x^*. These are the distance functions that are most widely used in this literature.

Recently, however, a generalization of these two distance functions has been introduced and employed to estimate productivity growth. We refer to these as *directional distance functions*, and it is useful to think of them as including the Shephard input and output distance functions as special cases; the directional distance function allows for scaling toward all of the points on the frontier that dominate the observation under evaluation. In figure 5.1, in evaluating (x^a, y^a), we could think of scaling to any of the frontier points between (x^a, y^*) and (x^*, y^a) that dominate (x^a, y^a). These would all be more profitable (with positive prices) than the combination at point a. In fact, the directional distance function is "dual" to the profit function, which is discussed in more detail in section 5.1.

These distance functions are the building blocks that allow us to aggregate outputs and inputs for the group of productivity measures that are the main focus of this chapter. The Shephard distance functions are the basis of the Malmquist productivity index, which was introduced as a theoretical index in 1982 by Caves, Christensen, and Diewert and has since then become a useful empirical tool in its own right with the introduction of methods to estimate the distance functions. Productivity measures based on distance functions have the advantage of directly telling us about productivity based on technology— no prices are required. This feature makes them useful for analysis of the public sector, for example, where price data may not be available—think of schools where we do not have price information on outcomes (outputs) in terms of student reading and writing skills. More generally, the Malmquist productivity index, as well as its distance-function–based relatives, the Hicks-Moorsteen and Luenberger productivity measures, is useful when prices are not available or do not reflect resource usage or shadow prices. This means that we can now measure productivity in almost any setting—see the list of novel applications in chapter 1 (table 1.1).

The role of distance functions as performance measures is also what facilitates the decomposition of productivity growth into components, including technical change and efficiency change, which we argue are of practical policy value. A vast literature, addressing both theoretical issues and empirical applications of the Malmquist productivity index, has appeared since the mid-1990s. These are the focus of section 5.2. Also included in that section are the Hicks-Moorsteen index, rediscovered by Bjurek (1994), which is also based on distance functions, and the Luenberger productivity indicator based on directional distance functions. These share the advantages cited above for the Malmquist productivity index.

Since Fried, Lovell, and Schmidt (1993), the directional distance function has been introduced and used to define the Luenberger productivity indicator mentioned above. It is called an indicator rather than an index[1] because it is defined in terms of differences in output and input usage rather than the ratios of output to input usage that characterize Malmquist productivity indexes and their traditional price-based aggregator relatives, including the Paasche, Laspeyres, Fisher, and Törnqvist productivity indexes. A distinguishing feature of the Luenberger indicator is its dual relationship to profit: It allows for simultaneous reduction of inputs and expansion of outputs. This characteristic also renders it useful as an environmental productivity measure: It can simultaneously seek increases in desirable outputs and reductions in undesirable outputs, which is discussed briefly in section 5.2 along with the other distance-function–based productivity measures. The Luenberger indicator also has a price-based relative, the Bennet-Bowley productivity indicator, which is discussed along with its price-based relatives in section 5.2.

Again, the heart of this chapter is the discussion of our distance function productivity measures, which explicitly link efficiency and productivity. These are the subject of section 5.2 and include

- Malmquist productivity indexes
- Hicks-Moorsteen productivity indexes
- Luenberger productivity indicators

Included is a discussion of the decompositions and properties of these indexes and indicators.

The latter half of section 5.2 turns to the more familiar, traditional price-aggregator indexes and indicators. These include

- Törnqvist productivity indexes
- Fisher productivity indexes
- Bennet-Bowley productivity indicators

Included here is a discussion of properties of these indexes and indicators.

As discussed here and in chapter 1, these more traditional price-aggregator measures of productivity can be derived as "approximations" of the distance-function–based productivity measures listed above. Caves, Christensen, and Diewert (1982a) pioneered this type of derivation for both outputs and inputs, relating the Malmquist productivity indexes based on Shephard-type distance functions to Törnqvist productivity indexes. This required appealing to duality to link shadow prices from the distance functions to observed prices, which are the basis of the weights in the Törnqvist indexes, as well as application of the quadratic and translog lemmas to arrive at the parameterization of technology for the Törnqvist indexes as translog. Similarly, there are links between the output- and input-based Malmquist productivity indexes and the Fisher productivity indexes, between the Hicks-Moorsteen productivity index (constructed from both Shephard input and output distance functions) and corresponding Törnqvist productivity index, and between the Luenberger productivity indicator (based on directional distance functions) and the Bennet-Bowley indicator. These relationships are summarized below and are discussed in more detail in section 5.2.

Starting at the top of figure 5.2, we have the directional distance function, which fully describes technology and allows for simultaneous contraction of inputs and expansion of outputs. The Luenberger productivity indicator is constructed as differences in directional distance functions, thus requiring information only on input and output quantities. We may approximate the Luenberger indicator with the Bennet-Bowley productivity indicator, which requires that we appeal to duality between the directional distance functions used to construct the Luenberger indicator and the profit function to link

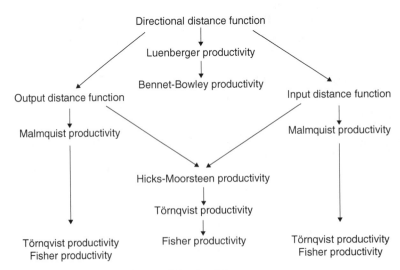

Figure 5.2. Distance Functions and Productivity

shadow prices to observed prices. This also requires assumption of a parametric form of technology to specify the final form of the Bennet-Bowley indicator, which then requires information on input and output quantities, as well as their prices.

Following the arrow from the directional distance function to the southwest leads us to the Shephard output distance function, $D_o(x, y)$. The output distance function is a special case of the directional distance function: It scales only on outputs rather than on outputs and inputs simultaneously. This is the building block used to define the output-based Malmquist productivity index. Similarly, if we take the arrow from the directional distance function to the southeast, we arrive at the Shephard input distance function, $D_i(y, x)$, which is another special case of the directional distance function: It scales only on inputs and is the building block for the input-based Malmquist productivity index. Both the output-based and input-based productivity indexes require data only on input and output quantities. As mentioned above, these were defined by Caves, Christensen, and Diewert (1982a), who then proceeded to show that they could be approximated by Törnqvist productivity indexes. Later, links were provided to show that the Fisher indexes could also be thought of as approximations of the Malmquist productivity indexes.

There are also arrows from the Shephard input and output distance functions leading to the Hicks-Moorsteen productivity index. This is constructed using both output and input distance functions and may also be approximated as a Törnqvist index.

One of the key advantages of the measures based on distance function is their ability to identify "new" sources of productivity growth. Nishimizu and Page (1982) were the first to isolate efficiency change and technical change components of productivity growth with a parametric specification of the Malmquist productivity index. Färe, Grosskopf, Lindgren, and Roos (1989) showed how these may be estimated using data envelopment analysis (DEA). Later Färe, Grosskopf, Norris, and Zhang (1994) extended this decomposition to include changes in scale efficiency. This was followed by a veritable flood of alternative decompositions of the Malmquist index; section 5.3 seeks to give a brief overview of what Bert Balk (2004) calls the "many decompositions" of the Malmquist productivity index; chapter 1 also includes a discussion of this topic.

Section 5.4 takes up issues of aggregation; that is, when can we simply add up (or average) individual productivity to arrive at aggregate productivity? As it turns out, aggregation is facilitated by focusing on optimizers. It is also facilitated by choosing the "same" direction in the case of the Luenberger productivity indicator, for example.

Obviously, these provide a large menu of possible choices for estimating productivity. Here, we follow the opening chapter and think of the Malmquist productivity index (and its additive cousin, the Luenberger productivity indicator) as benchmark theoretical concepts, which can be empirically framed in a number of ways, including index number "approximations" (our price-aggregator, traditional productivity measures), mathematical programming techniques, and econometric estimation of technology, where the latter two approaches have been customized to estimate inefficiency. Going from theory to practice requires assumptions, or what is called "approximation" in chapter 1; this may create a gap between the "true theoretical" measures of productivity and their empirical counterparts. The basic problem is that we do not know the true underlying technology.

Section 5.5 includes a discussion of empirical estimation of the distance-function–based productivity measures. Both nonparametric (DEA type) and parametric (stochastic frontiers) measures are described here. To make all this concrete, we provide an empirical example using data from U.S. agriculture to estimate the indexes and indicators itemized above. A brief discussion of computational issues is included here.

The concluding section discusses advantages and disadvantages of the various indexes and indicators and is intended to help the reader find an appropriate measure based on data issues, policy content, and index number properties. We also discuss what we consider to be unresolved issues and issues that are important but not addressed in this chapter.

5.1 Some Duality and Efficiency Theory

Productivity has an intimate connection to technology, which is where we begin. Economists have provided a wealth of tools that we can use to characterize technology, including quantity or primal concepts such as production functions and distance functions, as well as value or dual concepts, including profit, cost, and revenue functions. These provide a menu of options for the analyst since they are connected through duality theory, employ different types of data, and provide alternative objectives or frontiers by which to measure performance and productivity.

On the production side, duality theory was developed by Shephard (1953, 1970) from the insight that economic data may consist of quantity or primal information on inputs and outputs, or value or dual information on prices, leading to the representation of technology by profit, cost, or revenue functions. He argued (and showed) that economic properties of technology could be independent of whether they are derived from primal or dual information. For example, scale elasticity derived from a production function should not differ from scale elasticity derived from a cost function. Duality theory gives the researcher the freedom to work in quantity or price space, with the inner product connecting the two spaces (under the assumption of competitive markets).

Thus, duality theory provides a fundamental link between the traditional measures of productivity that are in value terms—typically, revenue and cost—and the distance function productivity measures, which are more directly linked to technology described in terms of input and output quantities. The dualities derived by Shephard are those between revenue and the Shephard output distance function and between cost and the Shephard input distance function. These also serve as the basis for the familiar Farrell decompositions of efficiency. Until recently, no analogous relationship was derived between profit and a distance function or primal representation of technology.[2] This, of course, would be useful since profit is a natural performance measure that includes cost minimization and revenue maximization as special cases, and thus could provide a unifying structure. What was missing was the dual distance function, which would mimic the fact that inputs and outputs are optimized simultaneously when we define the profit function. That distance function turns out to be what we call the directional (technology) distance function. It, too, provides a unifying structure since the Shephard distance functions are special cases: The Shephard output distance function optimizes over output quantities but not inputs, and the Shephard input distance function optimizes over input quantities but not outputs.

Figure 5.3 provides a general roadmap of this section. Although it is not as familiar as the dualities associated with the Shephard distance functions, we begin with the profit function and its dual the directional (technology) distance function, since the others are special cases that evolve naturally as we move from profit to revenue and cost. Profit maximization requires simultaneous adjustment of outputs and inputs, which is also characteristic of the directional (technology) distance function—it simultaneously adjusts in the direction of fewer inputs and greater outputs. When we focus on revenue maximization, then we are optimizing over output quantities, given input quantities and output prices. The Shephard output distance function mimics this idea by scaling in the direction of observed outputs, holding input quantities constant. Similarly, if we turn to cost minimization, we are optimizing over input quantities given output quantities and input prices. The Shephard input distance function scales in the direction of the observed inputs, holding output quantities constant. As we move through the diagram, we also show

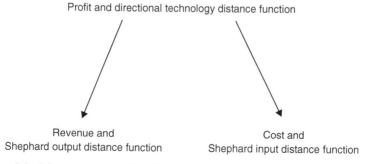

Figure 5.3. Distance Function Dualities

how to use the dualities to derive shadow prices, as well as the Farrell efficiency decompositions augmented with a new decomposition based on the duality between the profit and the directional (technology) distance function.

5.1.1 Profit and the directional (technology) distance function

We begin with some notation: Input quantities are denoted by

$$x = (x_1, \ldots, x_N) \in \Re^N_+,$$

and output quantities are denoted by

$$y = (y_1, \ldots, y_M) \in \Re^M_+.$$

The significance of assuming that the quantities of inputs and outputs are to be real numbers is that they become fully divisible: Inputs may be applied in any fraction, and outputs may be also be produced in any fraction.

Our most primitive characterization of technology is the technology set T, which is the set of all feasible input–output combinations; that is,

$$T = \{(x, y) : x \text{ can produce } y\}.$$

T is assumed to satisfy a set of reasonable axioms. Here we assume that T is a closed, convex, nonempty set with inputs and outputs freely disposable.[3] We illustrate the technology in figure 5.4, where the technology consists of the (x, y) vectors bounded by the curved line and the x-axis. The first duality relation we introduce is that between the profit function and the directional technology distance function (Chambers, Chung, and Färe, 1998) or shortage function (Luenberger, 1992). Denote output prices by

$$p = (p_1, \ldots, p_M) \in \Re^M_+$$

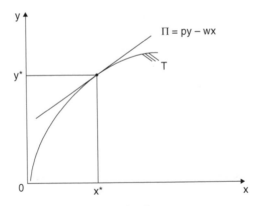

Figure 5.4. Profit Maximization and Technology

and input prices by

$$w = (w_1, \ldots, w_N) \in \Re_+^N.$$

Revenue and cost are defined as inner products; that is,

$$\text{observed revenue} = py = \sum_{m=1}^{M} p_m y_m$$

and

$$\text{observed cost} = wx = \sum_{n=1}^{N} w_n x_n,$$

respectively. The difference between observed revenue and cost is observed profit,

$$\text{observed profit} = py - wx = \sum_{m=1}^{M} p_m y_m - \sum_{n=1}^{N} w_n x_n.$$

The function $\Pi(p, w)$ is the profit function, which is the maximal profit feasible with prices (p, w) and technology T:

$$\Pi(p, w) = \max_{x,y} \{py - wx : (x, y) \in T\}^4 \qquad (5.2)$$

This function is homogeneous of degree $+1$ in prices in addition to being convex and continuous in positive prices.[5] The homogeneity in prices poses some problems when we wish to define some notion of profit efficiency; as we show below, some sort of normalization (which we show comes naturally from the duality with the directional distance function) is required. Profit maximization implies that

$$\Pi(p, w) = py^* - wx^* \geqq py - wx \quad \text{for all } (x, y) \in T. \qquad (5.3)$$

In words, the bundle (x^*, y^*) yields profits at least as high as any other feasible (x, y), or conversely, there exists no other feasible input–output vector that yields higher profits than (x^*, y^*). See figure 5.4, where the hyperplane $\{(x, y) : py - wx = \Pi(p, w)\}$ is tangent to technology T at the profit-maximizing bundle (x^*, y^*).

The quest for a dual to the profit function requires a functional representation of technology that completely represents technology (is equivalent to T) and that allows for adjustment of inputs and outputs simultaneously. This will also provide a measure of technical efficiency in this context. Thus, we turn to that dual function, namely, the directional (technology) distance function. To define it, we need to specify a directional vector. This vector—chosen by the researcher—determines the direction in which technical efficiency is assessed.

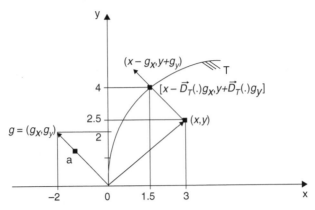

Figure 5.5. The Directional Technology Distance Function

Put differently, it is the path of projection of the observed data to the frontier of technology. Unlike the Shephard distance functions, that path is not necessarily determined by the observed bundle under observation (although that is a special case). The path or direction need not be the same for all inputs or all outputs as it is in the Shephard distance functions. That is, the direction is a vector rather than a scalar. Thus, for the general case, let $g = (g_x, g_y)$, where $g_x \in \Re_+^N$ and $g_y \in \Re_+^M$, and introduce

$$\vec{D}_T(x, y; g_x, g_y) = \sup\{\beta : (x - \beta g_x, y + \beta g_y) \in T\}. \tag{5.4}$$

We call this function the *directional technology distance function*, which we illustrate in figure 5.5. The technology is denoted by T, and the directional vector is in the fourth quadrant, indicating that inputs are to be contracted and outputs expanded simultaneously. The directional technology distance function projects the input–output vector (x, y) onto the technology frontier in the $(-g_x, g_y)$ direction, which in figure 5.5 is $g = (-2, 2)$. Intuitively or geometrically, the directional distance function subtracts g_x from the observed inputs x and adds g_y to the observed outputs y [here $(x, y) = (3, 2.5)$, which puts us at $(x - g_x, y + g_y) = (3 - 2, 2.5 + 2) = (1, 4.5)$, which projects us beyond the boundary of technology in figure 5.5. Next, we scale along this segment extending from (x, y) in the same direction—equivalently along the $0g$ vector—to the frontier of technology at $[x - \vec{D}_T(\cdot)g_x, y + \vec{D}_T(\cdot)g_y] = (1.5, 4)$ in figure 5.5. The value of the directional technology distance function for observation (x, y) is 0.75; that is, we must scale the bundle $(x - g_x, y + g_y)$ in figure 5.5 back to the boundary of T. The value of the directional technology distance function may be found here by solving

$$1.5 = 3 - \vec{D}_T(x, y; g_x, g_y) \cdot 2, \text{ (technically efficient input)},$$

$$4 = 2.5 + \vec{D}_T(x, y; g_x, g_y) \cdot 2, \text{ (technically efficient output)}.$$

If our original observation had been technically efficient, the value of the directional (technology) distance function would be zero.

In contrast, the familiar Shephard distance functions

$$D_o(x, y) = \min\{\theta : (x, y/\theta) \in T\}, \tag{5.5}$$

$$D_i(y, x) = \max\{\lambda : (x/\lambda, y) \in T\} \tag{5.6}$$

scale either in the output direction [the output distance function $D_o(x, y)$] or in the input direction [the input distance function $D_i(y, x)$], separately.[6] In figure 5.5, the Shephard output distance function would project (x, y) due north onto the boundary of T; the Shephard input distance function would project due west.

Before turning to the properties of the directional technology distance function, we take a slight detour to discuss the direction vector. Again, this is to be chosen by the researcher, which both presents an opportunity and, of course, raises the question, What direction do I choose? First of all, note that the direction vector *is* a vector: You can choose a different direction for each input and output. Also, the direction vector will be in the units you choose for your input and output data. If you change your labor input from workers to hours worked, the direction you choose for your labor input will also be in those units, just as the direction vector and observed vector are in the same units in figure 5.5. We return to the choice of direction vector later, but below we include some suggestions for choosing g:[7]

- $(g_x, g_y) = (x, y)$
- $(g_x, g_y) = (0, y)$ or $(g_x, g_y) = (x, 0)$
- $(g_x, g_y) = (\overline{x}, \overline{y})$, that is, the mean values of x and y
- $(g_x, g_y) = (1, 1)$
- (g_x, g_y) determined from a policy directive or social welfare function
- optimize (g_x, g_y) to minimize distance to frontier of technology

As we show below, choosing the direction in terms of the data under evaluation is the analog of what we do with the Shephard distance functions; each observation may be evaluated in a different "direction" based on its own input and output mix. The first option simultaneously scales in input and output directions. Next we can choose to scale either in the output direction as in the Shephard output distance function or in the input direction as in the Shephard input distance function. For example, if we choose $g = (0, y)$, then the amount by which we could increase outputs is $\vec{D}_T(x, y; 0, y) \cdot y$ units of outputs y, where y is a vector.

The next two options result in evaluation of all observations in the same direction. This is a little like assuming that all observations face the same prices in that it facilitates aggregation, which we discuss later in this chapter. If we choose $g = (1, 1)$, for example, then the amount by which we could increase outputs and decrease inputs would be $\vec{D}_T(x, y; 1, 1)$ units of x and y. Choosing

$g = (\bar{x}, \bar{y})$ implies that outputs may be increased by $\vec{D}_T(x, y; \bar{x}, \bar{y}) \cdot \bar{y}$ and inputs decreased by $\vec{D}_T(x, y; \bar{x}, \bar{y}) \cdot \bar{x}$.

Assuming a common direction would also be akin to an "egalitarian" evaluation, reflecting an underlying social welfare function, for example. We can imagine using the policy–motivated direction to evaluate environmental performance; later in this chapter we illustrate this idea. Finally, optimizing over the direction vector would provide the most favorable evaluation in terms of technical efficiency; that is, it seeks the minimum distance to the frontier of technology.

In terms of its properties, the directional distance function inherits these from the technology[8] and from its definition. From its definition, it has what we call the *translation property*

$$\vec{D}_T(x - \alpha g_x, y + \alpha g_y; g_x, g_y) = \vec{D}_T(x, y; g_x, g_y) - \alpha, \alpha \in \Re. \qquad (5.7)$$

Intuitively, this means that if we decide to double the size of the direction vector, everything else constant, then the associated value of the distance function will be reduced by 2. Returning to figure 5.5, the observed bundle (x, y) would be translated to $(x - \alpha g_x, y + \alpha g_y)$, requiring scaling by $[\vec{D}_T(\cdot) - \alpha]$ in the direction $(-g_x, g_y)$. This is the (additive) analog of the homogeneity property of the Shephard distance functions.

Another important property is the *representation property*

$$\vec{D}_T(x, y; g_x, g_y) \geq 0 \text{ if and only if } (x, y) \in T, \qquad (5.8)$$

which says that all feasible bundles (x, y) will have nonnegative values of the directional distance function. In turn, an observation is technically efficient when $\vec{D}_T(x, y; g_x, g_y) = 0$. In contrast, observations are technically efficient when the Shephard distance functions are equal to unity.

The directional distance function is also independent of unit of measurement, that is,

$$\vec{D}_T(\lambda \odot x, \theta \odot y; \lambda \odot g_x, \theta \odot g_y) = \vec{D}_T(x, y; g_x, g_y),$$
$$\lambda = (\lambda_1, \ldots, \lambda_N) > 0, \theta = (\theta_1, \ldots, \theta_M) > 0, \qquad (5.9)$$

where $\odot$ refers to componentwise multiplication; that is, $\lambda \odot x = (\lambda_1 x_1, \ldots, \lambda_N x_N)$. If, for example, we deflate inputs (outputs) and the associated direction vector by the same scalar, it will not change the value of the directional distance function.[9] These are the properties we focus on here; for more details, see Chambers, Chung, and Färe (1998) or Färe and Grosskopf (2004).

The representation property allows us to substitute $\vec{D}_T(x, y; g_x, g_y)$ for T in the definition of the profit function. Noting this as well as the feasibility of the projected vector, we have

$$[x - \vec{D}_T(\cdot)g_x, y + \vec{D}_T(\cdot)g_y] \in T. \qquad (5.10)$$

This says that the frontier bundle that consists of the original amount of x reduced by the amount $\vec{D}_T(\cdot)g_x$ and the original amount of y increased by $\vec{D}_T(\cdot)g_y$ is feasible. Then, if we take this bundle and compare its value to the profit maximum, we have the relationship

$$\Pi(p, w) \geq p[y + \vec{D}_T(\cdot)g_y] - w[x - \vec{D}_T(\cdot)g_x], \qquad (5.11)$$

where the right-hand side may be rewritten as

$$p[y + \vec{D}_T(\cdot)g_y] - w[x - \vec{D}_T(\cdot)g_x] = (py - wx) + \vec{D}_T(\cdot)(pg_y + wg_x). \qquad (5.12)$$

This says that the profit realized when we remove technical inefficiency (the left-hand side) is equal to the observed profit plus the gain realized by removing technical inefficiency (the right-hand side). The gain in profit from removing inefficiency is the value gained by adding the (value of the) direction vector $(pg_y + wg_x)$ to the observed bundle, and then scaling back to the frontier by the directional technology distance function, which gives the percentage of the gain that is feasible given technology.

If we substitute this into our profit inequality above and rearrange, we arrive at

$$\frac{\Pi(p, w) - (py - wx)}{pg_y + wg_x} \geq \vec{D}_T(x, y; g_x, g_y). \qquad (5.13)$$

On the left-hand side we have the *Nerlovian measure of profit efficiency*.[10] Note that this measure is independent of unit of measurement due to the normalization of the difference in maximum and observed profit by the total value of the direction vector. The denominator on the left-hand side comes from our relationship above between maximum profit and observed profit when we remove technical inefficiency, and tells us the profit associated with the direction vector.[11] This serves to normalize the difference between maximum and observed profit.[12] On the right-hand side is the directional technology distance function.

This inequality is in the family of what we call Mahler inequalities, which are the basis for the decompositions of "value efficiency" into technical and allocative components, where the directional technology distance function captures technical efficiency. If we add an allocative efficiency component $\vec{AE}_T$ to inequality (5.13), we arrive at our decomposition of profit efficiency as a strict equality:

$$\frac{\Pi(p, w) - (py - wx)}{pg_y + wg_x} = \vec{D}_T(x, y; g_x, g_y) + \vec{AE}_T \qquad (5.14)$$

The Mahler inequality (5.13) hints at the duality between the profit function and the directional technology distance function. Duality "closes" the inequality by optimization, that is, by removing allocative efficiency. Formally, the duality may be stated as

$$\Pi(p, w) = \max_{(xy)}\{p[y + \vec{D}_T(x, y; g_x, g_y)g_y] - w[x - \vec{D}_T(x, y; g_x, g_y)g_x]\}$$

$$= \max_{(xy)}\{py - wx + (pg_y + wg_x)\vec{D}_T(x, y; g_x, g_y)\},$$

$$\vec{D}_T(x, y; g_x, g_y) = \min_{(w,p)}\left\{\frac{\Pi(p, w) - (py - wx)}{pg_y + wg_x}\right\}. \quad (5.15)$$

This dual relationship allows us to identify the profit function if the directional technology distance function is known, or to retrieve the directional technology distance function if we know the profit function. The first relation shows that the profit function can be recovered from the directional technology distance function, and the second part shows how the directional technology distance function may be retrieved from the profit function. This duality is useful since it allows us to move from measures of productivity based on input–output quantities to measures of productivity based on input–output prices, which we demonstrate in section 5.3.

Another bonus of this duality result is that we can obtain shadow prices of inputs and outputs directly, by looking at the arg min problem

$$[w(x, y; g_x, g_y), p(x, y; g_x, g_y)] = \arg\min_{(w,p)} \frac{\Pi(p, w) - (py - wx)}{pg_y + wg_x}. \quad (5.16)$$

Given that the directional distance function is differentiable, the duality result may be used to derive normalized shadow prices where there are no market prices available; that is,

$$w(x, y; g_x, g_y)/(pg_y + wg_x) = \nabla_x \vec{D}_T(x, y; g_x, g_y),$$
$$p(x, y; g_x, g_y)/(pg_y + wg_x) = -\nabla_y \vec{D}_T(x, y; g_x, g_y) \quad (5.17)$$

(see, e.g., Chambers, 2002; Färe and Grosskopf, 2004). That is, the normalized shadow prices of inputs and outputs may be retrieved as the derivatives of the distance function. If one takes the ratio of two of the derivatives, then the normalization factor cancels and the relative prices so retrieved are equal to nonnormalized relative shadow prices. Note that to estimate stand-alone absolute shadow prices here, all we need is information on one absolute price, which can then be used to solve for the normalization factor. This is in contrast to the Lau and Yotopoulos (1971) approach discussed in chapter 1.

These shadow prices play a role in approximating the distance-function–based productivity measures such as the Malmquist productivity index by a value-based productivity index such as the Törnqvist productivity index.

Since profit maximization implies cost minimization and revenue maximization (but not the converse), we can derive duality results for the revenue and cost cases as special cases of our profit relationship. Eventually, we show that the traditional Shephard output and input distance functions, which capture technical efficiency in the revenue and cost cases, respectively, are in turn special cases of the directional technology distance function. Here, we provide an intermediate step that is defined in terms of a restricted directional distance function.

We begin with the revenue case and derive the duality between the revenue function and the directional output distance function, which is a special case of the directional technology distance function and is closely related to the Shephard output distance function. Define the revenue function as

$$R(x, p) = \max_{y}\{py : (x, y) \in T\} \tag{5.18}$$

and the directional output distance function as

$$\vec{D}_o(x, y; g_y) = \sup\{\beta : (x, y + \beta g_y) \in T\}. \tag{5.19}$$

The relationship between the directional technology distance function and the directional output distance function is simply

$$\vec{D}_o(x, y; g_y) = \vec{D}_T(x, y; 0, g_y). \tag{5.20}$$

That is, we set $g_x = 0$, which implies that we are projecting in the output direction only. In figure 5.5, we would be projecting northward to the frontier of T. Next, we make the assumption that $C(y, w) = wx$; that is, observed cost wx is equal to minimum cost defined as

$$C(y, w) = \min_{x}\{wx : (x, y) \in T\}. \tag{5.21}$$

Making these substitutions [including $\Pi(p, w) = R(x, p) - C(y, w)$] into our Nerlovian profit inequality, we have

$$\frac{R(x, p) - C(y, w) - (py - wx)}{pg_y} \geqq \vec{D}_o(x, y; g_y), \tag{5.22}$$

or

$$\frac{R(x, p) - py}{pg_y} \geqq \vec{D}_o(x, y; g_y). \tag{5.23}$$

The left-hand side is what we call the *revenue indicator of efficiency*[13], and the right-hand side is the directional output distance function, which is an indicator of output technical efficiency. If we add an allocative efficiency component $\vec{AE}_o$, we have the following decomposition of revenue efficiency:

$$\frac{R(x, p) - py}{pg_y} = \vec{D}_o(x, y; g_y) + \vec{AE}_o \tag{5.24}$$

Here, our normalization factor is pg_y.[14] If the direction vector is chosen to be $g_y = y$, then the normalization is observed revenue.[15] Similar arguments may be used to derive the cost efficiency indicator and its components as another special case of the profit relationship:

$$\frac{C(y, w) - wx}{wg_x} = \vec{D}_i(y, x; g_x) + \vec{AE}_i, \tag{5.25}$$

where

$$\vec{D}_i(y, x; g_x) = \vec{D}_T(x, y; g_x, 0) \tag{5.26}$$

is the directional input distance function, an indicator of input technical efficiency, and $\vec{AE}_i$ is the input allocative efficiency indicator. Here, if we choose $g_x = x$, then we normalize by observed cost.

5.1.2 Shephard and Farrell: Revenue efficiency and cost efficiency

Next we show how to derive the traditional Farrell-type cost and revenue efficiency measures and their decompositions from the above results.[16] Thus, we also illustrate the fact that the Shephard distance functions are special cases of directional distance functions.

The Shephard output distance function is defined as

$$D_o(x, y) = \sup\{\theta : (x, y/\theta) \in T\}, \tag{5.27}$$

which is homogeneous of degree +1 in outputs,[17] that is,

$$D_o(x, \lambda y) = \lambda D_o(x, y), \lambda > 0, \tag{5.28}$$

and which has the representation property

$$D_o(x, y) \leqq 1 \text{ if and only if } (x, y) \in T. \tag{5.29}$$

Moreover, one can show that the two output-oriented distance functions are related to each other as

$$\vec{D}_o(x, y; y) = \frac{1}{D_o(x, y)} - 1; \tag{5.30}$$

that is, Shephard's output distance function is a special case of the directional output distance function, namely, when the directional vector is defined as $g_y = y$, which is in the direction of the data of the observation under evaluation. To verify this claim, define

$$\vec{D}_o(x, y; y) = \sup\{\beta : (x, y + \beta y) \in T\}$$
$$= \sup\{\beta : D_o[x, y(1 + \beta)] \leq 1\}$$
$$= -1 + \sup\left\{(1 + \beta) : (1 + \beta) \leq \frac{1}{D_o(x, y)}\right\}$$
$$= \frac{1}{D_o(x, y)} - 1, \tag{5.31}$$

showing the relation between the directional output distance function and Shephard's output distance function.

Using this relation and revenue efficiency result given above, where we restrict the direction vector to the output direction; that is, $g = (0, y)$,

$$\frac{R(x, p) - py}{pg_y} \geqq \vec{D}_o(x, y; g_y) \tag{5.32}$$

yields

$$\frac{R(x, p)}{py} \geqq \frac{1}{D_o(x, y)}, \tag{5.33}$$

which is known as the output-oriented Mahler inequality. This is the basis for the Farrell (1957) indexes of output-oriented efficiency. The left-hand side is the revenue efficiency index, and the right-hand side is the index of Farrell output technical efficiency. Multiplication of the right-hand side by a residual allocative efficiency index yields the Farrell revenue efficiency decomposition

$$\frac{R(x, p)}{py} = \frac{1}{D_o(x, y)} \cdot AE_o. \tag{5.34}$$

Note that the Farrell decomposition is multiplicative, whereas our indicator decompositions are additive in structure.

The duality between the revenue function and the output distance function can be formulated using the Mahler inequality, namely,

$$R(x, p) = \max_y \frac{py}{D_o(x, y)},$$
$$D_o(x, y) = \max_p \frac{py}{R(x, p)}. \tag{5.35}$$

Again, the duality relationship eliminates allocative inefficiency through the optimization. In section 5.2.3, we use this duality result to show that the Malmquist output-oriented productivity index based on Shephard distance functions has a dual interpretation in terms of revenue functions.

The duality expression may also be used to create normalized output shadow prices; for example,

$$p(y, x) = \text{argmax}_p \frac{py}{R(x, p)}. \tag{5.36}$$

Among other uses, these normalized shadow prices may be used to create shares for aggregation or construction of traditional productivity indexes such as the Törnqvist output-based productivity index. Under differentiability of the Shephard distance function, we have

$$p(y, x)/R(x, p) = \nabla_y D_o(x, y). \tag{5.37}$$

The (revenue-deflated) output shadow prices are the derivatives of the output distance function. This observation was used by Färe and Grosskopf (1990) to evaluate price efficiency. We note that no data on prices are required to estimate the normalized shadow prices, $p(y, x)$.

Next we turn to the cost side. Starting with the profit and directional distance function duality relation, we can derive the cost and input distance function relationship. From the duality inequality between the profit function and the directional technology distance function, if we choose $g_y = 0$ and assume that observed revenue py equals maximum revenue $R(x, p)$, we have

$$\frac{wx - C(y, w)}{wg_x} \geqq \vec{D}_i(x, y; g_x), \tag{5.38}$$

where the directional input distance function

$$\vec{D}_i(x, y; g_x) = \vec{D}_T(x, y; g_x, 0) \tag{5.39}$$

is derived from the directional technology distance function.

By choosing $g_x = x$, we get the relation between the Shephard input distance function and the directional input distance function, namely,

$$\vec{D}_i(x, y; x) = 1 - \frac{1}{D_i(y, x)}, \tag{5.40}$$

where $D_i(y, x) = \max\{\lambda : (x/\lambda, y) \in T\}$ is the Shephard input distance function. This, together with the cost inequality above, yields the Mahler cost inequality, which is the basis of the Farrell cost-efficiency relationship:

$$\frac{C(y, w)}{wx} \leqq \frac{1}{D_i(y, x)} \tag{5.41}$$

and

$$\frac{C(y, w)}{wx} = \frac{1}{D_i(y, x)} \cdot AE_i \tag{5.42}$$

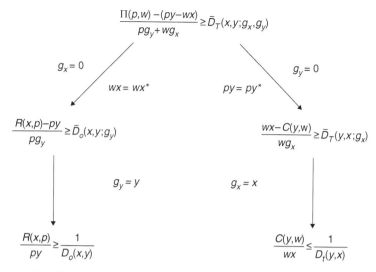

Figure 5.6. Efficiency Inequalities (reproduced from Färe and Grosskopf, 2004)

Figure 5.6 summarizes the relationships among the efficiency inequalities discussed in this section, demonstrating that the profit-directional technology distance function case includes the others as special cases. At the top of the diagram is the profit efficiency inequality. If we restrict our focus to scaling on either outputs or inputs (setting the appropriate directional vector equal to zero) and set observed cost (revenue) equal to its optimal value, we arrive at the middle-row relationships between an additive revenue efficiency indicator (additive cost efficiency indicator) and the associated directional distance function. If we set the restricted direction vector equal to the value of the observation under evaluation, our cost and revenue inequalities reduce to the familiar Farrell relationships using Shephard distance functions.

Summing up, we have given a brief overview of the relationships between the various distance functions and their value duals, including

- directional technology distance function and the profit function,
- Shephard output distance function and the revenue function, and
- Shephard input distance function and the cost function.

We also show that the Shephard dualities are special cases of the directional technology distance function and profit function duality. In addition, we have derived the Mahler inequalities for these cases, which lead to profit efficiency, revenue efficiency, and cost efficiency decompositions into allocative and technical efficiency components. Again, the Shephard-Farrell decompositions turn out to be special cases of the directional technology distance function profit decomposition. Along the way, we have shown how the dualities may be used to also retrieve shadow prices that link the value and distance functions.

These relationships are important for our discussion of productivity. First, they show that the distance functions and their duals both describe technology, but do so with different data, providing alternative building blocks to construct our productivity measures. The shadow price results are key to understanding the way in which we can link the traditional productivity measures, which use prices to aggregate inputs and outputs, to the distance-function–based productivity measures, which require only input and output quantity information.

5.2 Productivity

Let us begin with the simplest case: a world where one input is used to produce one output. And suppose that we have two observations (x^o, y^o) and (x^1, y^1), which could represent one production unit over time or two different production units in the same time period, for example. In this case, the level of productivity is understood to be the ratio of output to input or average product: y^1/x^1 and y^o/x^o. The corresponding productivity change is the ratio of these average products:

$$\text{productivity change} = \frac{y^1/x^1}{y^o/x^o} \tag{5.43}$$

Productivity has increased (or is higher for unit 1 than for unit o) if this ratio is greater than unity. We can rearrange this relationship as

$$\frac{y^1/x^1}{y^o/x^o} = \frac{y^1/y^o}{x^1/x^o}, \tag{5.44}$$

which says that change in average product is equal to the ratio of change in output to change in input. A discrete time approximation of the log difference gives us,

$$\text{productivity growth} = \frac{y^1 - y^o}{y^o} - \frac{x^1 - x^o}{x^o}, \tag{5.45}$$

which is the discrete time form of the familiar growth accounting relationship: Growth in outputs less growth in inputs gives us a residual measure of productivity growth. Here, values greater than zero signal improvements in productivity.

As noted above, this is all very straightforward in the single output–input case where we are measuring what might be called single-factor productivity, such as labor productivity. Things become more complicated when we allow for multiple inputs and multiple outputs and try to measure multiple factor or total factor productivity (TFP). We might also worry a bit about observed versus "best practice" or frontier performance and the need to distinguish efficiency change from technical change as a separate component of productivity growth.

Beginning with multiple outputs and inputs, we need to worry about aggregating apples and oranges and labor and capital, for example, to arrive at an "index" or scalar value for changes in total factor productivity. The production function provides an intermediate step toward aggregation and measurement of TFP; that was the contribution of Solow (1957). He showed that technical change could be measured as the change in observed output (scalar valued) minus the change in multiple inputs, where the latter could be aggregated based on the production function as an aggregator function. In practice, this required appealing to duality to employ cost shares as approximations of the marginal products derived from the production function, and assuming no technical inefficiency. In this section, we show how the Solow measure of technical change may be derived as a special case of the Malmquist index under these assumptions.

A long history of index number theory also provides means of aggregating inputs and outputs to measure productivity. Until the seminal contribution by Caves, Christensen, and Diewert (1982a), these index numbers, including Törnqvist, Fisher, Paasche, Laspeyres, and Bennet-Bowley, appeared to be somewhat ad hoc formulas for measuring productivity. Their suitability as measures of changes in productivity was typically evaluated on the basis of the tests or properties that they satisfied, which we discuss briefly below.[18] Caves, Christensen, and Diewert provided a link between a theoretical index of productivity defined directly on technology (what we know as the Malmquist productivity index) and the easily estimated Törnqvist index familiar from index number theory. This involved appealing to duality theory—linking technology and shadow prices, which they assumed were equal to observed prices—as well as the translog and quadratic lemmas, which allowed them to link the Törnqvist index to a translog technology and move from derivatives to discrete changes. Later, similar results were derived for the Fisher and Bennet-Bowley indexes, as well. This provided a new legitimacy to these classic index numbers, especially since the flexible functional forms to which they were now linked caused Diewert to dub these indexes not only exact (for the particular functional form under specific assumptions) but also superlative (providing the flexibility of a second-order approximation; see Diewert, 1976).

In introducing the Malmquist productivity indexes, Caves, Christensen, and Diewert (1982a) provided the framework for another group of productivity indexes that are based directly on the distance functions they used to define the Malmquist productivity indexes. These are the heart of this chapter. At the time Caves, Christensen, and Diewert thought of the Malmquist indexes as theoretical benchmarks. As it turns out, in the same year Nishimizu and Page (1982) published an empirical application of the Malmquist productivity index using the frontier production function model developed by Aigner and Chu (1968). This allowed them to estimate productivity change and identify efficiency change and technical change as separate components of productivity change. Eventually, Färe, Grosskopf, Lindgren, and Roos (1994) used DEA to estimate the component distance functions, providing another way to estimate Malmquist productivity and its components. There are other distance-function–based productivity indexes, as well; here, we include the Hicks-Moorsteen productivity index and the Luenberger productivity indicator.

Although not the main focus of this chapter, we also refer to some of the properties or tests that are associated with the index number approach to productivity measurement. Chapter 1 provides a more detailed list of those satisfied by the Malmquist indexes. The properties we find especially useful or well known in the literature include the following:

- **Identity**
  $$I(x, y, x, y) = 1$$
- **Proportionality**
  $$I(x^t, y^t, \lambda x^t, \mu y^t) = \mu/\lambda, \mu, \lambda > 0$$
- **Independence of unit of measurement**
  $$I(x^t, y^t, x^{t+1}, y^{t+1}) =$$
  $$I(\lambda_1 x_1^t, \dots, \lambda_N x_N^t, \mu_1 y_1^t, \dots, \mu_M y_M^t, \lambda_1 x_1^{t+1}, \dots \lambda_N x_N^{t+1},$$
  $$\mu_1 y_1^{t+1}, \dots, \mu_M y_M^{t+1}), \lambda_n, \mu_m, \forall m, n$$
- **Circularity**
  $$I(x^t, y^t, x^{t+1}, y^{t+1}) \cdot I(x^{t+1}, y^{t+1}, x^{t+2}, y^{t+2}) = I(x^t, y^t, x^{t+2}, y^{t+2}),$$

where $I(.)$ is the index number such as Malmquist or Törnqvist. The identity property is self-explanatory. The proportionality property relates to our definition of productivity as ratios of average products: If we scale inputs and outputs by λ and μ, respectively, between t and $t + 1$, then productivity will be equal to the ratio μ/λ. Independence of unit of measurement allows us to change from worker hours to worker days, for example, without affecting our measure. Circularity is a transitivity or path independence condition.

In the remainder of this section, we provide definitions and discussion of the aforementioned properties and derive relationships among the indexes and indicators. We begin with the distance-function–based productivity measures: Malmquist, Hicks-Moorsteen, and Luenberger. The last 10 years have witnessed an explosion of work in this area, especially with the Malmquist index. The rather lengthy discussion of the Malmquist productivity index reflects this. Some of this material is found in surveys of the Malmquist productivity index by Färe, Grosskopf, and Roos (1998), Lovell (2003), and Grosskopf (2003) and in a number of authoritative publications and papers by Bert Balk.[19] One of the major points of discussion in this growing literature is the decomposition of the distance-function–based productivity indexes, especially the Malmquist productivity index. Here, we touch briefly on the basic decomposition into efficiency and technical change and return to the quest for the "complete" decomposition of the Malmquist index later in this chapter.

After the introduction of the distance-function–based measures, we turn to a fairly brief discussion of three of the traditional productivity measures: Törnqvist, Fisher, and Bennet-Bowley. We sketch out the links to the distance function measures here, relying on our duality results from section 5.1.

5.2.1 Distance-function–based measures of productivity: Malmquist, Hicks-Moorsteen, and Luenberger

5.2.1.1 The Malmquist Productivity Index

Before turning to the specifics of the Malmquist index, we start with thinking about how distance functions can be used to arrive at our simple single output–input measure of productivity change,

$$\text{productivity change} = \frac{y^1/x^1}{y^o/x^o}. \qquad (5.46)$$

Let us illustrate with the Shephard output distance function

$$D_o(x, y) = \min\{\theta : (x, y/\theta) \in T\}, \qquad (5.47)$$

where for the moment we assume that technology does not change between period o and 1. As a generalization of the production function to multiple outputs, the Shephard output distance function will allow us to "aggregate" inputs and outputs. We note that, by definition, the output distance function is homogeneous of degree $+1$ in outputs. If, in addition, this function is homogeneous of degree -1 in inputs (which is guaranteed if we use a constant returns to scale reference technology), then we have (again, for the moment, with one input and output)

$$\frac{y^1/x^1}{y^o/x^o} = \frac{y^1/x^1}{y^o/x^o} \frac{D_o(1,1)}{D_o(1,1)} = \frac{D_o(x^1, y^1)}{D_o(x^o, y^o)}; \qquad (5.48)$$

that is, productivity change defined as ratios of average products may be expressed as ratios of output distance functions under constant returns to scale (see figure 5.7).

The technology T is bounded by the ray from the origin and the x-axis. The two observations are projected onto the reference technology (which reflects the highest average product feasible in period o) by the output distance function in the output direction, and the ratio of average products is equal to the ratio of the distance functions. Here, it is clear that productivity is higher for observation (x^1, y^1) than for observation (x^o, y^o); if we construct a ray through (x^1, y^1) from the origin and compare its slope [viz., the average product at (x^1, y^1)] to that of a similar ray constructed through (x^o, y^o), average product or productivity has increased going from (x^o, y^o) to (x^1, y^1).

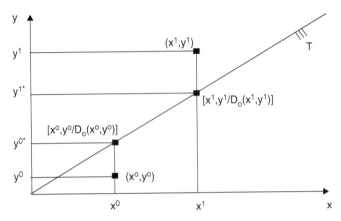

Figure 5.7. Productivity and Distance Functions

Since the output distance functions easily accommodate multiple inputs and outputs, the productivity index as ratios of output distance functions provides a natural generalization of the average product ratios. In fact,

$$M_o^o = \frac{D_o^o(x^1, y^1)}{D_o^o(x^o, y^o)} \tag{5.49}$$

is precisely the (base or period o) output-oriented Malmquist productivity index introduced by Caves, Christensen, and Diewert (1982a). Caves, Christensen, and Diewert conceived the Malmquist productivity index as a purely theoretical index that could not be empirically implemented;[20] they used it as a starting point and showed that the Törnqvist index (under certain conditions) is a very good approximation of the Malmquist index. Partly as a consequence, in their paper they made no assumptions concerning the scale properties of the technology and assumed that observations were on the frontier of their own period technology; that is, they assumed away what we would call technical inefficiency. Here, we relax the no-inefficiency assumption but employ a constant returns reference technology to maintain the link between the index as a measure of ratios of average products, which also means that our measure satisfies the proportionality property listed above.

Two other comments are in order at the outset: (i) The index above is defined as scaling on outputs only. Caves, Christensen, and Diewert also define an input-oriented analog that scales only on inputs. (ii) In this example, T is the single reference or benchmark technology. In the case of two periods, it is certainly possible that the reference technology changes over time; that is, we have T^o and T^1. The questions arise: Which reference should we choose, and does it matter?

The first comment leads to the natural idea that other directions could be chosen in which to project the data to the reference technology. Caves, Christensen, and Diewert proposed both input- and output-oriented directions.[21] Our discussion above suggests that using the directional distance function may be a useful generalization of the above-defined productivity index using traditional distance functions. In fact, the Luenberger productivity indicator, due to Chambers (1996), defines just such an approach, which we discuss later in this section.

The base period output-oriented Malmquist productivity index due to Caves, Christensen, and Diewert (1982a) is defined as

$$M_o^o = \frac{D_o^o(x^1, y^1)}{D_o^o(x^o, y^o)}. \tag{5.50}$$

As we show presently, a similar index could be defined relative to the period 1 technology.[22]

Recall that we showed above that, under constant returns to scale, the average product ratio index of productivity coincides with the Malmquist index.[23] Färe and Grosskopf (1996) showed that this is a necessary and sufficient condition. Formally:

Proposition. Suppose that one input is used to produce a single output. Then,

$$\frac{y^1}{x^1} \bigg/ \frac{y^o}{x^o} = D_o^\tau(x^1, y^1)/D_o^\tau(x^o, y^o), \tau = 0 \text{ or } 1,$$

if and only if the τ-period technology exhibits constant returns to scale.

One may translate the single input–output case in the multiple input–output case in the following way: Assume $x^\tau = \lambda^\tau \cdot x^o$ and $y^\tau = \mu^\tau \cdot y^o, \tau = t, t+1$. In this case, we have

$$D^\tau(x^{t+1}, y^{t+1})/D^\tau(x^t, y^t) = D^\tau(\lambda^{t+1}x^o, \mu^{t+1}y^o)/D^\tau(\lambda^t x^o, \mu^t y^o)$$

$$= \left(\frac{\mu^{t+1}}{\lambda^{t+1}} \bigg/ \frac{\mu^t}{\lambda^t}\right) D^\tau(x^o, y^o)/D^\tau(x^o, y^o)$$

$$= \frac{\mu^{t+1}}{\lambda^{t+1}} \bigg/ \frac{\mu^t}{\lambda^t}.$$

Thus, if inputs and outputs have been proportionally changed, under constant returns to scale the τ-period Malmquist index is the change in "average" product. It satisfies our proportionality property.

Above we introduced the base period Malmquist productivity index; Caves, Christensen, and Diewert (1982a) also introduced a period 1 index, namely,

$$M_o^1 = \frac{D_o^1(x^1, y^1)}{D_o^1(x^o, y^o)},$$
(5.51)

where the distance functions $D_o^1(x^1, y^1)$ and $D_o^1(x^o, y^o)$ are defined relative to the period 1 technology T^1.

In general, of course, M_o^o and M_o^1 yield different productivity numbers since the technologies T^o and T^1 may differ. One may show that $M_o^o = M_o^1$ if and only if the distance functions are of the form

$$D_o^\tau(x, y) = A(\tau)D_o(x, y), \tau = 0 \text{ or } 1,$$
(5.52)

which is demonstrated in appendix 5.1. This condition is referred to as Hicks output neutrality,[24] and it states that the output sets are shifted by the technology function $A(\tau)$.

The Hicks neutrality condition is quite restrictive, and we prefer not to impose it on the technology. Instead, one may arbitrarily choose period 0 or period 1 as the reference, or as in Färe, Grosskopf, Lindgren, and Roos (1989), one may take the geometric mean of the two.[25] They define the Malmquist output-oriented productivity index as

$$M_o = (M_o^o \cdot M_o^1)^{1/2}$$

$$= \left(\frac{D_o^o(x^1, y^1)}{D_o^o(x^o, y^o)} \frac{D_o^1(x^1, y^1)}{D_o^1(x^o, y^o)} \right)^{1/2}.$$
(5.53)

This is in the spirit of Fisher (1922), who defined his ideal price index as the geometric mean of the Laspeyres and Paasche indexes. We illustrate the index in figure 5.8.

One of the key advantages of the Malmquist index is that the component distance functions readily allow identification of movements toward the frontier, efficiency change (EC or catching up), and technical change (TC or shifts in the frontier); that is,

$$M_o = EC \cdot TC,$$
(5.54)

where

$$EC = D_o^1(x^1, y^1)/D_o^o(x^o, y^o)$$
(5.55)

is the efficiency change component and

$$TC = \left(\frac{D_o^o(x^1, y^1)}{D_o^1(x^1, y^1)} \frac{D_o^o(x^o, y^o)}{D_o^1(x^o, y^o)} \right)^{1/2}$$
(5.56)

captures technical change.

Intuitively, this index and its components take us from (x^o, y^o) to (x^1, y^1), taking account of technology; that is, we go from y^o to y^1 on the y-axis while traveling along technology and accounting for shifts in technology with associated movement from x^o to x^1 on the x-axis. Starting at (x^o, y^o) or point a on the y-axis, we first project to technology T^o and move from a to b. Moving along technology T^o by accounting for the increase in x^o to x^1 gives a movement on the y-axis from b to e. Accounting for technical change at x^1 moves us from e to f, and accounting for technical inefficiency of (x, y) relative to T^1 moves us from f to d. Alternative paths are possible—see the discussion in chapter 1.

Substituting for the distance functions in (5.52) and referring to figure 5.8 gives us

$$M_o = \left(\frac{0d}{0e} \Big/ \frac{0a}{0b} \cdot \frac{0d}{0f} \Big/ \frac{0a}{0c} \right)^{1/2}, \tag{5.57}$$

where

$$EC = \frac{0d/0f}{0a/0b}$$

$$\tag{5.58}$$

$$TC = \left(\frac{0d/0e}{0d/0f} \frac{0a/0b}{0a/0c} \right)^{1/2}.$$

This decomposition is due to Färe, Grosskopf, Lindgren, and Roos (1989, 1994); a similar decomposition was proposed by Nishimizu and Page (1982) in a parametric context. As mentioned in chapter 1, this simple decomposition may itself be decomposed to account for deviations from constant returns,

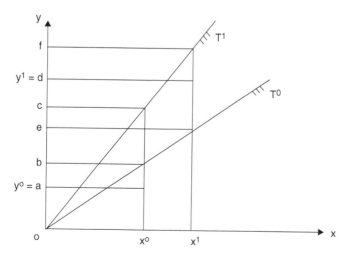

Figure 5.8. The Malmquist Productivity Index

among other factors. We return to a more detailed discussion of the many alternative decompositions of the Malmquist index in section 5.4.

Another nice feature of the Malmquist productivity index is that we may relate the above expression to the Solow (1957) measure of productivity change based on the aggregate production function. Assume that one output is produced according to the production function

$$F(x) = \max\{y : (x, y) \in T\}, \tag{5.59}$$

which, following Solow, we assume satisfies constant returns to scale. In terms of the distance function, this equals

$$F(x) = y/D_o(x, y) = y/\big[yD_o(x, 1)\big] = 1/D_o(x, 1), \tag{5.60}$$

or

$$D_o(x, y) = y/F(x). \tag{5.61}$$

Also assume, as in Solow, that technical change is disembodied and Hicks neutral, so that

$$y^\tau = F^\tau(x^\tau) = A(\tau)F(x^\tau), \tau = 0, 1,$$
$$D_o^\tau(x^\tau, y^\tau) = y^\tau/[A(\tau)F(x^\tau)], \tau = 0, 1, \tag{5.62}$$

Inserting these expressions into the Malmquist index yields

$$M_o = \left[\frac{y^1/\big[A(0)F(x^1)\big]}{y^0/\big[A(0)F(x^0)\big]} \frac{y^1/\big[A(1)F(x^1)\big]}{y^0/\big[A(1)F(x^0)\big]} \right]^{1/2}$$
$$= A(1)/A(0), \tag{5.63}$$

where we have substituted $A(\tau)F(x^\tau)$ for y^τ to arrive at the last relationship. This says that the Malmquist and Solow approaches coincide as measures of productivity change under these assumptions, which include technical efficiency; that is, $EC = 1$ in the Malmquist context. This follows since the production function is expressed as a strict equality,

$$y = A(\tau)F(x), \tag{5.64}$$

rather than an inequality and implies that productivity change is identical to technical change under these assumptions.

What properties does the Malmquist index satisfy? Førsund (1990) and Berg, Førsund, and Jansen (1992) pointed out that the Malmquist index,

$$M_o^\tau = \frac{D_o^\tau(x^1, y^1)}{D_o^\tau(x^0, y^0)}, \tau = 0, 1, \tag{5.65}$$

and its geometric mean version,

$$M_o = (M_o^1 M_o^0)^{1/2}, \tag{5.66}$$

do not satisfy the circularity test; that is, if t_1, t_2, and t_3 are three consecutive time periods and I is an index, then I satisfies the circularity test if

$$I(t_1, t_3) = I(t_1, t_2)I(t_2, t_3). \tag{5.67}$$

Aczél (1990) showed that an index satisfies the circularity test if and only if the index is multiplicatively separable; that is, if and only if

$$I(t_1, t_2) = I(t_1)I(t_2). \tag{5.68}$$

Färe and Grosskopf (1996) proved that this translates into

$$D_o^\tau(x, y) = A(\tau)D_o(x, y), \tau = 0, 1. \tag{5.69}$$

So once again, Hicks output neutrality must be imposed, this time to ensure circularity.[26] The Fisher productivity index also does not satisfy circularity. Following Fisher, one may argue that this is not an important property for productivity indexes since there is a natural order of time that makes productivity change inherently path dependent.

Nevertheless, Førsund (1990) and Berg, Førsund, and Jansen (1992) introduced a fixed-base Malmquist index in an effort to impose circularity; that is,

$$D_o^{t_o}(x^{t+1}, y^{t+1})/D_o^{t_o}(x^t, y^t), \tag{5.70}$$

where t_o is fixed for all $t = 1, 2, \dots$. Althin (1995) proved that this formulation of the Malmquist index is base independent if and only if the distance function takes the form

$$D_o^{t_o}(x, y) = A(t_o)D_o(x, y). \tag{5.71}$$

As we have already shown, when this Hicks output-neutrality condition holds, the Malmquist index satisfies the circularity test and implies that $M_o^o = M_o^1$.

In order to address the circularity issue without resorting to a fixed base, Balk and Althin (1996) created a Malmquist-type productivity index that depends on all time periods $t = 1, \dots, \bar{t}$. This index is independent of $\bar{t}$ provided that the distance function is again Hicks output neutral.

Our view is that, for analyzing productivity change where there is a time component, we should follow Fisher and use the natural order of time and not worry about circularity. For productivity comparisons where time does not play a role, circularity may be more important; we refer the reader to Caves, Christensen, and Diewert (1982b) for a discussion of multilateral comparisons.

5.2.1.2 The Hicks-Moorsteen productivity index

The Malmquist productivity index could be dubbed a technology index; in contrast to traditional productivity indexes such as the Törnqvist index, it is not a ratio of a quantity index of outputs to a quantity index of inputs. Rather, it compares observed input–output bundles to a given reference technology. One may, however, define a productivity index with distance functions, which is a ratio of a Malmquist quantity index of outputs to a Malmquist quantity index of inputs—this is the Hicks-Moorsteen index, which provides an interesting point of comparison to the Malmquist productivity index. The name we use here is due to Diewert; it was "rediscovered" by Bjurek (1994), who somewhat confusingly called it the Malmquist total factor productivity index.[27]

The connection to Malmquist is fairly direct: The Hicks-Moorsteen index is the ratio of output and input quantity indexes based on distance functions. Malmquist (1953) first proposed using distance functions to construct quantity indexes in the consumer context. In the production context, the Malmquist output quantity index is defined as ratios of Shephard output distance functions, where the general definition is

$$D_o(x, y) = \min\{\theta : (x, y/\theta) \in T\}. \tag{5.72}$$

The definition of the output quantity index requires a specific variation of this; that is, let $D_o^o(x^o, y^1)$ be the distance function given the (counterfactual) input–output vector (x^o, y^1), which is evaluated relative to T^o, and $D_o^o(x^o, y^o)$ be the distance-function–evaluating observed vector (x^o, y^o) relative to the same technology (see figure 5.9).

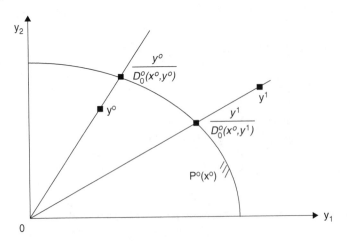

Figure 5.9. The Malmquist Output Quantity Index

The output set $P^o(x^o)$ is defined as

$$P^o(x^o) = \{y : (x^o, y) \in T^o\}, \tag{5.73}$$

and it consists of all output vectors $y = (y_1, y_2)$ that can be produced with the input vector x^o with the technology T^o; that is, $P^o(x^o)$ represents the same technology as T^o. The corresponding isoquant of the output set is defined as

$$\text{isoq}P^o(x^o) = \{y : y \in P^o(x^o), \lambda y \notin P^o(x^o), \lambda > 1\}, \text{ for } P^o(x^o) \neq \{0\}.$$

The isoquant is the curved line in figure 5.9, and the output set is bounded by the isoquant and the y-axis. The distance functions $D_o^o(x^o, y^o)$ and $D_o^o(x^o, y^1)$ project the output vectors y^o and y^1 onto the isoquant or boundary of the output set.

The Malmquist output quantity index is

$$Q_o^o = \frac{D_o^o(x^o, y^1)}{D_o^o(x^o, y^o)}. \tag{5.74}$$

In figure 5.9, the value of the quantity index is greater than one, reflecting the fact that output has "increased" relative to the isoquant between period 0 and period 1.[28] Malmquist's insight was to use the isoquant as a reference; without the isoquant, it is not obvious that output in period 1 "dominates" output in period 0. Note also that the input vector is held constant—at its value in period 0 (x^o)—in both distance functions in order to allow us to use the boundary of $P(x^o)$ as our reference; only the output vector changes, as is typical of output quantity index formulas such as the Törnqvist or Fisher output quantity indexes. Thus, in contrast to the Malmquist productivity index (5.50) or (5.51), we assess counterfactual observations, namely, (x^o, y^1) (see the numerator of the index). In the Malmquist index, we assess realized input–output bundles relative to realized technologies; the counterfactual in that case is the assessment of realized data from one period to technology in a different period.

Similarly, the Malmquist input quantity index is constructed as ratios of input distance functions, $D_i^o(y^o, x^o)$ and $D_i^o(y^o, x^1)$. The Malmquist input quantity index is defined as

$$Q_i^o = \frac{D_i^o(y^o, x^1)}{D_i^o(y^o, x^o)}, \tag{5.75}$$

which is illustrated in figure 5.10. The input set $L(y)$ is defined as

$$L^o(y^o) = \{x : (x, y^o) \in T^o\}, \tag{5.76}$$

and it consists of all input vectors $x = (x_1, x_2)$ that can produce output vector y^o with the technology T^o; that is, $L^o(y^o)$ represents the same technology

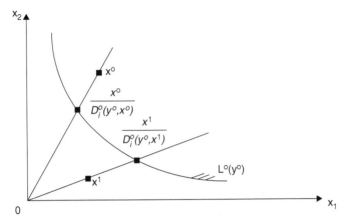

Figure 5.10. The Malmquist Input Quantity Index

as T^o. The corresponding isoquant of the input set is defined as

$$\text{isoq}L^o(y^o) = \{x : x \in L^o(y^o) \text{ and } \theta < 1 \text{ imply } \theta x \notin L^o(y^o)\}. \quad (5.77)$$

The isoquant is the curved line in figure 5.10 and is the boundary of the input set. The input distance functions $D_i^o(y^o, x^1)$ and $D_i^o(y^o, x^o)$ project the input vectors x^o and x^1 onto the isoquant or boundary of the input set, and the quantity index is the ratio of the corresponding distance functions. Here, we find that our index takes a value less than one, indicating that input usage has decreased between period o and period 1 relative to the input isoquant.[29]

The Hicks-Moorsteen base period productivity index is defined by the ratio of these quantity indexes:

$$\text{HM}^o = \frac{Q_o^o}{Q_i^o} = \frac{D_o^o(x^o, y^1)/D_o^o(x^o, y^o)}{D_i^o(y^o, x^1)/D_i^o(y^o, x^o)} \quad (5.78)$$

This is illustrated in figure 5.11. Here, we see that productivity has increased; the ray through the original observations has become steeper between period o and period 1. This is reflected in the value of the index, which here exceeds unity; that is, output change (the numerator) exceeds input change (the denominator). In figure 5.11, the net output growth is captured by the vertical difference between (x^o, y^o) and (x^o, y^1); that is, an increase. Net input growth is captured by the horizontal distance from (x^o, y^o) to (x^1, y^o), a decrease.

In the special case of a single output and single input, the index may be written

$$\text{HM}^o = \frac{D_o^o(x^o, 1)y^1/D_o^o(x^o, 1)y^o}{D_i^o(y^o, 1)x^1/D_i^o(y^o, 1)x^o} = \frac{y^1/x^1}{y^o/x^o}; \quad (5.79)$$

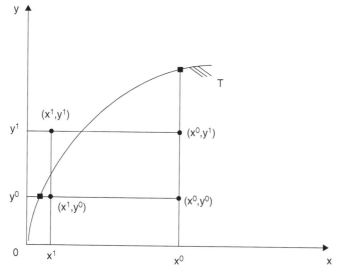

Figure 5.11. The Hicks-Moorsteen Productivity Index

that is, it reduces to the ratio of average products, as it should. Here, the assumption of constant returns to scale need not be imposed on the reference technology, in contrast to the Malmquist productivity index. One interesting feature of the Hicks-Moorsteen index (in contrast to the Malmquist index) is that it cannot be decomposed to include a meaningful scale effect.[30]

More formally, to compare the Malmquist and Hicks-Moorsteen productivity indexes, we need to introduce the concept of inverse homotheticity.[31] The technology is said to exhibit inverse homotheticity if the output distance function takes the form

$$D_o(x, y) = D_o(\bar{x}, y)/F\left[D_i(\bar{y}, x)\right],\qquad(5.80)$$

where F is increasing and the input–output vector $(\bar{x}, \bar{y})$ is an arbitrary fixed vector. The following proposition is due to Färe, Grosskopf, and Roos (1998):

Proposition. The Malmquist productivity index M_o^o coincides with the Hicks-Moorsteen index HM^o if and only if the technology is inversely homothetic and exhibits constant returns to scale.[32]

This proposition is informative in its own right, but also is of interest because of its implications for decompositions of productivity growth, which we address below. Nemoto and Goto (2004) show that the Hicks-Moorsteen index has no scale component and no input and output mix effect. Nevertheless, due to the equivalence between Malmquist and Hicks-Moorsteen in the special case of inverse homotheticity and constant returns to scale, we have the following decomposition of the geometric mean Hicks-Moorsteen index, which parallels the decomposition of the Malmquist productivity index into efficiency change and technical change components:

$$\text{HM} = (\text{HM}^1\text{HM}^o)^{1/2} = \text{HMEC} \cdot \text{HMTC} \tag{5.81}$$

Under inverse homotheticity and constant returns to scale, we can write HMEC as

$$\text{HMEC} = \left(\frac{D_o^1(\overline{x}, y^1)}{D_o^o(\overline{x}, y^o)} \right) \left(\frac{D_i^1(\overline{y}, x^1)}{D_i^o(\overline{y}, x^o)} \right), \tag{5.82}$$

where the expression in the first set of parentheses measures catching up in outputs, and the second captures catching up in inputs. The technical change component also consists of two parts, technical change in outputs and technical change in inputs,

$$\text{HMTC} = \left(\frac{D_o^o(\overline{x}, y^1)}{D_o^1(\overline{x}, y^1)} \frac{D_o^o(\overline{x}, y^o)}{D_o^1(\overline{x}, y^o)} \right)^{1/2} \left(\frac{D_i^1(\overline{y}, x^1)}{D_i^o(\overline{y}, x^1)} \frac{D_i^1(\overline{y}, x^o)}{D_i^o(\overline{y}, x^o)} \right)^{1/2}. \tag{5.83}$$

In the case of a scalar output, inverse homotheticity simplifies to standard homotheticity. Thus, by constant returns to scale, the geometric mean Hicks-Moorsteen index is the ratio of Solow residuals, as in the case of the Malmquist index.

As mentioned above, the Hicks-Moorsteen index, in general, does not allow identification; of a scale component in its decomposition; this has led Balk (2004) to suggest that the Hicks-Moorsteen index is "decomposition resistant." The Malmquist index allows us to identify such effects, which we discuss later in this chapter. There are some features of the Hicks-Moorsteen index that we assess in a more positive light. Of course, it shares with the Malmquist indexes the direct link to technology through the distance functions; thus, like the Malmquist indexes, it does not require price information. This index, given that it is defined as a ratio of output change to input change, allows ready identification of the separate contributions of output and input growth to productivity change, and in this sense it is more closely related to the more familiar price-related productivity indexes such as the Törnqvist indexes. In terms of estimation in the DEA context, it also has the advantage of avoiding problems with infeasibility that may arise when estimating the mixed period problems in the Malmquist case.

5.2.1.3 The Luenberger productivity indicator

The Malmquist productivity indexes as defined by Caves, Christensen, and Diewert (1982a) are either output oriented or input oriented, implying that they assess productivity growth as changes in either output or input, but not both. In contrast, the Hicks-Moorsteen index, as well as the traditional

Törnqvist and Fisher indexes, which are defined as ratios of output to input quantity indexes, take inputs and outputs into consideration separately.

The Malmquist and Hicks-Moorsteen productivity indexes have in common the feature that the direction(s) in which performance is assessed is given, and not a matter of choice by the researcher.[33] Also, since that direction depends on the individual observation's data under assessment, that direction may be different for each observation.

In this section, we discuss an alternative measure of productivity based on distance functions, namely, the Luenberger productivity indicator introduced by Chambers (1996). This measure differs from the aforementioned Malmquist-type indexes in two primary ways: (1) It is constructed from the directional technology distance functions, which simultaneously adjust outputs and inputs in a direction chosen by the investigator, and (2) it has an additive structure (inherited from the directional technology distance functions); that is, it is expressed as differences rather than ratios of distance functions. We follow Diewert (2005) and call these difference measures *indicators*, as opposed to *indexes*, which are in ratio form.

The fact that Luenberger productivity indicator is constructed from directional distance functions in which inputs and outputs may be simultaneously adjusted means that the Luenberger productivity indicator is a useful companion when profitability is the overall goal. The duality between the directional distance function and the profit function provides this crucial link. The Luenberger indicator also provides a useful basis for evaluating environmental performance; we can specify the underlying directional distance functions to allow for simultaneous reduction of undesirable outputs and expansion of desirable outputs. The link to profitability is explored in section 5.2.3; the "green" Luenberger productivity indicator is discussed briefly later in this section.

More formally, let (x^o, y^o) and (x^1, y^1) be two observations, and let the technology be T. The base period Luenberger productivity indicator is defined as

$$L^o = \vec{D}^o_T(x^o, y^o; g) - \vec{D}^o_T(x^1, y^1; g), \qquad (5.84)$$

where the $g = (g_x, g_y)$ and the distance functions are defined relative to the zero period technology T^o as

$$\vec{D}^o_T(x^\tau, y^\tau; g) = \sup\{\beta : (x^\tau - \beta g_x, y^\tau + \beta g_y) \in T^o\}, \tau = 0, 1. \quad (5.85)$$

Here, we have made no assumptions concerning returns to scale. As we show below, this facilitates the connection to profit maximization; imposing constant returns to scale would imply zero maximum profit.

Figure 5.12 illustrates our measure. As usual, the technology T^o is the area between the curved line and the x-axis. The directional vector, which is the same for both observations in our example (although that is not a necessary condition), is in the fourth quadrant, indicating that inputs are contracted

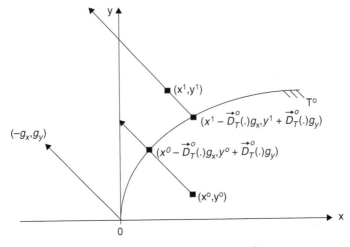

Figure 5.12. The Base Period Luenberger Productivity Indicator

and outputs expanded. The distance function projects both observations onto the boundary of the technology in the direction $(-g_x, g_y)$. The definition of productivity change as the difference between the value of the directional distance function using base period data and technology minus the value of the directional distance function using period 1 data appears at first to be reversed. Recall that the directional distance function takes values greater than or equal to zero for feasible data. Thus, in figure 5.12, $\vec{D}_T^o(x^o, y^o; g) > 0$. Since the data from period 1 lie outside the technology T^o, they are not feasible, in period o and the directional distance function takes on values less than zero; that is, in figure 5.12; $\vec{D}_T^o(x^1, y^1; g) < 0$. The difference is thus greater than zero, reflecting the fact that productivity has increased between period o and period 1.

We can also define a period 1–based Luenberger productivity indicator by choosing T^1 as the reference technology; that is,

$$L^1 = \vec{D}_T^1(x^o, y^o; g) - \vec{D}_T^1(x^1, y^1; g). \tag{5.86}$$

For the period o and period 1 indicators to coincide, the technology would have to be represented by

$$\vec{D}_T^\tau(x, y; g) = \vec{A}(\tau) + \vec{D}_T(x, y; g), \tag{5.87}$$

which is verified in appendix 5.1.

Rather than arbitrarily choosing between the two reference technologies T^o and T^1 or making overly strong restrictions on technology, we may instead define the (arithmetic) mean indicator

$$L = \frac{1}{2}(L^1 + L^o) = \left[\frac{1}{2}\vec{D}_T^1(x^o, y^o; g) - \vec{D}_T^1(x^1, y^1; g)\right.$$

$$\left. + \vec{D}_T^o(x^o, y^o; g) - \vec{D}_T^o(x^1, y^1; g)\right]. \qquad (5.88)$$

As shown by Chambers, Färe, and Grosskopf (1996), the Luenberger indicator, like the Malmquist index, may be decomposed into efficiency change (LEC) and technical change (LTC),

$$\text{LEC} = \vec{D}_T^o(x^o, y^o; g) - \vec{D}_T^1(x^1, y^1; g), \qquad (5.89)$$

and

$$\text{LTC} = \frac{1}{2}\left[\vec{D}_T^1(x^1, y^1; g) - \vec{D}_T^o(x^1, y^1; g) + \vec{D}_T^1(x^o, y^o; g) - \vec{D}_T^o(x^o, y^o; g)\right], \qquad (5.90)$$

respectively, where $L = \text{LEC} + \text{LTC}$.

Also like the geometric mean form of the Malmquist index, the arithmetic mean form of the Luenberger indicator does not require specification of a fixed base year; rather, it evaluates adjacent periods and satisfies (an additive version of) the circularity test only under restrictive conditions on technology that impose "neutrality".[34] To verify this claim, define an additive circularity test as

$$I(t_1, t_3) = I(t_1, t_2) + I(t_2, t_3), \qquad (5.91)$$

where t_1, t_2, t_3 are three periods. It then follows from Aczél (1990) that circularity holds if and only if

$$I(t_1, t_2) = I(t_1) + I(t_2). \qquad (5.92)$$

Implementing this for the Luenberger productivity indicator verifies our claim.

How are the Malmquist index and the Luenberger indicator related? Rather than taking the Boussemart, Briec, Kerstens, and Poutineau (2003) approximation approach, we follow Balk, Färe, Grosskopf, and Margaritis (2005) and show how the Luenberger productivity indicator can be transformed into the Malmquist productivity index.

We make use of the logarithmic mean, which states that for any positive real numbers a and b,

$$\text{LM}(a, b) = (a - b)/\ln(a/b), \text{ where } LM(a, a) = a. \qquad (5.93)$$

In addition we assume that $\vec{D}_T^o(x^o, y^o; 0, y^o) = 0$, that is, that (x^o, y^o) is on the boundary of technology, and that y^1 is strictly positive. These assumptions imply that

$$\vec{D}_T^o(x^o, y^o; 0, y^1) = 0 \tag{5.94}$$

(see Balk et al., 2005).

From the relation between the directional distance function and Shephard's output distance function, that is,

$$\vec{D}_T(x, y; 0, y) = 1/D_o(x, y) - 1, \tag{5.95}$$

and the assumptions above, using $g = (0, y)$, we have

$$\frac{1}{D_o^o(x^o, y^o)} - \frac{1}{D_o^o(x^1, y^1)} = L^o. \tag{5.96}$$

Thus, by the logarithmic mean, we have

$$\ln D_o^o(x^1, y^1) - \ln D_o^o(x^o, y^o) = L^o / \text{LM} \left[1/D_o^o(x^o, y^o), 1/D_o^o(x^1, y^1) \right], \tag{5.97}$$

or

$$M^o = e^{L^o / \text{LM}[(1/D_o^o(x^o, y^o), 1/D_o^o(x^1, y^1)]}. \tag{5.98}$$

A similar expression may be derived for the period one case. For the geometric mean formulation, we have

$$M = (M^o \cdot M^1)^{1/2}$$
$$= e^{1/2 \left(L^o / \text{LM} \left[1/D_o^o(x^o, y^o), 1/D_o^o(x^1, y^1) \right] + L^1 / \text{LM} \left[1/D_o^1(x^o, y^o), 1/D_o^1(x^1, y^1) \right] \right)}, \tag{5.99}$$

again assuming that

$$\vec{D}_T^\tau(x^\tau, y^\tau; 0, y^\tau) = 0, \tau = 0, 1, y^1 > 0. \tag{5.100}$$

Given the above-derived relationship between the Malmquist productivity index and the Luenberger productivity indicator, it is also of interest to develop the relationship between the Luenberger and Solow productivity models. For this purpose, we begin by specifying the directional distance function for the scalar output production function case by setting $g = (0, 1)$ and assuming scalar output, which yields

$$\vec{D}_T(x, y; 0, 1) = F(x) - y \tag{5.101}$$

and

$$\vec{D}_T(x, 0; 0, 1) = F(x). \tag{5.102}$$

If we assume that technical change is additive, then we can write

$$F^\tau(x) = F(x) + A(\tau), \tau = 0, 1; \tag{5.103}$$

then it follows that

$$L = A(1) - A(0). \tag{5.104}$$

Thus—analogous to the Malmquist productivity index—in the special case of single output, constant returns to scale, and Hicks neutrality, the Luenberger productivity indicator is equivalent to the Solow specification of technical change.

A noteworthy feature of the Luenberger productivity indicator is that inputs and outputs, although scaled simultaneously—they are all scaled by the same factor β—are not treated symmetrically since outputs are expanded and inputs are contracted. Put differently, the direction $(-g_x, g_y)$ is a vector, not a scalar. This feature may be exploited for the case of joint production of good and bad outputs, where contraction of bad outputs simultaneously with expansion of good outputs is a reasonable objective given environmental regulation, for example.[35]

To introduce a "green" Luenberger productivity indicator, some additional notation is required. Let the output vector be partitioned into good or desirable outputs and bad or undesirable outputs $y = (y_g, y_b)$. We say that a technology T is an environmental technology if it satisfies the following two axioms:

Nulljointness of (y_g, y_b):   if $y = (y_g, y_b) \in P(x)$, and $y_b = 0$, then $y_g = 0$, $$\tag{5.105}$$

Weak disposability: if $y \in P(x)$ and $0 < \theta \leq 1$, then $\theta y \in P(x)$. $$\tag{5.106}$$

Nulljointness, introduced by Shephard and Färe (1974), models the condition in which bads are byproducts of the production of good outputs. This definition (in its contrapositive form) states that positive good outputs are always accompanied by production or emission of bad outputs.

Weak disposability of outputs states that proportional reduction of good and bad outputs is always feasible; the disposability of individual outputs separately is not necessarily feasible. This axiom captures the idea that disposal of bad outputs is costly—at the margin, it requires diversion of inputs to "clean up" bad outputs or reduction of good outputs, which would reduce the byproduct bad outputs, as well.

We illustrate the environmental technology in figure 5.13. The environmental technology illustrated by the output set $P(x)$ satisfies the two axioms introduced above. Proportional contractions—one may scale back through point "*a*" to the origin, for example—are feasible, and if no bad output is produced, then the production of good output must also be zero. The latter implies that there are no feasible points on the good output axis other than the origin.

The next step toward defining a green Luenberger productivity indicator is to customize the directional distance function. Since our interest is on the output side, we set the input direction vector to zero, $g_x = 0$, and partition

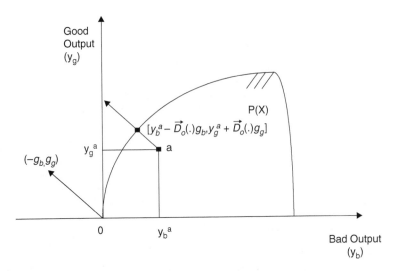

Figure 5.13. The Environmental Technology

the output vector and its associated direction vector into good and bad components $g_y = (g_g, g_b)$. Since we wish to credit expansion of good outputs and debit bad output production, $(g_g, -g_b)$ will typically be in the fourth quadrant (refer to figure 5.13). Again, one may choose this vector in a number of ways, including $(g_g, -g_b) = (y_g, -y_b), (g_g, -g_b) = (1, -1)$, or according to a particular policy goal, for example. Figure 5.13 illustrates the general case in which good output is increased and bad output decreased.

The observations (x^o, y_g^o, y_b^o) and (x^1, y_g^1, y_b^1) are projected onto the boundary of the output set according to

$$\vec{D}_o^\tau(x^t, y_g^t, y_b^t; g_y) = \sup\{\beta : (y_g^t + \beta g_g, y_b^t - \beta g_b) \in P^\tau(x^t)\}, \qquad (5.107)$$

with $\tau = 0, 1, t = 0, 1$. Inserting these four distance functions into the Luenberger indicator defined in (5.82) yields the green Luenberger indicator

$$GL = \frac{1}{2}\left[\vec{D}_o^1(x^o, y_g^o, y_b^o; g_y) - \vec{D}_o^1(x^1, y_g^1, y_b^1; g_y)\right.$$
$$\left. + \vec{D}_o^o(x^o, y_g^o, y_b^o; g_y) - \vec{D}_o^o(x^1, y_g^1, y_b^1; g_y)\right], \qquad (5.108)$$

where $(g_g, -g_b)$ is our partitioned directional vector. This indicator satisfies the same set of properties (suitably modified) as the technology indicator. An illustration of the green Luenberger indicator may be found in Ball, Färe, Grosskopf, and Nehring (2001) for U.S. agriculture. Illustration of the standard Luenberger productivity indicator may be found in Chambers, Färe, and Grosskopf (1996) for a comparison of productivity growth in Asian Pacific Economic Conference (APEC) countries.

Before turning to our price-related productivity measures, we should emphasize that the distance-function–based productivity measures share the advantage of minimal data requirements—no prices or shares are required. They also share the ability to readily model inefficiency, allowing identification of "catching up" among other factors that explain productivity growth. As we show below, their computation is slightly more demanding than the traditional measures of productivity growth, requiring frontier estimation. Typically, panel data are required to identify the frontier in each period.[36] Recent advances in frontier estimation and computer capability have rendered this disadvantage less of an obstacle.

5.2.2 Price-related productivity: Törnqvist, Fisher, and Bennet-Bowley

Until recently, the major contribution of Caves, Christensen, and Diewert (1982a) was thought to be the derivation of the link between what they conceived to be a purely theoretical index—the Malmquist productivity index[37]—and an empirically tractable and flexible approximation of that index that turned out to be the Törnqvist index (1936). The key result was achieved by applying duality and the Diewert (1976) quadratic identity lemma to the Malmquist productivity index, eventually arriving at the Törnqvist productivity index, which because of this equivalence, Diewert dubbed "exact".[38]

This idea was subsequently applied by Diewert (1992) to show the relationship between the Fisher productivity index and the Malmquist indexes, and by Chambers (1996, 2002, 2004) and Balk (1998) to do the same for the Bennet-Bowley productivity indicator, which is price dependent, and the Luenberger indicator, which is not. These approaches all rely on specification of a functional form for the distance functions: translog for the Törnqvist index, a Diewert functional form for the Fisher index, and a quadratic for Chambers's results. A different approach, not involving functional forms, was applied by Färe and Grosskopf (1992) and by Balk (1993). They showed that the Fisher productivity index is approximately equal to the Malmquist indexes.[39] A common feature of the Bennet-Bowley, Törnqvist, and Fisher productivity measures is that they are what Diewert (1993) calls superlative; that is, they are exact for a flexible functional form.

5.2.2.1 The Törnqvist productivity index

As is typical of the price-related productivity measures, the Törnqvist productivity index consists of two quantity indexes: an output quantity index and an input quantity index. The Törnqvist output and input quantity indexes are defined as

$$Y_T = \prod_{m=1}^{M} \left(\frac{y_m^1}{y_m^o} \right)^{1/2 \left(\frac{p_m^1 y_m^1}{p^1 y^1} + \frac{p_m^o y_m^o}{p^o y^o} \right)} \tag{5.109}$$

and

$$X_T = \prod_{n=1}^{N} \left(\frac{x_n^1}{x_n^o} \right)^{1/2 \left(\frac{w_n^1 x_n^1}{w^1 x^1} + \frac{w_n^o x_n^o}{w^o x^o} \right)}, \tag{5.110}$$

respectively. The Törnqvist productivity index is their ratio

$$Y_T / X_T. \tag{5.111}$$

The Törnqvist index often appears in its logarithmic form

$$\ln T = \sum_{m=1}^{M} \frac{1}{2} \left[\frac{p_m^1 y_m^1}{p^1 y^1} + \frac{p_m^o y_m^o}{p^o y^o} \right] (\ln y_m^1 - \ln y_m^o)$$

$$- \sum_{n=1}^{N} \frac{1}{2} \left[\frac{w_n^1 x_n^1}{w^1 x^1} + \frac{w_n^o x_n^o}{w^o x^o} \right] (\ln x_n^1 - \ln x_n^o).$$

This emphasizes the link to the Solow residual formulation of productivity change; that is, productivity change is estimated as the difference between the change in outputs (the first term on the right-hand side) and the change in inputs (the second term on the right-hand side).

As noted in chapter 1, this index, like the Bennet-Bowley productivity indicator and the Fisher productivity index, has the advantage that it can be implemented without estimating the true (unobserved) technology; rather, it is estimated using observable information on shares and quantities. Its ability to "approximate" the underlying Malmquist indexes depends on whether the assumptions imposed to derive the equivalence are valid. These include strictly positive input and output quantities and specification of technology as translog with second-order terms restricted to be constant across periods. Strictly positive quantities may cause problems in general, but are especially problematic with new and disappearing goods.

Optimizing behavior is also assumed in order to substitute observed prices for the derivatives of the technology (distance functions). As noted in chapter 1, this is perhaps the most restrictive assumption, that is, that prices reflect marginal productivities. If this is violated, then the Törnqvist index may no longer so closely approximate the Malmquist index. An obvious example in which observed prices do not reflect marginal cost is the case of imperfect competition. If observed prices are used in the Törnqvist index in this case, productivity change will be biased. As shown in Diewert and Fox (2004) and demonstrated for New Zealand by Fox (2005), one may adjust the Törnqvist productivity index to correct for imperfect competition; however, this requires estimation of the markup between price and marginal cost.

5.2.2.2 The Fisher productivity index

We turn now to another price-dependent productivity index, the Fisher productivity index, which is defined as

$$Y_F/X_F, \tag{5.112}$$

where Y_F is the Fisher ideal output quantity index and X_F is the Fisher ideal input quantity index. These are defined as

$$Y_F = \left(\frac{p^o y^1}{p^o y^o}\frac{p^1 y^1}{p^1 y^o}\right)^{1/2} \tag{5.113}$$

and

$$X_F = \left(\frac{w^o x^1}{w^o x^o}\frac{w^1 x^1}{w^1 x^o}\right)^{1/2}, \tag{5.114}$$

respectively. Each of these is a geometric mean of Paasche and Laspeyres quantity indexes.

Balk (1993, 1998) and Färe and Grosskopf (1992, 1996) applied a first-order approximation to relate the Malmquist and Fisher indexes. Diewert (1992) introduced a parametric formulation of the distance function and showed that the Fisher index is exact for the output-oriented geometric mean formulation of the Malmquist productivity index; again, this requires that the technology be of a specific functional form and that the realized data be consistent with optimizing behavior.

The fact that the Fisher productivity index is so closely related to the Malmquist productivity index provides arguments for its use given that the data are available and the underlying assumptions hold in terms of functional form and optimization (as in the Törnqvist case). Unlike the Törnqvist index, the Fisher index can accommodate zeros in the data, which is important in the case of entry and exit and new and disappearing goods. Diewert (1992, p. 196) argues in favor of the Fisher index: "Our recommended approach to productivity measurement in the general case is the approach ... where productivity change was defined as a Fisher quantity index of outputs divided by a Fisher quantity index of inputs." This conclusion is based in part on the fact that this index satisfies many desirable index number properties; at the end of the chapter, we include a discussion of these for all of the indexes and indicators discussed in this section.

5.2.2.3 The Bennet-Bowley productivity indicator

We end this section by introducing the Bennet-Bowley productivity indicator (BB). This indicator, named after Bennet (1920) and Bowley (1919), resembles the Luenberger productivity indicator in its additive structure, but uses prices to aggregate inputs and outputs instead of directional distance functions:

$$BB = \frac{1}{2}\left(\frac{p^o}{p^o g_y + w^o g_x} + \frac{p^1}{p^1 g_y + w^1 g_x}\right)(y^1 - y^o)$$

$$- \frac{1}{2}\left(\frac{w^o}{p^o g_y + w^o g_x} + \frac{w^1}{p^1 g_y + w^1 g_x}\right)(x^1 - x^o) \qquad (5.115)$$

The reader may have noticed the resemblance of the Bennet-Bowley indicator to the Törnqvist productivity index—the latter uses shares (cost or revenue rather than price shares) to aggregate inputs and outputs, but like the Malmquist index, it has a ratio rather than a difference form.[40]

The Bennet-Bowley productivity indicator is a price-weighted arithmetic mean of the difference in output and input changes in quantity. The price weights are normalized by the value of the direction vector, which is the same normalization as the profit efficiency measure from section 5.1 and serves to impose independence of unit of measurement. This normalization comes naturally from the duality between profit and the directional technology distance function. An intuitive choice to use in this normalization would be $g = (x, y)$, which would result in what might be called price share weights; that is, the difference in output $(y^1 - y^o)$ is weighted by $\frac{1}{2}\left(\frac{p^o}{p^o y^o + w^o x^o} + \frac{p^1}{p^1 y^1 + w^1 x^1}\right)$. If instead $g_y = 1$ and $g_x = 1$, then the nonnegative price weights sum to one.

Using the quadratic identity lemma, Chambers (2002) has followed up on the work by Caves, Christensen, and Diewert (1982a) and shows that the Bennet-Bowley productivity indicator is exact (in the sense of Diewert) for the Luenberger productivity indicator. As with the Caves, Christensen, and Diewert result for the Malmquist and Törnqvist indexes, this requires that the derivatives of the distance functions (in this case, the directional distance function) be proxied with observed prices. Thus, the Bennet-Bowley indicator is an approximation of the Luenberger indicator, just as the Törnqvist and Fisher indexes are approximations of the Malmquist index.

An interesting feature of the Bennet-Bowley productivity indicator is the role it plays in the decomposition of (normalized) change in profit. Grifell-Tatjé and Lovell (1999), following up on Miller (1984), who linked profitability and productivity, show that change in profit can be decomposed into a productivity change component and a price-related component. Following Färe and Grosskopf (2005), their result can be generalized to show that normalized profit change is equal to the Bennet-Bowley indicator of change in productivity and an indicator of price change.

We start with normalized change in profit defined as

$$\Pi C = \frac{\Pi^1}{p^1 g_y + w^1 g_x} - \frac{\Pi^o}{p^o g_y + w^o g_x}. \tag{5.116}$$

The normalization is the same as that used in the Bennet-Bowley productivity indicator. Next, we define a price change indicator as

$$PC = \frac{1}{2}(y^1 + y^o)\left(\frac{p^1}{p^1 g_y + w^1 g_x} - \frac{p^o}{p^o g_y + w^o g_x}\right)$$
$$- \frac{1}{2}(x^1 + x^o)\left(\frac{w^1}{p^1 g_y + w^1 g_x} - \frac{w^o}{p^o g_y + w^o g_x}\right), \tag{5.117}$$

which shares the same normalization as the Bennet-Bowley and profit change components. This term will have a favorable impact on profitability when output prices increase and input prices decrease (or output prices increase more than input prices, or input prices decrease more than output prices decrease):

$$\Pi C = BB + PC \tag{5.118}$$

The intuition is very appealing—changes in profit are both due to changes in the underlying fundamentals, namely, input and output quantities, and also due to changes in prices. This "decomposition" provides guidance to firms as to the sources of changes in profits.

Overall, we would argue that the Bennet-Bowley productivity indicator represents a useful addition to the productivity measurement toolbox. As long as data on quantities and prices are available, its computation is, at most, a spreadsheet operation. Its link to profitability is also a useful feature. Another advantage of this indicator is the fact that, due to its additive structure, it can accommodate identification of the effects of entry and exit in an industry and new and disappearing goods on productivity growth. Like the Törnqvist and Fisher indexes, its ability to approximate its primal cousin, in this case, the Luenberger productivity indicator, depends on the validity of the assumptions made concerning observed prices and functional form.

As mentioned above, these traditional measures are appealing in terms of estimation: These are simple spreadsheet calculations using observed data. These are especially well suited to time series data, which are problematic for our distance function measures of productivity. Price or share data are required here, which means that these price-related indexes are not appropriate where such data are missing or not consistent with optimizing behavior. The Bennet-Bowley indicator and Fisher index are robust to zeros in the data, whereas the Törnqvist index is not. In contrast to the distance-function–based measures of productivity, the traditional productivity measures generally face difficulties with respect to multilateral or cross-sectional comparisons. This reflects the fact that they do not satisfy the circularity test mentioned in chapter 1 and our introduction and do not have a natural benchmark—like the frontier of technology in the case of our distance-function–based measures—as a reference. In addition, the ability to capture deviations from frontier behavior is available only if we relax the assumption of optimizing behavior and instead estimate technology. That is not typical of these indexes, although an example of such an adaptation for the Fisher index is available in Ray and Mukherjee (1996) and for the Törnqvist index in Diewert and Fox (2004).

A discussion of the index number properties satisfied by these productivity measures is included in the summary section of this chapter.

5.2.3 Duality and productivity

Although one of the obvious advantages of the distance-function–based productivity measures discussed above is that they do not require data on input and output prices or shares to aggregate inputs and outputs—they are price independent—they are also dual to price-related concepts. Through duality, the distance-function–based productivity measures may be equivalently constructed as price-dependent measures when such data are available or by using shadow prices when such data are not available. For a discussion of a shadow price approach, see Kuosmanen et al. (2004). In section 5.1 we show how the profit function can be used to recover the directional technology distance function. We also show how the revenue (cost) function is related to Shephard's output (input) distance function. Below we use these and other duality results to derive new productivity measures.

As an example of dual formulations, suppose that data on revenue, input quantities, and output prices and quantities are available; then, one may use a revenue-based Malmquist index to measure productivity change. By duality, we have

$$D_o^\tau(x, y) = \max_p \frac{py}{R^\tau(x, p)};$$ (5.119)

thus, we may be substitute the revenue function for the distance functions in the Malmquist indexes defined previously;[41]

$$RM_o^\tau = \frac{R^\tau(x^o, p^o)\, p^1 y^1}{R^\tau(x^1, p^1)\, p^o y^o},$$ (5.120)

and for the geometric mean form,

$$RM_o = \frac{p^1 y^1}{p^o y^o} \left(\frac{R^o(x^o, p^o)\, R^1(x^o, p^o)}{R^o(x^1, p^1)\, R^1(x^1, p^1)} \right)^{1/2}.$$ (5.121)

The inner product $p^\tau y^\tau = \sum_{m=1}^M p_m^\tau y_m^\tau$ denotes observed revenue, and $R^\tau(\cdot)$, $\tau = 0, 1$ is the maximum revenue, or revenue function defined in (5.17). Note that by duality, separability of the distance function translates into revenue function separability, for example,

$$D_o^\tau(x, y) = A(\tau)D_o(x, y), \tau = 0, 1,$$ (5.122)

if and only if

$$R^\tau(x, p) = \frac{1}{A(\tau)} R(x, p).$$ (5.123)

See appendix 5.1 for verification.

Similarly, one may use the duality between the cost function and the Shephard distance function

$$D_i^\tau(y, x) = \min_w \frac{wx}{C^\tau(y, w)}$$ (5.124)

to derive a cost-based Malmquist productivity index,

$$CM = \frac{w^o x^o}{w^1 x^1} \left(\frac{C^o(y^1, w^1)}{C^o(y^o, w^o)} \frac{C^1(y^1, w^1)}{C^1(y^o, w^o)} \right)^{1/2},$$ (5.125)

where the inner product $w^\tau x^\tau$ is observed cost and $C^\tau(y, w)$ is minimum cost.

Another set of price-dependent representations of technology that we can use to define Malmquist productivity indexes are the "indirect" technologies such as the cost-indirect output correspondence

$$IP(w/C) = \{y : y \in P(x), wx \leq C\}$$ (5.126)

where $w \in \Re_+^N$ is a vector of input prices and C is the allowed cost or budget. This output set is distinguished from the direct output set $P(x)$ in that inputs (x) are not fixed; rather, output is constrained by a budget C and given input prices w. This allows for optimal allocation of costs $w_n x_n, n = 1, \ldots, N$ among usages.[42] Thus, $IP(w/C) \supseteq P(x)$ for $wx \leq C$. Since $IP(w/C)$ is an output set, we may define both a distance function and a revenue function relative to it, as well. The cost-indirect distance function is defined as

$$ID_o(w/C, y) = \min\{\theta : y/\theta \in IP(w/C)\}.$$ (5.127)

This function seeks to maximize outputs given a budget constraint C. This function is particularly well suited to modeling most public sector activities.[43]

The cost-indirect revenue function is defined as

$$IR(w/C, p) = \max_y \{py : y \in IP(w/C)\}.$$ (5.128)

Comparing the cost-indirect functions to the traditional output distance and revenue functions,

$$D_o(x, y) \text{ versus } ID(w/C, y) \qquad (5.129)$$

and

$$R(x, p) \text{ versus } IR(w/C, p), \qquad (5.130)$$

we see that there is a dual relation between inputs x and cost-deflated input prices w/C, the first arguments in these functions. One may use this duality to create both a cost-indirect Malmquist output productivity index[44] and a cost-indirect Malmquist revenue productivity index. One may also introduce revenue-indirect models among other price-dependent models, which we leave to the reader.[45]

As shown in section 5.1, the directional technology distance function is dual to the profit function,

$$\Pi(p, w) = \max_{x,y} p\left[y + \vec{D}_T(x, y; g)g_y\right] - w\left[x - \vec{D}_T(x, y; g)g_x\right]; \qquad (5.131)$$

thus, we may introduce the profit-based productivity indicator,

$$\Pi L = \frac{1}{2}\left(\frac{\Pi^1(p^o, w^o) + \Pi^o(p^o, w^o) - 2(p^o y^o - w^o x^o)}{p^o g_y + w^o g_x}\right)$$
$$- \frac{1}{2}\left(\frac{\Pi^1(p^1, w^1) + \Pi^o(p^1, w^1) - 2(p^1 y^1 - w^1 x^1)}{p^1 g_y + w^1 g_x}\right), \qquad (5.132)$$

where $(p^o y^o - w^o x^o)$ and $(p^1 y^1 - w^1 x^1)$ are observed profits in each period. As before, the denominators of the two terms are derived from the duality between profit and the directional distance function. If we choose $(g_x, g_y) = (x, y)$, the denominator would be the total value of the input–output bundle. Intuitively, this would be a reflection of the "size" of the observation under evaluation. Alternatively, we could follow Luenberger and choose g such that $p g_y + w g_x = 1$. See also Balk (1998) for a more detailed discussion of profit and productivity in this framework.

Here, the additive structure of profit lends itself more naturally to a difference productivity indicator rather than a ratio index such as Malmquist.[46]

5.3 Decomposition of Productivity

The reason for decomposing productivity change into components is, of course, so we can identify the sources of productivity growth and use this information to guide policy. Thus, it is important that the components are economically meaningful and that they can be estimated with some precision. The latter issue is taken up in chapter 4.

Before turning to what Balk (2004) calls the many decompositions of the Malmquist index, we first discuss a different kind of decomposition, which seeks to identify subgroups of inputs, outputs, input attributes, and output attributes to form subgroup indexes that are then used to construct Malmquist productivity indexes. This decomposition approach is motivated by the importance of isolating the role of quality changes on productivity growth. We then turn to the decomposition of technical change into bias and magnitude components. The final subsection is devoted to an overview of some of the other Malmquist decompositions.

5.3.1 Decomposition with quality change

The idea of isolating quality change as a component of productivity growth was, to our knowledge, pioneered by Fixler and Zieschang (1992) for the Törnqvist index. Here, we extend their approach to an output-oriented Malmquist productivity index. As usual, x and y denote inputs and outputs; the new variables are the input attributes $a \in \Re_+^A$ and output attributes $b \in \Re_+^B$. The enhanced technology is

$$T = \{(x, a, y, b) : (x, a) \text{ can produce } (y, b)\}. \tag{5.133}$$

The base period output distance function is

$$D_o^o(x, a, y, b) = \inf\{\theta : (x, a, y/\theta, b/\theta) \in T^o\}, \tag{5.134}$$

and the corresponding enhanced Malmquist productivity index is

$$M_o^o = \frac{D_o^o(x^1, a^1, y^1, b^1)}{D_o^o(x^o, a^o, y^o, b^o)}. \tag{5.135}$$

Following Fixler and Zieschang, our goal is to decompose this overall quality-enhanced index into four subindexes that depend only on the subvectors $x, a, y,$ and b, respectively. We begin by introducing four subvector distance functions:

$$\begin{aligned}
D_x(x, a, y, b) &= \sup\{\lambda : D_o(x/\lambda, a, y, b) \leq 1\} \\
D_a(x, a, y, b) &= \sup\{\lambda : D_o(x, a/\lambda, y, b) \leq 1\} \\
D_y(x, a, y, b) &= \inf\{\lambda : D_o(x, a, y/\lambda, b) \leq 1\} \\
D_b(x, a, y, b) &= \inf\{\lambda : D_o(x, a, y, b/\lambda) \leq 1\}
\end{aligned} \tag{5.136}$$

We say that the technology is subvector homothetic if the output distance function can be written as

$$D_o(x, a, y, b) = \left(\frac{D_b(1, 1, 1, b) D_y(1, 1, y, 1)}{F[D_x(x, 1, 1, 1) D_a(1, a, 1, 1)]} \right)^{1/2}, \tag{5.137}$$

where F is an invertible function normalized such that $F(1) = 1$. Subvector homotheticity generalizes Shephard's (1970) concept of inverse homotheticity, which allows us to write the output distance function as

$$D_o(x, y) = D_o(1, y)/F[D_i(1, x)], \qquad (5.138)$$

where $D_i(\cdot)$ is the input distance function for $y = 1$.[47] If the technology exhibits constant returns to scale, then the function F is the identity function.

Färe, Førsund, Grosskopf, Hayes, and Heshmati (2001) provided the following decomposition of the output-oriented Malmquist (base period) productivity index. The constant returns to scale Malmquist index M_o^o takes the form

$$M_o^o = \frac{\left(\frac{D_b^o(1,1,1,b^1)}{D_b^o(1,1,1,b^o)}\right)^{1/2} \left(\frac{D_y^o(1,1,y^1,1)}{D_y^o(1,1,y^o,1)}\right)^{1/2}}{\left(\frac{D_x^o(x^1,1,1,1)}{D_x^o(x^o,1,1,1)}\right)^{1/2} \left(\frac{D_a^o(1,a^1,1,1)}{D_a^o(1,a^o,1,1)}\right)^{1/2}} \qquad (5.139)$$

if and only if the technology is subvector homothetic. Note that each of the component indexes is a Malmquist quantity–quality index normalized by unit vectors. This result suggests that identification of quality change independent of other inputs and outputs requires that the underlying technology satisfy conditions—subvector homotheticity—that are perhaps unlikely to be satisfied in general. We conjecture that, while the Luenberger index with its additive structure might be more amenable to isolating quality change, nevertheless, some sort of separability will likely be required.

Since the subvector decomposition of the Malmquist index consists of four Malmquist quantity indexes, we note that if the corresponding distance functions are translog, then it follows from Diewert (1976) that each of these may be represented as a Törnqvist quantity index.

5.3.2 Decomposing Malmquist technical change into bias and magnitude

We leave further decompositions of the Luenberger and Hicks-Moorsteen index to the reader and focus on the Malmquist index technical change component.[48] But first note that, up to this point, constant returns to scale have played a role only in assuring that in the single output–input case the Malmquist index collapses to a ratio of average products as productivity change has traditionally been defined. The definition of the technical change component does not depend on any returns to scale assumption, but, of course, its empirical size depends on the choice of the reference technology when it is estimated.

Deferring the discussion of the specification of scale properties of the reference technology for the moment, we turn to a decomposition of technical change into three components:[49] (i) output-biased technical change OBTC,

(ii) input-biased technical change IBTC, and (iii) a magnitude or neutral component MATC:

$$TC = OBTC \cdot IBTC \cdot MATC \tag{5.140}$$

Identification of bias in technical change tells us about the pattern of shifts in the frontier of technology over time. If the shifts are "parallel" in the sense that OBTC and IBTC are equal to one, then $TC = MATC$ and we say that technical change is neutral.

The output-biased component of technical change is expressed in terms of the output distance function as

$$OBTC = \left(\frac{D_o^o(x^1,y^1)}{D_o^1(x^1,y^1)} \frac{D_o^1(x^1,y^o)}{D_o^o(x^1,y^o)} \right)^{1/2}. \tag{5.141}$$

Figure 5.14 illustrates our measure of output-biased technical change. The two output sets $P^1(x^1)$ and $P^o(x^1)$ differ in technology but not in input use. By holding input constant, we can separately identify output and input bias. In our example, the two output vectors y^1 and y^o belong to the corresponding isoquant, so we have $D_o^o(x^1,y^o) = D_o^1(x^1,y^1) = 1$. Clearly, the shift in technology is not parallel in our example. Specifically, in figure 5.14,

$$OBTC = \left(\frac{0c}{0d} \frac{0a}{0b} \right)^{1/2}, \tag{5.142}$$

which is greater than one; that is, technical change is output biased. Färe and Grosskopf (1996) proved that this component is equal to one if and only if the

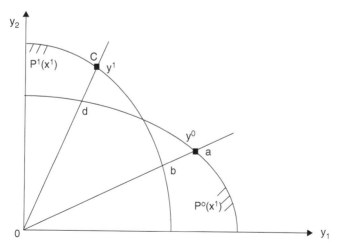

Figure 5.14. Output-Biased Technical Change

technology is implicitly Hicks output neutral,[50] that is,

$$D_o^\tau(x, y) = D_o(x, y)/A(\tau, x), \tau = 0, 1. \qquad (5.143)$$

The input-biased component is expressed in terms of the output distance functions as

$$\text{IBTC} = \left(\frac{D_o^1(x^o, y^o)}{D_o^o(x^o, y^o)} \frac{D_o^o(x^1, y^o)}{D_o^1(x^1, y^o)} \right)^{1/2}, \qquad (5.144)$$

where the only output vector that enters is the base period output y^o.

If constant returns to scale is assumed, then the input and output distance functions are reciprocals.[51] In this case, input-biased technical change equals

$$\text{IBTC} = \left(\frac{D_i^o(y^o, x^o)}{D_i^1(y^o, x^o)} \frac{D_i^1(y^o, x^1)}{D_i^o(y^o, x^1)} \right)^{1/2}, \qquad (5.145)$$

and one can show that it equals one if and only if the technology is implicitly Hicks input-neutral, that is,

$$D_i^\tau(x, y) = B(\tau, y)D_i(y, x), \tau = 0, 1. \qquad (5.146)$$

Finally, the magnitude component is

$$\text{MATC} = D_o^o(x^o, y^o)/D_o^1(x^o, y^o). \qquad (5.147)$$

Next, we turn to what Balk calls the "many decompositions" of the Malmquist index.

5.3.3 The many decompositions of the Malmquist index

The first decomposition of Malmquist productivity is due to Nishimizu and Page (1982), who used a parametric (translog) approach to separately identify efficiency change and technical change components of productivity change. This was probably also the first empirical application of the Malmquist index proposed by Caves, Christensen, and Diewert (1982a). The decomposition highlighted the fact that this was a generalization of the Solow model to allow for productivity change, which was not identical to technical change. It was nearly the end of the decade before this idea was taken up again and applied in a nonparametric, DEA context by Färe, Grosskopf, Lindgren, and Roos (first written in 1989, finally to appear in the 1994 volume edited by Charnes, Cooper, Levin, and Seiford). As mentioned above and in chapter 1, the first effort followed the Nishimizu and Page lead and arrived at the decomposition based on the geometric mean version of the Malmquist index:

$$M_o = \text{EC} \cdot \text{TC}$$

$$= D_o^1(x^1, y^1)/D_o^o(x^o, y^o) \left(\frac{D_o^o(x^1, y^1)}{D_o^1(x^1, y^1)} \frac{D_o^o(x^o, y^o)}{D_o^1(x^o, y^o)} \right)^{1/2}, \qquad (5.148)$$

where EC is efficiency change and TC is technical change. Initially, this decomposition was agnostic with respect to the scale properties of the technologies used to estimate the distance functions in the DEA context. In practice, we found that estimation of technical change, which includes what we refer to as *mixed period distance functions*, ran into computational problems (infeasibilities) when estimated relative to what is referred to in the DEA world as a variable returns to scale (VRS) technology, which allows for increasing, constant, and decreasing returns to scale. As a practical matter, this problem was "solved" by estimating these mixed period problems relative to a cone or constant returns to scale technology.

An interesting theoretical byproduct of specifying a "cone" version of the Malmquist index is that it resulted in the index satisfying what is referred to in chapter 1 and in Balk (2001) as the *proportionality property*. For the base period, Malmquist productivity index this may be written as

$$M_o^o(x^o, y^o, \lambda x^o, \mu y^o) = \mu/\lambda, \qquad (5.149)$$

which is the multiple input–output analog of the scalar input–output "definition" of total factor productivity change

$$M_o^o = \frac{y^1}{x^1} / \frac{y^o}{x^o}, \qquad (5.150)$$

as the change in the ratio of average products in adjacent periods. This was implicitly (but not explicitly) recognized by Caves, Christensen, and Diewert (1982a); they pointed out that the equivalence between Malmquist and Törnqvist (which satisfies the proportionality property) required constant returns to scale or a scale adjustment factor. Grifell-Tatjé and Lovell (1999) provided an empirical demonstration of the fact that the Malmquist index estimated under the VRS technology in DEA deviates from the average product definition of TFP.

In the meantime, in our 1994 book with Knox Lovell (Färe, Grosskopf and Lovell, 1994), we included a decomposition of the Malmquist index that included a scale efficiency component. Following the notation introduced in chapter 1, we denote distance functions estimated relative to a cone (constant returns to scale or "benchmark") technology with the subscript "c" and those estimated relative to a VRS (or "best practice") technology with the subscript "v". The decomposition from our book and that appears in Färe, Grosskopf,

Norris, and Zhang (1994) may be written

$$M_c = \frac{D_v^1(x^1, y^1)}{D_v^0(x^0, y^0)} \frac{S^1(x^1, y^1)}{S^0(x^0, y^0)} \left(\frac{D_c^0(x^1, y^1)}{D_c^1(x^1, y^1)} \frac{D_c^0(x^0, y^0)}{D_c^1(x^0, y^0)} \right)^{1/2}, \qquad (5.151)$$

where

$$SC = \frac{S^1(x^1, y^1)}{S^0(x^0, y^0)} = \left[\frac{D_c^1(x^1, y^1)}{D_v^1(x^1, y^1)} \bigg/ \frac{D_c^0(x^0, y^0)}{D_v^0(x^0, y^0)} \right], \qquad (5.152)$$

is the change in scale efficiency (SC), that is, the ratio of scale efficiency in period 0 and period 1.[52] Thus, productivity change may be decomposed into an efficiency change component defined relative to the VRS (best practice) technology and a scale efficiency change component that expands output up to most productive or efficient scale (the tangency between the VRS and constant returns to scale technologies in DEA), which leaves a technical change term evaluated at most productive scale size.

If we augment the technical change component to include its decomposition into magnitude-, input-, output-biased technical change as in Färe, Grifell-Tatjé, Grosskopf, and Lovell (1997) discussed in the preceding section, we have

$$M_c = EC_v \cdot SC \cdot TC_c$$
$$= EC_v \cdot SC \cdot OBTC \cdot IBTC \cdot MATC. \qquad (5.153)$$

The publication of the decomposition in (5.151) by Färe, Grosskopf, Norris, and Zhang (1994; FGNZ) started a small industry of alternative decompositions of the Malmquist productivity index.[53] Virtually all of these define the "summary" Malmquist productivity index as .

$$M_c^\tau = D_c^\tau(x^0, y^0)/D_c^\tau(x^1, y^1)$$

(or its geometric mean form), that is, the version that satisfies the proportionality property and that can be estimated directly using the cone technology, referred to as the benchmark technology in chapter 1. The alternative decompositions have in common the idea that efficiency change and technical change should be estimated relative to the VRS technology, referred to as the best practice technology in chapter 1. Since the various authors also insist on the ratio of average product interpretation of the overall index (the proportionality property), this leaves a residual that is variously attributed to changes in scale (variously defined) and input and output mix (see Balk, 2003). To illustrate the relationship between several of these and the FGNZ decomposition, we may rewrite the decomposition in (5.153) as

$$M_c = EC_v \cdot TC_v \cdot \frac{TC_c}{TC_v} \cdot SC, \qquad (5.154)$$

which can also be written as

$$M_c = M_v \cdot \frac{\text{TC}_c}{\text{TC}_v} \cdot \text{SC}, \qquad (5.155)$$

where $M_v = \text{EC}_v \cdot \text{TC}_v$, that is, a Malmquist index estimated relative to a VRS (best practice) technology.

The original FGNZ decomposition results by canceling the TC_v terms in (5.154). The Ray-Desli (1997) decomposition combines the last two terms as their change in the scale component. The complete decomposition in (5.154) was proposed by Simar and Wilson (1998) and implemented by Gilbert and Wilson (1998), Grifell-Tatjé and Lovell (1999), and Wheelock and Wilson (1999). Bert Balk has proposed several variations, including that in Balk (2001), which may be derived by rearranging the last two terms in (5.141) to yield a scale change and output mix change term:

$$\frac{\text{TC}_c}{\text{TC}_v} \cdot \text{SC} = \text{SEC}_o \cdot \text{OME}, \qquad (5.156)$$

where

$$\text{SEC}_o^\tau = \frac{S^\tau(x^1, \overline{y})}{S^\tau(x^o, \overline{y})}, \qquad (5.157)$$

with $\text{SEC}_o = [\text{SEC}_o^o \cdot \text{SEC}_o^1]^{1/2}, \tau = o, 1$, and

$$\text{OME}^\tau = \frac{S^\tau(\overline{x}, y^1)}{S^\tau(\overline{x}, y^o)}, \qquad (5.158)$$

where $\text{OME} = [\text{OME}^o \cdot \text{OME}^1]^{1/2}$. SEC_o^τ is a scale change term defined as the ratio of scale efficiency evaluated at input bundles x^o and x^1 relative to technology at τ. The output mix term is similarly defined by evaluating output bundles y^o and y^1 relative to technology at τ. The reader has probably noticed that it is the scale component that is defined in many different ways in these alternative decompositions. This component is generally used to isolate the change in productivity due to change in input usage (change in scale of production), which obviously may be accomplished in a number of ways. This is also true for the FGNZ decomposition; in that case, the scale term is used to capture gains from moving to most productive scale size in each period, with the associated technical change evaluated at that scale.

And there are more. Obviously all this may be repeated on the input-oriented side. De Borger and Kerstens (2000) include a capacity utilization component as part of the decomposition. Kumar and Russell (2002) provide a twist by decomposing labor productivity into a capital deepening component and the Malmquist components of efficiency and technical change, providing a more transparent link to the growth accounting literature. Henderson and Russell (2005) generalize this approach to include human capital. Färe,

Grosskopf, and Margaritis (2006) use this decomposition to study the contribution of these components to convergence of labor productivity in the European Union.

Where does this leave us? A smorgasbord of choices. Our advice is to consider several issues: What is the research question? Does it involve issues related to bias in technical change? Or scale effects? Or are you interested only in catching up? Choose the decomposition that focuses on your research question. Also keep in mind that your data may not allow you to identify statistically significant detailed components of productivity growth. See chapter 4 for a discussion of how to determine the statistical significance of the Malmquist index and its components.

5.4 Aggregation of Indexes and Indicators

We devote this section to aggregation of indexes and indicators of productivity and efficiency. Our focus in terms of aggregation is to say something about industry performance based on firm performance, for example. Aggregation over all inputs and outputs is, as pointed out by Blackorby and Russell (1999), a daunting task. This leads us to next focus on aggregating over the narrower category of optimizers (x^*, y^*)—cost minimizers, revenue maximizers, or profit maximizers, for example—and rely on results by Koopmans (1957) to yield more positive aggregation results. The result by Koopmans is an example of aggregation over optimizers; he shows that the sum of individual firm profits will yield industry profit, where the industry is defined as the sum of its firms.

5.4.1 Aggregation across firms

In this section, we focus on aggregation across firms, which we index as $k = 1, \ldots, K$. Their associated technologies are

$$T^k = \{(x^k, y^k) : x^k \text{ can produce } y^k\}, k = 1, \ldots, K. \qquad (5.159)$$

The aggregate technology is the sum of the firm technologies

$$T = \sum_{k=1}^{K} T^k. \qquad (5.160)$$

figure 5.15 illustrates.

In figure 5.15, the technologies for firms 1 and 2 are

$$T^1 = \{(x, y) : x \geq 2 \text{ and } 3 \geq y\},$$
$$T^2 = \{(x, y) : x \geq 5, \text{ and } 5 \geq y\}; \qquad (5.161)$$

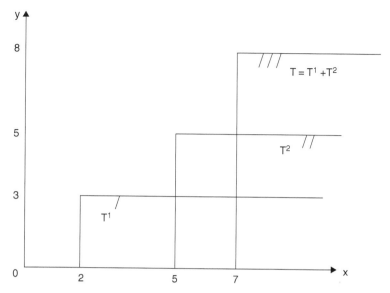

Figure 5.15. The Aggregate Technology

hence, the aggregate technology equals

$$T = T^1 + T^2 = \{(x, y) : x \geq 7 \text{ and } 8 \geq y\}. \tag{5.162}$$

If we assume that each firm faces the same prices, then the Bennet-Bowley productivity indicator aggregates; that is,

$$BB = \sum_{k=1}^{K} BB^k. \tag{5.163}$$

To see this, denote firm k's indicator in periods 0 and 1 by

$$BB^k = \frac{1}{2} \left(\frac{p^o}{p^o g_y + w^o g_x} + \frac{p^1}{p^1 g_y + w^1 g_x} \right) (y^{k,1} - y^{k,o}) \tag{5.164}$$

$$- \frac{1}{2} \left(\frac{w^o}{p^o g_y + w^o g_x} + \frac{w^1}{p^1 g_y + w^1 g_x} \right) (x^{k,1} - x^{k,o}) \tag{5.165}$$

and denote the industry or aggregate Bennet-Bowley indicator by

$$BB = \frac{1}{2} \left(\frac{p^o}{p^o g_y + w^o g_x} + \frac{p^1}{p^1 g_y + w^1 g_x} \right) \left(\sum_{k=1}^{K} y^{k,1} - \sum_{k=1}^{K} y^{k,o} \right) \tag{5.166}$$

$$- 1/2 \left(\frac{w^o}{p^o g_y + w^o g_x} + \frac{w^1}{p^1 g_y + w^1 g_x} \right) \left(\sum_{k=1}^{K} x^{k,1} - \sum_{k=1}^{K} x^{k,o} \right),$$

(5.167)

from which $\sum_{k=1}^{K} BB^k = BB$ follows directly.[54] In words, if we measure productivity growth using the Bennet-Bowley indicator and assume that all firms face the same prices, then industry productivity growth is the sum of the member firm productivity indicators.

The BB indicator requires data on prices and quantities; if price data are not available, the Luenberger indicator may be estimated. Let $L^k, k = 1, \ldots, K$ be the Luenberger firm productivity indicators and L be the industry or aggregate Luenberger indicator. We want to know under what conditions

$$L = \sum_{k=1}^{K} L^k,$$

(5.168)

where

$$L = 1/2 \left[\vec{D}_T^1 \left(\sum_{k=1}^{K} x^{k,o}, \sum_{k=1}^{K} y^{k,o}; g \right) - \vec{D}_T^1 \left(\sum_{k=1}^{K} x^{k,1}, \sum_{k=1}^{K} y^{k,1}; g \right) \right.$$

(5.169)

$$\left. + \vec{D}_T^o \left(\sum_{k=1}^{K} x^{k,o}, \sum_{k=1}^{K} y^{k,o}; g \right) - \vec{D}_T^o \left(\sum_{k=1}^{K} x^{k,1}, \sum_{k=1}^{K} y^{k,1}; g \right) \right]$$

(5.170)

and the distance functions are defined on the aggregate technology

$$T = \sum_{k=1}^{K} T^k.$$

(5.171)

For the indicator to aggregate, it is sufficient that

$$\vec{D}_T \left(\sum_{k=1}^{K} x^k, \sum_{k=1}^{K} y^k; g \right) = \sum_{k=1}^{K} \vec{D}_{T^k}(x^k, y^k; g).$$

(5.172)

This is a Pexider functional equation with the solution (see Aczél, 1966, p. 302)

$$\vec{D}_{T^k}(x^k, y^k; 1) = \sum_{n=1}^{N} a_n x_{kn} + \sum_{m=1}^{M} b_m y_{km} + c_k, k = 1, \ldots, K$$

(5.173)

and

$$\vec{D}_T \left(\sum_{k=1}^{K} x^k, \sum_{k=1}^{K} y^k; 1 \right) = \sum_{n=1}^{N} a_n \sum_{k=1}^{K} x_{kn} + \sum_{m=1}^{M} b_m \sum_{k=1}^{K} y_{km} + \sum_{k=1}^{K} c_k,$$

(5.174)

where we have set $g = 1$ for simplicity, and a_n, b_m, and c_k are arbitrary constants. This result shows that the distance functions must be linear and that the only difference across firms is the intercept coefficient c_k. This is essentially the pessimistic conclusion reached by Blackorby and Russell (1999). Recall that the directional distance functions must satisfy the translation property

$$\vec{D}_T(x - \alpha g_x, y + \alpha g_y; g_x, g_y) = \vec{D}_T(x, y; g_x, g_y) - \alpha. \tag{5.175}$$

In our case, $\vec{D}_T(\cdot)$ and $\vec{D}_{T^k}(\cdot)$ satisfy this property provided that

$$\sum_{m=1}^{M} b_m - \sum_{n=1}^{N} a_n = -1, \tag{5.176}$$

which reinforces the pessimistic result: In order to aggregate the Luenberger productivity indicator, if we insist on aggregating over all possible inputs and outputs (x, y), then that requires a very special and restrictive technology. If we focus on a narrower set of inputs and outputs over which we wish to aggregate—namely, economic optimizers—we find a happier result, which we turn to next.

5.4.2 Aggregation over optimizers

Referring to figure 5.15, if we look at the input output vectors $(5, 3) \in T^1$ and $(5, 3) \in T^2$, then both are boundary or technically efficient points. However, their sum $(10, 6) \in T$ is interior to the aggregate technology. Thus, even if we choose technically efficient points for the firms, they may not be technically efficient for the industry; that is, the sum of technically efficient firm bundles does not yield industry-efficient firm bundles. Overcoming this type of result requires some coordination; as it turns out, we can use prices to provide the required coordination. If we aggregate bundles that satisfy some sort of optimization given that all firms face the same prices, we can find a consistent result; that is, if all firms are maximizing profit, for example, the industry should also be achieving a profit maximum. Aggregation over optimizers proceeds with a definition of optimizers as profit maximizers. Define the industry or aggregate profit function as

$$\Pi_T = \max_{(x,y)} \left\{ py - wx : (x, y) \in T = \sum_{k=1}^{K} T^k \right\}, \tag{5.177}$$

where $x = \sum_{k=1}^{K} x^k, y = \sum_{k=1}^{K} y^k$. Koopmans (1957) proved the following aggregation theorem for profit functions:

$$\Pi_T = \sum_{k=1}^{K} \Pi^k(p, w) \tag{5.178}$$

In words, if each firm in the industry faces the same prices, then maximum industry profit is the sum of the firm maximum profits.

From this result, it follows directly that the profit-based Luenberger productivity indicator (ΠL defined in section 5.2.3) aggregates. To see, this note that

$$\sum_{k=1}^{K}\left[\frac{1}{2}\left(\frac{\Pi^{k,1}(p^o, w^o) + \Pi^{k,o}(p^o, w^o) - 2(p^o y^{k,o} - w^o x^{k,o})}{p^o g_y + w^o g_x}\right)\right.$$
$$\left. -\frac{1}{2}\left(\frac{\Pi^{k,1}(p^1, w^1) + \Pi^{k,o}(p^1, w^1) - 2(p^1 y^{k,1} - w^1 x^{k,1})}{p^1 g_y + w^1 g_x}\right)\right]$$
$$=\left[\frac{1}{2}\left(\frac{\sum_{k=1}^{K}\Pi^{k,1}(p^o, w^o) + \sum_{k=1}^{K}\Pi^{k,o}(p^o, w^o) - 2(p^o\sum_{k=1}^{K}y^{k,o} - w^o\sum_{k=1}^{K}x^{k,o})}{p^o g_y + w^o g_x}\right)\right.$$
$$\left. -\frac{1}{2}\left(\frac{\sum_{k=1}^{K}\Pi^{k,1}(p^1, w^1) + \sum_{k=1}^{K}\Pi^{k,o}(p^1, w^1) - 2(p^1\sum_{k=1}^{K}y^{k,1} - w^1\sum_{k=1}^{K}x^{k,1})}{p^1 g_y + w^1 g_x}\right)\right],$$

$$(5.179)$$

where the left-hand side (the first two lines) of the equality is the sum of the firm Luenberger profit productivity indicators and the right-hand side is the industry or aggregate indicator. Applying the Koopmans' result to the Nerlovian profit efficiency, recall (5.14) yields a relation between the industry and firm directional distance functions. In particular,

$$\vec{D}_T\left(\sum_{k=1}^{K}x^k, \sum_{k=1}^{K}y^k; g\right) + \vec{AE}_T = \frac{\Pi_T(p, w) - (p\sum_{k=1}^{K}y^k - w\sum_{k=1}^{K}x^k)}{pg_y + wg_x}$$

$$= \sum_{k=1}^{K}\frac{\Pi_k(p, w) - (py^k - wx^k)}{pg_y + wg_x}$$

$$= \sum_{k=1}^{K}\left[\vec{D}_{T^k}(x^k, y^k; g) + \vec{AE}_{T^k}\right]. \qquad (5.180)$$

Here the left-hand side is the industry profit efficiency and the right-hand side becomes the sum of the firm profit efficiencies. Thus, if industry allocative efficiency $\vec{AE}_T$ is equal to the sum of the firm allocative efficiencies, that is, if

$$\vec{AE}_T = \sum_{k=1}^{K}\vec{AE}_{T^k}, \qquad (5.181)$$

then the firm directional distance functions sum to the industry directional distance function

$$\vec{D}_T\left(\sum_{k=1}^{K}x^k, \sum_{k=1}^{K}y^k; g\right) = \sum_{k=1}^{K}\vec{D}_{T^k}(x^k, y^k; g), \qquad (5.182)$$

In turn, if these conditions hold in each period, then the Luenberger industry productivity indicator as defined in section 5.2.1 equals the sum of the firm Luenberger productivity indicators

$$L = \sum_{k=1}^{K} L_{T^k}, \qquad (5.183)$$

where L is the industry Luenberger indicator and L_{T^k} is the kth firm's Luenberger indicator. Furthermore, the decomposition into efficiency change and technical change also aggregates under these conditions:

$$\text{LEC} = \sum_{k=1}^{K} \text{LEC}_{T^k}$$

$$\text{LTC} = \sum_{k=1}^{K} \text{LTC}_{T^k} \qquad (5.184)$$

Following the same reasoning but using the revenue function rather than the profit function, it follows that the green Luenberger indicator discussed at the end of section 5.2.1 also aggregates.

Next, we take up the aggregation of the Malmquist productivity index: When can we aggregate the individual firm productivity indexes M_o^k to obtain the industry index M_o? We begin by looking at the Farrell output measures of efficiency.

Define the aggregate output set as

$$P(x^1, \dots, x^K) = \sum_{k=1}^{K} P^k(x^k), \qquad (5.185)$$

where we note that $y \in P(x^1, \dots, x^K)$ implies that there exist $y^k \in P^k(x^k), k = 1, \dots, K$ such that $y_m = \sum_{k=1}^{K} y_{km}, m = 1, \dots, M$. Thus, we aggregate outputs but not inputs; that is, the aggregate output set $P(x^1, \dots, x^K)$ depends on the given allocation of inputs across firms.

Next, define the aggregate revenue function as

$$R(x^1, \dots, x^K, p) = \max\{py : y \in P(x^1, \dots, x^K)\}, \qquad (5.186)$$

where $y = \sum_{k=1}^{K} y^k$ and all firms face the same prices p. The aggregate output distance function is defined as

$$D_o\left(x^1, \dots, x^K, \sum_{k=1}^{K} y^k\right) = \inf\left\{\theta : \sum_{k=1}^{K} y^k/\theta \in P(x^1, \dots, x^K)\right\}. \qquad (5.187)$$

The industry revenue efficiency inequality may be written as

$$\frac{R(x^1,\dots,x^K,p)}{py} \geqq 1/D_o\left(x^1,\dots,x^K,\sum_{k=1}^{K}y^k\right), \tag{5.188}$$

and by introducing an allocative efficiency component AE_o, we arrive at the Farrell decomposition of industry revenue efficiency into output-oriented technical and allocative efficiency:

$$\frac{R(x^1,\dots,x^K,p)}{py} = \frac{1}{D_o(x^1,\dots,x^K,\sum_{k=1}^{K}y^k)} \cdot AE_o \tag{5.189}$$

By an extension of the Koopmans profit aggregation result, the firm revenue functions aggregate into the industry function

$$R(x^1,\dots,x^K,p) = \sum_{k=1}^{K}R^k(x^k,p). \tag{5.190}$$

Applying this result to the Farrell revenue efficiency index yields

$$\frac{R(x^1,\dots,x^K,p)}{py} = \sum_{k=1}^{K}\frac{R^k(x^k,p)}{py^k}s^k, \tag{5.191}$$

where $y = \sum_{k=1}^{K}y^k$ and $s^k = py^k/py$ is firm k's share of industry revenue. Each s^k is nonnegative, and they sum to one.

The next issue is whether the technical and allocative components of Farrell output efficiency aggregate, as well. Like the Malmquist productivity index decomposition, the components of Farrell output efficiency have a multiplicative structure. Färe and Zelenyuk (2003) have shown that, to preserve the multiplicative structure, geometric mean weights must be adopted to obtain aggregation of the components (see also Färe and Grosskopf, 2004). The difficulty arises because our aggregation results are additive rather than multiplicative, which, as Fox (1999) demonstrated, may cause inconsistencies for cost efficiency. Färe and Grosskopf (2000) show that resolving the inconsistencies requires that the aggregation and performance measures "match," that is, both be additive in structure, for example.[55] This suggests the need for an "additive" Malmquist index, perhaps appealing to formulation in logarithmic mean form as discussed in Balk (2003).

Before closing this section, we note that if we are interested in average firm performance within an industry (as opposed to aggregation), we may retain the multiplicative form of the Malmquist index, to yield

$$\overline{M}_o = \prod_{k=1}^{K}\left(\frac{D_o^{k,o}(x^{k,1},y^{k,1})\,D_o^{k,1}(x^{k,1},y^{k,1})}{D_o^{k,o}(x^{k,o},y^{k,o})\,D_o^{k,1}(x^{k,o},y^{k,o})}\right)^{(s^{k,1}+s^{k,o})/2}, \tag{5.192}$$

where $s^{k,\tau}$ is firm k's revenue share

$$s^{k,\tau} = \frac{p^\tau y^k}{\sum_{k=1}^K p^\tau y^k} = \frac{p^\tau y^k}{p^\tau \sum_{k=1}^K y^k}, \tau = 0, 1. \qquad (5.193)$$

In the single-output case, this reduces to $s^k = y^k / \sum_{k=1}^K y^k$, which means that output prices are not required. Alternatively, in the multiple-output case, we may define

$$s^{k,\tau} = \frac{1}{M} \left(\sum_{m=1}^M \frac{y_{km}}{\sum_{k=1}^K y_{km}} \right), \quad k = 1, \ldots, K, \qquad (5.194)$$

which is the arithmetic mean of firm k's production share of each output, where each share is nonnegative and sums to one.

This averaging technique may be extended to the efficiency change and technical change components. The relative simplicity of this result (as opposed to our aggregation result for the Malmquist index) is due to the fact that we do not have to use the aggregation property

$$P(x^1, \ldots, x^K) = \sum_{k=1}^K P^k(x^k), \qquad (5.195)$$

but rather operate directly on the individual indexes.

5.5 Empirical Implementation

The productivity indexes and indicators in this section separate themselves into two groups, the group of superlative indexes and those that require some sort of optimization to estimate, including those using mathematical programming and econometric techniques. In the first group, we include the Bennet-Bowley indicator and the Fisher and Törnqvist indexes. Implementation of these requires data on inputs and outputs together with their associated prices. If such prices are not available, then shadow prices must be estimated.[56] How to estimate shadow prices using the appropriate distance functions and Shephard's dual lemma was discussed in section 5.1. One may view this first group of indexes as empirical approximations to the theoretical Malmquist (Törnqvist and Fisher) indexes and Luenberger indicators (Bennet-Bowley).

To empirically implement the Luenberger indicators, the Malmquist index, or the Hicks-Moorsteen index, one may use either an activity analysis approach or a parametric distance function approach. The same approaches may be used to estimate the dual forms of these indexes, for example, the profit-based Luenberger indicator, but, of course, the profit function rather than the distance function would be estimated and prices would be required. We begin with activity analysis methods and then turn to econometric approaches.

5.5.1 Activity analysis methods

Starting with the activity analysis approach or, as it is also called, the data envelopment analysis (DEA) approach, suppose that there are $k = 1, \ldots, K$ observations or activities $(x^k, y^k) = (x_{k1}, \ldots, x_{kN}, y_{k1}, \ldots, y_{kM})$. These are required to satisfy certain conditions to ensure solutions to the linear programming problems involved:

1. $x_{kn} \geq 0, y_{km} \geq 0, k = 1, \ldots, K, \ n = 1, \ldots, N, \ m = 1, \ldots, M,$
2. $\sum_{k=1}^{K} x_{kn} > 0, n = 1, \ldots, N,$
3. $\sum_{n=1}^{N} x_{kn} > 0, k = 1, \ldots, K,$
4. $\sum_{k=1}^{K} y_{km} > 0, m = 1, \ldots, M,$
5. $\sum_{m=1}^{M} y_{km} > 0, k = 1, \ldots, K.$

Condition 1 states that inputs and outputs are nonnegative, and condition 2 says that each input must be used by at least one activity. Condition 3 requires that each activity use at least one input. Conditions 4 and 5 mimic 2 and 3 for outputs. Together, these imply that the data (coefficient) matrix must have at least one positive element in each row and column. This is a much weaker condition than that originally assumed in Charnes, Cooper, and Rhodes (1978), which required all data elements to be strictly positive.

The activity analysis model makes use of intensity (activity) variables $z_k, k = 1, \ldots, K$, one for each activity or observation of data. These are nonnegative variables whose solution value may be interpreted as the extent to which an activity is involved in frontier production.

The programming approach allows for specifications of technology that can be customized to satisfy various (usually minimal) regularity conditions. For example, one may specify the following technology:

$$T_c = \left\{ (x, y) : \sum_{k=1}^{K} z_k x_{kn} \leq x_n, n = 1, \ldots, N, \right.$$

$$\left. \sum_{k=1}^{K} z_k y_{km} \geq y_m, m = 1, \ldots, M, z_k \geq 0, k = 1, \ldots, K \right\}. \quad (5.196)$$

This technology is convex with inputs and outputs freely disposable. In addition, it satisfies constant returns to scale, that is,

$$T_c = \lambda T_c, \lambda > 0,$$

and the intensity variables are only restricted to be non-negative.[57]

By adding restrictions to the intensity variables $z_k, k = 1, \ldots, K$, we can model different returns-to-scale properties. For example, by restricting the intensity variables to sum to one, what is called the variable returns to scale

(VRS) version[58] is obtained:

$$T_v = \left\{ (x,y) : \sum_{k=1}^{K} z_k x_{kn} \leqq x_n, n = 1, \ldots, N, \sum_{k=1}^{K} z_k y_{km} \geqq y_m, m = 1, \ldots, M, \right.$$

$$\left. z_k \geqq 0, k = 1, \ldots, K, \sum_{k=1}^{K} z_k = 1 \right\}. \qquad (5.197)$$

We can also modify the technology to satisfy our environmental conditions, weak disposability of outputs and nulljointness between good and bad outputs. Thus, our constant returns to scale environmental technology is specified as

$$T_{\text{env}} = \left\{ (x,y) : \sum_{k=1}^{K} z_k x_{kn} \leqq x_n, n = 1, \ldots, N, \sum_{k=1}^{K} z_k y_{kg_m} \geqq y_{g_m}, \right.$$

$$\left. m = 1, \ldots, M, \sum_{k=1}^{K} z_k y_{kb_j} = y_{b_j}, j = 1, \ldots, J, z_k \geqq 0, k = 1, \ldots, K \right\}$$

$$(5.198)$$

In the environmental technology, the bad output constraints $j = 1, \ldots, J$ hold with equality, which imposes weak disposability of outputs.[59] In order to impose nulljointness, the following conditions are required:

$$\sum_{k=1}^{K} y_{kb_j} > 0, j = 1, \ldots, J$$

$$\sum_{j=1}^{J} y_{kb_j} > 0, k = 1, \ldots, K \qquad (5.199)$$

These say that each firm k is required to produce some bad output, and each bad output is produced by some firm. If only one bad output is produced, then all firms with positive good output must produce positive bad output.

T_c, T_v, and T_{env} are the basic activity analysis models needed to estimate the productivity indexes and indicators discussed in this chapter. For example, beginning with the Malmquist productivity index, we may estimate the component Shephard output distance functions by solving the linear programming problems

$$\left[D_o^t \left(x^{k,\tau}, y^{k,\tau} \right) \right]^{-1} = \max \theta$$

$$\text{s.t. } (x^{k,\tau}, \theta y^{k,\tau}) \in T^t, \tau = o, 1, \ t = o, 1. \qquad (5.200)$$

The Luenberger productivity indicator requires estimating directional distance functions as solutions to the following linear programming problems:

$$\vec{D}_T^t(x^{k,\tau}, y^{k,\tau}; g) = \max \beta$$

$$\text{s.t. } (x^{k,\tau} - \beta g_x, y^{k,\tau} + \beta g_y) \in T^t, \tau = o, 1, \ t = o, 1$$

$$(5.201)$$

Note that we have not specified whether technology satisfies constant returns (benchmark) or VRS (best practice) in the problems above. Clearly, if the Malmquist index is to be interpreted as a ratio of average products, then T_c would be appropriate in estimating the Shephard distance functions for the Malmquist index. The relevant programming problems would then be

$$\left[D_o^t(x^{k,\tau}, y^{k,\tau})\right]^{-1} = \max \theta$$

$$\text{s.t. } \sum_{k=1}^{K} z_k^\tau x_{kn}^\tau \leq x_{k'n}^\tau, n = 1, \ldots, N,$$

$$\sum_{k=1}^{K} z_k^\tau y_{km}^\tau \geq \theta y_{k'm}^\tau, m = 1, \ldots, M,$$

$$z_k^\tau \geq 0, k = 1, \ldots, K; \tau = o, 1; t = o, 1. \quad (5.202)$$

The Luenberger indicator is clearly not designed for a ratio of average products interpretation; rather, it has a magnitude interpretation much like the notion of change in consumer surplus. Here, it is not clear what the appropriate reference technology should be. If the constant returns to scale technology is preferred, then the component directional distance functions may be computed as solutions to the following linear programming problems:

$$\vec{D}_T^t(x^{k,\tau}, y^{k,\tau}; g) = \max \beta$$

$$\text{s.t. } \sum_{k=1}^{K} z_k^\tau x_{kn}^\tau \leq x_{k'n}^\tau - \beta g_x, n = 1, \ldots, N,$$

$$\sum_{k=1}^{K} z_k^\tau y_{km}^\tau \geq y_{k'm}^\tau + \beta g_y, m = 1, \ldots, M,$$

$$z_k^\tau \geq 0, k = 1, \ldots, K; \tau = o, 1; t = o, 1. \quad (5.203)$$

Note how similar this is to the formulation of the Shephard output distance function; only the right-hand side is different. The distinctive difference is, of course, the additive form of the βg term and the inclusion of the direction vector $(-g_x, g_y)$. This raises the issue of how to choose the direction vector, which we discuss briefly in section 5.1. This depends, first of all, on the application. For example, in environmental applications (see below), the possibility of partitioning the output direction vector to allow for contraction of bad outputs $(-g_b)$ and expansion of good outputs (g_g) is generally appropriate. If equal "weights" for goods and bads are considered desirable, then $g_b = -1, g_g = 1$ is one possibility. This could also be considered a policy choice variable consistent with a social welfare function, for example. If we wish to have a measure that mimics the Shephard distance functions in evaluating individual observations in terms of their observed output (input) mix, then using the direction vector $(-x^k, y^k)$ would be appropriate in the nonenvironmental case. This allows every observation to be evaluated in its "own" direction. If we wish to evaluate all observations in the same direction, then direction vectors $(-1, 1)$ and $(-\bar{x}, \bar{y})$ are obvious choices. The "constant" direction vector facilitates aggregation, as well. Another possibility is to optimize over the direction—perhaps to minimize the distance to the frontier or to eliminate allocative efficiency.

If the Luenberger indicator is estimated in its dual profit form, a VRS technology T_v would be preferred—otherwise, zero profit would render the indicator meaningless. The component problems to be solved for the profit indicator would then be of the sort

$$\Pi(p^k, w^k) = \max_{(x,y)}\{p^k y - w^k x : (x, y) \in T_v\}, \qquad (5.204)$$

where prices may vary across observations.

Turning to the green Luenberger indicator, the environmental distance functions may be estimated according to

$$\vec{D}_{T_{\text{env}}}^t \left(x^{k,\tau}, y_g^{k,\tau}, y_b^{k,\tau}; g_g, g_b\right) = \max \beta$$

$$\text{s.t. } (x^{k,\tau}, y_g^{k,\tau} + \beta g_g, y^{k,\tau} - \beta g_b) \in T_{\text{env}}^t, \tau = 0, 1,$$

$$t = 0, 1. \qquad (5.205)$$

5.5.1.1 Accounting for slacks

It is probably fair to say that most of the applications of the various forms of the distance-function–based productivity measures use mathematical programming techniques to estimate the component functions. The cases in which the Malmquist productivity index is defined in terms of input or output distance functions and is not price dependent, the possibility arises that the data may be projected onto the isoquant and not the efficient subset of the technology; that is, there may be "slacks". More formally, the input and output distance functions assess efficiency relative to the isoquants of technology; that is,

$$D_i(y, x) = 1 \text{ if and only if } x \in \text{isoq} L(y), \qquad (5.206)$$

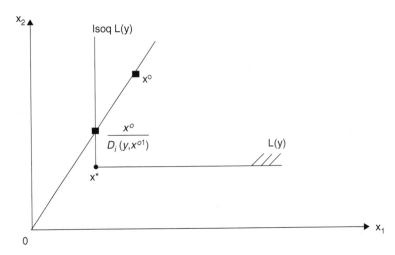

Figure 5.16. Isoquant and Efficiency

and

$$D_o(x, y) = 1 \text{ if and only if } y \in \text{isoq}P(x). \qquad (5.207)$$

These conditions imply that at the optimum, that is, when these functions take a value of unity, there may be slacks, which we illustrate for the input distance function in figure 5.16.

Figure 5.16 illustrates an input set $L(y)$ and its corresponding isoquant isoq$L(y)$. When radially contracted by the input distance function, the input vector x^o is projected onto the isoquant at $x^o/D_i(y, x^o)$; clearly, input usage could be further reduced to x^* and still produce y; that is, there is slack in x_2. In fact, x^* is the input bundle in the efficient subset of $L(y)$; thus, it is the only technically efficient input bundle in the sense of Pareto-Koopmans. As a consequence, some researchers have argued that productivity should be assessed relative to the efficient subsets rather than the isoquants of technology.[60] This can be achieved by using versions of the Russell measure of technical efficiency.[61] This may also be achieved by employing "dual" productivity measures such as the profit and revenue versions of productivity mentioned above. See also chapter 2 for other DEA specifications designed to eliminate slack.

Formally, technical efficiency of inputs is reflected in membership of the efficient subsets

$$\text{eff}\, L(y) = \{x : x \in L(y), x' \leqq x, x' \neq x, \text{ imply } x' \notin L(y)\}. \qquad (5.208)$$

In words, if x is in the efficient subset of $L(y)$, then any x' that is smaller than x in at least one component must not be able to produce y. Elements of $\text{eff}\, L(y)$

are the "smallest" input bundles capable of producing y. In figure 5.16, x^* is the only efficient input bundle in this sense. In general, as in our illustration, the isoquant and efficient subsets differ; an interesting case in which they coincide is the Cobb-Douglas function.

As mentioned above, the Russell measure uses the efficient subset rather than the isoquant as the efficient benchmark. Currently, there are two versions of the input-oriented Russell measure: the original using an "arithmetic mean" objective function and the second using a geometric mean objective,[62] which are defined, respectively, as[63]

$$R_A(y, x) = \min \left\{ \frac{1}{N} \sum_{n=1}^{N} \lambda_n : (\lambda_1 x_1, \ldots, \lambda_N x_N) \in L(y) \right\} \qquad (5.209)$$

and

$$R_G(y, x) = \min \left\{ \left(\prod_{n=1}^{N} \theta_n \right)^{1/N} : (\theta_1 x_1, \ldots, \theta_N x_N) \in L(y) \right\}. \qquad (5.210)$$

Both functions have the property that they equal one if and only if x belongs to the efficient subset $\text{eff} \, L(y)$.

One can obtain Malmquist productivity indexes based on the Russell measures by substituting the Russell measures for the distance functions in the original definition.[64]

A shortcoming of the Russell-based Malmquist indexes is that they do not have a "nice" dual setting. Färe, Grosskopf, and Zelenyuk (2003) provide a characterization of the dual, but it does not have an obvious familiar value counterpart.

5.5.2 Parametric methods

With respect to parameterizing and estimating the functions involved in the productivity measures, we can identify two major families of appropriate functional forms. The first group seeks to estimate functions that satisfy homogeneity, including the profit, cost, and revenue functions, as well as the Shephard distance functions. The second group is characterized by the translation property; these include the various directional distance functions.

For the homogeneous functions, the translog functional form is recommended; one can easily impose homogeneity with this form, but imposing translation is impossible. For the translation functions, the quadratic form readily allows for the translation property (but not homogeneity). [This form was used by Färe, Grosskopf, Noh, and Weber (2005) to estimate a stochastic frontier directional output distance function.]

Recall that the directional technology distance function satisfies the translation property while the output distance function is homogeneous of degree $+1$ in outputs. These conditions imply that the two distance functions require different parameterizations.[65] The directional distance function can be parameterized as a quadratic function; that is,

$$\vec{D}_T(x, y; g_x, g_y) = \alpha_o + \sum_{n=1}^{N} \alpha_n x_n + \sum_{m=1}^{M} \beta_m y_m + \frac{1}{2} \sum_{n=1}^{N} \sum_{n'=1}^{N} \alpha_{nn'} x_n x_{n'}$$

$$+ \frac{1}{2} \sum_{m=1}^{M} \sum_{m'=1}^{M} \beta_{mm'} y_m y_{m'} + \sum_{n=1}^{N} \sum_{m=1}^{M} \gamma_{mn} y_m x_n, \quad (5.211)$$

with symmetry $\alpha_{nn'} = \alpha_{n'n}$ and $\beta_{mm'} = \beta_{m'm}$, as well as the following restrictions to impose the translation property:

$$\sum_{n=1}^{N} \alpha_n g_{x_n} - \sum_{m=1}^{M} \beta_m g_{y_m} = -1,$$

$$\sum_{n=1}^{N} \alpha_{nn'} g_{x_n} = 0, \quad n' = 1, \ldots, N,$$

$$\sum_{m=1}^{M} \beta_{mm'} g_{y_m} = 0, \quad m' = 1, \ldots, M, \quad (5.212)$$

$$\sum_{n=1}^{N} \gamma_{mn} g_{x_n} = 0, \quad m = 1, \ldots, N,$$

$$\sum_{m=1}^{M} \gamma_{mn} g_{y_m} = 0, \quad n = 1, \ldots, N.$$

The traditional output distance function may be parameterized as a translog function

$$\ln D_o(x, y) = \alpha_o + \sum_{n=1}^{N} \alpha_n \ln x_n + \sum_{m=1}^{M} \beta_m \ln y_m + \frac{1}{2} \sum_{n=1}^{N} \sum_{n'=1}^{N} \alpha_{nn'} \ln x_n \ln x_{n'}$$

$$+ \frac{1}{2} \sum_{m=1}^{M} \sum_{m'=1}^{M} \beta_{mm'} \ln y_m \ln y_{m'} + \sum_{n=1}^{N} \sum_{m=1}^{M} \gamma_{mn} \ln y_m \ln x_n,$$

$$(5.213)$$

where symmetry is imposed and homogeneity of degree $+1$ is imposed by

$$\sum \beta_m = 1,$$

$$\sum_{m=1}^{M} \beta_{mm'} = 0, \quad m' = 1, \dots, M,$$

$$\sum_{m=1}^{M} \gamma_{mn} = 0, \quad m = 1, \dots, M. \tag{5.214}$$

5.5.3 Parameterizing the decomposition of Malmquist and Luenberger productivity

Beginning with the decomposition of the Luenberger productivity indicator, we need to include time in our specification of the directional distance function quadratic form:

$$\vec{D}_T(x, y; g_x, g_y, t, \theta) = \alpha_o + \sum_{n=1}^{N} \alpha_n x_n + \sum_{m=1}^{M} \beta_m y_m + \frac{1}{2} \sum_{n=1}^{N} \sum_{n'=1}^{N} \alpha_{nn'} x_n x_{n'}$$

$$+ \frac{1}{2} \sum_{m=1}^{M} \sum_{m'=1}^{M} \beta_{mm'} y_m y_{m'} + \sum_{n=1}^{N} \sum_{m=1}^{M} \gamma_{mn} y_m x_n$$

$$+ \delta_1 t + \frac{1}{2} \delta_2 t^2 + \sum_{n=1}^{N} \psi_n t x_n + \sum_{m=1}^{M} \mu_m t y_m, \tag{5.215}$$

where θ is a vector of parameters, and we also require that the symmetry and translation properties from the preceding section be imposed, as well as $\sum_{n=1}^{N} \psi_n g_{x_n} = 0, \sum_{m=1}^{M} \mu_m g_{y_m} = 0$ to preserve translation with our additional time terms.

The decompositions that we specify here include

$$L = LEC + LTC, \tag{5.216}$$

that is, Luenberger productivity is the sum of efficiency change; and technical change, and we can decompose technical change into input bias, output bias, and a (neutral) magnitude term:

$$LTC = LOBTC + LIBTC + LMATC \tag{5.217}$$

For the quadratic case above, these are

$$\text{LEC} = \vec{D}_T^o(x^o, y^o; g, t^o, \hat{\theta}) - \vec{D}_T^1(x^1, y^1; g, t^1, \hat{\theta})$$

$$= \sum_{n=1}^{N} \hat{\alpha}_n(x_n^o - x_n^1) + \sum_{m=1}^{M} \hat{\beta}_m(y_m^o - y_m^1)$$

$$+ \frac{1}{2} \sum_{n=1}^{N} \sum_{n'=1}^{N} \hat{\alpha}_{nn'}(x_n^o x_{n'}^o - x_n^1 x_{n'}^1) + \frac{1}{2} \sum_{m=1}^{M} \sum_{m'=1}^{M} \hat{\beta}_{mm'}(y_m^o y_{m'}^o - y_m^1 y_{m'}^1)$$

$$+ \sum_{n=1}^{N} \sum_{m=1}^{M} \hat{\gamma}_{mn}(y_m^o x_n^o - y_m^1 x_n^1) - \hat{\delta}_1 \Delta t$$

$$- \frac{1}{2}\hat{\delta}_2 \Delta t(t^o + t^1) + \sum_{n} \hat{\psi}_n(t^o x_n^o - t^1 x_n^1) + \sum_{m=1}^{M} \hat{\mu}_m(t^o y_m^o - t^1 y_m^1),$$

$$(5.218)$$

where $\Delta t = t^1 - t^o$.

$$\text{LTC} = \frac{1}{2}\Big[\vec{D}_T^1(x^1, y^1; g, t^1, \hat{\theta}) - \vec{D}_T^o(x^1, y^1; g, t^o, \hat{\theta})$$

$$+ \vec{D}_T^1(x^o, y^o; g, t^1, \hat{\theta}) - \vec{D}_T^o(x^o, y^o; g, t^o, \hat{\theta})\Big]$$

$$= \hat{\delta}_1 \Delta t + \frac{1}{2}\hat{\delta}_2 \Delta t(t^o + t^1) + \frac{1}{2}\sum_{n=1}^{N} \hat{\psi}_n \Delta t(x_n^o + x_n^1)$$

$$+ \frac{1}{2}\sum_{m=1}^{M} \hat{\mu}_m \Delta t(y_m^o + y_m^1), \qquad (5.219)$$

$$\text{LOBTC} = \frac{1}{2}\Big[\vec{D}_T^1(x^1, y^1; g, t^1, \hat{\theta}) - \vec{D}_T^o(x^1, y^1; g, t^o, \hat{\theta})$$

$$+ \vec{D}_T^o(x^1, y^o; g, t^o, \hat{\theta}) - \vec{D}_T^1(x^1, y^o; g, t^1, \hat{\theta})\Big]$$

$$= \frac{1}{2}\sum_{m=1}^{M} \hat{\mu}_m \Delta t(y_m^1 - y_m^o), \qquad (5.220)$$

$$\text{LIBTC} = \frac{1}{2}\Big[\vec{D}_T^o(x^o, y^o; g, t^o, \hat{\theta}) - \vec{D}_T^1(x^o, y^o; g, t^1, \hat{\theta})$$

$$+ \vec{D}_T^1(x^1, y^o; g, t^1, \hat{\theta}) - \vec{D}_T^o(x^1, y^o; g, t^o, \hat{\theta})\Big] \qquad (5.221)$$

$$= \frac{1}{2}\sum_{m=1}^{M} \hat{\psi}_n \Delta t(x_n^1 - x_n^o),$$

$$\text{LMATC} = \vec{D}_T^1(x^o, y^o; g, t^1, \hat{\theta}) - \vec{D}_T^o(x^o, y^o; g, t^o, \hat{\theta})$$

$$= \hat{\delta}_1 \Delta t + \frac{1}{2}\hat{\delta}_2 \Delta t (t^o + t^1) + \sum_{n=1}^{N} \hat{\psi}_n \Delta t x_n^o + \sum_{m=1}^{M} \hat{\mu}_m \Delta t y_m^o,$$

$$(5.222)$$

where $\hat{\theta}$ is the vector of estimated parameters.

The corresponding decompositions for the Malmquist index can be found in Fuentes et al. (2001, p. 84) for a translog parametric form. For completeness, we reproduce them here.[66] Their approach is to estimate the component distance functions econometrically and then substitute the forecasted values evaluated at the appropriate time period into the Malmquist index "formulas," resulting in a discrete change index. This is in contrast to the approach taken by Orea (2002) discussed in chapter 1, which relies on the Diewert quadratic lemma to go from the derivative-based approach to form the Malmquist index and its components (see the discussion in chapter 1).

The translog specification including time trends is given by

$$\ln D_o(x, y; t, \theta) = \alpha_o + \sum_{n=1}^{N} \alpha_n \ln x_n + \sum_{m=1}^{M} \beta_m \ln y_m + \frac{1}{2}\sum_{n=1}^{N}\sum_{n'=1}^{N} \alpha_{nn'} \ln x_n \ln x_{n'}$$

$$+ \frac{1}{2}\sum_{m=1}^{M}\sum_{m'=1}^{M} \beta_{mm'} \ln y_m \ln y_{m'} + \sum_{n=1}^{N}\sum_{m=1}^{M} \gamma_{mn} \ln y_m \ln x_n$$

$$+ \delta_1 t + \frac{1}{2}\delta_2 t^2 + \sum_{n=1}^{N} \psi_n t \ln x_n + \sum_{m=1}^{M} \mu_m t \ln y_m,$$

$$(5.223)$$

with the additional homogeneity restriction $\sum_{m=1}^{M} \mu_m = 0$. The decomposition that we include here is

$$M_o = \text{EC} \cdot \text{TC},$$

with

$$\text{TC} = \text{OBT} \cdot \text{IBTC} \cdot \text{MATC},$$

where

$$\text{EC} = \exp\left[\ln D_o^1(x^1, y^1; t^1, \hat{\theta}) - \ln D_o^o(x^o, y^o; t^o, \hat{\theta})\right], \qquad (5.224)$$

$$
\begin{aligned}
\text{TC} = \exp & \left\{ \frac{1}{2} \left[\ln D_o^o(x^1, y^1; t^o, \hat{\theta}) - \ln D_o^1(x^1, y^1; t^1, \hat{\theta}) \right. \right. \\
& \left. \left. + \ln D_o^o(x^o, y^o; t^o, \hat{\theta}) - \ln D_o^1(x^o, y^o; t^1, \hat{\theta}) \right] \right\} \\
= \exp & \left\{ - \left[\hat{\delta}_1 \Delta t + \frac{1}{2} \hat{\delta}_2 \Delta t (t^o + t^1) + \sum_{n=1}^{N} \hat{\psi}_n \Delta t \left(\frac{\ln x_n^o + \ln x_n^1}{2} \right) \right. \right. \\
& \left. \left. + \sum_{m=1}^{M} \hat{\mu}_m \Delta t \left(\frac{\ln y_m^o + \ln y_m^1}{2} \right) \right] \right\}
\end{aligned}
\tag{5.225}
$$

$$
\begin{aligned}
\text{OBTC} = \exp & \left\{ \frac{1}{2} \left[\ln D_o^o(x^1, y^1; t^o, \hat{\theta}) - \ln D_o^1(x^1, y^1; t^1, \hat{\theta}) \right. \right. \\
& \left. \left. + \ln D_o^1(x^1, y^o; t^1, \hat{\theta}) - \ln D_o^o(x^1, y^o; t^o, \hat{\theta}) \right] \right\} \\
= \exp & \left[- \sum_{m=1}^{M} \hat{\mu}_m \Delta t \left(\frac{\ln y_m^1 - \ln y_m^o}{2} \right) \right]
\end{aligned}
\tag{5.226}
$$

$$
\begin{aligned}
\text{IBTC} = \exp & \left\{ \frac{1}{2} \left[\ln D_o^1(x^o, y^o; t^1, \hat{\theta}) - \ln D_o^o(x^o, y^o; t^o, \hat{\theta}) \right. \right. \\
& \left. \left. + \ln D_o^o(x^1, y^o; t^o, \hat{\theta}) - \ln D_o^1(x^1, y^o; t^1\hat{\theta}) \right] \right\} \\
= \exp & \left[- \sum_{n=1}^{N} \hat{\psi}_n \Delta t \left(\frac{\ln x_n^1 - \ln x_n^o}{2} \right) \right]
\end{aligned}
\tag{5.227}
$$

$$
\begin{aligned}
\text{MATC} = & \exp[\ln D_o^o(x^o, y^o; t^o, \hat{\theta}) - \ln D_o^1(x^o, y^o; t^1, \hat{\theta})] \\
= \exp & \left\{ - \left[\hat{\delta}_1 \Delta t + \frac{1}{2} \hat{\delta}_2 \Delta t (t^o + t^1) + \sum_{n=1}^{N} \hat{\psi}_n \Delta t \ln x_n^o \right. \right. \\
& \left. \left. + \sum_{m=1}^{M} \hat{\mu}_m \Delta t \ln y_m^o \right] \right\}.
\end{aligned}
\tag{5.228}
$$

A number of specification and estimation issues arise in the parametric context. A specification that includes a time trend variable entered as a quadratic polynomial and interacted with both inputs and outputs allows for second-order flexibility (see Fuentes et al., 2001) and should, in general, be regarded as an adequate model of technical change by allowing for differences in technical change across firms and over time. An advantage of incorporating this type of time trend specification is that it is very economical in the use of degrees of freedom for panel-data models compared to fixed-effect models with dummy variables. Modeling time-varying inefficiency by explicitly incorporating an exponential function of time in the error term of the equation as proposed by Orea (2002) or by extending the error term specification to allow for different trends and levels in technical efficiencies across different firms as in Atkinson et al. (2003) adds more structure to the fixed-effects specification. Random-effects models impose impractical distributional assumptions by requiring strict exogeneity of the model's explanatory variables (see Atkinson et al., 2003). In fact, the inherent endogeneity features of these types of models favor the application of generalized method of moments estimators even under-fixed effects specifications as advocated by Atkinson et al. (2003).

Although not discussed here, an extensive econometric literature links productivity and the cost function, both in the frontier framework (see, for an early example, Bauer, 1990) and in many applications with extensive decompositions (e.g., in Morrison and Diewert, 1990). See also chapter 3.

5.5.4 Empirical illustration

In order to fix ideas, we include a simple empirical illustration of the main productivity indexes and indicators we have discussed in this chapter. These include our distance-function–based measures of productivity, Malmquist, Hicks-Moorsteen, and Luenberger, as well as the traditional price-based productivity measures: Törnqvist, Fisher, and Bennet-Bowley.

The data we use are publicly available at http://www.ers.usda.gov/data/agproductivity and consist of a time series of data for U.S. agriculture over the period 1948–2002.[67] The data consist of price indexes and implicit quantities[68] in millions of 1996 U.S. dollars. The price indexes are Törnqvist indexes. Output is divided into three categories: crops, livestock, and secondary output. Secondary output includes services such as machine services provided by farmers. The inputs include physical capital, land, labor, and intermediate inputs, which include materials such as pesticides and fertilizer. Land is the residual claimant; the rental rate for land satisfies the accounting identity.

This data set has the advantage of including information on both quantities and prices of multiple inputs and multiple outputs, which allows us to estimate our traditional price-related productivity indexes and indicators. These indexes are perfectly well suited to estimation of productivity with a single time series of data. On the other hand, these data are less well suited for our distance function measures of productivity, since their ability to identify benchmark and best-practice performance is facilitated by panel data; that is, the cross-section aspect of panel data is exploited to estimate the frontier of technology in each period. For an attempt to identify bounds on these in a time-series context, see Lynde and Richmond (1999). This allows for the ready identification of efficiency change and technical change, for example. Again, the distance-function–based productivity measures do not require price data, so the two sets of results will be based on different subsets of the variables in our data set.

Beginning with the price-related measures of productivity, we need to specify a direction for our Bennet-Bowley productivity indicator. In order to make it as closely comparable to its cousins the Törnqvist and Fisher productivity indexes, we choose the direction to be the observed data, that is, $(g_x, g_y) = (x, y)$, where these are vectors.[69] Thus, the Bennet-Bowley indicator is evaluated in each year in the direction of the observed three categories of output and four inputs; that is, we have

$$
\text{BB} = \frac{1}{2} \left(\frac{p^o}{p^o y^o + w^o x^o} + \frac{p^1}{p^1 y^1 + w^1 x^1} \right) (y^1 - y^o)
$$
$$
- \frac{1}{2} \left(\frac{w^o}{p^o y^o + w^o x^o} + \frac{w^1}{p^1 y^1 + w^1 x^1} \right) (x^1 - x^o), \quad (5.229)
$$

for each pair of years, o and 1.

The Törnqvist productivity index is specified as

$$
\ln Y_T - \ln X_T = \sum_{m=1}^{M} \frac{1}{2} \left(\frac{p_m^1}{p^1 y^1} + \frac{p_m^o}{p^o y^o} \right) (\ln y_m^1 - \ln y_m^o)
$$
$$
- \sum_{n=1}^{N} \frac{1}{2} \left(\frac{w^1}{w^1 x^1} + \frac{w^o}{w^o x^o} \right) (\ln x^1 - \ln x^o). \quad (5.230)
$$

Finally, the Fisher productivity index is

$$
Y_F / X_F = \left(\frac{p^o y^1}{p^o y^o} \frac{p^1 y^1}{p^1 y^o} \right)^{1/2} \Bigg/ \left(\frac{w^o x^1}{w^o x^o} \frac{w^1 x^1}{w^1 x^o} \right)^{1/2}. \quad (5.231)
$$

These are all calculated for each pair of years between 1948 and 2002 using *Excel*. We then cumulate them taking account of their multiplicative or additive structure. We also normalize so that the productivity changes all begin with the value one.[70] The results indicate that productivity has been increasing in U.S. agriculture over this period for all three price-related measures. The annual average productivity growth rate with the Fisher and Törnqvist productivity indexes are at about 1.8% per annum. The Bennet-Bowley indicator yields a weighted average annual increase of about 0.9 (not percent). The cumulated results are displayed in figure 5.17. The cumulative gains reflect the pattern of the average annual changes. One source of the difference between the Bennet-Bowley and the Fisher and Törnqvist time paths is that the direction vector of the Bennet-Bowley indicator is not mimicking the prices used in the other two productivity indices in this situation. In

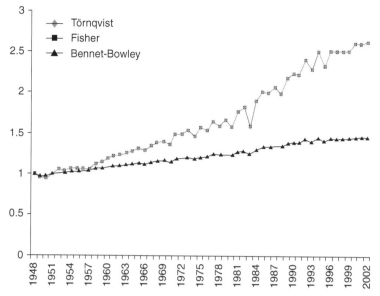

Figure 5.17. Törnqvist, Fisher and Bennet-Bowley Productivity

other words, there is a difference between the price shares used in the Bennet-Bowley and the cost or revenue shares used in the other two indices. This discrepancy stems from the difference in the time paths of input quantities, which, on average, show a slight decrease during the sample period, in contrast to input and output prices and output quantities, which are all increasing over time.

Turning to our distance-function–based frontier measures of productivity, we need to think about how to specify our reference technology. First of all, we use the benchmark or constant returns to scale technology for the Malmquist and Luenberger productivity measures and the VRS technology for the Hicks-Moorsteen. Since we do not have panel data, we also must decide which observations to include in the reference set for each period. In order to maintain the same number of observations in each period's reference, we use the entire time series to form our benchmark technology, what Tulkens (1991) and Tulkens and Vanden Eeckaut (1995) would call an intertemporal approach.[71] This would also be equivalent to what would be referred to as a very long window in the terminology of chapter 2.

We also need to choose a vector for the directional distance functions, which are the building blocks of the Luenberger productivity indicator; here, again, we choose the direction of the data $(-g_x, g_y) = (-x, y)$ to promote comparability with the Malmquist (Hicks-Moorsteen) index, which is based on Shephard output (and input) distance functions. Thus, the Luenberger productivity indicator is specified as

$$L = \frac{1}{2}[\vec{D}_T^1(x^o, y^o; x^o, y^o) - \vec{D}_T^1(x^1, y^1; x^1, y^1)$$
$$+ \vec{D}_T^o(x^o, y^o; x^o, y^o) - \vec{D}_T^o(x^1, y^1; x^1, y^1)], \qquad (5.232)$$

where the direction vectors $(-g_x, g_y)$ are from the same period as the data under evaluation. The general form of the linear programming problem to solve for the values of the various directional distance functions is

$$\vec{D}_T^t(x^{k,\tau}, y^{k,\tau}; g) = \max \beta$$

$$\text{s.t.} \sum_{k=1}^{K} z_k^\tau x_{kn}^\tau \leq x_{k'n}^\tau (1 - \beta), n = 1, \dots, N,$$

$$\sum_{k=1}^{K} z_k^\tau y_{km}^\tau \geq y_{k'm}^\tau (1 + \beta), m = 1, \dots, M,$$

$$z_k^\tau \geq 0, k = 1, \dots, K; \tau = o, 1; t = o, 1, \qquad (5.233)$$

where the summation over observations $k = 1, \dots, K$ is in practice the summation over $t = 1, \dots, T$ to form the benchmark technology from our time series data.

The output-oriented Malmquist productivity index

$$M_o = \left(\frac{D_o^o(x^1, y^1)}{D_o^o(x^o, y^o)} \frac{D_o^1(x^1, y^1)}{D_o^1(x^o, y^o)} \right)^{1/2} \qquad (5.234)$$

requires estimating Shephard output distance functions of the general form

$$[D_o^t(x^{k,\tau}, y^{k,\tau})]^{-1} = \max \theta$$

$$\text{s.t.} \sum_{k=1}^{K} z_k^\tau x_{kn}^\tau \leq x_{k'n}^\tau, n = 1, \dots, N,$$

$$\sum_{k=1}^{K} z_k^\tau y_{km}^\tau \geq \theta y_{k'm}^\tau, m = 1, \dots, M,$$

$$z_k^\tau \geq 0, k = 1, \dots, K; \tau = o, 1; t = o, 1, \qquad (5.235)$$

where again the summation over observations $k = 1, \dots, K$ is in practice the summation over $t = 1, \dots, T$ to form the benchmark technology from our time-series data.

Finally, the Hicks-Moorsteen index in its geometric mean form

$$\text{HM} = \left[\frac{D_o^o(x^o, y^1)/D_o^o(x^o, y^o)}{D_i^o(y^o, x^1)/D_i^o(y^o, x^o)} \cdot \frac{D_o^1(x^o, y^1)/D_o^1(x^1, y^1)}{D_i^1(y^o, x^1)/D_i^1(y^1, x^1)} \right]^{1/2} \quad (5.236)$$

also requires estimation of Shephard input distance functions

$$\left[D_i^t(x^{k,\tau}, y^{k,\tau}) \right]^{-1} = \min \lambda$$

$$\text{s.t.} \sum_{k=1}^K z_k^\tau x_{kn}^\tau \leq \lambda x_{k'n}^\tau, \ n = 1, \dots, N,$$

$$\sum_{k=1}^K z_k^\tau y_{km}^\tau \geq y_{k'm}^\tau, \ m = 1, \dots, M,$$

$$z_k^\tau \geq 0, k = 1, \dots, K; \tau = o, 1; t = o, 1. \quad (5.237)$$

The summation over observations is a summation over all the periods of our time-series data. Note that both the output and input distance functions in the numerator of this index require evaluation of "mixed" data, for example, (x^o, y^1).

These were estimated for each pair of years, starting with 1948–1949, and continuing to 2001–2002. The resulting measures are normalized to be comparable—the original formulation of the Luenberger productivity signals productivity gain with values greater than zero, whereas the others signal progress with values greater than one.[72] Annual average total factor productivity (TFP) growth was about 2.9% for the Malmquist index; the Hicks-Moorsteen was more modest, 1.2%. The average annual change for the Luenberger was 1.4 (not percent).[73] The cumulated results are displayed in figure 5.18.

Again, we see that these measures all agree that productivity has increased in U.S. agriculture over the 1948–2002 period. The Malmquist productivity index shows the largest cumulated productivity gains—its average rate of growth is 2.9%; the Hicks-Moorsteen index shows a more modest percent increase. There is a slight decline in productivity change in the early 1980s shown by the Luenberger indicator; however, overall cumulated productivity is still positive. The results for our distance function measures are intended for illustration; we do not recommend them in general if only time-series data are available. Nevertheless, although beyond the scope of this chapter, a more detailed study of the sources of the differences across the two types of measures would be of interest, especially with respect to possible distortions in the price-related measures if there is pervasive allocative inefficiency. This might be best investigated in the context of a Monte Carlo study. Also of interest would be a comparison of decompositions of the distance-function–based measures using panel data.

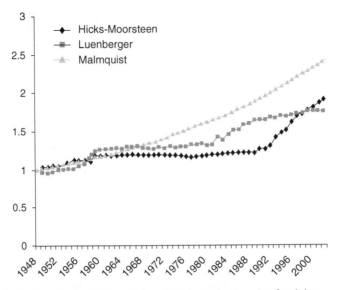

Figure 5.18. Luenberger, Malmquist, and Hicks-Moorsteen Productivity

There are a number of computational issues with respect to our distance function measures of productivity that are also important but have not been addressed here. Statistical significance, rates of convergence, identification of outliers (see Simar, 2003), and specification of inputs and outputs in a statistical sense are important; these are treated in detail in chapter 4. Alternative estimation procedures that are robust are also discussed in chapter 4 (see also Cazals, Florens, and Simar, 2002). Data smoothing through the application of windows techniques is sketched out in chapter 2; using moving averages may also be useful. Due to the wealth of results that are generated when estimating productivity and its components, we encourage more reliance on graphics to present these results.

5.5.5 Nonstationarity and nonlinear functional forms

The presence of integrated variables has received very little attention in parametric productivity analysis, yet it has far-reaching implications for model specification and estimation issues. As Granger (1995) emphasizes, sensible specifications can only be obtained if the underlying equations are balanced. For example, if both cost and output are either unit root or simple linear trend processes, then it is not sensible to express cost as a function of the square of output because the linear trend in the dependent variable (cost) cannot be balanced by the quadratic trends driving the independent variable (output square). A similar situation will apply in specifying a production function with quadratic terms on the right-hand side. More generally, the presence of several quadratic terms, for example, as in a translog specification, will typically require that the quadratic trends in the right-hand side variables somehow offset each other so that the overall model equation can be balanced. In this regard, it becomes an empirical question if, for example, balancing is achieved with or without the interaction terms capturing biased technical change in section 5.5.3 above. Clearly, the issue of balancing not only is a matter of concern for the econometrician but, as Granger points out, also presents a major challenge for the economic theorist to ascertain that the functional form and the variables used in theoretical constructs provide a meaningful apparatus for empirical work.

Additionally, it is not clear that a deterministic trend model of technical progress such as the translog specification with neutral technical progress will be adequate in most practical applications, as per standard practice, in the presence of stochastic trends in the data. Again, it is possible that adding interaction terms involving the product of deterministic terms times $I(1)$ variables yields a sufficient degree of balancing in the equation. The question, of course, is whether the significance of interaction terms in the estimation of production or cost models is evidence in support of biased technical progress or an artifact of stochastic trends.

Care also needs to be exercised in situations where restrictions on functional forms or other theoretical parametric restrictions are being tested in models with integrated variables. For example, the Lagrange multiplier test derived by regressing the residuals from a Cobb-Douglas equation on the extra terms appearing in a translog model will be biased against rejecting the null hypothesis that Cobb-Douglas is an acceptable model. The bias against the more general translog alternative will appear even if the Cobb-Douglas model is balanced (i.e., the equation cointegrates) because the right-hand side terms in the auxiliary (LM test) equation will involve integrated variables (see Granger, 1995).

Statistical analysis of time-series or panel models with integrated variables is very much limited to models that are linear in the variables. Granger (1995) emphasizes the importance of nonlinear cointegrating relationships, and Park and Phillips (2001) develop asymptotic theory for nonlinear regressions with integrated variables. Their results pertain to bivariate parametric nonlinear cointegrating relations. They recognize that multivariate extensions will involve vector Brownian approximations to the asymptotics of integrated time series that can behave very differently than a scalar Brownian motion. The situation will presumably be even more complex for panel-data applications. Their main finding is that convergence rates for nonlinear regressions with integrated time series can be both slower ($\sqrt[4]{n}$) and faster (powers of $\sqrt{n}$) compared to convergence rates for nonlinear regressions with stationary variables or linear cointegrating relations with nonstationary variables dependent upon whether the signal is attenuated or strengthened by the nonlinear transformations of the integrated regressors.

The convergence rate of the nonlinear estimator for regressions with homogeneous functions of integrated variables that include translog functional forms can be shown to converge faster than the standard $\sqrt{n}$ rate, but the estimator is unlikely to have a mixed normal limiting distribution except in the case where the error term of the equation is uncorrelated with the regressors (see Park and Phillips, 2001). The results of Park and Phillips can be extended to a nonparametric analysis of cointegration, although this is by no means a straightforward exercise. See chapter 4 for nonparametric results on convergence and limit distributions for frontier models with stationary variables. Understandably, extensions of the chapter 4 results from efficiency measurement to a probabilistic analysis of productivity measurement with integrated variables are highly cumbersome.

Table 5.1 shows the results of augmented Dickey-Fuller (ADF) unit root tests for the individual (log) price and quantity series used in the empirical illustration of section 5.5.4. The only variables for which the unit root hypothesis could possibly be rejected against the alternative of a stationary series around a deterministic time trend are the price (rental rate) of land and two of the output variables (crops and livestock). Although the theory of cointegration for nonlinear regressions with integrated time series is not well

Table 5.1
Unit Root (ADF) Tests

	Without Trend		With Trend	
	t-Static	p-Value	t-Static	p-Value
Land	1.678	0.436	−2.069	0.550
PLand	−1.594	0.479	−3.985	0.015
Capital	−1.180	0.676	−1.114	0.917
PCapital	−0.888	0.784	−1.630	0.767
Labor	−2.766	0.070	−0.545	0.978
PLabor	0.003	0.954	−2.571	0.295
Materials	−2.404	0.145	−2.796	0.205
PMaterials	−0.523	0.878	−2.071	0.594
Crops	−0.787	0.814	−5.841	0.000
Livestock	−2.424	0.140	−4.430	0.004
PLivestock	−0.511	0.881	−1.977	0.600
Secondary	−0.739	0.828	−1.611	0.776
PSecondary	−1.099	0.709	−1.143	0.911
Bennet-Bowley	−0.353	0.909	−6.527	0.000
Fisher	1.360	0.999	−1.593	0.782
Törnqvist	1.360	0.999	−1.593	0.782
Malmquist	1.141	0.997	−1.525	0.808
Luenberger	−0.230	0.928	−1.885	0.648
Hicks-Moorsteen	0.477	0.984	−0.936	0.944

developed, the residuals from the estimation of a translog function using the U.S. agriculture data appear to be a stationary series. To the extent that such a cointegrating relationship exists, it is possible that rates of convergence of estimates are faster than those in regressions with stationary variables. Furthermore, the presence of a cointegrating relationship helps overcome the usual endogeneity problems associated with the estimation of production models as discussed in section 5.5.3. Yet the presence of endogenous regressors complicates the limiting distribution of the model estimates, as also discussed above. There may be a case, again, to recommend estimating (dual) cost instead of production functions to the extent that these specifications are less suspect of endogeneity problems.

Table 5.1 also shows unit root test results for the six productivity indices. They confirm the persistent trends that are apparent in figures 5.17 and 5.18. It appears the only index that may be stationary around a deterministic trend is Bennet-Bowley; all other productivity indices appear to be driven by stochastic trends. As reported above, all indices show positive TFP growth, albeit at different rates. The question that needs to be asked is whether there is a mechanism by which the different productivity indices are kept together. To answer this, we carry out cointegration analysis. The results of a Johansen cointegration test are shown in table 5.2. They suggest the presence of three cointegrating vectors and therefore two common stochastic trends among the five series. The Törnqvist index was excluded because it is essentially identical to the Fisher index. We conclude that, although there is considerable variation in estimated TFP performance that in part reflects the effects of different methodologies and the nature of the data used to construct these TFP measures, there is also statistical evidence of common stochastic driving forces underlying the behavior of these series.

5.6 Comparisons Based on Index Number Properties

In this section, we summarize the properties or tests that the main productivity indexes and indicators discussed in this chapter satisfy. Specifically, we include the Malmquist, Hicks-Moorsteen, and Luenberger productivity measures along with their superlative approximations: the Fisher, Törnqvist, and Bennet-Bowley productivity measures.

We do not include the dual cost, revenue, and profit forms of productivity discussed above. That would require that we determine which of the tests or properties carry over through duality, a topic that we leave to others to explore. This problem is not straightforward. We know that differentiability does not carry over through duality; an example is the Leontief production function (nondifferentiable), which has a linear dual cost function.[74]

We consider the following tests:[75]

- Identity
- Proportionality

Table 5.2
Unrestricted Cointegration Rank Test (Trace)

Hypothesized No. of CE(s)	Eigenvalue	0.05			Normalized Cointegrating Coefficients				
		Trace Statistic	Crit Value	Prob.*	Hicks-Moorsteen	Malmquist	Luenberger	Bennet-Bowley	Fisher
None*	0.5475	96.32115	60.06141	0.0000	1.000	0.000	0.000000	0.000000	−0.824 (0.0279)
At most 1*	0.4356	55.0823	40.1749	0.0009	0.000	1.000	0.000000	0.000000	−1.684 (0.1358)
At most 2*	0.2831	25.34211	24.2759	0.0366	0.000	0.000	1.000000	0.000000	−0.716 (0.0397)
At most 3	0.14212	8.03675	12.3209	0.2338	0.000	0.000	0.000000	1.000000	−0.595 (0.048)
At most 4	0.00126	0.06559	4.12990	0.8336					

Trace test indicates three cointegrating equations (CEs) at the 0.05 level.
* Denotes rejection of the hypothesis at the 0.05 level.
** MacKinnon-Haug-Michelis (1999) p-values.

- Independence of unit of measurement (commensurability)[76]
- Circularity

We also include a comparison of these measures with respect to whether their estimation requires optimization and what their aggregation properties are.

The identity test ensures that, if nothing changes over time, the index or indicator also does not change. Formally, if I is an index, then

$$I(x, y, x, y) = 1. \tag{5.238}$$

If J is an indicator, then

$$J(x, y, x, y) = 0. \tag{5.239}$$

Proportionality applies only to indexes (ratio or multiplicative form rather than difference or additive form) and is defined as

$$I(x^t, y^t, \lambda x^t, \mu y^t) = \mu/\lambda, \mu, \lambda > 0. \tag{5.240}$$

Independence of unit of measurement or commensurability is defined as

$$I(x^t, y^t, x^{t+1}, y^{t+1}) = I(\lambda_1 x_1^t, \ldots, \lambda_N x_N^t, \mu_1 y_1^t, \ldots, \mu_M y_M^t), \lambda_n > 0, \mu_m > 0. \tag{5.241}$$

This says that if we change the way we define units of input and output—changing from pounds to kilos, for example—then our index should not change. In the case of the price-dependent measures, both quantity and price would behave in this way.

The circularity test has both a multiplicative (for indexes) and an additive (for indicators) formulation:

$$I(x^t, y^t, x^{t+1}, y^{t+1}) I(x^{t+1}, y^{t+1}, x^{t+2}, y^{t+2}) = I(x^t, y^t x^{t+2}, y^{t+2}) \tag{5.242}$$

$$I(x^t, y^t, x^{t+1}, y^{t+1}) + I(x^{t+1}, y^{t+1}, x^{t+2}, y^{t+2}) = I(x^t, y^t x^{t+2}, y^{t+2}) \tag{5.243}$$

The additional properties of optimization and aggregation are not traditionally included in the index number literature. With respect to optimization, we ask: To estimate the index or indicator, do we need to perform some form of optimization, for example, estimate technology using a distance function? With respect to aggregation, we have a fairly narrow interpretation. If we have indexes or indicators for firms $k = 1, \ldots, K$, we ask whether the associated industry index or indicator may be estimated by taking the sum of the firm measures.

These properties are summarized for our six productivity measures in table 5.3. This tells us that all of our indexes satisfy identity, proportionality, and independence of unit of measurement (our indicators do not have a proportionality property by definition). All of our measures fail with respect

Table 5.3
Comparison of Index Number Properties

	Identity	Proport-ionality	Indep-endence	Circularity	Optimality	Aggre-gation
Malmquist	Yes	Yes	Yes	No	Yes	No
Hicks–Moorsteen	Yes	?	Yes	No	Yes	Yes
Luenberger	Yes	No	Yes	No	Yes	Yes
Fisher	Yes	Yes	Yes	No	No	No
Törnqvist	Yes	Yes	Yes	No	No	No
Bennet-Bowley	Yes	No	Yes	No	No	Yes

to circularity. The distance-function–based measures require optimization, whereas their superlative approximations do not. Our indicators aggregate directly, whereas our indexes do not. Based on table 5.3, we think a case can be made for including the Bennet-Bowley index in our standard measures of productivity.

5.7 Summing Up

Productivity is one of our most basic and intuitive measures of performance; at the firm level, it is a component of profit growth (along with price changes), and at the aggregate level, it is a fundamental part of economic growth and welfare. In this chapter, we have tried to show how frontier methods and notions of efficiency can be integrated into our measures and understanding of productivity and its growth. The key building block is the distance function, which identifies a production frontier and assesses performance relative to that frontier. This provides a close link to the traditional definition of productivity as a ratio of output to input; that is, they are linked to technology. Because they explicitly seek to identify frontier performance, they readily allow us to identify shifts in the frontier (technical change) and movements toward the frontier as components of productivity growth. Because they do not require price data, they provide a means of evaluating productivity in the public sector and other applications where prices are absent or not meaningful. These advantages come at a cost—the Malmquist, Hicks-Moorsteen, and Luenberger productivity measures discussed here all require optimization in their estimation. In addition, to exploit the identification of efficiency change, technical change, and scale effects, panel data are generally required.

The traditional price-related productivity measures discussed here—Törnqvist, Fisher, and Bennet-Bowley—do not require solving an optimization problem for their computation and lend themselves readily to time-series data. In order to link them back to the distance function relatives that they are approximating, however, they require that the prices we observe and are used to aggregate outputs and inputs be generated by optimal behavior. This requirement that prices reflect optimization that underpins traditional price-related measures suggests that the distance function measures of productivity provide a useful complement when those conditions do not obtain.

Our focus here was to emphasize through duality theory the links between traditional productivity measures and our frontier-based measures. Naturally, this focus meant that there is much in the vast productivity literature that we did not address. Some omissions from earlier work include those related to growth accounting, such as Kendrick (1961) and Denison (1972), among others. We have also neglected the debate over the "residual" as captured in the growth accounting literature, and the work by Jorgenson and Griliches (1967), which argued for better measurement of inputs and outputs. There is also an interesting literature on using revealed preference techniques–linear programming approaches to identify productivity growth, including Varian (1984) and Chavas and Cox (1988, 1990). Also in that vein is the work associated with the Free Disposal Hull approach, which eschews the convexity of the DEA approaches, beginning with Deprins et al. (1984). We have also neglected discussions of stochastic technologies with uncertainty and dynamic technologies. The first is given a theoretical treatment in Chambers and Quiggin (2000), with applications found in Chambers (2004) and O'Donnell and Griffiths (2004). Chambers applies a state-contingent Bennet-Bowley indicator, while O'Donnell and Griffiths directly estimate the state-contingent technology. A treatment of dynamics in connection with DEA may be found in Färe and Grosskopf (1996).

A host of practical issues also merit attention, including the measurement of service output, the measurement of capital, the role of quality measurement and hedonics, how to exploit high-frequency sales data, the effect of entry and exit and new and disappearing goods on productivity growth, among many others. There has been considerable progress in these areas thanks to the efforts of among others, Erwin Diewert,[77] Who has made continued efforts to bring together those who produce our statistical data and the economists who work in both the theory and practice of productivity measurement.

Appendix 5.1

Demonstrate that $M_o^o = M_o^1$ if and only if the distance functions are of the form

$$D_o^\tau(x, y) = A(\tau)D_0(x, y), \tau = 0 \text{ or } 1. \tag{5.244}$$

Due to the representation property of the distance functions, for a technology satisfying Hicks output neutrality P^τ we have

$$P^\tau(x) = \{y : D_o^\tau(x, y) \leqq 1\} = \{y : A(\tau)D_o(x, y) \leqq 1\}. \tag{5.245}$$

By homogeneity of the distance function,

$$P^\tau(x) = \frac{1}{A(\tau)}\{A(\tau)y : D_o[x, A(\tau)y] \leqq 1\}$$

$$= [1/A(\tau)]P(x). \tag{5.246}$$

One may also show that if

$$P^\tau(x) = [1/A(\tau)]P(x), \tag{5.247}$$

then the output distance function takes the form

$$D_o^\tau(x, y) = A(\tau)D_o(x, y). \tag{5.248}$$

Thus, $M_o^o = M_o^1$ if and only if the technology is Hicks output neutral. We verify this by

$$D_o^\tau(x, y) = \inf\{\theta : y/\theta \in P^\tau(x)\}$$

$$= \inf\{\theta : y/\theta \in [1/A(\tau)]P(x)\}$$

$$= A(\tau) \inf \left\{\theta/A(\tau) : \frac{y}{\theta/A(\tau)} \in P(x)\right\}$$

$$= A(\tau)D_o(x, y), \tag{5.249}$$

where $D_o(x, y)$ is independent of τ. Q.E.D.
  To verify that

$$D_o^\tau(x, y) = A(\tau)D_o(x, y), \tau = 0, 1, \tag{5.250}$$

if and only if

$$R^\tau(x, p) = \frac{1}{A(\tau)}R(x, p), \tag{5.251}$$

we use the duality theorem between the output distance function and the revenue function

$$R^\tau(x, p) = \max_y \frac{py}{D_o^\tau(x, y)}$$

$$= \max_y \frac{py}{A(\tau)D_o(x, y)}$$

$$= \frac{1}{A(\tau)} \max_y \frac{py}{D_o(x, y)}$$

$$= \frac{1}{A(\tau)}R(x, p). \tag{5.252}$$

Conversely,

$$D_o^\tau(x, y) = \max_p \frac{py}{R^\tau(x, p)}$$

$$= \max_p \frac{py}{R^\tau(x, p)}$$

$$= \max_p \frac{pyA(\tau)}{R(x, p)}$$

$$= A(\tau) \max_p \frac{py}{R(x, p)}$$

$$= A(\tau) D_o(x, y). \tag{5.253}$$

Q.E.D.

To prove that $L^1 = L^o$ if and only if technology may be written as

$$\vec{D}_T^\tau(x, y; g) = \vec{A}(\tau) + \vec{D}_T(x, y; g), \tag{5.254}$$

we begin by substituting for the original definitions of L^1 and L^o and rearranging:

$$\vec{D}_T^1(x^1, y^1; g) = \vec{D}_T^o(x^1, y^1; g) - \vec{D}_T^o(x^o, y^o; g) + \vec{D}_T^1(x^o, y^o; g) \tag{5.255}$$

Fix (x^o, y^o) and T^o and then

$$\vec{D}_T^1(x^1, y^1; g) = \text{a constant} + \vec{D}_T(x^1, y^1; g) + \vec{A}(1), \tag{5.256}$$

or

$$\vec{D}_T^\tau(x^1, y^1; g) = \vec{A}(\tau) + \vec{D}_T(x, y; g) \tag{5.257}$$

by sign changes. Q.E.D.

Notes

1. This terminology was introduced by Diewert (2005).
2. Färe and Primont (1995) derive a conditional relationship between profit and the Shephard distance functions.
3. For a detailed discussion of these axioms, see Färe and Primont (1995). Note that inputs are freely disposable if $(x, y) \in T$, and $x' \geq x$ implies that $(x', y) \in T$. Outputs are freely disposable if $(x, y) \in T$, and $y' \leq y$ implies that $(x, y') \in T$. We introduce an alternative disposability axiom—weak disposability—later in our discussion of environmental productivity.
4. For a maximum to exist, some conditions in addition to the aforementioned axioms on technology are required; see Färe and Primont (1995).
5. For more properties, see a standard textbook, such as Varian (1992).

6. The hyperbolic efficiency measure, defined as $D_h(x, y) = \min\{\lambda : (\lambda x, y/\lambda) \in T\}$, is closely related to the directional technology distance function since it simultaneously contracts inputs and expands outputs. It does this along a hyperbolic path (rather than the linear path taken by the directional distance function) to the frontier. See Färe, Grosskopf, Lovell, and Pasurka (1989) for an example with the hyperbolic efficiency measure.

7. Typically, in describing the directional vector, we would multiply g_x by -1 to indicate that inputs are to be reduced.

8. See Chambers, Chung, and Färe (1998).

9. It is also possible to mean deflate the data without affecting the value of the directional distance function, as long as the associated direction subvector is also mean deflated by the same value [e.g., data variable $(x_1/\overline{x_1})$ and associated direction component $(g_{x1}/\overline{x_1})$].

10. See Chambers, Chung, and Färe (1998).

11. The use of $pg_y + wg_x$ as a normalization factor is neither arbitrary nor simply a matter of convenience. It is the value of the Lagrangean multiplier associated with the constrained profit maximization problem in which the directional technology distance function, representing the technology, is constrained to be greater than or equal to zero, and assuming an interior solution for which the constraint is binding as an equality.

12. Luenberger (1995) chooses the direction vector in this normalization such that $pg_y + wg_x = 1$.

13. We follow Diewert (2005) and refer to measures in ratio form as indexes and measures in difference form as indicators.

14. The normalization factor pg_y is the Lagrangean multiplier associated with the constrained revenue maximization problem in which the directional output distance function, representing technology, is constrained to be greater than or equal to zero, assuming an interior solution for which the constraint is binding as an equality.

15. In this case, choosing $g_y = 1$ would result in normalizing by $\sum_m p_m$. Again following Luenberger (1995), we may also choose g_y such that $pg_y = 1$.

16. The reader may consult Färe and Grosskopf (2004) for details.

17. This is the analog of the translation property for the directional distance functions. Homogeneity reflects the multiplicative form of the Shephard distance function, whereas translation reflects the additive form of the directional distance function.

18. For a detailed discussion, see especially Fisher (1922) and Diewert (1992, 2005).

19. For an overview of Malmquist productivity from an operations research point of view, see Tone (2004), and for a modern treatment of productivity, see Hulten, Dean, and Harper (2001).

20. They state that the Malmquist index could be computed if a functional form is specified for the structure of production and the parameters are "known." As they say, "However, without knowledge of the parameters," the index cannot be computed. "Thus the empirical usefulness of the Malmquist indexes is limited." (Caves, Christensen, and Diewert, 1982, 1982a, p. 1394).

21. Under constant returns to scale, i.e., $T = \lambda T, \lambda > 0$, the input and output distance functions are reciprocal to each other; in this chapter, we focus our attention on the output-oriented case.

22. This index may also be defined in terms of input distance functions. Let $D_i(y, x) = \inf\{\lambda : (x/\lambda, y) \in T\}$ be an input distance function; then,

the corresponding input-oriented Malmquist productivity index is $D_i^o(y^1, x^1)/D_i^o(y^o, x^o)$.

23. This was first observed by Berg, Førsund, and Jansen (1992). An example by Grifell-Tatjé and Lovell (1995) verified that they may not coincide if the reference technology does not satisfy constant returns to scale.

24. See Chambers and Färe (1994).

25. Färe, Grosskopf, Lindgren, and Roos were inspired by Caves, Christensen, and Diewert (1982a) who used the geometric mean definition to show the relationship between the Malmquist and Törnqvist productivity indexes.

26. This result holds for all $(x, y) \in \Re_+^{N+M}$.

27. Relevant references include Diewert (1992), Moorsteen (1961), Hicks (1932), Bjurek (1994), and Balk (2004).

28. Recall that feasible vectors have output distance function values less than one. Our observation in period 1 is not feasible and has an output distance function value greater than one.

29. Recall that the value of the distance function is greater than one for feasible bundles and less than one for those that lie below the isoquant.

30. See Balk (2004) for details.

31. This is due to Shephard (1970). See also Färe and Primont (1995) for some extensions.

32. Inverse homotheticity requires that the output distance function takes the form $D_o(x, y) = D_o(\overline{x}, y)/F[D_i(\overline{y}, x)]$. Constant returns to scale holds if and only if $F(\cdot)$ is the identity function.

33. One may choose an input or output orientation with the Malmquist index.

34. See Briec and Kerstens (2004) for a derivation of the relation between the Luenberger and Hicks-Moorsteen indexes.

35. For an application to agriculture, see Ball, Färe, Grosskopf, and Nehring (2001), and for an application to electric utilities, see Färe, Grosskopf, and Pasurka (2001).

36. For an attempt to estimate Malmquist productivity, including identifying bounds on efficiency change and technical change with time series data, see Lynde and Richmond (1999).

37. As noted above, they actually state that "the empirical usefulness of the Malmquist index is limited" (Caves, Christensen, and Diewert, 1982a, p. 1394).

38. This derivation also required assumptions concerning functional form of technology (translog), optimizing behavior (no technical inefficiency and revenue maximization and cost minimization under competitive conditions), and some specifics concerning parameterization of the translog distance function (identical second-order term parameters).

39. For an empirical comparison among some of these indexes, see Bureau, Färe, and Grosskopf (1995).

40. The Törnqvist index is often written in log difference form, however.

41. Recall that the duality result above is achieved through optimization; therefore, the resulting productivity index will coincide with the original Malmquist productivity index only when the data are consistent with such optimization.

42. See Balk (1998) and Färe and Grosskopf (1994) for theoretical treatments.

43. See Grosskopf, Hayes, Taylor, and Weber (1997, 1999) and Grosskopf and Moutray (2001) for applied examples.

44. See Färe, Grosskopf, and Lovell (1992) for a theoretical account.

45. The "duality diamond" in Färe and Primont (1995) may be used to create additional Malmquist productivity indexes. The same applies to the Hicks-Moorsteen index.

46. Balk (2004) notes that using profitability, i.e., the ratio of revenue to cost [or, as it was called by Georgescu-Roegen (1951), return to the dollar] rather than the difference, lends itself to the ratio form productivity index. See also Althin, Färe, and Grosskopf (1996) for a discussion of the relationship between profitability and Malmquist productivity.

47. In section 5.2.1, we fix inputs and outputs at $(\bar{x}, \bar{y})$ instead of normalizing them to unity.

48. For a decomposition of the Fisher index, see Ray and Mukherjee (1996) and Kuosmanen and Sapilänen (2004). For a decomposition of the Hicks-Moorsteen index see Nemoto and Goto (2004). Balk (2004) argues that the Hicks-Moorsteen index is "decomposition resistant." As noted above, the Hicks-Moorsteen index (when technology is not restricted to be constant returns and satisfy inverse homotheticity) will lack the scale-related components that may be isolated in the Malmquist index.

49. This decomposition is based on Färe, Grifell-Tatjé, Grosskopf, and Lovell (1997) and Färe and Grosskopf (1996).

50. See Chambers and Färe (1994) for a catalog of types of technical change.

51. See Färe and Lovell (1978).

52. This definition of scale efficiency—as the ratio of distance functions (technical efficiency) estimated under constant returns to scale and VRS at the observed input bundle—was first published in Färe, Grosskopf, and Logan (1983). It is often attributed to Banker (1984), who focuses on what he calls most productive scale size, i.e., the tangency between the VRS and constant returns to scale technologies, which is what we call scale efficient. The VRS form of the technology in an activity analysis context, as in DEA, is due to Afriat (1972).

53. The following discussion closely follows that in Grosskopf (2003).

54. This observation was made by Chambers and Pope (1996) and later by Färe and Primont (2003). We draw on Färe and Primont as well as on Färe and Grosskopf (2004).

55. Zelenyuk (in press) mixes the additive and multiplicative structure to achieve his aggregation results for the Malmquist productivity index.

56. For an early application of this approach to the Törnqvist index, see Pittman (1983).

57. See Shephard (1970) or Färe and Grosskopf (2004) for a more complete list of axioms and their representation in the activity analysis model.

58. This is often referred to the BCC model after Banker, Charnes, and Cooper (1984). However, it was first introduced by Afriat (1972) and first defined in the multiple-output case by Färe, Grosskopf, and Logan (1983).

59. This is under constant returns to scale. If variable returns to scale is imposed, the problem is more complicated, requiring an additional variable. See Färe and Grosskopf (2004).

60. See Fukuyama and Weber (2001) and Portela (2003) for examples.

61. This measure was introduced by Färe and Lovell (1978).

62. An example is found in Färe, Grosskopf, and Zelenyuk (2003).

63. For simplicity, we assume here that $x_n > 0, n = 1, \ldots, N$. This may be generalized.

64. The Portela (2003) version is a bit more sophisticated.

65. For a discussion of parameterizations of distance functions, see Färe and Sung (1986) and Färe and Lundberg (2005).

66. Our technical change terms differ slightly from those in Fuentes et al. (2001); ours are slightly more general and allow for geometric mean versions of technical change and its components.

67. We thank Eldon Ball for making us aware of these data and for his help in explaining the construction of the variables, which is the basis of the discussion here.

68. Implicit quantities are derived by dividing expenditures by a price index.

69. Using these same data, Chambers (2004) chooses the direction vector to be equal to the mean value of the inputs in the sample.

70. Note that in their original formulations, the Törnqvist and Fisher indexes signal productivity growth with values greater than unity; the associated value for the Bennet-Bowley index would be values greater than zero.

71. Alternatives include contemporaneous and sequential frontiers.

72. We typically use *OnFront2* for Malmquist estimation; we use *GAMS* to estimate the directional distance functions and Luenberger productivity indicators. There are a number of other packages available to estimate Malmquist indexes.

73. We also estimated a (dual) translog cost function yielding an estimate of about 1.7% average annual growth in technical progress. Adjusting this rate for scale effects gives an overall average rate of TFP growth of about 2.3%.

74. See Färe and Primont (1986) or Färe, Primont, and Samuelson (1990).

75. See chapter 1 for additional properties one might consider.

76. See Eichhorn and Voeller (1976) or Russell (1998).

77. See his home page for evidence of technical progress in this endeavor.

References

Aczél, J. (1990), Determining Merged Relative Scores, *Journal of Mathematical Analysis and Applications* 150:1, 20–40.

Aczél, J. (1966), *Lectures on Functional Equations and Their Applications*, New York: Academic Press.

Afriat, S. (1972), Efficiency Estimation of Production Functions, *International Economic Review* 13:3, 568–598.

Aigner, D.J., and S.F. Chu (1968), On Estimating the Industry Production Function, *American Economic Review* 58, 226–239.

Althin, R. (1995), *Essays on the Measurement of Production Performance*, Ph.D. Dissertation, Lund University.

Althin, R., R. Färe, and S. Grosskopf (1996), Profitability and Productivity Change: An Application to Swedish Pharmacies, *Annals of Operations Research* 66, 219–230.

Atkinson, S.E., C. Cornwell, and O. Honerkamp (2003), Measuring and Decomposing Productivity Change: Stochastic Distance Function Estimation versus Data Envelopment Analysis, *Journal of Business and Economic Statistics* 21:2, 284–294.

Balk, B.M. (1993), Malmquist Productivity Indexes and Fisher Ideal Indexes, Comment, *Economic Journal* 103, 680–682.

Balk, B.M. (1998), *Industrial Price, Quantity and Productivity Indices: The Microeconomic Theory and Application*, Boston: Kluwer.

Balk, B.M. (2001), Scale Efficiency and Productivity Change, *Journal of Productivity Analysis*, 15, 159–183.

Balk, B.M. (2003), The Residual: On Monitoring and Benchmarking Firms, Industries and Economies with Respect to Productivity, *Journal of Productivity Analysis* 20, 5–47.

Balk, B.M. (2004), The Many Decompositions of the Malmquist Index, Mimeo, Erasmus Research Institute of Management, Erasmus University Rotterdam and Methods and Informatics Department, Statistics Netherlands.

Balk, B.M., and R. Althin (1996), A New Transitive Productivity Index, *Journal of Productivity Analysis* 7, 19–27.

Balk, B.M., R. Färe, S. Grosskopf, and D. Margaritis (2005), The Equivalence Between the Luenberger Productivity Indicator and the Malmquist Productivity Index, mimeo, Oregan State University.

Ball, E., R. Färe, S. Grosskopf, and R. Nehring (2001), Productivity of the U.S. Agricultural Sector: The Case of Undesirable Outputs, in C.R. Hulten, E.R. Dean, and M.J. Harper (eds.), *New Developments in Productivity Analysis*, Chicago: University of Chicago Press, 541–586.

Banker, R.D. (1984), Estimating the Most Productive Scale Size Using Data Envelopment Analysis, *European Journal of Operational Research* 17, 35–44.

Banker, R.D., A. Charnes, and W.W. Cooper (1984), Some Models for Estimating Technical and Scale Inefficiencies in Data Envelopment Analysis, *Management Science* 30:9, 1078–1092.

Bauer, P.W. (1990), Decomposing TFP Growth in the Presence of Cost Inefficiency, Nonconstant Returns to Scale, and Technological Progress, *Journal of Productivity Analysis* 1:4, 287–301.

Bennet, T.L. (1920), The Theory of Measurement of Change in Cost of Living, *Journal of the Royal Statistical Society* 83, 455–462.

Berg, S.A., F.R. Førsund, and E.S. Jansen (1992), Malmquist Indices of Productivity Growth during the Deregulation of Norwegian Banking 1980–89, *Scandinavian Journal of Economics*, 94, 211–228.

Bjurek, H. (1994), Essays on Efficiency and Productivity Change with Application to Public Service Production, *Economiska Studier*, Göteborgs Universitet No. 52.

Blackorby, C., and R.R. Russell (1999), Aggregation of Efficiency Indices, *Journal of Productivity Analysis* 12:1, 5–20.

Boussemart, J.P., W. Briec, K. Kerstens, and J.C. Poutineau (2003), Luenberger and Malmquist Productivity Indices: Theoretical Comparisons and Empirical Illustration, *Bulletin of Economic Research* 55:4, 391–405.

Bowley, A.L. (1919), The Measurement of Changes in the Cost of Living, *Journal of the Royal Statistical Society* 82, 343–372.

Briec, W., and K. Kerstens (2004), A Luenberger-Hicks-Moorsteen Productivity Indicator: Its Relation to the Hicks-Moorsteen Productivity Index and the Luenberger Productivity Indicator, *Economic Theory* 23, 925–929.

Bureau, J.C., R. Färe, and S. Grosskopf (1995), Nonparametric Measures of Productivity Growth in European and U.S. Agriculture, *Journal of Agricultural Economics*, 46, 309–326.

Caves, D., L. Christensen, and W.E. Diewert (1982a), The Economic Theory of Index Numbers and the Measurement of Input, Output, and Productivity, *Econometrica* 50:6, 1393–1414.

Caves, D., L. Christensen, and W.E. Diewert (1982b), Multilateral Comparisons of Output, Input, and Productivity Using Superlative Index Numbers, *Economic Journal* 92, 73–86.

Cazals, C., J.P. Florens, and L. Simar (2002), Nonparametric Frontier Estimation: A Robust Approach, *Journal of Econometrics* 106, 1–25.

Chambers, R.G., Y.H. Chung, and R. Färe (1998), Profit, Directional Distance Functions and Nerlovian Efficiency, *Journal of Optimization Theory and Applications* 98, 351–364.

Chambers, R.G., and R. Färe (1994), Hicks Neutrality and Trade Biased Growth: A Taxonomy, *Journal of Economic Theory* 64, 554–567.

Chambers, R.G., R. Färe, and S. Grosskopf (1996), Productivity Growth in APEC Countries, *Pacific Economic Review* 1, 181–190.

Chambers, R.G., and R.D. Pope (1996), Aggregate Productivity Measures, *American Journal of Agricultural Economics* 78:5, 1360–1365.

Chambers, R.G., and J. Quiggin (2000), *Uncertainty, Production, Choice and Agency: The State-Contingent Approach*, New York: Cambridge University Press.

Charnes, A., W.W. Cooper, and E. Rhodes (1978), Measuring the Efficiency of Decision Making Units, *European Journal of Operational Research* 2, 429–444.

Chavas, J.-P., and T.L. Cox (1988), A Nonparametric Analysis of Agricultural Technology, *American Journal of Agricultural Economics*, 70, 303–310.

Chavas, J.-P., and T.L. Cox (1990), A Non-parametric Analysis of Productivity: The Case of U.S. and Japanese Manufacturing, *American Economic Review* 80:30, 450–464.

De Borger, B., and K. Kerstens (2000), The Malmquist Productivity Index and Plant Capacity Utilisation, *Scandinavian Journal of Economics* 102, 303–310.

Denison, E.F. (1972), Classification of Sources of Growth, *Review of Income and Wealth* 18, 1–25.

Deprins, D., L. Simar, and H. Tulkens (1984), Measuring Labor Efficiency in Post Offices, in M. Marchand, P. Pestieau, and H. Tulkens (eds.), *The Performance of Public Enterprises: Normative, Positive and Empirical Issues*, Amsterdam: North Holland, 243–267.

Diewert, W.E. (1976), Exact and Superlative Index Numbers, *Journal of Econometrics* 4, 115–145.

Diewert, W.E. (1992), Fisher Ideal Output, Input and Productivity Indexes Revisited, *Journal of Productivity Analysis* 3:3, 211–248.

Diewert, W.E. (2005), Index Number Theory Using Differences Rather Than Ratios, *American Journal of Economics and Sociology* 64:1, 347–395.

Diewert, W.E., and K. Fox (2004), On the Estimation of Returns to Scale, Technical Progress and Monopolistic Markups, paper presented at the SSHRC International Conference on Index Number Theory and Measurement of Prices and Productivity, Vancouver.

Diewert, W.E., and C. Morrison (1990), New Techniques in the Measurement of Multifactor Productivity, *Journal of Productivity Analysis* 1:4, 267–285.

Färe, R., F. Førsund, S. Grosskopf, K. Hayes, and A. Heshmati (2001), A Note on Decomposing the Malmquist Productivity Index by Means of Subvector Homotheticity, *Economic Theory* 17, 239–245.

Färe, R., E. Grifell-Tatjé, S. Grosskopf, and C.A.K. Lovell (1997), Biased Technical Change and the Malmquist Productivity Index, *Scandinavian Journal of Economics* 99:1, 119–127.

Färe, R., and S. Grosskopf (1990), A Distance Function Approach to Measuring Price Efficiency, *Journal of Public Economics* 43, 123–126.

Färe, R., and S. Grosskopf (1992), Malmquist Productivity Indexes and Fisher Ideal Indexes, *Economic Journal*, 102:4, 158–160.

Färe, R., and S. Grosskopf (1994), *Cost and Revenue Constrained Production*, Bilkent University Lecture Series, Springer-Verlag, Berlin.

Färe, R., and S. Grosskopf (1996), *Intertemporal Production Frontiers: With Dynamic DEA*, Boston: Kluwer.

Färe, R., and S. Grosskopf (2000), Outfoxing a Paradox, *Economics Letters*, 69, 159–163.

Färe, R., and S. Grosskopf (2004), *New Directions: Efficiency and Productivity*, Boston: Kluwer Academic Publishers.

Färe, R., and S. Grosskopf (2005), Comment: Profits and Productivity, mimeo, www.oregonstate.edu/dept/econ/research/working_papers.php.

Färe, R., S. Grosskopf, B. Lindgren, and P. Roos (1994), Productivity Developments in Swedish Hospitals: A Malmquist Output Index Approach, in A. Charnes, W. Cooper, A. Lewin, and L. Seiford, (eds.), *Data Envelopment Analysis: Theory, Methodology and Applications*, Boston: Kluwer, 253–272.

Färe, R., S. Grosskopf, and J. Logan (1983), The Relative Efficiency of Illinois Public Utilities, *Resources and Energy* 5, 349–367.

Färe, R., S. Grosskopf, and C.A.K Lovell (1985), *The Measurement of Efficiency of Production*, Boston: Kluwer-Nijhoff.

Färe, R., S. Grosskopf, and C.A.K. Lovell (1992), Cost Indirect Productivity Measurement, *Journal of Productivity Analysis* 2:4, 283–298.

Färe, R., S. Grosskopf, and C.A.K Lovell (1994), *Production Frontiers*, New York: Cambridge University Press.

Färe, R., S. Grosskopf, and D. Margaritis (2006), Productivity Growth and Convergence in the European Union, *Journal of Productivity Analysis*, 25:1/2, 111–141.

Färe, R., S. Grosskopf, D.W. Noh, and W. Weber (2005), Characteristics of a Polluting Technology: Theory and Practice, *Journal of Econometrics* 126, 469–492.

Färe, R., S. Grosskopf, M. Norris, and Z. Zhang (1994), Decomposition of Productivity Growth in Industrialized Countries into Technical Change and Change in Performance, *American Economic Review* 84:1, 66–83.

Färe, R., S. Grosskopf, and C. Pasurka (2001), Accounting for Air Pollution Emissions in Measuring State Manufacturing Productivity Growth, *Journal of Regional Science* 41:3, 381–409.

Färe, R., S. Grosskopf, and P. Roos (1998), Malmquist Productivity Indexes: A Survey of Theory and Practice, in R. Färe, S. Grosskopf, and R.R. Russell (eds.), *Index Numbers: Essays in Honour of Sten Malmquist*, Boston: Kluwer.

Färe, R., S. Grosskopf, and V. Zelenyuk (2003), Finding Common Ground, mimeo (www.oregonstate.edu/dept/econ/research/working_papers.php).

Färe, R., and C.A.K. Lovell (1978), Measuring the technical efficiency of production, *Journal of Economic Theory* 19, 150–162.

Färe, R., and A. Lundberg (2005), Parameterizing the Shortage Function, mimeo (http://www.oregonstate.edu/dept/econ/research/working_papers.php).

Färe, R., and D. Primont (1986), On Differentiability of the Cost Function, *Journal of Economic Theory*, 38, 233–237.

Färe, R., and D. Primont (1995), *Multi-output Production and Duality: Theory and Applications*, Boston: Kluwer.

Färe, R., and D. Primont (2003), Luenberger Productivity Indicators: Aggregation Across Firms, *Journal of Productivity Analysis* 20, 425–435.

Färe, R., and K.J. Sung (1986), On Second-Order Taylor's-Series Approximations and Linear Homogeneity, *Acquationes Mathematicae* 30, 180–186.

Farrell, M.J. (1957), The Measurement of Productive Efficiency, *Journal of the Royal Statistical Society, Series A, General*, 120:3, 253–281.

Fisher, I. (1922), *The Making of Index Numbers*, Boston: Houghton-Mifflin.

Fixler, D., and K. Zieschang (1992), Incorporating Ancillary Measures of Process and Quality Changes into a Superlative Productivity Index, *Journal of Productivity Analysis* 2, 245–267.

Førsund, F.R. (1990), The Malmquist Productivity Index, memorandum, no. 28, Department of Economics, University of Oslo, Oslo, Norway.

Fox, K. (1999), Efficiency at Different Levels of Aggregation: Public vs. Private Sector Firms, *Economics Letters* 65:2, 173–176.

Fox, K. (2005), Returns to Scale, Technical Progress and Total Factor Productivity Growth in New Zealand Industries, mimeo, School of Economics and CAER, University of New South Wales, Sydney, Australia.

Fried, H., C.A.K. Lovell and S. Schmidt (1993), *The Measurement of Productive Efficiency: Technologies and Applications*, Oxford University Press, Oxford.

Fuentes, H.J., E. Grifell-Tatjé, and S. Perelman (2001), A Parametric Distance Function Approach for Malmquist Productivity Estimation, *Journal of Productivity Analysis* 15, 79–94.

Fukuyama, H., and W.L. Weber (2001), Estimating Output Allocative Efficiency and Productivity Change: Application to Japanese Banks, *European Journal of Operational Research* 137, 177–190.

Georgescu-Roegen, N. (1951), The Aggregate Linear Production Function and Its Application to von Neumann's Economic Models, in T. Koopmans (ed.), *Activity Analysis of Production and Allocation*, New York: Wiley.

Gilbert, R.A., and P.W. Wilson (1998), Effects of Deregulation on the Productivity of Korean Banks, *Journal of Economics and Business* 50, 133–155.

Granger, C.W.J. (1995), Nonlinear Relationships Between Extended-Memory Variables, *Econometrica* 63, 265–280.

Grifell-Tatjé, E., and C. A. K. Lovell (1995), A Note on the Malmquist Productivity Index, *Economics Letters* 47:2, 169–175.

Grifell-Tatjé, E., and C. A. K. Lovell (1999), Profits and Productivity, *Management Science* 45, 1177–1193.

Grosskopf, S. (2003), Some Remarks on Productivity and Its Decompositions, *Journal of Productivity Analysis* 20, 459–474.

Grosskopf, S., K. Hayes, L. Taylor, and W. Weber (1997), Budget-Constrained Frontier Measures of Fiscal Equality and Efficiency in Schooling, *Review of Economics and Statistics* 79:1, 116–124.

Grosskopf, S., K. Hayes, L. Taylor, and W. Weber (1999), Anticipating the Consequences of School Reform: A New Use of DEA, *Management Science* 45:4, 608–620.

Grosskopf, S., and C. Moutray (2001), Evaluation of School Reform in Chicago Public Schools, *Economics of Education Review* 20:1, 1–14.

Henderson, D., and R.R. Russell (2005), Human Capital and Macroeconomic Convergence: A Production-Frontier Approach, *International Economic Review*, 46:4, 1167–1205.

Hicks, J.R. (1932), *Theory of Wages*. London: Macmillan.

Hulten, C.R., E.R. Dean, and M.J. Harper (eds.) (2001), *New Developments in Productivity Analysis*, Chicago: University of Chicago Press.

Jorgenson, D.W., and Z. Griliches (1967), The Explanation of Productivity Change, *Review of Economic Studies* 34:3, 249–282.

Kendrick, J.W. (1961), *Productivity Trends in the United States*, Princeton, NJ: National Bureau of Economic Research.

Koopmans, T.C. (1957), *Three Essays on the State of Economic Science*, New York: McGraw-Hill.

Kumar, S., and R.R. Russell (2002), Technological Change, Technological Catch-up, and Capital Deepening: Relative Contributions to Growth and Convergence, *American Economic Review* 92:3, 527–548.

Kuosmanen, T., T. Post, and T. Sipilänen (2004), Shadow Price Approach to Total Factor Productivity Measurement: With an Application to Finnish Grass–Silage Production, *Journal of Productivity Analysis* 22, 95–121.

Kuosmanen, T., and T. Sipilänen (2004), On the Anatomy of Productivity Growth: A Decomposition of the Fisher Ideal TFP Index, MTT Economic Research Paper no. 2004:17.

Lau, L.J., and P.A. Yotopoulos (1971), A Test for Relative Efficiency and Application to Indian Agriculture, *American Economic Review* 61:1, 94–105.

Lovell, C.A.K. (2003), The Decomposition of Malmquist Productivity Indexes, *Journal of Productivity Analysis* 20, 437–458.

Luenberger, D.G. (1992), Benefit Functions and Duality, *Journal of Mathematical Economics* 21, 461-481.

Luenberger, D.G. (1995), *Microeconomic Theory*, New York: McGraw-Hill.

Lynde, C., and J. Richmond (1999), Productivity and Efficiency in the UK: A Time Series Application of DEA, *Economic Modelling* 16, 105–122.

Malmquist, S. (1953), Index Numbers and Indifference Surfaces, *Trabajos de Estatistica* 4, 209–242.

Miller, D.M. (1984), Profitability Productivity + Price Recovery, *Harvard Business Review*, 62:3, 145–153.

Moorsteen, R.H. (1961), On Measuring Productive Potential and Relative Efficiency, *Quarterly Journal of Economics* 75, 451–467.

Morrison, C., and W.E. Diewert (1990), New Techniques in the Measurement of Multifactor Productivity, *Journal of Productivity Analysis* 1:4, 267–286.

Nemoto, J., and M. Goto (2004), Decomposition Analysis of Productivity Change Using a Hicks-Moorsteen Index, mimeo, Graduate School of Economics, Naguya University.

Nishimizu, M., and J.M. Page (1982), Total Factor Productivity Growth, Technological Progress and Technical Efficiency Change: Dimensions of Productivity Change in Yugoslavia 1965–78, *Economic Journal* 92, 920–936.

O'Donnell, C., and W.E. Griffiths (2004), Estimating State-Contingent Production Frontiers, Paper no. 02/2004, School of Economics, University of Queensland.

Orea, L. (2002), Parametric Decomposition of a Generalized Malmquist Productivity Index, *Journal of Productivity Analysis* 18, 5–22.

Park, J.Y., and P.C.B. Phillips (2001), Nonlinear Regressions with Integrated Time Series, *Econometrica* 69, 117–161.

Pittman, R. (1983), Multilateral Productivity Comparisons with Undesirable Outputs, *Economic Journal* 93:372, 883–891.

Portela, M.C.A.S. (2003), New Insights on Measuring Bank Branches Efficiency Through DEA: Transactional, Operational, and Profit Assessment, PhD Thesis, Ason Business School, Aston University, Birmingham, UK.

Ray, S., and E. Desli (1997), Productivity Growth, Technical Progress and Efficiency Change in Industrialized Countries: Comment, *American Economic Review* 87, 1033–1039.

Ray, S., and K. Mukherjee (1996), Decomposition of the Fisher Ideal Index of Productivity: A Non-parametric Dual Analysis of U.S. Airlines Data, *Economic Journal* 106, 1659–1678.

Shephard, R.W. (1953), *Cost and Production Functions.* Princeton, NJ: Princeton University Press.

Shephard, R.W. (1970), *Theory of Cost and Production Functions.* Princeton, NJ: Princeton University Press.

Shephard, R.W., and R. Färe (1974), The Law of Diminishing Returns, *Zeitschrift für Nationalökonomie* 34, 69–90.

Simar, L. (2003), Detecting Outliers in Frontier Models, *Journal of Productivity Analysis* 20, 391–424.

Simar, L., and P. W. Wilson (1998), Productivity Growth in Industrialized Countries, Discussion Paper 9810, Institute of Statistics, Louvain-la-Neuve, Belgium (http://www.stat.ucl.ac.be).

Solow, R.A. (1957), Technical Change and the Aggregate Production Function, *Review of Economics and Statistics* 39, 312–320.

Tone, K. (2004), Malmquist Productivity Index: Efficiency Change Over Time, in W.W. Cooper, L.M. Seiford, and J. Zhu (eds.), *Handbook on Data Envelopment Analysis,* Boston: Kluwer Academic Publishers.

Törnqvist, L. (1936), The Bank of Finland's Consumption Price Index, *Bank of Finland Monthly Bulletin* 10, 1–8.

Tulkens, H. (1991), Non-parametric Efficiency Measurement for Panel Data: Methodologies and an FDH Application to Retail Banking, July, mimeo, CORE, Louvain-la-Neuve, Belgium.

Tulkens, H., and P. Vanden Eeckaut (1995), Non-frontier Measures of Efficiency, Progress and Regress for Panel Data: Methodological Aspects, *European Journal of Operations Research* 80, 474–499.

Varian, H.R. (1992) *Microeconomic Analysis,* New York: W.W. Norton.

Varian, H. (1984), The Nonparametric Approach to Production Analysis, *Econometrica* 52:3, 579–597.

Wheelock, D.C., and P. W. Wilson (1999), Technical Progress, Inefficiency and Productivity Changes in U.S. Banking, 1984–1993, *Journal of Money, Credit and Banking* 31, 212–234.

Zelenyuk, V. (in press), On Aggregation of Malmquist Productivity Indexes, *European Journal of Operational Research.*

Index

Abad, C. 19
Abramovitz, M. 7
Absoft 124
Aczél, J. 551, 580
Adams, R. 136, 142
Adenzo-Diaz, B. 19, 374
Adler, N. 320, 321
Afriat, S. N. 48, 111
Agency theory 8–9, 13–15
Aggregation 7, 69, 523, 543, 578–585. *See also* indexes and indicators
Agrell, P. J. 17, 258
Aguilar, R. 110
Aida, K. 386
Aigner, D. J. 35, 36, 92, 94, 104, 107, 108, 118, 119, 120, 130, 219, 508, 515, 543
Airey, D. 17
Akhavein, J. 150
Albert, J. 129
Albright, T. 16
Albriktsen, R. 108
Alchian, A. A. 12, 13, 15
Ali, A. I. 263, 313, 333
Allen, K. 307

Allen, R. 301, 302, 320, 322, 323, 324, 326, 328, 329, 330, 331, 332, 337, 338, 339, 340
Alpar, P. 16, 479
Althin, R. 551
Álvarez, A. 100, 151, 153, 154, 166, 167, 220, 224, 361
Alves, C. 391
Ambec, S. 14
Amemiya, T. 112
Ammar, S. 16
Amos, D. 19
Amsler, C. 154, 166, 167, 220, 224
Andersen, P. 52, 316, 318, 338, 469, 503
Anderson, R. I. 19
Ang, B. W. 306
Angulo-Meza, L. 371, 372
Annaert, J. 128, 155
Anwandter, L. 386
Appa, G. 293, 295, 364
Aragon, Y. 479, 492, 494
Arcelus, F. J. 17
Arias, C. 100, 151, 153
Arickx, F. 190
Arocena, P. 17